UNITED NATIONS CONFERENCE ON TRADE AND DEVELOPMENT,
Geneva

The least developed countries.
1987 Report

Prepared by the UNCTAD secretariat

UNITED NATIONS
New York, 1988

NOTE

Symbols of United Nations documents are composed of capital letters combined with figures. Mention of such a symbol indicates a reference to a United Nations document.

*

* *

The designations employed and the presentation of the material in this publication do not imply the expression of any opinion whatsoever on the part of the Secretariat of the United Nations concerning the legal status of any country, territory, city or area, or of its authorities, or concerning the delimitation of its frontiers or boundaries.

*

* *

TD/B/1153

UNITED NATIONS PUBLICATION
Sales No. E.87.II.D.12
ISBN 92-1-112238-4 ISSN 0257-7550

06000P

Contents

Part One

THE LEAST DEVELOPED COUNTRIES IN THE WORLD ECONOMY

Chapter I

Chapter II

Chapter III

Chapter IV

SELECTED ISSUES – LDCs' POLICIES ON HUMAN RESOURCES AND SOCIAL DEVELOPMENT

Part Two

DEVELOPMENT OF THE ECONOMIES OF INDIVIDUAL LEAST DEVELOPED COUNTRIES

Annex

Abbreviations

AAAID	Arab Authority for Agricultural Investment and Development
ACP	African, Caribbean and Pacific
AfDB	African Development Bank
AfDF	African Development Fund
AFESD	Arab Fund for Economic and Social Development
AFTAAC	Arab Fund for Technical Assistance to African and Arab Countries
APEC	Action Programme for Economic Co-operation among Non-Aligned and other Developing Countries
BADEA	Arab Bank for Economic Development in Africa
CAEU	Council for Arab Economic Unity
CDCC	Caribbean Development and Co-operation Committee
CEAO	West African Economic Community
CEEAC	Communauté économique des Etats de l'Afrique centrale
CEPGL	Economic Community of the Great Lakes Countries
c.i.f.	Cost, insurance, freight
CILSS	Permanent Inter-State Committee on Drought Control in the Sahel
CMEA	Council for Mutual Economic Assistance
CRS	Creditor Reporting System (OECD)
D	Dalasis
DAC	Development Assistance Committee (of OECD)
DRS	Debtor Reporting System (World Bank)
ECOWAS	Economic Community of West African States
EDF	European Development Fund
EEC	European Economic Community
EEZ	Exclusive Economic Zone
EIB	European Investment Bank
FAO	Food and Agriculture Organization of the United Nations
FBu	Burundi franc
f.o.b.	Free on board
FY	Fiscal year
GATT	General Agreement on Tariffs and Trade
GDP	Gross domestic product
GNP	Gross national product
GSP	Generalized system of preferences
IBRD	International Bank for Reconstruction and Development (World Bank)
ICA	International Commodity Agreement
ICARA	International Conference on Assistance to Refugees in Africa
IDA	International Development Association
IDB	Inter-American Development Bank
IFAD	International Fund for Agricultural Development
IFC	International Finance Corporation
IMF	International Monetary Fund
IPC	Integrated Programme for Commodities

kg	Kilograms
km	Kilometres
km ^{2}	Square kilometres
Kwh	Kilowatt/hours
LCBC	Lake Chad Basin Commission
M	Maloti
m ^{3}	Cubic metres
MFN	Most favoured nation
MRU	Mano River Union
mt	Metric tons
OAPEC	Organization of Arab Petroleum Exporting Countries
OAU	Organization of African Unity
OCAM	African and Mauritian Common Organization
ODA	Official development assistance
OECD	Organisation for Economic Co-operation and Development
OKB	Organization for the Planning and Development of the Kagera River Basin
OLADE	Latin American Energy Organization
OMVG	Gambia River Development Organization
OMVS	Organization for the Development of the Senegal River
OPEC	Organization of the Petroleum Exporting Countries
pop.	Population
PTA	Preferential Trade Area for Eastern and Southern African States
RF	Rwanda franc
SAAFA	Special Arab Aid Fund for Africa
SADCC	Southern African Development Co-ordination Conference
SDR	Special drawing right
SELA	Latin American Economic System
SITC	Standard International Trade Classification, Revision 1
Tk	Taka
UDEAC	Central African Customs and Economic Union
UNDP	United Nations Development Programme
UNDRO	Office of the United Nations Disaster Relief Co-ordinator
UNHCR	Office of the United Nations High Commissioner for Refugees
UNICEF	United Nations Children's Fund
UNIDO	United Nations Industrial Development Organization
UNTA	United Nations technical assistance
UNPAAERD	United Nations Programme of Action for African Economic Recovery and Development
WFP	World Food Programme

Explanatory notes

The term "dollars" ($) refers to United States dollars unless otherwise stated. The term "billion" signifies 1,000 million.

Annual rates of growth and change refer to compound rates. Exports are valued f.o.b. and imports c.i.f. unless otherwise specified.

Use of a hyphen (-) between dates representing years, e.g. 1970-1979, signifies the full period involved, including the initial and final years.

An oblique stroke (/) between two years, e.g., 1980/81, signifies a fiscal or crop year.

The abbreviation LDC (or LDCs) refers, throughout this report, to a country (or countries) included in the United Nations list of least developed countries.

National currencies have been converted into United States dollars at the rates published by the IMF in *International Financial Statistics*. For flow figures (e.g., foreign trade, budgetary receipts and expenditures, debt service and aid statistics) the *average* exchange rate for the corresponding period was chosen. For stock figures (e.g., outstanding debt and exchange reserves) the exchange rate for the corresponding date was chosen.

In the tables:

Two dots (..) indicate that the data are not available, or are not separately reported.

One dot (.) indicates that the data are not applicable.

A dash (—) indicates that the amount is nil or negligible.

A plus (+) before a figure indicates an increase; a minus sign (-) before a figure indicates a decrease. Details and percentages do not necessarily add up to totals, because of rounding.

Foreword

(i) The group of least developed countries (LDCs), which currently comprises 40 countries with a combined population of nearly 350 million, are the weakest partners in the international community. They are particularly handicapped and ill-equipped to develop their domestic economies and to ensure adequate living standards for their population. Their average GDP per capita is slightly higher than $200, which is only about 2 per cent of that of the developed market-economy countries. Most of them suffer from one or more important geographical or climatic handicaps, such as land-lockedness (15 countries), remote insularity (8), drought and desertification (22) and high exposure to disasters such as cyclones, floods and earthquakes. Their economic and social development thus represents a major challenge for these countries as well as for their development partners.

(ii) To respond to this challenge, the international community unanimously adopted in 1981 the Substantial New Programme of Action for the 1980s for the Least Developed Countries (SNPA). The SNPA provides for action to be taken by the least developed countries at the national level, as well as for measures of international support. The SNPA also contains provisions for specific follow-up action at the country, regional and global levels.

(iii) UNCTAD, the institution in which consideration of the special problems of the LDCs started, is entrusted by the SNPA with the focal role of monitoring its implementation at the global level. UNCTAD's Intergovernmental Group on the Least Developed Countries met at a high level in 1985 to carry out the Mid-term Global Review of the SNPA and agreed on a set of conclusions and recommendations to speed up the implementation of the SNPA. Subsequently, the problems of the least developed countries constituted one of the four substantive items on the agenda for the seventh session of UNCTAD, which took place in Geneva in July 1987. The Conference adopted a Final Act which stresses the need for the full and expeditious implementation of the SNPA and of recommendations of the Mid-term Review, and sets out measures to attain this objective.

(iv) As a contribution to the global monitoring exercise, the UNCTAD secretariat prepares annual reports on the least developed countries. The present report, which is the fourth in the series, reviews recent socio-economic developments in the least developed countries and progress in the implementation of support measures in the context of the present international economic environment. The report also contains the Basic Data on the Least Developed Countries, which the UNCTAD secretariat has prepared periodically for several years.

(v) The UNCTAD secretariat would like to take this opportunity to express its appreciation to the Governments members of UNCTAD and to international organizations which, by replying to its questionnaire on the implementation of the SNPA, provided useful inputs to this report. It would also like to thank the organizations of the United Nations system for their co-operation, which has greatly facilitated the preparation of this volume.

Part One

THE LEAST DEVELOPED COUNTRIES IN THE WORLD ECONOMY

INTRODUCTION

The least developed countries are highly sensitive, and vulnerable, to the vagaries of the world economy. With an extremely limited savings capacity, they need to turn towards the outside world in search of the financial resources required for their economic development. With a narrow export base, a large number of them are at the mercy of world demand for traditional commodities. As their domestic markets are small, their ability to enlarge their industrial base is determined essentially by the possibility of expanding and diversifying their exports. Given their inadequate technological infrastructure, they can only enhance industrial development by acquiring and adapting foreign know-how and technology. Dependence, rather than any quantitative estimate, is indeed the most meaningful indicator of least developed country status. Hence the importance for these countries of a supportive international economic environment.

Yet, during the 1980s, the international economic environment, in which the least developed countries have been striving to accelerate economic development and achieve the structural transformation of their economies, has been characterized by slackening world demand, depressed commodity markets, growing protectionist pressures, insufficient expansion of concessional flows, high real interest rates, and the virtual collapse of commercial bank lending to developing countries. The foreign exchange receipts of LDCs have thus shrunk. Concomitantly, their mounting external debt and debt-service requirements have, despite reschedulings, resulted in a considerable increase in capital outflows, a phenomenon which has led both to a severe depletion of their reserve holdings and to a smothering compression of their imports. Against this background, it is no wonder that the economic performance of the LDCs throughout the 1980s has fallen short of expectations.

A. Foreign exchange earnings

The real prices of non-fuel primary commodities exported by the developing countries (including LDCs) declined steeply between 1980 and 1986, reaching their lowest level since the 1930s. The terms of trade of the LDCs deteriorated markedly during 1981-1983, but have improved somewhat since then. A modest recovery of world trade in volume terms was registered in 1983/84, and again in 1986. Yet the actual gains of such an expansion for the LDCs as a whole have been very small and concentrated on a few commodities only.

The LDCs as net energy importers have benefited from lower energy prices in so far as their import bill is concerned. But the net effects of the price decline on their economies has been less favourable, and even negative, if account is taken of the fact that it has adversely affected the remittances of LDC nationals working in oil-producing countries as well as the volume of OPEC aid flows to LDCs. Migrants' remittances have been declining steadily since 1983, and are estimated to have fallen in 1986 below the levels of the early 1980s.

B. External financial flows

The policy shift in the major developed market-economy countries (DMECs) in the early 1980s, involving tighter monetary control, has had numerous adverse repercussions upon the financial liabilities of the LDCs as well as upon the flow of resources towards these countries:

(a) Tighter monetary control has entailed a reversal of past inflation trends that dominated the world economy at the time when developing countries, including LDCs, contracted their now huge external debt. The expected real value of debt service, given the ongoing monetary erosion, was then much lower than turned out to be the case after the reversal of inflation rates. Thus, LDCs, like many other developing countries, are now facing a debt-service burden whose real value could not be anticipated at the time the debt was contracted.

(b) The combination of tighter monetary control with lenient (budget-deficit) fiscal policies in major DMECs have led to a crowding out in financial markets and to high real interest rates in the 1980s. The opportunity cost of mobilizing financial assistance has increased as a result. This phenomenon has contributed to the slow growth of ODA flows to the LDCs throughout the 1980s contrary to commitments embodied in the SNPA.

(c) Tighter monetary control with lenient fiscal policies in major DMECs have further entailed a dramatic reorientation of resource flows towards developed countries with commercial and fiscal deficits. World financial resources have thereby been diverted away from the developing world, including the LDCs.

As a result of all these factors, the net financial flows to the LDCs have fluctuated around a declining trend throughout the early 1980s, with an upturn in 1985 and 1986 due principally to substantial increases in 1985 in emergency aid to African countries and, in 1986, to the appreciation of the currencies of major donors against the United States dollar (in which aid flows are calculated).

C. Implications for LDCs' development

The adverse international economic environment of the 1980s has had profound implications for the economic development of the LDCs. Their serious economic and social problems have been aggravated, and the modest gains of past economic development eroded (cf. ch. I). Most LDCs have had to cut back imports, particularly of capital goods and intermediate products, to abandon national development programmes and to undergo a process of forced adjustment with austerity. The ensuing fall in investment, and deterioration of productive capacity and physical infrastructure, have impaired the LDCs' ability to resume growth and development and to meet the basic needs of their population. At the present time, more than six years after the SNPA was adopted, LDCs, are in many crucial respects, in a worse position than they were in 1981.

D. Action by LDCs

The least developed countries have not remained passive *vis-à-vis* their mounting economic problems (cf. ch. II). During the 1980s, far-reaching policy reforms have been undertaken by most LDCs with a view, in particular, to mobilizing domestic resources and creating a propitious socio-economic environment for development consonant with provisions of the SNPA. Greater attention is being given to strengthening economic and financial management and to expanding food and agricultural production. In a number of cases, measures have been taken in the context of stabilization and structural adjustment programmes. These countries need to persevere in their efforts and, in some cases and areas, to improve and intensify them. But action by these countries alone, courageous as it may be, will not be sufficient without complementary support measures by the international community.

E. Recent international policy initiatives

Several positive developments have recently taken place as a somewhat belated response to the urgent financial resource needs of the LDCs (cf. ch. III). Firstly, multilateral assistance to LDCs has been increasing, notably through World Bank and IMF facilities. Secondly, the Paris Club has been extending longer grace and repayment periods to LDCs in recent debt reschedulings, and the application of lower interest rates is under consideration. Thirdly, Japan has expressed its intention of stepping up significantly its role in international development and development assistance, an intention which it is hoped will have positive implications for the flow of resources towards the LDCs. Fourthly, new compensatory financing arrangements and measures are being instituted, in particular by the EEC (for those LDCs not signatories of the Lomé Convention) and by Switzerland (for commodity-exporting countries, including the poorest [1] of its trading partners). Finally, the seventh session

---

[1] Unlike the term "least developed countries", that of "poorest countries" (which is sometimes used by donor countries and institutions) does not have any specific official definition, nor is there any official list of countries in this regard. This latter term, however, generally includes all least developed countries or is used as a synonym therefor.

of UNCTAD adopted by consensus a Final Act which contains a section specifically devoted to the LDCs, with a comprehensive set of provisions regarding both national and supportive international efforts to promote the development of these countries.

All these initiatives allow the hope to be entertained that the international community will in the future be more forthcoming in responding to the difficult situation of the LDCs.

Chapter I

RECENT SOCIO-ECONOMIC TRENDS

A. Overall economic growth

Despite their development efforts,[2] the performance of the LDCs in the first half of the 1980s has been disappointing. Their average per capita GDP, after a modest increase in 1981, declined for four years in succession, reaching a level slightly above $200 in 1985, which is only about 2 per cent of the average per capita GDP of developed market-economy countries. This dismal growth performance has been widespread inasmuch as almost three-fifths of the 40 LDCs registered declines in per capita GDP during that period[3] (see table 1). However provisional data for 1986 indicate that the decline for the LDCs as a group was halted.

The overall economic performance of the LDCs has been to a large extent determined by the performance of the agricultural sector, which accounts for about two-fifths of GDP in these countries. Agricultural production declined in per capita terms in each of the first four years of the 1980s. The impact of the drought in Africa has been particularly catastrophic for the LDCs in the region.

The adverse external environment prevailing in the 1980s, notably the state of the primary commodities markets, is another major determinant of the poor growth performance of the LDCs. The large number of LDCs heavily dependent on agricultural or mineral exports (over two-thirds of the total) performed less well during the 1980s than those whose exports are not based mainly on primary commodities. Thus the median GDP growth rate between 1980 and 1985 of the services and mixed-basket-exporting LDCs was considerably higher than that of the LDCs exporting agricultural products, while the LDCs exporting mineral products fared even worse, albeit after an above-average performance during the 1970s (see table 2).

During the period 1980 to 1985, two individual LDCs – Botswana and the Maldives – were nevertheless able to surpass the growth rate of 7.2 per cent annually, the target established by the SNPA and required to double output in a decade. In terms of economic size, these countries are among the smallest of the LDCs. In Botswana, the expansion of exports (especially diamonds) and, in the Maldives, the development of services (tourism), contributed to this high rate of growth and helped release the foreign exchange constraint. The performance of these countries represented a continuation of a very fast growth path already established in the 1970s.

Two other LDCs – Bhutan and Cape Verde – managed to come close to the target, attaining annual rates of GDP growth of almost 7 per cent, while three LDCs – Lao PDR, Uganda and Yemen – recorded rates of around 5 per cent, and six countries achieved rates of nearly 4 per cent. The others (the majority) barely managed to keep their output ahead of population growth or, saw their GDP per capita decline (see table 1).[4]

---

[2] See chapter III where recent policy developments in LDCs are discussed.

[3] It should be noted that, in the 1980s, owing to increasing interest payments and deteriorating terms of trade, real national income (or GNP) of the LDCs performed even worse than GDP.

[4] However, the number of LDCs registering negative GDP growth rates has tended to decline; similarly the number of LDCs with GDP growth rates below the rate of population increase fell from over 20 in the early 1980s to 13 in 1985 and 9 in 1986.

TABLE 1

LDC: Population and GDP growth by country

	Population		GDP per capita (dollars)	Real GDP	
				Total	Per capita
	Level (mill.)	Growth (%)		(annual average growth rate (%))	
	1985	1980-1985	1985	1980-1985	1980-1985
Afghanistan	18.1	2.6	210[a]	2.9	0.3
Bangladesh	98.7	2.2	163	3.9	1.7
Benin	4.0	3.1	253	4.2	1.0
Bhutan	1.4	2.1	133	6.6	4.5
Botswana	1.1	3.9	855	10.8	6.6
Burkina Fasso	6.9	2.4	134	2.2	− 0.2
Burundi	4.7	2.9	232	3.1	0.3
Cape Verde	0.3	2.5	353	6.5	4.0
Central African Republic	2.6	2.4	259	0.6	− 1.8
Chad	5.0	2.2	128	− 4.4	− 6.4
Comoros	0.4	3.1	219	4.1	1.0
Democratic Yemen . . .	2.3	3.1	420[b]	1.9[e]	− 1.1[e]
Djibouti	0.4	3.3	567[c]	1.3	− 1.9
Equatorial Guinea. . . .	0.4	2.2	192	2.5	0.3
Ethiopia	43.4	2.8	109	− 0.0	− 2.8
Gambia	0.7	2.7	213	− 0.5	− 3.1
Guinea	6.1	2.4	349	0.7	− 1.6
Guinea-Bissau	0.9	1.9	152	3.5	1.6
Haiti	5.3	1.4	350[b]	− 0.4	− 1.8
Kiribati	0.1	2.0	317[c]	− 0.0	− 2.0
Lao People's Democratic Republic.	3.6	2.0	386	5.4	3.3
Lesotho	1.5	2.6	167	0.1	− 2.4
Malawi	6.9	3.1	156	1.2	− 1.9
Maldives	0.2	3.0	432[b]	10.0	6.8
Mali	8.1	2.8	143	− 0.4	− 3.1
Mauritania	1.9	3.0	366	1.5	− 1.4
Nepal	16.6	2.5	141	4.1	1.6
Niger	6.1	2.9	258	− 2.5	− 5.2
Rwanda	6.0	3.2	274[b]	4.2	0.9
Samoa	0.2	0.9	539	− 1.1	− 2.0
Sao Tome and Principe	0.1	2.9	324	− 3.6	− 6.3
Sierra Leone	3.6	1.8	324	1.8	0.0
Somalia	5.4	2.9	261[b]	4.1	1.2
Sudan	21.5	2.9	406	− 1.3	− 4.1
Togo	3.0	3.0	235	− 1.3	− 4.2
Tuvalu	0.0	1.2	245[c]	0.0	0.0
Uganda	15.5	3.4	220[d]	5.0	1.6
United Republic of Tanzania.	22.2	3.5	279	1.3	− 2.1
Vanuatu	0.1	2.8	499	2.4	− 0.4
Yemen	8.0	2.5	482[b]	5.6	3.1
ALL LDCs	333.5	2.6	215	2.0	− 0.8

Source: UNCTAD secretariat calculations based on data from the United Nations Statistical Office, the Economic Commission for Africa, the World Bank and other international and national sources.

[a] 1981.

[b] 1984.

[c] Income accruing to indigenous population.

[d] GNP per capita in 1984.

[e] 1980-1984.

TABLE 2

Median GDP growth rates of LDCs according to major exports[a]

Export category[b]	Number of LDCs in group		Annual growth (per cent)	
	1970–1980	1980–1985	1970–1980	1980–1985
Agricultural[c]	17	20	2.2	1.3
Mineral	7	7	3.9	0.7
Services[d]	4	5	2.2	5.6
Mixed[e]	5	6	2.3	4.0
TOTAL	33	38	3.3	1.5

Source: UNCTAD secretariat calculations based on data from the United Nations Statistical Office, the Economic Commission for Africa, the World Bank and other national and international sources.

[a] In the case of an even number of observations, the arithmetic mean between the two median rates is used.

[b] If none of the first three categories accounts for 50 per cent of the export value in 1980, the country is classified as mixed.

[c] Including forestry and fisheries.

[d] Excluding factor services.

[e] Including manufactures.

As regards future prospects, it has now become evident that the SNPA growth objective of doubling 1980 output by 1990 is realistic for a small minority of the LDCs only. Even the mere recovery of real per capita output to the levels prevailing in 1981, i.e. at the outset of the SNPA, would require the maintenance of a total GDP growth rate of 3.1 per cent throughout the remainder of the 1980s (on the assumption that the average population growth rate stabilizes at 2.6 per cent per annum). The high growth rates achieved by a few LDCs in the first half of the 1980s, however, demonstrated that the SNPA target is within reach given an appropriate domestic and external environment; a continuation of current adverse external conditions would, on the other hand, make it difficult for the LDCs to recover, let alone surpass, their 1981 per capita output levels by the end of this decade.

Recent short-term forecasts for the world economy by the secretariats of the OECD, the IMF and the United Nations all point to a continuation of the present slow pace of world output growth, although the United Nations Secretariat is slightly less pessimistic than those of the IMF and OECD.[5] As regards world trade, a small increase of between 3 and 4 per cent in volume terms is expected for the years 1987-1988.[6] The IMF also provides forecasts for the terms of trade and shows, for the category of small low-income countries, deteriorations of 3.6 and 1.3 per cent for 1987 and 1988 respectively.[7]

---

[5] OECD, *Economic Outlook* (July 1987); IMF, *World Economic Outlook*, (October 1987); United Nations, *World Economic Survey 1987.*

[6] GATT forecasts about 3 1/2 per cent in 1987 (GATT, *International Trade*, 1986/87).

[7] The IMF's country grouping of small low-income countries comprises 41 developing countries including 31 LDCs (see IMF, *World Economic Outlook* (April 1987), p. 112.

B. Investment and savings

The stark reality is that LDCs have been compressing their investment throughout the 1980s. Table 4 shows that only in the first year of the decade 1980-81 did LDCs as a whole register a growth in investment – of 3.6 per cent. For the 22 LDCs for which data are available, the rate of investment declined by 2.5 per cent during 1980-1985. For the LDCs as a group, the share of gross capital formation in GDP thus declined from 16 per cent in 1980 to 12 per cent in 1985. In the overwhelming majority of LDCs for which this information is available, the share declined or stagnated in relation to GDP. Provisional data for 1986 indicate that the declining trend for the LDCs as a group continued. As a result the per capita level of LDC investment in 1985 is pitifully low, at $30, with damaging effects on LDCs' medium-term growth prospects.

Many LDCs experiencing low or negative economic growth were obliged to compress their already limited domestic savings even further, so as to maintain minimal consumption levels. Moreover, with increasingly limited foreign exchange

TABLE 3

**Distribution of LDCs by average annual growth of GDP,
1970 – 1985[a]**

(*Number of countries*)

Growth of GDP	1970–1980	1980–1985	1980–1981	1981–1982	1982–1983	1983–1984	1984–1985	1985–1986
7.2 per cent and above	4	2	9	9	2	7	5	3
3 per cent up to 7.1 per cent . . .	14	13	9	9	14	8	15	11
0 per cent up to 2.9 per cent . . .	13	13	9	10	7	13	13	7
Below 0 per cent	3	11[b]	12	11	16	11	5	3
TOTAL	34	39	39	39	39	39	38	24
Below population growth	12	21	20	20	23	19	13	9

Source: UNCTAD secretariat calculations based on national and international sources.

[a] The growth rates for the period 1970-1980 are based on an exponential trend function.

[b] Including one country for the period 1980-1984.

availabilities, LDCs were forced to reduce their imports of capital goods and thus to cut back on their investment plans. The exports of capital goods from the developed market economies to the LDCs, expressed in constant values at 1980 prices, decreased from around $2.4 billion in 1980-1982 to $2.1 billion in 1983-1984. In 1985 they recovered to $2.4 billion, but fell again to a low of $2.0 billion in 1986 (see table 5).

The saving capacity of the LDCs continues to be constrained. The adverse effects of the critical world economic situation in the 1980s, as well as the economic hardship caused by famine and other disasters, have further limited the savings possibilities of these countries whose income levels are barely sufficient for them to survive. In addition, the institutional framework necessary for collect-

ing and channelling savings into productive investment is still rather rudimentary in many LDCs. Domestic savings thus represent in most LDCs only a small fraction of the total finance for investment. In a number of cases savings were negative, often for consecutive years (see table 6).

A major savings effort is made by LDC nationals working abroad, mainly in oil-exporting countries, with the result that the national savings of these LDCs are about twice the level of their domestic savings. It should be noted, however, that this form of savings is concentrated in a limited number of countries only, the most important ones being Bangladesh, Democratic Yemen, Lesotho, Sudan and Yemen, and that such revenue streams are sensitive to policy decisions taken by other Governments.

TABLE 4

Investment [a] in the LDCs

Country	Per capita levels ($) 1985	Annual average growth rates [b]					
		1980–1985	1980–1981	1981–1982	1982–1983	1983–1984	1984–1985
Afghanistan	..	..	..	..	..	..	..
Bangladesh	19	2.7	2.8	– 5.7	– 6.2	11.7	12.4
Benin	35	– 12.5	13.8	7.0	– 53.4	– 20.9	14.0
Bhutan.	..	..	..	..	..	..	..
Botswana	225	– 3.4	1.8	– 3.5	– 30.7	– 2.1	26.0
Burkina Faso	11	– 10.3	– 19.1	– 1.4	– 26.2	– 26.5	34.4
Burundi	36	22.0[h]	37.6	– 25.0	75.8	..	..
Cape Verde	178	10.4	56.7	4.3	5.9	– 9.6	4.8
Central African Republic	39	13.2	21.7	– 8.9	47.8	10.3	2.7
Chad	8	– 16.1	– 32.6	– 29.4	– 13.6	– 5.5	7.1
Comoros.	90	5.1	– 16.2	1.4	11.6	58.7	– 14.6
Democratic Yemen	..	..	..	..	..	..	..
Djibouti	132	5.3	27.8	10.1	1.8	– 6.1	– 3.8
Equatorial Guinea	28	1.4	5.2	3.6	– 7.0	3.3	2.6
Ethiopia	11	– 0.3	3.4	9.2	0.7	11.2	– 22.0
Gambia	46	– 6.2	– 2.3	– 17.6	7.6	– 32.6	24.3
Guinea.	33	– 7.8	– 9.1	– 1.3	2.8	– 23.1	– 6.1
Guinea-Bissau	61	4.3	– 16.5	28.3	– 3.9	3.8	15.5
Haiti	55[d]	0.9[i]	0.7	– 6.8	5.4	4.8	..

TABLE 4 *(continued)*

Investment [a] **in the LDCs**

Country	Per capita levels ($) 1985	Annual average growth rates [b]					
		1980–1985	1980–1981	1981–1982	1982–1983	1983–1984	1984–1985
Kiribati	..	..	..	..	..	..	..
Lao People's Democratic Republic	96	..	..	– 2.1	..	..	..
Lesotho	61	2.7	2.4	– 2.1	4.3	9.5	– 0.1
Malawi.	24	– 5.8 [i]	– 32.8	33.4	14.9	– 23.6	..
Maldives.	133 [d]	..	..	0.9	62.4	– 6.8	..
Mali	47	..	..	..	..	..	..
Mauritania	87	– 3.5	23.4	26.2	– 60.2	23.0	9.9
Nepal	29	6.7	4.3	– 0.6	18.4	3.0	9.5
Niger.	35	– 6.2 [h]	3.6	– 15.4	– 5.7	..	..
Rwanda	53 [e]	..	10.5	..	..	..	..
Samoa	168	– 13.1 [h]	5.3	– 33.7	– 5.9	..	..
Sao Tome and Principe	120	1.7	– 6.7	36.6	– 34.9	59.8	– 18.2
Sierra Leone	24	– 13.2	– 15.9	– 13.9	– 7.6	– 10.3	– 17.9
Somalia	70 [f]	88.3 [i]	261.8	– 2.0	..	..	..
Sudan	29	– 15.3	4.1	7.8	– 7.3	– 18.1	– 48.8
Togo	62	– 4.3	– 3.9	– 16.3	– 18.9	– 0.4	23.8
Tuvalu.	..	..	..	..	..	..	..
Uganda	18 [g]	21.4 [i]	22.3	20.5	..	..	..
United Republic of Tanzania . . .	41	0.1	12.3	– 4.7	– 19.2	– 10.6	30.1
Vanuatu	145	..	..	..	..	..	..
Yemen	101 [d]	– 14.9 [i]	– 13.9	– 6.8	– 28.7	– 8.2	..
ALL LDCs [c]	30	– 2.5	3.6	– 0.3	– 12.4	– 2.9	0.2

Source: UNCTAD secretariat calculations based on data from the United Nations Statistical Office, the Economic Commission for Africa, the World Bank and other international and national sources.

[a] Gross fixed capital formation plus increase in stocks.

[b] Real investment.

[c] Growth rates relate to countries for which data are available for all years (1980-1885).

[d] 1984.   [e] 1981.   [f] 1982.   [g] 1983.

[h] 1980-1983.   [i] 1980-1984.   [j] 1980-1982.

TABLE 5

Exports of capital goods from the developed market economies to the LDCs [a]

	1980	1981	1982	1983	1984	1985	1986 [b]
	(Millions of dollars)						
Developed market economies [c] . .	2 516	2 219	2 138	1 876	1 745	2 001	2 256
North America	287	303	268	222	257	249	233
Western Europe [d].	1 833	1 522	1 553	1 356	1 207	1 419	1 528
of which: EEC	1 685	1 401	1 389	1 244	1 097	1 294	1 358
Japan	384	385	307	287	270	320	482
	(Millions of dollars at 1980 prices)						
Developed market economies [c] . .	2 516	2 458	2 443	2 170	2 114	2 436	2 042

Source: UNCTAD secretariat calculations based on UN-COMTRADE data base and United Nations, *Monthly Bulletin of Statistics*, various issues.

[a] Capital goods are defined according to the System of National Accounts, by aggregating group 41 (machinery and other capital equipment) and group 521 (industrial transport equipment) of the United Nations classification, *Broad Economic Categories*, Series M, No. 53.

[b] Preliminary.

[c] Excluding Gibraltar, South Africa and Israel; including Australia and New Zealand.

[d] Excluding Gibraltar.

TABLE 6

Gross domestic savings as a percentage of investment

Country	1980	1981	1982	1983	1984	1985
Afghanistan	..	..	..	..	..	..
Bangladesh	22.3	15.0	16.0	34.5	41.7	51.7
Benin	− 78.2	− 77.4	− 7.7	0.5	− 95.2	− 6.1
Bhutan.	..	..	..	..	..	..
Botswana	69.6	51.4	17.5	57.2	97.5	97.2
Burkina Faso	− 95.7	− 125.9	− 104.1	− 184.0	− 228.1	− 138.4
Burundi	− 2.7	32.6	− 7.1	36.3	23.3	22.7
Cape Verde	− 81.3	− 36.1	− 27.1	− 26.9	− 19.2	− 22.7
Central African Republic	− 137.3	− 21.2	− 141.7	− 49.3	− 30.4	11.5
Chad.	− 35.3	− 42.0	− 65.4	− 38.3	− 24.9	3.6
Comoros.	36.6	33.8	39.2	37.9	19.4	20.8
Democratic Yemen	..	..	..	..	..	..
Djibouti	− 26.5	− 15.3	− 11.6	− 23.6	− 39.9	− 55.5
Equatorial Guinea	− 49.4	− 19.7	− 6.4	13.6	41.8	93.7
Ethiopia	48.1	44.9	25.3	17.6	11.6	− 61.1
Gambia	19.5	− 23.7	15.0	44.4	14.2	1.6
Guinea.	136.9	123.8	118.5	114.2	135.7	138.9
Guinea-Bissau	− 20.2	4.7	− 18.4	− 5.6	− 14.8	− 20.8
Haiti	28.1	− 11.0	19.3	20.8	26.6	..
Kiribati	..	..	..	..	..	..
Lao People's Democratic Republic	..	..	..	..	..	..
Lesotho	− 169.0	− 231.2	− 290.0	− 250.3	− 226.1	− 237.0
Malawi.	43.4	67.1	70.3	66.8	119.2	68.1
Maldives.	..	..	..	..	61.5	..
Mali	..	30.1	43.1	32.2	37.0	35.5
Mauritania	19.0	30.1	6.4	− 61.3	− 7.4	37.6
Nepal	60.7	61.9	41.9	42.9	53.1	57.5
Niger.	61.6	42.9	35.1	58.2	..	35.8
Rwanda	41.4	35.8	..	..	..	..
Samoa	− 13.8	− 41.6	− 36.5	− 7.1	0.7	− 22.1
Sao Tome and Principe	− 43.5	− 63.5	− 48.1	− 43.5	− 25.3	− 48.8
Sierra Leone	17.0	26.0	3.1	46.5	73.7	88.7
Somalia	− 255.8	47.9	− 9.4	..	..	..
Sudan	22.7	16.2	− 16.0	5.0	17.1	− 49.1
Togo	50.1	48.9	46.5	61.9	69.3	57.9
Tuvalu.	..	..	..	..	..	..
Uganda	..	..	..	..	..	..
United Republic of Tanzania . . .	41.1	63.2	49.2	52.5	41.7	18.3
Vanuatu	..	..	..	87.4	123.2	91.0
Yemen	− 60.9	− 53.8	− 76.0	− 112.2	− 107.1	..
ALL LDCs[a]	23.4	25.2	11.8	24.4	30.6	21.9

Source: UNCTAD secretariat calculations based on data from the United Nations Statistical Office, the Economic Commission for Africa, the World Bank and other international and national sources.

[a] Shares relate to those countries for which data are available for all years (1980-1985).

Investment is now in urgent need of revival through a restoration of international resource flows to supplement domestic savings. For most LDCs this can only be done through the provision of grants and soft loans from the official sector. It should be noted that LDCs in general have not been successful in attracting foreign direct investment.[8]

_____

[8] See section B.2 of chapter II below.

C. The external sector

1. *Exports*

(a) *General trends*

Although there has been a modest expansion in the volume of LDC exports during the 1980s, the value of their exports decreased from $8.0 billion in 1980 to $7.6 billion in 1986 (see table 7). The increase in export volume was mainly due to a recovery of production and exports of coffee to the levels of the early 1970s in a few countries, and to a sharp increase of diamond exports in one country. In 1986, the volume of world merchandise trade is estimated to have increased by 3 1/2 per cent, with an increase of similar magnitude expected in 1987.[9] But little of this recovery is being transmitted to developing countries. Commodity prices in general are at their lowest level in real terms for half a century. In 1986, the prices of primary commodities dropped to 21 per cent below the 1979-1981 average, and fell by another 8 per cent in the first half of 1987. For the LDCs, still highly dependent on exports of non-fuel primary commodities, the current world trade situation has been described as a "particularly worrying" development.[10]

The number of individual LDCs which succeeded in expanding the value of their exports in the 1980s has declined. For instance, in the first half of the 1980s, only 19 LDCs registered a positive annual average growth rate, as compared to 35 in the 1970s. In contrast, the number of LDCs with declining export value rose sharply to 18 as compared to only 2 in the 1970s (see table 8). Provisional figures for 1986 show that the value of exports decreased in more than one-third of the LDCs as compared to 1985.

Until 1985, the effect of declining export prices had been mitigated to some extent by declining import prices of capital goods and other manufactures. European and Japanese quotations declined in terms of dollars when the dollar rose sharply with respect to other major currencies. However, in 1986 and in the first half of 1987 when the dollar declined, dollar-denominated prices of manufactured imports rose accordingly, causing a further fall in primary commodity exporters' terms of trade. Information available for the first half of 1987 indicates that this downward trend can be expected to continue. The medium-term outlook for primary non-fuel commodity prices is not bright. There are indeed no indications that the factors that have been depressing such prices will be changing in the near future.[11] This prospect is particularly serious for LDCs. Over the period 1980-85, falling export earnings and other balance-of-payments difficulties obliged half of the LDCs to cut back on imports. This meant reducing their capital goods imports and therefore directly sacrificing future economic growth.[12]

---

[9] GATT, *International Trade 1986/87*, chapter 1, released on 25 September 1987, Geneva.

[10] *Ibid.*, p. 14.

[11] According to IMF projections, real commodity prices in 1991 will be about one third below their level in 1980. See IMF, *World Economic Outlook, 1987*, p. 96.

[12] A matter treated in greater detail in section 2 below (Imports).

TABLE 7

Growth of world merchandise exports by selected economic groupings, 1970-1986

	1970	1980	1985	1986[a]	1970–1980	1980–1985	1985–1986
		(billions of dollars)			(Annual average growth rate)		
World	316.9	2 027.3	1 150.8	1 930.3	20.4	− 0.9	− 1.1
Developing countries	58.3	582.6	474.7	433.8	26.1	− 4.3	− 8.6
Major petroleum exporters	21.1	343.0	194.3	143.1	31.8	− 11.6	− 26.3
Other developing countries	37.2	239.7	280.4	290.7	21.1	3.5	3.6
Major exporters of manufactures .	10.8	104.6	147.9	162.9	25.5	− 7.2	10.1
Least developed countries[b]	2.5	8.0	7.6	7.6	12.9	− 0.3	− 0.2
Remaining countries	23.8	127.1	124.9	120.2	19.1	0.2	− 3.8

Source: UNCTAD secretariat based on international and national sources.

[a] Preliminary estimates.

[b] Excluding Bhutan and Tuvalu.

TABLE 8

**Distribution of LDCs by average annual rate of growth of export
and import values, 1970-1986** [a]

(Number of countries)

	Exports			Imports		
	1970–1980	1980–1985	1985–1986	1970–1980	1980–1985	1985–1986
10 per cent and more	25	6	5	30	4	3
5 per cent up to 10 per cent . . .	7	8	4	4	5	1
0 per cent up to 5 per cent. . . .	3	5	13	2	9	21
–5 per cent up to 0 per cent. . . .	2	8	8	0	8	4
Less than –5 per cent	0	10	7	1	11	8
TOTAL [b]	37	37	37	37	37	37

Source: UNCTAD secretariat based on international and national sources.

[a] Exponential trend function.

[b] Excluding Bhutan, Kiribati and Tuvalu.

(b) *Developments in individual commodities*

Coffee is the LDCs' most important export product, representing in 1985 $1,076 million in value or 14.1 per cent of their total merchandise exports. Almost 90 per cent of their coffee exports originated in six countries – Burundi, Ethiopia, Haiti, Rwanda, Uganda and the United Republic of Tanzania. The unit value of LDCs' coffee exports in 1985 was 16 per cent below its 1980 level. World prices recovered in the beginning of 1986 to almost the record levels of 1977, but by the first half of 1987, prices were falling again, dropping to the lowest levels yet recorded in the 1980s.

Diamonds are the LDCs' second most important export product in terms of value, i.e. $648 million in 1985 or 8.5 per cent of total LDC exports. The LDCs' share in the 1980s amounted to about 20 per cent compared to 8 per cent at the beginning of the 1970s.[13] Diamond production has become increasingly concentrated in one country, Botswana. Sierra Leone's exports declined to only $24 million in 1985, while exports from the smaller LDC producers – the Central African Republic, Lesotho and the United Republic of Tanzania – have been stagnant or have declined in the 1980s. More recently, Guinea increased its production considerably, with exports rising in value to $26 million in 1985 and to $46 million in 1986.

With an export value of $515 million in 1985 or 6.7 per cent of the total, *cotton* is the LDCs' third export product. There was a 5.3 per cent annual expansion of the volume exported in the 1980s as compared to an average annual decline of 3.4 per cent in the 1970s. All LDC exporters, however, suffered from the severe world price falls for cotton in the first half of the 1980s, some responding with cutbacks in acreage planted. World prices improved in 1986-1987, but this may be only a temporary phenomenon.

The LDCs' exports of *raw jute* and *jute products* accounted in 1985 for $151 million and $350 million respectively, or altogether 6.6 per cent of total exports. These exports originated mainly in Bangladesh, with smaller amounts coming from Bhutan and Nepal. Jute prices, which were already in a long-standing decline, fell further at the onset of the world recession in 1981, but recovered in 1985. Thus, although the jute exported by LDCs in 1985 was 31 per cent below its 1980 level in terms of volume, its value remained the same. Producers may have overreacted to these high prices, by sharply increasing their volume of exports, which led again to extremely low prices in 1986. With respect to jute products, prices declined in the early 1980s but recovered in 1985 almost to their 1980 level.

With an export value of $414 million in 1985, representing 5.5 per cent of LDCs' total exports, *bauxite* is their fifth export product, the bulk of it coming from Guinea. Guinea also produces and exports alumina. In the 1980s the export volumes increased modestly, though at a lower rate than in the late 1970s, and world prices were also much lower. The world price for alumina however enjoyed a brief boom in 1987.

---

[13] In the 1970s and up to 1983, world production of natural rough diamonds had been about 47 million carats annually. Production increased by almost 22 per cent in 1983 and is estimated to have reached a level of 89 million carats in 1986.

Table 9

Principal export products of the LDCs

	Value in 1985			Average annual growth rate of volume in %		Volume index 1980=100	
	Millions of dollars	Share in per cent	Index 1980=100	1970-80	1980-85	1970	1985
COFFEE							
Burundi	94.2	8.8	162	0.0	9.1	112	184
Ethiopia	209.0	19.4	77	− 0.6	− 1.2	93	89
Rwanda	61.3	5.7	139	7.9	7.2	61	153
Uganda	420.5	39.1	124	− 5.9	4.5	174	138
United Republic of Tanzania .	113.6	10.6	79	0.4	− 1.2	104	98
Other LDCs[a]	177.5	16.5	94	− 3.8	1.4	118	114
All LDCs	*1076.1*	*100.0*	*103*	*− 2.7*	*2.6*	*125*	*121*
DIAMONDS							
Botswana	564.6	87.2	185	..	..	..	..
Other LDCs[b]	83.1	12.8	29	..	..	..	..
All LDCs	*647.7*	*100.0*	*109*	*2.0[c]*	*5.7[c]*	*82[c]*	*132[c]*
COTTON							
Benin	29.7	5.8	254	− 10.3	26.8	133	268
Burkina Faso	26.2	5.1	66	9.5	1.2	48	118
Chad	70.0	13.6	179	1.7	6.1	112	124
Mali	98.5	19.1	125	14.5	5.8	27	116
Sudan	163.6	31.8	69	− 4.9	8.3	174	76
United Republic of Tanzania .	40.8	7.9	84	− 5.6	− 4.3	193	85
Other LDCs[b]	85.9	16.7	86	− 8.4	− 0.3	192	99
All LDCs	*514.5*	*100.0*	*95*	*− 3.4*	*5.3*	*140*	*98*
JUTE PRODUCTS							
Bangladesh	339.1	96.8	91	4.2	− 1.3	84	97
Other LDCs[b]	11.3	3.2	123	1.5	12.6	106	141
All LDCs	*350.4*	*100.0*	*92*	*4.1*	*− 1.0*	*85*	*98*
JUTE							
Bangladesh	148.2	98.1	107	− 4.0	− 3.9	186	74
Other LDCs[b]	2.8	1.9	23	9.4	− 31.3	45	21
All LDCs	*151.0*	*100.0*	*100*	*− 3.3*	*− 5.9*	*173*	*69*
BAUXITE							
Guinea	390.0	94.2	115	40.5	5.9	8	134
Other LDCs[b]	23.9	5.8	72	1.5	− 4.4	85	83
All LDCs	*413.9*	*100.0*	*111*	*26.3*	*5.0*	*16*	*128*
BOVINE CATTLE							
Chad	81.7	33.9	115	2.2	− 5.6	78	67
Mali	52.0	21.6	65	4.0	− 7.2	48	57
Mauritania	20.0	8.3	91	− 1.7	− 3.0	111	89
Niger	51.0	21.2	161	1.6	1.2	115	120
Other LDCs	36.4	15.1	59	− 2.9	− 12.8	110	63
All LDCs	*241.0*	*100.0*	*90*	*0.8*	*− 5.7*	*83*	*72*
URANIUM							
Niger	213.5	100.0	46	..	− 4.3	0	80

Source: UNCTAD secretariat calculations based on FAO and other international and national sources.

[a] Calculated on the basis of an exponential trend function.

[b] LDCs with a value share in 1985 smaller than 5 per cent of the total.

[c] Estimates.

Bovine cattle exports declined in terms of volume by about one quarter in the first half of the 1980s. Their export value also declined, but less steeply, to $241 million in 1985, as prices improved. The declines were recorded by all major exporters except Niger.

Although *uranium ore* is exported by only one LDC, its export value in 1985 amounted to

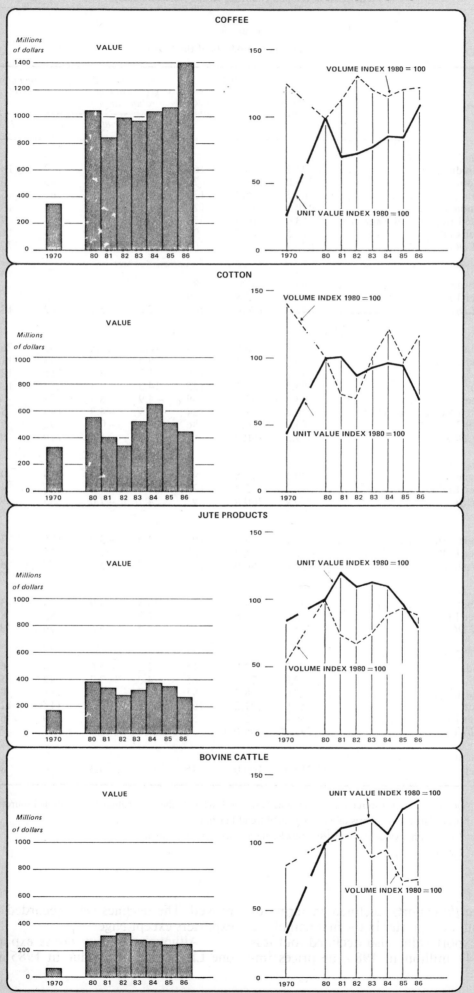

Source: UNCTAD secretariat calculations based on FAO and other international and national publications.

CHART 1b
Values and indices of volume and unit value for the LDCs' principal export products

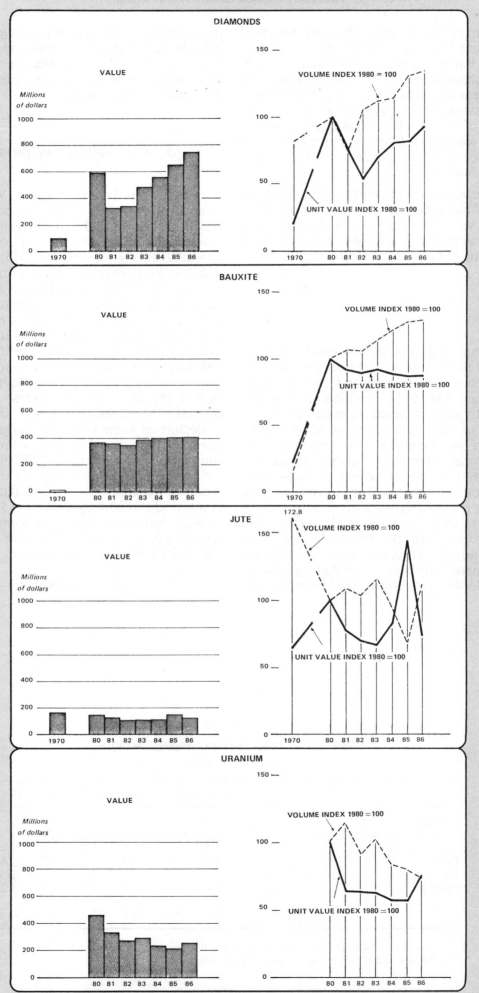

Source: UNCTAD secretariat calculations based on FAO and other international and national publications.

$214 million, or 2.8 per cent of the total exports of LDCs. In that same year Niger's production accounted for 9 per cent of the world total. In 1985, world production was 15 per cent lower than in the preceding year owing to increased energy conservation measures and to a virtual halt in the commissioning of new nuclear plants, while Niger's production was cut back by 27 per cent. In 1986, the unit value of Niger's exports was only 75 per cent of its 1980 level.

This brief description of the recent evolution of the LDCs' most important export products illustrates how varied the experience of individual LDCs has been in this area. For most of them, developments have been unfavourable.

2. *Imports*

The imports of the LDCs are more than twice the value of their exports if measured on an f.o.b. basis. In terms of value, imports declined from $16.1 billion in 1980 to $15.0 billion in 1986. This decline partly reflects the falling prices of imports from some of the major suppliers of the LDCs, especially in the case of fuels. In terms of volume, LDC imports have remained virtually stagnant. In table 10 estimates are presented for imports by major economic categories. The structure of these imports has changed significantly in recent years. Fuel imports were cut back in the early 1980s owing to economic shocks, but by the mid-1980s LDCs were adjusting to lower import volumes and benefiting marginally from the weakening in prices and in the dollar. On the other hand, as mentioned

in section B (Investment and savings) above, there have been significant cutbacks in capital goods imports since 1980. Such cutbacks may well have a direct negative impact on LDC growth rates, both now and in future years.

3. *The balance of payments*

In the first three years of the 1980s the LDCs' balance of payments showed a current account deficit of about $8.3 billion, while from 1983 onwards they were obliged to reduce this deficit to an annual average of some $6.7 billion. The reduction has been obtained mainly by compressing imports. Above all, the reduction from 1982 onwards of net capital flows has meant that LDCs are no longer able to finance such large current account imbalances. The balance of interest receipts and payments deteriorated considerably in the 1980s as receipts decreased owing to the decline in reserve holdings and the lower amounts of interest earned on them, while interest payments increased.[14] Migrants' remittances too have started to decline in some countries, largely as a consequence of the reduced demand in the oil-producing countries where many of the LDC migrant workers are employed (see table 11). For instance, remittances of workers to Bangladesh fell from $0.6 billion in 1983 to $0.4 billion in 1985, though rising to $0.5 billion in 1986; in Yemen the corresponding figures were $1.2, $0.9, and $0.8; and for Sudan $0.3, $0.3 and $0.1 billion.

---

[14] See section B of chapter III.

TABLE 10

Imports of the LDCs by broad economic categories

(Billions of dollars)

	1980	1981	1982	1983	1984	1985
Agricultural, forestry and fisheries products.	3.8	3.7	3.7	3.3	3.7	3.9
of which: cereals.	1.3	1.2	1.3	1.1	1.4	1.4
Fuels	3.2	2.9	2.9	2.8	2.7	2.3
Capital goods.	3.7	3.3	3.1	2.8	2.5	3.0
Other products.	5.4	6.3	6.4	6.2	6.9	6.3
TOTAL	16.1	16.2	16.1	15.1	15.8	15.5

Source: UNCTAD secretariat calculations and evaluation, based on FAO, IMF, UN-COMTRADE and other international and national sources.

TABLE 11
Balance of payments of the LDCs[a]

(Billions of dollars)

	1980	1981	1982	1983	1984	1985	1986[b]
Current account balance	− 0.1	− 8.3	− 8.5	− 6.7	− 6.5	− 6.5	− 7.2
Merchandise trade balance	− 8.0	− 8.5	− 8.7	− 7.1	− 6.9	− 6.4	− 6.3
Exports of goods f.o.b.[c]	8.1	8.0	6.9	7.0	7.6	7.4	8.2
Imports of goods f.o.b.	− 16.1	− 16.5	− 15.6	− 14.1	− 14.5	− 13.8	− 14.5
Non-factor services receipts . .	2.4	2.6	2.6	2.3	2.3	2.4	2.3
Non-factor services payments .	− 4.7	− 4.6	− 4.3	− 4.2	− 4.2	− 4.3	− 4.5
Net income from labour	0.3	0.3	0.4	0.4	0.4	0.3	0.3
Receipts of interest	0.6	0.5	0.5	0.4	0.3	0.3	0.4
Payments of interest.	− 0.7	− 0.8	− 0.9	− 1.0	− 0.9	− 1.0	− 1.0
Net direct investment income .	− 0.2	− 0.1	− 0.2	− 0.2	− 0.3	− 0.3	− 0.4
Net private transfers[d]	2.2	2.3	2.1	2.8	2.8	2.4	2.1
Capital account balance	7.4	7.5	7.8	6.7	6.5	6.5	7.9
Overall balance[e]	− 0.7	− 0.8	− 0.7	− 0.0	0.0	0.3	0.7

Source: UNCTAD secretariat calculations based on data from IMF.

[a] Excluding Kiribati and Tuvalu.

[b] Provisional estimates by the UNCTAD secretariat.

[c] The trade figures differ from those reported in the trade returns because of adjustments for coverage, evaluation, timing, inland freight, etc.

[d] Including migrants' transfers, workers' remittances and other transfers.

[e] Balanced by use of different types of reserve holdings and IMF credit.

D. Food and agriculture

1. *Overall performance*

The single most important recent development in this field relates to the recovery of agricultural and food production in African LDCs during the past two years, a phenomenon brought about by stronger domestic policies in support of agriculture but assisted by improvements in the weather (cf. section G below on Environment and disasters). Table 12 shows that the aggregate recovery of agricultural production was stronger in 1984/85, at 7.4 per cent for LDCs, than in 1985/86 (2.5 per cent). There was a major recovery in output after the crisis years 1983/84 which could not be fully sustained. Thus, the rate of growth of agricultural production per head, averaged over all LDCs, actually began to decline again in 1985/86. Although only marginal, this monitored decline is a worrying sign. However, with reference to SNPA food self-sufficiency objectives, it is a little more reassuring that rates of growth of per capita food

production remained positive in 1985/86, at 0.8 per cent (although the increase was much lower than in the previous season) while total LDC food production rose by 3.5 per cent.

2. *Cereals production*

Provisional estimates for the latest completed crop year (1986 or 1986/87) show a continuing upward trend, with above-normal cereals production recorded in 18 African LDCs (see table 13 below). Exportable surpluses were held in six African LDCs: Burkina Faso, Malawi,[15] Mali,

---

[15] However, even Malawi was planning to import 100,000 tonnes of maize at the end of 1987 in order to maintain strategic stocks after a poor harvest—a sign of how rapidly the food situation in LDCs can deteriorate.

TABLE 12

Annual average growth rates of agricultural and food production per capita in the LDCs

(*Percentages*)

Country	Agricultural production				Food production			
	1980–1986	1983–1984	1984–1985	1985–1986	1980–1986	1983–1984	1984–1985	1985–1986
Afghanistan	– 2.6	– 2.4	– 3.1	– 6.4	– 2.7	– 2.4	– 3.1	– 6.7
Bangladesh	0.2	– 0.8	4.5	– 2.0	0.3	– 0.5	2.3	0.6
Benin	3.5	19.6	1.9	3.4	2.8	18.3	2.1	1.8
Bhutan	0.2	0.1	0.2	0.1	0.2	0.1	0.2	0.1
Botswana	– 2.0	– 9.6	2.2	– 3.0	– 2.0	– 9.7	2.2	– 3.0
Burkina Faso	5.1	– 3.2	20.8	9.5	4.8	– 3.2	20.3	8.9
Burundi	0.4	– 7.5	5.9	– 1.0	0.0	– 5.3	4.7	0.4
Cape Verde	– 2.5	15.6	– 9.5	30.0	– 2.5	15.7	– 9.3	29.7
Central African Republic	– 1.1	– 2.4	– 7.5	6.6	– 1.2	– 4.4	– 7.7	7.3
Chad	0.6	– 13.8	20.8	– 1.6	0.8	– 11.0	21.5	0.4
Comoros	– 1.3	– 3.8	2.7	– 0.5	– 1.4	– 3.9	2.6	– 0.5
Democratic Yemen	– 2.8	– 2.5	– 3.7	– 4.9	– 3.1	– 2.4	– 3.7	– 5.1
Djibouti	..	..	..	..	..	..	..	..
Equatorial Guinea	..	..	..	..	..	..	..	..
Ethiopia	– 2.0	– 10.4	3.1	2.0	– 2.2	– 12.2	6.9	0.4
Gambia	4.0	7.5	20.4	– 3.1	4.0	7.1	20.5	– 3.1
Guinea	– 1.5	– 0.5	– 1.2	2.0	– 1.5	– 0.5	– 1.2	2.2
Guinea-Bissau	5.8	13.6	2.4	5.9	5.8	13.6	2.4	5.9
Haiti	0.4	0.7	– 2.0	1.8	0.3	1.3	– 2.0	1.7
Kiribati	..	..	..	..	..	..	..	..
Lao People's Democratic Republic	4.2	9.0	6.9	2.1	4.3	9.2	7.0	2.0
Lesotho	– 3.2	– 3.1	8.4	– 9.0	– 3.5	– 3.2	9.6	– 9.7
Malawi	– 1.0	0.6	– 2.4	– 1.4	– 1.8	– 2.0	– 2.7	– 1.9
Maldives	0.3	0.9	– 1.5	– 0.1	0.3	0.9	– 1.5	– 0.1
Mali	0.9	– 9.2	– 5.2	8.4	1.0	– 9.8	– 6.1	8.4
Mauritania	– 1.3	– 0.4	1.9	8.1	– 1.3	– 0.4	1.9	8.1
Nepal	– 1.0	– 3.1	– 1.2	– 5.8	– 0.9	– 2.8	– 1.3	– 6.3
Niger	– 1.9	– 22.1	23.9	0.5	– 1.9	– 22.2	23.9	0.5
Rwanda	– 1.5	– 18.6	1.4	– 0.8	– 1.9	– 21.1	2.5	– 0.4
Samoa	– 1.7	2.1	– 0.3	– 6.5	– 1.8	2.2	– 0.3	– 6.7
Sao Tome and Principe	– 5.0	– 15.4	– 1.6	– 2.0	– 5.0	– 15.5	– 1.6	– 2.0
Sierra Leone	– 0.0	– 12.0	– 1.7	8.6	– 0.0	– 10.9	– 5.3	8.7
Somalia	– 1.8	– 4.1	3.5	– 1.7	– 1.8	– 4.0	3.5	– 1.7
Sudan	0.8	– 9.3	16.8	1.0	0.8	– 10.8	20.2	3.4
Togo	– 2.5	7.2	0.2	– 7.6	– 2.8	8.8	– 3.2	– 7.8
Tuvalu	..	..	..	..	..	..	..	..
Uganda	4.0	– 25.6	47.6	0.2	4.0	– 27.0	50.0	0.7
United Republic of Tanzania	– 1.8	1.4	– 2.7	– 0.8	– 1.3	1.4	– 1.9	– 0.6
Vanuatu	1.6	10.3	– 6.7	3.2	1.7	10.7	– 6.8	3.2
Yemen	3.2	8.0	5.2	11.8	3.2	8.4	5.2	12.0
ALL LDCs[a]	– 0.2	– 4.6	4.8	– 0.2	– 0.3	– 5.3	4.8	0.8
Memo item:								
Total production, all LDCs[a]	2.4	– 2.1	7.4	2.5	2.4	– 2.8	7.5	3.5

Source: UNCTAD secretariat calculations, based on data from FAO.

[a] Excluding Djibouti, Equatorial Guinea, Kiribati, Mauritania and Tuvalu.

Niger, Sudan and Uganda. External assistance is required for the disposal of such food surpluses to neighbouring countries as well as for the internal movement of cereals – in these countries and in Chad – from surplus to deficit regions. Three African LDCs continued to face drought-induced food emergencies in 1987: Botswana, Ethiopia and Lesotho.

In Bangladesh, recurrent heavy floods have caused extensive damage to cereals and jute crops, and losses to the rice output as of August 1987 were provisionally estimated at about 2 million tonnes. In Nepal, owing to drought in the Terai, the aggregate production of cereals in 1986/87 (July/June) was reduced by some 350,000 tonnes compared to its level in the previous year, while floods and

TABLE 13

The cereal situation in the least developed countries in 1987

(As of mid-September 1987)

Country	Cereal self-sufficiency ratio (%) (normal year)[a]	Cereal production indexes for latest completed crop year		Cereal import requirements (1986/87 or 1987) (estimated or anticipated) ('000 tonnes)	
		As a percentage of the five-year moving average	As a percentage of normal[a] production	Total import requirements	of which food aid requirements
Afghanistan	97	99	..	250.0[d]	..
Bangladesh[1]	91[b]	107	..	1 900.0	1 600.0
Bénin	85	121	109	73.0	10.0
Bhutan	94[b]	..	..	30.0	..
Botswana[1 2]	27	156	50	188.0	48.0
Burkina Faso[3]	89	151	154	90.0	—
Burundi	94	109	103	20.0	8.0
Cape Verde	5	..	300	56.0	52.0
Central African Republic	69	132	128	25.0	5.0
Chad	94	167	126	47.0	35.0
Comoros	37	159	100	36.0	7.0
Democratic Yemen	28[b]	106	..	220.0	..
Djibouti[2]	—	.	.	50.0	10.0
Equatorial Guinea	—	.	.	7.0	3.0
Ethiopia[1]	91	106	92	765.0	611.0
Gambia	59	151	155	45.0	..
Guinea	80	109	108	100.0	30.0
Guinea-Bissau	78	130	132	17.0	16.0
Haiti	85	94	..	230.0	..
Kiribati		..	..	6.0	..
Lao PDR[1]	100[c]	117	75[d]	50.0[d]	—
Lesotho[1]	50	110	80	180.0[d]	40.0[d]
Malawi[1 2]	98	85	90	..	120.0[d]
Maldives	..	..	..	20.0	..
Mali[3]	88	131	107	80.0	20.0
Mauritania	31	178	119	155.0	75.0
Nepal[1]	101[c]	99	..	102.9	..
Niger[3]	97	113	106	25.0	15.0
Rwanda	89	105	101	40.0[d]	16.0[d]
Samoa	..	..	..	13.0	..
Sao Tome and Principe	2	100	100	11.0[d]	7.0[d]
Sierra Leone	85	103	104	85.0	40.0
Somalia[2]	59	136	129	217.0	170.0
Sudan[2 3]	87	142	115	530.0	365.0
Togo	81	96	95	85.0	10.0
Tuvalu		..	..	..	..
Uganda[2]	97	136	133	50.0	40.0
United Republic of Tanzania	93	122	104	265.0	..
Vanuatu		..	..	7.0	..
Yemen	52[b]	124	..	640.0	..

Source: FAO, *Foodcrops and shortages* (September 1986, April, May, August and September 1987); FAO, *Food supply situation and crop prospects in Sub-Saharan Africa* (April 1987); and UNCTAD secretariat calculations based on information contained in the above reports.

[a] Calculated on the basis of FAO estimations of normal levels of cereal production and imports. "*Normal*" *production* is defined by FAO as that level of production which would be harvested in the current year assuming no abnormal climatic conditions and no reductions in area planted or supply of inputs caused by civil disasters or other man-made causes. "*Normal*" *imports* of cereals are in turn defined as those quantities needed to meet domestic requirements in a year of "normal" production, including both commercial imports and food aid.

[b] 1984.　　[c] 1985/86 or 1986.　　[d] 1987/88.

[1] LDCs facing exceptional food emergencies.

[2] Emergency assistance is required to feed refugees, returnees and/or other displaced persons.

[3] LDCs with exportable cereal surpluses which could with donors' support be exchanged for other foodstuffs which these countries need.

landslides in August 1987 resulted in extensive damage to crops, thus affecting the next harvest prospects. In the Lao PDR, the harvest outlook for 1987/88 is poor on account of drought-stressed crops, official estimates indicating that crop losses could reach about 25 per cent of normal production.[16]

A problem arising from improved production in a number of African LDCs, however, relates to the downward movement of local prices for cereals and to the ensuing discouraging effects upon future plantings and the forthcoming harvests. In some countries, the effect of bumper crops has been to drive market prices for the main staples generally well below official prices (33 per cent and 55 per cent below official prices in Burkina Faso and Mali, respectively), though this effect can be moderated by judicious intervention buying and firm undertakings by the crop purchasing authorities where they either enjoy a monopoly position or have some limited powers of control over private traders.

3. *Other crops*

Drought-sensitive crops have been expanding again with the good rains in a number of LDCs. Groundnut production has been increasing in several LDCs; it doubled in Malawi in 1986 as compared to 1985, and increased in Mali from 37,600 tonnes in 1984/85 to 57,000 and 81,500 tonnes in the subsequent marketing years. In Niger groundnut production recovered massively from 8,500 tonnes in 1985 to 55,000 tonnes in 1986 (still representing only one half of local consumption needs), and in Sudan it doubled from 300,000 tonnes in 1984/85 to 600,000 tonnes in 1986/87.[17] Karité (shea) nut grew dramatically in Mali from a mere 60 tonnes in 1984/85 to 40,000 tonnes in 1985/86. Output of gum arabic in Sudan (which

had fallen from 38,000 tonnes in 1983/84 to 14,000 tonnes in 1984/85) is expected to reach a record 40,000 tonnes in 1986/87.

A continuing major problem faced by LDCs relates to the depressed conditions in world commodity markets (cf. section on external trade above). Low world prices have led to major losses of export earnings, notably in the cotton, jute, cocoa and clove sectors of LDCs. The average unit value of cotton exports declined by 53 per cent between 1984 and 1986. Losses incurred by Chad as a result of the negative difference between export prices for cotton and local production costs were estimated at CFAF 10.4 billion (around $30 million) in 1986. However, cotton prices staged a recovery in 1987 in a further indication of how LDCs dependent on a narrow range of commodity exports are highly vulnerable to world market fluctuations beyond their control. Malawi's sugar quota in the United States for 1987 was reduced by 47 per cent as compared to 1986. In addition, Malawi experienced severe transport problems in exporting the sugar across third countries. The international price for cloves, the main export item of Comoros, fell to a three-year trough of $2,641 per tonne in December 1986. The internal terms of trade of jute *vis-à-vis* rice in Bangladesh steadily declined by 40 per cent between 1980 and 1986.

4. *Livestock*

Livestock is also recovering from the drought in all western Sahelian LDCs. However, in Botswana (which has entered its sixth consecutive year of drought), cattle mortality rates rose from 20 per cent in 1985 to 25 per cent in 1986. The national stock of cattle has been reduced from 3 million in 1982 to 2.5 million in 1985 and to 2.3 million in 1986, whereas drought-resistant small stock increased by 25 per cent between 1985 and 1986 reaching 1.6 million head. Heavy livestock losses due to the dry spell are reported this year in Somalia, reaching up to 60 per cent in several areas. In Uganda, the rains have improved pastures, but outbreaks of animal diseases have been reported in several areas in 1987. The livestock sector of Bangladesh for its part has been seriously affected by floods.[18]

---

[16] See FAO, *Foodcrops and shortages* (September 1987).

[17] These figures are of monitored marketed production, and the very major shifts often reflect changes in policies (notably on pricing and payments to producers) more than changes in actual output. In the case of groundnuts, some output is directly consumed by the producers and so does not enter into marketed production, while many food and other crops can be traded across borders and so are not monitored as domestic marketed output. Changes in border prices thus induce shifts in figures for apparent output.

---

[18] FAO, *op. cit.*

E. Manufacturing

1. *Growth of manufacturing in 1985*

While the average growth rates of manufacturing for all 40 LDCs showed a modest improvement in 1985 in comparison with 1984, and the growth rates accelerated slightly for the second year running, performance was again very uneven among the different LDCs, ranging from an exceptional 49 per cent in Sao Tome and Principe to -11.8 per cent in Gambia and -11.0 per cent in Uganda (see table 14). These differences reflect not only a number of divergent influences that have marked manufacturing during the period under review, their effects depending on the particular industrial structure and environment of each country, but also wide variations in the industrial policies pursued by the different LDCs.

Industrial output of the LDCs consists mainly of consumer goods produced for domestic consumption; only a very small share of manufactured products is exported. With 32 per cent of total manufacturing output, textiles is the most important industrial sector, while food processing, which is the second largest sector, accounts for 24 per cent, and beverages and tobacco processing for 14 per cent. The textile sector has considerable export potential although, if production is aggregated for all LDCs, even this sector produces mainly for the local market. It is therefore predominantly developments on domestic markets which directly determine the prospects for manufacturing in most LDCs on the demand side, although developments on world markets play a role through the dependence of manufacturing production on imports. Moreover, world economic developments such as the level of interest rates and the commodity prices payable for LDCs' non-manufactured exports exert a crucial influence on the availability of foreign exchange to purchase and maintain capital equipment in the domestic manufacturing sector, and in creating effective demand, particularly in the rural sector, for domestically produced consumer goods, especially import substitutes.

The environment in which manufacturing operates, including conditions on domestic markets, has experienced important changes in recent years due in particular to the introduction by many LDCs of more active structural adjustment policies. While some of the measures introduced in this context have had stimulating effects on manufacturing activities, others have worsened the already insecure profit basis with which many companies have been working, especially when structural adjustment is preceded by a period of severe austerity (reductions in domestic credit, the damping down of local demand and cutbacks in government spending) as a means of reducing balance-of-payments deficits. A particularly decisive impact on conditions relevant for manufacturing has been made by the modifications to foreign currency policies introduced in many LDCs and by the policies designed to revitalize agricultural development.

2. *Effects of foreign exchange policies*

The constant scarcity of foreign exchange has remained a major limiting factor of manufacturing production which is heavily dependent on imports of raw materials, machinery and spare parts. It is often argued that the modern industrial sector has, at least in its start-up phase, been a heavy net absorber of foreign currency, both as regards investments and current operations although, according to a recent UNIDO study, the direct contribution of manufacturing industry to debt accumulation of sub-Saharan Africa has been small[19]. Similarly, policies directed at supposedly foreign-exchange-minimizing investment in the agricultural sector at the expense of manufacturing industry tend to neglect the obvious, and for LDCs often crucial, links between the two. The devaluation of domestic currency in many LDCs and the institution of currency auctions at which enterprises bid for currency at non-preferential rates has made foreign exchange available for manufacturing, but increased its price.

3. *Effects of agricultural policies on manufacturing*

(a) *Squeeze on new funding*

The priority given to agricultural development by a majority of LDCs has also had a major impact on the macro-economic parameters which

---

[19] "Industry and external debt in Africa: a preliminary analysis", *Industry and Development*, No. 17 (1986), p. 13.

TABLE 14

The manufacturing sector in LDCs

Country	Per-centage share in GDP 1985	Annual average growth rates (per cent) [a]					
		1980–1985	1980–1981	1981–1982	1982–1983	1983–1984	1984–1985
Afghanistan	..	..	..	..	..	..	..
Bangladesh	8	2.4	5.4	1.6	– 1.6	3.7	3.2
Benin	4	7.4	– 6.1	63.0	– 9.7	– 12.1	17.5
Bhutan.	4 c	..	..	– 1.5	16.1	4.8	..
Botswana	6	9.5	26.7	23.8	– 7.4	3.8	4.5
Burkina Faso	14	2.9	1.1	3.0	8.1	– 1.2	3.9
Burundi	12	7.5	14.1	– 2.9	6.6	4.1	16.6
Cape Verde	..	..	..	..	..	..	..
Central African Republic	7	– 2.3	– 9.8	– 5.4	1.4	1.4	1.4
Chad.	9	– 5.5	– 12.6	– 6.8	– 7.6	– 5.2	5.4
Comoros.	6	4.7	6.5	5.0	4.0	4.5	3.6
Democratic Yemen	11 c	4.4 g	22.6	– 11.2	..	..	..
Djibouti	10	0.6	– 0.3	3.3	0.9	– 1.6	0.9
Equatorial Guinea	5	4.9	3.7	3.3	– 6.4	6.8	18.7
Ethiopia	11 d	4.1 h	4.1	3.4	4.9	..	..
Gambia	10	..	..	35.8	5.8	– 0.8	– 11.8
Guinea.	2	1.2	0.8	– 2.0	3.0	5.6	– 1.0
Guinea-Bissau	4 d	0.3	– 4.0	3.0	– 1.7	1.0	3.4
Haiti.	(17) c	– 3.1 i	– 11.6	– 3.9	5.6	– 1.6	..
Kiribati	2 c	..	..	..	..	..	..
Lao People's Democratic Republic	(4)	2.2	0.9	1.1	– 3.3	– 8.5	23.9
Lesotho	7	4.9	– 3.4	27.5	– 25.4	25.9	10.0
Malawi	12 c	2.7	3.4	– 0.2	6.8	2.7	1.3
Maldives	5 c	14.6 i	26.2	21.9	6.3	5.5	..
Mali	7 c •	..	..	..	..	..	..
Mauritania	6 c	3.0	2.2	– 0.8	3.4	5.0	5.5
Nepal	4 d	..	..	..	..	..	..
Niger.	4	..	..	..	..	..	..
Rwanda	16 e	..	6.5	..	..	..	..
Samoa	6 d	9.4 h	7.2	3.6	17.7	..	..
Sao Tome and Principe	9	– 2.0	– 26.4	13.6	2.5	– 29.3	49.0
Sierra Leone	5	– 1.2	6.9	1.9	– 3.2	– 5.9	– 5.2
Somalia	6 f	– 0.8 g	– 0.8	– 0.7	..	..	..
Sudan	9	..	..	..	..	..	..
Togo.	7	– 1.6	9.1	4.2	– 7.4	– 18.2	7.1
Tuvalu.	2	..	..	..	..	..	..
Uganda	4 e	0.5	– 5.4	14.2	2.8	3.4	– 11.0
United Republic of Tanzania. . .	5	– 4.8	– 10.7	– 3.0	– 3.4	– 1.4	– 5.1
Vanuatu.	4	..	..	..	..	..	..
Yemen.	9 c	18.2 i	19.2	20.4	23.2	10.6	..
ALL LDCs [b]	8	1.1	1.0	2.6	– 1.4	1.1	2.4

Source: UNCTAD secretariat calculations based on data from the United Nations Statistical Office, the Economic Commission for Africa, the World Bank and other international and national sources.

[a] Value added at constant prices.

[b] Average relates to the 21 LDCs for which data are available for all years.

[c] 1984.

[d] 1983.   [g] 1980-1982.

[e] 1981.   [h] 1980-1983.

[f] 1982.   [i] 1980-1984.

influence manufacturing. On the one hand it has meant a drying up of new funds available for industrial development, as Governments as well as bilateral donors and multilateral institutions have channelled investments into programmes for the revival of agriculture. Whereas during the last two decades industry used to receive a major share of development funding, the sharp reduction of such investments has not only put a brake on industrial expansion but has also in many cases impaired current operations in need of modernization, rationalization and restructuring.

(b) *Impact on industrial production costs*

At the same time the increases in agricultural producer prices have also exerted a limiting influence on production by raising prices of inputs and thus production costs. For enterprises in the modern sector, in particular, this has meant a reduction of their products' competitiveness in regard to imported goods (which are usually preferred by consumers even at somewhat higher prices) or, in countries where markets are heavily protected and prices of domestic products could safely be increased, reduced sales. Manufacturing firms have found it increasingly difficult to pass on to local consumers the mounting production costs caused by higher prices of domestic raw materials and imports that have to be purchased with more expensive foreign currency.

(c) *Demand-side constraints*

Many of the consumer goods that form part of the output of the modern agricultural processing sector in the LDCs are geared to the small relatively better-off sector of the urban population and to foreigners. In many cases the former's purchasing power has suffered in absolute terms as a result of the austerity programmes many LDCs have pursued during 1985 and 1986 as well as in relative terms compared with the rural population which has benefited from increased development efforts on their behalf. A widening of the market to encompass large numbers of rural dwellers cannot be accomplished overnight though, with the assurance of steady demand growth, this is the direc-

tion in which the marketing of domestic manufactures is to be reorientated. Meanwhile, constraints on the demand side increasingly limit manufacturing performance. While, in recent years, attention had mainly focused on the supply side difficulties of industrial enterprises (scarcity of domestic inputs, interruptions of production due to lack of spare parts, irregular supply of electricity, transport difficulties, lack of skilled labour and experienced management, etc.), the growing recognition of the demand side constraints are increasing the pressures for a restructuring of industrial production to adapt it more successfully to the changing demand patterns in these countries.

4. *Impact on public enterprises*

Demand side constraints, scarcity of foreign exchange, higher production costs and the drying up of new funding have beset public enterprises (PEs), which dominate manufacturing output in practically all LDCs. The cost increases which many of these enterprises have had to accept have aggravated their operating losses. At the same time, the squeeze on State budgets has made it impossible for many Governments to continue their subsidies, let alone to extend greater credit to parastatal companies so as to enable them to maintain output while restructuring their operations. As a consequence, a number of PEs have had to close; others in better financial shape or operating in more attractive markets have been sold off to the private (often foreign) sector. This has tended to augment unemployment since many of these enterprises are judged by their new owners to be overstaffed.

F. Mining

The contribution of mining to the economies of LDCs as a group continues to be relatively modest. The mineral sector has accounted for less than 3 per cent of their GDP and around 20 per cent of exports during the 1980s. However, mineral resources play a significant role in several LDCs, namely Afghanistan, Botswana, Guinea, Mauritania, Niger, Sierra Leone and Togo (see table 15). For the Central African Republic, mineral production (diamonds) now vies with coffee as the leading export earner and contributor to government revenue. The prospects for economic growth for

these and some other LDCs could thus be enhanced by developing their mineral potential and production, thereby improving their export capacity, and by increasing the share of retained benefits from the sector through stronger national involvement in the marketing of raw minerals as well as through greater local processing of such minerals.

In the 1980s some LDCs have received external assistance for carrying out geophysical surveys, geological prospection and exploration. As a result of these efforts, the geological information on sev-

TABLE 15

Contribution of mining to the GDP and the exports of main mineral producing LDCs

(*Average 1981-1985*)

Country	Percentage share in		Leading mineral commodity
	GDP	Exports	
Afghanistan. . . .	..	45	Natural gas
Botswana	28	74	Diamonds
Guinea	15	91[a]	Bauxite, concentrate of alumina
Mauritania	11	52	Iron ore
Niger	8	89	Uranium ore
Sierra Leone . . .	10	71	Diamonds
Togo.	10	46	Phosphates

Source: Calculations based on data from the World Bank, IMF and other international and national sources.

[a] 1980-1984.

eral LDCs has increased and possible resource endowments of a number of them have been transformed into a useful set of reserve estimates. Such countries include, in addition to the traditional mineral-producing LDCs mentioned above, Burkina Faso, Central African Republic, Chad, Burundi, Bangladesh, Lao PDR, Benin, Ethiopia and Nepal, some of which have started exploitation of the various minerals concerned. Estimations are being made of the range of additional yearly output that could arise from such new discoveries.

Identifying and locating mineral deposits is only the first step. Further development and diversification of mining in all the above-mentioned and some other LDCs faces a number of internal and external constraints. Internal constraints include the lack of adequate physical infrastructure, often combined with a land-locked position inhibiting transportation to ports, few developed indigenous energy resources and high energy costs. The development of mining in many of the LDCs is also hampered by the lack of technical and economic knowledge of mining, minerals and metal markets, as well as by the absence of appropriate mining codes and of institutional arrangements for the formulation and implementation of realistic mineral policies as well as for facilitating investments in the mining sector. Technical co-operation, including the sharing of knowledge and skills among developing countries, can help to relieve such impediments.

The external constraints are intensifying, in part because of fundamental structural trends in the world economy and problems in world mineral markets (with the exception of precious and semi-precious minerals and metals). Structural trends relate to technological changes which have an adverse impact on the use of minerals and metals as a result of the substitution of materials and the shift in overall output towards services and products with a low raw materials content. Moreover, world markets are not only depressed because of such longer-term influences but also unstable because of the absence of short-term counter-cyclical and other necessary actions. While the short-term fluctuations can be addressed through recourse to an improved system of compensatory finance, plus more active dealings by LDCs on future markets, the issue of longer-term declines in demand has to be addressed structurally.

G. Environment and disasters

1. *The drought in Africa*

Good rains since late 1985 have brought relief to sub-Saharan Africa after the long drought from which most of that region had been suffering since the second half of the 1970s.[20] The drought persists, however, in southern Africa. Elsewhere, weather improvement has permitted a considerable increase in the production of food and drought-sensitive export staples (cf. section D on Food and agriculture above). The situation, however, is still far from normal. For instance, in early 1987 Lake Chad had not yet recovered its normal level, while river levels, though rising, were still below normal by August 1987. By April 1987, below-normal rainfall continued to affect some LDCs, notably in the cases of Botswana, where the effects of the

---

[20] The drought started in the western African region in 1968 and had a short-lived respite in 1974-1975. At its peak in 1984, the drought had extended to normally forested regions of Africa, which include Guinea and Guinea-Bissau. All in all, the drought has affected 22 LDCs: Benin, Botswana, Burkina Faso, Burundi, Cape Verde, Chad, Djibouti, Ethiopia, Gambia, Guinea, Guinea-Bissau, Lesotho, Malawi, Mali, Mauritania, Niger, Rwanda, Somalia, Sudan, Togo, Uganda and the United Republic of Tanzania (cf. A/40/392, E/1985/117, 24 June 1985, table 1; and UNCTAD, *The Least Developed Countries – 1986 Report* (TD/B/1120), United Nations publication, Sales No. E.86.II.D.7, paras. 130-135).

drought were felt for the sixth consecutive year, and Somalia, where an estimated 100,000 people were still affected by the drought. Moreover, it is by no means certain that a higher-rainfall pattern is now returning to the area. The recent precedent of the mid-1970s, when rainfall increased only temporarily, should be taken into account. In any event, the problems caused by the drought have not been dissipated automatically by the mere return of the rains: it will take many years for the drought-stricken LDCs to overcome the sequel of the drought in terms of environmental, economic and social disruption. Many of the African LDCs, which are still under severe economic pressures, are ill-equipped to cope alone with the consequences of drought and need extra external support for recovery. Moreover, national strategies in drought-prone areas must in the future take into account the possibility that Africa may be undergoing a permanent climatic change, in addition to demographic change, directly affecting the productive environment. This can involve a costly reappraisal of farming methods, output, research and settlement policy, none of which the LDCs are well-placed to finance or undertake on their own.

2. *Locust and grasshopper infestations*

Improved rainfall in the African region provided exceptionally favourable breeding conditions for the spread of grasshoppers and locusts in 1986. The greatest problem has been posed by grasshoppers, in particular the Senegalese grasshopper, *Oedaleus senegalensis*, in the Sahel. The countries most seriously affected were Burkina Faso, Chad, Mali, Mauritania, Niger and Senegal. Large grasshopper populations requiring control action also infested in Benin, Cameroon, Gambia, Ghana, Guinea-Bissau, Nigeria and the Sudan. In 1987, FAO has reported heavy infestations of grasshoppers, or threats thereof, in Benin, Burkina Faso, Cape Verde, Chad, Gambia, Guinea-Bissau and Niger, while rodents were threatening crops in Mauritania. As regards locusts, for the first time in 50 years high-density populations of all four African species of migratory locusts developed simultaneously: the desert locust, the African migratory locust, the red locust and the brown locust. By mid-1987, breeding of desert locusts continued to be reported from the Red Sea coasts of Sudan and northern Ethiopia, as well as from the Yemen Arab Republic. Control programmes currently implemented have had some success in reducing this threat, but it is not yet clear whether these programmes will be sufficient to prevent further increases in numbers.[21]

---

[21] See ECOSOC, *Fight against the locust and grasshopper infestation in Africa* (E/1987/57), 28 April 1987; and FAO, *Foodcrops and shortages* (June and September 1987).

3. *Other environmental events*

Various environmental phenomena have adversely affected LDCs located in other regions since January 1986. Drought in the Terai has led to losses in Nepal's agricultural production in 1986/87, and cereals output is forecast at 4.051 million tonnes as compared to 4.4 million tonnes in the previous year. Monsoon floods reportedly destroyed 2 million tonnes of rice in Bangladesh during the 1986/87 harvest. More flooding since September 1987 has caused the loss of further food and jute crops, and prompted the Bangladesh Government to declare a state of national emergency. Tropical storms or cyclones hit the Comoros, Vanuatu and Guinea-Bissau in January, February and September 1987, respectively.

4. *Desertification, deforestation and soil erosion*

A continuing environmental problem in the majority of LDCs is posed by the long-standing, cumulative interacting phenomena of desertification, deforestation and soil erosion arising to a large extent from man-made misuse or overuse of arid or semi-arid land. The LDCs are often arid, and land misuse or overuse in such cases is the inevitable response of a very poor rural population trying to cope with its immediate need for subsistence.

As indicated in the 1986 issue of this report (cf. paras. 139-140), high priority is being given in LDCs to forestry conservation and reforestation. Further measures towards this end have been taken in several LDCs since the preparation of that report. Nation-wide tree-planting was conducted in Chad in 1986, and in Cape Verde during 1986/87. In Nepal (where extinction of forestry resources is projected in about 30 years, at current depletion and reforestation rates), 11 governmental commissions have been established to monitor forestry problems. In January 1987, the exploitation and exportation of sandalwood was banned for five years in Vanuatu (where exports thereof had averaged 55 tonnes per year). In Niger, two decrees were issued in March 1987 to strengthen the control of forestry exploitation and to promote reforestation, and anti-desertification figures as one of the top priorities of the five-year development plan for 1987-1991 (published in April 1987). A soil management programme covering the next 15 years is under way in Burkina Faso with the purpose of enabling village communities to adopt better cultivation practices and protect the environment. To promote forestry development, the training programme at the Lao's Dongdok forestry school (established in 1980) is being upgraded to university level. A wide-ranging environment programme is under preparation in Ethiopia and is expected to be launched in FY 1988/89.

Initiatives to protect the environment have been taken recently by LDCs at the sub-regional level. A programme to protect plant life in 1988-1991 was adopted in January 1987 by the nine countries (of which eight are LDCs) members of the Permanent Inter-State Committee on Drought Control in the Sahel (CILSS), namely Burkina Faso, Cape Verde, Chad, Gambia, Guinea-Bissau, Mali, Mauritania, Niger and Senegal. A first meeting with donors was held in March 1987 by the recently established Inter-Governmental Authority on Drought and Development (IGADD),

which comprises six countries of eastern Africa (of which five are LDCs), namely, Djibouti, Ethiopia, Kenya, Somalia, Sudan and Uganda. Aid pledges amounting to more than $70 million were received for funding 217 projects (total cost $3.7 billion) relating to environmental protection and food self-sufficiency.

Of interest for African LDCs is the prospective establishment of a *Centre africain pour l'application de la météorologie au développement* (African Centre for the Application of Meteorology to Development) at Niamey, Niger, which is expected to start operations in early 1988. The Centre will try to channel meteorological information so as to improve agricultural production and water resource management and facilitate the development of new energy resources.

Chapter II

RECENT POLICY DEVELOPMENTS

A. Adjustment policies

1. *Basic features*

The continuing difficulties which LDCs face in regard to external disequilibrium have obliged many of them to adopt stabilization programmes to address what are ostensibly short-term balance-of-payments problems. Many of them have also opted to undertake more fundamental policy reforms aimed at enhancing the efficiency and productivity of the national economy, including improved management of public resources, and the correction of price and intersectoral distortions which may have discouraged rural production and exports in particular. The distinction between stabilization and adjustment is conceptually useful (see Box 1) although in practice the two are not mutually-exclusive policy categories. LDCs are, however, particularly vulnerable to the danger that excessive attention to short-term balance-of-payments measures can be inimical to successful longer-term adjustment.

In most cases, the package of stabilization and adjustment measures includes: liberalization of the pricing and marketing of agricultural commodities as a means of stimulating production; streamlining, liquidating or privatising parastatal enterprises; promoting and facilitating the activities of the non-governmental sector; reducing public consumption and subsidies; restricting the money supply and increasing interest rates; increasing public revenues by improving tax collection and raising tax rates and fees charged for public services; and currency depreciation.

Since mid-1981, 19 LDCs have formulated a stabilization programme supported by a stand-by arrangement (typically of 12-24 months' duration) with the IMF; and 12 have done so for more or less consecutive periods (see table 16);[22] another LDC (Guinea-Bissau) implemented a programme of this nature with a purchase of the first credit tranche. One of these LDCs benefited from an extended arrangement with IMF.[23] Of the above-mentioned 19 LDCs, several have received structural adjustment loans (SALs) from the World Bank [24] (five in the year ending 30 June 1986) i.e. Burundi, Guinea, Malawi, Niger and Togo.[25]

---

[22] It may be seen from table 16 that the typical adjustment package usually contains the same type of measures. Such information, however, is not to be considered comprehensive. For instance, many LDCs instituted policies to facilitate the role of the private sector even before the establishment of the adjustment programme. Measures in this regard, therefore, did not explicitly form part of the adjustment programme itself. Similarly, devaluation is not an autonomous option for countries members of the CFA franc zone, as the exchange rate is adjusted through fluctuations and realignments of the French franc *vis-à-vis* other major currencies.

[23] Extended arrangements with the Fund are normally designed to run for three years. Altogether, five LDCs have had extended arrangements with the IMF, four of which were concluded before mid-1981. The fifth was cancelled before expiry in 1986. In recent years LDCs have not had easy access to this facility, although the new low-interest Structural Adjustment Facility (SAF) of the Fund is possibly more appropriate to their needs.

[24] In 1980 the World Bank established a structural adjustment lending programme, designed to support programmes of broad policy reform in developing countries. Lending under this programme spans five or more years and may involve up to five separate loans.

[25] In two cases these followed earlier SALs for the same countries.

TABLE 16

Main measures taken in the context of IMF-supported adjustment programmes in selected LDCs[a]

	Year of agreement or period covered by stand-by or extended agreements with IMF	Main measures taken						
		Liberalization of prices and marketing of commodities	Improving the efficiency of public enterprises	Expanding the role of the private sector	Containing or reducing government expenditure	Tightening monetary and credit policies	Improving tax collection and/ or raising rates	Depreciation and/or exchange rate flexibility
Bangladesh	1980-1982, 1983, 1985-1987	×	×	×	×	×	×	×
Central African Republic	1980-1981-1982, 1983-1984,1984-1985, 1985-1987,1987-1988		×		×			
Gambia	1982-1983,1984-1985, 1986-1987	×	×	×	×	×	×	×
Haiti	1978-1981,1982-1983, 1983-1985				×		×	
Malawi.	1980-1982,1982-1983, 1983-1986	×	×		×	×	×	×
Mali	1982-1983,1983-1985, 1985-1987	×	×	×				×
Niger	1983-1984,1984-1985, 1985-1986,1986-1987	×	×		×	×	×	
Samoa	1981,1983-1984, 1984-1985		×		×	×	×	×
Somalia	1980-1981,1981-1982, 1982-1984,1985-1986, 1987-1989	×	×		×	×		×
Sudan	1979-1982,1982-1983, 1983-1984,1984-1985	×			×		×	×
Togo	1981-1983,1983-1984, 1984-1985,1985-1986, 1986-1988	×	×	×	×	×	×	
Uganda	1980,1981-1982, 1982-1983,1983-1984	×			×	×		×

Source: IMF press releases and information available in the UNCTAD secretariat.

[a] LDCs having implemented IMF-supported adjustment programmes over consecutive periods since mid-1981.

Thus, structural adjustment programmes are increasingly twinned with stabilization arrangements and the two measures are now often linked with efforts to secure fresh donor funding or debt relief.

2. *Elements affecting growth*

Like many other developing countries, LDCs have been attempting to design and implement adjustment policies that are not only compatible with but also supportive of their development efforts. Existing adjustment policies and prescriptions have been subject to careful scrutiny, both by the international institutions and by the LDCs concerned. This has led recently to a reappraisal of adjustment. Several elements of the policies appear to have adverse effects on the economies of the LDCs concerned as well as on the living conditions of their population. These elements relate in particular to the deflationary and pro-cyclical effects of the demand management measures embodied in the programmes.

Some of the measures contained in the adjustment packages tend to give priority to demand management aimed at reducing deficits in the public sector and on current account in the short term, as well as at containing monetary expansion. While such measures appear to be necessary to secure an efficient use of resources, they may provoke undesirable contractionary effects upon the level of economic activity, notably in the form of shortages of imported inputs and spare parts, capacity under-utilization, a slow-down in the implementation of productive projects, and discouragement of potential new projects and investments. Some of the measures involved (notably price increases, tightening of credit and of public expenditures, and currency depreciation) also tend to have immediate adverse effects upon the standard of living and bring additional hardship to the rural and urban poor through a restricted or more expensive supply of food, of agricultural inputs such as fertilizers and of other basic necessities. Similarly, they tend to raise the cost and restrict the supply of essential social services.

Moreover, the deflationary measures appear to contain a pro-cyclical bias. Stabilization programmes are normally resorted to as a means of coping with balance-of-payments disequilibria which arise to a large extent from shortfalls or a deteriorating trend in export earnings and from unanticipated levels of debt service. The programmes are thus often adopted at times, as at present, when external demand remains depressed. The deflationary measures embodied in such programmes therefore reduce the ability of the domestic markets of LDCs to provide the stimulus to local production that world markets are failing to generate.

The adoption of these deflationary measures constitutes a critical element of the conditionality clauses and the often quite wide-ranging performance criteria embodied in stand-by arrangements and related credits provided by IMF. LDCs have in some cases been unable to meet such criteria. The non-fulfilment of conditionality clauses and/or performance criteria has led to the suspension of the credit lines agreed to under stand-by arrangements negotiated by Gambia, Haiti, Sierra Leone and Sudan. Similarly, out of the five extended agreements in force at some point during the 1980s, four were cancelled before the foreseen expiry date. Access to other forms of credit may also be withdrawn as a result of the collapse of such arrangements, further limiting the financial resources available with which to implement structural reforms.

In other cases, negotiations between LDCs and international financial institutions have been stalled as conditionality requirements have been regarded by LDCs as jeopardizing unduly both their development prospects and the living conditions of their population. Some LDCs have thus pressed ahead with their own adjustment programmes without such external credits and outside the framework of internationally negotiated agreements, this having been the case in particular of Burkina Faso, Djibouti, Rwanda and Yemen.

3. *An evolving policy perspective: adjustment with growth*

Least developed countries have been endeavouring to ensure what has been called "adjustment with growth" or "growth-oriented adjustment". Measures adopted in this connection relate to increased mobilization of domestic resources (both financial and human) and to the allocation of resources in such a way as to develop the productive basis as well as to protect the poor from undue hardship. The measures are taken in the context of the macroeconomic and sectoral policies which are discussed below in this chapter.

At the same time, there appears to be an emerging perception within the international community of the need to support adjustment with growth. As regards financial institutions, the new perception has been translated into the expansion or establishment of lending facilities, such as the Special Facility for Sub-Saharan Africa of the World Bank and the Structural Adjustment Facility of the IMF, which provide credits of a longer-term nature than the traditional stand-by arrangements of the IMF, and thus more suitable to the promotion of the long-term development programmes of LDCs (for more details, see chapter III, section A below). There has also been some recognition that, especially for LDCs, a narrower range of economic criteria, monitored over a longer period, would be more appropriate. The mere fact that the last comprehensive review of conditionality criteria was carried out by the IMF in 1978-79, namely before the outbreak of the current debt crisis, is in itself an indication that the time has arrived for a fresh reappraisal of such criteria.

The new perception has manifested itself in promising initiatives put forward during the 1987 meetings of the World Bank and the IMF. At its meeting in April 1987, the World Bank Development Committee requested the Bank and the Fund to continue examining additional measures to refine and strengthen the implementation of growth-oriented programmes and to submit a report with possible recommendations for consideration at a future meeting of the Committee. Further recommendations were made at the September meetings of the IMF:

(i) The Ministers of the Group of 24, after commissioning a study on this matter from an experts' working group,[26] urged that "a thorough review of the design and implementation of structural adjustment programmes be undertaken and that, where country circumstances render implementation of a full structural adjustment programme inappropriate, the approach of undertaking a series of investment projects and sector adjustment programmes be adopted".[27]

(ii) The Managing Director of the IMF stated that "in certain cases our conditionality might lose nothing of its vigour, and indeed could gain in effectiveness, if it were predicated on a smaller number of essential variables with somewhat longer time frames. Ten years have passed since the Fund last reviewed in comprehensive fashion its policies on the conditional use of its resources, and it is time we reviewed them again."[28]

(iii) The Interim Committee of the Board of Governors of the IMF welcomed the

decision to carry out a comprehensive examination of adjustment programmes and of supporting Fund arrangements in the context of growth-oriented strategies. The Committee further stated that "[such] an examination will also provide an opportunity to consider whether the Fund's policies regarding conditionality need to be re-examined in light of changes in the conditions facing member countries since the last comprehensive review in 1978-79, and in light of the increased emphasis being placed on growth-oriented adjustment."[29]

Increased attention is also being paid to the need to protect the poor from hardships arising out of adjustment measures. A distinct initiative in this regard relates to the special study prepared by UNICEF entitled *Adjustment with a human face.* The study ascertains that there do exist adjustment strategies other than programmes involving a deterioration of the living conditions of the national population, including children. The study brings out examples of developing countries where measures towards this end have been taken. Such measures relate in particular to a more efficient use of social expenditure, more focused on the poor, and to the adoption of nutrition and employment programmes aimed at compensating the poor during the adjustment period. The study emphasizes, however, that such measures have to be complemented with adequate international support in particular in regard to debt rescheduling, improved aid flows, increased lending and greater access to the rich world's markets for the poor world's goods. In the April 1987 meeting of the World Bank/IMF Development Committee, Ministers urged that, in the design and implementation of policy reforms, Governments and international institutions should give special attention to protecting the most vulnerable groups. Such considerations are crucial to the LDCs as these countries have a very large proportion of their population in this category.

The seventh session of UNCTAD, in July 1987, provided a sound occasion for the international community to review the progress in, and the requirements of, the implementation of growth-oriented adjustment programmes in LDCs. The Conference adopted by consensus a Final Act which contains a number of relevant provisions. In particular, the Final Act:

(i) welcomes the efforts made by many LDCs to improve the effectiveness of

[26] See *IMF Survey,* supplement, 10 August 1987.

[27] *Communiqué of the Ministers of the Intergovernmental Group of Twenty-Four,* 26 September 1987, para. 37.

[28] Board of Governors – 1987 Annual Meetings – Washington D.C., *Press Release No.3,* 29 September 1987.

[29] *Communiqué of the Interim Committee of the Board of Governors of the International Monetary Fund,* 28 September 1987, point No. 10.

domestic resource mobilization and use;

(ii) deems it imperative to design structural adjustment and diversification programmes or other more specific measures suited to each LDC's particular social and economic conditions;

(iii) stresses that the volume and forms of aid should be supportive of and commensurate with the growing requirements of the LDCs' adjustment programmes and broader development efforts;

(iv) calls upon relevant international institutions to continue their concerted efforts to increase the share of concessional assistance to LDCs;

(v) invites the IMF to continue to keep under review the principles on which its conditionality rests, in such a way as to reflect the peculiar social, economic and political priorities of the LDCs;

(vi) specifies that the debt-servicing burden of the poorest countries, including LDCs, the majority of which are in sub-Saharan Africa, which are undertaking adjustment efforts, should be eased by longer repayments and grace periods, especially in the Paris Club.

It is salutary to note that within the months after the seventh session of UNCTAD, positive consideration is being given by the relevant authorities to both the last two specific provisions, as reflected in the above-mentioned initiatives put forward at the September 1987 meetings of the IMF, and that the spirit and practical implications of the remainder are being addressed by the international community.

Box 1

STABILIZATION AND ADJUSTMENT

All economies have to adjust to changes in the world economy, notably with respect to relative prices for goods and services, so as to exploit judiciously their own dynamic comparative advantage or to establish the required national mix between self-reliance and openness. LDCs are no different from other countries in this, except that they have particular problems and deficiencies in implementing policy change. In this sense "adjustment" is little other than the formulation and execution of a set of policies to ensure sustained growth and development, or at least recovery after a recession. Sensible domestic policies would have to take proper account of both external and internal shocks, but not address one set of shocks at the expense of other perhaps equally important developments, or allow short-term preoccupations to distort or damage the longer-term policies. Such adjustment policies would arise naturally from the policy-making process of the country concerned, though it may also seek advice and support from outside bodies.

Adjustment in the 1980s has, for LDCs in particular, come to mean a rather different set of parameters and constraints. LDCs now have to adjust *instead of* pursuing their development policies. They have to erect countervailing forces to limit the economic and social damage caused by adjustment. Whereas in the past their main objective would have been to proceed in linear fashion towards the elimination of poverty and need through economic growth and development, now there is much concern to prevent the poor getting poorer or the nation as a whole suffering from the adjustment process. As a further twist, LDCs – of whom it was once thought normal that they should run a managed balance-of-payments deficit, as capital importers in the early stages of development – now are proposed adjustment packages comprising finance plus a set of required policy reforms essentially affecting their external economic relationships, largely to reduce or eliminate both their current account and their overall balance-of-payments deficits as rapidly as possible. In other words, they are assured that such adjustment is in their interest, but in case they fail to be convinced they are offered a financial inducement. This has occurred, however, when their aid flows have stagnated, when the availability of compensatory finance has become more constrained, and their access to commercial credit – already modest – has almost completely vanished owing both to the prevailing high real interest rates and to the reluctance of creditors to lend, given the "crowding-out" effect of other financial markets. LDCs are thus having to adjust to recession with or without external help. The question, which remains to be tested in an adequate sample of LDCs, is what part of the deterioration in their economic and social life is the result of adjustment rather than the recession itself; whether the country would be worse off without adjustment (some policy changes would be implemented without any external agency); and whether policies which urgently address problems of short-run instability and external balance end by damaging or delaying the real process of structural adjustment that will eventually take place.

Stabilization policies operate on demand management through fiscal and monetary restraint. They aim to achieve balance-of-payments stability and lower domestic price inflation by reducing real

(Continued on next page.)

Box 1 (continued)

incomes and therefore domestic demand for imports (and exportables). As well as expenditure cut-backs, especially in the public sector (often a major contributor to demand in LDC economies), the instrument of devaluation is often used to limit import demand and encourage exports. However, in LDCs, which mainly export primary commodities, devaluation is not always a simple or rapid means of stimulating the production of traded goods that, in addition, are facing depressed world demand.

Most stabilization policies are designed to work in the short term (between one and two years). It is argued that a brief period of austerity permits the attainment of internal and external balance and so provides the basis for the restoration of long-term growth including future credit-worthiness. In practice, in many LDCs the austerity generated by stabilization programmes (often repeated three or four times in succession, see section A.1 of this chapter) has undermined growth prospects and discouraged both domestic and foreign investment.

Structural adjustment policies aim at reducing current account deficits over the medium term (3-5 years) by making the whole economy more efficient, primarily through expanding and diversifying the production of tradeables (exports and import substitutes). This is done by altering (or "restoring appropriate") price relationships, both between the domestic and the external economy (i.e. changing the exchange rate to correspond to the hitherto unadjusted deterioration in the terms of trade) or within the economy itself (e.g. adjusting producer prices among sectors and among products, altering the mix between producer and consumer prices to provide incentives to the former, and perhaps within the former to lay stress on export production or import substitutes such as food in a food deficit country), or by raising the prices of (reducing the subsidies to) government services relative to the private production sector. Establishing better price relations and making them work, in this way, is deemed to support an efficient reallocation of resources by encouraging investment to flow into the key sectors identified under the structural adjustment programme. There are of course major controversies as to whether output within a particular sector – especially the agricultural sector, of special interest to most LDCs – can respond in aggregate over the short-to-medium term, though it is clearly possible to get specific supply responses within sub-sectors. Another problem, even with medium-term, adjustment is that if similar export-oriented prescriptions are being offered to all deficit developing countries, including LDCs, simultaneous success in implementing the programme requirements would rapidly run into the fallacy of composition conundrum – world prices would fall as a result of over-supply.

Lastly, though many LDCs have carefully followed structural adjustment programmes of this sort, they have been disappointed with the levels of resources mobilized externally by Governments and official bodies and by the private sector for credit and investment alike.

All this has meant that, after nearly a decade of adjustment, the subject remains firmly on the international agenda while the particular forms of adjustment programmes prescribed are undergoing a reappraisal. At the autumn 1987 World Bank/IMF meetings it became clear that the reappraisal ought to take four forms;

– of the type and range of policies included in the adjustment package, with particular emphasis on setting priorities for and so limiting the number of targets to be set and monitored, and on allowing adequate time for stabilization measures to work though in conjunction with structural adjustment.

– of the financial terms: given that a large number of developing countries already have unserviceable scheduled external debt burdens, it makes little sense to continue to demand of them negative capital flows to the institutions that are supposedly facilitating their adjustment towards eventual creditworthiness. For the LDCs in particular, the precedent set by low-interest SAF credits (and IDA credits as finance under SAL programmes) needs to be extended to other forms of adjustment finance, including compensatory arrangements to make up for export deficiencies.

– of the correct dosages of the micro-macro policy prescription mix, with particular attention to protecting vulnerable groups which may otherwise be harmed by the adjustment process. This can be done by countervailing programmes, counterpart financing, or by building monitoring and protection of the poor into the adjustment programme itself. The UNICEF proposals (see section A.3 of this chapter) address this question by developing a new level of "meso-policies".

– lastly it makes sense to reappraise the contribution of the North to the adjustment process, especially as regards co-ordination, with respect to its markets as well as its finance. LDCs can only export their way out of recession if there are markets available; they cannot attract international capital if other financial markets have already crowded it out.

B. Mobilization of financial resources

For most LDCs, the fact of their overall poverty (an average per capita income of barely more than $200 per annum) is the main constraint on domestic resource mobilization, at least as regards finance. Necessary consumption, in the form of the basic needs of households and a substantial part of Governments' recurrent budgets, absorbs in most cases a large amount of local financial resources. As a result, LDCs' domestic savings rates are very low: in 1985, 10 LDCs had negative rates (see table 6), and many of them have been dissaving for a number of years. The bulk of the financial resources for investment, therefore, have to be raised abroad, though it follows that, given the prevalence of low or negative domestic savings rates, not all such external finance should necessarily be channelled into investment, as a judicious targeting of consumption in certain LDCs and in certain circumstances can not only save lives but also assist the longer-term process of development by embodying a preinvestment consumption phase.[30]

Financial resources raised abroad fall into three main categories. First, there are the external savings of nationals. In the case of a small but significant number of LDCs, the repatriated earnings of migrant workers form a substantial part of the national (but not domestic) savings. In many cases where an LDC has a negative domestic savings rate, its external savings by expatriates are high, thus providing a compensatory factor to low domestic savings. In the period 1986-87, LDCs dependent on migrants' remittances were faced with the contraction of the host countries' demand for labour. LDCs have responded to these difficult conditions by introducing policies to ensure that a larger proportion of the remitted incomes stays with the LDC economy concerned in the form of investment where possible but also as domestic consumption of locally-produced goods (see section II.E, below).

Second, external resources can be raised through borrowing abroad or by attracting direct or portfolio investment to the country. LDCs are particularly badly placed to succeed in the competition for funds, not just with other developing countries but with the developed countries too, on any of these fronts. They start by being the least creditworthy countries in the world, in the view of banks and of risk assessment agencies. Their already small creditworthiness has in many cases been eroded, as many of the *official* credits contracted in recent years (notably from the IMF) are now proving difficult to service and are in some cases falling into arrears, further damaging their prospects for new borrowing. Furthermore, following the onset of the debt crisis in 1981-82, the commercial banks are reluctant to lend to third world countries in general, and the volume of bank lending to developing countries has slumped from the relatively high levels of the late 1970s, when recycling was in vogue. Lastly, the persistence of high real interest rates limits the LDCs' capacity to take on commercial borrowing. Direct investment, which is of some importance to LDCs, is dealt with in detail below, although it must be recognized that the poor growth performance of most LDCs and their restricted local markets place them among the least promising candidates for direct investment.

All these factors strengthen the importance for the LDCs of the third category of external resource mobilization, i.e. foreign aid in the form of official grants, loans and debt relief. This is dealt with extensively in Chapter III of this report. Here it suffices to note, that of all the possible external flows, LDCs more than any other developing countries are dependent on official concessional flows. While this remains a reality which Governments both of the LDCs and of the donor countries (and the international institutions which they govern) must acknowledge, it must also be recognized that the LDCs' dependence on aid flows is in itself a manifestation of their vulnerability.

1. *Domestic savings*

Although domestic savings represent only a modest share of total investment finance for most LDCs,[31] many LDCs have introduced policies to encourage the growth of domestic savings by households and by Governments. They have also introduced measures to reduce capital flight, though it is recognized that a sound, growing domestic economy and a realistic, managed exchange rate are the best ingredients for discouraging such outflows. The efforts to enhance domestic savings rates can be classified under two main approaches:

---

[30] Examples of such expenditures in the public sector, and in the social services in particular, are given in a recent publication of UNICEF, *Adjustment with a human face.*

[31] See chapter I, section B.

(i) reducing operation costs, cutting back on expenditures, streamlining enterprise management and identifying spending priorities whether for investment or consumption more efficiently. These approaches are most appropriate to Government services and parastatals, where increased efficiency can release substantial public savings for channelling into priority public investments;

(ii) raising revenues for Government and mobilizing resources from private households or groups. In the former case this can be secured through increased taxation, the replacement of inefficient or counterproductive fiscal measures by new forms of taxation, greater efficiency in tax and excise revenue collection, an increase in the tax base, and charging to parastatals the economic cost of the government services they use. In the private sphere, it can be done through the stimulation of corporate and household savings by tapping the human collateral which can often stand in the stead of the physical capital which in LDCs is such a scarce resource. A specific example of the latter is given in Box 2 on Rural finance in Bangladesh. The more general issue of recent national policies on domestic savings mobilization is treated under four separate heads below.

(a) Taxation

In most LDCs the tax base is rather narrow. Taxes on imports and sales and excise taxes on a very limited range of consumer items provide the bulk of tax revenues. Direct taxes, with income and payroll taxes as the principal components, contribute only a small fraction to the overall tax revenue. There is usually a potential for greater taxation of, and tax collection from, capital gains as well as business and property income.

To redress some of these weaknesses, many LDCs have made efforts to make the tax system simpler and more broadly based. Efforts have also been made to reduce tax leakages by streamlining the tax administration and by reinforcing customs departments. However, a serious problem arises from the reduction in tax revenue ensuing from import-compressing measures. Lower imports not only affect the volume of import taxes but also have negative consequences for investment in pro-

ductive capacities, thus adding losses in income, either as taxes or as non-tax revenues, to the direct losses in import duties.

Many LDCs have undertaken a thorough revision of their tax systems in order, *inter alia*, to reduce the dependence of government revenue on import taxes. Samoa introduced in 1986 a goods and service tax and undertook a detailed review of income tax in 1987. With a view to encouraging the declaration of taxable income and to broadening the base of income taxpayers, Bangladesh lifted the ceiling under the self-assessment scheme for income tax by 20 per cent in FY 1985/86.

(b) Non-tax revenues

Non-tax revenues derive mainly from earnings of public enterprises and revenue from services provided by the Government. Several LDCs have instituted measures aimed at increasing the revenue from public enterprises and reducing budgetary support requirements by improving their performance. These programmes focus mainly on fees and prices of public sector goods and services as well as on recruitment policies. In several LDCs measures have been taken for the rationalization, including liquidation where appropriate, of public and parastatal enterprises. While these measures do not contribute to the generation of additional resources, they will alleviate the pressure on the budget and free resources for higher-priority activities.

(c) Recurrent expenditures

In addition to the steps already taken to make public enterprises self-financing, efforts have been undertaken to limit recurrent expenditures by streamlining administrative services, by introducing user participation [32] in the cost of social services, particularly health services, and by rescheduling external debt. During the period 1981-1987 a number of LDCs (Bangladesh, Benin, Botswana, Bhutan, Burundi, Burkina Faso, Central African Republic, Haiti, Malawi, Lesotho, Nepal, Rwanda, Sierra Leone, United Republic of Tanzania) announced and implemented measures to restrain non-essential public consumption and thus limit recurrent budget expenditures. Several adjustment programmes also contain elements designed to reduce recurrent expenditure.

---

[32] It has to be remembered that the introduction of or increases in user charges for basic needs services in LDCs, however desirable as a means of revenue mobilization, necessarily mean the rationing by income of such services to the poorer sectors of the population, which in many LDCs represent the vast majority.

(d) *Private savings*

Some LDCs have launched two-pronged initiatives with a view both to mobilizing corporate and household savings for development and to increasing the volume of these savings through the development of credit institutions in urban as well as rural areas. These programmes include expanding commercial banks and their branches, improving depository functions of non-bank financial institutions, issuing new financial instruments and establishing postal saving banks, national insurance companies and employees' provident funds.

Given the specific socio-economic conditions prevailing in the LDCs, Governments have explored unconventional ways to mobilize domestic savings. Particularly in rural areas, lending and saving schemes have been set up or developed from grassroots schemes which target social groups who were widely believed not to be able to participate in the saving process. In Bangladesh, a scheme for landless men and women has been functioning successfully for several years. Its members contribute regularly to the scheme's assets. Conversely, credits are extended to participants who otherwise would have difficulties in borrowing in the absence of material collateral (see also Box 2).

Along with the expansion of the institutional network, policies have been implemented in several LDCs to encourage the holding of financial assets and their channelling into the national banking system. Interest rates have been raised to levels above the inflation rates. Currency devaluations recently undertaken in several LDCs should help to stem capital flight. Furthermore, special investment packages, as well as an attractive portfolio of financial assets, provide incentives for migrants to invest their savings in their home countries.

Box 2

RURAL FINANCE IN BANGLADESH: THE GRAMEEN BANK

As Bangladesh is a country where 75 per cent of the population depends on farming for subsistence, credit programmes have at various times been implemented in rural areas. These policies have included the rural group lending and savings schemes. One such scheme is the Grameen Bank (GB), established in 1983, which organizes landless men and women for the mobilization of small rural savings and offers them loans. Seventy five per cent of the shares of the Grameen Bank are held by its borrowers, landless men and women, and the rest by the Bangladesh Government. By August 1987, total membership had reached 291,136 (males 61,872, females 229,264), with the number of centres reaching 12,706, covering 6,570 villages through 347 branches.

The GB has created a variety of fund saving schemes. For example, under a group fund arrangement every member deposits one taka each week as a personal saving. In addition to this saving, each member also pays a 5 per cent obligatory group tax upon receipt of a loan from the GB. This group tax is also deposited in group saving. Over and above this, an emergency fund has been created by the members for insurance against default, death, disability and other accidents, with additional payments of 25 per cent of the interest due on the loan after the loan is fully paid. The proceeds of the Emergency Fund can be used to repay the loan of a member who becomes unable to repay owing to accident or other unforeseen reasons.

The GB members saved TK 183.6 million ($5.6 million) both in group saving and in the Emergency Fund as of August 1987. The average saving per member (the total number of members is 291,136) has thus been TK 631 ($19) which, although seemingly very little, is actually quite significant given socio-economic conditions in rural Bangladesh.

This kind of group mechanism has been particularly valuable for mobilizing savings on a regular basis among the rural poor. The country's experience has attested that the poor can and do save. Regularity of savings has been an important factor in developing the rural poor's asset base. In most cases the savings are both contractual and compulsory in the sense that every group member is expected to make a weekly deposit, however small it may be. Group responsibility and group pressure have been extremely valuable in developing the necessary discipline.

Credits for groups are handled by loans extended either to individual members of the group or to the group as a whole. In some instances, a risk guarantee fund is created with the implementing bank in order to cover possible defaults and the absence of security.

(Continued on next page.)

Box 2 *(continued)*

In most group-based operations, it has been noted that the repayment record has been highly satisfactory, in fact even better than the average repayment record in rural banking operations. For example, as of end August 1987, arrears amounted to TK 0.151 million only, while disbursed loans outstanding were as high as TK 1,958 million. This challenges the familiar contentions that the poor are not creditworthy under present circumstances or that it is always risky to lend without material collateral.

As a result, group savings in the Grameen Bank serve a wide range of purposes other than the immediate investment:

(*a*) The system imposes a discipline on the group members in developing a savings habit which did not exist before;

(*b*) Savings enhance self-confidence. Having been a non-saver or adissaver all his or her life, an individual in a group finds it a great source of encouragement to become a habitual saver;

(*c*) Savings cover normal business risks, seasonal variations in income, natural calamities like flood, famine, cyclone and drought, disease and even political disturbances. Members of the group can take riskier decisions because they are cushioned to some extent by the savings;

(*d*) Group savings of the poor demonstrate that the ordinary people can be a great source of strength to themselves and to the nation. If each poor person saves a tiny amount each week regularly, the cumulative amount mobilized as savings will be enormous because the poor are so numerous. The Bangladesh example is thus worthy of emulation in other LDCs.

2. *Foreign direct investment*

Faced with a very limited savings capacity, a mounting debt-service burden, slow growth and even stagnation of export earnings and concessional flows, as well as with the virtual collapse of commercial bank lending, LDCs have been turning towards foreign direct investment as a means of securing financial resources for their economic development and structural transformation. Many LDCs have thus undertaken a reform of their investment codes, or are in the process of doing so, with a view to encouraging the establishment of foreign enterprises and to allowing the employment of foreign manpower. Countries which have revised their investment codes since 1984 include Burkina Faso, Burundi, Cape Verde, Comoros, Gambia, Guinea, Guinea-Bissau (in process), Sierra Leone, and Sao Tome and Principe. A number of LDCs Governments are also providing a variety of production incentives to attract foreign investment such as the liberalization of profit-repatriation rules, the offer of tax holidays, and the granting of special foreign-exchange and tax privileges to enclave assembly operations for exports.

Some LDCs have approached foreign investors directly or developed special promotional policies. In the beginning of 1987, the Bangladesh Government, for example, organized an investors' forum at which it introduced projects calling for an overall investment of $530 million. Representatives of 168 companies from 15 developed and developing countries attended. Seventy memoranda of understanding were signed with prospective foreign investors interested in joint ventures, which, if realized, will mobilize a total investment of $300 million, including $200 million in foreign exchange. The Government has further announced its intention of joining the World Bank-supported Multilateral Investment Guarantee Agency which is to promote and guarantee foreign investments in developing countries.

Lesotho has continued its policy of seeking foreign investment through the Lesotho National Development Corporation (LNDC), signing at the beginning of 1987 a draft agreement involving an investment of M 13 million ($6.227 million) for a joint venture with a Shanghai Corporation. The latter will scour and spin the whole Lesotho output of wool and mohair and produce in successive stages wool fabrics and a range of garments. Several LNDC teams have conducted promotional campaigns in key developed countries to convince selected groups of entrepreneurs to come to Lesotho to set up manufacturing plants. During the two-year period ending March 1986, a total of 136 industrialists visited Lesotho to discuss industrial investment opportunities.

The Botswana Government also provides substantial investment incentives. The Botswana Development Corporation builds "factory shells" which it then sells or leases to investors, and has even been prepared to lease whole plants and equipment. Financial incentives under the Financial Assistance Policy (which emphasizes labour-intensive activities), include tax reimbursements and net subsidies. The country's liberal foreign exchange policy is a further incentive for foreign investors.

In Mauritania, a new fisheries policy involving the promotion of joint ventures has been successfully implemented during the 1980s. Mauritanians have become substantially involved in fishing activities through joint ventures with local majority control. The Government has raised considerable revenue through licensing, and the programme has virtually eliminated illegal fishing along the Mauritanian coast. Fish exports thus increased from $14 million in 1979 to $278 million in 1986.

LDC Governments can clearly see the distinctions between management, ownership and control. Some are prepared to allow foreign investors to take a majority stake in locally-based companies while others insist on retaining at least a 51 per cent stake. It is reasonable to expect a wide range of responses from the 40 LDCs, which naturally have different political perceptions and ownership régimes.

Be that as it may, despite some positive developments in this field, LDCs have in general not been successful in attracting foreign direct investment: in the period 1980-1985, direct investment flows from the DAC member countries to the LDCs amounted to only $407 million. Small domestic markets, lack of skilled labour, inadequate infrastructure and, in the case of a number of LDCs, landlockedness and remoteness from the main world markets, are among the factors which have undermined the attractiveness of LDCs to foreign investors. Because of these structural and geographical handicaps, the incentives offered by LDCs do not often lead to substantial foreign investment inflows. In these circumstances, concessions to foreign investors may even bring about losses in government revenue and foreign exchange. LDCs must therefore be cautious about their expectations of the extent to which they can influence the foreign investment climate to their advantage by fiscal measures or by selling off State assets at a loss.

C. Food and agriculture

1. *Past shortcomings*

Least developed countries, like many other developing countries, have a record of inadequate domestic policy support for local agriculture and food production in the past. Prices to farmers for foodstuffs and other crops have been kept artificially low through price controls and/or the procurement and sales policies of commodity-marketing boards, the main purpose being to ensure adequate nutrition standards among certain, usually urban, income groups and to generate surpluses for use elsewhere in the economy. Such low prices, however, have discouraged production as well as investment in the agricultural sector. In cases where subsidies have been granted to farmers to promote agricultural output this has mostly led to financial strain on the national marketing boards, thus jeopardizing their ability to finance services to or carry out investment in the agricultural sector.

Macroeconomic policies, too, have entailed discrimination against agricultural and food production. Import restrictions have been resorted to, notably through customs duties and/or quotas, so as to cope with external trade imbalances and to provide protection to the local manufacturing sector. Exchange rates have been kept overvalued. The implications of currency overvaluation for agricultural and food production are twofold. First, the local prices for exported commodities are kept high as compared to prevailing international prices, thus reducing the incentives to domestic exporters. Second, exchange rate overvaluation implies low prices for imported foodstuffs, which in turn tend to discourage local agricultural production. The depressing effects of exchange rate overvaluation also tend to nullify the incentives provided to agricultural production such as annual producer price rises and subsidies to the supply of agricultural inputs.

2. *FAO's programme of action for African agriculture*

Increasingly, however, governments have undertaken to implement major reforms in support of the agricultural sector, particularly in the African LDCs, many of which are food deficit countries.

Of particular relevance for agricultural development in LDCs is the programme of action for African agriculture proposed by the Director-General of FAO in 1986.[33] While the programme is addressed to African countries, the analysis and recommendations contained therein are applicable more widely to the least developed countries in general. The programme focuses on four major lines of action:

(a) *Priority to agriculture*, which should involve, *inter alia*, assigning 20-25 per cent of aggregate public investment to this sector, as provided for in *Africa's Priority Programme for Economic Recovery, 1986-1990* (APPER), and endorsed by the United Nations Programme of Action for African Economic Recovery and Development (UN-PAAERD).

(b) *Improvements in the four "i's" of agricultural development*:

(i) *incentives*: increasing producer prices; opening up new marketing channels; adjusting the ratio of producer prices to the cost of inputs;

(ii) *inputs*: priority to agricultural inputs in the allocation of foreign exchange; increasing production of improved seeds; promoting mechanization through the introduction of water pumps, ox or donkey carts and simple processing machinery;

(iii) *institutions*: improving practical training and research and extension services; land reform;

(iv) *infrastructure*: better transport systems, more efficient use of existing transport and communications.

(c) *Adoption of a conservation strategy* aimed at limiting soil erosion, safeguarding communal grazing, overcoming the fuelwood crisis, developing small-scale irrigation, and promoting involvement of the population in anti-desertification tasks.

(d) *Improving the international economic environment*: dismantling agricultural protectionism wherever it occurs, including in the countries of the North which are the leading markets for LDC agricultural exports.[34]

---

[33] See FAO, *A programme of action for African agriculture, proposed by the Director-General of FAO*; and main report, annexes I-IV and executive summary (ARC/86/3) (1986).

[34] See in particular the 1986 World Bank *World Development Report* which analyses world agricultural policies.

3. *New policy trends in LDCs*

A tendency towards the readjustment of agricultural strategies and policies can be clearly perceived in LDCs. The LDCs are giving higher priority than in the past to agricultural development and are adapting their policies to the need to overcome insufficient food production and falling export earnings from the agricultural sector. Increasing self-sufficiency in food is one of the top priorities of the national development plans of virtually all of them. The new policies are generally in consonance with the above-mentioned recommendations proposed by the FAO. Policies regarding agricultural development naturally vary from one LDC to another according to their individual needs, priorities and economic systems. *The Least Developed Countries – 1986 Report* discussed the major features of the new policies (cf. paras. 50-60). The sub-sections below give an account of recent developments in this regard, further to the measures discussed in the 1986 issue of this report.

(a) *More effective use of the market mechanism*

LDCs are resorting increasingly to price incentives and to the liberalization of commodity markets as a means of encouraging agricultural and food production (cf. paras. 50-51 of the 1986 report). During 1986, producer prices for cereals were raised in Gambia, Guinea, Guinea-Bissau and Sudan, and those for export crops in Uganda (coffee, tea, cocoa, beans and tobacco). Liberalization of commodity marketing is under way in Bangladesh (for jute), Botswana (for sorghum), Malawi (for oilseeds used in domestic consumption and for export items), Sao Tome and Principe (for palm kernels) and Sudan (for cotton). Trade in rice was privatized in Sierra Leone in January 1987. In the United Republic of Tanzania, the private sector is expected to play an expanded role in the internal commercial distribution of cereals. Various livestock services currently provided by the public sector are being privatized in Guinea. Starting in 1985 the pig herd of Sao Tome and Principe, which is being reconstituted with FAO/UNDP assistance, is being sold to private farmers. In some LDCs, the good cereals harvests registered during the past two years have tended to depress local prices, and governments have had to intervene to prevent prices from falling, thereby encouraging cereals production in the period ahead. Thus, in Mauritania, producer prices for rice and cereals are to be kept in 1987/88 at the same high levels as during the two previous marketing years; whereas the Government of Burkina Faso is engaged in reconstituting stocks through the purchase of cereals.

(b) *Diversification efforts: fisheries and other sectors*

The fisheries sector is being developed in a number of LDCs particularly through foreign assistance and in the context of joint ventures or international fisheries agreements. Expansion of the fishing fleet and related infrastructure is under way in Cape Verde, with assistance from the USSR. Two separate fishing agreements were entered into in the summer of 1986 by the European Communities with Equatorial Guinea and Guinea. In Guinea, further to the measures described in the 1986 report, a joint venture fishing enterprise was set up in 1986 with French participation and is being expanded with assistance from the European Development Fund (credit totalling ECU 8 million, equivalent to $9.1 million). A regional committee for the development of fishing in the Gulf of Guinea was created in May 1987, comprising five countries of which two are LDCs (Equatorial Guinea and Sao Tome and Principe, plus Congo, Gabon and Zaire).

In Mauritania, where fishing and fisheries licensing have become a major source of foreign exchange earnings, second only to iron ore, international support has been secured for the feasibility studies of projects relating to fisheries development (totalling $60 million); and negotiations are under way for a fishing agreement with the EC. In Democratic Yemen, external assistance has been secured for the development of manpower resources in the fisheries sector, and a fishing agreement with the USSR is in force for the period 1986-90. Modernization of this sector led to a fish catch estimated at 90,000 tonnes in 1986, which is 8 per cent above the planned target. A new fishing port is being built up at Hodaida, Yemen Arab Republic. In land-locked Malawi (where the fish catch grew from 62,100 tonnes to 73,000 tonnes between 1985 and 1986), measures have been taken to promote both the processing of prawns and the experimental farming of crabs.

The development of the fisheries sector in LDCs has been accompanied by measures aimed at securing national control over the rate of exploitation of the fishing resources; and such measures relate to the promotion of local participation in joint ventures, the strengthening of local companies, the protection of territorial waters from poachers, the development of the fishing fleet and landing facilities, and the granting of fishing licences on a more stringent basis.

Import substitution activities involving agricultural products are being promoted in several LDCs. Efforts are being made in a number of LDCs to expand sugar production for domestic use. These confront a situation of world oversupply with sugar trading as low as $US 0.05 per lb for much of 1986/87, but may be justifiable in terms of national self-sufficiency planning. Developing countries are now the main (if not the only) expanding market for sugar. In Bangladesh, sugar output is expected to increase from 60,000 tonnes in 1986 to 140,000 tonnes in 1987. In Mali, sugar production (which is being developed with assistance from China) reached 18,000 tonnes in 1985/86, which is three times the 1982/83 level (while still far short of the annual local consumption level of 50,000 tonnes). Sugar storage facilities are being built up at Port Sudan. A palm oil mill is being set up to meet domestic needs in Sao Tome and Principe (capacity 1,400 tonnes a year) with the assistance of the European Investment Bank, subsequent to the expansion of plantations with the assistance of the European Development Fund. Several measures have been taken during 1987 in Burkina Faso to promote import substitution of agricultural goods and inputs. These measures include encouraging production of cotton to be used by the local textile industry, increasing the content of locally produced maize flour in domestic bread, and diverting expensively produced wheat and sugar to alternative uses.

(c) *Rehabilitation of the commodity export sector*

Several LDCs have undertaken programmes to streamline the operation of their commodity export sector, particularly with a view to reducing production costs, enhancing producer and national revenues, and alleviating the financial burdens on their marketing boards. In Chad, a programme of rehabilitation of *Cotontchad* (the State-owned board dealing with the production, marketing and exports of cotton) has been continuing since 1986, involving the closing of one-half of the ginning mills, personnel cuts and reduction of producer subsidies. Rehabilitation of the cocoa sector is under way in Sao Tome and Principe, where production of this commodity – which represents 80-90 per cent of exports – had fallen from 11,600 tonnes in 1973 to 3,500 tonnes in 1985. Under the rehabilitation programme, foreign companies have been charged with the management of State-owned plantations, and are allowed to retain up to 30 per cent of export earnings for the importation of raw materials and of consumer goods for their workers. Malawi has moved to a leading world position as a producer of burley tobacco, which is now the dominant variety produced in a country over 50 per cent dependent on tobacco for its export earnings.

The Comoros made arrangements with neighbouring States collectively to limit the supply and enhance the price of some exotic commodities on the world market, notably vanilla and cloves, though both products face declining demand trends, the former being undermined by cheaper substitutes while the latter (also produced for export by the United Republic of Tanzania, another LDC) faces falling demand in its major market, Indonesia, following a self-sufficiency drive.

Box 3

GUINEA-BISSAU'S EFFORTS TO ACHIEVE FOOD SELF-SUFFICIENCY

With the launching of an economic recovery programme in December 1983, a market-oriented agricultural development strategy started to be implemented in Guinea-Bissau. Positive results have already been achieved due both to better weather conditions after the 1983 drought and to the new production incentives introduced by the recovery programme. After a decline of 5 per cent in 1983, agricultural production rose by 2.4 per cent in 1984 and 3.0 per cent in 1985. Growth rates were impressive in regard particularly cereals production, which increased by 24.5 per cent in 1984, by 16.3 per cent in 1985 and by 14.5 per cent in 1986. The volume of cereals thus increased from 132,000 tonnes in 1983 to a record of 200,000 tonnes in 1986. Consequently, the food self-sufficiency ratio in cereals was equivalent to about 97 per cent in 1986. Cereal import requirements for 1987 were estimated at 17,000 tonnes, as against an average of 37,000 tonnes during preceding years.

As regards production incentives introduced by the recovery programme, producer price increases ranged from 53 to 92 per cent in 1984, and again from 63 to 66 per cent in 1985. The provision of inputs such as seeds and fertilizers, and of essential consumer goods, was improved in rural areas thanks to balance-of-payments assistance and to a more efficient management of retail trade which resulted, *inter alia*, from the transfer to the private sector of the activities of Socomin and Armazens do Povo, the two State-owned wholesale and retail companies.

Improvement in food self-sufficiency has not been achieved at the expense of agricultural exports, as a similar positive trend has been registered for the production of export cash crops. In 1984, the total export value rose sharply to $17.4 million from $8.6 million in 1983, even though it declined subsequently due to exogenous, world market conditions (fall in international commodity prices). A particularly impressive improvement has been achieved in regard to the production and exports of cashew nuts, which have been expanding steadily: from a volume of 950 tonnes exported in 1983, 6,000 tonnes was reached in 1986, equivalent to 50 per cent of the total value exported last year by Guinea-Bissau. In view of this success, the Government intends to expand the cashew plantations from 3,000 ha to 5,000 ha in the next few years.

The implementation of the recovery programme, however, has had to confront a number of difficulties, particularly in 1986. The full elimination of internal and external price distortions was not achieved because of implementation delays and of insufficient producer price rises. It was estimated that in spite of weekly exchange rate devaluations since December 1983, domestic inflation kept the ratio between parallel market and official exchange rates unchanged, at about 3 to 1. Producer prices for cashew nuts and palm kernels were equivalent to only 50 per cent of the official export parity price. Producer prices for rice were equivalent to three-quarters of the import parity price. Furthermore, in order to shift income in favour of the rural sector, the change of the rural-urban terms of trade remains an unfulfilled objective of the structural adjustment programme adopted in May 1987.

The new agricultural development strategy attaches greater importance than past policies to promoting the production of small farmers, who account for most of the crop. The decision to direct public investments in agriculture primarily towards providing basic support to small private farmers, and developing low-cost infrastructure, permits an optimistic forecast for Guinea-Bissau's efforts to achieve food self-sufficiency in spite of the acute economic difficulties which the country is still facing.

(d) *Other recent policy initiatives*

Other initiatives relate principally to improvement of food reserve schemes, irrigation, and training and research in the field of agriculture. Developments in these matters were discussed in the 1986 report. A further development in early 1987 was the establishment of a food security reserve scheme of 200,000 tonnes of wheat and rice by seven developing countries of southern Asia, which include four LDCs: Bangladesh, Bhutan, India, Maldives, Nepal, Pakistan and Sri Lanka. A grain silo and warehouses are being built up in Botswana. As regards irrigation, the first stage of the Marib dam was opened in Yemen in 1986. It is expected to irrigate initially 4,000 ha and to reach 20,000 ha by 1988.

D. Manufacturing

Least developed countries have been reviewing their industrial policies with a view to overcoming past shortcomings and enhancing the contribution of the manufacturing sector to their national economic development. As indicated in the 1986 report, the instruments used for this purpose vary among LDCs, but several policy trends are clearly discernible:

- privatization and efforts to attract foreign investment;

- rationalization of public enterprises (PEs);

- encouragement of small- and medium-scale enterprises (SMEs).

1. *Privatization*

Privatization efforts are continuing in a number of LDCs, including Togo, Guinea, Central African Republic, Gambia, and Nepal. Problems, however, have arisen in this connection, notably as regards valuation of assets, reductions of the labour force and identification of potential investors, thereby causing delays in reaching divestiture targets. In Nepal, fiscal and monetary incentives are being designed to attract private investors. The Government of Malawi, which has assigned a high priority to preserving the role of the private sector in industrial enterprises, is introducing export promotion schemes and credit facilities. Both Rwanda and Burundi have recently embarked on limited exercises in divestiture of State corporations, with mixed results.[35]

Although the governments of LDCs pursuing privatization policies have been turning to domestic business circles with their proposals, it has generally become apparent that, given the limited savings capacity of these countries, the capital outlays required for the take-over of usually large PEs could hardly be provided by domestic sources. Hence the search for foreign investors. But even this alternative encounters serious limitations in the case of the LDCs, as their ability to attract foreign investment is impaired by their small domestic markets, lack of skilled labour and inadequate infrastructure (cf. section B.1 above).

In any event, privatization based on foreign investment does not offer a simple solution to the manufacturing problems of LDCs. Given the great number of PEs in need of rehabilitation, governments must decide how much, if any, of the country's manufacturing sector they want to see in foreign hands, and at which discounts they are prepared to sell the enterprises built up with substantial capital outlays. Unlike equivalent policies in developed countries, such as France and the United Kingdom, where privatization of powerful monopolies or internationally competitive major firms has raised enormous sums for the national treasuries, very large concessions usually have to be made in LDCs to induce private buyers to take on State assets. Thus in Togo, for instance (see Box 4), where State corporations were sold to the private sector at very low valuations, the immediate, once-and-for-all benefits to the national budget may be outweighed by the longer-term effects on the economy as a whole. In addition, for a number of LDCs with a heavily subsidized public enterprise sector, privatization through foreign investment is hardly a viable option, as no investor is likely to be prepared to buy loss-making enterprises whose long-term profit prospects are doubtful without enormous local subsidies and long-term concessions.

[35] For more details, see J. T. Winpenny, "The divestiture of public enterprises in developing countries", *Development Policy Review*, vol. 5, No. 4 (1987).

It can also be argued that it is not the form of ownership which determines the economic viability of an enterprise, i.e. public or private, but the degree to which it is efficiently managed and responds to market forces. Monopolies, whether public or private, can contribute to the national economy or can be a drag on it, depending on policies and the efficiency of management. Moreover, in their business operations, public enterprises are able to take into consideration social and broader development objectives and can thus make an important contribution to the well-being of the population which a more narrowly profit-oriented enterprise may be unable to provide.

2. *Rationalization of public enterprises (PEs)*

Divestiture, or the form of privatization considered in the foregoing section, is only one way of approaching the issue of reform of public enterprises, the other form being their streamlining and rationalization. Since possibilities of attracting domestic or foreign private investment for manufacturing activities appear limited, many LDCs are resorting to the second alternative through a thorough reform of their PEs, on the understanding that these will continue to remain the main source of industrial output in the foreseeable future. Measures introduced for this purpose include the establishment of special mechanisms for monitoring the enterprises' financial performance; introduction of improved supervisory systems; and strengthening of administrative and financial management, including greater autonomy for boards of directors and managers in formulating policies relating to staffing, salary structures and bonuses, pricing, and choice of suppliers and distributors. An example of a thorough overhaul of the legal framework governing PEs is provided by Gambia, which is in the process of adjusting the relevant regulations in such a way as to ensure consistency with modern patterns of commercial company law.

3. *Encouragement of small- and medium-scale enterprises (SMEs)*

The problems governments are experiencing with their PEs have put into sharp focus the contribution which small- and medium-scale enterprises (SMEs) can make to domestic manufacturing. Many governments are thus making renewed efforts to mobilize this potential. Nevertheless, the need to concentrate on the rehabilitation of PEs, given limited public resources, has often meant a *de facto* lower priority for measures to encourage the establishment and expansion of SMEs. Bangladesh, Bhutan, Botswana, Burkina Faso, Central African Republic, Guinea, Malawi, Mauritania, Nepal, Togo and Rwanda are among the countries which have in recent years introduced special incentives for SMEs. Togo, for example, is launching a large co-ordinated programme, backed jointly by the Government and private sector, to stimulate and expand the SME sector. Measures are being designed to encourage the start of new companies, improve management training, launch new products and create more employment. A new Togolese Centre for Investment and a Club for Entrepreneurs are being established, and special services are created to help businessmen start new companies. In addition, some LDCs have taken measures to curb the quasi-monopoly power of large enterprises by facilitating the entry or establishment of new companies as entrepreneurs, in the same way that agricultural produce marketing is also being liberalized in these countries. Such measures, together with policies to liberalize the economy – often introduced in the context of structural adjustment programmes [36] – are improving the general environment for business activity in the LDCs and positively affecting many of those elements of the business climate that influence the decisions of (potential) entrepreneurs and investors.

---

[36] The World Bank's 1987 *World Development Report* focused on industrialization and trade liberalization policies, citing developing countries with a strong outward orientation and sound industrial diversification, such as the Republic of Korea and Mauritius as exemplars. It should not, however, be suggested that LDCs could automatically follow the same path, even of that of a small country like Mauritius, which reduced its commodity export dependence by diversifying into *both* manufactures and services, in the late 1980s. Present world trading conditions and the starting-point of LDCs make this a very difficult path to follow. Most LDCs remain best advised not to neglect the SNPA recommendations on the satisfaction of key domestic needs as a priority.

Box 4

PRIVATIZATION: THE EXPERIENCE OF TOGO

Restructuring of the public enterprise sector in Togo began in 1984 with support by the IMF which had made such reforms a condition for the release of the second tranche of its Structural Adjustment Loan. Public enterprises were classified into four categories: (*a*) enterprises of strategic importance which were to remain in the Government's portfolio; (*b*) enterprises to be privatized; (*c*) enterprises to be restructured and privatized; (*d*) enterprises to be liquidated.

To promote the involvement of local and foreign enterprises in the national economy, a new Investment Code was introduced in 1985, including generous tax and import duty advantages, as well as measures to facilitate the repatriation of capital and profits. A stable and convertible currency, the CFA franc, is another decisive asset, in this case shared by several other LDCs.

A 10 year lease of the steel company *Sociéte nationale de sidérurgie* was granted to an American concern. In 1985, a year after signing the agreement, the company, renamed *Société togolaise de sidérurgie*, had a turnover of CFAF 1.5 billion on which it made a profit of at least CFAF 112 million, contributing CFAF 319 million to the State in taxes.

The Government also succeeded in finding a private buyer for its two textile companies, TOGOTEX and ITT. The two factories are to be operated by the Pan Atlantic Textile Corporation, 90 per cent of which is owned by the Pan Africa Textile Corporation, a private firm registered in the United States which is in the hands of a group of private American and Republic of Korean investors. The purchase price for this, the largest privatization project so far, was around $30 million. To assist the take-over by United States and Korean interests, long-term loans have been arranged with West African development institutions and the IFC, which is providing a $1 million equity investment and a $7 million loan.

The companies will be modernized and begin limited production of African wax prints for sale in Togo and West African markets; as production increases, polo and tee shirts will be produced for export which are planned eventually to account for 60 per cent of production. The experience of the company's technical partner, a Republic of Korea textile firm specializing in the manufacturing and export of knitted and woven apparel, will be used to secure export markets in the United States and in Europe. The project is expected to create 5,000 new jobs and become profitable in 1988, producing earnings of $15 million by 1991. To restore local ties the new owners, Pan Africa, are being encouraged to sell 25 per cent of its shares to the Togolese public when the operation moves into profits.

Other privatizations include a company manufacturing agricultural implements that has been acquired by a French firm, and the *Société de produits laitiers*, which was renamed Fanmilk after the Danish company Emidan bought it. The marble quarrying and processing company SOTOMA has been bought by the Norwegian cement company Norcem while a German-Dutch-Danish group has bought 58 per cent of the shares of the Lomé-based enterprise *Industries togolaises des plastiques* (ITP) which manufactures tubes; the remaining shares continue to be held mainly by the Government. A French company has acquired 51 per cent of the shares of the cotton seed oil processing firm *Industries oléagineux du Togo*, with the rest of the capital being provided by local investors. Foreign business concerns have also shown interest in a few other PEs.

Sotocon, a clothing manufacturing concern, has been taken over by a domestic businessman, providing so far the only example of a private Togolese entrepreneur taking advantage of the privatization.

The earliest privatization deals, including the leasing of the steel mill, were negotiated on generous terms to set the process in motion. The Government is now, however, adopting a somewhat tougher negotiating stand, reducing, for example, tax holidays from five to two years. So far only very few Togolese entrepreneurs have been able to take advantage of the take-over offers. The corollary is that LDCs do not as yet have a sufficiently developed private sector to take advantage of privatization policies.

E. External sector

The scarcity of foreign exchange constitutes one of the major economic constraints of the LDCs which particularly limits their possibilities of importing the intermediate products and capital goods required for their economic development and structural transformation. The need to devote increasing amounts of scarce foreign exchange to debt service has impaired the performance of the LDCs' economies even further. The sources of these problems can be classified in three main categories: structural handicaps, including those of a geographic or historical nature; an adverse international economic environment in terms notably of depressed demand, high interest rates and insufficient resource flows; and inadequate domestic policies in the LDCs themselves, this last category of problems being the only one in respect of which LDC governments can individually take direct action.

Governments of LDCs have to determine, on the basis of the existing economic structures, the appropriate degree of outwardness and hence of export orientation of their respective countries. Given this constraint, national trade policies should be geared towards the creation of an environment that would permit exporters to exploit whatever comparative advantages the LDC enjoys, and to expand accordingly into new areas. This requires the adoption of appropriate pricing policies, both internally and as regards foreign exchange, an attractive and supportive tax régime and, where relevant, some element of subsidy to encourage the initial development of exports and import competing products. Above all, the institutional environment in which agents of the external sector operate should be supportive rather than obstructive. Many LDCs have been taking meaningful policy initiatives in regard to the external sector, and these are outlined below.

1. *Pricing policies*

Agricultural production of export crops has been stimulated in many LDCs through the overhaul of producer prices which are now set at more remunerative levels, and/or through the elimination of export taxes levied on these products. The African LDCs in particular have almost all substantially revised their producer price structures so as to provide greater incentives to exports, in line with the recovery programme for Africa endorsed by the United Nations General Assembly (UN-PAAERD). Some LDCs have also introduced modifications to their fiscal policies so as to make such policies supportive of the efforts to enhance the performance of the external sector. Thus, under the Public Investment Programme for the period 1982/83-1984/85, *Sudan* removed in 1983 export taxes on 25 export commodities. More recently the price for Sudan's cotton has been delinked from the high Egyptian price, thus making that commodity more competitive in world markets. Similarly, the new *Haitian* Government reduced in 1987 the export tax on coffee, while taxes on all other agricultural products were abolished. In 1985 the Copra and Cocoa Board of *Samoa* established prices at a level somewhat below world prices, but guaranteed the stabilization of the producers' export earnings.

2. *Exchange rate policies*

The disadvantages of exchange rate overvaluation have been widely recognized. An overvalued rate tends to discourage investment in exporting and import-competing activities, makes imports artificially cheap and stimulates their demand in excess of the national purchasing power, thus requiring rationing. The local prices of exportable and import-competing domestic products may become so low as compared to costs that their production may have to be discontinued. The ensuing distortion of the price structure creates a suboptimal allocation of resources.

On the other hand, because of the relatively undiversified structure of production and the low supply elasticities of traditional exports, the usefulness of devaluation in promoting LDCs exports is limited. In some cases, the supply constraints may be such that higher prices in domestic currency resulting from a devaluation would not lead to increased output and exports but rather would imply a higher producers' rent. Moreover, for a few, price-inelastic primary products of which LDCs are important suppliers in world markets, the effects of devaluation might be perverse and volume gains nullified by declines in export values.[37] Yet, allocation of the scarce foreign exchange among different sorts of imports, as well as

---

[37] See M. Godfrey, "Trade and exchange rate policy: A further contribution to the debate", in Tore Rose (ed.), *Crisis and Recovery in Sub-Saharan Africa* (Paris, OECD, 1985).

the choice between domestic production and importing, requires that the exchange rate be set, or allowed to be set, at an appropriate level.

While there may have been, in the past, a tendency among LDCs to keep the exchange rate at an overvalued level, more realistic exchange rate policies are being adopted by them in recent years. In fact, the number of LDCs that depreciated the real value of their currency with respect to the dollar increased from two in the period 1970-75 to 31 in 1980-85.

More recently, a number of LDCs have carried out devaluations of their national currencies, some of which were of a sweeping nature. In Sierra Leone, the floating of the national currency resulted in a depreciation by 85 per cent against the US dollar. Sudan devalued by 44 per cent against the US dollar in October 1987. In the United Republic of Tanzania, the exchange rate fell by 68 per cent against the US dollar, and in Gambia by 53 per cent in 1986. Somalia introduced an auction system for the allocation of foreign currencies, which resulted in a considerable *de facto* devaluation. In Guinea, the Government implemented a set of monetary measures which entailed a significant depreciation, the launching of a new national currency and the use of auctions for allocating foreign exchange. As of mid-1986, the value of the new currency had depreciated by 94 per cent against the SDR as compared to the December 1985 rate. All these devaluations were undertaken in the context of negotiations with the IMF. In addition, Yemen devalued its currency against the dollar by 28 per cent, and Burundi and Vanuatu did so against the SDRs (to which their respective currencies are pegged).

3. *Establishment of bonded warehouse facilities and export processing zones*

The Government of *Bangladesh* has established a system of bonded warehouses, which allows producers of garments, specialized textiles and knitwear destined exclusively to export markets to import industrial materials free of duty. Under the duty drawback system, export units that do not have access to the bonded warehouse facility are entitled to a refund of import duties on intermediate products. In 1985, Bangladesh further established an export processing zone. The enterprises set up in this zone are fully exempt from customs and excise duties, and they are given a tax holiday and a rebate on income tax payments. More recently, the rules determining the role and function of the authorities of the zone have been modified to enhance investment and to ensure greater autonomy for the authorities of the zone.

Similarly, the *Maldives* has established an export processing zone, at present consisting of two garment factories. It must, however, be remembered that the net export earnings from EPZs are only a small proportion of the gross earnings because of the high import intensity of the activities in these zones and their often minimal linkages with the domestic economy (other than through the use of unskilled labour).

4. *Import policies*

During the 1980s, a number of LDCs have adopted measures to facilitate the flow of imports required for the production of exports. In *Bangladesh*, schemes are in operation to release import restrictions applied to inputs needed for direct and indirect exports. In the *Lao PDR* the measures adopted in 1985 to improve the management of public enterprises included authorisation for firms to retain export earnings to finance imports of intermediate goods.

Measures have been taken in other LDCs with a view to restricting imports. In *Sudan*, under the Public Investment Programme for the period 1982/83-1984/85, measures were implemented to discourage imports, particularly of luxury goods, and to encourage domestic production. Such measures include: (i) elimination of subsidies; (ii) bans on imports of a wide range of luxury and non-essential goods (the list included 39 items which, in 1981, accounted for 12 per cent of total imports); (iii) obligation for importers to deposit the full value (instead of 40 per cent as in the past) of the letter of credit from their own sources; and (iv) promotion of the production of import substitutes, particularly sugar, cement and textiles. In 1985, *Samoa* tightened its exchange control measures to reduce import demand: the value limit on imports requiring letter of credit facilities was lowered by 50 per cent, while imports of motor vehicles were further discouraged by the imposition of non-interest-bearing advance deposits.

5. *Credit policies*

Exports can also be stimulated by extending credit at concessional rates. In this connection, *Bangladesh* has established a credit system which consists of the following set of measures:

(i) bank credit up to 90 per cent of the f.o.b. value of export orders is available at subsidized interest rates of 9 per cent for non-traditional exports, and of 12 per cent for traditional exports;

(ii) export credits extended by commercial banks can be refinanced at a concessional interest rate through the Bangladesh Bank;

(iii) concessional credits can be obtained for imports of raw materials for the clothing industries;

(iv) priority is given to export-oriented projects in the allocation of investment credit provided by development financing institutions; and

(v) the credit ceiling for the export sector is determined by export performance and is not subject to other restrictions.

Similarly, in *Nepal* there exists a comparable package of measures in the area of credit:

(i) loans at concessional interest rates by the Nepal Industrial Development Corporation and commercial banks are available to investors in export-oriented industries;

(ii) a restricted amount of pre-shipment and post-shipment credit by commercial banks is available for exporters;

(iii) commercial banks have preferential interest rates for discounting export bills;

(iv) the Nepal Rastra Bank and the Nepal Industrial Development Corporation have jointly established the Credit Guarantee Corporation to extend guarantees on export credits;

(v) the Nepal Insurance Corporation provides insurance for export credits.

6. *Private transfers*

In several LDCs, the remittances from nationals working abroad constitutes an important source of foreign exchange. The recent trend to-wards more flexible exchange rate policies by the LDCs has contributed to encouraging the inflow of foreign exchange through remittances and to ensuring that some of the foreign exchange benefits accrue to the migrants' home country. Various LDCs have adopted further specific measures to achieve these aims. For example in *Cape Verde* the time deposits of emigrants receive as an incentive a higher interest than those of residents. In *Lesotho*, 60 per cent of the miners' earnings go directly from the South Africa companies to Lesotho and these workers can only draw on this portion in Lesotho. In *Bangladesh*, the emigration of workers has been encouraged through measures such as the establishment of technical training centres and orientation centres for migrant workers.

7. *Conditions for the success of the above policies*

The implementation of all these policies relating to the external sector needs to be carried out with the maximum degree of automaticity and administrative simplicity. This is particularly important for LDCs, where government structures are often already overextended and cannot be expected to administer efficiently a system consisting of complex regulations requiring frequent decisions.

These examples of policy initiatives in selected LDCs serve to illustrate the attempts which have been made to streamline LDC policies to improve their external sector. However, more often than not, the structural handicaps and the adverse international economic environment are so overwhelming that no overall improvement of the LDCs' external sector has yet taken place. It should in fact be recognized that these countries have been facing very unfavourable external conditions during the 1980s. Their efforts to adjust to these circumstances by improving their national trade policies should, therefore, receive strengthened support from the international community.

Box 5

STRENGTHENING THE EXTERNAL SECTOR – RECENT POLICY INITIATIVES IN MALAWI

Malawi was one of the first among the LDCs to institute a major programme of policy reform; it last had a balance-of-payments surplus in 1979. As early as 1980, the Government adopted, with IMF advice, an economic stabilization arrangement and in 1981 began the first of a series of structural adjustment programmes. These had the aim of (*a*) restoring internal and external balance to the economy, and (*b*) achieving longer-term structural change through an expansion and diversification of

Box 5 (continued)

tradeables, enhanced performance of key development institutions and improved resource mobilization and allocation in the public sector. The various phases of the programme have been supported by stand-by agreements and an extended arrangement with the IMF, and by structural adjustment lending in the form of World Bank loans and IDA credits. Malawi has also sought and obtained debt rescheduling in the Paris and London Clubs in 1982 and 1983 although the pressure of external debt was again severe in 1987. Major elements in the programme aimed specifically at strengthening the external sector include the following:

– Maintenance of a liberal trade and exchange system and an active *exchange rate policy*. The Malawi Kwacha was first devalued by 15 per cent in April 1982 and then by 12 per cent in September 1983. In January 1984 the Kwacha was tied to a basket of the currencies of Malawi's major trading partners. Reviews of the exchange rate and subsequent devaluations of 15 per cent, 10 per cent and 20 per cent respectively were again carried out in April 1985, August 1986, and February 1987. Measured against the SDR, the Malawi Kwacha was reduced to a third of its 1979 value by 1987; this depreciation exceeded the deterioration of Malawi's terms of trade over the period, indicating that Malawi took exchange rate management policies very seriously. As a result, imports in 1986 were only 65 per cent of 1980's already depressed levels;

– Various *supply-oriented* measures, notably substantial increases in producer prices for smallholder export crops (though it is significant that a major increase in maize producer prices *preceded* the export crop price rises and the IMF/World Bank programmes themselves). Steps to improve agricultural marketing and input supply have also been taken, including the elimination of some marketing monopolies. Moreover, various measures have been introduced to increase flexibility in the economy e.g. a programme of price liberalization, encouraging private sector activity, etc.

– *Export-promotion* efforts. The Malawi Export Promotion Council is to be reorganized and its management strengthened. Technical assistance has been mobilized to formulate a strategy for trade promotion and export diversification and to identify new products and markets and requisite export incentives. A new export financing facility is to be aimed particularly at the small exporter. The facility will provide pre- and post-shipment financing and export credit insurance. Preparations for its start-up were to be completed by the end of 1987;

– A limitation of non-concessional borrowing and improved *external debt management*. An investment co-ordinating committee has been established to oversee all major investments and an external borrowing plan prepared;

– Attempts to *strengthen aid mobilization and co-ordination*. To this end, Malawi organized an International Conference of Partners in Economic Development in 1984 and in 1986 set up a Consultative Group under World Bank sponsorship. Internal aid co-ordination machinery has also been strengthened.

Among new measures announced in the presentation of the budget proposal for fiscal year 1987/88 were the elaboration of a comprehensive *agricultural credit* programme and a *tax reform* programme to be implemented over two to three years, and aimed *inter alia*, at providing incentives to industry through a substantial reduction in customs duties for raw materials and capital goods.

The difficult external transport situation has in recent years been a major constraint for the country's economic progress. Freight traffic, which at the beginning of the decade was shipped almost exclusively through Malawi's natural ports in Mozambique, had, by 1986, to be diverted to the extent of some 90 per cent through South African ports, vastly increasing the c.i.f. cost of exports and rendering some Malawi exports, like sugar, non-competitive. The Government has attempted to alleviate the situation by improving co-ordination of shipments and traffic flows, building up the country's own road haulage capacity and developing a new transit route through the United Republic of Tanzania to the port of Dar-es-Salaam.

This broad reform programme has not yet led to the improvement hoped for in the balance-of-payments. The 1987 balance of payments outturn was expected to be the worst this decade, and real GDP fell in 1986 after a brief recovery. External constraints are currently the most important limiting factor to economic performance. Factors beyond the country's control such as commodity prices, the external transport situation and a very heavy debt burden have obstructed Malawi's adjustment efforts despite a tradition of openness to the world economy which has been further strengthened by the reforms. Its situation thus illustrates both the determining role of external factors in the outcome of the LDCs' adjustment programmes, as well as the long time period likely to be required for adjustment with growth in these countries.

Chapter III

INTERNATIONAL SUPPORT MEASURES

A. Financial assistance

---

1. *Recent trends and prospects*

LDCs' total net external resource flows reached US$ 8.8 billion in 1985, exceeding for the first time the 1980 level. Between 1980 and 1984, their external resource flows had fluctuated around a declining trend, and in 1984 the level reached had been 6 per cent below that of 1980.

The sluggish flow of ODA, which has constituted over 90 per cent of LDCs' external resource receipts during the 1980s, and the slump in non-concessional lending (export credits as well as bank lending and direct investment) brought about a flow of external finance which was inadequate to support the far-reaching structural adjustment reforms which most LDCs engaged upon at some point during the first half of the 1980s. In 1985 there was a welcome increase in ODA due to emergency relief and structural adjustment aid to African countries, but ODA (at constant prices and exchange rates) is forecast to increase only at a modest rate during the remainder of the decade. Provisional figures for total ODA to LDCs for 1986 indicate what appears to be a substantial rise to some $11 billion – a nominal increase of more than 25 per cent. However, the bulk of this increase is attributable to the appreciation of other currencies against the US dollar.[38] The prospects for

LDCs outlined below are on the whole rather bleak, although improving multilateral allocations and the attention given in 1986 to debt relief measures for at least the African countries among the LDCs offers some prospect of slightly improved net resource flows in the future.

(a) *Official development assistance*

LDCs have traditionally and increasingly relied on ODA. In 1985 concessional flows accounted for 96 per cent of their external resource flows. The bulk of it (79 per cent of total external flows) has been provided by DAC donors and multilateral agencies essentially financed by them, mainly IDA and EEC. In terms of their combined GNP, ODA from DAC countries to LDCs remained at 0.08 per cent. For some LDCs, the socialist countries of Eastern Europe and OPEC countries are major donors.

(i) *Donors' performance*

Individual donors' performance (including bilateral flows as well as imputed flows through multilateral channels) indicate that efforts have been made to reach either one of the aid targets embodied in the SNPA. In 1985, seven DAC countries, namely Norway, Denmark, Netherlands, Sweden, Belgium, France and Canada, provided 0.15 per cent or more of their GNP as ODA to LDCs. In that same year, four other DAC mem-

---

[38] Without the depreciation of the US dollar, the increase in ODA of the Western donors to all developing countries would have been only 2.6 per cent (at constant 1985 prices and exchange rates) instead of the apparent 26 per cent. A similar downward adjustment would need to be made to ODA flows to LDCs. See OECD, *Financing and external debt of developing countries, 1986 survey* (Paris, 1987), p. 6.

TABLE 17

The flow of external resources to LDCs, 1980-1985

(Net disbursements)

	Millions of dollars						Percentage of total					
	1980	1981	1982	1983	1984	1985	1980	1981	1982	1983	1984	1985
Concessional flows	7 184	6 875	7 305	7 333	7 435	8 431	85.9	91.8	89.8	93.4	93.8	95.7
of which:												
DAC	5 508	5 361	5 557	5 424	5 935	6 996	65.8	71.6	68.3	69.1	74.9	79.4
Bilateral [a]	3 491	3 333	3 559	3 284	3 479	4 210	41.7	44.5	43.8	41.8	43.9	47.8
Multilateral [a]	2 017	2 028	1 998	2 140	2 456	2 786	24.1	27.1	24.6	27.3	31.0	31.6
OPEC	1 090	961	1 139	1 023	798	561	13.0	12.8	14.0	13.0	10.1	6.4
Bilateral [b]	950	742	963	863	698	479	11.4	9.9	11.8	11.0	8.8	5.4
Multilateral [b]	140	219	176	160	100	82	1.7	2.9	2.2	2.0	1.3	0.9
Non-concessional flows	1 181	612	829	521	490	380	14.1	8.2	10.2	6.6	6.2	4.3
of which:												
Multilateral [a]	89	88	103	116	65	147	1.1	1.2	1.3	1.5	0.8	1.7
Guaranteed private export credits [c]	863	193	187	103	91	122	10.3	2.6	2.3	1.3	1.1	1.4
Direct investment [c]	52	102	168	30	32	23	0.6	1.4	2.1	0.4	0.4	0.3
Total external flows	8 365	7 487	8 134	7 853	7 925	8 811	100.0	100.0	100.0	100.0	100.0	100.0
Memo items:												
Per capita ODA												
In current dollars [d]	24.5	22.9	23.7	23.1	22.9	25.3						
In 1980 dollars [d]	24.5	24.0	25.7	25.9	26.0	28.6						
Per capita total external flows												
In current dollars [d]	28.5	24.9	26.3	24.8	24.4	26.4						
In 1980 dollars [d]	28.5	26.1	28.6	27.8	27.7	29.9						

Source: Data from the OECD secretariat, the World Bank and data of the UNCTAD secretariat.

[a] Multilateral agencies mainly financed by DAC member countries.

[b] Multilateral agencies mainly financed by OPEC member countries.

[c] DAC sources only.

[d] External flows in real terms are expressed in terms of LDCs' command over imports at 1980 prices.

bers, namely Austria, Finland, Italy and Ireland, achieved the alternative target of doubling their ODA to LDCs in current dollars.

Of the remaining DAC countries that have committed themselves to the SNPA aid targets (the Federal Republic of Germany, Japan and the United Kingdom), none has accepted any precise time frame. The United States, Australia and New Zealand have not endorsed the SNPA aid targets. It should be noted, however, that the Federal Republic of Germany is not too far from reaching the 0.15 per cent target (in 1985 it provided 0.13 per cent of its GNP as ODA to LDCs) and the United States and Japan have substantially increased their aid to the LDCs (by 84 per cent and 71 per cent respectively as compared to the average level in 1976-1980), although such aid remained small in terms of donors' GNP (0.04 per cent and 0.06 per cent respectively). DAC donors' aid ratios are shown in full in table 18.

Japan's aid to LDCs is expected to increase further [39] but uncertainties remain with respect to other DAC donors including major donors to LDCs.[40] The Final Statement from the Venice economic summit of the Group of Seven major industrialized countries [41] held in June 1987 underlines the importance of ODA and contains an implicit call for increased resources for the poorest countries by recognizing that they deserve special treatment. Most LDCs are to benefit from such treatment. The Statement does not contain, however, any specific sub-target for aid to these countries, although it recalls the general target of providing 0.7 per cent of GNP to developing countries (already endorsed in 1970 by the General Assembly but not yet met by any of the seven major industrialized countries).

Among the socialist countries of Eastern Europe, two countries namely the USSR and Czechoslovakia, reported that they have reached or exceeded the 0.15 per cent target. The USSR reported that it provided 1.7 billion roubles (US$ 2.2 billion) or 0.22 per cent of its GNP, as net transfers to LDCs in 1985 as compared to 1.1 billion roubles ($1.5 billion) or 0.18 per cent of GNP in 1981. For 1986, it reported estimated net transfers to LDCs of 2 billion roubles ($3.2 billion).

In the context of South-South co-operation, LDCs have been receiving aid from OPEC donors, China and other developing countries. OPEC concessional assistance to LDCs has continued to exceed 0.15 per cent of their combined GNP. In 1985 Kuwait and Saudi Arabia provided respectively 1.1 per cent and 0.38 per cent of GNP. The United Arab Emirates also continued to exceed the target by providing 0.16 per cent of its GNP to LDCs in 1985. However, in absolute terms, aid to LDCs from OPEC donors other than Kuwait generally started to decline in 1983. It is expected to continue to decline in 1986 and 1987, given the fall in oil prices and revenues (see table 19).

In summary, although efforts have been made by many donors to meet the 0.15 per cent target, or substantially to increase ODA to LDCs when the level of ODA was relatively small in terms of GNP, these efforts have not led to the substantial overall ODA increase called for in the SNPA.[42] This raises, *inter alia*, the question of the adequacy of the alternative aid targets [43] embodied therein, especially now that six years have elapsed since the adoption of the SNPA by the Paris Conference and that the number of countries included in the list of LDCs has been increased from 35 to 40.

(ii) *Multilateral aid*

During the period 1980-1985, contributions to multilateral agencies essentially financed by DAC countries have fluctuated around a rising trend, and the share allocated to LDCs in the programmes of such agencies, in particular IDA and UNDP, has on the average increased, exceeding one third in 1985. Thus LDCs' recourse to these multilateral agencies increased notably, from 24 per cent in 1980 to 32 per cent in 1985 (see table 17). The institution of the World Bank Special Facility for Sub-Saharan Africa (which became effective on 1 July 1985) and of the IMF Structural Adjustment Facility (established in March 1986), as well as the agreement in 1987 on a US$ 12.4 billion IDA-8 replenishment, should mean a continuation of the above trends during the remainder of the decade. In particular, the share of LDCs in total IDA lending is now projected to exceed 40 per

---

[39] The Japanese Government has recently announced measures to double its ODA to developing countries in five years, i.e., by 1990, and to recycle some $US 30 billion over the next three years to developing countries; within the framework of these measures, special measures will be made to increase grants and other assistance to the least developed countries.

[40] "Taking into account the uncertainties not only for United States aid, but also for other countries, the average annual rate of growth for total DAC aid [to all developing countries] up to around 1990 may fall to the vicinity of 2 per cent in real terms." OECD, *Development co-operation, 1986 report*, pp. 51-53.

[41] Namely Canada, the Federal Republic of Germany, France, Italy, Japan, the United Kingdom and the United States.

[42] Calculations based on donors' interpretation of the SNPA aid targets and intentions in this respect, as known from official statements or replies to the UNCTAD secretariat's questionnaire, suggest that if, in 1985, those donors who had accepted at the Paris Conference either of the two alternative targets had met them, the level of ODA from that group of donors to LDCs would not have been substantially higher than the actual levels. However, if all donors had provided 0.15 per cent of their GNP as ODA to LDCs, such ODA would have been almost 80 per cent higher than the actual level.

[43] UNCTAD VII, in its Final Act (para. 117), urged developed countries once again to attain 0.15 per cent of GNP for ODA to LDCs or double their ODA to these countries as soon as possible.

TABLE 18

**Net ODA[a] as a percentage of donors' GNP and as ratio to average ODA in 1976-1980
from individual DAC member countries to LDCs as a group**

Donor country[b]	Percentage of GNP					Ratio to average ODA in 1976-1980				
	1981	1982	1983	1984	1985	1981	1982	1983	1984	1985
Norway	0.29	0.37	0.35	0.31	0.35	1.32	1.64	1.53	1.34	1.58
Denmark	0.25	0.29	0.27	0.29	0.31	1.06	1.20	1.11	1.15	1.31
Netherlands	0.30	0.29	0.24	0.30	0.26	1.37	1.32	1.04	1.20	1.06
Sweden	0.26	0.31	0.25	0.22	0.22	1.14	1.18	0.87	0.78	0.86
Belgium	0.17	0.15	0.13	0.14	0.18	1.28	1.03	0.84	0.89	1.16
France	0.13	0.13	0.12	0.15	0.15	1.64	1.52	1.36	1.60	1.74
Canada	0.11	0.12	0.13	0.13	0.15	1.13	1.19	1.47	1.52	1.80
Finland	0.08	0.08	0.10	0.12	0.13	1.59	1.55	1.92	2.24	2.67
Italy	0.06	0.07	0.08	0.13	0.13	2.02	2.28	2.46	4.00	4.04
Germany, Federal Republic of .	0.13	0.12	0.12	0.12	0.13	1.26	1.19	1.19	1.08	1.14
United Kingdom	0.12	0.11	0.10	0.10	0.10	1.49	1.34	1.10	0.99	1.12
Switzerland	0.09	0.08	0.10	0.10	0.10	1.54	1.42	1.91	1.72	1.77
Ireland[c]	0.03	0.04	0.08	0.09	0.09	2.44	2.72	5.47	6.03	6.44
Australia	0.06	0.10	0.08	0.07	0.08	1.30	2.30	1.70	1.78	1.59
Japan	0.05	0.05	0.06	0.06	0.06	1.26	1.23	1.51	1.74	1.71
Austria	0.04	0.04	0.03	0.03	0.05	2.02	1.80	1.43	1.67	2.43
New Zealand	0.04	0.04	0.04	0.03	0.04	1.08	0.99	0.87	0.88	0.99
United States	0.03	0.05	0.04	0.04	0.04	1.18	1.74	1.71	1.70	1.84
TOTAL DAC	0.08	0.08	0.08	0.08	0.08	1.32	1.42	1.38	1.44	1.54

Source: UNCTAD secretariat calculations, based on information provided by the OECD secretariat.

[a] Including imputed flows through multilateral channels.

[b] Ranked in descending order of the ODA/GNP ratio in 1985.

[c] Ireland became a member of DAC at the end of 1985.

TABLE 19

**Net ODA[a] as a percentage of donors' GNP and as ratio to average ODA in 1976-1980
from individual OPEC member countries to LDCs as a group**

Donor country[b]	Percentage of GNP					Ratio to average ODA in 1976-1980				
	1981	1982	1983	1984	1985	1981	1982	1983	1984	1985
Kuwait	0.77	0.96	1.03	1.04	1.10[c]	1.24	1.29	1.41	1.41	1.50
Saudi Arabia	0.34	0.61	0.76	0.71	0.38[c]	0.96	1.66	1.48	1.25	0.67
United Arab Emirates .	0.35	0.39	0.28	0.13	0.16[c]	0.74	0.76	0.50	0.23	0.29
Qatar	0.43	0.31	0.25	0.12	0.10[c]	1.41	0.92	0.70	0.32	0.28
Libyan Arab Jamahiriya	0.22	0.09	0.19	0.03	0.06[c]	1.56	0.69	1.35	0.25	0.43
Algeria	0.09	0.08	0.06	0.07	0.03	1.60	1.54	1.17	1.57	0.84
Nigeria	0.12	0.03	0.03	0.04	0.03	3.63	0.93	0.70	1.12	0.78
Venezuela	0.05	0.04	0.07	0.01	0.01	1.96	1.84	2.74	0.31	0.18
Iran (Islamic Republic of)	0.00	0.00	0.00	—	0.00[c]	0.01	0.00	0.27	—	0.00
Iraq	0.06	0.07	0.01	−0.01	−0.08[c]	0.30	0.32	0.02	−0.04	−0.35
TOTAL OPEC	0.21	0.25	0.24	0.21	0.15	1.05	1.31	1.22	0.99	0.68

Source: UNCTAD secretariat estimates.

[a] Including imputed flows through multilateral channels.

[b] Ranked in descending order of the ODA/GNP ratio in 1985.

[c] 1985 ODA as a percentage of GNP in 1984.

cent during fiscal years 1986-1989. Additional resources to LDCs are also to come from the African Development Fund, in view of the expected substantial increase in its fifth replenishment (for the years 1988-1990).

The growing importance for LDCs of multilateral resources must not be viewed only in terms of the volume of the flow which, after all, will still need to be much complemented by other resources in order to meet LDCs' requirements.[44] Of great significance is the fact that these resources should increasingly consist of fast-disbursing non-project assistance, in particular assistance in support of adjustment programmes.[45] On the other hand, conditionality provisions can delay, if not impair to a certain extent, access to such resources.[46]

As regards support to adjustment programmes, the World Bank had already instituted in 1980 structural adjustment lending designed to support programmes of policy changes and institutional reforms to achieve a more sustainable balance of payments in the medium and long-term. Up to June 1986, however, only five LDCs (namely, Burundi, Guinea, Malawi, Niger and Togo) had been able to obtain agreement for structural adjustment loans (SALs) to the overall amount of US$ 381 million. During the following year, Malawi received an additional amount of $10 million and further SALs were approved for six more LDCs, namely the Central African Republic, Gambia, Guinea-Bissau, Mauritania, Nepal and Sao Tome and Principe, totalling US$ 161 million. Other types of credits, such as import financing or sector adjustment credits, have also been extended in support of structural adjustment programmes of LDCs. Some of these loans are partly financed from the Special Facility for Sub-Saharan Africa which has been specially designed to provide fast-disbursing concessional financing over a three-year period to countries in Africa committed to

undertaking significant adjustment programmes aimed at increasing production in key sectors and in the economy at large. Operations in LDCs financed from the Special Facility for Sub-Saharan Africa, other than SAL programmes as such, include reconstruction import credits (approved for Equatorial Guinea, and Guinea-Bissau) as well as sector credits for transport (Niger, Rwanda) and agriculture (Somalia). It should also be noted that the Special Facility for Sub-Saharan Africa has been instrumental in attracting additional resources for structural adjustment from certain bilateral donors through co-financing.

The Structural Adjustment Facility (SAF) of the IMF was established to provide additional assistance on concessional terms to low-income countries[47] facing protracted balance-of-payments problems and to present medium-term macro-economic and structural adjustment programmes intended to overcome such problems. During the period since its inception up to end July 1987, structural adjustment arrangements were agreed with 11 LDCs (Bangladesh, Burundi, Central African Republic, Gambia, Guinea, Haiti, Mauritania, Niger, Sierra Leone, Somalia and Uganda) for a total amount of SDR 362 million, of which about SDR 138 million were already disbursed during that period. The Managing Director of the IMF is requesting a tripling of the Facility (originally set at SDR 2.7 billion, equivalent to US$ 3.1 billion) over the three years from 1 January 1988.[48] At their September meetings, the IMF Interim Committee and the World Bank Development Committee strongly endorsed the initiative of the Managing Director of the IMF for a substantial increase in the resources of the SAF to support adjustment programmes. The Development Committee emphasized that enhancement of SAF resources should be based on genuine *additionality* in availability of concessional resources to low-income countries. It expected that the realization of such enhancement would result in substantial benefits to the LDCs. The consultations with potential contributors to the SAF are to be concluded during 1987.

(b) *Non-concessional finance including private flows*

LDCs' recourse to those multilateral agencies (mainly financed by DAC countries) which provide flows on non-concessional terms also in-

---

[44] Moreover, a large part of such multilateral assistance is provided in the form of loans which, concessional as they may be, will still mean a substantially increased debt burden for the LDCs as outlined in section B below.

[45] At its 31st meeting in April 1987, the Development Committee encouraged the World Bank to increase its lending programme to support growth and reform efforts. IDA's eighth replenishment provides that $3 to 3.5 billion be made available for adjustment lending. A feature of the IMF's Structural Adjustment Facility (available only to the lower income member countries, including almost all LDCs) is the large proportion of funding distributed at the beginning of the adjustment period.

[46] In its study of "The role of the IMF in adjustment with growth", the Working Group commissioned by the Intergovernmental Group of 24 on International Monetary Affairs calls for more flexibility in IMF conditionality provisions, in particular with regard to the principles governing performance criteria (see IMF *Survey*, 18 May 1987, p. 155). A review of these provisions will be considered in the context of the comprehensive examination of adjustment programmes, to be carried by IMF (see chapter II, section A.3 of this report).

[47] Of the 40 LDCs all but three (Botswana, Kiribati and Vanuatu) are eligible for assistance under this Facility.

[48] In his speech to the United Nations Economic and Social Council on 26 June 1987.

creased during the 1980s, but there was a slump in all other non-concessional flows to LDCs. Altogether they fell by 70 per cent between 1980 and 1985. This is due to a number of concomitant interrelated factors. On the side of the LDCs, economic difficulties including severe problems of indebtedness led them to reduce their vulnerability by minimizing new borrowing, especially borrowing on commercial terms. Adjustment programmes undertaken by many of them implied substantial cuts in imports, hence less recourse to export credits. On the other hand, LDCs' shortage of liquidity accompanied by the erosion of their creditworthiness, and more restrictive policies instituted by export credit agencies and banks, curtailed the extension of export credits and bank lending to LDCs and also direct investment.

A resumption of non-concessional borrowing (never a very significant factor for most LDCs) is not to be encouraged in the immediate future because it would only aggravate an often already unsustainable debt situation. As for direct investment – a non-debt-creating flow – prospects remain dim. Despite incentives provided by some donors and the LDCs' own efforts to improve the investment climate in their own country, LDCs, with their limited market potential, low income and weak human, physical and institutional infrastructure, have little attraction for direct investors. Borrowing from multilateral agencies is, however, likely to continue to increase. In particular the recent agreement on a 200 per cent increase in the capital of the African Development Bank (from $6.3 billion to $19.6 billion)[49] should translate into additional resources for LDCs.

(c) *Scope for future action*

Already in the SNPA it was recognized that only a substantial increase in ODA would enable the LDCs to achieve their development objectives and priorities.[50] The need for adequate financial and technical support to complement national efforts has increasingly been stressed since then, especially as many of these countries undertook courageous far-reaching economic restructurings with a view to improving their financial positions and resuming economic growth. UNCTAD VII, in its Final Act, urged donors to substantially enlarge financial assistance to the LDCs in the volume and on terms which correspond to their immediate and longer-term development needs. The volume and forms of aid should be supportive of and commen-

surate with the growing requirements of the LDCs' adjustment programmes and broader development efforts.[51]

In many cases adjustment programmes have been undertaken with policy advice from the IMF and/or the World Bank. How adequate and successful such reforms are is as yet difficult to assess, however, because the structural changes needed to achieve growth take a long time to yield results. In addition to a number of shortcomings in design and orientation,[52] a major deficiency often referred to is the inadequacy of supporting finance.[53] Hence the concern expressed in various international fora. For example, the Communiqué of the Interim Committee of the IMF [54] stated: "The Committee members expressed special concern about the plight of low-income countries. The Committee emphasized that it is crucial for these countries to implement major reforms which, to be fully effective, will need to be accompanied by additional financing on concessional terms".[55] The OECD Ministerial Communiqué of May 1987 (para. 36) stresses that "For poorer developing countries, provision of adequate concessional finance is essential ... The volume and reforms of aid must be commensurate with the growing requirements of policy reform programmes and broader development efforts".[56] The communiqué of the Development Committee of the World Bank [57] is also explicit on this issue, stating that "the financing needs of low-income countries should largely be met through assistance on appropriately concessional terms" and urging donors "to find ways and means to increase the concessional element of their support in order to strengthen the efforts of this

---

[49] See *Financial Times* of 15 June 1987.

[50] See, in particular, SNPA, para. 63.

[51] See TD/350, para. 116.

[52] In its study of "The Role of the IMF in Adjustment with Growth" the Working Group established by the Intergovernmental Group of 24 on International Monetary Affairs concludes that "Fund-supported adjustment programmes have generally relied heavily on demand-management policies to correct external payments imbalances, which has led to a decline in levels of output and rates of growth and increased unemployment, and has adversely affected income distribution in developing countries". See IMF *Survey*, 18 May 1987, p. 154. For a discussion of adjustment policies, see chapter III, section A.

[53] "There are some indications that the availability of concessional funding for adjustment programmes is lagging behind the pace of policy reform in eligible developing countries. In order to support programmes for policy reform and structural adjustment in Sub-Saharan Africa and Least Developed Countries in other regions, adequate multilateral and bilateral concessional flows must be provided". OECD, *Towards shared policy perceptions for development* (Paris, March 1987), p. 14.

[54] IMF Press Release No. 87/5, 10 April 1987, p. 3.

[55] Many LDCs are considered low-income countries in IMF/World Bank listings.

[56] OECD PRESS/A(87), Paris, 13 May 1987.

[57] Press Communiqué of the Development Committee of 28 September 1987.

group of countries". Given the particular economic and social conditions of LDCs, policy conditions need to be highly flexible to allow for external shocks beyond the control of the country concerned. Such conditions need of course to be distinguished from the normal loan repayment conditions.

As noted earlier, the LDCs may benefit in the years to come from increased multilateral resources. To what extent multilateral arrangements such as the World Bank Facility for Sub-Saharan Africa and the IMF Structural Adjustment Financing facility will be instrumental in catalysing *additional* bilateral aid is still open to question. Prospects for larger bilateral aid are dim in view of the expenditure constraints prevailing in most donor countries, although there are some notable exceptions. Moreover, the provision of aid increasingly depends on successful policy dialogue between donors and recipients, that is on undertakings, by recipients of structural adjustment policies, that are credible to donors.

An encouraging feature is the increased emphasis that is being placed in internationally agreed adjustment programmes on establishing conditions for sustainable growth – rather than merely on restoring the balance of payments through expenditure cutbacks and the like. Equally important is the wide recognition of the crucial need for the timely provision of adequate financing on concessional terms to support agreed reforms. In addition to quick-disbursing assistance to meet immediate financing requirements and ensure the implementation of medium-term adjustment programmes, the financing of longer-term programmes in education, health, environment, etc. will also have to be secured. Where once a major objective of assistance policy was to eliminate poverty, under current conditions donors must at least ensure that the poor do not grow poorer under the effect of adjustment. This aspect is particularly pertinent to LDCs, which have a very large proportion of their population among the poorer strata.[58]

Agreement on such issues now needs to be translated into concrete action. For donor governments, this implies taking a political decision to raise budget appropriations for aid to the LDCs. As a first step, meeting the 0.15 per cent target appears an ever more imperative requirement.

2. *Aid modalities and co-ordination*

(a) *Terms and conditions of aid*

No major changes were evident in the terms and conditions on which concessional assistance was extended to the LDCs in the first half of the 1980s. LDCs continued to receive aid largely in grant form or as loans on very soft terms. Available information points to little change in policies and practices regarding the procurement conditions attached to this aid during the same period.

As regards the terms of aid, the most noticeable developments were the shift to grant or increasingly grant-like terms by several DAC donors in their aid programmes with LDCs, and a higher grant share in OPEC bilateral aid after 1981. In 1985 Italy and Japan for the first time met the norms for aid to LDCs – that is a minimum grant element of at least 90 per cent for the LDCs as a group – laid down in the Recommendation on Terms and Conditions of Aid adopted by the DAC.[59] (see table 20).

In the first half of the 1980s, around 40 per cent of total concessional aid received by the LDCs from all sources continued nevertheless to be in the form of loans. This form of aid has been used by a few DAC countries (mainly France, the United States, Italy and Japan), by multilateral development financing institutions, in OPEC bilateral aid programmes as well as in the aid programmes of socialist countries of Eastern Europe and China.[60] Moreover, non-concessional loans – that is lending on terms which are not sufficiently soft to qualify the loans as concessional assistance according to the standard ODA definition – are to some extent extended to LDCs by both bilateral and multilateral donors. The economic situation of the LDCs, however, is such that the scope for borrowing on non-concessional or less concessional terms is extremely limited. Thus, the Ministerial Meeting of the Group of 77 in April 1987 requested that immediate steps be taken to provide ODA to the LDCs fully in the form of grants and to provide loans without discrimination on highly concessional terms, at least as concessional as those provided by IDA.

---

[58] See TD/329, chapter III, section D., para. 95.

[59] See TD/B/1120, para. 232.

[60] Over the period 1981-1985, average loan terms of DAC bilateral concessional lending to the LDCs corresponded to a grant element of just below 60 per cent. For OPEC countries the corresponding grant element was in the range of 50 to 55 per cent, and in the concessional loan programmes of multilateral OPEC agencies the range was 40 to 50 per cent. In the future, the overall concessionality of aid to LDCs from the multilateral lending institutions mainly financed by DAC countries is likely to be affected following the envisaged reduction of IDA credit maturities from the current level of 50 years, in the case of least developed recipients, to 40 years.

TABLE 20

**Grant element[a] of concessional commitments and concessional loans
to LDCs, 1981-1985**

(Percentages)

Donor or donor group	1981	1982	1983	1984	1985
Australia	100	100	100	100	100
Austria	94	95	99	100	100
Belgium	99	98	96	98	95
Canada	100	100	100	100	100
Denmark	95	97	99	100	99
Finland	93	99	100	100	100
France	89	83	80	77	77
Germany, Federal Republic of .	99	99	96	99	100
Italy	55	70	90	80	95
Japan	86	82	88	89	91
Netherlands	98	100	99	100	98
New Zealand	100	100	100	100	100
Norway	100	100	100	100	100
Sweden	100	100	100	100	100
Switzerland	100	100	100	100	100
United Kingdom	100	100	100	100	100
United States	96	98	96	98	97
DAC countries[b]	94	93	94	94	95
of which: loans	58	60	57	58	58
Multilateral agencies mainly financed by DAC	92	90	89	89	90
of which: loans	82	82	82	82	82
OPEC countries	64	77	91	82	75
of which: loans	54	56	54	54	51
Multilateral agencies mainly financed by OPEC	49	51	42	52	52
of which: loans	46	47	40	48	46

Source: UNCTAD secretariat estimates mainly based on OECD/DAC and UNCTAD data.

[a] The grant element, used as a standard measure of the concessionality of aid programmes, reflects the grant share of new commitments as well as the financial terms of loans (i.e. their interest rate, maturity and grace period). See TD/B/1120, footnote 86, p. 300.

[b] Excluding Ireland, which joined the DAC in November 1985. Irish aid is provided entirely in grant form.

Tying practices continue to pose problems for the LDCs, entailing as they may higher costs and inefficient use of aid resources as well as possible distortions in investment, programming and negative implications for the availability of funding for local costs, efforts to standardize equipment, training and maintenance requirements, choice of technology, etc. Moreover, the complexity and diversity of procurement rules of various donors is an additional administrative burden on the LDCs.

Available information (see table 21) points to relative overall stability in the first half of the 1980s in tying practices and patterns with regard to the concessional assistance extended to LDCs from DAC countries bilaterally and from multilateral agencies mainly financed by them. Well over half of total aid from these sources was reported to be free from procurement restrictions in 1984-85. Slightly over one-fifth of bilateral commitments from DAC countries was reported to be untied, and technical assistance and food aid shipments together accounted for a significant part of tied aid. At the mid-term review of the implementation of the SNPA (in September-October 1985), representatives of LDCs indicated that in their experience the tying of bilateral aid had increased since 1981.

TABLE 21

Tying status of concessional commitments to LDCs from DAC countries
and multilateral agencies, 1981-1982 and 1984-1985

(Percentages)

	1981[b]	1982[b]	1984[b]	1985[b]
1. *Concessional commitments from DAC countries[a] and multilateral agencies* .	100	100	100	100
Multilateral and untied bilateral . . .	57	56	56	55
Partially untied bilateral	8	6	8	5
Tied bilateral, including technical co-operation and food aid	35	38	36	40
2. *DAC bilateral concessional commitments[a]*	100	100	100	100
Untied	29	24	21	22
Partially untied	12	12	13	9
Tied, including technical co-operation and food aid	59	64	66	69
of which: technical co-operation . .	29	29	28	27
food aid	9	10	13	11

Source: UNCTAD secretariat estimates based on data provided by the OECD secretariat in mid-1987. The conceptual basis of these data is presently under review at OECD.

[a] Excluding commitments from Ireland, which joined the DAC in November 1985.

[b] Data for 1981 and 1982 exclude aid to Kiribati, Mauritania, Tuvalu and Vanuatu. The figures in this table should be interpreted bearing in mind that data for 1984-1985 are not directly comparable with those for the earlier years 1981-1982 because of a change in reporting methods. The figures are likely to reflect this change as well as improved coverage.

Recently several DAC countries have reported taking steps of relevance to LDCs to increase forms of untied assistance.[61] Work has also been undertaken in the DAC to improve policies and procedures for aid procurement, and to strengthen the distinction between trade and aid financing as well as the development orientation of the latter. In November 1986 the committee approved a set of principles intended to contribute to improved procurement practices under tied aid.[62] Moreover, in April 1987 the DAC adopted revised guiding principles for associated financing and new arrangements for exchange of information and consultations among members also on tied and partially untied projects and programmes falling under the ODA definition,[63] with provisions for the review of the developmental priority of tied aid projects and programmes. As regards the LDCs specifically, the guiding principles state that to the extent associated financing or tied or partially untied ODA is provided to these countries, DAC members will ensure that such transactions take place on favourable terms.

(b) *Forms of aid*

A large number of the LDCs have now initiated economic recovery and adjustment programmes (see chapter II, section A above). Typical of these countries' situation is their need for increased amounts of flexible and quick-disbursing assistance and various forms of non-project aid. Many of them need generous debt relief. The

---

[61] See TD/B/1120, para. 241. Sweden has reported that in the context of joint efforts to reduce obstacles for utilization of aid resources the proportion of tied aid to the most needy African countries is diminishing.

[62] OECD, *Good procurement practices for official development assistance* (Paris, 1986). Annexed to these were a description of actual practices followed by DAC members and the international financial institutions, including information on training opportunities available to recipients in the field of procurement. Also set out were minimum conditions for efficient international competitive bidding which recipient countries are encouraged to apply in appropriate situations.

[63] In this context, the concepts of tied and partially untied aid were redefined and the definitions sharpened. See OECD Press Release (Press/A(87)23) of 28 April 1987.

resource constraints currently faced by the LDCs also call for special efforts from donors to help finance local costs and recurrent expenditure in the LDCs.

In 1981-84, the share of recorded programme aid (mainly current imports financing and debt relief) in total DAC aid commitments to LDCs remained around 10 per cent or below. The recorded share of food aid and emergency relief programmes in new commitments rose until 1984, then dropped in 1985 (although disbursements under previous commitments for such programmes still rose). In the first half of the 1980s the bulk of DAC aid continued to be in the form of project or sector-related aid and technical assistance.[64] In contrast, the share of general economic (especially budget and balance-of-payments) support in OPEC aid programmes with the LDCs has always been very high, accounting for well over half of total concessional commitments to LDCs in 1981-85.

Towards the mid-1980s donors started to more examine more closely ways of adapting aid in support of policy reforms. The high-level meeting of the DAC in December 1986 adopted conclusions regarding aid for improved development policies and programmes[65] which, inter alia, acknowledged the need for adequate and quick-disbursing funding in support of such programmes and the high priority of aid for rehabilitation as well as of provisions for recurrent cost and maintenance requirements. In practical terms, DAC countries have responded by supporting new multilateral initiatives for programme lending (such as the World Bank's special facility for Africa and the IMF Structural Adjustment Facility), extending or setting up bilateral facilities for similar purposes, or shifting orientations in their aid programmes to meet the specific needs of LDCs.[66] On the part of non-DAC donors, increased provision of import financing (e.g. oil grants and credits) to LDCs has also been reported.

Scope remains for further strengthening donors' capacity to provide resources – especially bilateral – in support of policy reforms in LDCs. Issues pertaining to the adequacy of structural adjustment assistance to LDCs have been discussed above (see chapter II). This is also a question of providing appropriate forms of aid, and of timing. The LDCs need the right type of aid, at the right time. However, shortfalls, notably in non-project financing intentions, were noted in some of the recent country reviews for LDCs. There is a need for close monitoring of the adequacy of various forms of assistance to the LDCs and for enhancing the flexibility of aid programmes and donor procedures to ensure that LDCs' emerging requirements are expeditiously met.

It must also be underlined that the need for increased aid in flexible, quick-disbursing forms is not restricted to those LDCs which are implementing structural adjustment programmes under formal agreements with the IMF and the World Bank. Other LDCs suffer from the same type of budget and balance-of-payments constraints and have taken similar steps to rehabilitate their economies. These countries equally need support from donors adapted to their special requirements, including support for local and recurrent costs.

Special aid requirements for LDCs also exist as regards technical assistance, to enhance skills and strengthen administrative capacity, and as regards various types of emergency-related aid. LDCs are highly prone to drought and/or other disasters. Apart from relief in emergency situations, special support is required for disaster prevention and preparedness and for rehabilitation efforts. LDCs also host substantial numbers of refugees. The LDCs concerned need help by the international community to surmount the additional major difficulties in the development process caused by the presence of such large numbers of displaced persons.

(c) Aid co-ordination and country review mechanisms in the LDCs

(i) The evolution of the country review process since 1981

The setting up of review mechanisms at the country level in pursuance of paragraph 111 of the SNPA, and the concomitant strengthening of policy dialogue with donors and of aid co-ordination machinery in LDCs, is one of the areas of implementation of the SNPA where developments have been most dynamic. By the end of 1985, review meetings had already been held for 27 LDCs.[67] For the majority of them this type of consultation with donors was arranged for the first time. The UNDP (through round-table meetings) and the World Bank (through consultative and aid groups) acted as the main lead agencies for these consultations.

During 1986 and the first half of 1987 new consultative groups were set up for Guinea and Malawi and the group for the United Republic of

---

[64] However, an unusually large amount of new commitments in 1985 for unattributed purposes may indicate a shift towards increased programme assistance.

[65] See OECD, Development Co-operation, 1986 report (Paris, 1987), pp.105-110. See also pp.25-26 and pp.111-112.

[66] See TD/B/1120, paras. 246-247 and 254-259.

---

[67] Not counting Mauritania.

Tanzania was re-established. The consultative and aid groups for Bangladesh, Nepal, Somalia and Uganda also met during this period. The Caribbean Group for Co-operation in Economic Development, which also covers Haiti, was convened in January 1987. A special session was devoted to this country's economic recovery programme during a preparatory donors' meeting.

As regards the UNDP-sponsored mechanisms, four of the Asian LDCs (Bhutan, Lao PDR, Maldives and Samoa) as well as Cape Verde held their second round-table meetings in 1986. The first round tables for the Central African Republic and Niger were convened in June 1987. The first such meeting for Sierra Leone was under preparation, as well as a second round table for Equatorial Guinea. A meeting for Burkina Faso was also under consideration. Various follow-up meetings, in particular at the sectoral level, were arranged or in preparation for other LDCs on the basis of round-table arrangements.

Of the three new countries designated as LDCs by the forty-first session of the General Assembly, Mauritania has a consultative group which was set up in 1985 and round-table arrangements were under consideration in Kiribati and Tuvalu. In mid-1987, country review mechanisms had thus been constituted or were under preparation for all but a very few of the 40 LDCs.

Salient features in aid co-ordination efforts since 1981 have been the attempts to adapt and improve both round-table and consultative and aid group mechanisms, and the growing co-operation between the two main lead agencies in the preparation of meetings. The Governing Council of the UNDP in 1985 adopted a new format for the round tables, now under implementation, which *inter alia* gives more weight than previously to overall policy reform and to selectivity as regards countries and participants.[68] The country review process has come to be linked fairly closely to such reform and structural adjustment programmes. Other trends have been the fostering of in-country follow-up and supportive co-ordinative processes at the local level; an increased emphasis on sector programmes;[69] the introduction of more streamlined investment programming;[70] and efforts to strengthen economic and aid management ca-

pacity in the LDCs. For the African LDCs, review of the implementation of the United Nations Programme of Action for African Economic Recovery and Development (UNPAAERD) for 1986-90 adds a new dimension to the country review process during the second half of the SNPA decade.

(ii) *The mobilization of resources through the country review process*

Available evidence does not indicate that the country review process gave any strong impetus to increasing aid commitments to the LDCs in the first half of the decade, though it may have helped to sustain them. The average level of new aid commitments to the LDCs as a group from DAC and OPEC donors in 1983-85 was practically the same as in the preceding three-year period (see table 22). Of the six LDCs which arranged round-table consultations in 1982, four could register on average increased aid commitments in 1983-85. Of the four LDCs with long-standing consultative or aid group arrangements (Bangladesh, Haiti, Nepal and Sudan) three received more aid commitments in 1983-85 than in the preceding three-year period. However, for many of the LDCs which arranged country review meetings, there was no immediate pay-off in the form of a higher level of commitments up to 1985.

The new format for the round tables sponsored by UNDP was designed to improve the mobilization of resources for the LDCs, and improvements in the consultative and aid groups have also been sought for the same purpose. The first country review meeting organized fully under the new round table format, by Cape Verde in 1986, was judged by UNDP to be successful from the point of view of resource mobilization, since donor financing intentions then expressed were deemed to be sufficient to cover the country's requirements during its second five-year development plan period.[71] Similarly donor financing indications given at the first round tables for the Central African Republic and for Niger in 1987 were reported to have met, or in the case of the Central African Republic even surpassed, the expressed minimum external financing needs. However, the element of additionality in funding secured at round table meetings is difficult to assess.

As regards recent experience from consultative and aid groups, increased amounts of assistance have also been pledged at some of them (e.g. Bangladesh, Haiti, Nepal). It was likewise reported from the 1986 meeting of the consultative group for the United Republic of Tanzania that the over-

---

[68] See TD/B/1120, paras. 290-298.

[69] By mid-1987 sectoral programme consultations had taken place as a follow-up to round tables in, for instance, Chad, Gambia, Guinea-Bissau, Sao Tome and Principe and Togo. A number of consultations of this type were planned or in preparation for other LDCs. Consultative group countries are also increasingly introducing the modality of sectoral follow-up. Examples are Guinea, Malawi, Mauritania, Somalia and the United Republic of Tanzania.

[70] Three-year public investment programmes which can serve also as a framework for aid co-ordination in general form part of structural adjustment programmes sponsored by the World Bank.

[71] DP/1987/18, para. 18.

TABLE 22

Concessional commitments to the LDCs,[a] 1980-1982 and 1983-1985

	Average concessional commitments in $ million	
	Average 1980-1982	Average 1983-1985
First country review meeting held in 1982		
Cape Verde	69.5	81.3
Chad	67.1	153.5
Equatorial Guinea	17.6	29.9
Mali	281.5	378.6
Rwanda	211.3	196.4
Yemen	476.9	369.3
First country review meeting held in 1983		
Afghanistan	15.6	17.0
Benin	129.9	110.9
Bhutan	13.2	41.5
Djibouti	107.0	105.2
Lao PDR	50.8	40.1
Maldives	21.0	14.7
Samoa	29.5	25.0
First country review meeting held in 1984		
Burundi	179.9	173.9
Comoros	62.1	39.4
Gambia	74.4	59.0
Guinea-Bissau	63.4	83.5
Lesotho	108.9	106.2
Malawi	146.4	212.1
First country review meeting held in 1985		
Sao Tome and Principe . . .	6.9	13.3
Togo	115.0	176.5
Consultative or aid groups that met in 1981-85		
Bangladesh	1 860.3	1 625.6
Mauritania	244.1	190.3
Nepal	247.3	358.0
Somalia	510.9	385.3
Sudan	845.7	1 045.2
Uganda	212.2	252.1
Haiti	137.6	149.2
No country review meeting in 1981-85		
Botswana	131.4	108.3
Burkina Faso	291.6	233.3
Central African Republic . .	124.5	120.6
Democratic Yemen	157.7	136.9
Ethiopia	276.7	584.0
Guinea	176.5	182.3
Kiribati	13.3	13.4
Niger	272.7	285.8
Sierra Leone	94.9	85.6
Tuvalu	4.7	3.7
United Republic of Tanzania	793.6	505.7
Vanuatu	45.4	27.5
TOTAL	8 689.9	8 721.8

Source: UNCTAD secretariat estimates mainly based on OECD/DAC and UNCTAD data.

[a] From DAC and OPEC countries and multilateral agencies mainly financed by these countries.

all target for external support for this country's economic recovery programme was largely met.[72]

(iii) *Policy issues in aid co-ordination*

Major work has been done over the recent past in various organizations and by donor groups to identify the basic principles for and needed improvements in aid co-ordination. Studies have been undertaken and recommendations made on this subject, notably by DAC [73], the World Bank [74] and UNDP [75] as well as by ECOSOC and the General Assembly.[76] Some of this work has been focused on co-ordinating aid more effectively in support of structural adjustment efforts in low-income countries. Even when not limited to the LDCs, these studies and the recommendations they have prompted address issues of the utmost relevance to this group of countries. The LDCs are most desperately in need of increased resources, and their administrative capacity is in general weak. LDCs thus stand to greatly benefit from better focused, more effective aid efforts, and from any reduction in the administrative burden of aid.

Attention has now been shifting to follow-up at the field level. The United Nations Director-General for Development and International Economic Co-operation was invited by the Economic and Social Council and the General Assembly to conduct country case studies on the functioning of the operational activities for the development of the United Nations system. Two LDCs were selected for such studies (Nepal and Togo). In conjunction with this work, UNDP was to prepare an assessment of aid co-ordination arrangements at the field level, to be presented to its Governing Council in 1988. Another exercise was being undertaken by the Joint Consultative Group on Policy [77] to explore a more co-ordinated approach to programming. Of four African countries selected for this exercise, two were LDCs (Mali and the United Republic of Tanzania).

---

[72] *World Bank News,* various issues.

[73] The above-mentioned conclusions from the December 1986 high-level meeting of the DAC contains a set of guiding principles for aid co-ordination with developing countries.

[74] A report on aid co-ordination in Sub-Saharan Africa was submitted by the Bank to the September 1986 meeting of the Development Committee.

[75] See in particular the report submitted to the UNDP Governing Council for the annual review of thematic programmes established by the Council, (DP/1987/15/Add.1).

[76] See A/41/350-E/1986/108, ECOSOC resolution 1986/74 and General Assembly resolution 41/171.

[77] In which UNDP, UNFPA, WFP and UNICEF are represented.

The intensive debate and definition of the principal issues in aid co-ordination that have taken place in different fora over the past few years, and the various studies carried out at the policy and field level, should now lead to actual and tangible improvements in practices. At the same time the responsibility and central role of LDCs in aid co-ordination needs to be constantly restressed, and their capacity to carry out these functions strengthened. The tendency to increase conditionality in the provision of assistance has added another layer to the already complex requirements with which LDCs are confronted. They now have to deal not only with a large number of donors with widely varying practices and procedures at the project level, but they increasingly have to negotiate reform programmes and satisfy various policy conditions and requirements of both bilateral and multilateral donors – without necessarily being assured of the sustained long-term backing essential to the success of their undertaking.

Certain areas where further aid co-ordination efforts could be most effective and are most needed, are the following:

– matching of LDCs' willingness to discuss reform measures and of their commitment to make far-reaching policy changes by corresponding longer-term aid commitments from the donors' side;

– effective monitoring of aid flows. This may indeed be the weakest link in the country review mechanisms set up so far; [78]

– simplification and harmonization of terms and procedures;

– broadening the scope of policy discussions. The LDCs' reform efforts are not likely to be sufficient to ensure the success of their adjustment and development programmes. As the focus of country reviews has shifted from project financing to broader policy discussions, a critical analysis of the supportiveness of the external environment (including debt and trade issues) may be needed for a fair assessment of LDCs' performance and prospects;

– systematic monitoring of the impact of economic developments and adjustment measures on the most needy population groups in the LDCs, given that the provision of "fully adequate and internationally accepted minimum standards for the poor" is after all one of the major objectives of the SNPA.

---

[78] Some steps towards building up procedures for monitoring aid pledges and aid flows were being taken in 1986-87 (see DP/1987/18, para. 13). In addition, in-country joint monitoring committees have been set up for some consultative group countries. These arrangements may still leave gaps in monitoring for countries with less active groups or that have not had recent round-table meetings.

Box 6

AID MODALITIES IN PRACTICE – THE LAMOSANGU-JIRI ROAD PROJECT IN NEPAL

The Lamosangu-Jiri road project in Nepal, financed in part by Swiss bilateral aid, exemplifies the application in practice of many of the recommendations concerning aid modalities set down in the SNPA, and is an illustration of how donors, by adapting their practices to LDCs' needs, can help these countries to overcome constraints in aid implementation and render more effective assistance.

The project was first conceived as part of an integrated hill development project and is intended to be the back-bone of development activities in the region. A feasibility study and the first survey work was undertaken in 1971-72, and an agreement on the project was signed by His Majesty's Government of Nepal and the Swiss Government in 1974. A loan of 15 million Swiss francs was provided by Switzerland for the project.

Implementation of the project started in 1975. It was originally envisaged to complete the road by 1981. However, a number of changes in project design were introduced, postponing completion of the construction work. The most important of these was the decision to upgrade the construction standard of the road and take up additional erosion protection works to counter maintenance problems and recurring costs that would otherwise have been involved. These changes as well as some other additional provisions, together with the effects of inflation, raised the cost estimate from the original NRs 94 million to NRs 225 million. In 1978, the Swiss Government *converted the original loan into a grant* and later provided *additional aid* through a grant of 16.9 million Swiss francs to cover the cost increases due to changes in project design and to inflation. The road was inaugurated in 1985, and upon completion of the construction works the project moved into the maintenance stage.

Box 6 (continued)

Aid to Nepal from Switzerland is *untied* and foreign procurement for the project has been undertaken on the basis of international competition. From the outset provisions were also made for covering *local costs* of the project. Direct transfers were made by the Swiss for this purpose to the project budget to cover such items as road construction, local equipment and land compensation. Nepal's counterpart contribution consisted of hiring a Nepalese project manager and other local staff and participating in local equipment, labour and maintenance costs. Flexibility has been shown by both sides e.g. in recruitment and procurement, which contributed to lessening delays and to successful performance of the project.

In two aspects the project was particularly innovative and introduced new aid practices in Nepal. From the outset, a tentative *maintenance* schedule was worked out looking beyond the construction phase up to the year 1992, eight years after the scheduled completion. The donor country undertook to meet all maintenance costs for the first four years of the post-construction period. During the next four years Swiss assistance will be phased out with Nepal gradually taking over full responsibility for maintenance costs. An additional feature in this stage of the project is the elaboration of an economically and socially viable maintenance concept, in which the donor and the Nepalese Government are currently engaged. Switzerland has also made *advance payments* for project expenditure whereby any burden on Nepal for providing bridging finance between actual expenditure and reimbursement from the donor was removed, and delays which might otherwise have occurred due to resource constraints avoided. This required from the Nepalese side the institution of exceptional procedures whereby the donor paid funds directly to a separate account operated by the project management, instead of to the general revenue account of the Ministry of Finance. Both parties have thus shown flexibility in adapting procedures for more effective project management.

Institution-building involving human-resource development was made an important part of the project. The agreement on project implementation stipulated that planning techniques and construction methods be such that the maximum possible number of Nepalese engineers, supervisors and draftsmen could participate in the project and increase their experience in adopting appropriate technology. On-the-job training of local people for maintenance work was also provided for. The intention is now to use the experience gained in the implementation of the Lamosangu-Jiri road project – as regards construction principles, institution-building and maintenance concepts – in other similar projects.

Broader socio-economic considerations were also taken into account in the implementation of the project. The tendency in Nepal is generally to award major contracts for earthwork in road construction to big contractors in order to minimize supervision and administration, and this principle was followed at the beginning in the Lamosangu-Jiri road project as well. However, the Government later decided that the project should adopt the piecework system involving small local entrepreneurs in earthwork, a proposal aiming at channelling benefits to the poor local population and readily accepted by the donor. Moreover, food has been provided to project workers at subsidized prices through WFP assistance. The counterpart funds generated by this food aid were allocated to general development activities for the integrated hill development project under which the road was built.[79]

B. Coping with debt

There has been a growing recognition that debt problems strike seriously not only at the so-called "highly indebted countries",[80] but also at those low-income countries, including in particular the LDCs which, because of their structurally limited capacity to service debt, find themselves in an increasingly difficult situation. Unlike the major debtors, however, whose external debt is mainly owed to commercial banks, the LDCs' debt burden is chiefly due to borrowing from governments and international institutions. A particular feature of LDCs is, moreover, the high proportion of debt owed to multilateral institutions.

---

[79] Features of the Lamosangu-Jiri road project are discussed in greater detail in *Aid modalities – practices and management: A case study of aid modalities in Nepal* (TD/B/AC.21/11).

[80] Seventeen countries that account for nearly half of all developed countries' debts. See World Bank, *World debt tables*, 1986-1987 edition.

This recognition of a separately identifiable debt problem of the LDCs is due to a considerable worsening of their situation during the 1980s. Indeed, the rate of growth of their debt, which had tended to decelerate up to 1984, rose again in 1985 and in 1986. A substantial part of the increase in those years was due to the revaluation of loans denominated in currencies other than US dollars. Thus, LDCs had to face increasingly unsustainable debt ratios. Low and sometimes negative economic growth, as experienced by most LDCs, and sluggish demand for their exports, as well as the fall in commodity prices, which further reduced their export earnings, impaired their debt servicing capacity. A good number of them accumulated arrears and had to seek debt relief. On the other hand, the preponderance of official debt among the LDCs has given governments more opportunity to intervene; during 1987 some promising debt relief initiatives were introduced, extendable to LDCs, which have generally focused on low-income countries, primarily in sub-Saharan Africa, that are undertaking adjustment efforts. Furthermore, from the middle of 1987 onwards, certain LDCs have begun to benefit from much more generous rescheduling terms in the Paris Club (see section 2 (b) above).

1. *Evolution of LDCs' debt and debt service*

In all, LDCs' total external debt is estimated to have reached $US 41.7 billion at the end of 1985. This amount may appear small in absolute terms, but it is well over 50 per cent of the LDCs' combined GDP, thus imposing a very severe burden on these countries. Of the $US 41.7 billion, almost $US 2.9 billion consist of short-term debts and another $US 2.3 billion arise from the use of IMF credit. More than two-thirds of long and medium-term debt is concessional. Multilateral agencies are increasingly the main ODA creditors of LDCs (see table 23). According to provisional estimates, LDCs' total external debt attained $45 billion at the end of 1986.[81]

Bangladesh and Sudan are the biggest debtors with debts corresponding, if taken together, to a third of the total debt of LDCs. Another 12 LDCs have accumulated debts exceeding $1 billion (see table 24).

LDCs' long and medium-term debt service payments and estimated interest on short-term debt exceeded $2.2 billion in 1985, being equivalent to somewhat less than a quarter of their com-

bined exports of goods and services. This ratio should be viewed against the fact that LDCs on the average can finance only half of their imports with their export earnings. In addition, during that year LDCs' repurchases to the IMF amounted to SDR 277 million (exceeding purchases by SDR 34 million). Despite the high and increasing share of concessional debt, the greatest part (almost 60 per cent in 1985) of debt service payments has continued, although to a lesser extent, to arise in respect of non-concessional borrowing (for the major part export credits extended by OECD countries).

After stagnating at about $1.5 billion during the years 1981 to 1983, debt service payments (excluding repurchases to the IMF) rose by nearly 18 per cent in 1985 following a rise of 23 per cent in 1984. In 1986 a further jump to $ 2.5 billion is estimated to have taken place, due to the appreciation of service on loans not denominated in dollars. In general, during the 1980s, debt service payments have been contained by debt relief operations (see below). Projected debt service payments falling due in the second half of the decade (based upon debt outstanding, including undisbursed debt as of end 1985) point to considerably higher levels in the absence of rescheduling or other forms of debt relief.

2. *Debt relief*

(a) *Retroactive terms adjustment (RTA) measures*

LDCs have traditionally been ODA-reliant. Their main creditors are governments (although multilateral agencies have now become almost as important). Thus, of particular benefit to LDCs has been action taken in implementation of UNCTAD Board resolution 165 (S-IX). Since its adoption in 1978, 33 LDCs have benefited from retroactive terms adjustment measures provided by 15 DAC countries, for an overall nominal value of $4.1 billion, of which $3.0 billion was in the form of debt cancellation (see table 25). Some socialist countries of Eastern Europe also appear to have taken debt relief measures benefiting major LDC recipients.

At present, the scope of further debt relief under Board resolution 165 (S-IX), which is addressed to developed bilateral donors only, mainly concerns a few creditor countries. The United States and Japan account for over 80 per cent of LDCs' outstanding ODA debt to DAC countries. To ease LDCs' payments, the United States has allowed, on a case-by-case basis, repayment in

---

[81] See OECD, *Financing and external debt of developing countries, 1986 survey* (Paris, 1987), p. 68.

TABLE 23

Total external debt and debt service of LDCs, by source and terms of lending, 1982-1985

Creditor	Outstanding debt disbursed at year-end								Debt Service							
	$ billion				Percentage of total				$ million				Percentage of total			
	1982	1983	1984	1985	1982	1983	1984	1985	1982	1983	1984	1985	1982	1983	1984	1985
OECD countries and capital markets	10.2	10.9	11.0	13.0	31.3	29.7	29.5	31.3	710	802	920	1 024	47.4	51.2	47.8	45.1
of which:																
ODA	4.0	4.0	4.7	5.7	12.1	10.8	12.5	13.8	110	109	157	190	7.4	7.0	8.2	8.4
Official and officially supported	4.3	5.2	4.4	5.4	13.2	14.1	11.8	13.0	389	461	533	533	25.9	29.4	27.7	23.5
Financial markets	1.9	1.7	1.9	1.8	5.8	4.7	5.0	4.4	208	229	222	294	13.9	14.6	11.5	12.9
Other private	0.1	0.1	0.1	0.1	0.2	0.2	0.2	0.1	3	3	8	7	0.2	0.2	0.4	0.3
Multilateral	8.4	9.6	10.8	12.6	25.8	26.1	28.9	30.1	270	296	391	536	18.0	18.9	20.3	23.6
of which:																
Concessional	7.3	8.4	9.5	11.2	22.3	22.8	25.4	26.9	130	147	206	338	8.6	9.4	10.7	14.9
Non-concessional	1.1	1.2	1.3	1.4	3.5	3.3	3.5	3.3	140	149	185	198	9.3	9.5	9.6	8.7
Non-OECD creditor countries	10.0	11.6	11.3	10.9	30.5	31.5	30.3	26.2	335	284	400	501	22.3	18.1	20.7	22.1
of which:																
Socialist countries of Eastern Europe	3.4	4.3	4.1	4.4	10.4	11.8	11.1	10.6	..	..	..	..	..	..	..	..
OPEC	4.6	5.1	5.3	4.6	14.0	14.0	14.2	11.1	..	..	..	..	..	..	..	..
Other countries and unspecified	2.0	2.1	1.9	1.9	6.1	5.8	5.0	4.5	..	..	..	..	..	..	..	..
Total long and medium-term	28.6	32.1	33.0	36.6	87.6	87.3	88.7	87.6	1 315	1 382	1 711	2 060	87.7	88.1	88.8	90.9
of which:																
Concessional	19.5	21.9	23.5	26.4	59.7	59.7	63.1	63.3	450	459	678	932	30.0	29.3	35.2	41.1
Non-concessional	9.1	10.2	9.5	10.2	27.9	27.6	25.5	24.4	865	923	1 033	1 128	57.7	58.8	53.6	49.7
Short-term	2.2	2.4	2.2	2.9	6.6	6.5	5.8	6.9	185	186	216	207	12.3	11.9	11.2	9.1
IMF credit	1.9	2.2	2.1	2.3	5.8	6.1	5.5	5.4								
Total external debt, including IMF credit[a]	32.7	36.7	37.3	41.7	100.0	100.0	100.0	100.0	1 500	1 568	1 927	2 267	100.0	100.0	100.0	100.0

Source: UNCTAD secretariat calculations based on information from the OECD secretariat and IMF, *International Financial Statistics.*

[a] Debt service excludes repurchases from IMF.

TABLE 24

LDCs: debt[a] indicators by country, 1982 and 1985

| | Debt disbursed ($ million) | | Debt service[b] ($ million) | | Share of non-concessional debt in: | | | | Ratio of: | | | | Share of long-term debt in total: | |
| | | | | | Total debt (per cent) | | Total debt service[b] (per cent) | | Debt to GDP (per cent) | | Debt service to exports[c] (per cent) | | Debt (per cent) | Debt service[b] (per cent) |
	1982	1985	1982	1985	1982	1985	1982	1985	1982	1985	1982	1985	1985	1985
Afghanistan	1 410	1 429	40	47	2	1	8	49	(40)	(38)	5	7	100	99
Bangladesh	4 942	6 845	161	294	17	13	38	44	37	43	16	23	93	98
Benin	623	777	30	41	67	60	85	81	60	76	14	17	87	86
Bhutan	9	6	2	9	85	7	99	5	6	3	6	24	94	99
Botswana	340	441	62	56	70	71	97	84	40	47	10	6	95	97
Burkina Faso	390	551	27	33	34	31	83	79	38	59	15	20	92	92
Burundi	252	461	18	24	23	23	87	51	25	42	16	20	94	94
Cape Verde	57	102	2	5	47	40	94	80	53	87	4	14	99	99
Central African Republic	262	349	7	18	53	40	85	50	40	52	6	10	87	93
Chad	157	167	2	9	46	37	89	68	23	26	3	9	93	97
Comoros	81	135	2	3	19	10	61	57	82	139	9	12	97	90
Democratic Yemen	843	1 573	35	133	10	18	40	25	111	(163)	18	84	91	94
Djibouti	47	244	4	35	65	65	55	62	23	118	2	23	89	94
Equatorial Guinea	124	141	4	4	75	77	99	93	179	187	22	18	92	95
Ethiopia	1 239	1 911	69	125	29	27	69	66	28	40	12	22	94	96
Gambia	212	248	13	15	45	42	87	69	102	158	16	18	80	84
Guinea	1 440	1 432	102	78	36	35	52	44	82	68	22	15	93	93
Guinea-Bissau	152	253	3	19	30	39	73	25	75	188	19	100	88	91
Haiti	667	833	27	39	55	45	84	77	45	(45)	10	11	74	75
Kiribati	8	11	0	1	94	94	100	9	47	52	—	..	99	91
Lao People's Democratic Republic	321	528	2	26	5	14	12	22	87	38	4	34	87	85
Lesotho	117	177	14	19	34	19	94	76	34	69	3	6	99	99
Malawi	882	987	76	86	55	46	90	79	75	91	29	31	78	94
Maldives	48	81	2	13	27	53	31	70	80	(104)	3	14	84	89
Mali	855	1 504	33	52	10	17	85	37	68	130	18	23	89	89
Mauritania	1 201	1 509	55	96	45	43	66	60	160	218	18	23	94	94
Nepal	352	589	13	18	15	10	60	32	15	25	5	6	94	90
Niger	891	1 058	172	96	67	58	93	78	46	67	39	31	85	92

TABLE 24 *(continued)*

LDCs: debt[a] indicators by country, 1982 and 1985

| | Debt disbursed ($ million) | | Debt service[b] ($ million) | | Share of non-concessional debt in: | | | | Ratio of: | | | | Share of long-term debt in total: | |
| | | | | | Total debt (per cent) | | Total debt service[b] (per cent) | | Debt to GDP (per cent) | | Debt service[b] to exports[c] (per cent) | | Debt (per cent) | Debt service[b] (per cent) |
	1982	1985	1982	1985	1982	1985	1982	1985	1982	1985	1982	1985	1985	1985
Rwanda	221	369	10	24	14	16	39	61	15	(22)	6	14	93	89
Samoa	64	75	3	5	29	26	73	63	59	85	12	18	87	100
Sao Tome and Principe .	22	31	0	3	26	27	94	40	63	89	3	35	96	96
Sierra Leone	615	693	37	39	60	65	93	81	48	59	24	24	63	62
Somalia	1 266	1 725	24	91	31	37	63	43	73	(123)	9	71	90	97
Sudan	6 367	6 484	147	184	66	62	75	79	73	74	16	22	77	71
Togo	1 046	1 010	59	94	72	68	95	64	127	145	13	27	84	93
Tuvalu	—	0	—	0	—	—	—	—	—	5	—	..	100	100
Uganda	879	1 076	66	118	55	52	68	72	27[d]	(32)[d]	17	30	72	98
United Republic of Tanzania . . .	2 740	3 374	93	102	43	44	81	77	44	54	17	23	92	83
Vanuatu	14	128	2	11	72	96	67	94	(26)	195	4	13	83	79
Yemen	1 541	2 399	82	207	19	28	43	49	44	(63)	24	92	89	90
TOTAL LDCs	32 698	41 706	1 500	2 267	40	37	70	59	49	58	14	22	88	91

Source: UNCTAD secretariat calculations based on information from the OECD secretariat, the World Bank, the IMF and other international and national sources.

[a] Total external debt including short-term debt and use of IMF credit.

[b] Excluding repurchases to the IMF.

[c] Exports of goods and services.

[d] As a percentage of GNP.

local currency of the dollar debt obligation arising from purchases of agricultural commodities. Japan gives LDCs cash grants to offset debt servicing regarding ODA loans on which an exchange of notes was concluded before 31 March 1978. In the case of debt to the socialist countries of Eastern Europe, 90 per cent of the LDCs' debt is owed to the USSR.

(b) Multilateral renegotiations of debt

The other form of debt relief to which LDCs have had access is that provided under debt renegotiations. Renegotiations for debts to governments (concessional as well as non-concessional) and for officially guaranteed export credits take place in the framework of the Paris Club, while debts to banks (not covered by export credit insurance) are renegotiated by *ad hoc* commercial bank advisory committees often referred to as the "London Club". Up to December 1986, 13 LDCs had rescheduled their outstanding obligations at the Paris Club, namely the Central African Republic (3 times), Equatorial Guinea, Gambia, Guinea, Malawi (twice), Mauritania (twice), Niger, Sierra Leone (3 times), Somalia, Sudan (3 times), Togo (4 times), Uganda (twice) and the United Republic of Tanzania. Moreover, five of them also renegotiated their commercial debts at the London Club, namely Malawi, Niger, Sierra Leone, Sudan (5 times) and Togo (twice). 1983 was a peak year for reschedulings and commercial restructurings for LDCs. The levels rescheduled under the aegis of the Paris Club in the following years were significantly lower.

Experience has shown that reschedulings, like restructurings, have had relatively little effect in ameliorating LDCs' debt situation. LDCs' outstanding debt obligations have not thereby decreased. In several cases such operations have led to repeated renegotiations. As regards Paris Club reschedulings, even the temporary relief provided has proved to be of limited scope to LDCs, in so far as these negotiations do not include multilateral creditors to which LDCs have a high and increasing level of obligations, nor do they include the OPEC members and socialist countries of Eastern Europe, which are the principal bilateral creditors for some LDCs.

In this area, however, progress appears to be made at least with regards to improving terms. The Paris Club has begun to implement a lengthening of the repayment period up to 20 years, instead of the current limit of 10 years, including longer grace periods (the Venice communiqué refers to a grace period of up to 10 years). Such exceptional treatment was granted for the first time to Mozambique (not an LDC) in June 1987. Then Uganda's official and officially guaranteed debt was rescheduled over 15 years, with a 6-year grace period, in June. Also in June 1987, Mauritania arranged to have its debts rescheduled at the Paris Club over 15 years. In July 1987 Somalia obtained a 20-year rescheduling with a 10-year grace period. Second, the possibility of applying lower interest rates to existing debts is under consideration.[82] The granting of concessional terms for the amounts renegotiated has already been agreed by a few creditor countries.[83] UNCTAD VII, in its Final Act, agreed that the debt-servicing burden of the poorest countries, including LDCs, the majority of which are in sub-Saharan Africa, which are undertaking adjustment efforts, should be eased by longer repayments and grace periods, especially in the Paris Club. It urged that consideration should also be given to the possibility of applying lower interest rates to their existing debts.[84]

On the other hand, the provision of commercial restructurings on a multi-year basis (so-called MYRAS) is increasingly questioned and has not yet been agreed with any LDC.[85] The IMF Interim Committee, in its communique of 28 September 1987, "encouraged private creditors to continue their efforts to find realistic responses to the debt-servicing difficulties and efforts of adjustment" of low-income countries.

---

[82] See Communiqué of the IMF Interim Committee of 28 September 1987. At its September 1987 meeting, the World Bank Development Committee considered proposals for debt relief by reducing interest rates, noting that for some of the highly indebted low-income countries continued reliance on rescheduling at commercial interest rates did not provide a solution to the difficulties facing them (see Press Communiqué of the Development Committee of 28 September 1987).

[83] In connection with the follow-up to the General Assembly's special session on Africa, the Italian Government has recently announced its intention to alleviate the debt burden of African countries through the rescheduling of debt repayments over a number of years at concessional terms, which will include substantially reduced interest rates (1.5 per cent), long periods of repayment (20 years) and a 10-year grace period. In its reply to the UNCTAD secretariat's questionnaire, the Federal Republic of Germany has indicated that, with regard to bilateral rescheduling operations subsequent to multilateral reschedulings in the Paris Club, concessional loans are rescheduled at concessional rates of interest, while commercial claims backed by guarantees are rescheduled at market rates of interest; as a rule, rates of interest are to remain constant throughout the period of the rescheduling agreement. The United Kingdom, with France, now favours lower interest rates (below the market rate i.e. implying subsidies) on the remaining official debt outstanding owed by the poorer African countries that are pursuing satisfactory reform programmes. By late 1987 the United Kingdom was endeavouring to gain wider acceptance of this principle among the remaining OECD Governments. See the statement of Mr. Nigel Lawson, Chancellor of the Exchequer, to the United Kingdom All-Party Parliamentary Group on Overseas Development, reported in the *Financial Times*, 23 July 1987.

[84] See TD/L.316/Add.5.

[85] See World Bank, *World Debt Tables*, 1986-1987 edition, p. XIV.

3. *Debt strategy*

The perpetuation of the debt crisis of the early 1980s has led to the view that a lasting solution to debt problems requires adjustment and sustainable growth in indebted countries. This is the core of the debt strategy initiative proposed by United States Treasury Secretary Baker in October 1985, which has received wide support. The strategy is primarily addressed to the highly indebted developing countries which are mainly market borrowers, but the growing awareness of the need to deal with the problems of poor countries as well has led to further initiatives specially geared to the needs of this group of countries, which materialized with the establishment of the World Bank Special Facility for Sub-Saharan Africa and the IMF Structural Adjustment Facility. The resumption of growth in these countries, has, however, been hampered *inter alia* by the inadequacy of the present flow of concessional aid to support structural adjustment efforts, as already outlined above. Creditor governments are nevertheless being forced to conclude that both increased concessional flows and special relief measures to reduce the existing burden of LDCs' debt and its accruing arrears are necessary.

4. *Scope for future action*

Despite measures taken so far – adjustment measures on the part of LDCs and debt relief measures on the part of creditors – the debt situation of the LDCs has worsened, mainly because of factors beyond their own control. Acute poverty, limited domestic and external resources to invest, adverse terms of trade, have rendered their debt burden unmanageable. Poor prospects for an improvement in the external environment and the scheduled levels of service due in the years ahead point to debt ratios which could entail not only interruptions in creditor-debtor relationships, but also economic and social strains leading to severe political disturbances.

Clearly, additional innovative measures, including measures of an exceptional nature, are urgently called for. These are not beyond reach. It must be remembered that LDCs' problems are not of a magnitude to threaten the financial stability of their creditors which, moreover, are principally governments and international financial institutions, not private lenders.

A number of specific proposals, generally intertwined within the framework of debt relief plans, have been put forward recently by creditor countries.[86] These and other types of action needed are set out below.

The first type of action – also perhaps relatively the easiest to achieve by governments – is the writing off of all LDCs' remaining bilateral ODA loans. Such action has already been taken by a good number of governments within the framework of UNCTAD Board resolution 165 (S-IX) [87](see table 25).

The second type of action concerns other bilateral official and officially guaranteed debts (loans and export credits). It has been proposed that the terms of such debts be lowered substantially below market rates through government subsidies and that these debts be rescheduled over longer periods.[88] The practice of rescheduling such debts over 20 years should be currently adopted in the case of LDCs' debts. Partial write-offs may also be considered.[89]

Thirdly, solutions to cope with LDCs' debt service due to multilateral financial institutions are to be urgently devised. Arrangements such as interest subsidy schemes and refinancing schemes would allow past loans that are non-concessional to be converted to IDA terms. For instance, an

---

[86] In particular, by the United Kingdom and France as well as the Nordic countries at the recent meetings of the IMF Interim Committee and the World Bank Development Committee. The OECD Ministerial Communiqué of May 1987 refers to proposals recently made by OECD countries for "additional action to reduce the debt servicing burden of the poorest countries, especially in Sub-Saharan Africa, undertaking strong growth-oriented adjustment programmes" and states that "early results from the current discussions among creditor governments will be urgently sought" (OECD/PRESS/A(87) 27), Paris, 13 May 1987. In their final statement at the Venice economic summit, the seven major industrialized countries again urged a conclusion of discussions on the various proposals made in this area within 1987.

[87] The conversion of outstanding loans to the poorest African debtors into grants is a key element of the plan proposed by Mr. Nigel Lawson, Chancellor of the Exchequer of the United Kingdom.

[88] Longer grace periods and maturities for official debts and the lowering of interest on existing debts of the poorest African debtors, are the elements of the Lawson Plan. The British Government has confirmed that if the plan is approved any costs will not be drawn from the aid programme.

[89] For instance, the Swedish Government accorded partial forgiveness for officially guaranteed export credits and official loans to Guinea-Bissau in February 1987. The World Bank has recently proposed an international programme of assistance to a group of highly indebted low-income African countries undertaking adjustment programmes, which calls for concessional debt relief in the Paris Club, including lowered interest rates and extended grace periods and maturities as well as continued conversion of loans into grants (see the address by the President of the World Bank of 29 September 1987 (Board of Governors, 1987 Annual Meetings, Washington, D.C., Press release No. 2)

TABLE 25

Action taken under section A of Trade and Development Board resolution 165 (S-IX) in favour of LDCs

I. SUMMARY OF DEBT CANCELLATIONS

(Millions of dollars)

Creditor / Debtor	Australia	Canada	Denmark	Finland	France	Germany, Fed. Rep. of	Italy	Japan	Luxembourg	Netherlands	New Zealand	Sweden	Switzerland	United Kingdom	Total[a]
Afghanistan		1.2						×						2.1	3.3
Bangladesh		16.8	39.1	6.7	14.4	472.5		×		43.1		10.0	7.7	33.3	643.6
Benin		14.1	6.2		4.0	20.4	0.8								45.5
Botswana		34.0	2.7			33.7						6.1		42.9	119.4
Burkina Faso		0.9	3.5		17.8	92.7				7.5					122.4
Burundi					0.3	30.1									30.4
Central African Republic					1.6	13.3									14.9
Chad			1.8		15.2	6.1									23.1
Comoros					5.0										5.0
Democratic Yemen			2.7												2.7
Djibouti					11.1	3.4		×							14.5
Ethiopia				1.8			9.8					10.9			22.5
Gambia						10.9								11.0	21.9
Guinea					2.8	23.6	6.4			1.0					33.8
Guinea-Bissau										9.8					9.8
Haiti						8.4									8.4
Kiribati	×														×
Lao People's Democratic Republic		2.4						×							2.4
Lesotho						12.0								0.6	12.6
Malawi		36.8	15.8			49.1		×		7.2				64.3	173.2
Mali		1.9			13.2	93.8	1.5	×							110.4
Nepal		2.4	2.8			43.1		×					5.8	4.6	58.7
Niger		37.7	7.6		6.2	98.0		×							149.5
Rwanda						56.2		×	0.3		×				56.5
Samoa	×													0.4	0.4
Sierra Leone						47.5				5.5				18.2	71.2
Somalia						56.8	28.7								85.5
Sudan			7.6			237.0	7.4			16.9		10.2		20.4	299.5
Togo			9.3		3.7	101.0									114.0
Tuvalu	×														×
Uganda		2.2	7.3			26.6		×		3.6				25.2	64.9
United Republic of Tanzania		37.7	114.6	26.5		188.5	12.2			53.3		50.7		5.3	488.8
Yemen						107.0		×		17.2					124.2
TOTAL LDCs	..	188.1	221.0	35.0	95.3	1 831.7	66.8[b]	56.3[b]	0.3	165.1	..	87.9	13.5	228.3	2 989.3

Source: For source and footnotes, see Part II of the table.

TABLE 25 *(continued)*

**Action taken under section A of Trade and Development Board
resolution 165 (S-IX) in favour of LDCs**

II. NOMINAL VALUE OF OTHER MEASURES TAKEN WITH RESPECT TO ODA DEBT

(Millions of dollars)

Creditor Debtor	Belgium A	Canada A	France A	Germany, Fed. Rep. of A	Netherlands A	Sweden A	United Kingdom A	Total A	USA B
Afghanistan		×						×	
Bangladesh	2.0^c	×	4.6	×	13.7	2.0		22.3	317.3
Benin		×	2.0	×				2.0	
Botswana		×		×		1.2	1.1	2.3	
Burkina Faso		×	8.3	×	2.2			10.5	
Burundi			0.2	×				0.2	
Central African Republic			1.9	2.7				4.6	
Chad			8.4	0.9				9.3	
Comoros			3.0					3.0	
Democratic Yemen								—	
Djibouti			3.1	0.3				3.4	
Ethiopia						2.0		2.0	
Gambia				×				×	
Guinea			0.8	×	0.2			1.0	27.0
Guinea-Bissau					0.7			0.7	
Haiti				1.6				1.6	53.0
Kiribati								—	
Laos People's Democratic Republic		×						×	
Lesotho				×			0.2	0.2	
Malawi		×		×	1.4		1.5	2.9	2.4
Mali		×	5.6	×				5.6	
Nepal		×		×				×	
Niger		×	3.2	×				3.2	
Rwanda				×				×	
Samoa								—	
Sierra Leone				9.2			4.0	13.2	10.1
Somalia				×				—	78.2
Sudan				×	5.9	1.8	0.8	8.5	175.0
Togo			0.9	21.1				22.0	
Tuvalu								—	
Uganda		×		5.0	0.6		3.7	9.3	
United Republic of Tanzania	0.2	×		×	12.3	9.5	1.9	23.9	25.0
Yemen				×	0.6			0.6	3.0
TOTAL LDCs	2.2	30.0	42.0	311.1	37.6	16.5	13.2	452.6	691.0

Source: Information supplied by creditor countries to the UNCTAD secretariat up to end September 1986. Ireland and Norway have been providing their ODA to LDCs in the form of grants and are therefore not shown in this table. No debt relief operations have been reported for Bhutan, Cape Verde, Equatorial Guinea, Maldives, Mauritania, Sao Tome and Principe, and Vanuatu.

NOTE: × indicates action taken by the creditor country in favour of the indivudal debtor country but amounts are not allocable by debtor country. The totals for LDCs include some unallocated amounts.

A = Waiving of interst payments

B = Agreement to allow payment of debt in local currency.

^a Excluding amounts not allocable by debtor country (see general note to this table).

^b Including interests payments.

^c Including 50.05 million for refinancing of debt interest.

TABLE 26

LDCs: multilateral debt renegotiations

(Millions of dollars)

	1977-1981	1982	1983	1984	1985	1986
			Paris Club[a]			
Central African Republic ..	55 (50)	—	13 (19)	—	14 (14)	—
Equatorial Guinea	—	—	—	—	29 (38)	—
Gambia	—	—	—	—	—	25 (25)
Guinea	—	—	—	—	—	196 (190)
Malawi	—	24 (25)	30 (20)	—	—	—
Mauritania	—	—	—	—	77 (70)	27 (30)
Niger	—	—	33 (30)	39 (30)	32 (35)	39 (39)
Sierra Leone	68 (49)	—	—	88 (60)	—	50 (60)
Somalia	—	—	—	—	142 (140)	—
Sudan	373 (475)	174 (105)	502 (540)	179 (280)	—	—
Togo	262 (452)	—	114 (150)	51 (70)	22 (31)	—
Uganda	56 (50)	22 (20)	—	—	—	—
United Republic of Tanzania	—	—	—	—	—	40 (110)
TOTAL	814 (1076)	220 (150)	692 (759)	357 (440)	316 (328)	377 (454)
			Commercial banks			
Malawi	—	—	57	—	—	—
Niger	—	—	—	27	—	—
Sierra Leone	—	—	—	20	—	—
Sudan	638	55	790	838	920	—
Togo	69	—	84	—	—	—
TOTAL	707	55	931	885	920	—

Source: World Bank, *World Debt Tables,* 1986-1987 edition and OECD, *Financing and external debt of developing countries, 1986 Survey.*

NOTE: Figures indicate renegotiated amounts as reported by the country or estimated by the World Bank. Figures in parentheses are estimated by OECD.

[a] No renegotiation of LDCs' debt took place prior to 1977.

improvement of the IMF Compensatory Financing Facility in order to make it more concessional is highly desirable.[90]

The establishment of a new exceptional facility for debt relief for the poorest indebted countries, possibly within the framework of the World Bank, has also been proposed for consideration. Its resources would be used for refinancing various types of official debts on highly concessional terms.[91]

Measures to reduce LDCs' commercial debt stocks, which, despite the limited amounts involved, are a major burden for some LDCs, should also be considered, including write-offs to be financed out of bank profits,[92] improvements in terms and conditions, and in appropriate cases conversion of debt into equity or domestic loan claims. The establishment of a debt reconstruction facility to buy the commercial debt of developing countries has been proposed by the World Institute for Development Economics Research (WIDER), a body of the United Nations University. The facility would be funded primarily through recycling part of Japan's external surplus and would also receive financial support from other countries.[93]

[90] The purpose of the Compensatory Financing Facility (CFF) of the IMF is to compensate for losses in export revenues due mainly to the fall in the price of commodities. However, because interest rates are so high and the repayment period is so short, few LDCs have drawn on the Facility in recent years despite the fall in commodity prices. (In 1984 only Malawi, in 1985 only Bangladesh, Chad and Somalia and in 1986 only Ethiopia.) Given the service of outstanding CFF drawings, LDCs' total net purchases under the CFF were negative in 1983 and 1984, very small (SDR 1.8 million) in 1985, and again heavily negative (SDR -64.3 million) in 1986. See table 31, in section F of this chapter.

[91] At the Spring 1987 meetings of the Development and Interim Committees of the World Bank and IMF, the Nordic countries argued for consideration of a multilateral facility or arrangement under the auspices of the World Bank designed to provide special assistance to the poorest indebted countries, including possible debt relief on their debts to the Bank.

[92] To the extent that the spreads charged by commercial banks in their loans to LDCs are higher than those charged to borrowers from other countries, where risks of default are considered to be less, finance could be set aside and made available for this purpose.

[93] See WIDER, *Mobilizing international surpluses for world development: A Wider plan for a Japanese initiative,* Study group series No. 2, 7 May 1987.

Last, but not least, an essential element for containing the mounting debts are the efforts of the LDCs themselves. Careful borrowing and the strengthening of debt management have become a major preoccupation in many of these countries. In this area also co-operation and assistance from donors is crucial. Moreover, to ensure effective debt management, LDCs will require technical assistance.[94]

[94] UNCTAD has developed a debt monitoring and financial analysis system (DMFAS) for the use of debt managers in developing countries, and is providing technical assistance for the installation thereof to five LDCs (Burundi, Djibouti, Haiti, Togo and Uganda).

C. NGOs in the LDCs

At UNCTAD VII, the contribution of the NGOs to the development of LDCs, as well as in providing valuable disaster relief, was recognized. In its Final Act, the governments of LDCs and donors were called upon to encourage active participation of the local population, both women and men, through non-governmental entities. The NGOs were invited to comply with national policies and legislation of the host countries while preserving their character and to contribute to the development priorities of the LDCs, co-operating with appropriate authorities and organizations in order to implement effective development programmes. The NGOs of the donor countries were invited to reinforce their role in consciousness-raising in their countries of origin and in mobilizing increased private and public resources for the benefit of the LDCs.

1. *Volume of NGO assistance to the LDCs*

Unlike official aid, most of which is monitored according to international norms, the aid channelled by NGOs to the developing countries has traditionally been difficult to quantify. According to OECD, total financial and technical assistance provided by private voluntary agencies from DAC countries to developing countries exceeded $3.3 billion in 1985, adding more than 10 per cent to total DAC official aid.[95] However, no breakdown exists of the overall volume or share of funds channelled to the LDCs. This share may vary considerably among individual NGOs, depending *inter alia* on their home country's historical ties with certain recipient countries, the existence of counterpart voluntary agencies through which

they can channel their funding, and the policy of governments in recipient countries regarding the work of voluntary agencies.

From the replies to a questionnaire sent by UNCTAD to key NGOs in DAC countries,[96] a total of $325 million was provided by 63 NGOs to 37 LDCs in 1985. This amount broadly corresponds to about one third of the assistance provided by IDA or by United Nations agencies as a whole to all LDCs in that year. Although this figure is likely to underestimate the actual level of NGO assistance directed towards the LDCs, since the UNCTAD survey was selective, and the rate of response limited,[97] it throws some light on the issue of NGO assistance to the LDCs, particularly as most of the important donor NGOs replied to the questionnaire.

Three countries, namely Ethiopia, Sudan and the United Republic of Tanzania, reportedly received 54 per cent of the total assistance provided by the NGOs in the UNCTAD survey. The substantial amounts of development assistance channelled to Ethiopia and Sudan were mostly used for emergency assistance to the drought vic-

[95] See OECD, *Development Co-operation, 1986 Report* (Paris, 1987), p. 21.

[96] In July 1986 a detailed questionnaire was sent to 130 NGOs asking for the amount of grants channelled to LDCs (excluding Kiribati, Mauritania and Tuvalu, which were not included in the list of LDCs at that time) in 1985. NGOs were selected on the basis of their assistance to developing countries: the overwhelming majority of the NGOs to which the questionnaire was sent had reported having provided more than $1 million aid in 1978 and 1979 (see *Directory of Non-Governmental Organizations in OECD Countries Active in Development Co-operation*, vol. I (Paris, 1981)). Fifteen sectors of assistance were specified in the questionnaire: namely agriculture and rural development; industry, mining and construction; small-scale industry and handicrafts; energy; roads and transport, storage, communications; health and nutrition; water supply and sanitation; education and training; housing and urban programmes; community development/social services; women's programming; food aid; refugees; other emergency assistance.

[97] Replies to the questionnaire were received from about half of the NGOs contacted.

tims. Other important beneficiaries were Bangladesh, Haiti, Burkina Faso and Mali (see table 27). As regards the relative importance of donor NGOs, more than half of the funds (55.9 per cent) mentioned in the replies to the UNCTAD questionnaire came from the NGOs of two countries, the United States and the Federal Republic of Germany.[98] The NGOs from the United Kingdom and Switzerland were the second most important DAC donors to the LDCs. Swiss together with Irish NGOs, however, appear to have been the most generous in terms of their contribution as a share of gross national product.

2. *Main types of assistance*

According to the replies to the UNCTAD questionnaire, the contribution of NGOs to the different sectors are as follows: health and nutrition, 18.19 per cent; agriculture and rural development, 14.98 per cent; education and training, 14.25 per cent; community development, 9.18 per cent; water supplies and sanitation, 8.33 per cent; women's programmes, 7.04 per cent; and small-scale industry and handicrafts, 5.57 per cent. The rest of the NGO funding has benefited seven other areas as well as "diverse activities".

In the field of health, on the basis of the information provided, the NGOs surveyed engaged in primary health care including maternal and preventive health care. They often funded mobile health teams, and put heavy emphasis on education and training of paramedical personnel. In the area of education and training, they supported in particular vocational training and informal training activities in order to provide basic productive skills.

In the field of agriculture and rural development, the attainment of food self-sufficiency received a high priority among the NGOs replying to the UNCTAD survey. In this context, the larger agencies have often channelled assistance to long-term programmes for the rehabilitation of rural areas which addressed a large range of basic needs of the local population. With their funds they have in particular encouraged local initiatives and self-help groups. The 1985 programmes included expansion and improvement of agricultural production, reafforestation, soil improvement, and protection against erosion, water conservation, animal husbandry and settlement projects for semi-nomadic families. The training of rural animators and community development personnel was considered essential for the success of many programmes.[99]

Contributions to small-scale industries and handicrafts ranked seventh of the 15 possible activities in the responses to the questionnaire. In this context, NGOs reported channelling assistance into the informal sector in small towns and in the countryside and helping co-operatives, associations of craftsmen, women's groups and groups of handicapped persons to start and expand productive activities. Technology acquired with NGO funds was usually of the traditional type for which spare parts could be obtained locally. NGOs have also supported the organization of seminars to help co-operatives and groups of potential entrepreneurs launch commercially viable activities.

The UNCTAD survey also shows that NGO contributions have varied considerably in size, from very small contributions for the purchase of a few vital tools for a production group to the financing of a fully integrated development project.

NGOs funds have usually been channelled to the target groups through local NGOs or other comparable bodies domiciled in the respective LDCs, the character of the national counterparts depending largely on the nature and working habits of the donor NGOs. Thus, a large number of church-related NGOs of DAC countries have often channelled their funds through national ecumenical organizations or national councils of churches in the respective LDCs, or organizations related to them.

Other large NGOs have stimulated the creation of specific counterpart organizations in the developing countries, including LDCs. This applies for example to the International Planned Parenthood Federation, which has its specific national counterparts in the form of family planning associations in the LDCs. The FAO Freedom from Hunger Campaign, which stimulated the foundation of numerous NGOs in the OECD countries, has at the same time encouraged the creation of counterpart NGOs in the developing countries, including LDCs. Other NGOs that did not have counterpart NGOs in LDCs have worked with a great variety of recipient organizations and bodies there, including self-help groups, peasants' associations, local interest groups, *ad hoc* associations and, on occasions, with State and parastatal bodies. This has been the case, for example, of organizations like Oxfam and other secular NGOs. Such

---

[98] This result is congruent with the DAC statistics regarding total NGO funding to all developing countries in 1985, according to which NGOs from the United States and the Federal Republic of Germany contributed 67.6 per cent of all NGO funding to developing countries. According to DAC statistics, Irish NGOs give most in terms of national GNP.

[99] The NGO orientation to rural development is underlined in the study prepared by Bertrand Schneider for the Club of Rome. See Bertrand Schneider, *La révolution aux pieds nus: Rapport au Club de Rome* (Paris, 1985).

TABLE 27

Assistance of DAC NGOs to individual LDCs in 1985 [a]

Recipient country	Total (thousands of dollars)	Per capita (dollars)	As a percentage of the total
Afghanistan	1 127	0.06	0.35
Bangladesh	21 638	0.22	6.66
Benin	1 095	0.27	0.34
Bhutan	1 885	1.33	0.58
Botswana	2 624	2.37	0.81
Burkina Faso	12 410	1.79	3.82
Burundi	3 695	0.78	1.14
Cape Verde	4 831	14.47	1.49
Central African Republic	2 044	0.78	0.63
Chad	7 128	1.42	2.20
Comoros	217	0.49	0.07
Democratic Yemen	761	0.33	0.23
Djibouti	124	0.34	0.04
Equatorial Guinea	477	1.22	0.15
Ethiopia	120 959	2.79	37.26
Gambia	4 455	6.04	1.37
Guinea	651	0.11	0.20
Guinea-Bissau	2 507	2.82	0.77
Haiti	18 017	3.42	5.55
Lao People's Democratic Republic	549	0.15	0.17
Lesotho	2 376	1.55	0.73
Malawi	4 006	0.58	1.23
Maldives	374	2.06	0.12
Mali	9 453	1.17	2.91
Nepal	7 615	0.46	2.34
Niger	1 884	0.31	0.58
Rwanda	2 819	0.47	0.87
Samoa	61	0.38	0.02
Sao Tome and Principe	273	2.53	0.08
Sierra Leone	4 673	1.30	1.44
Somalia	4 090	0.76	1.26
Sudan	33 193	1.54	10.23
Togo	4 053	1.37	1.25
Uganda	10 270	0.66	3.16
United Republic of Tanzania	29 501	1.33	9.09
Vanuatu	104	0.80	0.03
Yemen	2 683	0.34	0.83
TOTAL	324 622	0.98	100.00

Source: Replies to the UNCTAD questionnaire.

[a] Excluding Kiribati, Mauritania and Tuvalu.

agencies have often executed their own development projects and sent their own experts to the LDCs. Donor NGOs have indicated paying great attention to institution-building at the grass-roots level in LDCs, trying to create and strengthen local associations.

The UNCTAD survey did not evaluate the effectiveness of NGO programmes, but the Box on NGOs below provides an example of a joint evaluation of NGO activities in a particular country, from which a number of lessons can be drawn for the future.

Box 7

EFFORTS TO IMPROVE NGO/GOVERNMENT CO-OPERATION:
THE CASE OF GUINEA-BISSAU

As a follow-up to a country review meeting, the Government of Guinea-Bissau arranged, in November 1985 in Bissau, an NGO Conference, chaired by the Minister of Planning and Economic Co-operation, with the purpose of evaluating the work of the NGOs in the country and of drawing lessons for the future. A number of problems were identified by the NGOs as well as by the host Government.

Among the problems mentioned by the NGOs were: (a) lack of clear demarcation of responsibilities among the various ministries with which NGOs were in contact; (b) insufficient project preparation and follow-up by local authorities; (c) the fact that commitments regarding inputs and funds were not always kept; (d) numerous administrative problems which had hampered and delayed project implementation (customs clearance of project inputs, the provisions of entry and exit visas for project personnel, lack of housing for project personnel, validation of drivers' licenses, etc.); (e) lack of guarantees regarding the holding of foreign exchange earmarked for the import of spare parts and of raw materials necessary for the functioning of the projects.

To remedy these problems the NGO proposed the facilitation and speeding up of certain administrative procedures, the adoption of an official status for NGO personnel and clear rules regarding foreign currency for project purposes. They asked for assurances in this respect that a certain percentage of the earnings resulting from the productive activities of a project could be exchanged in foreign currency. In their view this was often essential to maintain the vitality of projects, which in many cases could only exist if a certain amount of key imports were guaranteed.

The problems described by the Government related in turn to: (a) insufficient integration of the NGO projects into the national development plans and strategies; (b) insufficient monitoring of projects by NGOs; (c) excessive delays in providing the agreed funding; (d) insufficient awareness by NGOs of how much financing had gone into their projects, which had made decisions regarding new projects difficult; (e) difficulties often encountered by NGOs in ordering materials sufficiently in advance, and last-minute changes; (f) the inadequate preparation of foreign NGO personnel; and (g) the fact that some NGOs preferred to work on their own, without sufficiently explaining their initiatives and plans to the relevant Government services. The Government officials recognized that so far there existed no listing or summary of the areas and sectors where NGOs could and should become active, or a catalogue of projects that could be presented to them. They also felt that Government officers had not always come up with project proposals themselves and had clearly experienced difficulty in providing the necessary backstopping and inputs.

Accordingly, the Government made several proposals aimed at improving NGOs' co-operation: NGOs should refrain from transplanting concepts and ideas that were alien to the people of the country; they should give greater emphasis to the training of local personnel, even if this meant slowing down project implementation; they should try to strengthen their administrative structures so as to be able to honour their financial and other commitments; they should provide precise requests for the materials they needed and hold discussions in advance with the relevant offices before making changes in their original requests. Also, their project planning and evaluation should be improved and projects should be planned for a duration of at least three years to make them worthwhile.

The newly established NGO liaison office, Solidami, designed to rationalize and formalize co-operation with the NGOs, is to provide the institutional framework that should enable NGO activities to be better planned and co-ordinated, and the necessary guidelines for their development in Guinea-Bissau. Solidami is expected to create a better knowledge and understanding of the NGOs within government departments and offices, to help in mobilizing the desired NGO support for the execution of projects, and also to help in the search for finance. It is further expected to assist the NGOs in their search for appropriate areas of work and in their efforts to perform this work to the best advantage of the country. Another important task ahead for Solidami will be to encourage the creation and organization of national NGOs.

D. Economic co-operation among developing countries

LDCs have been increasingly involved in regional and subregional co-operation groupings. New groupings have been established with the participation of LDCs, the most recent cases being the South Asian Regional Co-operation (SARC), with four LDCs out of seven members (Bangladesh, Bhutan, Maldives, Nepal), and the Intergovernmental Authority on Drought and Development (IGADD), comprising six countries of Eastern Africa of which five are LDCs (Djibouti, Ethiopia, Somalia, Sudan, Uganda). In other cases, LDCs have been joining existing groupings, examples of this being the accession of Benin to the West African Economic Community (CEAO), of Chad and Equatorial Guinea to the Central African Customs and Economic Union (UDEAC), and of Guinea to the Mano River Union. Moreover, increasing attention is being paid within groupings to the particular development needs of the LDCs in fields such as trade liberalization, transit-transport and transit-traffic for land-locked LDCs, industrial and agricultural development, energy, and money and finance.

The share of LDCs in intra-grouping trade, however, has continued to decrease. Correspondingly, between 1981 and 1985, the value and share of intra-subregional trade in total LDCs' exports and imports declined, respectively, from $451 million (or 6.4 per cent) to $365 million (or 5.1 per cent), and from $1,214 million (or 7.7 per cent) to $1,032 million (or 7.0 per cent).[100] During the same period, the share of developing countries in LDCs' exports also decreased, from 30.1 per cent to 24.0 per cent. Hence the importance for LDCs of the establishment of a global system of trade preferences among developing countries (GSTP), which is currently under negotiation. Article 17 of the proposed GSTP agreement already envisages special concessions for LDCs to be granted on a non-reciprocal basis.

In the context of South-South co-operation, LDCs have been receiving financial assistance from OPEC countries, China and other developing countries, a matter dealt with in section A of chapter III.

Economic co-operation among developing countries involving LDCs can further be promoted through the establishment of joint ventures as well as through agreements concerning the exchange of technological skills. Agreements of this type have been concluded, for instance, between developing countries of the Mediterranean region (Egypt, Maghreb countries, Cyprus) and some African LDCs, as well as between Liberia and Sierra Leone.[101] In the commercial sphere, firms from relatively advanced developing countries (such as Brazil, India, the Republic of Korea and the Philippines) perform contract work, often as a result of international competitive bidding, in LDCs. Some skill and technology transfer among developing countries thus occurs through these channels.

In the field of education and training, about 20,000 students of LDCs have been enrolled in universities of 20 other developing countries.[102]

E. Access to markets

The efforts of the LDCs to expand their exports have been hampered by the tariff and non-tariff barriers that exist against the products from these countries in the principal import markets. This remains true despite the preference schemes established by the developed market-economy and socialist countries, and the imminent emergence of the GSTP among developing countries (see section D above). Rare instances of positive differential treatment in favour of the LDCs do exist, such as Sweden's recent liberalization measures for all imports from LDCs (see below), but they need to be emulated by some other preference-giving countries.

---

[100] Estimations made on the basis of available national data and of IMF, *Direction of Trade*, 1984, 1986.

[101] See TD/B/1128, p. 12.

[102] See UNESCO, *Statistical Yearbook*, 1985, pp. III-418 to 447.

1. *Tariff barriers*

Several mechanisms have been established by developed countries with the purpose of promoting imports from developing countries through preferential tariff treatment. The most important of them is the generalized system of preferences (GSP), which is open to all developing countries. Nevertheless, the product coverage of the system has since its inception tended to be focused on industrial products, on the basis that one of the main objectives of the GSP is to promote industrial development. This makes it less useful generally to LDCs – which are defined *inter alia* by their narrow manufacturing base – than for the more advanced developing countries. Moreover, most preference granting countries exclude, or impose tariff quotas or equivalent measures upon, a large number of agricultural products covered by their GSP schemes (in addition to those on selected sensitive industrial products), precisely those products in which LDCs have a comparative advantage. On the other hand, many LDCs have not been able to take full advantage of the schemes, because of the complexities involved in complying with rules of origin.[103]

A recent study shows that LDCs and other relatively small developing countries have not benefited from competitive need exclusions, a criterion applied in the schemes of some preference-giving countries and leading to the exclusion from the scheme of beneficiaries which surpass a certain value or a defined share of the total imports, ostensibly leaving more room under the scheme for emerging exporters.[104] In the study, which refers exclusively to the United States scheme, annual market shares were calculated for each of the 340 products affected by competitive need exclusions in one or more years. The LDCs increased the mean market shares with respect to only four out of the affected beneficiaries; but even in three of these four cases the major share of the benefits accrue to suppliers other than LDCs.[105]

These various factors more than justify the adoption of special measures in favour of LDCs by preference-giving countries. In the recent past, however, only modest steps have been taken in this direction. The EEC added one product to its scheme in 1986 and another in 1987, for the ben-efit of the least developed countries.[106] In 1986, *Finland* added four products in favour of these countries.[107] *Japan* has announced that it will add in fiscal year 1989 one product for the benefit of LDCs.[108] A hopefully path-breaking step in this regard was taken in February 1987 by *Sweden* which, like Norway in 1976, decided to extend duty-free treatment to all imports originating in the 40 least developed countries, subject to fulfilment of the notification procedure.

2. *Non-tariff barriers*

Slackening world economic growth, with its adverse repercussions on international trade, has triggered a recrudescence of protectionist pressures particularly in developed market economies, a phenomenon which jeopardizes the chances for LDCs to expand and diversify their export base. In this connection, the 1987 GATT report expresses concern over a worrying "increased tendency to regard imports as threatening".[109] With a narrow, short-term perspective, major importing countries have been turning towards the application of non-tariff measures to protect their own industries and employment. This hardly enhances the relevance of the tariff preferences which they simultaneously grant to exports of developing countries, including LDCs. Attempts by LDCs to penetrate new markets and to sell their industrial products have thus been encountering a wide variety of non-tariff obstacles in the major industrialized countries, which has further hampered their export performance.

(a) *Developed market-economy countries*

The UNCTAD secretariat has established a data base on non-tariff measures applied in most developed market-economy countries, including volume constraints, price controls and automatic import authorizations. The information gathered thereby shows that an important share of the LDCs' exports is subject to such measures, particularly to quantitative restrictions. These measures are widely used in regard to the agricultural sector, which is of paramount importance to the LDCs.

---

[103] Notification is required with respect to the names and addresses of governmental authorities empowered to issue the certificate of origin (Form A) together with an impression of the stamps used by such authorities.

[104] See "Effects of competitive need exclusions and redesignations under the United States scheme of generalized preferences", study by Craig R. MacPhee (UNCTAD/ST/MD/29), English only.

[105] Calculations were possible for only 40 of the total number of 43 affected beneficiaries.

[106] For 1986: asparagus (ex 07.01K); for 1987: grape juice (20.07 B. II. a).

[107] Sheep and lamb skin leather (41.03); goat and kid skin leather (41.04); jute shopping bags (ex 42.02); and hanging flower pots (ex 62.02).

[108] Jute yarn (57.06).

[109] GATT, *International Trade 1986/87*, chapter 1 (Geneva, 25 September 1987).

TABLE 28

Imports of clothing (SITC 84) by the developed market economies[a]
from the world, the developing countries and the LDCs

	1980	1981	1982	1983	1984	1985	1986[b]
IMPORTS FROM THE WORLD *(millions of dollars)*							
Developed market economies	34 768	33 567	33 278	33 845	39 475	42 156	55 587
North America	7 655	8 961	9 633	11 447	15 901	17 495	20 237
Europe	25 225	22 363	21 367	20 531	21 172	22 279	32 042
of which: EEC	20 485	18 151	17 202	16 525	16 976	17 735	25 538
Japan	1 530	1 802	1 832	1 501	1 949	1 995	2 853
IMPORTS FROM THE DEVELOPING COUNTRIES *(millions of dollars)*							
Developed market economies	14 405	15 584	15 723	16 429	20 674	21 601	26 978
North America	6 247	7 261	7 686	9 052	12 387	13 402	14 926
Europe	7 092	6 911	6 596	6 263	6 766	6 749	9 973
of which: EEC	6 267	6 079	5 754	5 490	5 913	5 899	8 796
Japan	853	1 127	1 144	879	1 237	1 184	1 808
IMPORTS FROM THE LDCs *(millions of dollars)*							
Developed market economies	99.6	115.8	123.1	156.8	207.0	383.3	404.8
North America	63.4	75.5	84.4	99.5	158.8	336.9	357.4
Europe	19.7	21.6	20.7	30.1	26.0	25.4	44.0
of which: EEC	16.1	18.2	17.7	27.0	22.0	20.8	30.0
Japan	0.2	0.1	0.1	0.1	0.1	0.1	0.3
SHARE OF LDCs IN WORLD *(per thousand)*							
Developed market economies	2.86	3.45	3.70	4.63	5.24	9.09	7.28
North America	8.28	8.43	8.76	8.69	9.99	19.26	17.66
Europe	0.78	0.96	0.97	1.46	1.23	1.14	1.37
of which: EEC	0.79	1.00	1.03	1.63	1.29	1.17	1.17
Japan	0.13	0.08	0.08	0.05	0.07	0.07	0.09

Source: UNCTAD secretariat calculations based on UN-COMTRADE data base.

[a] Excluding Gibraltar, South Africa and Israel; including Australia and New Zealand.

[b] Provisional and excluding Spain.

Agricultural commodities affected by these measures represented in 1986 more than 45 per cent of the total exports of LDCs in value terms. As regards the industrial sector, 84 per cent of LDCs' exports from the clothing industry were subjected to this sort of measure, as compared to 78 per cent in the case of the developing countries as a whole; this suggests that, in terms of non-tariff-barriers, the LDCs did not receive preferential treatment with respect to other developing countries in this sector. Non-tariff measures on imports of clothing from LDCs is a particularly worrisome feature, inasmuch as these countries have succeeded in expanding their share in the world market for this item (see Box 8 on the Bangladesh experience below). In textiles, however, the situation appears to be less detrimental to LDCs, as only 15 per cent of their trade was affected by non-tariff measures, as compared to 60 per cent for all developing countries.

During the 1980s, the LDCs have been able to increase their exports of a limited number of industrial products. An example of a successful export experience is *clothing* (SITC 84), for which the value of DMEC imports from the LDCs increased more than four-fold, from $100 million in 1980 to $405 million in 1986 (see table 28). More than two-thirds of this increase was connected to the establishment of clothing industries for exports in Bangladesh (see Box 8 below), where the value of exports increased from virtually nil in 1980 to $214 million in 1986. Although the share of the LDCs in the total is still extremely low, the increase in their share (which multiplied by 2.5 between 1980 and 1985) is highly significant. Yet provisional estimates for 1986 point to a retreat in the LDCs' market share. Total imports into the North American market continued to grow at the rapid pace of 15 per cent, while those from the LDCs increased by only 6 per cent. As regards market

Box 8

THE EXPERIENCE OF BANGLADESH

Traditionally, Bangladesh's exports have been dominated by primary commodities and manufactured products with limited processing, the jute industry being a key sector. In the past 20 years, world demand for jute products, at first sluggish, eventually declined mainly because of competition from synthetic fibres. This trend has prompted the country to explore alternative exports. Towards the end of the 1970s, the establishment of companies for the production of garments for exports was stimulated, notably through the transfer of production technology and marketing experience from businessmen of, *inter alia*, the Republic of Korea to local producers. Thus, during the first half of the 1980s the country managed to diversify and increase considerably its non-traditional exports, particularly of ready-made garments. For the production of these exports a free-trade environment has been promoted, with the institution of bonded warehouses and with duty-free treatment of imported inputs and credit on favourable terms. Initially Bangladesh enjoyed relatively liberal access to export markets, especially in the United States, through unfulfilled quotas under the Multi-fibre Arrangement. United States imports of clothing (SITC 84) from Bangladesh thus increased from $0.1 million in 1980 to $173.1 million in 1986. Nevertheless, the successful and accelerated penetration of this and other export markets was halted by the imposition of restrictions on the part of the United Kingdom and France in 1984, and then more recently also by the United States and Canada. Such restrictions have been imposed in spite of the fact that Bangladesh's share in the total imports of clothing in these markets in 1986 in no case exceeded 1 per cent, the United States figure being by far the highest at 0.9 per cent; total 1986 import values being respectively $2.3 million for the United Kingdom, $3.1 million for France, $173.1 million for the United States and $7.9 million for Canada. The clothing exports of this LDC therefore can hardly be deemed to have posed a serious threat to the textile industries of the importing countries concerned.

Such restrictions, although strictly speaking in accordance with specific rules of the Multi-fibre Arrangement and the bilateral agreements contained in it, could be said to be at variance with the spirit of the accord. Moreover, they are, in the case of Bangladesh, jeopardizing the development potential of one of the poorest countries in the world. Their imposition has, in fact, caused the closure of factories that were producing competitively and has rendered thousands of workers unemployed, making the country more dependent on foreign aid. Paragraph III of Annex A of the first MFA of 1974 notes that "account shall be taken of the interests of the exporting country, especially in regard to its stage of development... the employment situation... and overall balance of payments". Considering these three elements, it is easy to conclude with Spinanger that "It would be difficult to find a country which should be treated more favourably than Bangladesh".[110]

penetration, the share of LDCs is particularly high in the North American market, representing 17.66 per million of the total in 1986, as compared to 1.37 per million and 0.09 per million, respectively, in the European and the Japanese markets. Thus, if the share of the LDCs in the Japanese market in 1986 were to have been equivalent to that in the North American market, LDCs' exports to Japan would have amounted to $50.4 million instead of only $0.3 million. Similarly, those to Europe would have amounted to $566 million instead of $44 million. This obviously leaves plenty of scope for special access measures for LDCs, given the requisite political will in the importing country.

(b) *Socialist countries of Eastern Europe*

The trade relations of the socialist countries of Eastern Europe with the LDCs have often been determined by intergovernmental trade agreements, including long-term ones. These agreements help to make trade more predictable for both partners and allow the LDCs to develop stable outlets for their products. Nevertheless, the LDCs also encounter, in their efforts to expand trade with the socialist countries of Eastern Europe, quantitative constraints whose effects on exports can be assimilated to conventional non-tariff trade measures.

---

[110] D. Spinanger, "Will the Multi-Fibre Arrangement keep Bangladesh humble", in *The World Economy*, vol. 10, No.1 (March 1987).

F. Compensatory finance

As a large number of LDCs mainly export primary commodities, the instability of their commodity export earnings figures prominently among their more serious problems.[111] Calculated on the basis of a 10-year exponential trend and measured in terms of dollars, the average annual export earnings shortfall for the non-fuel commodity sector of the LDCs in the period 1980-1984 amounted to $925 million. These shortfalls were partly compensated by the Compensatory Financing Facility (CFF) of the IMF and the STABEX scheme administered by the EEC. The compensations accorded to the LDCs on account of the IMF-CFF and the STABEX in the period 1980-1984 were $91 and $46 million respectively, implying a total shortfall coverage rate of 15 per cent only (measured in terms of SDRs the instability in export earnings is less marked and the coverage rate improves to 20 per cent). The experience of individual LDCs has been extremely varied. In fact, in the period of five years, there were 11 LDCs which did not receive any compensation, while two LDCs were fully compensated (see table 29). It should be noted that the commodity export earnings shortfall of the LDCs represented 7 per cent of the shortfall for all developing countries in the period 1980-1984, while the LDCs' share in IMF-CFF drawings and STABEX transfers was 6 and 34 per cent respectively.

1. *EEC schemes*

The STABEX scheme covers the 66 developing countries members of the Group of African, Caribbean and Pacific States (ACP Group), of which 31 are LDCs. The scheme, which covers 48 agricultural products, aims at stabilizing the earnings from exports of each of these products to EEC by means of compensation paid to individual producing countries in the case of earnings shortfalls.[112] In 1986, the financial resources transferred to participating LDCs within the STABEX scheme amounted to SDR 81 million (see table 30).

A welcome recent initiative has been the establishment by the EEC of a scheme for LDCs that are not signatories of the Lomé agreement. This new scheme, which unofficially is called COMPEX or "extra-ACP STABEX", is a STABEX-type arrangement designed to compensate the non-ACP LDCs for foreign exchange earnings shortfalls on their commodity exports to the EEC.[113] The system became operational in the beginning of 1987. The eligibility criteria for COMPEX funds are more restrictive than for transfers under STABEX. The total resources that will be available under COMPEX for the period 1987-1992 amount to ECU 50 million.

It should be noted that the COMPEX scheme also includes jute in the list of products, as a means of making it relevant to the non-ACP LDCs to which it is addressed, particularly Bangladesh and Nepal. However, jute products – exports of which are twice as large as those of raw jute in Bangladesh and which too suffer wide earnings fluctuations – are not included in the EEC COMPEX scheme. By mid-1987, Bangladesh, Nepal and Yemen had secured transfers of ECU 5.6 million, ECU 0.2 million and ECU 0.4 million, respectively, under the new scheme, on account of shortfalls on exports to the EEC of jute and tea, hides and skins and coffee.

The relatively limited overall amount of resources available under STABEX is, along with its restricted product and trade coverage, its major shortcoming. This means that only part of the export earnings shortfalls incurred can be compensated. However, STABEX as well as COMPEX are relatively generous with respect to financial terms. The LDCs specifically are exempted from repayment, while, in principle, the ACP countries that

---

[111] The Intergovernmental Group of Experts on the Compensatory Financing of Export Earnings Shortfalls, at its second session held in Geneva in September 1987, agreed that: "shortfalls have a severe negative impact on economic and social development, especially on the least developed countries", and "were a matter of concern to the international community as a whole" (TD/B/AC.43/L.4).

[112] In principle, transfers under the STABEX system are accorded only in relation to exports to the Community. However, where an ACP State exports the bulk of its production of commodities covered by the system to destinations other than the Community, the system provides for the possibility of a derogation to cover all exports

to all destinations. This derogation has already been accorded to nine ACP-LDCs: Burundi, Cape Verde, Comoros, Ethiopia, Guinea-Bissau, Lesotho, Rwanda, Tuvalu and Samoa. It should also be noted that several export products of considerable interest to ACP-LDCs are not eligible for compensation, specifically, fish, live animals and tobacco.

[113] See the *Official Journal of the European Communities*, 13 February 1987, No. L43. In annex II of Council Regulation No. 429/87, the following non-ACP-LDCs are defined as eligible for the system: Bangladesh, Bhutan, Democratic Republic of Yemen, Haiti, Lao People's Democratic Republic, the Maldives, Nepal and Yemen Arab Republic.

TABLE 29

Annual average shortfall in LDCs' non-fuel commodity sector export earnings on the basis of a 10-year exponential trend and a 4-year arithmetic average, as well as finance provided under the IMF-CFF and Stabex in the period 1980-1984[a]

[In millions of dollars (in millions of SDRs)]

| | Shortfall[b] | | | | IMF-CFF drawings[c] | | Stabex transfers[d] | |
	4-year arithmetic average		10-year exponential trend					
Benin	2.9	(1.3)	1.5	(0.7)			0.9	(0.8)
Botswana	13.4	(3.7)	57.9	(39.0)				
Burkina Faso	4.6	(1.3)	9.5	(5.7)			0.2	(0.2)
Burundi	5.9	(4.5)	19.1	(11.9)			3.3	(2.6)
Cape Verde			0.3	(0.2)			0.1	(0.1)
Central African Republic	1.4		9.4	(4.1)	2.3	(1.8)	0.8	(0.7)
Chad	3.6	(1.0)	14.5	(8.0)	1.8	(1.4)	1.4	(1.2)
Comoros	0.5	(0.2)	1.4	(1.1)			1.2	(1.0)
Djibouti	n.a.	(n.a.)	n.a.	(n.a.)				
Equatorial Guinea	0.7	(0.7)	0.4	(0.3)	2.7	(2.1)		
Ethiopia	4.5		43.7	(17.6)	4.2	(3.6)	1.8	(1.7)
Gambia	6.2	(4.8)	6.6	(4.7)	2.1	(1.8)	4.0	(3.3)
Guinea	6.5		127.9	(82.4)				
Guinea-Bissau	1.7	(1.1)	4.0	(2.9)	0.4	(0.4)	0.7	(0.6)
Kiribati	6.6	(5.2)	2.4	(1.8)			0.3	(0.3)
Lesotho	n.a.	(n.a.)	n.a.	(n.a.)			0.3	(0.2)
Malawi	3.2		26.2	(12.4)	6.0	(5.5)	1.0	(0.9)
Mali	1.0		34.7	(19.1)			2.2	(1.9)
Mauritania								
Niger	70.8	(35.0)	187.7	(142.0)	5.2	(4.8)		
Rwanda	11.3	(7.2)	29.3	(19.7)			2.2	(1.8)
Samoa	1.4	(0.7)	1.8	(1.1)	0.7	(0.6)	1.3	(1.1)
Sao Tome and Principe	5.5	(3.6)	5.0	(3.5)			1.4	(1.3)
Sierra Leone	12.6	(7.5)	8.6	(5.2)	4.6	(4.1)	2.5	(2.3)
Somalia	20.5	(13.7)	22.0	(16.6)	6.7	(6.5)	0.8	(0.7)
Sudan	23.2	(13.3)	47.3	(19.3)	22.5	(18.5)	8.4	(7.1)
Togo	23.3	(11.3)	36.5	(23.8)			4.8	(4.5)
Tuvalu	n.a.	(n.a.)	n.a.	(n.a.)				
Uganda	54.9	(46.6)	43.3	(29.8)	10.6	(9.0)		
United Republic of Tanzania	37.9	(26.2)	57.6	(34.1)	3.9	(3.0)	3.9	(3.4)
Vanuatu	3.8	(2.3)	4.5	(2.7)			2.1	(1.7)
ACP LDCs[e]	327.9	(191.2)	803.1	(509.8)	74.0	(63.1)	45.7	(39.5)
Afghanistan	41.7	(19.7)	70.1	(46.5)				
Bangladesh			16.6	(2.5)	10.4	(9.4)		
Bhutan	n.a.	(n.a.)	n.a.	(n.a.)				
Democratic Yemen . . .	5.3	(3.0)	5.3	(3.4)				
Haiti	17.9	(8.8)	20.5	(13.5)	4.0	(3.4)		
Lao People's Democratic Republic	1.5	(0.9)	1.1	(0.7)				
Maldives			0.5	(0.3)				
Nepal	5.8	(5.4)	3.8	(2.8)	2.7	(2.1)		
Yemen Arab Republic .	2.0	(0.7)	3.9	(2.5)				
Non-ACP LDCs	74.2	(38.5)	121.8	(72.2)	17.1	(15.0)		
All LDCs	402.1	(229.8)	925.5	(582.0)	91.1	(78.1)	45.7	(39.5)
All Developing Countries	4 818.5	(1 862.0)	14 859.9	(8 366.2)	1 603.2	(1 425.5)	132.9	(115.2)

Source: TD/B/AC.43/5, and TD/B/AC.43/5/Add.1.

   [a] The commodity sector includes all food, agricultural raw materials and mineral and metal commodities, but excludes petroleum and precious stones and metals. Figures may not add up exactly owing to rounding.

   [b] The 10-years exponential trend formula has been recommended by the Intergovernmental Group of Experts on the Compensatory Financing of Export Earnings Shortfalls. The 4-year arithmetic average formula corresponds to the one used in Stabex.

   [c] Drawings by year of shortfall and not by year of drawing. Finance relates to shortfalls in total merchandise exports and excludes purchases of excesses in cereal imports under cereal decision EBD No. 6860 (81/81).

   [d] Transfers by year of shortfall. Finance relates to the list of products covered by Stabex under the third ACP-EEC Convention.

   [e] The third ACP-EEC Convention specifies as least developed countries 43 States, of which 31 are included in the United Nations category of the least developed countries used in this report.

TABLE 30

**Transfer of resources under the Stabex scheme to ACP-LDCs
in the period 1980-1986** [a]

(In millions of SDR)

	1980	1981	1982	1983	1984	1985	1986 [b]
Benin	—	0.9	—	0.4	0.7	—	3.0
Botswana	—	—	—	—	—	—	—
Burkina Faso	—	—	0.9	—	—	—	4.0
Burundi	11.1	—	—	—	2.0	—	—
Cape Verde	0.2	—	—	—	0.2	—	—
Central African Republic.	0.1	1.4	1.5	—	0.7	—	1.4
Chad	2.5	—	3.2	—	0.4	—	10.7
Comoros	1.1	0.8	0.3	—	3.0	1.6	2.5
Djibouti	—	—	—	—	—	—	—
Equatorial Guinea	—	—	—	—	—	—	0.9
Ethiopia	—	0.9	—	3.7	3.9	5.2	5.3
Gambia	8.1	3.9	1.7	—	2.7	3.5	3.9
Guinea	—	—	—	—	—	—	—
Guinea-Bissau	1.5	—	0.4	1.1	0.1	0.1	2.1
Haiti	—	—	—	—	—	—	—
Kiribati	0.5	—	0.9	—	0.1	—	1.4
Lesotho	0.2	0.3	0.6	—	—	—	—
Malawi	1.3	0.7	2.4	—	0.1	—	2.0
Mali	2.6	0.7	3.1	2.5	0.6	—	11.9
Mauritania	—	—	—	—	—	—	—
Niger	—	—	—	—	—	4.4	—
Rwanda	6.6	0.7	—	0.4	1.1	—	2.8
Samoa	1.2	1.9	1.3	—	1.1	—	3.9
Sao Tome and Principe .	—	0.9	2.4	2.6	0.4	—	—
Sierra Leone	0.9	1.0	5.5	—	4.2	—	—
Somalia	1.8	0.9	—	—	0.6	—	—
Sudan	13.5	10.0	—	6.1	6.0	31.8	14.6
Togo	—	—	6.3	10.6	5.6	7.0	0.5
Tuvalu	—	—	—	—	—	—	0.1
Uganda	—	—	—	—	—	—	—
United Republic of Tanzania	6.2	0.7	—	4.2	6.0	3.2	—
Vanuatu	4.2	0.3	3.9	—	0.3	—	9.6
TOTAL	63.6	26.0	36.8	31.2	39.8	56.9	80.6

Source: UNCTAD secretariat calculations based on information from the EEC.

[a] The third ACP-EEC Convention specifies 43 States as least developed countries, of which 31 are included in the United Nations category of least developed countries in this report.

[b] In July 1987 three requests were still under consideration.

are not LDCs have to repay. In contrast, the IMF's CFF drawings are charged at the IMF's standard rate of interest (around 8 per cent) for LDCs and all other drawing members alike, including developed countries.

Another significant development in 1987 was the announcement made by Switzerland at UNCTAD VII, "to share in the efforts of the international community with regard to compensatory financing by committing funds for the poorest countries suffering from export earnings shortfalls in their commodity trade with Switzerland". For this purpose the Swiss Government will commit up to SF 40 million during the years 1987-1990.

2. IMF's Compensatory Financing Facility (CFF)

The purpose of this IMF Facility is to provide financial assistance to countries that have balance-of-payments difficulties owing to overall export earnings shortfalls of a temporary character, largely attributable to factors beyond the country's control. The coverage of the Facility was extended in 1981 to include compensation for excesses in the costs of imports of cereals. The number of LDCs using the Facility as well as the foreign exchange purchases by them under this scheme have been rather limited and have fallen over time. Whereas in 1981 drawings on this Facility were made by 12 LDCs, with purchases totalling SDR 150.3 million, in 1986 only one LDC made use of it, purchasing SDR 30.8 million. Moreover, in 1983, 1984 and 1986, the repayments by the LDCs as a group within the CFF surpassed their drawings (see table 31). Increased conditionality as well as the reduction of the limit of access to the applicant's quotas in the Fund have proven to be major impediments to a wider use of the CFF by LDCs. The disturbing net position of the LDCs *vis-à-vis* the CFF – a Facility purportedly designed as an automatic short-term adjustment measure – gives greater urgency to the need for LDCs to have special treatment within the CFF.[114]

_____

[114] See TD/B/1078, B.XIV, and also section B of this chapter.

TABLE 31

Net finance made available to LDCs under the IMF compensatory financing facility, 1981 to 1986[a]

(In millions of SDR)

Country	1981	1982	1983	1984	1985	1986
Afghanistan						
Bangladesh	−10.4	108.1	−19.3		34.6	−44.4
Benin						
Bhutan						
Botswana						
Burkina Faso						
Burundi			−4.8	−4.8		
Cape Verde						
Central African Republic	7.6		−0.2	−3.3	−4.4	−1.1
Chad	2.2			−2.7	3.5	−0.9
Comoros						
Democratic Yemen						
Djibouti						
Equatorial Guinea	4.1			−4.8	−4.5	−1.2
Ethiopia	18.0	−2.2	−18.0	−20.3	−9.0	30.8
Gambia	9.0	−2.2	−2.2	−1.1	−2.3	−0.9
Guinea						
Guinea-Bissau	1.9	−0.3	−0.4	−0.4	−0.9	−0.9
Haiti	17.0				−6.4	−10.6
Kiribati						
Lao People's Democratic Republic	−1.6					
Lesotho						
Malawi	12.0	−11.7	2.7	5.3	−0.7	−5.2
Maldives						
Mali			−1.3	−3.2	−0.6	
Mauritania	−3.4		−3.9	−5.3	−1.3	
Nepal	−0.2	−4.8	−4.9	−5.2	−3.9	
Niger			24.0			−1.5
Rwanda						
Samoa	1.3	−0.6	0.5	−0.5	−1.0	−0.8
Sao Tome and Principe						
Sierra Leone	−4.5		20.7			−7.8
Somalia					32.6	
Sudan	36.8	−24.8	10.5	−14.5	−4.5	
Togo						
Tuvalu						
Uganda	35.0	−0.6	−11.9	−25.6	−25.6	−11.3
United Republic of Tanzania	5.4	−7.1	−24.0	−12.6	−3.7	−3.8
Vanuatu						
Yemen Arab Republic						
TOTAL	130.2	53.8	−32.5	−99.0	1.8	−59.6

Source: IMF reply to the UNCTAD questionnaire, and IMF, *International Financial Statistics* (various issues).

[a] Including arrears.

The UNCTAD Intergovernmental Group on LDCs, meeting at a high level in 1985, invited the IMF to explore, within its existing rules, ways and means of improving the use of its Compensatory Financing Facility by least developed countries.[115] Similarly, the report of the Intergovernmental Group of 24 called for major design changes in the IMF-CFF, making it less conditional and extending its coverage to all external sources of disturbances in the balance of payments. The Group also asked for an increase in the access limit for CFF drawings, using the shortfall as the basis for determining access instead of quotas as present, and suggested giving relatively larger compensation to the poorer countries, and easing the repayment periods for them.[116] In the light of the above, the changes that may be made in the functioning of the IMF-CFF as a result of its current review should take into account the special needs and problems of the LDCs.

---

[115] See TD/B/1078, B.XIV, para. 15.

[116] This report was adopted by the Group of 24 at the forty-ninth meeting of Deputies on 4-5 June, 1987, in Washington D.C. (see IMF *Survey*, 10 August 1987).

Chapter IV

SELECTED ISSUES–LDCs' POLICIES ON HUMAN RESOURCES AND SOCIAL DEVELOPMENT

The mobilization of human resources and the improvement of social conditions constitute a major component of the development plans and programmes that LDCs have been implementing in pursuance of the SNPA. The importance of measures in these fields has increased along with the adoption of adjustment and stabilization policies (see section A of chapter II), as there exists an ineluctable need to prevent the burden of the latter from falling unduly on the poorer strata of the LDCs' population. This chapter presents a brief discussion of the issues at stake as well as of the policies that LDCs have been adopting in this regard.

A. Population

The LDCs currently comprise nearly 350 million people, who constitute 6.7 per cent of world population and 13.2 per cent of that of the developing countries. More than 84 per cent of the total population of the LDCs live in rural areas. The population size of individual LDCs varies widely, from about 100,000 (Sao Tome and Principe, Vanuatu) to 100 million (Bangladesh). The population density varies too, from 66 persons per square kilometre of arable land in Botswana to 1,003 in Bangladesh, 1,439 in Bhutan, 4,867 in Maldives and 6,000 in Sao Tome and Principe (see table 32). Approximately half of the LDCs have a population density in excess of the carrying capacity of the land and resources.

One half of the LDCs are reportedly giving active support to family planning, and UNFPA reports that family planning is in operation in almost all LDCs. However, between 1980 and 1985, the crude birth rate in LDCs declined very slightly from 47.8 to 47.0. In the same period, the population of the LDCs grew at an average annual rate of 2.8 per cent. In the LDCs average life expectancy at birth increased during the 1980s, but remains low (46 years).

The population of LDCs is young, with the under-15 age groups representing more than 45 per cent of the total.

As of 1985 the economically active population constituted 38 per cent of the total. This ratio varies widely from country to country, from less than 30 per cent in both Yemen and Bangladesh to over 50 per cent in Burkina Faso, Burundi, Central African Republic, Niger and Rwanda.

TABLE 32

Least developed countries: literacy and schooling

	Adult literacy rate (%)		Gross school enrolment ratios (%)					
			Primary schooling		Secondary		Tertiary	
	1970	1985	1970	1984	1970	1984	1970	1984
Afghanistan	7.6	23.7	24.4	16	5	8	0.7	1.3
Bangladesh	24.5	33.1	56.0	60[b]	16	18[b]	2.2	5.0[b]
Benin	15.3	25.9	34.9	64	5	20	0.1	2.1
Bhutan	..	..	5.8	25	0.6	4	..	0.1
Botswana	42.0	70.8	62.4	99	7	28	0.7	1.6
Burkina Faso	7.9	13.2	13.7	29	1.5	5	0.1	0.7
Burundi	8.9	33.8	34.7	49	1.7	4	0.2	0.6
Cape Verde	30.8	47.4	93.0	110[a]	11	11.5	..	..
Central African Republic	15.4	40.2	63.8	74	4	16	0.1	1.2
Chad	10.6	25.3	34.6	38	2	6	0.1	0.4
Comoros	..	..	93.0	..	3	24	..	..
Democratic Yemen	19.9	41.4	61.4	66[a]	4	19[a]	0.1	2.3[c]
Djibouti	..	..	..	..	..	..	..	..
Equatorial Guinea	..	..	..	108[a]	..	..	..	..
Ethiopia	6.3	55.2[a]	16.4	39[a]	4	11	0.2	0.4
Gambia	10.7	25.1	25.8	73	9	21	..	..
Guinea	14.3	28.3	32.9	32	13	13	0.6	2.1
Guinea-Bissau	9.6	31.4	38.2	62[a]	8	11[a]	..	..
Haiti	21.2	37.6	49.6	76[a]	5	16[a]	..	1.1
Kiribati	..	..	..	..	..	..	..	..
Lao People's Democratic Republic	32.4	83.9	62.8	90[a]	4	19[a]	0.1	1.4[a]
Lesotho	62.2	73.6	97.6	111[a]	6.5	22	0.4	1.8
Malawi	29.1	41.2	37.3	62	3	4	0.3	0.7
Maldives	..	..	..	..	..	..	..	..
Mali	7.2	26.8	22.4	24[d]	5	7[d]	0.2	0.9[b]
Mauritania	..	..	14.0	37[d]	..	13[d]	..	..
Nepal	12.6	25.6	26.2	77	10	23	1.7	4.8[a]
Niger	3.8	13.9	14.2	28[a]	1	7[a]	0.1	0.5[a]
Rwanda	31.8	46.6	53.1	62[a]	2.5	2[a]	0.2	0.3[a]
Samoa	..	..	..	..	..	..	..	..
Sao Tome and Principe	..	..	..	..	..	..	..	..
Sierra Leone	..	29.3	33.6	58[d]	8	17[d]	0.5	0.8
Somalia	3.2	11.6	11.7	25[a]	3	17[a]	0.4	1.2
Sudan	17.0	..	37.9	49[a]	7	19[a]	1.1	2.0[a]
Togo	..	41.7	70.9	97	7	21	0.5	1.8
Tuvalu	..	..	..	..	..	..	..	..
Uganda	41.1	57.3	58.1	58[d]	6	8[d]	0.5	0.6[d]
United Republic of Tanzania . . .	32.4	..	34.0	87[a]	3	3[a]	0.2	0.4
Vanuatu	..	..	..	..	..	..	..	..
Yemen	4.6	13.7	12.4	67[a]	1	10[a]	..	1.3
ALL LDCs	19.4	32.4	39.1	54	9	15	0.9	2.6

Sources: UNESCO, *Statistical Yearbook*, 1985 and 1986; UNESCO, *The current literacy situation in the world* (Paris, 1987) and other international and national sources.

[a] 1983. [b] 1985. [c] 1981. [d] 1982.

About 80 per cent of the economically active population of the LDCs is engaged in agriculture and only 6 per cent in industry. The highest level of labour force concentration in rural activities is to be found in Bhutan (93 per cent), Nepal (92) and Rwanda (88); and the lowest in Democratic Yemen (36 per cent), Maldives (46) and Cape Verde (45).

B. Mobilization of the labour force

LDCs in general suffer from an acute shortage of educated and skilled labour and from a surplus of able-bodied but untrained persons seeking work. Many LDCs are thus adopting policies aimed at creating employment for the unskilled labour force. These policies are being implemented mainly in the rural areas, to provide off-season employment and build rural infrastructure (Bangladesh and Nepal). Some of the LDCs' labour mobilization policies include food-for-work programmes (Cape Verde, Sierra Leone, Uganda). Other policies of relevance in this context relate to land reform and development of co-operatives.

The public sector in the LDCs has an important role to play in mobilizing human resources for economic and social development. A number of LDCs (Afghanistan, Bangladesh, Benin, Ethiopia, Guinea-Bissau, Malawi, Mali, Nepal, Niger, Rwanda, Somalia, United Republic of Tanzania)

have taken measures to improve the use of labour resources in their public sector. A potentially important source of employment in these countries is the private sector, the development of which is being promoted in many LDCs. The development of co-operatives is another form of mobilizing entrepreneurial skills, and is being resorted to in LDCs.

The above-mentioned policies and instruments for mobilizing human resources are, of course, not sufficient to improve the quality of those resources. An elementary knowledge of reading, writing and numeracy is necessary for most jobs and for performing social duties and improving health. Therefore the improvement of the quality of LDCs' manpower through policies of human resource development depends particularly on education and training in required skills, a matter dealt with below.

C. Eradication of illiteracy [117]

1. *Adult literacy*

One of the three major criteria to qualify for least developed country status relates to the level of adult illiteracy, the threshold of which was set at 80 per cent. Adult literacy rates in the LDCs are considerably lower than those of the other major country groupings. The rate in the LDCs was 32 per cent in 1985 as compared to 58 per cent in the developing countries as a group (see table 32).

Adult literacy campaigns combining literacy programmes with the development of basic vocational skills are under way in several LDCs, i.e. Ethiopia, Sudan, the United Republic of Tanzania and the Lao People's Democratic Republic; and

some experimental campaigns connected to vocational training in agriculture have been launched in Botswana, Mali and Bangladesh.[118]

Adult illiteracy rates have decreased extensively in almost all LDCs. Decreases of more than 20 percentage points between 1970 and 1985 were achieved in Botswana, the Central African Republic, Democratic Yemen, Ethiopia, Guinea-Bissau and the Lao People's Democratic Republic. The average literacy rate for all LDCs increased steadily from 1970 to 1985 (see table 32). Nevertheless, the absolute number of illiterate adolescents and adults (aged 15 or older) in the LDCs grew from 95.2 million in 1970 to 112.6 million in 1985. This trend persisted during the first half of the present decade, even though the average illiteracy rate

---

[117] This section includes the input of Dr. Dorothy Winifred Courtney, a consultant whose work was commissioned by the UNCTAD secretariat.

[118] See Sarah Colton, *Education in the LDCs – Problems, priorities and programmes*, Reports studies S.106. UNESCO (Paris, 1983), p. 9; Paul Lengrand, *L'alphabétisation des adultes dans les PMA*, S.98, UNESCO (Paris, 1982), p. 3; documents for Asian-Pacific Round Table Meeting, Geneva, April 1986, vol. 1.

TABLE 33

Illiteracy rates among population aged 15 and over, 1985

(Percentages)

Region	Both sexes	Males	Females	Female-male differential
WORLD	27.7	20.5	34.9	14.4
Industrial countries	2.1	1.7	2.6	0.9
Developing countries:	38.2	27.9	48.9	21.0
of which: LDCs	67.6	56.9	78.4	21.5

Source: UNESCO, Office of Statistics, *The Current literacy situation in the world* (Paris, May 1987), p. 4.

decreased by 5.2 per cent for all LDCs while the number of illiterates increased by 2.3 million. All LDCs except Benin and Rwanda saw their illiteracy rate fall between 1980 and 1985, but the number of illiterates decreased only in nine of them (Afghanistan, Botswana, Central African Republic, Democratic Yemen, Ethiopia, Guinea-Bissau, Haiti, Lao People's Democratic Republic and Lesotho).

The female illiteracy rate is higher than the total rate in all LDCs except Lesotho.[119] The difference between the male and female illiteracy rates averages 21.5 percentage points (see table 33).

Based on these rates, it appears difficult for LDCs to attain a substantial degree of adult literacy, say, 70 to 80 per cent, by the year 2000, with the exception of those LDCs whose adult literacy rates had already attained 50 per cent in 1985, namely Botswana, Ethiopia, Lao People's Democratic Republic, Lesotho and Uganda.

Post-literacy activities are very important for maintaining the recently acquired skill of the newly literate population. Post-literacy comprises all measures which enable the neo-literate to put into practice the skills acquired and to strengthen and increase the knowledge obtained during the previous stage. Post-literacy programmes are, however, frequently hindered by the scarcity of written texts. Mali, the Central African Republic and the United Republic of Tanzania use newspapers as a partial solution, while other countries have established educational centres or popular development colleges (Benin, The United Repub-

lic of Tanzania) which aim at utilizing neo-literates in national development tasks and programmes of collective interest.[120]

Stronger co-operation between neighbouring countries can be particularly effective, in particular as regards the following areas: training and study tours in adult education, dissemination of information and documentation, and research.[121]

2. *Primary schooling*

While LDCs still have low gross school enrolment ratios (GERs) considerable improvement has been made in recent years (see table 32). The GER's present rate of increase in many LDCs, however, is not sufficient to make it likely that universal primary education (UPE) will be attained by the year 2000, and greater efforts will need to be deployed to attain such an objective. LDCs that are likely to be in a position to attain this objective with international support are Botswana, the Central African Republic, Democratic Yemen, Haiti, Lao People's Democratic Republic, Lesotho and Togo (which had more than half their school age population in schools in 1970), and Benin and the United Republic of Tanzania (which had only a third of that population in school in 1970 but have made considerable progress in increasing primary school enrolments).

According to information available at the UNCTAD secretariat (UNESCO sources), the ratio of females in total enrolment is one third or less in eight LDCs: Afghanistan, Benin, Bhutan, Chad, Democratic Yemen, Guinea, Nepal and Yemen. Female enrolment is virtually as high as that of males in six LDCs (Cape Verde, Haiti, Rwanda, Samoa, Sao Tome and Principe and the

---

[119] The exceptional situation in Lesotho, where the female illiteracy rate is lower than the total rate is largely explained by the fact that girls outnumber boys in both primary and post-primary schooling, as many rural boys have to spend their early years herding and later seeking wage employment. The opportunity to attend school is thereby restricted. A similar pattern is emerging in Botswana.

[120] Paul Lengrand, *op.cit.*, p. 35.

[121] See Sarah Colton, *op.cit.*, p. 33.

United Republic of Tanzania), and higher in two other LDCs (Lesotho and Botswana).

3. *The outlook*

Taking into account both the potential gains in literacy and the likely increases in primary enrolment, it appears that except in a few countries, i.e. Botswana, Democratic Yemen, Lao People's Democratic Republic, Haiti and the United Republic of Tanzania, the chances of reaching the twin objectives of full adult literacy and universal primary education by the year 2000 in the LDCs are not very bright.

D. Post-primary schooling

1. *Secondary education*

The graduates of the secondary level provide medium- and high-level manpower, the lack of which constitutes a major constraint on economic development. Enrolment at the secondary level has increased in developing countries, from 22.4 per cent of the school age population in 1970 to 37.7 per cent in 1984, whereas in the LDCs it has almost doubled, from 8.8 per cent to 16 per cent.[122] Information available at the UNCTAD secretariat (UNESCO sources) indicates that a large majority of LDCs have doubled their gross enrolment rates at the secondary level since 1970, and many have even tripled them.

2. *Vocational training*

According to calculations based on UNESCO data, the number of pupils enrolled in vocational training in the LDCs more than doubled between 1970 and 1980 from around 51,800 to 123,680 in 1984. The share of vocational education in total secondary education of the LDCs remains very modest: 1.7 per cent in 1970, 2.8 per cent in 1980 and 2.2 per cent in 1984, with large variations among LDCs.

As regards teacher training, the number of pupils enrolled in teacher training in the LDCs appear to have risen by nearly 80 per cent between 1970 and 1980, from 42,400 to 75,200, reaching 77,000 in 1984. However, the average share of teacher training in total enrolment in secondary education of the LDCs declined from 1.7 per cent in 1970 to 1.5 per cent in 1980 and to 1.1 per cent in 1984. This share varies among individual LDCs.[123]

3. *Higher education*

The number of students at the tertiary level in LDCs grew from 187,000 in 1970 to 416,000 in 1980 and reached 580,000 in 1984. The third level teaching staff in the LDCs has been growing more slowly than the number of students enrolled. The average student-teacher ratio in the LDCs has thus increased from 14.1 in 1970 to 15.5 in 1980 and to 21.0 in 1984.[124]

In order to make tertiary education more relevant to the national needs, many LDCs attempt to reorient students among the different fields of study and to reform courses and programmes with a view to enhancing their practical utility. The general aim of the reform of third level education is the expansion of professional training with a direct impact on development. Such a reform generally involves the creation of university institutes for economics, engineering, technical sciences, transport, agriculture, administration, law, etc. Some LDCs such as Benin, Burkina Faso, Burundi, Ethiopia, Malawi, Mali, Rwanda, Somalia and Sudan have established, within their academic institutions, departments concerned with subjects such as agricultural development, forestry, zootechnology and livestock administration and management.

4. *Cost of formal education*

The share of education in total GDP averages 6 per cent in industrial countries and 4 per cent in the developing countries as a whole. Ten LDCs spend 5 per cent or more of their GDP on education: Botswana, Cape Verde, the Central African Republic, the Comoros, Democratic

---

[122] TD/B/AC.17/26/Add.16, p. 24.

[123] Estimates on the basis of the UNESCO *Statistical Year-book 1986*, pp. III-141 to III-186.

[124] The figures are considerably influenced by Bangladesh. The share of Bangladesh alone in total enrolment in the LDCs was 58 per cent in 1980 and 75 per cent in 1984.

Yemen, the Gambia, Sao Tome and Principe, Togo, the United Republic of Tanzania and Yemen. Most of the other LDCs spend less than 4 per cent, while Bangladesh, Haiti, Lao People's Democratic Republic, the Maldives and Uganda spend less than 2 per cent. On the other hand, in all but a few LDCs, education takes more than 10 per cent of the government budget, with this share reaching more than 15 per cent in the case of Botswana, Burkina Faso, Burundi, the Central African Republic, the Comoros, Democratic Yemen, Mali, Niger, Rwanda, Togo and the United Republic of Tanzania.

Although primary enrolment in LDCs accounts for between 80 per cent and 90 per cent of total enrolment, most of these countries spend only 40 to 50 per cent of their education budget on primary education. This reflects the higher unit costs of secondary and tertiary schooling. Most LDCs spend between 20 and 30 per cent of their education budget on higher education alone, which has only about 1 per cent of total enrolment (and where the GER is only between 1 and 2 per cent (see table 32). The extreme cases in this regard, are on the one hand, Bhutan, Democratic Yemen, Guinea-Bissau, Haiti and Rwanda, which spend less than 13 per cent of their budget on this level, and, on the other, Guinea and Nepal, which spend more than 30 per cent (but they also have a high 4 per cent of enrolment at this level).

E. International support measures

LDCs develop their human potential with the assistance of international organizations and bilateral donors. Country review meetings have provided a suitable framework for a joint evaluation of the education and training needs of LDCs. Such evaluation includes:

– examining shortages of skilled labour;

– assessing the ability of existing training facilities to meet manpower needs and identifying training needs in priority sectors;

– identifying methods for assessing available education and training facilities;

– developing and harmonizing education and training policies at the national level and of enhancing co-operation among institutions at subregional and regional levels.

Bilateral donors' co-operation in LDCs in the field of training includes the building of sec- ondary and third level educational establishments and of vocational training centres, the training of local personnel with the assistance of foreign specialists as well as admission of LDC nationals in educational institutions in donor countries. Each year 20,000 third level students from LDCs are accepted by developed market-economy countries; another 20,000 students are accepted in 20 developing countries; and 300 are accepted in China. Czechoslovakia, Poland and Hungary together accept about 2,000 students from LDCs. Information regarding other socialist countries of Eastern Europe, which are host to many foreign students, is not disaggregated on a country-by-country basis.[125]

---

[125] See UNESCO *Statistical Yearbook 1986*, pp. III-425 to III-449.

F. Health

The SNPA, in paragraph 37, calls for the formulation and implementation by LDCs of national policies, strategies and plans of action in the field of health through the mobilization of all available resources as part of the Global Strategy for Health for All by the Year 2000 adopted unani- mously at WHO.[126] The SNPA further stresses that: "These strategies and actions should be based

---

[126] World Health Assembly resolution 34.36. See also WHO, *Evaluation of the strategy of health for all by the year 2000 – seventh report on the world health situation*, vol. I, *Global Review*.

on the concept of primary health care and particular importance should be placed on efforts to provide by 1990 safe drinking water and adequate sanitation, immunization of all children against major infectious diseases, as well as the necessary caloric and protein intake". LDCs have been preparing and implementing their health plans and programmes in line with the above recommendations, as discussed below.

1. *Life expectancy at birth*

Life expectancy at birth – LEB – is the average number of years that will be lived by those born alive within a given population if the current age-specific mortality rates persist. The average LEB in the LDC has changed very little in the last decade. It was 45 years for the male and 46 years for the female population in 1980-1985, as compared to 44 and 45 years, respectively, during 1975-1980. On the other hand, the 1980-1985 average LEB for all developing countries was estimated at 55 years for males and 57 years for females, whereas in the developed countries the average LEB for both sexes was estimated at 72.4 years.[127]

2. *Infant mortality rate*

The infant mortality rate in 38 LDCs for which data are available has shown some improvement in the past decade: it was estimated at an average 138.0 per 1,000 live births in 1980-1985, as compared to an average rate of 145.0 in 1975-1980.[128] Despite improvements, more than one quarter of the newborn do not survive their fifth birthday in Burkina Faso, Ethiopia, Gambia, Malawi, Mali, Sierra Leone and Somalia, or in Afghanistan. Between 20 and 25 per cent of infants die before the age of five in some Central and Western African LDCs (Benin, Burundi, Central African Republic, Chad, Equatorial Guinea, Guinea-Bissau and Mauritania), as well as in Yemen and Democratic Yemen, and in parts of South and East Asia including LDCs such as Bangladesh, Bhutan and Nepal. In Haiti, between 15 and 20 per cent of infants do not survive their fifth birthday.

3. *Birth weight*

The birth weight of an infant is the single most important determinant of its chances of survival and healthy growth and development. The coverage of low birth weight infants in LDCs, for

which data are available, is 24.8 per cent compared to 20.8 per cent in all developing countries.[129] On the other hand, the incidence of LBW in developed countries seems to have stabilized at between 4 per cent and 8 per cent.

4. *Common diseases in LDCs*

High prevalence and incidence of infectious and parasitic diseases as well as acute diseases of the upper respiratory tract are reported by the majority of the LDCs. Nearly all LDCs list diarrhoeal diseases, respiratory diseases and malaria as major causes of morbidity and mortality, affecting particularly the health of their child population. Low birth weight and malnutrition aggravate the risk of death from these. Malaria remains a major public health problem in 25 out of 40 LDCs, including 15 African LDCs, and it appears that the malaria situation deteriorated in several LDCs between 1979 and 1983.[130] Schistosomiasis, another common disease, particularly in sub-Saharan Africa, is basically related to heavy parasite loads in children, acquired by constant contact with freshwater transmission sites. Furthermore, cholera, tuberculosis, leprosy and onchocerciasis are still important public health problems in a number of LDCs. Many of these diseases can be overcome by improvements in environmental and living conditions and by specific preventive action.

5. *Health infrastructure and manpower development*

In a number of LDCs, the national health system is still characterized by the skewed distribution of health resources.[131] Physicians, nurses and other health personnel, when available, are concentrated in one or two main urban centres. Investment in physical facilities has in many cases been largely devoted to the construction of one or more highly sophisticated hospitals in the largest city, while ambulatory care units are few. The allotment of public funds to health activities forms a very small proportion of the overall government budget and of the GNP, with a declining trend in some LDCs. These seem unable to devote more than 1 per cent of GNP to health and their ratios of hospital beds and physicians per 10,000 population are exceedingly low (see table 34).

---

[127] WHO, *World Health Statistics Annual 1986 – Analysis of data on the global indicators.*

[128] *Ibid.*

[129] WHO, 1984, "The incidence of low birth weight: an update", *Weekly Epidemiological Record 59(27)*:205, and table 53C.

[130] See Map 1.

[131] Kleczkowski, B. *et al.* "National health systems and their reorientation towards health for all", *Public Health Papers*, No. 77, WHO, 1984.

Epidemiological assessment of the status of malaria, 1985

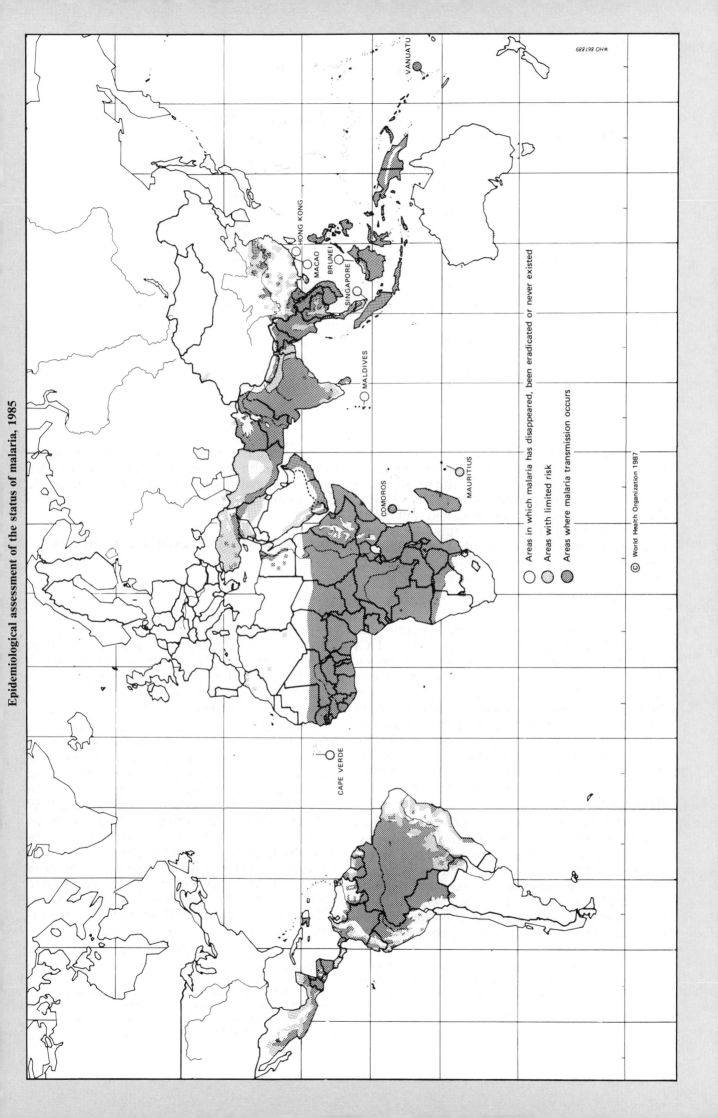

○ Areas in which malaria has disappeared, been eradicated or never existed

◔ Areas with limited risk

◉ Areas where malaria transmission occurs

© World Health Organization 1987

VANUATU

HONG KONG

MACAO

BRUNEI

SINGAPORE

MALDIVES

MAURITIUS

COMOROS

CAPE VERDE

688198 OHM

TABLE 34

Health infrastructure and manpower in selected LDCs

Countries	Years	Health expenditure[a] as a percentage of GDP	Number of hospitals	Ratios	
				Hospital beds 10 000 persons	Physicians 10 000 persons
Afghanistan	1984	0.67	n.a.	3.0[b]	0.86
Bangladesh	1985	2.00	70[c]	n.a.	0.50
Ethiopia	1983	1.80	86	2.7	0.01
Nepal	1985	1.40	70	2.0	n.a.
Sudan	1983	4.0	n.a.	8.2	0.9
United Republic of Tanzania . .	1982	5.4	150	n.a.	[d]

Source: WHO 1987a., *op. cit.*, country reports.

[a] Relates to government expenditure.

[b] For settled population.

[c] Plus 464 health complexes.

[d] Health manpower ratios: 3.5/1,000 in better served regions and 1.5/1,000 in relatively under-served regions.

Several other LDCs have been giving higher priority to the development of health resources in accordance with the strategy of health for all by the year 2000 and with provisions of the SNPA. Efforts are being made to establish and staff health centres for ambulatory care in rural areas, and local communities are encouraged to assume responsibility for a number of activities relating to primary health care. Foreign assistance has been gradually integrated into the overall health system.

The coverage of the rural and nomadic population has been increased in some LDCs (Afghanistan, Sudan), and significant improvements in health manpower development have been registered in Bangladesh, Nepal and the United Republic of Tanzania. However, the majority of African LDCs continue to experience enormous difficulties in implementing their national health plans, especially the development of local health centres and the training of health personnel, mainly because of the shortage of financial and human resources.

Mention should be made of some problems connected to the development of health resources, which have been highlighted and discussed in specialized, technical reports prepared for WHO.[132] Organized arrangements are necessary to bring such health resources as manpower, facilities, equipment and knowledge into effective relationships, and also to bring individual patients or community groups into contact with the resources through health care delivery mechanisms. Adequate national planning and budgeting for health systems are also required.

6. *Availability of primary health care*

(a) *Safe drinking water and sanitation*

Since the launching of the international drinking water supply and sanitation decade (1981-1990), most LDCs have taken steps to accelerate the provisions of potable water supplies and proper sanitation, especially to the under-served rural and fringe urban areas.[133]

The population coverage in the LDCs in terms of a safe drinking-water supply shows some improvement in the first half of the present decade and noticeable differences between urban and rural areas. The average coverage of the urban population was increased from 49 per cent in 1980 to 53 per cent in 1985, with only 27 per cent of the rural population being covered in 1980 as compared to 33 per cent in 1985. The corresponding average coverage rate for all developing countries increased from 72 per cent in 1980 to 74 per cent in 1985 for urban inhabitants and from 32 per cent in 1980 to 42 per cent in 1985 for the rural population.

Coverage in the LDCs as regards sanitation facilities developed positively between 1980 and

[132] See, *inter alia*, the following WHO documents: "Research for the reorientation of national health systems", *Technical Report Series*, No. 694 (1983); Kleczkowski, B. *et al.*, *op. cit.*; "Community-based education of health personnel" *Technical Report Series*, No. 746 (1987); and "Hospitals and health for all", *Technical Report Series*, No. 744 (1987).

[133] Safe water supply and sanitary facilities measure the percentage of the population with access to drinking water within 15 minutes walking distance, as well as the coverage by adequate sanitary facilities in the home or its immediate vicinity.

1985, increasing from 40 per cent to 46 per cent in urban areas and from 8 per cent to 15 per cent in rural areas. The situation in all developing countries, by comparison, registered a similar trend of development, with increases from 50 per cent in 1980 to 57 per cent in 1985 in the case of urban areas, and from 11 per cent in 1980 to 15 per cent in 1985 in the rural areas.

The developed countries reported 95.8 per cent coverage as regards a safe water supply and 76.6 per cent for sanitation.[134]

(b) *Immunization of children during the first year of life*

Immunization coverage (against tuberculosis (BCG), DPT (triple vaccine), poliomyelitis, measles and tetanus (single vaccine)) is also an important indicator of effective health infrastructure. Although the present immunization situation in the LDCs represents a major public health gain, there is no room for complacency. For example, out of five LDCs for which the information is available, only one is near to achieving the goal of universal childhood immunization by the year 1990 (see table 35). Furthermore, immunization coverage is less than 15 per cent in 15 LDCs.[135] The likelihood of reaching the 1990 goals without extraordinary external support and special national efforts is remote. Programme acceleration requires two complementary actions: social mobilization and improved management of immunization services.

---

[134] WHO, 1986, *op. cit.*

[135] WHO, 1987b, "Expanded programme on immunization. Global status report", *Weekly Epidemiological Record 62(33)*:241.

(c) *Availability of local health care*

According to the above-mentioned first evaluation of the health-for-all strategy, some progress is reported in regard to the availability of treatment for common diseases and injuries and of essential drugs at the first level of contact. Lack of human, material and financial resources, along with poor transport and communications in rural areas, are identified as the major obstacles. On the basis of replies covering 55 per cent of the world's population, WHO estimated the coverage rates for reporting countries in 1986 as follows: 48.5 per cent of the population in the LDCs and 72.8 per cent of the population in other developing countries.[136] Local health care is provided to 99.8 per cent of the population in developed countries.

(d) *Trained personnel for attending women in pregnancy and childbirth and for child care*

According to the 1986 WHO statistics, 33.3 per cent of women in 36 LDCs are attended during pregnancy as compared to 47.8 per cent in other developing countries. On the other hand, attendance at childbirth is provided to 36.7 per cent of mothers in LDCs, as compared to 44.5 per cent in other developing countries.[137] In developed countries this coverage had almost reached 100 per cent even prior to the formulation of the strategy.

---

[136] WHO, 1986, *op. cit.*

[137] *Ibid.* and WHO, 1987a, *op. cit.*

TABLE 35

Estimated immunization coverage with BCG, DPT, poliomyelitis, measles and tetanus vaccines in the five largest LDCs and in all developing countries, based on data available as of June 1987

Country	Year of coverage data	Infants surviving to 1 year of age (millions)	Immunization coverage (percentage)				
			Children under one year				Pregnant women, tetanus
			BCG	DPT3	Polio 3	Measles	
Bangladesh . . .	1986	3.17	5	5	4	3	5
Burma	1986	1.02	32	20	4	3	21
Ethiopia	1984	1.92	12	7	6	13	3
Sudan	1986	0.91	23	14	14	11	6
United Republic of Tanzania .	1984-1985	1.03	84	65	65	68	32
All developing countries (including China)		103.01	49	50	51	39	18

Source: WHO, *Weekly Epidemiological Record No. 33*, 14 August 1987, table 1.

G. Nutrition

1. *Review of recent trends*

Endemic hunger and chronic malnutrition are permanent conditions for a large number of people in many LDCs. Severe malnutrition has recently become widespread in sub-Saharan Africa and is, in numerical terms, the most serious condition affecting the health of children.

According to recent estimates,[138] the average world per capita food supplies, measured as dietary energy, were 2,660 kcal/day during the three-year period 1981-1983. The gap between the LDCs and both developed and developing countries, remains wide: the per capita dietary energy supplies (DES) of the LDCs stood at 61.3 per cent of those of developed countries and at 86.6 per cent of developing countries. Thus, the stagnating trend of the 1970s persisted in the LDCs, with per capita DES at the very low levels of 2,070-2,080 kcal/day, during the early 1980s. As FAO has stated: "the average inhabitant of the developed countries had nearly two thirds more to eat in 1981-1983 than the average inhabitant of the LDCs".

The FAO *Survey* ascertained that malnutrition does not hit all population groups with equal severity and, in general, the poorest people suffer the most because of their lack of resources. Within the poorest groups, young children and pregnant and lactating women are the most vulnerable because of their extra nutritional requirements. High correlation co-efficients were obtained by FAO between the percentage of the population that is undernourished and both the infant mortality rate and per capita income. Significant correlations were also obtained between access to a safe water supply and female illiteracy rates with low weight-for-height data in children.[139]

[138] FAO, *Fifth World Food Survey* (1987), table 2.6

[139] Pellet, Peter, "The determinants of nutritional status" in FAO, *Food and Nutrition*, vol. 13, No. 1 (1987).

Anaemia in women, also an indicator of malnutrition, partly reflects dietary inadequacies (primarily iron deficiency) and the incidence of malaria and other parasitic infections that increase blood loss. This acute problem contributes significantly to maternal morbidity and mortality and is estimated to affect nearly two thirds of the pregnant and half the non-pregnant women in developing countries, including LDCs.

2. *Review of nutritional policies*

There is a common understanding that the speed at which malnutrition is reduced depends primarily upon efforts made at the national level. FAO's *Survey* recommends a combination of four types of measures to achieve that goal: (i) measures to increase overall food demand and supplies; (ii) measures to improve income distribution and thus the effective demand for food among the poorest groups; (iii) direct nutrition-intervention programmes; and (iv) the introduction of nutritional considerations into rural and agricultural development programmes.

On the other hand, international financial and technical assistance are likely to remain, for a long time to come, essential inputs into the efforts made by the LDCs to improve their nutritional situation. Substantially more assistance is required for the poorest countries, especially in Africa, where the nutrition situation is the worst. Policies and projects that not only stimulate and expand production growth but also alleviate poverty and improve nutrition in the most effective ways should receive the priority attention of donors and the international community.

Part Two

DEVELOPMENT OF THE ECONOMIES
OF INDIVIDUAL LDCs

Introduction

The notes on individual countries which make up this part bring out the salient features of recent economic events in each LDC as well as of the policies adopted by these countries to cope with their economic problems and accelerate their development.

For each LDC, a statistical table presents information on some key socio-economic indicators. The sources for the data in these tables are the same as those used for the tables in part one and in the annex. The explanatory notes to the annex also apply to the tables in this chapter.

1. Afghanistan

A. *Recent socio-economic developments*

1. *Overall economy*

The political difficulties which have affected the economic performance in Afghanistan since the start of the 1980s continued throughout FY 1985/86.[140] Despite this constraint, GNP is reported to have grown by 1 per cent in FY 1985/86 compared to 3.7 per cent in the previous fiscal year. After a 7.7 per cent consumer price increase in 1984, prices fell during the middle of 1985, largely owing to lower food prices, but the year-to-year increase of the consumer price index was over 9 per cent in 1985 as a whole.

2. *Main sectors*

Chiefly because of the internal instability, the output of the agricultural sector, which employs about 60 per cent of the working population and provides 60 per cent of GNP, is reported to have declined in FY 1985/86. Total grain production of 4.5 million tonnes was reported for FY 1985/86, which is equivalent to the preceding year. Nevertheless, there are conflicting reports on food self-sufficiency. In the industrial sector, output increased by 8 per cent in FY 1985/86 compared to the previous fiscal year, thereby exceeding the planned growth target of 5.5 per cent. Major industrial and mining growth rates for FY 1985/86 as compared to the previous fiscal year included 10.7 per cent for electricity generation, 0.8 per cent for coal, 7.0 per cent for natural gas and 5.9 per cent for concrete. In addition, Af 2.6 billion ($51 million) were reported to have been spent on construction activities in FY 1985/86, reflecting a 100 per cent increase over the previous year.

3. *Trade and payments*

Between FY 1984/85 and 1985/86, exports declined by 12 per cent to $556.8 million, while imports were cut by 14 per cent, lowering the trade

---

[140] The fiscal year (FY) ends on 21 March.

deficit to $472 million in FY 1985/86 as compared to $523 million in the previous fiscal year. During the first three quarters of FY 1986/87, the value of overall exports again declined by 16.9 per cent (to $388.3 million) compared to the corresponding period of the previous fiscal year. Nevertheless, during the first half of that fiscal year, the value of natural gas exports increased by 6 per cent, while fruit and carpet exports grew by 89 and 19 per cent respectively compared to the first half of FY 1985/86. While overall import figures for FY 1986/87 are not yet available, so-called "commercial imports" (i.e. trade settled in convertible currencies) increased by 34.5 per cent to $607.5 million during the first half of FY 1986/87 as against the corresponding period of FY 1985/86, implying a substantial widening of the trade deficit, at least as far as convertible currency trade is concerned.

The country has continued to receive increased grant aid from the USSR and other CMEA countries in the form of various infrastructural projects. The debt service exports ratio with the convertible-currency area was modest compared to other LDCs. As for the debt with socialist countries, much of it has been rescheduled by the CMEA creditors owing to the present political difficulties. Non-gold foreign exchange reserves fluctuated moderately within the range of $240-$300 million during 1985 and 1986.

B. *Recent policy developments*

1. *Macro-economic policies*

A five-year plan covering the period FY 1986/87-1990/91 was recently announced by the Government. The major objectives are rehabilitation and reconstruction of institutions, increased exploration activities for mineral resources, particularly natural gas, implementation of land and water reforms, improvement of the tax collection and education systems and expansion of foreign trade. In view of the very low level of the country's ODA receipts, the Government has recognized

AFGHANISTAN

1. Population, total and per capita GDP, growth of agricultural and manufacturing output

Year and periods	Population Millions	GDP[a] Total Millions of dollars	GDP[a] Per capita Dollars	GDP[a] Per capita Per cent of LDC average	Agricultural production Total	Agricultural production of which: Food	Manufacturing value-added Total
1985	18.1	(3806)	210[b]	97.7			
			Real growth rates, per cent per annum				
1980-1985	2.6	2.9	0.3		0.7	0.7	..
1984-1985	2.7	3.7	1.0		-0.5	-0.5	..
1985-1986	2.6	..	..		-4.0	-4.3	..

2. Area, demographic indicators and labour force share in agriculture

Area Total	Area Share of arable land under permanent crops	Area Share covered by forestry and woodlands	Density	Average life expectancy at birth M	Average life expectancy at birth F	Average life expectancy at birth T	Infant mortality as share of live births	Share of population In urban areas	Share of population Economically active	Labour force Share in agriculture
		1984	1985		1980-1985		1980-1985		1985	
000 km2	Per cent		Pop/km2		Years		Per 1,000		Per cent	
647.5	12.4	2.9	28	37	37	37	194	19	30	58

3. Origins and uses of output; investment

Years	Sectoral origin of GDP Agriculture	Sectoral origin of GDP Mining	Sectoral origin of GDP Manufacturing	Sectoral origin of GDP Services	Uses of GDP Private consumption expenditure	Uses of GDP Government consumption expenditure	Uses of GDP Gross domestic savings	Investment
				Per cent of total GDP				
1980	61.8	..	..	12.1	..	..	..	..
1985	57.7	..	..	13.5	..	..	..	..

4. Balance of payments, debt and external assistance

Years	Balance of payments Merchandise trade balance	Balance of payments Balance on services	Balance of payments Balance on current account	Debt service Amortization	Debt service Interest	Debt service Total	Debt service As ratio of exports of goods and services	Debt Amount outstanding at year-end	External assistance Total	External assistance of which: ODA
		Millions of dollars					Per cent		Millions of dollars	
1980	..	..	..	8.8[c]	30.8[c]	39.6[c]	4.6[c]	1410.4[c]	335.4	324.4
1985	..	..	..	25.7	20.3	46.6	6.7	1429.2	235.1	257.7

5. Trade

Years and periods	Exports Value Mill. of dollars	Exports of which: share of Natural gas Per cent	Imports Value Mill. of dollars	Imports of which: share of food Per cent	Terms of trade
1980	670	32.2	552	8.5	100
1985	557	55.6	999	..	105

	Value	Volume	Purchasing power	Value	Volume	Index
			Growth rates, per cent per annum			
1980-1985	-3.6	-2.0	-1.1	12.6	15.6	0.9
1984-1985	-12.0	-5.1	-12.8	-13.6	-14.4	-8.1
1985-1986	-3.6	0.5	-6.3	-4.9	-7.6	-6.8

6. Other economic and social indicators

Energy Commercial energy consumption per capita	Transport & communication Commercial vehicles	Transport & communication Telephones	Education Adult literacy rate	Education School enrolment ratio share of relevant age group Primary M	Education Primary F	Education Primary T	Education Secondary M	Education Secondary F	Education Secondary T	Health Attendance at childbirth by trained personnel	Health Share of population Immunized against DPT (3 doses)	Health Share of population With access to safe water	Food and nutrition Cereals Consumption per capita	Food and nutrition Cereals Self-sufficiency ratio	Food and nutrition Average daily calorie intake per capita Total	Food and nutrition Average daily calorie intake per capita Share of requirements
1984	1980	1980	Around 1985			1984				1984	1984	1985		1985	1985	Between 1982&1985
kg of coal equiv.	Per 1,000 pop.								Per cent				kg	Per cent	Calories	Per cent
56	1.8	2.0	24	22	10	16	10	5	8	5.0	16.0	20	252	99	..	..

a/ Years beginning 21 March.   b/ 1981.   c/ 1982.

that increased domestic resource mobilization is an important element in Afghanistan's rapid development. Accordingly, measures aiming at increasing revenue from public enterprises, reducing subsidies on certain items, widening the tax base and controlling expenditures have been introduced. Moreover, out of total planned budget expenditures of $2.26 billion for the five-year period FY 1986/87-1990/91, $1.76 billion has been allocated to development projects, of which $988 million will be mobilized from domestic resources. In addition, the Government has recently emphasized the role of the private sector in the economy, which already accounts for over 50 per cent of the "general volume of products", including a 12 per cent share of the industrial sector. Measures in this direction include financial facilitation of land purchases by enterprises, special bank credits, preferential customs duties for imported investment goods, the establishment of industrial estates and tax holidays. Foreign and local investors can enjoy the same incentives.

2. *International support measures*

Due to political differences, Afghanistan receives very limited amounts of ODA and other financial support from DAC member countries. Although Afghanistan remains a member of the IMF, it has not benefited from the Structural Adjustment Facility (SAF), since it has been unable to meet applicable criteria. On the other hand, the United Nations system continues to provide assistance to it.

3. *SNPA follow-up*

The last Round Table Meeting for Afghanistan with its development partners was held in Geneva in May 1983. No follow-up meeting has been convened to date.

2. Bangladesh

A. *Recent socio-economic developments*

1. *Overall economy*

Bangladesh's economy remains vulnerable in two major ways. Firstly, agriculture, which accounts for about one hàlf of GDP, is heavily dependent on weather. Secondly, the economy is vulnerable to world economic fluctuations, since the modern industrial sector is still heavily dependent on a single industry – jute textiles. Within these constraints, FY 1985/86,[141] the first year of the Third Five-Year Plan – 1985-1990 – showed mixed results. GDP grew by 4.9 per cent as compared to the 5.4 per cent Plan target. Among the reasons for this lower economic growth were: (*a*) the overproduction of jute, which resulted in price declines and thus had adverse effects on farmers' incomes and export earnings; and (*b*) a 15 per cent cut in public development expenditures, due to budgetary and balance-of-payments constraints. The rate of inflation during FY 1985/86 remained at about 10 per cent, which was somewhat lower than during the preceding year.

2. *Main sectors*

The real growth rate of the agricultural sector as a whole declined between FY 1984/85 and FY 1985/86, largely owing to a disappointing performance in food grain production. Jute production increased to about 7.6 million bales. Industrial expansion at only 1 per cent was well below expectations. On the other hand, in the energy sector, output of natural gas increased by 13 per cent, while a small quantity of oil was discovered in the North-East, from which a commercial flow began in December 1986.

3. *Trade and payments*

The terms of trade in 1986 declined by 29 per cent compared to 1985, more than reversing the gain of 13 per cent obtained between 1984 and 1985. This was largely caused by a drop of 29 per cent in average dollar export prices, partly due to the drop of more than 50 per cent in the dollar price of the major primary export commodity, i.e. raw jute. However, the export value shortfall could be limited to 4.4 per cent in terms of national cur-

---

[141] The fiscal year (FY) ends on 30 June.

BANGLADESH

1. Population, total and per capita GDP, growth of agricultural and manufacturing output

Year and periods	Population Millions	GDP[a] Total Millions of dollars	Per capita Dollars	Per cent of LDC average	Agricultural production Total	of which: Food	Manufacturing value-added Total
1985	98.7	16069	163	75.8			
				Real growth rates, per cent per annum			
1980-1985	2.2	3.9	1.7		2.8	2.4	2.4
1984-1985	2.0	4.1	2.1		6.6	4.3	3.2
1985-1986	2.2	..	..		0.1	2.9	3.2

2. Area, demographic indicators and labour force share in agriculture

	Area			Demographic indicators						Labour force
Total	Share of arable land under permanent crops	Share covered by forestry and woodlands	Density	Average life expectancy at birth M F T			Infant mortality as share of live births	Share of population In urban areas	Economically active	Share in agriculture
	1984		1985	1980-1985			1980-1985		1985	
000 km2	Per cent		Pop/km2	Years			Per 1,000	Per cent		
144.0	63.3	14.6	687	48	47	48	128	18	29	71

3. Origins and uses of output; investment

Years	Sectoral origin of GDP				Uses of GDP			Investment
	Agriculture	Mining	Manufacturing	Services	Private consumption expenditure	Government consumption expenditure	Gross domestic savings	
				Per cent of total GDP				
1980	50.3	..	9.9	34.9	91.3	6.2	2.5	11.3
1985	50.1	..	8.3	35.7	87.7	6.1	6.2	11.9

4. Balance of payments, debt and external assistance

Years	Balance of payments			Debt service				Debt	External assistance	
	Merchandise trade balance	Balance on services	Balance on current account	Amortization	Interest	Total	As ratio of exports of goods and services	Amount outstanding at year-end	Total	of which: ODA
		Millions of dollars					Per cent	Millions of dollars		
1980	-1558.8	-263.0	-1521.0	75.4[b]	85.9[b]	161.3[b]	15.9[b]	4941.9[b]	1254.4	1289.0
1985	-1297.4	-352.5	-1200.5	169.8	124.0	293.7	22.9	6844.7	1113.5	1162.4

5. Trade

Years and periods	Exports Value Mill. of dollars	of which: share of Jute goods Per cent	Imports Value Mill. of dollars	of which: share of food Per cent	Terms of trade
1980	738	49.8	1973	23.6	100
1985	927	41.6	2170	24.3	99

	Value	Volume	Purchasing power	Value	Volume	Index
			Growth rates, per cent per annum			
1980-1985	4.7	7.5	7.4	1.9	4.6	-0.1
1984-1985	-0.7	-1.6	-0.3	6.3	6.8	1.3
1985-1986	-2.9	-4.9	-5.1	-10.1	-12.2	-0.2

6. Other economic and social indicators

Energy	Transport & communication		Education				Health			Food and nutrition			
Commercial energy consumption per capita	Commercial vehicles	Telephones	Adult literacy rate	School enrolment ratio share of relevant age group Primary M F T		Secondary M F T	Attendance at childbirth by trained personnel	Share of population Immunized against DPT (3 doses)	With access to safe water	Cereals Consumption per capita	Self-sufficiency ratio	Average daily calorie intake per capita Total	Share of requirements
1984	1981	1984	Around 1985	1985			1984	1983-1984	1985	1985		1985	Between 1982&1985
kg of coal equiv.	Per 1,000 pop.					Per cent				kg	Per cent	Calories	Per cent
54	0.4	1.4	33	70 50 60		26 10 18	..	1.5	44	264	90	1899	81

a/ Years ending 30 June.   b/ 1982.

rency as compared to 1985, mainly thanks to the good performance of non-traditional exports (such as frozen shrimps and garments), from which earnings increased by 17 per cent. Total imports, measured in national currency terms, increased by 6 per cent, but declined in dollar terms, largely due to lower import bills for food grains and petroleum. The rise of import unit values was negligible. Private unrequited transfers in 1986 increased by 16 per cent to $521 million compared to 1985. Nevertheless, the current account deficit (excluding ODA) grew from $1,190 million in 1985 to $1,249 million in 1986, owing to the increased deficits on both trade and services accounts. However, this was entirely financed by ODA, which increased to $1,380 million in 1986. International non-gold reserves, which had declined to around $285 million in September 1985, increased to $460 million by June 1986 and reached $700 million at the end of July 1987, equivalent to more than three months' imports. Although most of the country's borrowing has been on concessional terms, debt service is increasing. Thus the debt service exports ratio rose to 31 per cent in FY 1985/86 from 19 per cent in FY 1984/1985.

4. *Budget*

The domestic fiscal revenue increase of 15 per cent in FY 1985/86 was lower than expected. This shortfall was largely due to lower-than-expected receipts on account of customs duties, sales taxes and other import duties as a result of the lower level of imports. On the other hand, the total expenditure level grew by only 11 per cent in the same period. Nevertheless, due to its far higher level, even this moderate rise in expenditure caused the budget deficit to increase in national currency terms from Tk 31.69 billion ($1.19 billion) to Tk 33.94 billion ($1.12 billion), equivalent to 7.1 per cent of GDP.

B. *Recent policy developments*

1. *Macro-economic policies*

The Government has been implementing far-reaching structural adjustment policies since 1985. These include revenue measures, including a

number of stringent measures to recover overdue loans; liberalization of trade and industrial policies; exchange rate adjustments; moderation of the rate of inflation through strict monetary and credit policies; as well as support to the private sector. Moreover, in efforts to realize increased domestic resource mobilization, a number of changes in fees and prices of public sector goods and services were introduced. At the same time, efforts to promote private savings and investment resulted in an increase of the savings rate from 4.2 per cent of GDP in FY 1984/85 to 4.8 per cent in FY 1985/86.

2. *International support measures*

In February 1987 the IMF approved drawings of SDR 77.8 million ($98.2 million) under the Compensatory Financing Facility (CFF). Additional drawings of SDR 135.1 million ($170.5 million) were approved over the subsequent three years under the Structural Adjustment Facility (SAF), of which SDR 57.5 million could be drawn during the first year. Moreover, Bangladesh also had a stand-by arrangement amounting to SDR 180 million during the period December 1985 to July 1987. Under the EC's so-called Compex system of compensation for export earnings shortfalls, Bangladesh will receive ECU 5.6 million in 1987.

3. *SNPA follow-up*

At the Consultative Group meeting held in Paris in April 1987, donor governments and institutions met under the chairmanship of the World Bank. The aid group concluded that it would be necessary for the country to attain a rate of growth in excess of 5 per cent during the period 1988-1990 to meet its development needs. Donors attending the meeting indicated that their aid contribution to Bangladesh would amount to $1.9 billion in 1987 compared with $1.85 billion in 1986.

3. Benin

A. *Recent socio-economic developments*

1. *Overall economy*

Official figures indicate that GDP in 1985 rose by 10 per cent in nominal terms. Since statistics on inflation are not available, GDP growth in real terms can only be estimated. Recent estimates for 1986 give a picture of a stagnant or even declining economy, with GDP estimated to have risen by 3 per cent in nominal terms, which is likely to have produced a further decline in real terms, inasmuch as the rate of inflation is thought to have been about 10 per cent.

2. *Main sectors*

The climatic conditions in Benin have been favourable since the end of the drought in 1984, so that agricultural production in 1985 exceeded the pre-drought levels. The major food crops have performed well: sorghum/millet production was better than average, maize production was far above average, and the production of manioc and yams attained record levels. The two main cash crops – cocoa and cotton – performed particularly well in 1985. Production of cocoa more than doubled over the 1984 level, while cotton production continued to grow, attaining a level four to five times as high as at the beginning of the decade.

The other cash crops showed a much weaker performance. The coffee harvest is officially reported to have been minimal. Groundnuts production fell back to a very low level, after having peaked in 1984. Palm oil production had suffered gravely during the drought period, and the aging plantations of Benin show no evidence of revival yet, although national output is expected to grow after new plantations in the South mature. The situation in 1986 was generally comparable to that of 1985: yields of all food crops went up substantially, while among the cash crops only cotton production continued to increase. No official figures are available for the other cash crops (cocoa, coffee and palm products), which may indicate a disappointing performance.

3. *Trade and payments*

The good agricultural outturn has had a positive impact on Benin's exports. In the absence of national data, analysis must be based on partners' trade data, which may have a wide margin of error. These data indicate that in 1985 Benin's exports rose by 21 per cent in dollar terms, while imports rose by 29 per cent (to about $400 million). The faster growth of imports led to a widening trade deficit. In 1986 exports stagnated, accompanied by a rise in imports of 2.5 per cent.

No official figures on Benin's services balance have been published since 1982, but indications exist that Benin is losing its importance as a transit country. The low level of activity in neighbouring Nigeria has damped the important transit trade with that country, and Benin also appears to be losing its transit trade with Niger and Burkina Faso to neighbouring Togo.

Benin's debt (including short-term debt and use of IMF credits) rose from $641 million at the end of 1984 to $777 million one year later. Measured in local currency, however, this corresponds to a decrease from CFAF 307 billion to CFAF 293 billion. Debt service payments in 1985 amounted to $41.4 million, corresponding to almost 17 per cent of the country's estimated exports of goods and services, i.e. an improvement, as against the 20 per cent estimated for 1984. As the country runs a structural trade deficit, Benin has great difficulties in servicing its debt. Arrears are accumulating, and debt service payments for 1987 are forecast at over $100 million, which is clearly beyond the country's capacity to pay, given that export of goods in 1986 were estimated at only $40 million. But debt rescheduling depends on a prior agreement with the IMF on the country's macro-economic policies.

In 1982 Benin had started to exploit the offshore Semé oil field, which reached a maximum production of 8,500 b/d in 1985. The development rights had been given successively to two different foreign companies, but both agreements aborted. Production is reported to have fallen thereafter by 50 per cent.

The development of the Nangbeto Dam, a joint venture between Benin and Togo, is progressing on schedule. The work should terminate by the end of 1987. The electricity plant will have a capacity of 62 MW. A feasibility study has been commissioned for a second joint Beninese-Togolese hydro-electric plant with a capacity of 15 to 20

BENIN

1. Population, total and per capita GDP, growth of agricultural and manufacturing output

Year and periods	Population Millions	GDP Total Millions of dollars	GDP Per capita Dollars	GDP Per capita Per cent of LDC average	Agricultural production Total	Agricultural production of which: Food	Manufacturing value-added Total
1985	4.0	1021	253	117.7			
				Real growth rates, per cent per annum			
1980-1985	3.1	4.2	1.0		6.8	6.2	7.4
1984-1985	3.1	4.3	1.2		5.1	5.3	17.5
1985-1986	3.1	..	..		6.6	4.9	..

2. Area, demographic indicators and labour force share in agriculture

Area Total	Area Share of arable land under permanent crops	Area Share covered by forestry and woodlands	Density	Average life expectancy at birth M	Average life expectancy at birth F	Average life expectancy at birth T	Infant mortality as share of live births	Share of population In urban areas	Share of population Economically active	Labour force Share in agriculture
		1984	1985		1980-1985		1980-1985		1985	
000 km2	Per cent		Pop/km2		Years		Per 1,000		Per cent	
112.6	16.1	33.5	36	42	46	44	120	35	48	64

3. Origins and uses of output; investment

Years	Sectoral origin of GDP Agriculture	Sectoral origin of GDP Mining	Sectoral origin of GDP Manufacturing	Sectoral origin of GDP Services	Uses of GDP Private consumption expenditure	Uses of GDP Government consumption expenditure	Uses of GDP Gross domestic savings	Investment
					Per cent of total GDP			
1980	47.8	0.3	5.8	40.0	103.9	10.6	-14.5	18.6
1985	47.8	4.7	4.4	36.5	92.1	8.7	-0.8	13.7

4. Balance of payments, debt and external assistance

Years	Balance of payments Merchandise trade balance	Balance of payments Balance on services	Balance of payments Balance on current account	Debt service Amortization	Debt service Interest	Debt service Total	Debt service As ratio of exports of goods and services	Debt Amount outstanding at year-end	External assistance Total	External assistance of which: ODA
				Millions of dollars			Per cent		Millions of dollars	
1980	..	..	..	10.0[a]	20.1[a]	30.1[a]	14.0[a]	622.5[a]	393.2	91.7
1985	..	..	..	13.9	27.5	41.3	16.9	777.1	175.4	95.7

5. Trade

Years and periods	Exports Value Mill. of dollars	Exports of which: share of Palm products Per cent	Imports Value Mill. of dollars	Imports of which: share of food Per cent	Terms of trade
1980	63	27.8	331	26.3	100
1985	40	24.1[a]	400	14.8[b]	103

	Value	Volume	Purchasing power	Value	Volume	Index
			Growth rates, per cent per annum			
1980-1985	-8.7	-6.7	-6.1	3.9	6.8	0.6
1984-1985	21.2	39.6	20.7	29.0	28.5	-13.5
1985-1986	0.0	39.9	-3.8	2.5	-1.4	-31.2

6. Other economic and social indicators

Energy Commercial energy consumption per capita	Transport & communication Commercial vehicles	Transport & communication Telephones	Education Adult literacy rate	Education School enrolment ratio share of relevant age group Primary M	Primary F	Primary T	Secondary M	Secondary F	Secondary T	Health Attendance at childbirth by trained personnel	Health Share of population Immunized against DPT (3 doses)	Health Share of population With access to safe water	Food and nutrition Cereals Consumption per capita	Food and nutrition Cereals Self-sufficiency ratio	Food and nutrition Average daily calorie intake per capita Total	Food and nutrition Average daily calorie intake per capita Share of requirements
1984	1984	1984	Around 1985			1984				1982	1984	1985		1985	1985	Between 1982&1985
kg of coal equiv.	Per 1,000 pop.								Per cent				kg	Per cent	Calories	Per cent
43	..	4.4	26	86	42	64	28	11	19	34.3	15.8	57	153	92	2173	83

a/ 1982.   b/ 1983.

MW at Adjarra on the Mono river. In addition to the work on hydro-electric plants, the conventional thermal station of Parakou has had its capacity increased from 2.7 to 4.5 MW. Completion of these projects will bring Benin's electricity generating capacity to one half the nation's needs.

The project is financed by the European Investment Bank, the French Caisse Centrale de Coopération Economique, the OPEC Fund and the Société Beninoise d'Electricité et d'Eau. The project will provide clean drinking water for 560,000 persons and work should commence at the beginning of 1988.

B. *Recent policy developments*

1. *Macro-economic policies*

Benin is changing its policy towards the private sector. Assisted by the World Bank, the country has embarked upon a privatization programme of public enterprises. In the first phase, State enterprises will be examined as to their intrinsic viability, so as to identify those to be closed down and those to be reorganized. The programme includes an education and redeployment plan for employees who will become redundant. The total cost of the project is $31.5 million, to which IDA will contribute $15 million.

A project is planned to improve the water supply in Cotonou and Porto Novo. The project includes the drilling of boreholes, construction of water treatment plants and rehabilitation of reservoirs. A network of 280 km of distribution pipelines is included, with 23 km of feeder pipeline.

2. *International support measures*

Benin has received support for a rehabilitation project for the port of Cotonou and for the road network connecting Benin with its northern neighbours. IDA gave a $19.5 million credit for the $70.5 million project, while $44.8 million has been received in pledges from other development banks and funds.

3. *SNPA follow-up*

A sectoral Round Table Conference dealing with Benin's infrastructure programme was convened in March 1987. The meeting agreed on CFAF 19.2 billion ($64 million) of funding for construction and rehabilitation of rural roads and rehabilitation of some of the major transit highways. A sectoral meeting on civil aviation and food policies was planned for the end of 1987.

4. Bhutan

A. *Recent socio-economic developments*

1. *Overall economy*

The GDP for 1986 was estimated at Nu 2,020.1 million ($154.32 million); with an estimated population of 1.4 million, this yielded a per capita GDP of Nu 1,628 ($133). The real GDP growth rate between FY 1984/85[142] and FY 1985/86 amounted to 4 per cent, i.e. one percentage point less than the previous year's growth rate.

However, by all available indications, economic performance during the Fifth Plan period (FY 1981/82 – 1986/87) has been favourable.

2. *Main sectors*

In 1986, the agricultural sector contributed just over one half of GDP, but employed over 90 per cent of the economically active population. The service sector's share in GDP amounted to about one third in 1986, which was slightly higher than in the preceding years. Manufacturing in Bhu-

---

[142] The fiscal year (FY) ends on 31 March.

BHUTAN

1. Population, total and per capita GDP, growth of agricultural and manufacturing output

Year and periods	Population Millions	GDP[a] Total Millions of dollars	GDP[a] Per capita Dollars	GDP[a] Per capita Per cent of LDC average	Agricultural production Total	Agricultural production of which: Food	Manufacturing value-added Total
1985	1.4	189	133	61.9			
				Real growth rates, per cent per annum			
1980-1985	2.1	6.6	4.5		2.3	2.3	..
1984-1985	2.1	5.0	2.9		2.2	2.3	..
1985-1986	2.2	..	..		2.2	2.2	..

2. Area, demographic indicators and labour force share in agriculture

Area Total	Area Share of arable land under permanent crops	Area Share covered by forestry and woodlands	Density	Average life expectancy at birth M	Average life expectancy at birth F	Average life expectancy at birth T	Infant mortality as share of live births	Share of population In urban areas	Share of population Economically active	Labour force Share in agriculture
		1984	1985		1980-1985		1980-1985		1985	
000 km2	Per cent		Pop/km2	Years			Per 1,000	Per cent		
47.0	2.1	69.9	30	47	45	46	139	4	45	91

3. Origins and uses of output; investment

Years	Sectoral origin of GDP Agriculture	Mining	Manufacturing	Services	Uses of GDP Private consumption expenditure	Uses of GDP Government consumption expenditure	Uses of GDP Gross domestic savings	Investment
					Per cent of total GDP			
1980	63.2	0.8	3.3	30.6	..	..	..	..
1985	50.5[b]	0.3[b]	3.9[b]	31.8[b]	..	..	..	..

4. Balance of payments, debt and external assistance

Years	Balance of payments Merchandise trade balance	Balance of payments Balance on services	Balance of payments Balance on current account	Debt service Amortization	Debt service Interest	Debt service Total	As ratio of exports of goods and services	Debt Amount outstanding at year-end	External assistance Total	External assistance of which: ODA
	Millions of dollars						Per cent	Millions of dollars		
1980	..	..	..	0.0[c]	1.8[c]	1.8[c]	6.2[c]	9.4[c]	8.3	8.3
1985	..	..	..	0.3	8.8	9.0	23.7	5.7	24.2	24.2

5. Trade

Years and periods	Exports Value Mill. of dollars	Exports of which: share of Cement Per cent	Imports Value Mill. of dollars	Imports of which: share of food Per cent	Terms of trade
1980	..	20.8[d]	..	..	100
1985	..	25.0[e]	..	15.3[e]	..

	Value	Volume	Purchasing power	Value	Volume	Index
	Growth rates, per cent per annum					
1980-1985	..	..	..	..	..	..
1984-1985	..	..	..	..	..	..
1985-1986	..	..	..	..	..	..

6. Other economic and social indicators

Energy Commercial energy consumption per capita	Transport & communication Commercial vehicles	Transport & communication Telephones	Education Adult literacy rate	Education School enrolment ratio share of relevant age group Primary M	Primary F	Primary T	Secondary M	Secondary F	Secondary T	Health Attendance at childbirth by trained personnel	Health Share of population Immunized against DPT (3 doses)	With access to safe water	Food and nutrition Cereals Consumption per capita	Self-sufficiency ratio	Average daily calorie intake per capita Total	Share of requirements
1984	1984	1985	Around 1985			1984				1984	1984	1985	1985		1985	Between 1982&1985
kg of coal equiv.	Per 1,000 pop.									Per cent			kg	Per cent	Calories	Per cent
11	..	1.3	12	32	17	25	6	1	4	3.4	8.7	19[f]	142	89	2571	..

a/ Years beginning 1 April.   b/ 1984.   c/ 1982.   d/ 1981.   e/ 1983.   f/ Rural only.

tan is still at an early stage, with a GDP share for 1984 of about 4 per cent. Bhutan's forests, which cover 46.4 per cent of its area, constitute the country's most valuable natural resource. It is likely that the forestry sector will grow significantly during the Sixth Plan period (FY 1987/88-1991/92), with an expansion of logging and wood-based industries. In the energy sector, the 336 MW Chukha hydro-electric project, the first phase of which was put into full operation in mid-1986, will be a reliable source of power for domestic industrial development and its surplus for export to India will provide the country with substantial export earnings.

3. Trade and payments

India remains Bhutan's predominant trading partner: out of Bhutan's total exports of Nu 272.00 million ($22.23 million) during FY 1985/86, over 99 per cent were directed to that country. Although import dependence on India was slightly less pronounced, the latter increased considerably during FY 1985/86 as compared to previous years, having reached 90.1 per cent of the total imports of Nu 888.40 million ($72.60 million) as compared to 87.9 per cent in FY 1984/85. Bhutan traditionally runs large trade deficits both with India and the rest of the world. Vis-à-vis the rest of the world, this deficit in FY 1985/86 was more than offset by inflows of aid receipts ($15.59 million) and tourism earnings ($2 million). The large trade deficit with India was mainly financed by grants and concessional loans ($60.15 million), particularly ad hoc budgetary grants. The current account deficit (excluding official grants) improved from Nu 966.09 million ($81.27 million) in FY 1984/85 to Nu 847.36 million ($69.24 million) during FY 1985/86. On the other hand, total concessional loans and grants also declined from Nu 984.08 million ($82.79 million) in FY 1984/85 to Nu 926.81 million ($75.74 million) in FY 1985/86. During the latter fiscal year, Bhutan ran an overall balance-of-payments surplus of Nu 67.33 million ($5.5 million). Indian rupee reserves, which did not change during the fiscal year ending in March 1986, were equivalent to about six months' imports from India, while the convertible currency reserves on that date covered about thirty-four months' imports from other countries, as against twenty months' imports one year earlier. Such reserve-import ratios are high compared to those of other LDCs. Bhutan's total debt increased from $2.98 million on 31 March 1985 to $10.40 million one year later, while the debt service exports ratio increased from 1.9 per cent between FY 1984/85 to 3.2 per cent during FY 1985/86, which is still modest compared to most LDCs.

4. Budget

During the latter part of the Fifth Plan period, the Government was able to increase budget revenues to Nu 263.9 million ($21.57 million) during FY 1985/86, compared to Nu 123.5 million ($15.65 million) in FY 1981/82. This was done largely from increased taxes on company profits and trading companies' gross turnover and rising after-tax earnings of public enterprises. On the expenditure side, the growth of maintenance (recurrent) expenditures was kept under 10 per cent annually. Development expenditure for the Sixth Plan is projected to be $497.5 million, of which domestic resource mobilization is targeted at $48.5 million. The Planning Commission's projection of external resources available comes to $383 million, which leaves a shortfall of $66 million.

5. Social developments

While school enrolment grew by almost 11 per cent in FY 1983/84 compared to FY 1982/83, this growth rate fell to 7 and 5 per cent respectively in the two subsequent years. The educational development objective has been to consolidate and improve existing programmes and facilities and to develop a sophisticated cadre of manpower rather than to expand physical infrastructure. Considerable resources have been devoted to the public health sector, and the Government is determined to continue its efforts as regards preventive measures, safe water supplies, the extension of the network of basic health units (BHUs) and an increase in the number of village health workers. As of 1985, three new hospitals had been built, a total of 22 BHUs established and 11 new dispensaries opened. Health services have suffered generally from a shortage of trained manpower.

B. Recent policy developments

1. Macro-economic policies

The underlying objectives of the Sixth Plan (FY 1987/88-1991/92) are to create a well-integrated and just society through social and economic development and to attain national self-reliance through sustained economic growth. The broader policy initiatives aim at establishing a simple and progressive tax system; optimizing public-sector enterprise revenues and private savings for domestic resource mobilization; encouraging private sector development; and controlling public expenditures. The Government is conscious of the looming problems of debt servicing. Therefore efforts are being made to increase the country's convertible-currency-earning capabilities through third country exports and tourism from the rest of the world.

2. International support policies

Bhutan depends upon external assistance to implement its Sixth Plan. The capital costs are high, especially because of its land-locked position. In order to ensure effective planning and co-ordination of development assistance, external assistance is programmed on a medium- to long-term basis. India still remains the largest single donor, accounting for over 69 per cent of total budgetary aid flows, but the United Nations system (including IDA), the Asian Development Bank, the Kuwait Fund and new bilateral donors have substantially increased their assistance, particularly in jointly-financed development projects.

· 3. SNPA follow-up

Sectoral follow-up consultations to the Round Table Meeting held in April 1986 in Geneva have not yet been planned owing to the finalization process of the Sixth Plan. However, several high-level bilateral consultations have taken place both in the country's capital as well as in the donor capitals. As a result, several donors, including international funding agencies, have either committed or assured substantial increases in their assistance to Bhutan for the present Plan period.

---

5. Botswana

A. Recent socio-economic developments

1. Overall economy

The economy of Botswana continued to perform well in 1985 and 1986, although drought conditions persisted. According to preliminary estimates, the real rate of growth of total GDP was 6 per cent in the national accounts year 1984/85 [143] and around 12 per cent in 1985/86. The upturn in the latter year was largely due to improved conditions in the diamond markets. However, relatively satisfactory overall growth was also maintained outside the mining sector. The inflation rate, which had started to accelerate in 1985, was kept at a level of around 10 per cent in 1986, substantially lower than in neighbouring South Africa.

Botswana's overall economic performance over the past two decades has been impressive. A reading of aggregate indicators may nevertheless give a misleading picture of the economy's basic strength. Performance has been diamond-led and the health of the economy is closely linked to international economic conditions and vulnerable to changes in these. Commercial and industrial diversification has only made limited progress. The employment situation, the prolonged drought, a high rate of population growth and environmental degradation remain causes of serious concern. Rainfall in the first quarter of 1987 was again far below normal and in April Botswana had to appeal for international aid to help combat the effects of the sixth consecutive year of drought.

2. Main sectors

Grain output in 1986 was estimated at around 20,000 tonnes, one-third of normal pre-drought crop yields and one-tenth of annual cereal requirements. Harvest expectations for 1987 were only marginally better. Mortality continued to rise in the cattle herd, and there was another drop in the number of slaughtered cattle in 1986. The mining sector continues to dominate the country's economy, and now accounts for around two-fifths of total output. Diamond prices were raised twice in 1986. Botswana was able to sell all its diamond output that year as well as a portion of the stockpile accumulated in earlier years. However, the markets for copper and nickel, mined in Botswana at Selebi-Phikwe, continued to be depressed. Preliminary estimates indicated that developments in

---

[143] The national accounts year (NAY) ends on 30 June.

BOTSWANA

1. Population, total and per capita GDP, growth of agricultural and manufacturing output

Year and periods	Population Millions	GDP[a] Total Millions of dollars	Per capita Dollars	Per capita Per cent of LDC average	Agricultural production Total	Agricultural production of which: Food	Manufacturing value-added Total
1985	1.1	946	855	397.7			
				Real growth rates, per cent per annum			
1980-1985	3.9	10.8	6.6		2.0	2.0	9.5
1984-1985	3.6	5.9	2.2		5.8	5.9	4.5
1985-1986	4.1	..	..		1.0	1.0	-2.2

2. Area, demographic indicators and labour force share in agriculture

Area Total 000 km2	Area Share of arable land under permanent crops 1984 Per cent	Area Share covered by forestry and woodlands 1984 Per cent	Demographic indicators Density 1985 Pop/km2	Average life expectancy at birth M 1980-1985 Years	F 1980-1985 Years	T 1980-1985 Years	Infant mortality as share of live births 1980-1985 Per 1,000	Share of population In urban areas	Economically active 1985 Per cent	Labour force Share in agriculture
581.7	2.3	1.6	2	53	56	55	76	20	34	60

3. Origins and uses of output; investment

Years	Sectoral origin of GDP Agriculture	Mining	Manufacturing	Services	Uses of GDP Private consumption expenditure	Government consumption expenditure	Gross domestic savings	Investment
				Per cent of total GDP				
1980	11.9	30.0	4.2	46.6	51.1	20.1	28.9	41.5
1985	5.2	36.3	6.1	46.4	46.8	27.6	25.6	26.3

4. Balance of payments, debt and external assistance

Years	Balance of payments Merchandise trade balance	Balance on services	Balance on current account	Debt service Amortization	Interest	Total	As ratio of exports of goods and services	Debt Amount outstanding at year-end	External assistance Total	of which: ODA
	Millions of dollars						Per cent	Millions of dollars		
1980	-58.0	-148.0	-207.3	4.6[b]	57.0[b]	61.6[b]	9.6[b]	340.5[b]	53.4	106.1
1985	233.8	-191.5	39.2	26.7	28.9	55.6	6.3	441.0	161.6	99.8

5. Trade

Years and periods	Exports Value Mill. of dollars	of which: share of Diamonds Per cent	Imports Value Mill. of dollars	of which: share of food Per cent	Terms of trade
1980	503	60.8	691	15.7	100
1985	727	75.8	596	17.5	..

	Value	Volume	Purchasing power	Value	Volume	Index
			Growth rates, per cent per annum			
1980-1985	7.6	..	10.3	-2.9	-0.5	..
1984-1985	7.9	..	7.4	-12.2	-12.6	..
1985-1986	-7.8	..	-9.1	2.3	1.0	..

6. Other economic and social indicators

Energy Commercial energy consumption per capita 1984 kg of coal equiv.	Transport & communication Commercial vehicles 1983	Telephones 1984 Per 1,000 pop.	Education Adult literacy rate 1985 Around	School enrolment ratio share of relevant age group Primary M	F	T	Secondary M	F	T	Health Attendance at childbirth by trained personnel 1984	Share of population Immunized against DPT (3 doses) 1982	With access to safe water 1985	Food and nutrition Cereals Consumption per capita 1985 kg	Self-sufficiency ratio 1985 Per cent	Average daily calorie intake per capita Total 1985 Calories	Share of requirements Between 1982&1985 Per cent
..	19.2	17.9	71	94	104	99	26	30	28	..	82.0	54	149	12	2219	93

a/ Years ending 30 June.   b/ 1982.

other sectors were uneven in NAY 1984/85 and 1985/86: manufacturing, which accounts for only 6 per cent of GDP, showed little growth in real terms and there was a downturn in construction activity.

3. *Trade and payments*

Botswana's balance-of-payments position remained strong in 1985 and 1986, surpluses on the current and capital accounts in both years leading to substantial increases in the country's international reserves. This performance was largely explained by the recovery in the diamond markets and improved terms of trade, which were partly due to exchange rate developments in the currencies of the country's principal trading partners. Copper-nickel matte and beef both contributed to export growth in 1985, but earnings from copper-nickel matte declined substantially in 1986.

4. *Budget*

Budgetary developments in Botswana have in recent years been characterized by simultaneous and rapid increases in revenue, expenditure and Government cash balances. Buoyant mineral revenue has contributed to larger-than-anticipated increases in revenue, while there has been a tendency to underspend, particularly in the development budget. Overall budgetary surpluses were increasing between FY 1983/84 and FY 1985/86, but the surplus for FY 1986/87 was expected to be similar to the one produced in the preceding fiscal year.[144]

5. *Social developments*

Rural incomes and welfare have been severely affected by the long period of drought. The Government has attempted to alleviate the impact through labour-based relief programmes and supplementary feeding programmes. Employment in the formal sector grew by 9 per cent and 6.5 per cent in 1984 and 1985 respectively. These increases fell far short of absorbing the new entrants into the labour force, estimated at over 20,000 annually. The abolition of secondary school fees with effect from 1988 was announced in the 1987 budget speech.

---

[144] The fiscal year (FY) ends on 31 March.

B. *Recent policy developments*

1. *Macro-economic policies*

Botswana's Sixth National Development Plan (1985/91) came into operation in FY 1985/86. The Government continues to adopt a cautious policy stance, aimed at maintaining substantial international reserves as well as domestic cash balances in view of Botswana's continuing external vulnerability and of expected changes in budgetary trends during the later years of the Plan period.

Budgetary estimates presented for FY 1987/88 projected a stagnation in revenue, a moderate increase in expenditure over actual spending in the previous fiscal year, and a corresponding reduction in the overall budgetary surplus. Following a review of the tax system undertaken in 1986, a number of tax reforms were proposed, involving notably a simplification and rationalization of the income tax system, an increase in the company tax rate, and the introduction of a general sales tax in 1988.

A major review of monetary and credit policies was also carried out in 1986, with a view to encouraging economic activity through increased credit creation and lower interest levels. Consequently a realignment and a general reduction of interest rate levels were undertaken in September 1986. Other initiatives in the financial sector in 1986 were the institution of an agricultural credit guarantee scheme and of a mortgage guarantee scheme designed to promote home-owning and property development.

2. *International support measures*

The net inflow of concessional aid to Botswana decreased in the first half of the 1980s, from a peak of $106 million in 1980 to $100 million in 1985. Main sectors of co-operation in 1985, apart from humanitarian and relief programmes, were natural resources development, education, and transport and communications. Non-concessional development finance to Botswana from both multilateral agencies and bilateral sources, as well as private capital inflows, have also played an important role in external financing in recent years.

6. Burkina Faso

A. *Recent socio-economic developments*

1. *Overall economy*

Following rainfall improvement, provisional estimates for 1985 point to a 4.3 per cent increase in real GDP per capita after three consecutive years of decline.

2. *Main sectors*

Improved weather conditions have continued, leading to a record cereal crop of 1.9 million tonnes in 1986, which is 15 per cent above the already good harvest of the preceding year and 50 per cent above the 1981-1985 average. For 1987, the country is reported to have an exportable surplus of 60,000 tonnes of maize, millet and white sorghum, as compared to an import deficit in wheat and rice of 90,000 tonnes. External assistance has been requested for the marketing of the exportable surplus as well as for the internal movement of cereals towards deficit areas. Grasshoppers proliferated at the beginning of the return of rains, but the danger has been contained, notably by means of appropriate spraying and other control measures.

With the bumper crop, market prices for cereals have tended to decline: in early 1987, millet was trading at CFAF 60-65 per kg as compared to the official price of CFAF 94. The Government, however, has been actively engaged in reconstituting depleted stocks through the purchase of cereals at above-market prices, in order to counteract the disincentive to future production levels caused by the low market prices.

Gold production (interrupted in 1966) resumed in late 1984, reaching an estimated 3.5 tonnes in 1986, or more than double the 1985 volume. In addition, small-scale gold mining in the desert regions of the North is being promoted. New gold reserves, of an unspecified magnitude, have been discovered in the past two years.

3. *Trade and payments*

Foreign exchange earnings have been constrained by depressed conditions in the world market for cotton, whose share in total exports ac-

counted for around one-half of the country's total exports in the period 1983-1985. Import compression in 1983 and 1984 made it possible to improve the ratio of coverage of (c.i.f.) imports by (f.o.b.) exports from a trough of 16 per cent in 1982 to 38 per cent in 1984, but this ratio deteriorated again to 29 per cent in 1985. However, the record cereal crop of 1986 is expected to alleviate the import burden, while herd recovery (in terms of numbers) resulting from weather improvement should boost exports of live animals and products, which account for over one-tenth of total exports. Import substitution of clothing is being promoted, notably through the use of local garments among public employees.

B. *Recent policy developments*

1. *Macro-economic policies*

A five-year development plan for 1986-1990 was launched on 3 August 1986, following a preliminary *Programme populaire de développement*, which covered the period October 1984 – December 1985. The five-year plan places the emphasis on meeting basic needs and gives top priority to agricultural development, particularly through the mobilization of the rural population.

A major review of parastatal enterprises was undertaken in 1986 with a view to improving their efficiency, and measures taken include management changes and cuts in personnel expenditures and in other operating costs. To promote the involvement of the private sector in national economic development, the Government took several initiatives in 1986 such as the organization of seminars and the promotion of co-operatives, following the introduction in 1984 of a new investment code.

A programme of fiscal reform was put into effect in February 1987, consisting essentially of expenditure cutbacks (particularly with regard to the civil service) and the imposition of a turnover tax, which would compensate for the reduction in customs revenue resulting from import compression.

A programme involving the mobilization of the local population was initiated in 1986 with the purpose of establishing a primary health care unit in each of the 7,000 villages of the country. In

BURKINA FASO

1. Population, total and per capita GDP, growth of agricultural and manufacturing output

Year and periods	Population Millions	GDP Total Millions of dollars	GDP Per capita Dollars	GDP Per capita Per cent of LDC average	Agricultural production Total	Agricultural production of which: Food	Manufacturing value-added Total
1985	6.9	927	134	62.3			
				Real growth rates, per cent per annum			
1980-1985	2.4	2.2	-0.2		6.7	6.5	2.9
1984-1985	2.3	6.7	4.3		23.6	23.1	3.9
1985-1986	2.8	..	..		12.6	11.9	..

2. Area, demographic indicators and labour force share in agriculture

Area Total 000 km2	Area Share of arable land under permanent crops 1984 Per cent	Area Share covered by forestry and woodlands 1984 Per cent	Demographic indicators Density 1985 Pop/km2	Demographic indicators Average life expectancy at birth M 1980-1985 Years	Demographic indicators Average life expectancy at birth F 1980-1985 Years	Demographic indicators Average life expectancy at birth T 1980-1985 Years	Demographic indicators Infant mortality as share of live births 1980-1985 Per 1,000	Demographic indicators Share of population In urban areas Per cent	Demographic indicators Share of population Economically active 1985 Per cent	Labour force Share in agriculture
274.2	9.6	25.4	25	44	47	45	150	8	54	86

3. Origins and uses of output; investment

Years	Sectoral origin of GDP Agriculture	Sectoral origin of GDP Mining	Sectoral origin of GDP Manufacturing	Sectoral origin of GDP Services	Uses of GDP Private consumption expenditure	Uses of GDP Government consumption expenditure	Uses of GDP Gross domestic savings	Investment
					Per cent of total GDP			
1980	44.3	0.2	11.8	39.5	96.4	15.3	-11.7	12.2
1985	46.5	0.0	13.8	36.2	96.4	14.7	-11.1	8.0

4. Balance of payments, debt and external assistance

Years	Balance of payments Merchandise trade balance	Balance of payments Balance on services	Balance of payments Balance on current account	Debt service Amortization	Debt service Interest	Debt service Total	Debt service As ratio of exports of goods and services	Debt Amount outstanding at year-end	External assistance Total	External assistance of which: ODA
	Millions of dollars						Per cent	Millions of dollars		
1980	..	..	..	14.8a/	12.0a/	26.8a/	14.6a/	390.1a/	234.8	218.5
1985	..	..	..	19.4	13.5	33.0	20.2	551.1	205.5	207.4

5. Trade

Years and periods	Exports Value Mill. of dollars	Exports of which: share of Cotton Per cent	Imports Value Mill. of dollars	Imports of which: share of food Per cent	Terms of trade
1980	90	43.9	358	20.5	100
1985	66	45.2b/	225	25.5c/	115

	Value	Volume	Purchasing power	Value	Volume	Index
			Growth rates, per cent per annum			
1980-1985	-6.0	-6.3	-3.6	-8.9	-6.5	2.9
1984-1985	-16.5	-15.3	-16.9	8.7	8.1	-1.9
1985-1986	-1.5	-1.9	-3.8	2.2	-0.2	-1.9

6. Other economic and social indicators

Energy Commercial energy consumption per capita 1984 kg of coal equiv.	Transport & communication Commercial vehicles 1981 Per 1,000 pop.	Transport & communication Telephones 1984 Per 1,000 pop.	Education Adult literacy rate Around 1985 Per cent	Education School enrolment ratio share of relevant age group Primary M 1984	Education Primary F 1984	Education Primary T 1984	Education Secondary M 1984	Education Secondary F 1984	Education Secondary T 1984	Health Attendance at childbirth by trained personnel 1984 Per cent	Health Share of population Immunized against DPT (3 doses) 1982 Per cent	Health Share of population With access to safe water 1985 Per cent	Food and nutrition Cereals Consumption per capita 1985 kg	Food and nutrition Cereals Self-sufficiency ratio 1985 Per cent	Food and nutrition Average daily calorie intake per capita Total 1985 Calories	Food and nutrition Average daily calorie intake per capita Share of requirements Between 1982&1985 Per cent
29	2.6	2.1	13	37	22	29	6	3	4	..	2.0	65	257	89	1924	85

a/ 1982.   b/ 1984   c/ 1983.

addition, a nation-wide vaccination campaign was launched between November 1986 and January 1987, covering pregnant women and children under two years of age.

A national anti-desertification plan was launched in July 1986, and local tree-planting is strongly encouraged and facilitated by the Government (which provided *inter alia* transport and tools).

2. *International support*

Negotiations with IMF have been under way, but no agreement had been reached at the time this report was prepared.

A UNDP-sponsored round table was expected to be held some time in 1987.

7. Burundi

A. *Recent socio-economic developments*

1. *Overall economy*

After the stagnation of GDP growth in 1984, when agriculture suffered from drought, Burundi's economic situation improved in 1985. GDP at constant factor cost grew by an estimated 7.7 per cent in 1985. This yielded an increase of about 5 per cent in per capita GDP, breaking the trend of falling per capita income during the previous three years. With food supply returning to normal, the rate of inflation slowed down in 1985. Overall GDP growth was expected to remain relatively satisfactory in 1986.

2. *Main sectors*

The recovery in agriculture in 1985 affected the output both of food crops and of cash crops, whose values increased by some 5 per cent and one-third respectively. Production of coffee, the main export crop and a major source of fiscal revenue, rose from 27,000 tonnes in 1984/85 to over 32,000 tonnes in the 1985/86 crop year, making it the third best coffee harvest ever recorded in Burundi. Coffee output reportedly fell slightly in the crop year 1986/87. Of the other main sectors in the economy, industrial production and modern services both registered over 10 per cent growth rates in 1985, while modern construction contracted.

3. *Trade and payments*

Burundi's terms of trade worsened significantly in 1985, as export prices fell by close to 4 per cent, while import prices increased by close to 5 per cent. The country was not able to take full advantage of the rise in world coffee prices which began in November 1985, as a large share of its coffee crop had already been sold by then. Nevertheless the balance on merchandise trade improved in 1985, as the volume of exports increased (in particular of coffee, tea and hides and skins), while the volume of imports fell. On the other hand, the balance on services account deteriorated, owing in large part to increased interest payments on external debt. Available indicators pointed to an improvement in the overall balance of payments in 1986 due to a significant increase in the value of exports and to capital inflows under the Government's economic adjustment programme.

4. *Budget*

Burundi has two separate budgets, the ordinary budget and the extraordinary investment budget. Largely due to increased receipts from coffee, the ordinary budget surplus more than doubled between 1984 and 1985, but this was more than offset by increased debt reimbursement, both domestic and foreign. On the other hand, resources earmarked for the extraordinary budget continued

BURUNDI

1. Population, total and per capita GDP, growth of agricultural and manufacturing output

Year and periods	Population Millions	GDP Total Millions of dollars	GDP Per capita Dollars	GDP Per capita Per cent of LDC average	Agricultural production Total	Agricultural production of which: Food	Manufacturing value-added Total
1985	4.7	1097	232	107.9			
				Real growth rates, per cent per annum			
1980–1985	2.9	3.1	0.3		3.5	2.8	7.5
1984–1985	2.7	7.7	4.9		8.7	7.5	16.6
1985–1986	3.1	..	..		2.1	3.5	..

2. Area, demographic indicators and labour force share in agriculture

Area Total	Area Share of arable land under permanent crops 1984	Area Share covered by forestry and woodlands 1984	Density 1985	Average life expectancy at birth M	Average life expectancy at birth F	Average life expectancy at birth T	Infant mortality as share of live births 1980–1985	Share of population In urban areas	Share of population Economically active 1985	Labour force Share in agriculture
000 km2	Per cent		Pop/km2	Years			Per 1,000	Per cent		
27.8	47.0	2.3	170	45	48	47	124	2	53	92

3. Origins and uses of output; investment

Years	Sectoral origin of GDP Agriculture	Sectoral origin of GDP Mining	Sectoral origin of GDP Manufacturing	Sectoral origin of GDP Services	Uses of GDP Private consumption expenditure	Uses of GDP Government consumption expenditure	Uses of GDP Gross domestic savings	Investment
					Per cent of total GDP			
1980	61.8	0.3	9.0	24.0	87.8	12.6	-0.4	13.3
1985	56.6	1.0	11.7	24.6	82.6	13.8	3.5	15.5

4. Balance of payments, debt and external assistance

Years	Balance of payments Merchandise trade balance	Balance of payments Balance on services	Balance of payments Balance on current account	Debt service Amortization	Debt service Interest	Debt service Total	Debt service As ratio of exports of goods and services	Debt Amount outstanding at year-end	External assistance Total	External assistance of which: ODA
	Millions of dollars						Per cent	Millions of dollars		
1980	..	..	..	12.8[a/]	4.9[a/]	17.7[a/]	16.4[a/]	252.3[a/]	132.4	128.0
1985	..	..	..	13.6	10.7	24.3	20.1	461.0	157.8	139.9

5. Trade

Years and periods	Exports Value Mill. of dollars	Exports of which: share of Coffee Per cent	Imports Value Mill. of dollars	Imports of which: share of food Per cent	Terms of trade
1980	65	89.0	168	10.5	100
1985	110	84.3	186	16.4	..

	Value	Volume	Purchasing power	Value	Volume	Index
			Growth rates, per cent per annum			
1980–1985	11.1	..	13.9	2.1	4.6	..
1984–1985	12.2	..	11.8	0.0	-0.4	..
1985–1986	111.8	..	109.0	10.8	9.3	..

6. Other economic and social indicators

Energy Commercial energy consumption per capita 1984 kg of coal equiv.	Transport & communication Commercial vehicles 1984 Per 1,000 pop.	Transport & communication Telephones 1983	Education Adult literacy rate 1982	Education School enrolment ratio share of relevant age group Primary 1984 M	Education Primary 1984 F	Education Primary 1984 T	Education Secondary 1983 M	Education Secondary 1983 F	Education Secondary 1983 T	Health Attendance at childbirth by trained personnel 1984	Health Share of population Immunized against DPT (3 doses) 1982	Health Share of population With access to safe water 1985	Food and nutrition Cereals Consumption per capita 1985 kg	Food and nutrition Cereals Self-sufficiency ratio 1985 Per cent	Food and nutrition Average daily calorie intake per capita Total 1985 Calories	Food and nutrition Average daily calorie intake per capita Share of requirements Between 1982&1985 Per cent
								Per cent								
16	1.1	1.3	34[b/]	58	40	49	5	3	4	12.0	38.0	26	100	96	2116	102

a/ 1982.   b/ Age group 10+.

to fall. Investment expenditures, most of which have been financed by money creation, dropped to the lowest level in the 1980s. This combination of trends caused the overall Treasury position to be strengthened, although a considerable deficit remained.

B. *Recent policy developments*

1. *Macro-economic policies*

In 1986 the Government launched a new economic adjustment programme to restore external and internal balance and revitalize the economy, which supplements the country's Fourth Five-Year Economic and Social Development Plan (1983-1987). The programme aims at improving the balance of payments and reconstituting foreign exchange reserves, improving public finances and supporting investment and growth. Over the longer term, the objective is also to lessen dependence on coffee, which accounted for 84 per cent of exports in 1985. Austerity measures intended to restore financial equilibrium had already been instituted in Burundi starting in 1983, but the new programme is more comprehensive and envisages a wide range of measures, many of them aiming at liberalizing the economy. The measures envisaged include a flexible exchange-rate and price policy, liberalization of import and exchange controls, tariff reform, the containment of Governmment spending, reform of public enterprises, and monetary policies designed to encourage savings and improve credit allocation. Implementation of the programme started with a 15 per cent devaluation of the Burundi franc *vis-à-vis* the SDR in July 1986, an adjustment of interest rates, removal of price controls and import licences for a number of products, a revision and simplification of the tariff schedule, revision of the country's investment code, elaboration of a new public investment programme and measures to strengthen external debt management. Producer prices for coffee and tea were raised by 28 and 20 per cent respectively for the 1986/87 crop year.

2. *International support measures*

The initial phase of the Government's adjustment programme was to be supported by a structural adjustment credit of $31 million from IDA and its special facility for sub-Saharan Africa, accompanied by joint financing of $19 million from bilateral donors; a stand-by arrangement with the IMF amounting to SDR 21 million and running from August 1986 to March 1988; and a loan of SDR 20 million under the IMF's Structural Adjustment Facility. Concessional development assistance received from official sources was estimated at $140 million in 1985 ($138 million in 1984).

3. *SNPA follow-up*

Sectoral follow-up consultations to the Round Table held in Bujumbura in February 1984 were planned in the areas of rural development, energy and education.

8. Cape Verde

A. *Recent socio-economic developments*

1. *Overall economy*

According to national sources, GDP in constant prices increased by an average of 6.5 per cent over the period 1980-1985. From a high of 14.6 per cent in 1982, GDP growth slowed down to 3.5 per cent in 1984, but provisional data for 1985 indicate a recovery for that year. The GNP of Cape Verde is higher than GDP, mostly because of the high level of private transfers from Cape Verde nationals living abroad. However, these have declined in constant prices since 1980, particularly between 1983 and 1984 when they dropped by 32 per cent from C.V. Esc. 2.4 billion ($33.5 million) to C.V. Esc. 1.8 billion ($21.2 million). In 1985, the level of remittances was maintained in constant prices at its depressed 1984 level. Between 1980 and 1985, per capita private consumption levels have hardly increased.

CAPE VERDE

1. Population, total and per capita GDP, growth of agricultural and manufacturing output

Year and periods	Population Millions	GDP Total Millions of dollars	GDP Per capita Dollars	GDP Per capita Per cent of LDC average	Agricultural production Total	Agricultural production of which: Food	Manufacturing value-added Total
1985	0.3	118	353	164.2			
				Real growth rates, per cent per annum			
1980-1985	2.5	6.5	4.0		-5.7	-5.7	..
1984-1985	2.5	4.0	1.5		-7.2	-7.1	..
1985-1986	2.4	..	..		33.1	32.9	..

2. Area, demographic indicators and labour force share in agriculture

Total 000 km2	Area Share of arable land under permanent crops Per cent	Area Share covered by forestry and woodlands 1984 Per cent	Density 1985 Pop/km2	Average life expectancy at birth M 1980-1985 Years	Average life expectancy at birth F 1980-1985 Years	Average life expectancy at birth T 1980-1985 Years	Infant mortality as share of live births 1980-1985 Per 1,000	Share of population In urban areas 1985 Per cent	Share of population Economically active 1985 Per cent	Labour force Share in agriculture
4.0	9.9	0.2	81	57	61	59	75	5	37	45

3. Origins and uses of output; investment

Years	Sectoral origin of GDP Agriculture	Mining	Manufacturing	Services	Uses of GDP Private consumption expenditure	Government consumption expenditure	Gross domestic savings	Investment
				Per cent of total GDP				
1980	34.5	0.3	..	54.5	110.5	23.9	-34.4	42.3
1985	19.7	0.5	..	63.2	89.9	21.6	-11.5	50.5

4. Balance of payments, debt and external assistance

Years	Balance of payments Merchandise trade balance	Balance on services	Balance on current account	Debt service Amortization	Interest	Total	As ratio of exports of goods and services	Debt Amount outstanding at year-end	External assistance Total	External assistance of which: ODA
	Millions of dollars						Per cent	Millions of dollars		
1980	..	..	..	0.1[a]	1.7[a]	1.9[a]	6.3[a]	56.5[a]	62.5	62.5
1985	..	..	..	2.2	3.2	5.3	13.6	102.4	74.4	73.5

5. Trade

Years and periods	Exports Value Mill. of dollars	Exports of which: share of Fish fresh, simply preserved Per cent	Imports Value Mill. of dollars	Imports of which: share of food Per cent	Terms of trade
1980	4	22.0	68	35.1[b]	100
1985	5	54.8[c]	113	39.7[c]	..

	Value	Volume	Purchasing power	Value	Volume	Index
	Growth rates, per cent per annum					
1980-1985	4.6	..	7.2	10.7	13.5	..
1984-1985	0.0	..	-0.4	34.5	34.0	..
1985-1986	0.0	..	-1.3	1.8	0.4	..

6. Other economic and social indicators

Energy Commercial energy consumption per capita 1984 kg of coal equiv.	Transport & communication Commercial vehicles 1984 Per 1,000 pop.	Transport & communication Telephones 1984 Per 1,000 pop.	Education Adult literacy rate Around 1985	Education School enrolment ratio share of relevant age group Primary M 1983	Education Primary F 1983	Education Primary T 1983	Education Secondary M 1983	Education Secondary F 1983	Education Secondary T 1983	Health Attendance at childbirth by trained personnel 1983	Health Share of population Immunized against DPT (3 doses) 1984	Health Share of population With access to safe water 1985	Food and nutrition Cereals Consumption per capita 1985 kg	Food and nutrition Cereals Self-sufficiency ratio 1985 Per cent	Food and nutrition Average daily calorie intake per capita Total 1985 Calories	Food and nutrition Average daily calorie intake per capita Share of requirements Between 1982&1985 Per cent
							Per cent						kg	Per cent		Per cent
169	2.2	7.5	47	113	107	110	13	10	11	10.0	..	63	204	1	2535[d]	111

a/ 1982.   b/ 1981.   c/ 1984.   d/ Year other than 1985.

2. *Main sectors*

The share of agriculture within GDP has continued to decline, falling to 13 per cent in 1985, as compared to 22 per cent in 1980. Satisfactory rainfall in 1986 has caused a significant increase in the production of food crops: maize output reached 12,000 tonnes, compared to an average of 2,800 tonnes in the period 1981-85, and output of beans was 6,000 tonnes, compared to the 1981-1985 average of 2,600 tonnes. However, these figures are still far below the country's food requirements, inasmuch as the consumption of cereals for 1987 is estimated at almost 80,000 tonnes. In spite of a good potential, fishing catches have stagnated around 10,000 tonnes in the 1980s. This sector has not been able to contribute substantially to exports, as anticipated by the First National Development Plan (1982-1985). Although a number of import-substituting industries have been created in the 1980s, value added in manufacturing only accounted for 4 per cent of GDP in 1985, while commerce, transport and other services accounted for 60 per cent.

3. *Trade and payments*

Exports of traditional products (bananas, salt, fish products) declined throughout the 1980s. Although some new products (garments, pharmaceuticals) have started to be exported since 1985, merchandise exports (f.o.b.) covered less than 5 per cent of imports (c.i.f.) in 1985, as compared to 6 per cent in 1980. The services account, on the other hand has been positive, mainly owing to supply and service activities at the airport of Sal and the port of Mindelo, but this surplus is far smaller than the merchandise trade deficit. Income on services account reached a peak in 1983, but declined in 1984 and 1985 in spite of the entry into operation of the Cabnave shipyard in 1984. In 1986, sanctions by the United States against South African Airways flights that stopped over at Sal Airport further affected earnings from this source. In spite of the negative balance of goods and services, the overall balance of payments continued to be positive in 1984 and 1985, owing to substantial private transfers (remittances) and public transfers. The external debt increased from $39 million in 1981 to $101 million in 1985, equivalent to 85 per cent of GDP. Correspondingly, debt servicing payments increased very rapidly from 1.3 per cent of exports of goods and services in 1981 to 14.5 per cent in 1985.

4. *Budget*

The Central Government's recurrent expenditure (C.V. Esc. 2.3 billion in 1985, equivalent to $26 million) continues to be financed from domestic revenue, but the larger share of expenditure (C.V. Esc. 4.4 billion in 1985, equivalent to $50 million), classified as capital expenditure, is largely financed by foreign grants including proceeds from food aid. In spite of this external assistance, the overall fiscal deficit increased from 8 per cent of GDP in 1984 to 11.8 per cent in 1985.

5. *Employment*

Out of a population of 334,900 in 1985, the economically active population is estimated at 107,000, of whom only about 30 per cent are permanently employed. A larger percentage (more than 44 per cent) has what is called "temporary employment", "or indeterminable employment" referring mostly to labour-intensive activities financed directly or indirectly by foreign aid. Twenty-five per cent of the economically active population was reported as wholly unemployed.

B. *Recent policy developments*

1. *Macro-economic policies*

The Second National Development Plan (1986-1990) was approved by the National Assembly in December 1986. During this period an average annual GDP growth rate of 4.5 per cent is forecast, with industry growing at more than 11 per cent per year, fishing and services by about 8 per cent and tourism by 4 per cent. Although the creation of 10,000 new jobs is envisaged (of which, 3,500 will be permanent), this still implies an unemployment rate as high as 25 per cent. In the course of the Second Development Plan, major reforms are to be implemented in land tenure, administration and the education system.

2. *Relations with donors*

A restricted consultation between Cape Verde and its main development partners took place in Geneva on 22-23 October 1986. This was followed by an enlarged Round Table Meeting in Praia from 30 November to 3 December 1986. At these meetings, the Government presented its policies and programmes for the Second Development Plan, as well as its requirements for external assistance for the five-year period covered by the Plan ($562 million). At both meetings, the overall orientations of the Government received general support by donors, while the Government was able to give further details on its policies for export development, transport, population and emigration matters. At the Geneva meeting, several donors gave broad indications of their intended level of support, and at the Praia meeting it was estimated that commitments were made in excess of the requirements for 1987 and 1988 ($224 million). Following these meetings, a number of bilateral aid agreements were signed, some of them on a pluri-annual basis in response to the Indicative Co-operation Programme (PIC) requested by Cape Verde.

9. Central African Republic

A. *Recent socio-economic developments*

1. *Overall economy*

Real GDP of the Central African Republic grew by about 3 per cent in 1985, resulting in a slight improvement of GDP per capita. In 1986 the combined effect of the decline of dollar-denominated commodity prices and of the CFA franc-dollar exchange rate caused export earnings to fall, resulting in low GDP growth.

2. *Main sectors*

Agriculture is the most important sector of the economy, representing 40 per cent of GDP, employing two-thirds of the active population and providing 60 per cent of export revenues. Following years of drought, the 1985/86 harvest of coffee, one of the major export crops, almost recovered its 1982/83 peak production of over 16,500 tonnes. Assisted by the World Bank, coffee production is being rehabilitated, with particular reliance on production by smallholders. Production of the two major food crops – cassava and maize – has also reached pre-drought levels. The production of diamonds has been recovering steadily since its 1982 low; by 1985 it had already exceeded its 1980 level, and by 1986 diamonds recovered their former position as the country's leading export earner.

3. *Trade and payments*

Exports in 1985 grew by 2 per cent, while imports augmented by 25 per cent, thus widening the trade deficit considerably. In 1986 the growth of diamond production was accompanied by rising dollar prices, resulting in a 12 per cent growth of the dollar value of diamonds and offsetting the losses incurred by other commodities. The sharp drop of cotton prices measured in dollars compounded by the exchange rate developments caused export earnings of this item to fall by 35 per cent, despite a small growth in volume. Coffee exports constituted the weakest area: revenues therefrom decreased by 45 per cent, in terms of CFA francs, largely owing to a decline in volume of over 40 per cent. Exports of wood also were disappointing: their CFA franc value fell by 12 per cent, owing to smaller volumes (reflecting weak demand on the world market), as well as the depreciation of the dollar.

The balance of payments in 1985 was distinguished by a worsening trade deficit and unusually large short-term and unidentified capital outflows. In 1986, the deterioration of the trade deficit continued, but appears to have been offset by larger ODA and other capital inflows, inasmuch as official exchange reserves in 1986 recovered to levels well above those prevailing during the previous two years. In contrast to the sharply rising debt level of the early 1980s, the country's foreign debt, expressed in local currency, grew by less than 5 per cent during 1986, reaching CFAF 131 billion ($406 million) at the end of that year; however, debt service mounted to CFAF 10.7 billion ($31 million) in that year, which corresponds to a debt service/exports ratio of around 30 per cent, as compared to 20 per cent in 1985.

CENTRAL AFRICAN REPUBLIC

1. Population, total and per capita GDP, growth of agricultural and manufacturing output

Year and periods	Population Millions	GDP Total Millions of dollars	GDP Per capita Dollars	GDP Per capita Per cent of LDC average	Agricultural production Total	Agricultural production of which: Food	Manufacturing value-added Total
1985	2.6	675	259	120.5			
				Real growth rates, per cent per annum			
1980-1985	2.4	0.6	-1.8		-0.2	-0.5	-2.3
1984-1985	2.4	2.8	0.4		-5.3	-5.4	1.4
1985-1986	2.4	..	..		9.1	9.8	..

2. Area, demographic indicators and labour force share in agriculture

	Area			Demographic indicators								Labour force
Total	Share of arable land under permanent crops	Share covered by forestry and woodlands	Density	Average life expectancy at birth			Infant mortality as share of live births	Share of population In urban areas	Economically active		Share in agriculture
	1984		1985	M	F	T	1980-1985	1980-1985	1985		
000 km2	Per cent		Pop/km2	Years			Per 1,000	Per cent			
623.0	3.2	57.6	4	41	45	43	142	45	50		66

3. Origins and uses of output; investment

Years	Sectoral origin of GDP Agriculture	Mining	Manufacturing	Services	Uses of GDP Private consumption expenditure	Government consumption expenditure	Gross domestic savings	Investment
				Per cent of total GDP				
1980	40.0	8.3	7.2	35.1	94.5	15.1	-9.6	7.0
1985	37.2	5.3	7.3	40.2	86.5	11.8	1.7	15.0

4. Balance of payments, debt and external assistance

Years	Balance of payments Merchandise trade balance	Balance on services	Balance on current account	Debt service Amortization	Interest	Total	As ratio of exports of goods and services	Debt, Amount outstanding at year-end	External assistance Total	of which: ODA
	Millions of dollars						Per cent	Millions of dollars		
1980	-37.9	-85.9	-140.6	2.0[a]	5.4[a]	7.3[a]	4.3[a]	261.8[a]	127.4	111.0
1985	-36.7	-65.5	-114.0	8.9	8.7	17.6	9.5	349.4	116.8	109.2

5. Trade

Years and periods	Exports Value Mill. of dollars	of which: share of Coffee Per cent	Imports Value Mill. of dollars	of which: share of food Per cent	Terms of trade
1980	115	27.4	81	20.9	100
1985	88	31.4	109	18.0[b]	95

	Value	Volume	Purchasing power	Value	Volume	Index
	Growth rates, per cent per annum					
1980-1985	-5.2	-2.0	-3.0	6.1	8.6	-1.1
1984-1985	2.3	4.0	1.3	25.3	24.1	-2.6
1985-1986	36.4	17.3	27.4	12.8	5.4	8.6

6. Other economic and social indicators

Energy Commercial energy consumption per capita	Transport & communication Commercial vehicles	Telephones	Education Adult literacy rate	School enrolment ratio share of relevant age group Primary M	F	T	Secondary M	F	T	Health Attendance at childbirth by trained personnel	Share of population Immunized against DPT (3 doses)	With access to safe water	Food and nutrition Cereals Consumption per capita	Self-sufficiency ratio	Average daily calorie intake per capita Total	Share of requirements
1984	1983	1985	Around 1985	1982						1984	1982	1985	1985		1985	Between 1982&1985
kg of coal equiv.	Per 1,000 pop.		rate							Per cent			kg	Per cent	Calories	Per cent
38	1.5	2.7	40	98	51	74	24	8	16	..	21.0	13[c]	55	86	2050	91

a/ 1982.   b/ 1983.   c/ Urban only.

B. *Recent policy developments*

1. *Macro-economic policies*

In preparation for the Round Table Conference (Geneva, June 1987) a new Five-Year Plan was drafted, outlining the policies to be followed through 1990. About one-half of the investment programme is directly or indirectly allocated to agriculture. Among the reforms planned for this sector, the most important is the restructuring of cotton production, since current yields per hectare are only around one-half as high as in other countries of the region. With the assistance of the World Bank, SOCADA, which is involved in the marketing of cotton, is being reorganized, while cotton production is being temporarily reduced to make it more efficient. Current subsidization of cotton production is expected to end once production becomes more efficient and world prices return to higher levels. Thereafter production can be expanded.

The cornerstone of the Government's economic policy is the reorganization of the public sector, comprising both the Government itself and the parastatals, from which the Government wants to withdraw. The budget should improve through stricter tax collection and the recovery of tax and customs arrears. Major relief on the expenditure side is expected to come from the freeze of civil service salaries, which has been in force over the last five years. Moreover, the size of the civil service is being reduced, until expenses on salaries are cut to 50 per cent of budget receipts. Incentives are given to civil servants to leave the service and to set up private businesses. Recruitment of staff is governed by a "one for three" rule: for every franc spent on new staff, three francs should be saved elsewhere on the wage bill. In 1986, 2,690 civil servants out of a total of 21,000 were dismissed. In pursuance of this policy the Government intends to set up a data bank covering the civil service so as to spot redundancies more easily. A training programme, designed to improve performance of the remaining officials, will be carried out.

In order to achieve the GDP growth target of 3.5 per cent per year in the period 1986-1990, the Government wants to create an environment that stimulates private investment. To achieve this, the Government intends to disengage from productive and commercial activities, and concentrate on playing a supportive role for the productive sector. In order to counteract the very low level of savings, the Government is stimulating the growth of financial institutions in the rural sector, so that the savings thus mobilized can be used to finance small- and medium-size enterprises.

The Government is trying to stabilize and increase officially-registered diamond and gold exports, the former of which usually rank among the country's two major export-revenue earners. This is being attempted by lowering export taxes, which were reduced by 60 per cent between 1983 and 1985 in the case of diamonds, and by 75 per cent in the case of gold. In fact, an upward trend in officially-recorded exports of diamonds and gold has been recorded since these measures were taken.

2. *Social policies*

Reforms in the educational sector will be geared towards a rehabilitation of the existing system. Access to higher education will be ruled by a quota system, and major departments *(facultés)* will be transformed into separate institutes. While overall supply of and demand for labour are about equal, they do not match qualitatively, implying a need for vocational training, a task put under the aegis of the Ministry of Social Affairs.

To fight the high infant mortality rate (200 per 1,000 before the age of one, and 100 per 1,000 between ages one to five), and the short life expectancy in general, the Plan intends to take the following measures: a mother-and-child health care project is already in the process of execution, and two studies on primary health care will help to identify further measures that must be taken in this field. A project against endemic diseases will entail a vaccination programme and a programme against hepatitis. A subprogramme of the Plan aims at improving the water supply in rural and urban areas, which should prevent the spread of the many water-borne diseases in the Central African Republic.

2. *International support policies*

In September 1986 the World Bank supported the country's structural adjustment programme with credits from IDA and from the Special Facility for Sub-Saharan Africa, totalling $30 million. In 1987 the World Bank granted a further $15 million sectoral adjustment credit to the cotton sector. In June 1987 the International Monetary Fund gave its support with a 12-month stand-by arrangement worth SDR 8 million and a three-year loan from the Structural Adjustment Facility amounting to SDR 14.3 million.

4. *SNPA follow-up*

A Round Table Conference was organized in June 1987 in Geneva, during which the new Five-Year Plan for the period 1986-1990 was presented. The Government's request for support for this Plan was favourably met, and first indications of development aid ($170 million per year) matched the country's stated requirements.

10. Chad

A. *Recent socio-economic developments*

1. *Overall economy*

Good rains since 1985 have permitted some improvement in economic performance. Provisional estimates for that year point to a 4.6 per cent increase in real GDP per capita, a reversal of the negative trend of the past three years. However, the 1985 level of real GDP per capita is still 20 per cent below the 1977 peak.

2. *Main sectors*

Self-sufficiency in coarse grains was achieved in 1986 (as compared to only 50 per cent in 1984), with a record output of 690,000 tonnes. Provisional estimates for 1987 point to a further 9 per cent increase. Donor financial assistance is required for the internal movement of 30,000 tonnes of grains as well as for imports of 35,000 tonnes of wheat and rice (a less than normal deficit in these items). The national herd is expected to regain the pre-drought (1980) level by mid-1987. Grasshopper infestations occurred in 1986 along with the rainfall increase, but damage was reduced by timely spraying. A more serious danger of infestation, exists for 1987, however, if rains approach last year's level.

Oil drilling by a foreign-led consortium, which had started in 1985, was suspended in June 1986, as low world prices made exploitation unprofitable. Drilling, however, was reportedly to resume some time during 1987 and production is expected to reach 120,000 tonnes per year, thereby covering domestic needs. The country is seeking international support for the establishment of a small oil refinery to refine the domestic crude production.

The cumulative impact of the drought has not yet been fully overcome: in late 1986, the level of Lake Chad was still below normal, and the limit of the desert zone remained at 200 km south of the 16th parallel.

3. *Trade and payments*

Cotton normally accounts for nearly 80 per cent of exports. Therefore, foreign exchange earnings have been considerably affected by the low world price for this commodity. The 53 per cent decline of the average unit value of cotton exports between 1984 and 1986 was partly due to the fact that cotton is traded in dollars, a currency which depreciated by over 20 per cent against the French franc (to which the CFA franc is linked) between 1984 and 1986 and by as much as 33 per cent between January 1985 and January 1987. Export prices are thus well below production costs, and losses in this regard during 1986 were estimated at CFAF 10.4 billion (around $30 million), while Treasury losses in terms of revenue foregone were estimated at CFAF 4 billion ($11.6 million). The trade deficit, which almost doubled in 1985, is expected to be even wider in 1986. An encouraging development relates to the modest recovery in world cotton prices since the last quarter of 1986.

B. *Recent policy developments*

1. *Macro-economic policies*

A programme of fiscal reform was launched in 1986, involving increased taxes on oil and luxury goods as well as a reduction in public expenditures. The streamlining of *Cotontchad*, the State-

CHAD

1. Population, total and per capita GDP, growth of agricultural and manufacturing output

Year and periods	Population Millions	GDP Total Millions of dollars	GDP Per capita Dollars	GDP Per capita Per cent of LDC average	Agricultural production Total	Agricultural production of which: Food	Manufacturing value-added Total
1985	5.0	641	128	59.5			
				Real growth rates, per cent per annum			
1980-1985	2.2	-4.4	-6.4		3.2	3.1	-5.5
1984-1985	2.2	6.9	4.6		23.4	24.2	5.4
1985-1986	2.2	..	..		0.6	2.6	..

2. Area, demographic indicators and labour force share in agriculture

	Area		Demographic indicators							Labour force
Total	Share of arable land under permanent crops	Share covered by forestry and woodlands	Density	Average life expectancy at birth			Infant mortality as share of live births	Share of population In urban areas	Economically active	Share in agriculture
	1984		1985	M	F	T	1980-1985	1980-1985	1985	
000 km2	Per cent		Pop/km2	Years			Per 1,000	Per cent		
1284.0	2.5	10.3	4	41	45	43	143	27	36	79

3. Origins and uses of output; investment

Years	Sectoral origin of GDP				Uses of GDP			Investment
	Agriculture	Mining	Manufacturing	Services	Private consumption expenditure	Government consumption expenditure	Gross domestic savings	
					Per cent of total GDP			
1980	40.5	0.8	9.1	46.4	80.1	24.5	-4.7	13.2
1985	46.7	0.5	8.5	42.1	78.9	20.9	0.2	6.6

4. Balance of payments, debt and external assistance

Years	Balance of payments			Debt service			As ratio of exports of goods and services	Debt Amount outstanding at year-end	External assistance Total	of which: ODA
	Merchandise trade balance	Balance on services	Balance on current account	Amortization	Interest	Total				
	Millions of dollars						Per cent	Millions of dollars		
1980	15.7	-27.5	-15.9	0.2a/	1.9a/	2.1a/	3.4a/	156.8a/	33.9	35.3
1985	-104.5	-123.5	-221.0	6.4	2.7	9.1	9.1	167.0	182.7	182.0

5. Trade

Years and periods	Exports Value Mill. of dollars	Exports of which: share of Cotton Per cent	Imports Value Mill. of dollars	Imports of which: share of food Per cent	Terms of trade
1980	71	76.6	74	(23.0)	100
1985	80	81.3b/	190	(18.1)c/	114

	Value	Volume	Purchasing power	Value	Volume	Index
			Growth rates, per cent per annum			
1980-1985	2.4	1.9	4.6	20.8	23.3	2.6
1984-1985	-27.3	-30.7	-28.1	11.1	9.8	3.8
1985-1986	6.2	16.7	3.5	2.6	0.0	-11.3

6. Other economic and social indicators

Energy Commercial energy consumption per capita	Transport & communication Commercial vehicles	Transport & communication Telephones	Education Adult literacy rate	School enrolment ratio share of relevant age group Primary M	Primary F	Primary T	Secondary M	Secondary F	Secondary T	Health Attendance at childbirth by trained personnel	Share of population Immunized against DPT (3 doses)	Share of population With access to safe water	Food and nutrition Cereals Consumption per capita	Cereals Self-sufficiency ratio	Average daily calorie intake per capita Total	Average daily calorie intake per capita Share of requirements
1984	1984	1985	Around 1985	1984						1984	1984	1985	1985		1985	Between 1982&1985
kg of coal equiv.	Per 1,000 pop.						Per cent						kg	Per cent	Calories	Per cent
21	..	0.6	..	55	21	38	11	2	6	..	1.1	..	158	87	1504d/	68

a/ 1982.   b/ 1984.   c/ 1983.   d/ Year other than 1985.

owned cotton marketing board, has been under way since 1986: this programme includes the closing of one-half of the 26 ginning mills, the laying off of 450 employees and the reduction of producer subsidies.

A major tree-planting campaign at the village level was conducted in 1986 under Government supervision.

2. *International support*

Foreign aid to Chad is mostly in the form of grants: 95.5 per cent of total ODA in 1984 as compared to 70.4 per cent for the LDCs as a group, on the basis of OECD estimates. Therefore, total external debt, which amounted to $167 million at the end of 1985, is relatively small as compared to other LDCs (25 per cent of GDP in that year); correspondingly, debt service during the year ($9 million, 77 per cent of which consisted of amortization) represented 10 per cent of merchandise exports.

ODA from all sources peaked in 1985 at $181.7 million as compared to $95 million and $115 million in the two preceding years. Much of the increase, however, was related to drought relief and other emergency assistance and may, therefore, subside along with the improvement in weather conditions.

International assistance to support the above-mentioned streamlining of *Cotontchad* and to finance cotton crop purchases, totalling CFAF 17 billion francs ($47.4 million), was secured in 1986 from France, IDA, the European Development Fund and the Netherlands.

3. *SNPA follow-up*

As a follow-up to the Round Table held in December 1985, sectoral consultations were held in 1986 on transport, cotton and the agro-sylvo-pastoral sector. Two in-country conferences were expected to take place in 1987 on transport infrastructure and human resources, respectively.

11. Comoros

A. *Recent socio-economic developments*

1. *Overall economy*

Growth of GDP slowed down in 1985 to 3.4 per cent in real terms, which is close to the rate of population growth. This was due mostly to the relative stagnation of the agricultural sector and to the completion of major investment projects. In January 1987, a cyclone swept the archipelago, killing a dozen persons and destroying crops and infrastructure.

2. *Main sectors*

Agriculture's share in GDP has declined slightly in the 1980s to about 42 per cent in 1985. Although food output increased in 1985, it did not keep pace with food consumption. The main cash and export crops – vanilla, cloves, and ylang-ylang

– represent about 30 per cent of value added in agriculture. Output of vanilla and ylang-ylang increased in 1985 and 1986, while that of cloves, which had risen in 1985, fell in 1986 mainly because of unfavourable prices. Manufacturing, including handicrafts, accounted for only 6 per cent of GDP in 1985. In 1986, a new addition to this sector was a soap factory using copra as a raw material. Construction and public works, which had accounted for an increasing share of GDP in the period 1980-1984, have decreased in relative importance with the completion, in 1985, of the surfacing of major roads and of the deep water port at Mutsamudu (Anjouan). In spite of its fairly good potential, the tourist industry is still in its infancy. In 1985, there were 162 rooms in the three islands, but the occupancy rate was only about 25 per cent. However, in order to try and reach a critical minimum size in tourism, a new hotel is being built at Malouja (Grand Comoro), which will double the country's hotel room capacity by 1988.

COMOROS

1. Population, total and per capita GDP, growth of agricultural and manufacturing output

Year and periods	Population Millions	GDP Total Millions of dollars	GDP Per capita Dollars	GDP Per capita Per cent of LDC average	Agricultural production Total	Agricultural production of which: Food	Manufacturing value-added Total
1985	0.4	97	219	101.9			
				Real growth rates, per cent per annum			
1980-1985	3.1	4.1	1.0		1.6	1.5	4.7
1984-1985	2.7	3.4	0.7		5.4	5.3	3.6
1985-1986	2.7	..	..		2.1	2.2	..

2. Area, demographic indicators and labour force share in agriculture

Area Total	Area Share of arable land under permanent crops	Area Share covered by forestry and woodlands	Density	Average life expectancy at birth M	Average life expectancy at birth F	Average life expectancy at birth T	Infant mortality as share of live births	Share of population In urban areas	Share of population Economically active	Labour force Share in agriculture
		1984	1985		1980-1985		1980-1985		1985	
000 km2	Per cent		Pop/km2		Years		Per 1,000		Per cent	
2.2	43.3	16.1	205	48	52	50	88	25	46	81

3. Origins and uses of output; investment

Years	Sectoral origin of GDP Agriculture	Sectoral origin of GDP Mining	Sectoral origin of GDP Manufacturing	Sectoral origin of GDP Services	Uses of GDP Private consumption expenditure	Uses of GDP Government consumption expenditure	Uses of GDP Gross domestic savings	Investment
					Per cent of total GDP			
1980	49.3	..	5.2	34.8	65.9	21.5	12.6	34.4
1985	42.1	..	5.8	38.4	70.1	21.4	8.6	41.3

4. Balance of payments, debt and external assistance

Years	Merchandise trade balance	Balance on services	Balance on current account	Amortization	Interest	Total	As ratio of exports of goods and services	Debt Amount outstanding at year-end	External assistance Total	External assistance of which: ODA
	Millions of dollars						Per cent	Millions of dollars		
1980	-9.2	-11.1	-20.2	0.8[a]	1.3[a]	2.1[a]	9.1[a]	81.0[a]	42.8	41.8
1985	-10.0	-35.6	-46.3	0.7	1.9	2.5	12.5	135.1	50.7	47.5

5. Trade

Years and periods	Exports Value Mill. of dollars	Exports of which: share of Vanilla Per cent	Imports Value Mill. of dollars	Imports of which: share of food Per cent	Terms of trade
1980	20	..	33	(22.2)	100
1985	25	66.5	30	(22.2)[b]	..

Years and periods	Value	Volume	Purchasing power	Value	Volume	Index
			Growth rates, per cent per annum			
1980-1985	4.6	..	7.2	-1.9	0.6	..
1984-1985	19.0	..	18.6	0.0	-0.4	..
1985-1986	0.0	..	-1.3	0.0	-1.3	..

6. Other economic and social indicators

Energy Commercial energy consumption per capita	Transport & communication Commercial vehicles	Transport & communication Telephones	Education Adult literacy rate	Education School enrolment ratio share of relevant age group Primary M	Primary F	Primary T	Secondary M	Secondary F	Secondary T	Health Attendance at childbirth by trained personnel	Health Share of population Immunized against DPT (3 doses)	Health Share of population With access to safe water	Food and nutrition Cereals Consumption per capita	Food and nutrition Cereals Self-sufficiency ratio	Food and nutrition Average daily calorie intake per capita Total	Food and nutrition Average daily calorie intake per capita Share of requirements
1984	1984	1982	Around 1985			1980				1981	1984	1985		1985	1985	Between 1982&1985
kg of coal equiv.	Per 1,000 pop.						Per cent						kg	Per cent	Calories	Per cent
42	..	7.9	..	109	78	93	31	16	24	24.0	31.0	..	92	54	2214 [c]	91

a/ 1982.   b/ 1983.   c/ Year other than 1985.

3. *Trade and payments*

In value terms, exports showed an increase in 1985 over 1984, but stagnated in 1986. They are dominated by vanilla (69 per cent of merchandise exports in 1985, 77 per cent in 1986). In 1984, the volume of vanilla exports had been abnormally low, due to delayed shipment following the signature in May 1984 of the three-year Vanilla Agreement (jointly with Madagascar) with importers. "Normal" exports are considered to be 200 tonnes per annum; this figure was almost reached in 1985 (181 tonnes) and was exceeded in 1986 (257 tonnes). Exports of cloves had stabilized at about 1,100 tonnes over the period 1983-1985, but fell to 865 tonnes in 1986. This was mostly due to the decline in world prices in 1986, when Indonesia, by far the world's biggest market for cloves, became a net exporter. Although exports of ylang-ylang essence (used in the perfume industry), increased in volume in 1985 and 1986, when a record 86 tonnes were exported, the value of this export, expressed in Comoros francs, was lower in 1986 than in 1985 and substantially less than in 1982. The lower prices obtained are due partly to competition from synthetic substitutes and partly to the larger share of lower quality products in total exports. The value of total imports declined in national currency terms in both 1985 and 1986 due to the combined effect of lower prices (e.g. of petroleum products) and smaller volumes of imported capital goods. Despite the considerable improvement of exports in 1985 and, 1986, the trade balance remains negative. The invisible account continues to be in structural deficit owing to high freight and insurance costs and the purchase of other services, while the remittances of Comorians living abroad are insufficient to offset the remittances out of the country, including those by expatriate technical assistance personnel.

4. *External debt*

The external debt of the Comoros continued to increase rapidly, from about 44 per cent of GDP in 1981 to over 100 per cent in 1985. Debt servicing has also increased rapidly in the 1980s; for 1985 it amounted to almost 13 per cent of exports of goods and services, and, given the growing amortization payments falling due, all projections show debt service ratios in excess of 30 per cent for the rest of the decade.

5. *Government finance*

In spite of substantial ordinary and extra-ordinary (e.g. STABEX) budgetary assistance from abroad (e.g. through STABEX payments), the global Government deficit remained high in 1985 and 1986. This had to be financed by external and internal borrowing, while arrears to suppliers and on external debt servicing are thought to have increased.

6. *Education*

Several measures have been taken to improve the quality of education, but the strict selection criteria resulting therefrom have led to the reduction of the number of pupils at various levels. Thus, the numbers admitted to secondary school diminished between 1985 and 1986, while the number of teachers in the school system had to be reduced from 3,900 in 1985 to 3,200 in 1986, when the employment of unqualified teachers was discontinued.

B. *Recent policy developments*

1. *Development planning*

Recent macro-economic policies have been guided by the first Interim Plan for Economic and Social Development 1983-1986, published in mid-1984. The main objective has been to lessen food dependency and to improve internal and external transport links. A new Plan was in preparation in 1987.

2. *The Investment Code*

In 1984, the Government adopted an Investment Code which accords privileged status *(régime privilégié)* to entreprises, including foreign ones, whose activities are considered to be particularly beneficial to the economy. Among the many requests received for such privileged status, 21 had been conditionally approved by early 1987, pending a final decision by the Council of Ministers.

3. *Utilization of Mutsamudu harbour*

The construction of the deep water port at Mutsamudu was completed in 1985. This was an expensive investment, costing 13 billion Comoros francs ($29 million), equivalent to more than 25 per cent of GDP, but was justified by the need to reduce the international transport costs for the country. However, by 1987 the complex logistical problems of using this facility as a transshipment harbour for the archipelago had not yet been solved.

4. *SNPA follow-up*

The first Round Table Meeting (Solidarity Conference) for the Comoros was held in May 1984. The dates of a follow-up meeting had not yet been determined when this report was prepared.

12. Democratic Yemen

A. *Recent socio-economic developments*

1. *Overall economy*

In 1986, economic performance deteriorated further as a result of: (*a*) the adverse effects of the violent internal conflict in January 1986 on the productive sectors and infrastructure, and (*b*) the decline in external assistance and workers' remittances. Although no estimates for real GDP growth are available since 1984, the small decline of per capita GDP registered in the latter year probably accelerated to a much more significant deterioration of per capita GDP in the two subsequent years.

2. *Main sectors*

A major constraint on increased agricultural production is the small size of arable land, which is less than 1 per cent of the country's total area, while the area actually under cultivation only covers about 0.17 per cent. The fish catch was estimated at 90,000 tonnes in 1986, i.e. 8 per cent over the planned target, although still below the peak of 162,000 tonnes achieved in 1977. This outturn was due to the modernization of the fishing fleet and the related infrastructure. In 1986, production in the manufacturing sector declined by 10 per cent. The Aden oil refinery, the main manufacturing enterprise, was operating at about 20 per cent of capacity, as compared to 40 per cent in 1985. Petroleum has been discovered in commercial quantities in the Shabwa region. Furthermore oil exploration and sharing agreements covering an area of about 36,000 km ^{2} have been signed with two foreign firms. In the infrastructure sector, a sum of $60 million was provided by Arab development funds to finance the Aden Port Development Scheme, including the construction of four deep-water berths and cargo handling equipment. The second stage of the Hiswah thermal power station is to be implemented at a total cost of $138 million, all of which is to be provided by the USSR.

3. *Trade and payments*

The target for domestic export earnings in 1986, including value added by the refinery, was set at $57 million. However, according to balance-of-payments figures (which include the value added of re-exported petroleum products, but exclude the large crude oil component in both directions), export earnings amounted to $29 million only. Thus the 1986 exports not only fell short of the target, but were below the 1985 level of $40.9 million. This was mainly due to the decline in the earnings of the oil refinery. Imports in 1986, estimated at $483 million, were 30 per cent below their 1985 level. In 1987, exports are projected at about $60 million, i.e. 5.3 per cent above the previous year's target, while imports are planned to remain at their 1986 level. Total external debt was estimated at about $1.5 billion at the end of 1985, as compared to $1.1 billion at the end of 1984. Debt service in 1985 were estimated to correspond to 99 per cent of exports of goods and services as compared to 79 per cent in 1984.

4. *Budget*

The 1987 Investment Programme allocates a total of $428 million to be distributed among energy, agriculture, industry and communications sectors. Domestic resources will provide about 40 per cent of the total outlay.

DEMOCRATIC YEMEN

1. Population, total and per capita GDP, growth of agricultural and manufacturing output

Year and periods	Population Millions	GDP Total Millions of dollars	GDP Per capita Dollars	GDP Per capita Per cent of LDC average	Agricultural production Total	Agricultural production of which: Food	Manufacturing value-added Total
1985	2.3	(964)	420[a]	195.3			
				Real growth rates, per cent per annum			
1980-1985	3.1	1.9[b]	1.1[b]		0.6	0.3	4.4[c]
1984-1985	3.1	..	..		-0.7	-0.7	..
1985-1986	3.1	..	..		-2.0	-2.2	..

2. Area, demographic indicators and labour force share in agriculture

Area Total 000 km2	Area Share of arable land under permanent crops 1984 Per cent	Area Share covered by forestry and woodlands 1984 Per cent	Density 1985 Pop/km2	Average life expectancy at birth M 1980-1985 Years	Average life expectancy at birth F 1980-1985 Years	Average life expectancy at birth T 1980-1985 Years	Infant mortality as share of live births 1980-1985 Per 1,000	Share of population In urban areas Per cent	Share of population Economically active 1985 Per cent	Labour force Share in agriculture 1985 Per cent
333.0	0.5	4.7	6	47	50	48	135	37	26	36

3. Origins and uses of output; investment

Years	Sectoral origin of GDP Agriculture	Mining	Manufacturing	Services	Uses of GDP Private consumption expenditure	Government consumption expenditure	Gross domestic savings	Investment
				Per cent of total GDP				
1980	16.0	..	10.1	60.6	..	..	..	..
1985	10.5[a]	..	11.3[a]	61.1[d]	..	..	..	..

4. Balance of payments, debt and external assistance

Years	Balance of payments Merchandise trade balance	Balance on services	Balance on current account	Debt service Amortization	Interest	Total	As ratio of exports of goods and services Per cent	Debt Amount outstanding at year-end	External assistance Total	External assistance of which: ODA
		Millions of dollars						Millions of dollars		
1980	..	..	..	24.8[d]	10.0[d]	34.8[d]	18.1[d]	842.5[d]	255.7	129.8
1985	..	..	..	102.9	29.6	132.5	83.9	1573.4	350.6	348.3

5. Trade

Years and periods	Exports Value Mill. of dollars	Exports of which: share of Petroleum products Per cent	Imports Value Mill. of dollars	Imports of which: share of food Per cent	Terms of trade
1980	779	94.8	652	(14.0)	100
1985	690	95.9[a]	1290	(24.3)[e]	..

	Value	Volume	Purchasing power	Value	Volume	Index
			Growth rates, per cent per annum			
1980-1985	-2.4	..	0.0	14.6	17.5	..
1984-1985	7.0	..	6.5	-16.4	-16.7	..
1985-1986	0.0	..	-1.3	-10.9	-12.0	..

6. Other economic and social indicators

Energy Commercial energy consumption per capita 1984 kg of coal equiv.	Transport & communication Commercial vehicles 1981	Transport & communication Telephones 1984 Per 1,000 pop.	Education Adult literacy rate Around 1985	Education School enrolment ratio share of relevant age group Primary M 1983	Primary F 1983	Primary T 1983	Secondary M 1983	Secondary F 1983	Secondary T 1983	Health Attendance at childbirth by trained personnel 1982	Health Share of population Immunized against DPT (3 doses) 1984	Health Share of population With access to safe water 1983	Food and nutrition Cereals Consumption per capita 1985 kg	Food and nutrition Cereals Self-sufficiency ratio 1985 Per cent	Food and nutrition Average daily calorie intake per capita Total 1985 Calories	Food and nutrition Average daily calorie intake per capita Share of requirements Between 1982&1985 Per cent
										Per cent						
851	10.1	11.7	41	96	35	66	26	11	19	10.0	7.0	50	199	25	2337	94

a/ 1984   b/ 1980-1984   c/ 1980-1982   d/ 1982   e/ 1983.

B. *Recent policy developments*

1. *Macro-economic policies*

The Third Five-Year Development Plan (1986-1990) was approved by the Council of Ministers in April 1987. The total investment outlay in the Plan is estimated at $1.7 billion. The Plan gives priority to increasing production in industry, agriculture, and fisheries, and improving infrastructure facilities, but the highest priority is accorded to industry, to which almost 46.6 per cent of the investment volume is allocated. Total budgetary revenue during the Plan period is estimated at $2.88 billion, 62.7 per cent of which is to be provided from domestic sources.

2. *International support measures*

Concessional financial flows were estimated at $348.3 million in 1985, an increase of 80 per cent over the previous year's level. The USSR has agreed to provide 50,000 tonnes of crude oil annually for three years, starting in 1987, on a grant basis.

13. Djibouti

A. *Recent socio-economic developments*

1. *Overall economy*

Real GDP declined in 1986 by about 1.5 per cent as compared to an average annual growth rate of 1.3 per cent between 1980 and 1985. This reflects the continuing stagnation in the activities of the transport, construction and services sectors, which together account for over 70 per cent of GDP. The decline in per capita income experienced since 1980 thus worsened in 1986. The consumer price index, reflecting the expatriate consumption basket, increased by an annual rate of 11.6 per cent in 1985 and 22.5 per cent in 1986.

2. *Main sectors*

Value added in the tertiary sector increased by 1 per cent in 1985 as compared to 1.6 per cent in 1984. The Port of Djibouti is to be further improved by expanding the container terminal, rehabilitating the petroleum berth and building a repair and maintenance workshop and a warehouse for containers. The total cost of these projects is estimated at $22 million, to be provided mainly by Arab funds. Agricultural production, chiefly livestock, fruits and vegetables, increased by 3.7 per cent, while industrial production, concentrated in textiles and bottling of mineral water, only increased by 0.9 per cent.

3. *Trade and payments*

The pressure on the balance of payments persisted due to declining external assistance, increasing debt service payments and the drop in trade and transit earnings. Export earnings, excluding re-exports and services, fell between 1985 and 1986 to a level of $25 million, i.e. by 3.8 per cent. Imports are estimated to have increased by 4.5 per cent, reaching a level of $115 million. The balance on current account has been in deficit since 1984, but the deficit increased almost three-fold between 1984 and 1986. Total external debt was estimated to have grown by 70 per cent to a level of $244 million at the end of 1985, while debt service payments were estimated to have doubled between 1984 and 1985 to reach $35 million, which is equivalent to 25 per cent of total export earnings for goods and services.

4. *Budget*

Government expenditure projected in the 1987 budget is estimated at DF 22.2 billion ($125 million), i.e. about 3.1 per cent below actual outlays in 1986. This is due to the freeze of salaries, which constitute the major item in recurrent expenditure, and the stagnation of the capital budget, which had already been cut by 27 per cent in 1986. Direct budgetary assistance, provided mainly by France, increased by 25 per cent between 1986 and 1987 to a level of FFr 82.5 million

DJIBOUTI

1. Population, total and per capita GDP, growth of agricultural and manufacturing output

Year and periods	Population Millions	GDP Total Millions of dollars	GDP Per capita Dollars	GDP Per capita Per cent of LDC average	Agricultural production Total	Agricultural production of which: Food	Manufacturing value-added Total
1985	0.4	205	567[a]				
				Real growth rates, per cent per annum			
1980-1985	3.3	1.3	-1.9		..	..	0.6
1984-1985	2.8	0.6	-2.2		..	..	0.9
1985-1986	3.2	..	..		..	..	..

2. Area, demographic indicators and labour force share in agriculture

Area Total	Area Share of arable land under permanent crops 1984	Area Share covered by forestry and woodlands 1984	Density 1985	Average life expectancy at birth M	Average life expectancy at birth F	Average life expectancy at birth T 1982-1985	Infant mortality as share of live births 1980-1985	Share of population In urban areas	Share of population Economically active 1985	Labour force Share in agriculture
000 km2	Per cent		Pop/km2	Years			Per 1,000	Per cent		
22.0	..	0.3	17	..	..	48	..	77	..	2[b]

3. Origins and uses of output; investment

Years	Sectoral origin of GDP Agriculture	Mining	Manufacturing	Services	Uses of GDP Private consumption expenditure	Government consumption expenditure	Gross domestic savings	Investment
					Per cent of total GDP			
1980	4.4	..	10.2	75.6	67.1	37.8	-4.9	18.5
1985	5.8	..	10.2	70.9	76.8	36.1	-12.9	23.2

4. Balance of payments, debt and external assistance

Years	Balance of payments Merchandise trade balance	Balance on services	Balance on current account	Debt service Amortization	Interest	Total	As ratio of exports of goods and services	Debt Amount outstanding at year-end	External assistance Total	External assistance of which: ODA
	Millions of dollars						Per cent	Millions of dollars		
1980	..	..	..	2.8[c]	1.3[c]	4.0[c]	2.3[c]	47.0[c]	71.1	71.2
1985	..	..	..	26.2	8.5	34.7	23.1	243.5	99.4	77.7

5. Trade

Years and periods	Exports Value Mill. of dollars	Exports of which: share of Clothing Per cent	Imports Value Mill. of dollars	Imports of which: share of food Per cent	Terms of trade
1980	19	..	125	(32.9)	100
1985	26	7.4[d]	110	(24.5)[d]	..

	Value	Volume	Purchasing power	Value	Volume	Index
			Growth rates, per cent per annum			
1980-1985	6.5	..	9.1	-2.5	-0.1	..
1984-1985	0.0	..	-0.4	0.0	-0.4	..
1985-1986	-3.8	..	-5.1	4.5	3.2	..

6. Other economic and social indicators

Energy Commercial energy consumption per capita 1984 kg of coal equiv.	Transport & communication Commercial vehicles 1984 Per 1,000 pop.	Transport & communication Telephones 1985	Education Adult literacy rate Around 1985	Education School enrolment ratio share of relevant age group Primary M	Primary F	Primary T	Secondary M	Secondary F	Secondary T	Health Attendance at childbirth by trained personnel 1984	Health Share of population Immunized against DPT (3 doses) 1985	Share of population With access to safe water 1985	Food and nutrition Cereals Consumption per capita 1985 kg	Cereals Self-sufficiency ratio 1985 Per cent	Average daily calorie intake per capita Total 1985 Calories	Average daily calorie intake per capita Share of requirements Between 1982&1985 Per cent
				between 1982 & 1985												
									Per cent							
263	18.9	22.2	..	..	..	32	..	..	8	73.0	20.0	43	172	..	..	..

[a] Income accruing to indigenous population.   [b] Year other than 1985.   [c] 1982.   [d] 1983.

(about $13.8 million) and represented 11 per cent of total budgetary expenditure. This has helped the Government to replenish the Reserve Fund, which had been drawn down heavily in 1986.

5. *Social developments*

As part of the WHO's expanded immunization campaign, the Government has continued its mass vaccination programme focusing on children aged between two months and five years and women between 14 and 45 years. A project to improve the production capacity, storage and distribution of safe drinking water will be implemented at a cost of $16.1 million provided by the African Development Bank.

B. *Recent policy developments*

1. *Macro-economic policies*

Austerity measures were introduced in 1986 to counter the previous decline in the budgetary assistance provided by France and Arab States and the fall in income generated by the tertiary sector. A 10 per cent cut in public expenditure and stretchout of budgetary commitments were implemented in 1986. To increase revenue, a 25 per cent surtax on luxury goods was imposed and measures to improve tax collection were introduced. The Djibouti franc has been pegged to the US dollar at the rate of DF 177.721 per dollar since 1973. As a result it appreciated considerably against the French franc, the currency of Djibouti's major donor, from an average of DF 42.1 per French franc in 1980 to DF 19.8 per French franc in 1985. Accordingly the level of French assistance in local currency terms declined in those years. However, this level was at least partially reversed, inasmuch as the exchange rate of the Djibouti franc to the French franc fell again to DF 29.2 during the first half of 1987.

2. *International support measures*

The net inflow of concessional aid to Djibouti in 1985 amounted to $77.7 million, about 33 per cent below the 1984 level.

3. *SNPA follow-up*

The sectoral consultations for the energy sector, planned for early 1987, were rescheduled for late 1987.

14. Equatorial Guinea

A. *Recent socio-economic developments*

1. *Overall economy*

Equatorial Guinea faced serious difficulties in 1986. Cocoa production, the main economic activity of the country, fell severely, while the crisis of the banking system culminated in an almost total lack of liquidity during 1986. The two commercial banks of the country, the State-owned Banco de Credito y Desarrollo and the Banco Exterior de Guinea Ecuatorial [Guinextebank], did not fully respect the credit limits established by the Bank of Central African States [BEAC]. This in turn led to large-scale capital flight, made possible by the convertibility of the national currency, the CFA franc, within the French franc area. This crisis of confidence was partially alleviated by (*a*) the establishment of a branch of the Banque Internationale pour l'Afrique Occidentale [BIAO], a joint venture of the Government with private domestic investors, as well as (*b*) Spain's agreement to cover a part of the deficit of Guinextebank.

2. *Main sectors*

The decline of cocoa production was due to climatic conditions, depressed world market prices, and lack of incentives to producers while the four-fold increase in the price of chemical inputs during the 1985/86 crop year as a result of

EQUATORIAL GUINEA

1. Population, total and per capita GDP, growth of agricultural and manufacturing output

Year and periods	Population Millions	GDP Total Millions of dollars	GDP Per capita Dollars	GDP Per capita Per cent of LDC average	Agricultural production Total	Agricultural production of which: Food	Manufacturing value-added Total
1985	0.4	75	192	89.3			
				Real growth rates, per cent per annum			
1980-1985	2.2	2.5	0.3		..	..	4.9
1984-1985	2.1	7.3	5.1		..	..	18.7
1985-1986	2.4	..	..		..	..	..

2. Area, demographic indicators and labour force share in agriculture

	Area Total	Area Share of arable land under permanent crops 1984	Area Share covered by forestry and woodlands 1984	Density 1985	Demographic indicators Average life expectancy at birth M	Demographic indicators Average life expectancy at birth F	Demographic indicators Average life expectancy at birth T 1980-1985	Demographic indicators Infant mortality as share of live births 1980-1985	Share of population In urban areas	Share of population Economically active 1985	Labour force Share in agriculture
	000 km2	Per cent	Per cent	Pop/km2	Years	Years	Years	Per 1,000	Per cent	Per cent	
	28.1	8.2	46.2	14	42	46	44	137	60	43	61

3. Origins and uses of output; investment

Years	Sectoral origin of GDP Agriculture	Sectoral origin of GDP Mining	Sectoral origin of GDP Manufacturing	Sectoral origin of GDP Services	Uses of GDP Private consumption expenditure	Uses of GDP Government consumption expenditure	Uses of GDP Gross domestic savings	Investment
				Per cent of total GDP				
1980	40.6	..	5.1	47.6	73.4	36.2	-9.6	19.4
1985	45.7	..	4.6	43.7	57.7	28.7	13.6	14.5

4. Balance of payments, debt and external assistance

Years	Balance of payments Merchandise trade balance	Balance of payments Balance on services	Balance of payments Balance on current account	Debt service Amortization	Debt service Interest	Debt service Total	Debt service As ratio of exports of goods and services	Debt Amount outstanding at year-end	External assistance Total	External assistance of which: ODA
	Millions of dollars						Per cent	Millions of dollars	Millions of dollars	
1980	..	..	..	1.7a/	2.3a/	4.0a/	22.2a/	124.0a/	10.0	9.3
1985	..	..	..	1.0	3.3	4.4	18.3	140.8	20.8	20.4

5. Trade

Years and periods	Exports Value Mill. of dollars	Exports of which: share of Cocoa Per cent	Imports Value Mill. of dollars	Imports of which: share of food Per cent	Terms of trade
1980	14	69.1	26	27.8	100
1985	20	68.9b/	30	23.5b/	..

	Value	Volume	Purchasing power	Value	Volume	Index
			Growth rates, per cent per annum			
1980-1985	7.4	..	10.1	2.9	5.5	..
1984-1985	0.0	..	-0.4	0.0	-0.4	..
1985-1986	0.0	..	-1.3	0.0	-1.3	..

6. Other economic and social indicators

Energy Commercial energy consumption per capita	Transport & communication Commercial vehicles	Transport & communication Telephones	Education Adult literacy rate	Education School enrolment ratio share of relevant age group Primary M	Education Primary F	Education Primary T	Education Secondary M	Education Secondary F	Education Secondary T	Health Attendance at childbirth by trained personnel	Health Share of population Immunized against DPT (3 doses)	Health Share of population With access to safe water	Food and nutrition Cereals Consumption per capita	Food and nutrition Cereals Self-sufficiency ratio	Food and nutrition Average daily calorie intake per capita Total	Food and nutrition Average daily calorie intake per capita Share of requirements
1984	1984	1981	1980	1983			1982			1984	1984	1983	1985		1985	Between 1982&1985
kg of coal equiv.	Per 1,000 pop.			M F T			M F T			Per cent			kg	Per cent	Calories	Per cent
91	..	3.1	37	 108			 10			..	..	47c/	19	..	..	..

a/ 1982.　　　b/ 1984.　　　c/ Urban only.

the general domestic inflation registered in 1985 caused these inputs to represent about 50 per cent of the total production cost. Timber production of around 138,000 m^3 in 1986 represented an increase of 54 per cent over 1985. Progress in raising production of coffee has been slow.

3. *Trade and payments*

In 1986, the value of cocoa exports fell by 24 per cent, causing a considerable decline in tax revenues and aggravating the crisis of the banking system due to the non-reimbursement of credits. However, timber exports increased by 50 per cent, more than offsetting the decline in cocoa exports. Debt service payments due in 1986 were estimated at $5 million, equivalent to one quarter of merchandise export earnings. Equatorial Guinea's total external debt amounted to $141 million at the end of 1985, as compared to $104 million at the end of 1984. Preliminary figures indicate that the current account deficit of the balance of payments in 1986 was equivalent to about 20 per cent of the value of exports, compared to 55 per cent in 1985.

4. *Budget*

Current revenues were almost 30 per cent lower than expected owing to the reduction of receipts from cocoa export duties; moreover, the usability of tax revenue was limited by the liquidity problem, since commercial banks were unable to honour cheques representing government revenue. In spite of a sharp reduction in current and capital expenditures, it was not possible to avoid a major budget deficit. Foreign debt obligations constitute an important constraint on fiscal policy, i.e., interest and amortization were equivalent to almost 80 per cent of current revenue in 1986.

B. *Recent policy developments*

1. *Macro-economic policies*

Prevailing socio-economic and financial problems have confirmed the need for structural adjustment. During 1986, the Government continued its efforts to restructure its economic policy with a view to greater participation by the private sector in economic development. One of the Government's major concerns has been the achievement of fiscal and balance-of-payments equilibria,

while keeping up external debt service. Measures have been taken to co-ordinate short- and medium-term policies. The monitoring of the self-imposed discipline in fiscal and monetary policies and practices is one of the important results of the country's membership in the Central African Economic and Customs Union (UDEAC) and the Bank of Central African States (BEAC).

2. *International support policies*

Equatorial Guinea continued to depend heavily on external assistance. In 1986, 58 per cent of public consumption as well as 85 per cent of public investment were financed by external sources. Equatorial Guinea's first stand-by arrangement with the IMF expired in June 1986, with the entire amount available (SDR 9.2 million) having been drawn. Loans from IDA ($6 million) and the Sub-Saharan African Facility ($4 million) were approved by the World Bank to aid the country in its attempt to increase productive capacity and exports during a critical phase of the Government's economic rehabilitation programme. Spain extended Ptas 1,925 million ($13.75 million) in credits to Equatorial Guinea in 1986 under the Bilateral Co-operation Programme, after a year of relative disengagement attributed to Equatorial Guinea's increased co-operation with France. Under the United States foreign aid bill for FY 1987/88.[145] Equatorial Guinea was to receive $1.94 million in economic assistance, twice as much as the allocation for FY 1986/87. The European Fund for Development (EDF) approved a total aid package of ECU 10 million (about $11.5 million) until 1990, of which ECU 2 million ($2.3 million) will consist of risk capital from the European Investment Bank and ECU 1 million ($1.15 million) of compensatory financing under the STABEX scheme. The emphasis of the EDF projects will be placed on forest road construction. A three-year fishing agreement with the EC adopted in January 1987 includes a licensing fee of ECU 20 per tonne.

The Government has continued its efforts to expand and diversify the external sources of finance. In this respect, a new agreement was signed with Italy for the financing of projects, and consultations with Japan are well advanced. Some African countries, such as Morocco, Nigeria, Gabon, and Zaire among others, have also shown interest in supporting Equatorial Guinea. It should be noted that France has increased its assistance, with particular emphasis on infrastructural sectors,

---

[145] The US fiscal year (FY) ends on 30 September.

such as transport, communications and energy, apart from fiscal and financial policy formulation and monitoring.

3. *SNPA follow-up*

An important element in the Government's pursuit of economic policy adjustment has been a UNDP-assisted Donors' Round Table. Although a Round Table meeting has not yet taken place, donors have already shown interest in some projects that support these policies. In preparation for such a Round Table, the Government has formulated global and sectoral development strategies for the period 1987-1991. Government priorities have been established and coherent development initiatives have been defined. In this manner, co-ordination between the Government and donors as well as among the latter – both bilateral and multilateral – has been strengthened.

15. Ethiopia

A. *Recent socio-economic developments*

1. *Overall economy*

In FY 1985/86 [146] the Ethiopian economy recovered from the disastrous drought of the previous year. Sufficient rains led to a revival of agriculture, the mainstay of the economy, which activated a variety of economic activities closely linked to it. As a result GDP grew by 11.3 per cent over its level in FY 1984/85, more than recouping that year's 7 per cent fall in GDP. However, with a population growth of 2.9 per cent per annum, per capita GDP remained 2 per cent below the level of two years earlier. The rate of inflation dropped from 18 per cent in the previous year to 4.6 per cent in FY 1985/86. Food prices, which had soared by 25 per cent in 1984/85, rose by a relatively modest 5 per cent. On the assumption of good climatic conditions, it may take another three years to overcome the impact of the drought and achieve a full recovery of the economy.

2. *Main sectors*

In FY 1985/86 agriculture grew by more than 22 per cent over the previous year's level. Although food production performed well, it did not reach pre-drought harvest figures and fell short of requirements. Increases in cash crop production – largely coffee – were partly due to more acreage under cultivation. Generally the agricultural sector still suffers from inadequate supplies of inputs,

poor infrastructural facilities, especially as regards the distribution network, an ineffective credit system and a generally low level of investment. In addition, producer price increases have been inadequate. The performance of industry has been positive, with 4 per cent growth as against FY 1984/85, while the service sector grew by 4.5 per cent. Manufacturing, especially agro-industries, benefited from the upturn of agricultural production, while import-dependent industries faced difficulties due to foreign exchange shortages.

3. *Trade and payments*

Export earnings have been favourably influenced by an increased volume of output and higher world market prices for coffee, the country's major foreign-currency earner. Coffee export receipts in FY 1985/86 grew by 27.4 per cent as against FY 1984/85, contributing 72 per cent to total export earnings, well above the 62 per cent share of previous years. As imports could be kept at about the same level as in the previous year – a consequence of lower commercial food imports and stricter import controls – it was possible to reduce the huge trade deficit of Birr 1.4 billion ($676 million) incurred during FY 1984/85 to Birr 939 million ($454 million) in the subsequent fiscal year.

As a result of the substantial famine relief mobilized by the international community for the victims of the drought, Ethiopia experienced an unprecedented influx of financial flows in 1985, amounting to $906.3 million, or 70 per cent more than in 1984, which placed Ethiopia in the third rank among LDC aid beneficiaries (behind Ban-

_____
[146] The fiscal year (FY) ends 7 July.

ETHIOPIA

1. Population, total and per capita GDP, growth of agricultural and manufacturing output

Year and periods	Population Millions	GDP[a] Total Millions of dollars	GDP[a] Per capita Dollars	GDP[a] Per capita Per cent of LDC average	Agricultural production Total	Agricultural production of which: Food	Manufacturing value-added Total
1985	43.4	4729	109	50.7			
			Real growth rates, per cent per annum				
1980-1985	2.8	-0.0	-2.8		-0.0	0.1	4.1[b]
1984-1985	2.8	-7.0	-9.6		5.9	9.9	..
1985-1986	2.8	..	..		4.9	3.2	..

2. Area, demographic indicators and labour force share in agriculture

Area Total	Area Share of arable land under permanent crops	Area Share covered by forestry and woodlands	Density	Average life expectancy at birth M	Average life expectancy at birth F	Average life expectancy at birth T	Infant mortality as share of live births	Share of population In urban areas	Share of population Economically active	Labour force Share in agriculture
		1984	1985		1980-1985		1980-1985		1985	
000 km2	Per cent		Pop/km2		Years		Per 1,000		Per cent	
1221.9	11.4	22.7	35	39	43	41	155	15	44	77

3. Origins and uses of output; investment

Years	Agriculture	Mining	Manufacturing	Services	Private consumption expenditure	Government consumption expenditure	Gross domestic savings	Investment
	Sectoral origin of GDP				Uses of GDP			
				Per cent of total GDP				
1980	50.6	0.1	10.9	33.9	80.0	15.2	4.8	10.1
1985	44.3	0.1[c]	11.1[c]	35.9[c]	86.5	19.7	-6.2	10.2

4. Balance of payments, debt and external assistance

Years	Merchandise trade balance	Balance on services	Balance on current account	Amortization	Interest	Total	As ratio of exports of goods and services	Amount outstanding at year-end	Total	of which: ODA
	Balance of payments			Debt service				Debt	External assistance	
	Millions of dollars						Per cent	Millions of dollars		
1980	..	..	..	40.9[d]	28.2[d]	69.1[d]	11.9[d]	1239.3[d]	269.9	270.2
1985	..	..	..	84.3	40.4	124.7	22.3	1911.1	953.1	884.1

5. Trade

Years and periods	Value Mill. of dollars	of which: share of Coffee Per cent	Value Mill. of dollars	of which: share of food Per cent	Terms of trade
	Exports		Imports		
1980	425	64.1	722	7.9	100
1985	333	62.8	996	29.8	95

	Value	Volume	Purchasing power	Value	Volume	Index
			Growth rates, per cent per annum			
1980-1985	-4.8	-1.9	-2.8	6.6	8.8	-1.0
1984-1985	-20.1	-14.9	-20.3	5.7	5.5	-6.4
1985-1986	77.2	32.6	83.5	7.4	11.3	38.5

6. Other economic and social indicators

Energy Commercial energy consumption per capita	Transport & communication Commercial vehicles	Transport & communication Telephones	Adult literacy rate	School enrolment ratio share of relevant age group Primary M	Primary F	Primary T	Secondary M	Secondary F	Secondary T	Attendance at childbirth by trained personnel	Immunized against DPT (3 doses)	With access to safe water	Cereals Consumption per capita	Cereals Self-sufficiency ratio	Average daily calorie intake per capita Total	Average daily calorie intake per capita Share of requirements
				Education							Health Share of population		Food and nutrition			
1984	1982	1985	1983			1983				1984	1982	1985		1985	1985	Between 1982&1985
kg of coal equiv.	Per 1,000 pop.							Per cent					kg	Per cent	Calories	Per cent
17	0.4	2.8	55[e]	48	29	39	14	8	11	58.0	6.0	14	140	88	1681	93

a/ Years ending 7 July.   b/ 1980-1983.   c/ 1983.   d/ 1982.   e/ Age group 10+.

gladesh and Sudan). Most of the resources (93 per cent) were provided in the form of grants and concessional loans. ODA from DAC countries and multilateral institutions largely financed by them more than doubled, accounting for 78 per cent of the total inflow, while the socialist countries of Eastern Europe also raised their assistance by 16 per cent to $196.3 million.

Total external debt stood at $1,868.7 million at the end of 1985, an increase of about 21 per cent over the end of 1984. All but 4 per cent of this debt was long term, and all of it was public or publicly guaranteed. The growth in debt was largely due to concessional and commercial loans contracted with OECD donors and creditors to import food during the famine. The ratio of debt service to exports of goods and services fell from 13.8 per cent in 1984 to 10.9 per cent in 1985 and remained manageable. During 1985 international reserves recovered from their historical low of $30 million, approaching $150 million by the end of that year and growing to $250 million by the end of 1986. The latter amount covered nearly three months of import requirements.

4. *Budget*

Government finances in FY 1985/86 were dominated on both the income and expenditure sides by the effects of the drought, which necessitated higher expenditures for famine relief and agricultural rehabilitation, while further eroding the already weak tax base and inadequate tax collection system. In 1985, the Government introduced drastic austerity measures consisting of expenditure cuts and compulsory contributions for famine relief. The latter amounted to one month's wages/income for urban employees and farmers, 1 per cent of public company turnover and shareholder profits, and 2 per cent of turnover of private entrepreneurs. As a result, non-tax revenues increased by 39 per cent and total domestic revenues also grew slightly, despite the income losses of large parts of the population. But inasmuch as total expenditures, especially capital expenditures, also increased, the budget deficit almost doubled compared with the previous year, to reach 10.6 per cent of GDP. Nevertheless, money supply grew by only about 16 per cent owing to tight Government control on domestic credit.

B. *Recent policy developments*

1. *Macro-economic policies*

The Government has concentrated on the consolidation of its resettlement and villagisation programme. In the context of the resettlement pro-

gramme, food crops were planted and requirements of food, drinking water, health care, sanitation, roads and energy in a number of areas effectively met. Another 180,000 families are to be moved to more fertile areas by FY 1988/89. The villagisation programme for FY 1986/87 aims at establishing 5,146 new villages, for which nearly 1 million houses are being built. This will increase the number of villagised peasants to more than 8.5 million out of a total peasant population of an estimated 37 million. The emphasis of the three-year Development Plan for FY 1986/87-1988/89, which is a part of the Ten-Year Perspective Plan, focuses on the alleviation of food shortages through an increase in the production of food crops and measures against drought. It also stipulates efforts to enhance export capacity and diversification. Of the projected fixed capital investments, the lion's share (24.4 per cent) going to agriculture, while transport and communications together are to receive 14.5 per cent. Energy, industry and water resources come next in the order of priority. Total gross fixed investments will increase from 9.4 per cent of GDP in FY 1985/86 to 16.4 per cent in 1988/89, of which domestic resources are expected to finance 47.6 per cent. The Plan projects an annual GDP growth rate of 6.3 per cent, with agricultural output growing by 6.8 per cent annually, industry by 8.3 per cent and the service sector by 4 per cent. During the Plan period the Government will also embark upon the preparatory stage of a wide-ranging environmental programme to begin in FY 1988/89, which is designed to eradicate drought permanently.

2. *International support policies*

The Government considers that during FY 1986/87 6.7 million people were still dependent on food aid, estimated at 1.7 million tonnes of grain. Of this, donors were expected to contribute 70 per cent, while the rest was to be provided internally through the Relief and Rehabilitation Commission. By September 1986, donor pledges had amounted to 995,000 tonnes, of which 615,000 tonnes had been delivered. In 1986 IDA approved a credit of SDR 39.6 million ($45 million) to improve the supply of firewood and building poles in an attempt to halt the deforestation, and another credit of SDR 53.7 million ($62 million) for the rehabilitation of the energy sector. Ethiopia receives the largest single country allocation under Lomé III – ECU 230 million (about $265 million) – of which the major part will be devoted to agriculture.

16. Gambia

A. *Recent socio-economic developments*

1. *Overall economy*

GDP recorded an impressive real growth of 8.4 per cent in FY 1985/86,[147] producing the first positive per capita growth in three years. The momentum was maintained in FY 1986/87 when real GDP grew further by 5.3 per cent. This is due in large measure to the economic and financial reforms undertaken under the Economic Recovery Programme (ERP) as well as the strong recovery of agricultural output. The currency was floated in January 1986 and by the end of six months it had undergone a depreciation of 54 per cent against the US dollar, but remained virtually stable during the subsequent nine months. Inflation rose to an estimated rate of 56 per cent between 1985 and 1986.

2. *Main sectors*

Agricultural production, which contributes about one-third of GDP, consists mainly of rain-fed food crops and groundnuts. Good rainfall helped the recovery of agricultural output, which expanded by 18.1 per cent between FY 1984/85 and FY 1985/86. However, a strong impetus was also given by the special measures aimed at stimulating this sector. Producer prices were raised before the planting season and efforts were made to enhance the availability of credit, to improve deliveries of high-yielding seeds, to improve extension services and to assure the supply of inputs. The output of the industrial sector – mainly groundnut crushing and food-processing – also recovered, growing by 16 per cent in FY 1985/86 as compared to a decline of 3.1 per cent in the previous fiscal year. Value added generated by tourism tripled between 1981 and 1985 in real terms, making this the country's fastest growing sector. However, the sector's linkage with the local industries is still very low and it contributed only about 20 per cent to the country's net foreign-exchange earnings.

3. *Trade and payments*

In FY 1985/86 groundnut exports fell by about 40 per cent in dollar terms, largely owing to a fall in volume exported. Although groundnuts traditionally account for over 90 per cent of domestic merchandise exports, total exports increased by about 6 per cent, as the decline in groundnut exports appears to have been offset by an increase in other exports and re-exports. World prices for groundnut oil during FY 1986/87 were about 27 per cent lower than during the preceding 12-month period. This will continue to exert a depressive effect on the country's exports. In FY 1986/87 exports stagnated, while sharply rising imports (in dollar terms) led to a widening of the FOB/FOB trade deficit from $15.5 million in FY 1985/86 to an estimated $32.6 million in FY 1986/87. Owing to substantial increases in net earnings on account of tourism, the deficit on service account is expected to fall from $21 million in FT 1985/86 to $13.4 million in FY 1986/87. However, this improvement could not offset the deterioration on trade account; therefore the current-account deficit (excluding official transfers), which had hovered around $35 million in FY 1984/85 and 1985/86, rose to an estimated $46 million in FY 1986/87. As a result of substantial increases in ODA (from $22 million to $60 million), the overall balance is expected to produce a surplus of $14 million in FY 1986/87 as against a deficit of $14.8 million in the previous fiscal year. This improvement was reflected in a sharp recovery of official exchange reserves, which rose from $1.6 million at the end of FY 1985/86 to $25 million one year later. The improved reserve position will enable the country to cover about 14 weeks of its c.i.f. imports as compared to one week's imports a year earlier.

4. *Budget*

In FY 1984/85 the budget deficit (excluding grant receipts) amounted to 17.0 per cent of GDP. Stringent control over recurrent expenditures, and a slow-down in development expenditures on the one hand and an improvement of tax collection on the other, was expected to bring down the fiscal deficit/GDP ratio to 9 per cent in FY 1985/86. However, the Government's policy of sustaining groundnut producer prices in order to boost production and stem the illegal cross-border outflow

---

[147] The fiscal year (FY) ends 30 June.

GAMBIA

1. Population, total and per capita GDP, growth of agricultural and manufacturing output

Year and periods	Population Millions	GDP[a] Total Millions of dollars	Per capita Dollars	Per cent of LDC average	Agricultural production Total	of which: Food	Manufacturing value-added Total
1985	0.7	157	213	99.1			
				Real growth rates, per cent per annum			
1980-1985	2.7	-0.5	-3.1		8.3	8.3	..
1984-1985	2.6	-8.7	-11.0		23.5	23.7	-11.8
1985-1986	2.7	..	..		-0.4	-0.4	22.2

2. Area, demographic indicators and labour force share in agriculture

	Area			Demographic indicators							Labour force
Total	Share of arable land under permanent crops	Share covered by forestry and woodlands	Density	Average life expectancy at birth			Infant mortality as share of live births	Share of population In urban areas	Economically active	Share in agriculture
	1984		1985	1980-1985			1980-1985		1985	
000 km2	Per cent		Pop/km2	M	F	T	Per 1,000		Per cent	
11.3	14.6	17.0	64	34	37	35	174	20	48	83

3. Origins and uses of output; investment

Years	Sectoral origin of GDP				Uses of GDP			Investment
	Agriculture	Mining	Manufacturing	Services	Private consumption expenditure	Government consumption expenditure	Gross domestic savings	
					Per cent of total GDP			
1980	31.2	..	3.8	55.4	73.3	21.4	5.2	26.7
1985	32.7	..	10.2	51.8	78.9	20.8	0.3	21.7

4. Balance of payments, debt and external assistance

Years	Balance of payments			Debt service				Debt	External assistance	
	Merchandise trade balance	Balance on services	Balance on current account	Amortization	Interest	Total	As ratio of exports of goods and services	Amount outstanding at year-end	Total	of which: ODA
		Millions of dollars					Per cent	Millions of dollars		
1980	..	..	..	9.8[b]	3.5[b]	13.3[b]	16.4[b]	211.7[b]	86.3	58.7
1985	..	..	..	6.9	7.9	14.9	18.2	248.0	58.4	49.0

5. Trade

Years and periods	Exports Value Mill. of dollars	of which: share of Groundnut products Per cent	Imports Value Mill. of dollars	of which: share of food Per cent	Terms of trade
1980	31	54.2	163	(23.2)	100
1985	43	19.8	93	40.3[c]	167

	Value	Volume	Purchasing power	Value	Volume	Index
			Growth rates, per cent per annum			
1980-1985	6.8	-0.4	10.4	-10.6	-7.6	10.8
1984-1985	-8.5	-11.2	-8.5	-5.1	-5.1	3.0
1985-1986	4.7	-22.0	-0.1	2.2	-2.5	28.1

6. Other economic and social indicators

Energy Commercial energy consumption per capita	Transport & communication Commercial vehicles	Telephones	Education Adult literacy rate	School enrolment ratio share of relevant age group Primary			Secondary			Health Attendance at childbirth by trained personnel	Share of population Immunized against DPT (3 doses)	With access to safe water	Food and nutrition Cereals Consumption per capita	Self-sufficiency ratio	Average daily calorie intake per capita Total	Share of requirements
				M	F	T	M	F	T							
1984	1984	1985	Around 1985		1984					1983	1983	1985		1985	1985	Between 1982&1985
kg of coal equiv.	Per 1,000 pop.						Per cent						kg	Per cent	Calories	Per cent
114	1.8	4.8	..	91	55	73	29	13	21	80.0	87.8	59	273	64	2257[b]	95

a/ Years ending 30 June.   b/ 1982.   c/ 1984/85.   d/ Year other than 1985.

led to a 100 per cent increase in these prices during FY 1985/86, and further increases in FY 1986/87. The budget deficit for FY 1986/87 on a partial commitment basis (excluding grant receipts) was forecast to rise to 17.5 per cent of GDP, one-half of which was due to these groundnut producer price subsidies.

B. *Recent policy developments*

1. *Macro-economic policies*

The ERP launched in August 1985 was complemented by a structural adjustment programme with the IMF for FY 1986/87, under which the private sector is to provide the basis for medium-term growth and diversification of the economy. A flexible exchange rate was adopted in January 1986 coupled with liberalization of exchange control, so as to curb the parallel exchange market. Pricing and fiscal incentives were introduced to stimulate the productive sectors. The Investment Code was revised and the National Investment Board embarked on an aggressive drive to promote investments in export-oriented industries, which bore fruit in fishing and agro-processing. The financial and institutional structures of the Gambia Commercial Development Bank were overhauled, so as to make this institution more responsive to the development needs of the country's productive sector. Interest rates on deposits were raised and guidelines to regulate commercial bank credit to the private sector were implemented.

Significant changes were made with regard to parastatals. The reform strategy involves divestiture of certain public enterprises and an improved performance of the remainder through the use of performance contracts, technical assistance and tariff adjustments to make them financially self-sufficient. The fisheries and tourism sectors came under the first phase of the divestiture programme. Tight control was exercised over public expenditure. The civil service was reduced and in January 1986 a moratorium was placed on the creation of new public enterprises or joint ventures with Government equity participation of more than 10 per cent, as well as on the provision of loan guarantees to private or public enterprises, except in special cases. Stringent criteria for investment selection were imposed. Priority was to be given to: (*a*) projects with net foreign-exchange-generating or saving potential; (*b*) the rehabilitation and main-

tenance of existing capital assets rather than expansion or creation of new ones; and (*c*) long-term investment in human resource development. For the period beyond FY 1986/87 the Government has adopted a three-year "rolling" investment programme with strengthened links to the annual recurrent budget.

2. *International support measures*

The World Bank agreed on a $30 million structural adjustment loan (SAL) in August 1986, the first tranche of which, amounting to $17 million, was immediately released. The remaining $13 million was to be disbursed over a 15-month period ending about December 1987, depending on the Government's performance with respect to the ERP. This credit would finance about 24 per cent of the Gambia's merchandise imports over the period. This credit was complemented by a combined package of SDR 17.88 million ($21.6 million) agreed to by the IMF, which included a stand-by arrangement that expired in October 1987 and a Structural Adjustment Facility loan worth SDR 8.04 million ($9.7 million) over three years. Other project and non-project financing included a balance-of-payments support commitment of about $7.7 million from the United Kingdom (for the period October 1985 to June 1987), $3 million from the Netherlands, and STABEX compensation of about $4 million from the EC.

Debt service payments (on long- and short-term debt), including repayments of IMF drawings, rose by about 40 per cent in 1985 to $19.9 million, representing about 24 per cent of the exports of goods and services, as against 15 per cent in 1984. Moreover, payments arrears had accumulated to a level equivalent to 35 per cent of GDP by September 1986. At that time the Gambia negotiated its first debt rescheduling within the framework of the Paris Club, which provided for a repayment schedule of 9 1/2 and 10 1/2 years (including five and six years of grace) on debt falling due between October 1986 and September 1987 and on accumulated arrears respectively.

3. *SNPA follow-up*

As a follow-up to the Round Table Meeting in November 1984, sectoral consultations for the agricultural sector and water were scheduled for the end of 1987.

17. Guinea

A. *Recent socio-economic developments*

1. *Overall economy*

Real GDP growth in 1986 was estimated at 2.5 per cent, a modest improvement in economic performance during the first year of implementation of a comprehensive reform programme with the financial support of the World Bank and the IMF, but still implying stagnant real per capita income. Consumer price inflation for 1986 was estimated at 70 per cent, according to the index introduced in January 1986.

2. *Main sectors*

Agriculture remains the basis of Guinea's economy, accounting for 45 per cent of GDP in 1986, and employing some 80 per cent of the population. Since rice is the principal mass consumption staple and its cultivation accounts for 42 per cent of the arable land, grain production is an important barometer for the success of overall agricultural policy. Grain production in 1986 amounted to 445,000 tonnes, a 9.4 per cent increase compared to 1985. Nevertheless, mainly because of the consumption needs of Conakry, which comprises 13 per cent of Guinea's population, rice imports rose to 160,000 tonnes, equivalent to one-quarter of the value of total imports, as compared to 120,000 tonnes in 1985.

3. *Trade and payments*

Guinea has recorded a substantial surplus on visible trade during recent years, but its export base is narrow. Bauxite and aluminum still account for over 90 per cent of exports. Moreover, one quarter of bauxite exports goes to the USSR on a barter basis and therefore does not yield convertible foreign exchange. Substantial growth in diamond and gold earnings is expected over the next few years. The net deficit on services account, largely connected with the operations of the mining companies and their expatriate staff, has much more than offset the trade surpluses. The resulting current account deficits have been compounded by net capital outflows on the part of the mining sector, leaving a substantial deficit to be financed by foreign assistance as well as debt accumulation.

At the end of 1985, Guinea's external debt, including short-term debt and use of IMF credits was estimated at $1,430 million, equivalent to two-thirds of GDP. Total debt service was equivalent to 17 per cent of freely-convertible export earnings in 1985, as compared to 27 per cent in 1984 but was expected to rise to 29 per cent in 1986 to $155 million. This figure must be set against gross official development assistance estimated at $141 million in 1985.

4. *Budget*

Government revenues in 1986 amounted to about $275 million and were equivalent to 16.5 per cent of GDP, based mainly on mining activities. Current spending amounted to $155 million and represented 59 per cent of the budgeted expenditures, while most of the rest was devoted to investment outlays, leaving a budget deficit of $35.5 million, equivalent to about 21.1 per cent of GDP, which was entirely financed by external inflows.

B. *Recent policy developments*

1. *Macro-economic policies*

Overall economic reforms continued to be implemented in 1986, although more slowly than officially foreseen by the Government. A medium-term recovery programme covering the period 1987-1991 was adopted by the Guinean Government and received broad approval in the World Bank-sponsored Consultative Group (Paris, 18-19 March 1987). The programme's main targets are: (*a*) to achieve an annual growth rate of 4.6 per cent, principally through private sector initiatives; (*b*) to curb the rate of inflation; (*c*) to build up foreign exchange reserves; and (*d*) to raise the national savings rate to counteract the projected drop in bauxite earnings and to meet the expected rise in gross domestic investment. The most dynamic sectors are expected to include fishing, manufacturing, construction and public works. Agricultural production is expected to grow by 3.6 per cent per year – over 1 per cent in excess of the

GUINEA

1. Population, total and per capita GDP, growth of agricultural and manufacturing output

Year and periods	Population Millions	GDP Total Millions of dollars	Per capita Dollars	Per cent of LDC average	Agricultural production Total	of which: Food	Manufacturing value-added Total
1985	6.1	2117	349	162.3			
				Real growth rates, per cent per annum			
1980-1985	2.4	0.7	-1.6		0.1	0.1	1.2
1984-1985	2.2	2.6	0.4		1.0	1.0	-1.0
1985-1986	2.6	..	..		4.7	4.9	..

2. Area, demographic indicators and labour force share in agriculture

Total	Area Share of arable land under permanent crops	Share covered by forestry and woodlands	Density	Average life expectancy at birth M F T	Infant mortality as share of live births	Share of population In urban areas	Economically active	Labour force Share in agriculture
		1984	1985	1980-1985	1980-1985		1985	
000 km2	Per cent		Pop/km2	Years	Per 1,000		Per cent	
245.9	6.4	41.7	25	39 42 40	159	22	47	78

3. Origins and uses of output; investment

Years	Sectoral origin of GDP Agriculture	Mining	Manufacturing	Services	Uses of GDP Private consumption expenditure	Government consumption expenditure	Gross domestic savings	Investment
					Per cent of total GDP			
1980	42.4	14.1	2.2	35.0	57.6	20.8	21.6	15.8
1985	44.0	13.5	2.1	34.4	72.5	14.5	13.0	9.4

4. Balance of payments, debt and external assistance

Years	Balance of payments Merchandise trade balance	Balance on services	Balance on current account	Debt service Amortization	Interest	Total	As ratio of exports of goods and services	Debt Amount outstanding at year-end	External assistance Total	of which: ODA
	Millions of dollars						Per cent	Millions of dollars		
1980	..	..	..	67.0a/	34.6a/	101.7 a/	22.4a/	1439.7a/	153.8	100.5
1985	..	..	..	49.7	28.7	78.4	15.1	1432.5	140.6	135.8

5. Trade

Years and periods	Exports Value Mill. of dollars	of which: share of Bauxite Per cent	Imports Value Mill. of dollars	of which: share of food Per cent	Terms of trade
1980	390	..	270	11.9	100
1985	430	95.0b/	420	12.8b/	..

	Value	Volume	Purchasing power	Value	Volume	Index
			Growth rates, per cent per annum			
1980-1985	2.0	..	4.5	9.2	12.0	..
1984-1985	0.0	..	-0.4	16.7	16.2	..
1985-1986	0.0	..	-1.3	2.4	1.0	..

6. Other economic and social indicators

Energy Commercial energy consumption per capita	Transport & communication Commercial vehicles	Telephones	Education Adult literacy rate	School enrolment ratio share of relevant age group Primary M F T	Secondary M F T	Health Attendance at childbirth by trained personnel	Share of population Immunized against DPT (3 doses)	With access to safe water	Food and nutrition Cereals Consumption per capita	Self-sufficiency ratio	Average daily calorie intake per capita Total	Share of requirements
1984	1984	1982	Around 1985	1984		1984	1983	1985	1985		1985	Between 1982&1985
kg of coal equiv.	Per 1,000 pop.								kg	Per cent	Calories	Per cent
					Per cent							
72	..	2.4	..	44 20 32	20 7 13	..	4.0	20	120	81	1728	84

a/ 1982.   b/ 1983.

growth of the population, but even higher growth rates have been planned for certain products, such as rice (6 per cent), cotton (14 per cent) and coffee (10 per cent). At the beginning of 1987, the Government announced major changes in the interest rate policy to strengthen incentives for investment and saving. A minimum annual interest rate of 15 per cent for bank deposits, and a maximum 20 per cent on bank credits, were introduced. In view of an annual inflation rate of 70 per cent in 1986, these still constituted highly negative real rates of interest. Monetary authorities have estimated that some 60 per cent of the money supply remained outside the banking system. In June 1986, the dual exchange rate was abolished, leaving a single rate of GF 360 = $1, which decreased gradually in value to GF 412 = $1, in mid-March 1987. This caused the virtual disappearance of the parallel exchange market, which had previously assumed major proportions. Prospects for an increase in foreign investment improved after the adoption in January 1987 of an investment code which includes, *inter alia*, waivers of import duties on capital equipment, deductions on tax revenues, special incentives to small and medium-size firms, to enterprises using more than 70 per cent local inputs and to those located outside Conakry.

2. *International support measures*

Over the period 1987-1989, Guinea will need $670 million to carry out its public investment programme and an additional $200 million in balance-of-payments support. Indicative pledges were made at the Consultative Group by aid donors for the full $670 million requested to support the three-year public investment programme. Priority will be given to fishing, manufacturing industry, construction and public works.

3. *SNPA follow-up*

After reviewing Guinea's financial requirements, the above-mentioned Consultative Group, chaired by the World Bank, agreed that sustained external assistance will be essential to support the completion of the recovery programme and to achieve Guinea's growth objectives. Participants included the IMF, UNDP, EC, African Development Bank, Canada, France, the Federal Republic of Germany, Italy, Japan, Saudi Arabia, Switzerland and the United States.

18. Guinea-Bissau

A. *Recent socio-economic developments*

1. *Overall economy*

Guinea-Bissau's economy continued to deteriorate in 1986. The economic recovery programme, initiated in 1983, lost its momentum in 1985 and 1986. Available data show that GDP growth in the 1980s has been weak and erratic, with an average negative growth rate of 1.1 per cent over the period 1982-1985. The critical shortage of foreign exchange resulted in a loss of import capacity. Most public enterprises ceased to operate. Only two mixed enterprises were working satisfactorily by 1986.

2. *Main sectors*

The primary factor explaining the poor growth performance during the first half of the 1980s, was the inadequacy of production incen-

tives in agriculture. Agricultural production, which represents about one half of GDP, grew at an average rate of 7.8 per cent per annum between 1980 and 1985. The production of cereals increased by 24 per cent, 16 per cent and 14 per cent during 1984, 1985 and 1986 respectively. This series of improvements continued into the 1986/87 agricultural year. The cereal deficit in 1987 was brought down to 17,000 tonnes, as against an average of 37,000 tonnes during preceding years. Although this positive trend is partly due to better weather conditions since the 1983 drought, it is also due to the new production incentives introduced by the recovery programme. Producer prices increased by 53 to 92 per cent in 1984, and again by 63 to 66 per cent in 1985. The provision of inputs, such as seeds and fertilizers for development projects and of essential consumer goods, was improved in rural areas thanks to balance-of-payments assistance and to the progressive withdrawal of the public sector from retail trade. Nevertheless, negative trends prevailed in other sectors of the economy. Industrial output, which represents less than 10 per cent of GDP, stagnated

GUINEA-BISSAU

1. Population, total and per capita GDP, growth of agricultural and manufacturing output

Year and periods	Population Millions	GDP Total Millions of dollars	GDP Per capita Dollars	GDP Per capita Per cent of LDC average	Agricultural production Total	Agricultural production of which: Food	Manufacturing value-added Total
1985	0.9	135	152	70.7			
				Real growth rates, per cent per annum			
1980-1985	1.9	3.5	1.6		7.8	7.8	0.3
1984-1985	1.8	1.5	-0.3		4.3	4.3	3.4
1985-1986	2.2	..	..		8.2	8.2	..

2. Area, demographic indicators and labour force share in agriculture

Area Total	Area Share of arable land under permanent crops	Area Share covered by forestry and woodlands 1984	Density 1985	Average life expectancy at birth M	Average life expectancy at birth F	Average life expectancy at birth T 1980-1985	Infant mortality as share of live births 1980-1985	Share of population In urban areas	Share of population Economically active 1985	Labour force Share in agriculture
000 km2	Per cent	Per cent	Pop/km2	Years	Years	Years	Per 1,000	Per cent	Per cent	Per cent
36.1	8.0	29.6	25	41	45	43	143	27	48	81

3. Origins and uses of output; investment

Years	Sectoral origin of GDP Agriculture	Mining	Manufacturing	Services	Uses of GDP Private consumption expenditure	Government consumption expenditure	Gross domestic savings	Investment
				Per cent of total GDP				
1980	44.3	..	7.4	36.1	77.0	29.0	-6.0	29.6
1985	42.4a/	..	4.4a/	46.2a/	79.7	28.7	-8.4	40.1

4. Balance of payments, debt and external assistance

Years	Merchandise trade balance	Balance on services	Balance on current account	Amortization	Interest	Total	As ratio of exports of goods and services	Debt Amount outstanding at year-end	External assistance Total	External assistance of which: ODA
	Millions of dollars						Per cent	Millions of dollars		
1980	..	..	..	2.2b/	1.1b/	3.4b/	19.4b/	151.5b/	90.0	78.7
1985	..	..	..	14.5	4.2	18.6	100.0	253.3	70.4	65.0

5. Trade

Years and periods	Exports Value Mill. of dollars	Exports of which: share of Cashew nuts Per cent	Imports Value Mill. of dollars	Imports of which: share of food Per cent	Terms of trade
1980	11	3.5	55	(18.3)c/	100
1985	14	41.4	60	(23.3)c/	..

	Value	Volume	Purchasing power	Value	Volume	Index
			Growth rates, per cent per annum			
1980-1985	4.9	..	7.6	1.8	4.3	..
1984-1985	-22.2	..	-22.5	25.0	24.5	..
1985-1986	7.1	..	5.7	0.0	1.3	..

6. Other economic and social indicators

Energy Commercial energy consumption per capita 1984 kg of coal equiv.	Transport & communication Commercial vehicles 1984	Transport & communication Telephones 1981 Per 1,000 pop.	Education Adult literacy rate Around 1985	Education School enrolment ratio share of relevant age group Primary M	Primary F	Primary T 1983	Secondary M	Secondary F	Secondary T	Health Attendance at childbirth by trained personnel 1984	Health Share of population Immunized against DPT (3 doses) 1983	Health Share of population With access to safe water 1985	Food and nutrition Cereals Consumption per capita 1985 kg	Food and nutrition Cereals Self-sufficiency ratio 1985 Per cent	Food and nutrition Average daily calorie intake per capita Total 1985 Calories	Food and nutrition Average daily calorie intake per capita Share of requirements Between 1982&1985 Per cent
				Per cent										Per cent		Per cent
42	..	2.7	31	84	40	62	19	4	11	..	24.0	21	225	85	..	97

a/ 1983.   b/ 1982.   c/ Import f.o.b.

during the period 1980-1985. A second Four-Year Development Plan (1988-1991) is being prepared: agriculture, fishing, forestry and mining will be the priority sectors for investment.

3. *Trade and payments*

The balance of payments has deteriorated, as the current account deficit rose from $11.3 million in 1985 to $48.6 million in 1986. The rate of financing of imports by exports declined from 37 per cent in 1984 to 23 per cent in 1985, but rose slightly in 1986 when their respective values were estimated at $60 million and $15.4 million. External debt and debt payment arrears have increased and continue to be the principal constraint to development. At the end of 1986, Guinea-Bissau's external debt was estimated at $253.3 million. Although about three-quarters of this is on concessional terms, total debt service is forecast to rise from $15.7 million in 1986 to $27 million in 1990. As far as the estimated $50 million debt to Portugal is concerned, negotiations undertaken in October 1986 resulted in an agreement to reschedule commercial debt over a period of 10 years and to convert $5 million of public debt into Guinea-Bissau pesos to be used for the financing of projects to be implemented by Portugal. At the Paris Club Meeting held in October 1987, exceptional treatment of Guinea-Bissau's bilateral debt was decided by creditor countries. However, this scheduling covers at most a fifth of the external debt. Thus, repayment will be made by the Government over a 20-year period including a grace period of ten years for debts rescheduled.

4. *Budget*

The overall government deficit rose from 30.9 per cent of GDP in 1984 to 36.4 per cent in 1985, essentially owing to the growth in the capital budget, whose share in GDP increased from 41.4 per cent in 1984 to 48.4 per cent in 1985. The second Four-Year Development Plan includes measures on fiscal and monetary policies designed to reduce expenditure and increase State revenue.

B. *Recent policy developments*

1. *Macro-economic policies*

In November 1986, the Government adopted a new policy aimed at the progressive disengagement of the State from most economic sectors, the liberalisation of trade and a new system of prices. The overall objective is to transform the present rigid economic system into a free-market economy. Following the new policy, a package of austerity measures was adopted in May 1987, which included a 59 per cent devaluation of the Guinea-Bissau peso (from 265 per dollar to 650 per dollar); increases in export and import taxes, fuel and electricity prices; and a reduction of the budget deficit, partly by way of cuts in the number of civil servants. The monopoly powers of parastatals in foreign and domestic trade are being phased out: private traders are increasingly involved in Government export deals and retail trade is being progressively re-privatized. Foreign investment remains minimal but a new investment code is expected to be drafted shortly, setting out the areas in which foreign investment is welcome and providing guarantees on the repatriation of profit and capital.

2. *International support policies*

Sweden has continued its support to the country by allocating Skr. 140 million (about $10 million) annually for 1986 and 1987 to rural development, small-scale fishing, industry, commerce and telecommunications. France, Japan, the United Kingdom and the United States approved credits in 1986 to support Guinea-Bissau's agricultural development, particularly the production of cereals. Pakistan will supply food aid in 1987, and will train agricultural experts to help solve the difficulties created by drought. In the face of its difficult financial situation, Guinea-Bissau has collaborated closely with the World Bank, the IMF and other donors to introduce a new Structural Adjustment Programme for the period 1987-1989, in support of which the country has received pledges totalling $44.0 million.

3. *SNPA follow-up*

As part of the follow-up to the Round Table Meetings (Lisbon, 1984 and Bissau, 1985), the Government requested assistance from UNDP to prepare discussions for non-project assistance with the principal development partners. Sectoral consultations on agriculture, fisheries and human resources have been held in 1987.

19. Haiti

A. Recent socio-economic developments

1. Overall economy

GDP growth continued to be very sluggish over the period 1983-86, averaging less than 0.5 per cent per annum. Total GDP in 1986 in constant prices is estimated to have been below the 1980 level. With a population growing at about 1.5 per cent per annum, per capita consumption levels declined by over 13 per cent between 1980 and 1986, particularly in the rural areas.

2. Main sectors

Agriculture has continued to stagnate. The industrial sector, including the formerly dynamic assembly activities, has stopped growing and probably declined in 1986. This is mostly as a result of the civil disturbances which preceded and followed the change of régime in February 1986. The tourist industry, which has a good potential, has been similarly affected by this and other factors, the number of visitors arriving by air having continued declining (from 134,000 in FY 1980/81 [148] to fewer than 112,000 in FY 985/86).

3. Trade and payments

The 6.8 per cent increase, according to recently revised data, of exports in 1986 more than offset the decline of 2.7 per cent during the previous year. Light manufactures represented 58 per cent of exports in both years, mostly from assembly industries, whose value added had increased in 1985, but declined somewhat in 1986. For coffee, the main domestic export, production and export volumes declined in 1985 and 1986, but higher prices led to an increase in export values of coffee. The contribution of other agricultural exports combined (sisal, cocoa, essential oils, sugar) has normally been less than 7 per cent of total merchandise exports. A contraction of imports took place in both FY 1984/85 and FY 1985/86, so that the current account deficit was significantly reduced in FY 1985/86. With the increase in official transfers in that year, the overall balance of pay-

ments turned positive for the first time in the 1980s. As a result, the exchange rate discount of the gourde in the parallel market *vis-à-vis* the official rate fell from 20 in early 1986 to 5-7 per cent later that year. The total external debt rose by 25 per cent between 1982 and 1985, reaching $833 million at the end of the latter year. However, most of this is concessional. The ratio of debt service to exports of goods and services is estimated to have been about 16 per cent in 1986. Official grants (including those channelled through NGOs and food aid) are reported to have increased significantly in FY 1984/85 and 1985/86, reaching $117 million in the latter year.

4. Budget

Following the change of régime in February 1986, the provisional National Government Council (CNG) reorganized the management of public finance. Almost one-fifth of the appropriations contained in the FY 1985/86 budget was cancelled, and about one-half of the cancelled portion reallocated to health, education, agriculture and internal security. A number of taxes (particularly excise duties on basic consumption items) were also reduced, but, with the increase in the grants received from abroad, the overall fiscal deficit was reduced to 1.2 per cent of GDP, the lowest level for ten years. In FY 1986/87, the deficit is expected to increase, owing in part to increases in Government salaries. The budget expenditures are fully allocated, ending the past practice under which large sums were reserved for unspecified purposes.

B. Recent policy developments

1. Macro-economic policies

Since February 1986, the provisional CNG initiated an Economic Recovery Programme and implemented a number of important policy and institutional reforms, besides the budgetary management measures mentioned above. The formerly overprotected and inefficient public entreprises – an oilseed extraction plant, two sugar refineries, the cement plant and the flour mill – have either been closed or restructured, and the sectors in which they operate have been opened to competi-

---

[148] The fiscal year (FY) ends on 30 September.

HAITI

1. Population, total and per capita GDP, growth of agricultural and manufacturing output

Year and periods	Population Millions	GDP[a] Total Millions of dollars	GDP[a] Per capita Dollars	GDP[a] Per capita Per cent of LDC average	Agricultural production Total	Agricultural production of which: Food	Manufacturing value-added Total
1985	5.3	(1848)	350[b]	162.8			
				Real growth rates, per cent per annum			
1980-1985	1.4	-0.4	-1.8		1.6	1.4	-3.1[c]
1984-1985	1.4	1.7	0.3		-0.6	-0.6	..
1985-1986	1.6	..	..		3.4	3.3	..

2. Area, demographic indicators and labour force share in agriculture

	Area			Demographic indicators								Labour force
Total	Share of arable land under permanent crops	Share covered by forestry and woodlands	Density	Average life expectancy at birth M	Average life expectancy at birth F	Average life expectancy at birth T	Infant mortality as share of live births	Share of population In urban areas	Share of population Economically active		Share in agriculture
	1984		1985	1980-1985			1980-1985		1985		
000 km2	Per cent		Pop/km2	Years			Per 1,000	Per cent			
27.8	32.6	1.9	190	51	54	53	128	27	43		68

3. Origins and uses of output; investment

Years	Sectoral origin of GDP Agriculture	Mining	Manufacturing	Services	Uses of GDP Private consumption expenditure	Government consumption expenditure	Gross domestic savings	Investment
				Per cent of total GDP				
1980	32.2	1.2	18.2	42.3	85.2	10.1	4.8	16.9
1985	31.8[b]	0.1[b]	16.6[b]	45.0[b]	84.0[b]	11.8[b]	4.2[b]	15.8[b]

4. Balance of payments, debt and external assistance

Years	Balance of payments Merchandise trade balance	Balance on services	Balance on current account	Debt service Amortization	Interest	Total	As ratio of exports of goods and services	Debt Amount outstanding at year-end	External assistance Total	of which: ODA
	Millions of dollars						Per cent	Millions of dollars		
1980	-103.0	-89.0	-139.9	11.1[d]	15.4[d]	26.5[d]	9.7[d]	667.5[d]	117.8	105.1
1985	-123.8	-120.3	-194.7	10.7	27.9	38.6	11.0	833.1	144.7	152.6

5. Trade

Years and periods	Exports Value Mill. of dollars	of which: share of Coffee Per cent	Imports Value Mill. of dollars	of which: share of food Per cent	Terms of trade
1980	226	34.4	354	26.1[e]	100
1985	174	26.0	470	28.1[f]	..

	Value	Volume	Purchasing power	Value	Volume	Index
			Growth rates, per cent per annum			
1980-1985	-5.1	..	-2.7	5.8	8.5	..
1984-1985	-2.8	..	-3.2	-0.4	-0.8	..
1985-1986	-2.3	..	-3.6	-4.3	-5.5	..

6. Other economic and social indicators

Energy Commercial energy consumption per capita	Transport & communication Commercial vehicles	Transport & communication Telephones	Education Adult literacy rate	Education School enrolment ratio share of relevant age group Primary M	Primary F	Primary T	Secondary M	Secondary F	Secondary T	Health Attendance at childbirth by trained personnel	Share of population Immunized against DPT (3 doses)	Share of population With access to safe water	Food and nutrition Cereals Consumption per capita	Self-sufficiency ratio	Average daily calorie intake per capita Total	Share of requirements
			around													Between
1984	1981	1981	1985		1983					1983	1984	1985	1985		1985	1982&1985
kg of coal equiv.	Per 1,000 pop.			M	F	T	M	F	T				kg	Per cent	Calories	Per cent
65	2.5	4.2	38	81	72	76	16	16	16	20.0	12.0	38	97	57	1855	84

a/ Years ending 30 September.   b/ 1984.   c/ 1980-1984.   d/ 1982.   e/ 1981/82.   f/ 1984/85.

tion. In order to lower prices and remove price distortions, a comprehensive programme of trade liberalization has been enacted. By February 1987, almost all quantitative restrictions on imports had ended, specific tariffs had been replaced by *ad valorem* ones at relatively low rates (between 0 and 40 per cent), while almost all price controls had been dismantled. Export taxes on coffee have been greatly reduced (from around 25 per cent to 10 per cent), and those on cocoa and sisal fibre eliminated.

2. *Relations with donors*

At the November 1986 meeting of the Haiti Sub-Group of the Caribbean Group for Co-operation and Economic Development (chaired by the World Bank), donors expressed their support for the Government's Economic Recovery Programme and announced substantial increases in their intended levels of financial support to Haiti. The Government also presented to the Sub-Group a list of 26 small new projects costing $43 million which concentrate on productive employment generation in the short term. These will be included in the public development programme, as and when they receive financing commitments. In December 1986, a three-year structural adjustment arrangement involving the allocation of SDR 20.7 million ($24.9 million) was approved under the IMF Structural Adjustment Facility, and in early 1987, the IDA approved a concessional credit of $40 million to support the Economic Recovery Programme.

20. Kiribati

A. *Recent socio-economic developments*

1. *Overall economy*

After a negative growth rate of 9.3 per cent of real GDP in 1985, when exports fell by more than one half compared with 1984, Kiribati's economic situation improved slightly in 1986. Real GDP growth during the latter year was expected to be positive for the third time since 1980. However, the positive growth rates in 1982, 1984 and probably in 1986 were far too modest to offset the dramatic halving of GDP between 1979 and 1981, which was caused by the cessation of phosphate mining. The annual inflation rate oscillated around 5 per cent during the period 1985-86.

In addition to its handicapped communication ties with the outside world because of the country's geographical isolation and remoteness, Kiribati faces tremendous internal transportation problems. They are due to the dispersed nature of the country, whose land mass of about 750 km^2 is scattered across a vast ocean territory extending about 3,780 km from east to west and 2,050 km from north to south.

2. *Main sectors*

Agriculture experienced a severe setback in 1985. The yield of coconuts, the only cash crop, was adversely affected by the severe deterioration of world copra prices in 1985 and 1986, during each of which they fell by nearly one-half. Food production is virtually a subsistence activity. The expansion of the fishing sector harnessing abundant tuna resources in the waters surrounding the islands, was hampered by weather-related production cuts in 1985. Mining activity ceased with the exhaustion of the phosphate resources in 1979. The share of manufacturing output in GDP is insignificant.

3. *Trade and payments*

Between 1984 and 1985, exports more than halved from $10.7 million to $4.5 million, of which copra accounted for 80 per cent. Fish is the second most important export item, having contributed $0.7 million in the latter year. Total imports amounted to $13 million in 1985, composed largely of food, fuel, transport equipment and capital goods, with Australia as the main supplier.

In contrast to the trade balance, the balance on account of services and private transfers was in surplus, improving from $3.0 million in 1984 to $6.3 million in 1985. This surplus was the combined result of a net income on services of $4.5 million and private net transfers of $1.8 million, although the latter have been showing a downward trend since 1982. Major sources for service income and private transfers are fees paid by foreign long-

KIRIBATI

1. Population, total and per capita GDP, growth of agricultural and manufacturing output

Year and periods	Population	GDP				Agricultural production		Manufacturing value-added
		Total	Per capita				of which:	
	Millions	Millions of dollars	Dollars	Per cent of LDC average	Total	Total	Food	Total
1985	0.1	20	317a/	147.4				
			Real growth rates, per cent per annum					
1980-1985	2.0	-0.0	-2.0		..	..	..	..
1984-1985	2.0	-9.3	-11.1		..	..	..	..
1985-1986	2.0	..	..		..	..	..	..

2. Area, demographic indicators and labour force share in agriculture

Area			Demographic indicators							Labour force
Total	Share of arable land under permanent crops	Share covered by forestry and woodlands	Density	Average life expectancy at birth			Infant mortality as share of live births	Share of population		Share in agriculture
								In urban areas	Economically active	
		1984	1985	M	F	T	1980-1985	1980-1985	1985	
000 km2	Per cent		Pop/km2	Years			Per 1,000	Per cent		
0.7	52.1	2.8	89	..	..	..	..	34	..	..

3. Origins and uses of output; investment

Years	Sectoral origin of GDP				Uses of GDP			Investment
	Agriculture	Mining	Manufacturing	Services	Private consumption expenditure	Government consumption expenditure	Gross domestic savings	
				Per cent of total GDP				
1980	18.3	..	1.5	73.9	..	..	..	..
1985	37.1b/	..	2.1b/	55.2b/	..	..	..	..

4. Balance of payments, debt and external assistance

Years	Balance of payments			Debt service				Debt	External assistance	
	Merchandise trade balance	Balance on services	Balance on current account	Amortization	Interest	Total	As ratio of exports of goods and services	Amount outstanding at year-end	Total	of which: ODA
	Millions of dollars						Per cent	Millions of dollars		
1980	..	..	..	-c/	0.0c/	0.0c/	..c/	8.5c/	19.2	19.2
1985	..	..	..	-	0.5	0.5	..	10.5	12.0	12.1

5. Trade

Years and periods	Exports		Imports		Terms of trade
	Value	of which: share of Oil seeds, nuts, kernels	Value	of which: share of food	
	Mill. of dollars	Per cent	Mill. of dollars	Per cent	
1980	2.7	..	17	(31.5)	100
1985	4.5	91.7d/	13	(18.7)d/	..

	Value	Volume	Purchasing power	Value	Volume	Index
			Growth rates, per cent per annum			
1980-1985	10.8	..	13.5	-5.2	-2.8	..
1984-1985	-57.9	..	-58.1	-7.1	-7.5	..
1985-1986	..	..	..	15.4	11.9	..

6. Other economic and social indicators

Energy	Transport & communication		Education						Health		Food and nutrition			
Commercial energy consumption per capita	Commercial vehicles	Telephones	Adult literacy rate	School enrolment ratio share of relevant age group					Attendance at childbirth by trained personnel	Share of population		Cereals		Average daily calorie intake per capita
				Primary			Secondary			Immunized against DPT (3 doses)	With access to safe water	Consumption per capita	Self-sufficiency ratio	Total
				M	F	T	M	F	T						Share of requirements
1984	1984	1985	around 1985			1984				1984	1982	1985	1985		1985	Between 1982&1985
kg of coal equiv.	Per 1,000 pop.							Per cent					kg	Per cent	Calories	Per cent
210	..	17.4	..	..	..	..	..	..	..	..	53.0	..	94	..	2633e/	..

a/ Income accruing to indigenous population.   b/ 1984.   c/ 1982.   d/ 1983.   e/ Year other than 1985.

distance fleets fishing in the country's EEZ and remittances from I-Kiribati working abroad on foreign ships or in the Nauru phosphate mine.

Income from the Revenue Equalization Reserve Fund, a facility set up by the Government in 1956 and which was valued at $108.4 million in mid-1986, was about $6.3 million in that year.

Foreign aid, largely in the form of official grants, averaging about $14.2 million between 1983 and 1985, was the equivalent of about 60 per cent of GDP. It constitutes Kiribati's largest single source of foreign exchange, financing as much as 75 per cent of imports. Moreover, foreign aid represents the principal source of financing for development projects.

During 1985 the external debt increased slightly to 10.5 but debt service as a percentage of current receipts tripled in that year.

4. *Budget*

During the period 1983-1986, the Government successfully managed to finance all current budget expenditures from domestic sources. To this end, it cut expenditure on wages and salaries (in real terms) as well as on subsidies for unprofitable public enterprises. Furthermore, it refrained from investments with high current costs during the first half of the 1980s. The current budget for 1987 is again being financed without outside financial assistance, but the Government does draw on interest earned from the Reserve Fund for this purpose.

B. *Recent policy developments*

1. *Macro-economic policies*

The Government is making serious efforts to enhance the use of domestic resources for development. In 1986, it was decided to use only part of the interest earned on investments of the Reserve Fund for financing the current budget and to re-invest the remainder. In the same year, the Government renounced requesting a budgetary grant from the United Kingdom, which had been annually extended since independence. An agreement on the exploitation of the fish resources in the country's EEZ was concluded with the United States. However, the Government did not renew the fishing agreement with the Soviet Union.

Kiribati joined the IMF and the World Bank in 1986.

2. *International support policies*

Kiribati relies heavily on external assistance, particularly for development projects. Foreign grants are the principal source for financing development expenditures. Kiribati has succeeded in diversifying its sources of assistance from almost exclusive reliance on the United Kingdom, to include Japan, New Zealand and the EEC as well as several other multilateral institutions.

21. Lao People's Democratic Republic

A. *Recent socio-economic developments*

1. *Overall economy*

The economy grew at an estimated annual rate of 5 per cent during the 1981-1985 Plan Period, but a growth rate of 7 per cent was estimated for 1985.

2. *Main sectors*

The improved 1985 performance was largely due to the agricultural sector, which represents over 75 per cent of total output and which achieved a 11.2 per cent growth rate in 1984, followed by an estimated 9 per cent increase in 1985. The recovery in this sector in 1985 resulted in a reported grain production level of 1.4 million tonnes, equiv-

LAO PEOPLE'S DEMOCRATIC REPUBLIC

1. Population, total and per capita GDP, growth of agricultural and manufacturing output

Year and periods	Population Millions	GDP Total Millions of dollars	GDP Per capita Dollars	GDP Per capita Per cent of LDC average	Agricultural production Total	Agricultural production of which: Food	Manufacturing value-added Total
1985	3.6	1398	386	179.5			
				Real growth rates, per cent per annum			
1980-1985	2.0	5.4	3.3		6.8	6.9	2.2
1984-1985	2.2	7.2	4.9		9.3	9.3	23.9
1985-1986	2.0	..	..		4.1	4.0	..

2. Area, demographic indicators and labour force share in agriculture

Area Total	Area Share of arable land under permanent crops 1984	Area Share covered by forestry and woodlands 1984	Density 1985	Average life expectancy at birth M 1980-1985	Average life expectancy at birth F 1980-1985	Average life expectancy at birth T 1980-1985	Infant mortality as share of live births 1980-1985	Share of population In urban areas	Share of population Economically active 1985	Labour force Share in agriculture
000 km2	Per cent	Per cent	Pop/km2	Years	Years	Years	Per 1,000	Per cent	Per cent	Per cent
236.8	3.8	56.2	16	48	51	50	122	16	49	74

3. Origins and uses of output; investment

Years	Agriculture	Mining	Manufacturing	Services	Private consumption expenditure	Government consumption expenditure	Gross domestic savings	Investment
	Sectoral origin of GDP				Uses of GDP			
	Per cent of total GDP							
1980	62.2	..	4.6	31.0	83.9[a]	16.2[a]	..	24.6[a]
1985	61.6	..	4.0	30.2	..	..	..	24.9

4. Balance of payments, debt and external assistance

Years	Merchandise trade balance	Balance on services	Balance on current account	Amortization	Interest	Total	As ratio of exports of goods and services	Amount outstanding at year-end	Total	of which: ODA
	Balance of payments			Debt service				Debt	External assistance	
	Millions of dollars						Per cent	Millions of dollars		
1980	..	..	..	1.2[a]	1.2[a]	2.4[a]	4.4[a]	321.5[a]	87.8	88.8
1985	..	..	..	3.3	22.5	25.8	33.9	527.7	154.0	126.9

5. Trade

Years and periods	Value Mill. of dollars	Exports of which: share of Hydroelectric power Per cent	Value Mill. of dollars	Imports of which: share of food Per cent	Terms of trade
1980	31	46.8[b]	131	(20.8)[b]	100
1985	29	57.4	160	..	..

	Value	Volume	Purchasing power	Value	Volume	Index
	Growth rates, per cent per annum					
1980-1985	-1.3	..	1.1	4.1	6.7	..
1984-1985	141.7	..	140.7	10.3	9.9	..
1985-1986	3.4	..	2.1	0.0	-1.3	..

6. Other economic and social indicators

Commercial energy consumption per capita 1984	Commercial vehicles 1984	Telephones 1985	Adult literacy rate Around 1985	Primary M 1983	Primary F 1983	Primary T 1983	Secondary M 1983	Secondary F 1983	Secondary T 1983	Attendance at child-birth by trained personnel 1984	Immunized against DPT (3 doses) 1984	With access to safe water 1983	Consumption per capita 1985	Self-sufficiency ratio 1985	Total 1985	Share of requirements Between 1982&1985
Energy	Transport & communication		Education							Health			Food and nutrition			
kg of coal equiv.	Per 1,000 pop.									Per cent			kg	Per cent	Calories	Per cent
29	..	2.1	84[c]	103	77	90	22	15	19	..	..	21	409	98	2228[d]	90

a/ 1982.   b/ 1981.   c/ Age group 15-45.   d/ Year other than 1985.

alent to the target set by the 1981-1985 Five-Year Plan, making the country self-sufficient in rice. The Lao PDR is endowed with rich forestry resources: it is estimated that out of a total forested area of 11 million ha, 4.4 million ha could be economically exploited. However, the timber output for 1984 of 170,000m^3 fell considerably short of the planned target of 400,000 m^3, and in 1985 the estimated output was no more than 200,000 m^3. Among the country's numerous mineral deposits, exploitation has been limited to gypsum and tin; production of the latter increased by 19 per cent in 1985 over the previous year. In the industrial sector, a new sugar refinery and pharmaceutical plants were established in 1986.

3. Trade and payments

The trade deficit in 1985 remained large, with export earnings (including electricity) amounting to less than 20 per cent of imports. The current account deficit in 1985 has been estimated at $95.3 million compared to $84 million in the previous year. The debt service exports ratio in 1985 amounted to 33.7 per cent, as compared to 15.6 per cent in 1983. Well over one-half of the total debt of $528 million outstanding at the end of 1985 was owed to the socialist countries of Eastern Europe.

B. Recent policy developments

1. Macro-economic policies

In 1985 the Government launched a reform of the public enterprise management system, which embodied steps such as rises in official retail prices with the intention of eliminating subsidies and improving the profitability of State enterprises. Under these reforms, the individual enterprise will determine production and investment levels. Moreover, the wages of State employees were increased, causing the annual inflation rate to rise to more than 50 per cent between 1982 and 1985. In mid-November 1986, the Government announced the overall and sectoral objectives of the Second Plan (1986-1990). The priorities of this Plan include an increased food supply, the promotion of forestry-based industries, the launching of an industrial programme, a master plan for urban and rural construction, the development of transport and communications, an increased role for the State sector, the expansion of educational and health facilities, and the promotion of science and technology. The Government renewed its efforts in 1986 to introduce new socialist accounting techniques into State enterprises and other industrial organizations.

2. International support measures

The Lao PDR has been heavily dependent on foreign assistance to cover current and development expenditure. At a Round Table Meeting with its development partners (Geneva, April 1986), the Government received commitments of approximately $300 million from bilateral and multilateral donors for the period covered by the Second Plan. Moreover, in 1986 the Government was invited to take advantage of financial assistance available under the IMF Structural Adjustment Facility (SAF).

22. Lesotho

A. Recent socio-economic developments

1. Overall economy

After consecutive decreases in real GDP in 1982 and 1983, the economy showed signs of recovering in 1984 and 1985, when real GDP growth was estimated at 3.7 per cent and 2.4 per cent respectively. Remittances from migrant workers in South Africa currently surpass domestic output in Lesotho, but the rate of growth of migrant labour income has slowed down considerably since the beginning of the decade. Consequently, the estimated increase of real GNP [149] in 1985 (2.2 per

---

[149] Gross national product (GNP) includes migrant labour income, while gross domestic product (GDP) does not.

LESOTHO

1. Population, total and per capita GDP, growth of agricultural and manufacturing output

Year and periods	Population Millions	GDP a/ Total Millions of dollars	Per capita Dollars	Per cent of LDC average	Agricultural production Total	of which: Food	Manufacturing value-added Total
1985	1.5	257	167	77.7			
				Real growth rates, per cent per annum			
1980–1985	2.6	0.1	−2.4		0.6	0.4	4.9
1984–1985	2.6	2.4	−0.2		11.2	12.5	10.0
1985–1986	2.6	..	..		−6.7	−7.3	..

2. Area, demographic indicators and labour force share in agriculture

Area Total 000 km2	Share of arable land under permanent crops 1984 Per cent	Share covered by forestry and woodlands Per cent	Density 1985 Pop/km2	Average life expectancy at birth M F T 1980–1985 Years	Infant mortality as share of live births 1980–1985 Per 1,000	Share of population In urban areas	Economically active 1985 Per cent	Labour force Share in agriculture
30.4	9.8	..	50	46 52 49	111	17	48	84

3. Origins and uses of output; investment

Years	Sectoral origin of GDP Agriculture	Mining	Manufacturing	Services	Private consumption expenditure	Government consumption expenditure	Gross domestic savings	Investment
				Per cent of total GDP				
1980	23.1	7.7	5.5	52.5	138.7	28.5	−67.2	39.8
1985	20.5	0.6	7.2	58.7	158.0	28.1	−86.1	36.3

4. Balance of payments, debt and external assistance

Years	Merchandise trade balance	Balance on services	Balance on current account	Amortization	Interest	Total	As ratio of exports of goods and services	Amount outstanding at year-end	External assistance Total	of which: ODA
	Millions of dollars						Per cent	Millions of dollars		
1980	−366.4	247.6	−116.7	6.7 b/	7.0 b/	13.7 b/	3.3 b/	117.3 b/	94.2	94.3
1985	−282.8	232.0	−49.8	14.2	4.6	18.8	6.3	176.7	119.7	94.5

5. Trade

Years and periods	Exports Value Mill. of dollars	of which: share of Diamonds Per cent	Imports Value Mill. of dollars	of which: share of food Per cent	Terms of trade
1980	58	54.6	464	26.5	100
1985	21	1.6 c/	250	25.1 b/	..

	Value	Volume	Purchasing power	Value	Volume	Index
			Growth rates, per cent per annum			
1980–1985	−18.4	..	−16.3	−11.6	−9.4	..
1984–1985	0.0	..	−0.4	−19.9	−20.2	..
1985–1986	0.0	..	−1.3	4.0	2.6	..

6. Other economic and social indicators

Energy Commercial energy consumption per capita 1984 kg of coal equiv.	Transport & communication Commercial vehicles 1982	Telephones 1985 Per 1,000 pop.	Education Adult literacy rate Around 1985	School enrolment ratio share of relevant age group Primary M F T 1983 Per cent	Secondary M F T	Health Attendance at childbirth by trained personnel 1984	Share of population Immunized against DPT (3 doses) 1984	With access to safe water 1985	Food and nutrition Cereals Consumption per capita 1985 kg	Self-sufficiency ratio 1985 Per cent	Average daily calorie intake per capita Total 1985 Calories	Share of requirements Between 1982&1985 Per cent
..	10.8	9.0	..	97 126 111	17 26 21	28.0	69.0	35	212	59	2358	104

a/ Years beginning 1 April.   b/ 1982.   c/ 1984.

cent) was slightly lower than that of GDP.[149] In per capita terms, there was no real income growth in 1985. Inflation appeared to be slowing down somewhat in 1986. The year-to-year increase in retail prices (which closely follow price developments in South Africa) was measured at 16 per cent in October 1986, as compared to 20 per cent in January of that year.

2. *Main sectors*

Drought conditions still prevailed in 1984, but in 1985 the ending of the drought led to a recovery in agricultural output. However, the 1986 harvest was again poor with most crop production substantially down compared with the previous year. Manufacturing registered significant growth in both 1984 and 1985 and increased its share in GDP marginally to 7 per cent in 1985. A number of new manufacturing ventures were again created in 1986 and others were expanded, notably in the footwear and clothing industry. Industrial promotion efforts continue. A draft agreement on the establishment of a wool and mohair scouring plant and a wool-top-making mill, which would process Lesotho's main traditional export commodities, was signed in December 1986.

3. *Trade and payments*

Although still in surplus, Lesotho's current account weakened in 1985, since increased imports were not fully offset by the increased income from migrant labour abroad. The overall surplus was correspondingly somewhat lower than in the previous year. In 1986 a marked decline in net foreign assets of the banking system indicated a further weakening of the balance of payments. The loti (pegged at par with the South African rand) continued to depreciate in the first half of 1986, but then started to move up against the dollar.

4. *Budget*

The budgetary situation deteriorated sharply in FY 1985/86,[150] after the progressive narrowing of the budget deficit over the previous three-year period. Accelerating recurrent expenditure and debt payments, in conjunction with much slower growth in customs receipts – the Government's major source of revenue – contributed to the large budget deficit in FY 1985/86, estimated to corre-

spond to some 5 per cent of GNP. A new record level deficit was projected for FY 1986/87, partly due to customs revenues, which were projected to decrease after four years of growth. During the nine months up to the end of 1986, domestic borrowing to finance the deficit had already achieved the level budgeted for the whole fiscal year ending March 1987.

5. *Social developments*

The population growth rate has steadily increased over the past three decades. According to the preliminary 1986 census results, the *de facto* population increased by some 3 per cent per annum and the *de jure* population by 2.6 per cent between 1976 and 1986. Population is projected to be close to 2 million by the end of the 1990s. In 1986, an estimated 84 per cent of the population were living in the rural areas. Analysis of the census results continues. Preliminary findings show, *inter alia*, an increase in the number of landless rural households.

B. *Recent policy developments*

1. *Development policies*

Lesotho's Third Five-Year Development Plan (FY 1980/81-1984/85) was extended to allow additional time for the preparation of the Fourth Plan. The basic objectives laid down in the Third Plan were expected to remain in the new Plan: reduction of the country's vulnerability to external economic and political pressures, and an increase in domestic employment.

The signing of a water treaty with South Africa in October 1986 paved the way for the start-up of the engineering design phase for the water export and hydropower Lesotho Highlands Water Scheme, the largest development project ever undertaken in the country. This phase of the project is expected, *inter alia*, to bring employment opportunities through major road works in the mountain areas.

2. *International support measures*

The net inflow of concessional assistance to Lesotho in 1985 contracted for the second consecutive year, falling to $95 million from $108 million in 1983. Over the same period, non-concessional development financing from multilateral agencies gained in importance, rising to over $10 million in 1985. The cost of the engineering phase

---

[150] The fiscal year (FY) ends on 31 March.

of the Lesotho Highlands Water Scheme (to be completed by 1990) is estimated at over $50 million. Co-financing has been obtained from the World Bank through an IDA credit, from the European Development Fund and from the European Investment Bank. Advisers and training programmes are to be provided by UNDP and by bilateral donors.

3. *SNPA follow-up*

Lesotho's latest Donor Round Table was held in May 1984. Special sectoral consultations on employment generation in the rural sector and problems related to migrant labour were planned for 1987.

23. Malawi

A. *Recent socio-economic developments*

1. *Overall economy*

A deteriorating external environment thwarted Malawi's adjustment efforts in 1986. The years 1982 to 1985 had seen the beginning of recovery in Malawi's economy. GDP at constant factor cost had grown by around 3 per cent annually on the average. However, the external position started to worsen in 1985 with a drop in tobacco prices. In 1986 the balance of payments deteriorated further and there was a sharp downturn in overall economic performance. GDP contracted by an estimated 0.3 per cent in real terms, leading to a decline of per capita income of around 3 per cent in 1986.

The transport situation remained very difficult in 1986, with the virtual closure of Malawi's traditional trade routes through Mozambique and the necessity of freighting the country's sea-borne trade via long road routes. The influx of displaced persons moving from Mozambique over the border into Malawi was increasing rapidly in the beginning of 1987. Their total number was estimated to have more than doubled in the first three months of the year to reach 200,000 by mid-April.

2. *Main sectors*

Malawi has achieved self-sufficiency in basic food staples and has even produced exportable surpluses of maize. However, unfavourable weather in 1987 led to a need for renewed maize imports. Overall agricultural performance deteriorated in 1985 and 1986, as compared with the real growth of 5 per cent on average estimated for the

period 1982/1984. Manufacturing also stagnated in 1986, and there was a downturn in construction activity.

3. *Trade and payments*

Foreign exchange constraints became increasingly severe in 1986. While tobacco prices rose in 1986, world market prices for Malawi's next two principal export commodities – tea and sugar – declined. The transport situation contributed to the deficit on services account and there were heavy debt payments. Capital inflows under the structural adjustment programme cushioned, but did not fully offset, the effect of these developments. Consequently, the overall deficit further widened in 1986. The debt service ratio was estimated at close to 50 per cent of export earnings in 1986. As part of a policy of periodic exchange rate adjustments, the kwacha was devalued by 10 per cent in August 1986 and by a further 20 per cent in February 1987 *vis-à-vis* the currency basket to which it is pegged.

4. *Budget*

A record budget deficit was recorded in FY 1986/87,[151] due to a shortfall in revenue, spending beyond budgeted levels and a sharp rise in external and internal debt payments. A major contributory factor to the overspending was the financial support which the Government has had to extend for the stocking of maize, as export markets were lost in 1986. However, there was an improvement in overall parastatal performance in 1986.

---

[151] The fiscal year (FY) ends on 31 March.

MALAWI

1. Population, total and per capita GDP, growth of agricultural and manufacturing output

Year and periods	Population Millions	GDP Total Millions of dollars	GDP Per capita Dollars	GDP Per capita Per cent of LDC average	Agricultural production Total	Agricultural production of which: Food	Manufacturing value-added Total
1985	6.9	1081	156	72.6			
				Real growth rates, per cent per annum			
1980-1985	3.1	1.2	-1.9		2.2	1.2	2.7
1984-1985	3.0	1.8	-1.1		0.5	0.2	1.3
1985-1986	3.6	..	..		2.2	1.7	0.3

2. Area, demographic indicators and labour force share in agriculture

Area Total 000 km2	Area Share of arable land under permanent crops 1984 Per cent	Area Share covered by forestry and woodlands 1984 Per cent	Density 1985 Pop/km2	Average life expectancy at birth M 1980-1985 Years	Average life expectancy at birth F 1980-1985 Years	Average life expectancy at birth T 1980-1985 Years	Infant mortality as share of live births 1980-1985 Per 1,000	Share of population In urban areas 1985 Per cent	Share of population Economically active 1985 Per cent	Labour force Share in agriculture Per cent
118.5	19.8	39.1	59	44	46	45	163	12	44	78

3. Origins and uses of output; investment

Years	Sectoral origin of GDP Agriculture	Sectoral origin of GDP Mining	Sectoral origin of GDP Manufacturing	Sectoral origin of GDP Services	Uses of GDP Private consumption expenditure	Uses of GDP Government consumption expenditure	Uses of GDP Gross domestic savings	Investment
					Per cent of total GDP			
1980	35.0	..	10.9	41.0	70.4	19.0	10.6	24.5
1985	37.9a/	..	12.5 a/	45.3 a/	73.8	15.5	10.7	15.7

4. Balance of payments, debt and external assistance

Years	Balance of payments Merchandise trade balance	Balance of payments Balance on services	Balance of payments Balance on current account	Debt service Amortization	Debt service Interest	Debt service Total	Debt service As ratio of exports of goods and services	Debt Amount outstanding at year-end	External assistance Total	External assistance of which: ODA
				Millions of dollars			Per cent	Millions of dollars		
1980	..	..	..	32.6 b/	43.3 b/	75.8 b/	28.5 b/	882.1 b/	188.1	143.3
1985	..	..	..	53.3	32.3	85.6	31.0	987.5	111.5	113.0

5. Trade

Years and periods	Exports Value Mill. of dollars	Exports of which: share of Tobacco Per cent	Imports Value Mill. of dollars	Imports of which: share of food Per cent	Terms of trade
1980	285	44.2	440	7.5	100
1985	252	43.6	284	8.2 c/	142

	Value	Volume	Purchasing power	Value	Volume	Index
			Growth rates, per cent per annum			
1980-1985	-2.4	-7.2	-0.5	-8.4	-6.6	7.3
1984-1985	-19.5	-23.1	-20.3	5.6	4.6	3.7
1985-1986	-3.6	-8.7	-5.7	-11.3	-13.3	3.2

6. Other economic and social indicators

Energy Commercial energy consumption per capita 1984 kg of coal equiv.	Transport & communication Commercial vehicles 1983 Per 1,000 pop.	Transport & communication Telephones 1985 Per 1,000 pop.	Education Adult literacy rate Around 1985	Education School enrolment ratio share of relevant age group Primary M 1984	Education Primary F 1984	Education Primary T 1984	Education Secondary M 1984	Education Secondary F 1984	Education Secondary T 1984	Health Attendance at childbirth by trained personnel 1984 Per cent	Health Immunized against DPT (3 doses) 1984 Per cent	Health With access to safe water 1985 Per cent	Food and nutrition Cereals Consumption per capita 1985 kg	Food and nutrition Cereals Self-sufficiency ratio 1985 Per cent	Food and nutrition Average daily calorie intake per capita Total 1985 Calories	Food and nutrition Average daily calorie intake per capita Share of requirements Between 1982&1985 Per cent
43	2.2	5.8	..	71	53	62	6	2	4	58.6	66.0	55	224	106	2448	95

a/ 1984.   b/ 1982.   c/ 1983.

B. *Recent policy developments*

1. *Macro-economics policies*

The Government continues to pursue the economic stabilization and structural adjustment programme launched in 1981. Policy reforms which have been undertaken so far under this programme have aimed *inter alia* at: (*a*) providing incentives for increased smallholder agricultural and industrial production, (*b*) restructuring and strengthening of the parastatal sector, (*c*) price liberalization, (*d*) prudent exchange rate and interest rate policies, and (*e*) strengthening of economic planning and debt management. The country's public sector investment programme is reviewed and revised annually in the light of changing needs and priorities and expected resource availabilities. Agriculture and transport together account for over one half of planned expenditure under the current programme.

A new Statement of Development Policies, a longer-term development strategy, was under preparation and tentatively scheduled for release in late 1987. Previously, sectoral plans for education and health had been adopted for the decade 1985-1995. New policy measures announced in the 1987 budget statement were the setting up of an export financing facility to aid small exporters, a strengthening of export promotion activities, and reform and liberalization of the agricultural marketing system.

The FY 1987/88 budget foresaw greater expenditure control, notably cuts in recurrent spending. A number of new tax measures were announced for FY 1987/88, among them an increase of surtax rates and the imposition of an additional duty on luxury goods.

2. *International support measures*

The net inflow of concessional aid to Malawi declined in 1985 to $113 million, moderately lower than the average levels received in the period 1980 through 1983, but substantially lower than the aid inflow of $159 million in 1984, when IDA disbursements were boosted by drawings on loans received in support of Malawi's structural adjustment programme. A new financial package, amounting to $114 million, was arranged by IDA in support of this programme in December 1985. Supplementary funding of $10 million to support further reform efforts in agricultural marketing and pricing was granted in January 1987 under the World Bank's Special Facility for Sub-Saharan Africa. In the latter context an additional $30 million in special joint financing from bilateral donors was announced. IDA credits in support of the Government's education and health programmes were also approved early in 1987. On the other hand, the three-year extended agreement concluded with the IMF in 1983 came to an end in 1986.

3. *SNPA follow-up*

Since the inception of the SNPA, Malawi arranged a Round Table Conference of Partners in Economic Development in 1984, and set up a consultative group arrangement with the World Bank. The first meeting of the group was held in January 1986 and a second meeting was scheduled for late 1987 or early 1988. Local donor consultations have been arranged, notably for the transport and health sectors.

24. Maldives

A. *Recent socio-economic developments*

1. *Overall economy*

Real GDP grew by 14.1 per cent in 1985, representing a further improvement over the rates of 12.9 per cent and 5.9 per cent reported in 1984 and 1983 respectively. As a result GDP reached a level close to $80 million in 1985.

2. *Main sectors*

The share of the primary sector in GDP was 39.7 per cent in 1985, of which fisheries alone constituted 26.9 per cent. The latter registered a growth rate of 20.8 per cent in 1985, making it one of the faster-growing sectors of the economy. The secondary sector's growth rate amounted to 4.5 per cent from 1984 to 1985, but its share in GDP in 1985 was only 11.2 per cent. The tertiary sector,

MALDIVES

1. Population, total and per capita GDP, growth of agricultural and manufacturing output

Year and periods	Population Millions	GDP Total Millions of dollars	GDP Per capita Dollars	GDP Per capita Per cent of LDC average	Agricultural production Total	Agricultural production of which: Food	Manufacturing value-added Total
1985	0.2	(78)	432 a/	200.9			
				Real growth rates, per cent per annum			
1980-1985	3.0	10.0	6.8		3.5	3.5	14.6 b/
1984-1985	3.0	14.1	10.7		1.5	1.5	..
1985-1986	3.0	..	..		2.9	2.9	..

2. Area, demographic indicators and labour force share in agriculture

Area Total	Area Share of arable land under permanent crops 1984	Area Share covered by forestry and woodlands 1984	Density 1985	Average life expectancy at birth M 1980-1985	Average life expectancy at birth F 1980-1985	Average life expectancy at birth T 1980-1985	Infant mortality as share of live births 1980-1985	Share of population In urban areas 1985	Share of population Economically active 1985	Labour force Share in agriculture
000 km2	Per cent	Per cent	Pop/km2	Years	Years	Years	Per 1,000	Per cent	Per cent	
0.3	10.0	3.3	611	..	..	53	82	20	44	46

3. Origins and uses of output; investment

Years	Sectoral origin of GDP Agriculture	Sectoral origin of GDP Mining	Sectoral origin of GDP Manufacturing	Sectoral origin of GDP Services	Uses of GDP Private consumption expenditure	Uses of GDP Government consumption expenditure	Uses of GDP Gross domestic savings	Investment
				Per cent of total GDP				
1980	34.2	1.7	4.4	50.5	..	..	-3.2 c/	..
1985	29.2 a/	1.2 a/	4.7 a/	57.3 a/	62.6 a/	18.4 a/	18.9 a/	30.7 a/

4. Balance of payments, debt and external assistance

Years	Balance of payments Merchandise trade balance	Balance of payments Balance on services	Balance of payments Balance on current account	Debt service Amortization	Debt service Interest	Debt service Total	Debt service As ratio of exports of goods and services	Debt Amount outstanding at year-end	External assistance Total	External assistance of which: ODA
	Millions of dollars						Per cent	Millions of dollars		
1980	-31.2	6.6	-24.9	1.4 d/	1.0 d/	2.3 d/	3.0 d/	48.4 d/	22.8	22.9
1985	-36.0	25.6	-12.4	8.6	4.1	12.7	13.9	81.5	10.0	10.1

5. Trade

Years and periods	Exports Value Mill. of dollars	Exports of which: share of Fresh fish, simply preserved Per cent	Imports Value Mill. of dollars	Imports of which: share of food Per cent	Terms of trade
1980	10	71.5	29	31.4	100
1985	32	44.7 e/	53	16.9 e/	..

	Value	Volume	Purchasing power	Value	Volume	Index
	Growth rates, per cent per annum					
1980-1985	26.2	..	29.4	12.8	15.6	..
1984-1985	28.0	..	27.5	0.0	-0.4	..
1985-1986	-6.2	..	-7.5	3.8	2.4	..

6. Other economic and social indicators

Energy Commercial energy consumption per capita 1984 kg of coal equiv.	Transport & communication Commercial vehicles 1984 Per 1,000 pop.	Transport & communication Telephones 1985	Education Adult literacy rate Around 1985	Education School enrolment ratio share of relevant age group Primary M between 1982 and 1985	Education Primary F	Education Primary T	Education Secondary M	Education Secondary F	Education Secondary T	Health Attendance at childbirth by trained personnel 1984	Health Share of population Immunized against DPT (3 doses) 1984	Health Share of population With access to safe water 1985	Food and nutrition Cereals Consumption per capita 1985 kg	Food and nutrition Cereals Self-sufficiency ratio 1985 Per cent	Food and nutrition Average daily calorie intake per capita Total 1985 Calories	Food and nutrition Average daily calorie intake per capita Share of requirements Between 1982&1985 Per cent
											Per cent			Per cent		Per cent
68	0.8	13.7	..	..	..	61	..	..	..	..	23.0	24	85	1	..	91

a/ 1984.   b/ 1980-1984.   c/ 1981.   d/ 1982.   e/ 1983.

which remains the largest sector in the economy (with a share in GDP of 60.7 per cent in 1985), recorded a growth rate of 16 per cent. Within this sector, the growth rate of tourism was 32.9 per cent between 1984 and 1985, making this the fastest-growing sector of the economy and raising its share in GDP from 15.8 per cent in 1984 to 18.3 per cent in 1985.

3. Trade and payments

As a result of tighter fiscal and monetary policies and increased tourism receipts, the balance-of-payments position improved noticeably in 1985, with the current-account deficit (excluding official transfers) declining from $24.0 million in 1984 to $12.4 million in 1985, equivalent to 12 per cent of GDP. The trade deficit was cut by $7 million, reflecting a considerable improvement in the export performance in the former year. The flow of concessional loans and grants increased from $7.3 million in 1984 to $10.1 million in 1985. Despite the improvements, the outstanding medium- and long-term external debt increased from $59 million at the end of 1984 to $68 million by the end of 1985. However, the debt/service merchandise exports ratio fell sharply from 31 per cent in 1984 to about 14 per cent in 1985, owing to lower amortization requirements.

4. Budget

Government revenue increased marginally from $24.3 million in 1984 to $25.0 million in 1985, while current expenditures climbed from $25.9 million to $27.9 million raising the budget deficit from $1.6 million to $2.9 million. The higher expenditures were more than accounted for by the heavier debt servicing burden, whose share of total expenditures increased from 7.5 per cent in 1984 to 15.9 per cent in 1985.

5. Social developments

While the literacy rate of 86.6 per cent (1983) in the Maldives may be high, given the country's traditional education system, only 24 per cent (1985) receive formal post-primary education in Government schools, which highlights the country's shortage of trained manpower. One of the major health hazards is still the shortage of proper drinking-water facilities, so water-borne diseases are epidemic, contributing to the high

infant mortality rate of 63 per thousand. According to the mid-1986 census, the population of the Maldives (189,400) had grown at an annual rate of 3.3 per cent during the period 1977-1985. The labour force constitutes 78 per cent of the population of working age (15-59), partly because of a rate of female participation far higher than in many developing countries.

B. Recent policy developments

1. Macro-economic policies

The National Development Plan for 1985-1987 provided for an allocation of over 30 per cent of the country's GDP to economic and social development. Projected Plan outlays at current prices were expected to be approximately $107 million, of which $29.6 million were to be spent through the private sector and $76.6 million by the Government and public enterprises. External resource requirements were set at $55.6 million, of which the ODA component was projected at $43.0 million, one-half in grant form.

2. International support policies

The Government anticipates a substantial increase in ODA from traditional donors. It hopes to utilize external technical assistance to carry out pre-investment surveys in the fields of transport, communications, tourism, manpower development, fisheries, etc.

3. SNPA follow-up

At the second UNDP Round Table Meeting held in Geneva in April 1986, the Government's policies and economic management were commended. It was noted that the country's acute balance-of-payments disequilibrium had resulted from increased debt service obligations and decreases in net external aid, which justified increased donor assistance to help ensure continued economic growth. As a follow-up to the meeting, the Government is preparing in-country sectoral meetings to be held with bilateral donors.

25. Mali

A. *Recent socio-economic developments*

1. *Overall economy*

Real GDP per capita declined for the third consecutive year in 1985 (by 4.2 per cent, according to provisional estimates), owing mainly to a continuing fall in export earnings and despite a considerable improvement in agricultural production resulting from good rains.

2. *Main sectors*

Rainfall improvement has permitted two successful cereal harvests since late 1985. The September-November 1986 harvest, which determines the aggregate production for the marketing year November 1986/October 1987, reached a record of 1.8 million tonnes, i.e. 7 per cent above the already high level registered in the preceding harvest. In 1987, the country will have an exportable surplus in coarse grains estimated at 100,000 tonnes, against an import requirement of wheat of 50,000 tonnes. However, improved crops have led to lower local prices for cereals. Thus millet – the main staple – was trading at CFAF 25 per kg in January 1987, as compared to the indicative official price of CFAF 55. The low level of actual trading prices may discourage plantations and thereby affect the forthcoming harvest.

Rainfall improvement has also led to significant increases in drought-sensitive export items, such as groundnuts (from 37,600 tonnes in 1984/85 to 57,000 tonnes and 81,500 tonnes in the subsequent marketing years) and karité (shea) nut (from a mere 60 tonnes in 1984/85 to 40,000 tonnes in 1985/86).

A meat processing factory started operations in late 1986. Sugar production was estimated at 18,000 tonnes in 1985/86, which tripled the 1982/83 level, but was still far short of the annual local consumption level of 50,000 tonnes. Expansion of sugar production is being supported by assistance from China.

3. *Trade and payments*

Cotton accounted for over 40 per cent of total exports during most of the early 1980s. World dollar prices for this commodity fell by 40 per cent between 1984 and 1986, thus impairing the country's export earnings. Imports first continued to rise between 1984 and 1985, but then fell again, to below the 1984 level in 1986. An encouraging development relates to the partial recovery of world cotton prices since the third quarter of 1986: these had reached 8.25 French francs per kg (c.i.f. Europe) by the end of March 1987 as compared to the trough of 5.65 French francs at the end of August 1986.

Total outstanding debt (including short-term debt and use of IMF credit) reached $1,500 million by the end of 1985 (equivalent to 130 per cent of GNP), while debt service remained at a modest 23 per cent of total exports of goods and services mainly due to the long maturity profile and to the concessional terms of most of the debt.

B. *Recent policy developments*

1. *Macro-economic policies*

Mali has been implementing IMF-supported structural adjustment programmes since 1982. In the context of these programmes, four public enterprises were dismantled in early 1987. On the other hand, the activities of the import-export company SOMIEX, which had been terminated in 1983, resumed in August 1986, while private export businesses were still allowed to operate; and Air Mali, whose operation had been suspended in 1985, resumed internal flights in May 1987.

A balanced budget amounting to CFAF 78.5 billion (about $260 million) was approved for 1987, representing a 13.6 per cent increase *vis-à-vis* the 1986 budget. Personnel expenditures have been contained and account for 54 per cent of the total, as against 70 per cent in 1986. The previous budget had also been in balance when approved, but terminated with a realized deficit corresponding to 15 per cent of the planned level.

A five-year development plan for 1987-1991 is under preparation. Since the expiry of the pre-

MALI

1. Population, total and per capita GDP, growth of agricultural and manufacturing output

Year and periods	Population Millions	GDP Total Millions of dollars	GDP Per capita Dollars	GDP Per capita Per cent of LDC average	Agricultural production Total	Agricultural production of which: Food	Manufacturing value-added Total
1985	8.1	1154	143	66.5			
				Real growth rates, per cent per annum			
1980–1985	2.8	-0.4	-3.1		2.4	2.4	..
1984–1985	2.7	-1.6	-4.2		-2.6	-3.6	..
1985–1986	3.2	..	..		11.8	11.8	..

2. Area, demographic indicators and labour force share in agriculture

Area Total 000 km2	Area Share of arable land under permanent crops 1984 Per cent	Area Share covered by forestry and woodlands 1984 Per cent	Demographic indicators Density 1985 Pop/km2	Average life expectancy at birth M 1980–1985 Years	Average life expectancy at birth F 1980–1985 Years	Average life expectancy at birth T 1980–1985 Years	Infant mortality as share of live births 1980–1985 Per 1,000	Share of population In urban areas Per cent	Share of population Economically active 1985 Per cent	Labour force Share in agriculture
1240.0	1.7	7.0	7	40	44	42	180	20	32	83

3. Origins and uses of output; investment

Years	Sectoral origin of GDP Agriculture	Mining	Manufacturing	Services	Uses of GDP Private consumption expenditure	Government consumption expenditure	Gross domestic savings	Investment
				Per cent of total GDP				
1980	59.0 a/	..	4.2 a/	31.3 a/	83.0 a/	9.6 a/	7.4 a/	24.5 a/
1985	45.9	..	6.9 b/	36.4 b/	77.3	11.0	11.7	32.8

4. Balance of payments, debt and external assistance

Years	Balance of payments Merchandise trade balance	Balance on services	Balance on current account	Debt service Amortization	Interest	Total	As ratio of exports of goods and services	Debt Amount outstanding at year-end	External assistance Total	External assistance of which: ODA
	Millions of dollars						Per cent	Millions of dollars		
1980	-103.5	-170.9	-233.9	2.6 c/	30.9 c/	33.4 c/	17.6 c/	855.0 c/	269.0	269.5
1985	-111.9	-168.0	-258.7	25.1	26.6	51.8	22.7	1503.7	390.7	389.0

5. Trade

Years and periods	Exports Value Mill. of dollars	Exports of which: share of Cotton Per cent	Imports Value Mill. of dollars	Imports of which: share of food Per cent	Terms of trade
1980	205	47.3	440	11.5	100
1985	170	40.4	410	15.4 d/	119

	Value	Volume	Purchasing power	Value	Volume	Index
			Growth rates, per cent per annum			
1980–1985	-3.7	-4.8	-1.4	-1.4	0.9	3.5
1984–1985	-12.8	-15.5	-13.7	9.3	8.3	2.2
1985–1986	12.9	15.1	11.0	-9.8	-11.3	-3.6

6. Other economic and social indicators

Energy Commercial energy consumption per capita 1984 kg of coal equiv.	Transport & communication Commercial vehicles 1984 Per 1,000 pop.	Transport & communication Telephones 1982 Per 1,000 pop.	Education Adult literacy rate Around 1985	Education School enrolment ratio share of relevant age group Primary M 1982	Education Primary F 1982	Education Primary T 1982	Education Secondary M 1982	Education Secondary F 1982	Education Secondary T 1982	Health Attendance at childbirth by trained personnel 1984	Health Share of population Immunized against DPT (3 doses) 1980	Health Share of population With access to safe water 1985	Food and nutrition Cereals Consumption per capita 1985 kg	Food and nutrition Cereals Self-sufficiency ratio 1985 Per cent	Food and nutrition Average daily calorie intake per capita Total 1985 Calories	Food and nutrition Average daily calorie intake per capita Share of requirements Between 1982&1985 Per cent
30	..	1.5	17	30	17	24	10	4	7	..	17.5	17	201	84	1788	68

a/ 1981.   b/ 1984.   c/ 1982.   d/ 1983.

ceding plan in 1985, the macro-economic policy of the country has been determined to a large extent by the above-mentioned structural adjustment programmes.

A 1986 revision of the investment code provides for reduced taxes and duties on export businesses as well as for some incentives to industries established in disadvantaged regions.

2. *International support*

Total ODA continued increasing to reach $389 million in 1985, up from $219 million and $328 million in 1983 and 1984, respectively. However, much of the increase was related to drought relief and related assistance, which appears to be diminishing along with rainfall improvement.

A STABEX grant amounting to ECU 5 million (about $5.5 million) was extended by the EC in early 1987 to compensate for export earnings losses caused by the drought and by the fall in world cotton prices.

Negotiations are under way with the IMF for a new stand-by agreement to replace the one which expired in March 1987.

26. Mauritania

A. *Recent socio-economic developments*

1. *Overall economy*

Mauritania faced a multiplicity of economic and financial problems up to 1984. Growth performance was weak: per capita GDP declined by 0.6 per annum in real terms between 1980 and 1984, despite a very high investment rate (32 per cent of GDP on average). In 1984, the critical situation was characterized by budgetary and balance-of-payments deficits, equivalent to 7.9 per cent and 26 per cent of GDP respectively. Mainly as a result of the the good performance in fishing and the recovery of the rural sector following good rainfall in mid-1985, real GDP grew by 3.1 per cent in 1985. Preliminary estimates put real GDP growth at 4 per cent in 1986, largely due to increased agricultural production. The general consumer price index rose by 7 per cent in 1986, as compared to a 12 per cent inflation rate in 1985.

2. *Main sectors*

As a result of the chronic drought which started in 1973 and low world commodity prices, the structure of Mauritania's GDP changed radically. Whereas agriculture and livestock used to account for more than 40 per cent of GDP in the 1960s, the effects of the drought have slashed their share drastically. Crop cultivation is severely restricted by the limited area of arable land. Greatly improved rainfall in 1985 and 1986 pushed production of grains up from 67,500 tonnes in 1985 to 95,000 tonnes in 1986, raising the self-sufficiency ratio to 32 per cent as compared to only 12 per cent during the period 1981-1984. Fishing is now one of the driving forces of Mauritania's economy. It has averaged 11 per cent growth a year during the 1980s and has been the most significant foreign-exchange earner since 1983, followed by iron ore, output of which averaged 9 million tonnes during the period 1984-1986.

3. *Trade and payments*

In 1986 fish exports were worth about $280 million and those of iron ore $150 million. The depressed world market for iron ore led the State Mining Company to concede price reductions of up to 11 per cent for 1987 deliveries to main customers. Consequently, the burden of generating additional export revenues fell primarily on the fisheries sector. Fish exports rose 43 per cent between 1985 and 1986 to reach 390,000 tonnes. Despite these efforts, the level of 1985 exports could not be sustained in 1986. Prospects for 1987 are more promising, with the value of fish exports almost twice as high during the first quarter as compared to the same period of 1986. Earnings from other exports such as gypsum and plaster, are also expected to increase. Tight control over imports, together with the increase in fish exports produced trade surpluses during recent years. The main drain on the external account has come from service payments, including those associated with the fisheries and mining sectors. The annual current account deficits of around $110 million during 1984 and 1985 were financed by aid and an

MAURITANIA

1. Population, total and per capita GDP, growth of agricultural and manufacturing output

Year and periods	Population Millions	GDP Total Millions of dollars	GDP Per capita Dollars	GDP Per capita Per cent of LDC average	Agricultural production Total	Agricultural production of which: Food	Manufacturing value-added Total
1985	1.9	691	366	170.2			
			Real growth rates, per cent per annum				
1980-1985	3.0	1.5	-1.4		-0.2	-0.2	3.0
1984-1985	2.8	3.1	0.3		4.7	4.7	5.5
1985-1986	3.3	..	..		11.7	11.7	14.2

2. Area, demographic indicators and labour force share in agriculture

Area Total	Area Share of arable land under permanent crops	Area Share covered by forestry and woodlands	Density	Average life expectancy at birth M	Average life expectancy at birth F	Average life expectancy at birth T	Infant mortality as share of live births	Share of population In urban areas	Share of population Economically active	Labour force Share in agriculture
	1984	1984	1985	1980-1985	1980-1985	1980-1985	1980-1985		1985	
000 km2	Per cent	Per cent	Pop/km2	Years	Years	Years	Per 1,000	Per cent	Per cent	Per cent
1030.7	0.2	14.6	2	42	46	44	137	31	31	59

3. Origins and uses of output; investment

Years	Agriculture	Mining	Manufacturing	Services	Private consumption expenditure	Government consumption expenditure	Gross domestic savings	Investment
				Per cent of total GDP				
1980	30.4	11.5	6.9	43.6	67.8	25.3	6.9	36.2
1985	28.7	11.6	5.6a/	45.9a/	75.7	15.4	9.0	23.8

4. Balance of payments, debt and external assistance

Years	Merchandise trade balance	Balance on services	Balance on current account	Amortization	Interest	Total	As ratio of exports of goods and services	Debt Amount outstanding at year-end	External assistance Total	External assistance of which: ODA
	Millions of dollars						Per cent	Millions of dollars	Millions of dollars	
1980	-124.9	-98.1	-251.2	22.1 b/	33.2 b/	55.3 b/	18.1 b/	1200.6 b/	146.3	157.6
1985	37.7	-257.0	-240.1	55.2	40.7	95.9	23.2	1508.7	215.2	198.0

5. Trade

Years and periods	Exports Value Mill. of dollars	Exports of which: share of Iron ore Per cent	Imports Value Mill. of dollars	Imports of which: share of food Per cent	Terms of trade
1980	194	77.7	286	29.6	100
1985	374	40.2	234	36.3	96

	Value	Volume	Purchasing power	Value	Volume	Index
			Growth rates, per cent per annum			
1980-1985	14.0	18.7	17.8	-3.9	-0.8	-0.8
1984-1985	25.9	27.6	26.4	-4.9	-4.5	-0.9
1985-1986	-25.1	-24.7	-27.8	2.6	-1.1	-4.0

6. Other economic and social indicators

Energy Commercial energy consumption per capita	Transport & communication Commercial vehicles	Transport & communication Telephones	Education Adult literacy rate	Education School enrolment ratio Primary M	Education School enrolment ratio Primary F	Education School enrolment ratio Primary T	Education School enrolment ratio Secondary M	Education School enrolment ratio Secondary F	Education School enrolment ratio Secondary T	Health Attendance at childbirth by trained personnel	Health Share of population Immunized against DPT (3 doses)	Health Share of population With access to safe water	Food and nutrition Cereals Consumption per capita	Food and nutrition Cereals Self-sufficiency ratio	Food and nutrition Average daily calorie intake per capita Total	Food and nutrition Average daily calorie intake per capita Share of requirements
1984	1984	1983	Around 1985	1982	1982	1982	1982	1982	1982	1984	1984	1985	1985	1985	1985	Between 1982&1985
kg of coal equiv.	Per 1,000 pop.					Per cent							kg	Per cent	Calories	Per cent
158	..	2.7	..	45	29	37	19	6	12	22.6	21.4	73c/	160	16	2078	98

a/ 1984.   b/ 1982.   c/ Urban only.

accumulation of arrears on external debt. According to the World Bank, Mauritania's public and publicly-guaranteed medium- and long-term external liabilities stood at about $1,400 million at the end of 1985. The ratio of debt service (estimated at $96 million in 1985) to export of goods and services has remained relatively low, as a result of the high proportion of concessional foreign loans. The debt negotiations at the Paris Club in March 1986, covering 95 per cent of the debts to the creditor countries represented, rescheduled repayment over a period of nine years, including four years of grace. Special treatment to Mauritania was granted at the Paris Club meeting held in June 1987. Thus, payments of interest and principal due between March 1987 and May 1988 will now be made over a period of 15 years including 5 years of grace. The rescheduling applies to all public and publicly-guaranteed loans.

4. *Budget*

The central Government budget for 1986 foresaw balanced ordinary revenues and expenditures. This basic objective was probably achieved, inasmuch as by October of that year ordinary revenues and expenditures had reached about 72 per cent of the amount budgeted for the year as a whole. The 1987 budget aims at achieving a surplus of about $12.8 million for partial financing of capital expenditures. The 1987 Finance Act, pursuing a policy of austerity, revised custom tariffs and strengthened the tax collection services.

B. *Recent policy developments*

1. *Macro-economic policies*

The basic statement of the Government's development policy is the "Economic and Financial Recovery Programme 1985-1988", prepared with the World Bank's assistance, whose main macro-economic goals are: (*a*) to maintain an annual growth rate of 4 per cent; (*b*) to improve the productivity of investments; (*c*) to bring the central Government budget into balance; and (*d*) to reduce the balance-of-payments deficit. Policies required to achieve these goals include a flexible exchange rate, tightening of budgetary and credit policies, fiscal austerity, progressive liberalization of pricing and marketing, rehabilitation of the public enterprise sector and a major rationalization of the investment programme to support productive activities in fisheries, agriculture, mining and public services.

2. *International support measures*

At the end of 1986, Mauritania was formally designated as a least developed country by the United Nations General Assembly. Multilateral and bilateral assistance from OPEC countries normally constitute the bulk of Mauritania's development aid. But drought relief, combined with IMF support of the Recovery Programme and debt rescheduling, raised commitments to $231.9 million in 1985. The IMF supported the Recovery Programme with three successive stand-by arrangements (the last of which is worth SDR 10 million and expires in May 1988), as well as a three-year arrangement of SDR 15.93 million under the Fund's Structural Adjustment Facility expiring in September 1989.

3. *SNPA follow-up*

The Recovery Programme 1985-1988 was presented to the Consultative Group organized by the World Bank in Paris on 26 and 27 November 1985, where the requirements of $616 million of net external aid were favourably received by donors. Sectoral meetings on assistance to the fisheries and mining sectors took place during the first quarter of 1987.

27. Nepal

A. *Recent socio-economic developments*

1. *Overall economy*

The 4.2 real growth rate achieved by Nepal in FY 1985/86 [152] can be regarded as satisfactory. Although the economy showed signs of further improvement during the first seven months of FY 1986/87, real growth is expected to fall to 2.0 – 2.5 per cent over the latter year as a whole, owing to prolonged drought, floods and damage to major irrigation facilities. Inflation accelerated from 8 per cent in 1985 to approximately 19 per cent in 1986, partly due to the devaluation of November 1985. However, since mid-1986 there had been a marked price stabilization, so that the year-to-year increase was reduced to less than 9 per cent by May 1987.

2. *Main sectors*

The still dominant agricultural sector remains vulnerable to the vagaries of the weather. Owing to the disappointing performance of food crops, total agricultural production shrank in FY 1985/86. Non-agricultural output rose by 3.4 per cent but, subsumed within the latter, industrial output grew by as much as 7.2 per cent. Other sectors, such as tourism and construction, also performed satisfactorily during FY 1985/86.

3. *Trade and payments*

According to original figures, exports stagnated in 1986. However, recent revisions point to a drop in exports of 11.2 per cent during that year. According to these revised figures, imports rose marginally, causing the trade deficit to widen by 8 per cent. There was a considerable increase in income on account of services, which reduced the deficit on current account (excluding official transfers) from $207 million in 1985 to $182 million in 1986. Despite a $30 million decline in recorded ODA and other capital inflows, the overall balance recorded a surplus of $27.3 million in 1986 as compared to a deficit of $33 million in the preceding year, partly due to upward valuation changes in the dollar value of foreign exchange reserves. Non-gold reserves more than recovered their 1985 losses during the course of 1986, and increased further to $106 million by the end of May 1987, i.e. the equivalent of three months' imports. Nevertheless, this improved level was still considerably below the levels maintained during the early 1980s. The total long-term debt increased by 24 per cent and reached $555 million by the end of 1986. Although the debt service merchandise exports ratio increased from 3.5 per cent in FY 1984/85 to 5.8 per cent in FY 1985/86, this was a modest figure compared to LDCs as a whole.

4. *Budget*

Government revenues grew by 17 per cent between FY 1984/85 and FY 1985/86 to NRs 4,504.4 million ($230.4 million), while recurrent expenditures grew slightly faster (18.7 per cent) to NRs 3,230.1 million ($165.2 million). Meanwhile, development expenditures were estimated to have grown to NRs 5,992.6 million ($306.5 million) for a nominal growth rate of only 9.2 per cent, but implying a negative real growth rate. As a result, the overall budgetary deficit has been lowered from 4.1 per cent of GDP in FY 1984/85 to 2.4 per cent of GDP in 1985/86. Virtually all the deficit was financed by domestic borrowing, which dropped correspondingly.

5. *Social developments*

Efforts to upgrade the educational level and increase student enrolment by establishing primary, middle and high schools continued in FY 1985/86. The literacy rate of about 30 per cent is viewed by the Government as unsatisfactory. Similarly, in the area of community health, additional health services were established in 1986. The population growth rate of 2.6 per cent continued to be a challenge to the Government.

---

[152] The fiscal year (FY) ends on 15 July.

NEPAL

1. Population, total and per capita GDP, growth of agricultural and manufacturing output

Year and periods	Population Millions	GDP a/ Total Millions of dollars	Per capita Dollars	Per cent of LDC average	Agricultural production Total	of which: Food	Manufacturing value-added Total
1985	16.6	2347	141	65.6			
				Real growth rates, per cent per annum			
1980-1985	2.5	4.1	1.6		2.5	2.8	..
1984-1985	2.6	2.8	0.2		1.4	1.3	..
1985-1986	2.5	..	..		-3.4	-3.9	..

2. Area, demographic indicators and labour force share in agriculture

	Area		Demographic indicators							Labour force
Total	Share of arable land under permanent crops	Share covered by forestry and woodlands	Density	Average life expectancy at birth			Infant mortality as share of live births	Share of population In urban areas	Economically active	Share in agriculture
	1984		1985	M 1980-1985 F		T	1980-1985	1985		
000 km2	Per cent		Pop/km2	Years			Per 1,000	Per cent		
140.8	16.5	16.4	117	47	45	46	139	7	42	93

3. Origins and uses of output; investment

Years	Sectoral origin of GDP				Uses of GDP			Investment
	Agriculture	Mining	Manufacturing	Services	Private consumption expenditure	Government consumption expenditure	Gross domestic savings	
				Per cent of total GDP				
1980	61.8	0.2	4.3	26.3	84.0	4.9	11.1	18.3
1985	56.2 b/	0.2 b/	4.3 b/	31.7 b/	79.6	8.5	11.9	20.7

4. Balance of payments, debt and external assistance

Years	Balance of payments			Debt service				Debt	External assistance	
	Merchandise trade balance	Balance on services	Balance on current account	Amortization	Interest	Total	As ratio of exports of goods and services	Amount outstanding at year-end	Total	of which: ODA
		Millions of dollars					Per cent	Millions of dollars		
1980	-226.1	78.9	-113.6	6.7 c/	6.8 c/	13.5 c/	5.1 c/	352.4 c/	161.5	163.1
1985	-288.5	44.8	-207.0	8.9	9.4	18.3	5.7	588.7	247.1	237.1

5. Trade

Years and periods	Exports Value Mill. of dollars	of which: share of Clothing Per cent	Imports Value Mill. of dollars	of which: share of food Per cent	Terms of trade
1980	80	1.0	342	4.3	100
1985	161	21.5	460	14.0	..

	Value	Volume	Purchasing power	Value	Volume	Index
			Growth rates, per cent per annum			
1980-1985	15.0	..	17.9	6.1	8.8	..
1984-1985	25.8	..	25.3	10.6	10.1	..
1985-1986	-0.6	..	-1.9	-2.2	-3.5	..

6. Other economic and social indicators

Energy	Transport & communication		Education							Health			Food and nutrition			
Commercial energy consumption per capita	Commercial vehicles	Telephones	Adult literacy rate	School enrolment ratio share of relevant age group Primary			Secondary			Attendance at childbirth by trained personnel	Share of population Immunized against DPT (3 doses)	With access to safe water	Cereals Consumption per capita	Self-sufficiency ratio	Average daily calorie intake per capita Total	Share of requirements
			Around	M	F	T	M	F	T							Between
1984	1984	1984	1985		1984					1985	1983-1984	1985		1985	1985	1982&1985
kg of coal equiv.	Per 1,000 pop.							Per cent					kg	Per cent	Calories	Per cent
17	..	1.1	26	104	47	77	35	11	23	10.0	26.4	28	251	102	2034	93

a/ Years ending 15 July.   b/ 1983.   c/ 1982.

B. *Recent policy developments*

1. *Macro-economic policies*

At the end of 1985, the Government introduced a series of economic measures to accelerate growth and stabilize the economy. These measures included a devaluation of the Nepalese rupee by 15 per cent, the liberalization of interest rates and the limitation of the public sector's external borrowing capacity. In the fiscal domain, the programme involved a combination of higher tax rates, better tax collection and real declines in development expenditures. As part of the programme to support broader private sector participation in the economy, shares of public enterprises were floated for private acquisition. In the agricultural sector, measures were introduced by the Government to promote private sector initiative, limiting the public sector's role to providing essential support functions. Moreover, farmers were assured of more remunerative prices for their produce by the announcement of support prices for food grains and cash crops well ahead of the harvesting season. In pursuance of the objectives of its structural adjustment programme, the Government has adopted measures to provide industrial producers with improved incentives both for exports and import substitution. In the field of foreign trade, cash and other incentive mechanisms were introduced as a part of an export promotion programme. Although these measures assisted the Government to correct short-term fiscal and external payments imbalances, the continuation of the programme may jeopardize the long-term growth of the economy if it is not complemented by appropriate growth-oriented strategies.

2. *International support measures*

The stand-by arrangement entered into by Nepal with the IMF in December 1985 expired in April 1987. Discussions have begun with the IMF to obtain support from the Structural Adjustment Facility (SAF) during FY 1987/88. Similarly, an agreement for an IDA structural adjustment credit worth $50 million was signed with the World Bank in early 1987.

3. *SNPA follow-up*

The 7th meeting of the Nepal Aid Group was held in Paris on 25 April 1987 under the auspices of the World Bank. In commending the Government for the steps taken since the January 1986 meeting held in Tokyo, the participants reaffirmed their strong support for the country's development priorities by pledging a $570 million aid package, representing a 65 per cent nominal increase over the amount pledged at the previous meeting. However, if account is taken of late pledges for 1986, and deducting a major project long under discussion but formally included among the 1987 pledges, the increase amounts to only 12 per cent.

28. Niger

A. *Recent socio-economic developments*

1. *Overall economy*

Following rainfall improvement, provisional estimates for 1985 point to a significant recovery of real GDP per capita (4.3 per cent growth, as compared to a decline of 18.4 per cent in 1984).

2. *Main sectors*

Despite some grasshopper damage, two good harvests were achieved consecutively in 1985 and 1986, thus allowing the country to regain its pre-drought self-sufficiency in cereals. For the marketing year October 1986/September 1987, the country has achieved an exportable surplus of coarse grains of 50,000 tonnes, as compared to a deficit of

NIGER

1. Population, total and per capita GDP, growth of agricultural and manufacturing output

Year and periods	Population Millions	GDP Total Millions of dollars	GDP Per capita Dollars	GDP Per capita Per cent of LDC average	Agricultural production Total	Agricultural production of which: Food	Manufacturing value-added Total
1985	6.1	1577	258	120.0			
				Real growth rates, per cent per annum			
1980-1985	2.9	-2.5	-5.2		0.5	0.4	..
1984-1985	2.7	7.1	4.3		27.2	27.2	..
1985-1986	3.3	..	..		3.7	3.7	..

2. Area, demographic indicators and labour force share in agriculture

Area Total	Area Share of arable land under permanent crops	Area Share covered by forestry and woodlands	Density	Average life expectancy at birth M	Average life expectancy at birth F	Average life expectancy at birth T	Infant mortality as share of live births	Share of population In urban areas	Share of population Economically active	Labour force Share in agriculture
	1984		1985	1980-1985			1980-1985		1985	
000 km2	Per cent		Pop/km2	Years			Per 1,000	Per cent		
1267.0	3.0	2.1	5	41	44	43	146	15	52	89

3. Origins and uses of output; investment

Years	Sectoral origin of GDP Agriculture	Sectoral origin of GDP Mining	Sectoral origin of GDP Manufacturing	Sectoral origin of GDP Services	Uses of GDP Private consumption expenditure	Uses of GDP Government consumption expenditure	Uses of GDP Gross domestic savings	Investment
					Per cent of total GDP			
1980	42.6	12.6	3.7	29.7	67.1	10.3	22.6	36.7
1985	46.8	7.6	3.8	33.0	83.1	12.0	4.9	13.7

4. Balance of payments, debt and external assistance

Years	Balance of payments Merchandise trade balance	Balance of payments Balance on services	Balance of payments Balance on current account	Debt service Amortization	Debt service Interest	Debt service Total	Debt service As ratio of exports of goods and services	Debt Amount outstanding at year-end	External assistance Total	External assistance of which: ODA
		Millions of dollars					Per cent	Millions of dollars		
1980	..	..	..	98.8 a/	73.1 a/	171.9 a/	39.0 a/	891.1 a/	251.8	170.5
1985	..	..	..	43.2	52.6	95.8	31.4	1058.2	301.2	316.8

5. Trade

Years and periods	Exports Value Mill. of dollars	Exports of which: share of Uranium Per cent	Imports Value Mill. of dollars	Imports of which: share of food Per cent	Terms of trade
1980	566	84.3	594	14.3	100
1985	223	82.7 b/	400	..	85

	Value	Volume	Purchasing power	Value	Volume	Index
			Growth rates, per cent per annum			
1980-1985	-17.0	-12.3	-15.1	-7.6	-5.5	-3.2
1984-1985	-2.2	-5.0	-2.6	21.2	20.7	2.5
1985-1986	-26.0	-23.1	-24.1	2.5	5.1	-1.3

6. Other economic and social indicators

Energy Commercial energy consumption per capita	Transport & communication Commercial vehicles	Transport & communication Telephones	Education Adult literacy rate	Education School enrolment ratio share of relevant age group Primary M	Education Primary F	Education Primary T	Education Secondary M	Education Secondary F	Education Secondary T	Health Attendance at childbirth by trained personnel	Health Share of population Immunized against DPT (3 doses)	Health Share of population With access to safe water	Food and nutrition Cereals Consumption per capita	Food and nutrition Cereals Self-sufficiency ratio	Food and nutrition Average daily calorie intake per capita Total	Food and nutrition Average daily calorie intake per capita Share of requirements
1984	1984	1985	Around 1985			1983				1983	1983	1985		1985	1985	Between 1982&1985
kg of coal equiv.	Per 1,000 pop.								Per cent				kg	Per cent	Calories	Per cent
56	3.6	1.9	..	..	..	28	..	..	7	46.5	5.0	46	344	88	2250	97

a/ 1982. b/ 1983.

wheat and rice estimated at 25,000 tonnes. Although groundnut production increased dramatically from 8,500 tonnes in 1985 to 55,000 tonnes in 1986 (with ensuing depressive effects on domestic prices), it still remained well below local consumption needs (estimated at 100,000 tonnes per year). The national herd, unrecorded exports of which appear to be significant, is expanding again after being halved by the drought. A matter of concern is the danger of extensive grasshopper infestations which, based on recent egg pod surveys, is expected to be more serious in 1987 than in the preceding year.

3. Trade and payments

Exports of uranium, which generally account for more than four-fifths of total exports, continue to be affected by depressed world market conditions. The adverse impact of such conditions is mitigated by the fact that around one-half of the national production is purchased by France, Niger's main client, at preferential prices. The continuing decline in export earnings, combined with a moderate import expansion from the extremely depressed 1984 level, led to a deterioration of the trade balance in 1985, which, according to balance-of-payments figures, recorded a deficit of $50.9 million as compared to a $6 million surplus in 1984. During 1986, the trade deficit was brought back to about $41 million. At the end of 1985, total outstanding debt (including short-term debt and use of IMF credit) amounted to $1.1 billion (as compared to $930 million one year earlier), and debt service, excluding repurchases to the IMF, represented 31.4 per cent of the exports of goods and services in that year.

B. Recent policy developments

1. Macro-economic policies

Since 1983, Niger has been implementing IMF-supported adjustment programmes which involve liberalization of prices and marketing of commodities, streamlining of the parastatal sector, the promotion of private sector activities, and increased public investment, notably in the productive sectors.

A three-year, interim recovery programme for 1987-1989 has been launched, while a five-year development plan for 1987-1991 was completed in April 1987. For the sake of being realistic, the five-year development plan aims at an annual growth rate of 3.1 per cent, which is equivalent to the population growth rate. Priority is given to anti-desertification measures, agricultural development and stronger private sector involvement. Moreover, there is a clear intention to reduce the country's dependence on uranium sales through the promotion of other exports, notably agricultural commodities.

A programme of fiscal reform was announced in May 1987, providing for a reduction of the value added tax (VAT) as well as of other indirect taxes such as those on cigars, cigarettes and petroleum products.

2. International support

Official development assistance from all sources nearly doubled in 1985 at $318 million, as compared to $166 million in 1984. Much of the increase, however, related to drought relief and other emergency assistance, which appears to be shrinking along with rainfall improvement.

A package of adjustment programme support, totalling SDR 25.9 million ($31.3 million) was accorded by the IMF in December 1986, following three successive stand-by arrangements. The package includes a new stand-by credit of SDR 10.1 million ($12.2 million) and a loan of SDR 15.8 million ($19.1 million) under the newly established Structural Adjustment Facility (SAF). It complements two structural adjustment loans of $60 million and $80 million granted by the World Bank in February 1986 and June 1987, respectively.

Six multilateral reschedulings have been negotiated at the Paris and London Clubs since 1983. The most recent rescheduling was agreed upon at Paris in November 1986, relating to the officially-guaranteed debt falling due between December 1986 and November 1987 ($39 million). The agreement provides for a 10-year rescheduling including a 5-year grace period.

An EC grant from the Sysmin facility, amounting to ECU 120 million ($134.4 million), was accorded in early 1987 to compensate for depressed uranium sales. The grant is to be used to develop the non-uranium sector.

3. SNPA follow-up

A Donor Round Table was held in Geneva from 30 June to 1 July 1987. The round table ascertained that the external resources required for the implementation of the five-year development plan 1987-1991 amounted to $350 million per year. Assistance already secured for the first two years goes beyond this amount. As a follow-up to the round table, three sectoral meetings were to be held before the end of 1987 on rural development, the private sector and the transport sector, respectively.

29. Rwanda

A. *Recent socio-economic developments*

1. *Overall economy*

After a modest economic performance in 1984 (2.9 per cent), real growth of GDP in 1985 was estimated at 3.4 per cent. Since annual population growth is around 3.5 per cent, per capita income remained constant. Inflationary tendencies reached a low that had not been witnessed since the early 1970s, as the consumer price index only advanced by 1.7 per cent in 1985 and actually declined by almost 4 per cent during the first half of 1986. The relative price stability is not only due to stable – and for some items, even decreasing – food prices, but also reflects the depreciation since early 1985 of the United States dollar against the SDR, to which the Rwanda franc is tied.

2. *Main sectors*

Good rains in 1985 and the subsequent recovery of agriculture has affected output of both food and cash crops. Food production increased by 6 per cent as compared to 1984. Production of coffee, the main export crop and an essential revenue-earner for the Government, increased by 20 per cent, to exceed 40,000 tonnes in 1985, but this did not begin to be reflected in higher export volumes until the last quarter of the year, when prices were higher.

Output of tea, the second leading export, grew by 30 pr cent in 1985, while that of pyrethrum and cinchona, also produced for export, stagnated. Output of mining declined sharply, while the manufacturing sector experienced a growth of 12.5 per cent. Although the continuous decline of the construction sector has come to a halt, 1985 did not show any positive growth. The service sector as a whole was marked by favourable development, in particular of transport, which grew by 33 per cent.

Tourism also experienced a modestly favourable development, with hotels and restaurants increasing their receipts by 4.3 per cent.

3. *Trade and payments*

In 1985, the trade deficit reached its peak level during the 1980s. Both declining merchandise exports and – even more importantly – growing import values were responsible for this development. The increase in the price of coffee exports was nearly offset by the decline in export volume lasting for most of the year, leaving receipts from coffee exports virtually unchanged between 1984 and 1985. But during the first half of 1986 these receipts were 72 per cent above the corresponding 1985 period, reflecting the sharp price increase through mid-1986. However, by early 1987 the situation had been fundamentally reversed, with coffee prices falling to a 12-year low. Unfavourable world market prices of minerals in 1985 resulted in a 10 per cent fall of export receipts from tin as compared with 1984. More important, however, was the one-third fall in tea export receipts following the decline in world tea prices. The deteriorating trade balance reflects the worsening of Rwanda's terms of trade by 10 per cent between 1984 and 1985. The long-standing deficit on the service account increased in 1985, due mainly to the increased weight of transport costs which Rwanda has to bear as a landlocked country. In fact, these costs account for more than 60 per cent of total non-debt service payments abroad, adding no less than 21 per cent to the total cost of imports.

Rwanda's total external debt amounted to $370 million at the end of 1985, which corresponded to about 20 per cent of GDP. The debt service for 1985 amounted to 15 per cent of exports of goods and services. As the concessional portion of Rwanda's debt is high (estimated at 72 per cent), nearly three-quarters of the existing stock of debt does not necessitate debt servicing. In

RWANDA

1. Population, total and per capita GDP, growth of agricultural and manufacturing output

Year and periods	Population Millions	GDP Total Millions of dollars	GDP Per capita Dollars	GDP Per capita Per cent of LDC average	Agricultural production Total	Agricultural production of which: Food	Manufacturing value-added Total
1985	6.0	(1651)	274 a/	127.4			
				Real growth rates, per cent per annum			
1980-1985	3.2	4.2	0.9		1.5	1.0	..
1984-1985	3.2	3.4	0.2		4.7	5.8	..
1985-1986	3.2	..	..		2.4	2.8	..

2. Area, demographic indicators and labour force share in agriculture

	Area		Demographic indicators							Labour force
Total	Share of arable land under permanent crops	Share covered by forestry and woodlands	Density	Average life expectancy at birth			Infant mortality as share of live births	Share of population In urban areas	Share of population Economically active	Share in agriculture
	1984		1985	M	F	T	1980-1985	1980-1985	1985	
000 km2	Per cent		Pop/km2	Years			Per 1,000	Per cent		
26.3	38.3	19.3	230	45	48	47	132	5	50	92

3. Origins and uses of output; investment

Years	Sectoral origin of GDP Agriculture	Mining	Manufacturing	Services	Uses of GDP Private consumption expenditure	Government consumption expenditure	Gross domestic savings	Investment
					Per cent of total GDP			
1980	45.3	1.7	15.6	32.7	74.8	15.6	9.7	23.4
1985	..	..	..	..	..	..	..	..

4. Balance of payments, debt and external assistance

Years	Balance of payments Merchandise trade balance	Balance on services	Balance on current account	Debt service Amortization	Interest	Total	As ratio of exports of goods and services	Debt Amount outstanding at year-end	External assistance Total	of which: ODA
	Millions of dollars						Per cent	Millions of dollars		
1980	-62.2	-90.1	-155.4	4.6 b/	5.2 b/	9.8 b/	6.2 b/	220.6 b/	155.8	155.4
1985	-93.2	-87.2	-176.2	16.2	7.7	24.0	14.1	369.0	186.0	181.5

5. Trade

Years and periods	Exports Value Mill. of dollars	of which: share of Coffee Per cent	Imports Value Mill. of dollars	of which: share of food Per cent	Terms of trade
1980	112	37.2	243	12.2	100
1985	112	64.6 a/	343	16.5 a/	74

	Value	Volume	Purchasing power	Value	Volume	Index
			Growth rates, per cent per annum			
1980-1985	0.0	8.8	2.4	7.1	9.7	-5.9
1984-1985	-22.8	-24.8	-22.9	16.3	16.0	2.4
1985-1986	5.4	-3.5	2.0	2.6	-0.7	5.6

6. Other economic and social indicators

Energy Commercial energy consumption per capita	Transport & communication Commercial vehicles	Telephones	Education Adult literacy rate	School enrolment ratio share of relevant age group Primary			Secondary			Health Attendance at childbirth by trained personnel	Share of population Immunized against DPT (3 doses)	With access to safe water	Food and nutrition Cereals Consumption per capita	Self-sufficiency ratio	Average daily calorie intake per capita Total	Share of requirements
				M	F	T	M	F	T							
1984	1984	1985	Around 1985		1983					1984	1983	1985	1985		1985	Between 1982&1985
kg of coal equiv.	Per 1,000 pop.						Per cent						kg	Per cent	Calories	Per cent
34	0.9	1.5	47	64	60	62	3	1	2	..	32.0	49	56	92	1919	98

a/ 1984.   b/ 1982.

contrast, suppliers' credits, which have been contracted at market-related rates, accounted for nearly one-third of total debt service in 1985, despite the fact that they constituted less than 3 per cent of the total stock of disbursed debt at the end of that year. Total gross ODA in 1985 came to $181.5 million, of which $132.2 million was in the form of grants. Rwanda has been successful in keeping up the level of aid commitments at a time of generally declining levels of aid. Belgium has been one of the key donor countries.

4. *Budget*

The policy of financial austerity followed since the beginning of 1984 has had a salutary effect on the ordinary (current) budget, which showed a surplus for the first time since 1981. The main source of growth of receipts was the coffee export tax, although consumption, property and direct taxes also contributed. The development budget, which covers domestically-financed projects and local-currency inputs for foreign assistance projects, also showed a surplus. Its resources come from a levy on imports, the profits of the National bank and domestic borrowing through development bonds.

B. *Recent policy developments*

1. *Macro-economic policies*

The achievement of food self-sufficiency has been given top priority within the current development strategy. In July 1986, producer price rises for food products and coffee were announced by the President. While the country has been fairly successful with its agricultural policies, the developments in other productive sectors give rise for concern, in particular in connection with the deter-

ioration of the trade balance. To improve the performance of the non-agricultural sector, the Government launched a "Programme de Relance" in 1985, whose measures include: (*a*) a rationalization of the industrial incentives system; (*b*) improved management of the public sector; and (*c*) a rehabilitation of the mining sector. A three-year (1986-88) Public Investment Programme worth RF 72.4 billion (about $825 million) has been launched, which is expected to be covered by foreign aid to the extent of about 60 per cent.

In the context of the development of import substitution industries, the Government has announced support for local artisans, handicraft and small-scale industries. Given the collapse of the mining company Somirwa and the consequent loss of as many as 10,000 jobs, the Government is laying particular stress on small-scale production of tin. It is studying a project to group the miners into co-operatives under the umbrella of a national corporation. The EC will be providing a loan of ECU 2.84 million on soft terms for a revitalization of small-scale mining, which should provide 320 new jobs and double small-scale production by 1988.

2. *International support measures*

In December 1985 the World Bank announced a financing credit of $11 million from IDA and $15 million from the Special Facility for Sub-Saharan Africa, and reallocated $50 million from an earlier IDA credit for the sixth highway project (1986-1988). The Ministry of Public Works has calculated that the road, which is due for completion in June 1988, will accommodate 85 per cent of the country's imports and 65 per cent of its exports. As regards bilateral aid, Rwanda is one of the four sub-Saharan African countries which currently qualify for United States financial support from a fund established for the promotion of economic reforms.

30. Samoa

A. *Recent socio-economic developments*

1. *Overall economy*

In 1986, Samoa's economy continued the modest recovery which had already occurred in 1985. Growth in real GDP was estimated at about 2 to 3 per cent. An ample supply of local food, an increase in the volume of consumer goods available as well as greater competition in retail trade contributed to the further abatement of the rate of inflation to 5.8 per cent, as compared to 9.1 per cent in 1985. With a view to avoiding potential problems connected with the currency's previous link to the New Zealand dollar and providing greater exchange rate flexibility, the tala was pegged to a trade-weighted basket of currencies as of 1 March 1985, with the US dollar acting as the intervention currency.

2. *Main sectors*

Agricultural production recovered moderately in 1985. As a result of good weather and high producer prices, copra production expanded from 26,300 tonnes in 1984 to 33,400 tonnes in the following year. Rebounding after two successive years of crop failure, the cocoa output increased by almost 60 per cent in 1985. Other agricultural products showed mixed results. Production was either stagnant, as in the case of taro, or declined (bananas, passion fruit).

The domestic fish catch in 1985, although higher than in 1984, remained far below the yield in both 1982 and 1983. The small manufacturing sector performed in line with the overall economic trend. However, the coconut oil mill, which dominates the sector, experienced financial difficulties with the decline in the world price in late 1985. As a new hydro-power station came on stream, the dependence on imported fuel for electricity generation could be markedly reduced.

The tourism industry developed favourably in 1985. The number of tourist arrivals rose by 9 per cent, and tourism receipts improved from WS$ 6.0 million ($3.3 million) in 1984 to WS$ 11.9 million ($5.3 million) in the following year. This trend extended into 1986, with tourist arrivals rising by 12 per cent and tourism income to WS$ 15.5 million ($6.9 million).

3. *Trade and payments*

Although import prices tended to fall in 1986, the steeper slump of export prices (–41 per cent) resulted in a further deterioration of Samoa's terms of trade. The precipitous decline in the world market price for coconut oil, the country's major export commodity, could not be offset by the increased export volume of 15 per cent. Whereas in previous years other export items could still make up for the resulting decline in export earnings at least in local currency terms, the 60 per cent fall of coconut oil exports in 1986 was compounded by price declines in other items, causing total export receipts to fall by over a fifth.

While overall export earnings fell between 1984 and 1985, imports rose slightly in dollar terms. This meant a widening of the trade deficit to record levels. But in 1986 imports fell by 6 per cent, keeping the deficit at about the 1985 level. However, the (cif) import-export ratio approached 4.5, well in excess of the corresponding ratio for the previous four years.

4. *Budget*

The overall adjustment strategy aimed at reducing inflation and improving the balance of payments had positive effects on the Government's fiscal position. The budget deficit narrowed to WS$1.0 million ($0.5 million) in 1985, compared with WS$8.0 million ($4.4 million) in 1984. While current expenditure rose somewhat faster than in 1984, development expenditure slowed in line with a policy of containing foreign borrowing. A higher proportion of development expenditure was financed by the Government from domestic revenues in 1985 than in the previous year.

B. *Recent policy developments*

1. *Macro-economic policies*

The Government introduced financial measures in September 1985 to exercise tighter control on foreign trade. With a view to stemming the import spree, the threshold import value, above which funding against letter of credit is mandato-

SAMOA

1. Population, total and per capita GDP, growth of agricultural and manufacturing output

Year and periods	Population Millions	GDP Total Millions of dollars	GDP Per capita Dollars	GDP Per capita Per cent of LDC average	Agricultural production Total	Agricultural production of which: Food	Manufacturing value-added Total
1985	0.2	88	539	250.7			
				Real growth rates, per cent per annum			
1980-1985	0.9	-1.1	-2.0		0.2	0.2	9.4 a/
1984-1985	1.2	2.6	1.4		0.9	0.9	..
1985-1986	1.0	..	..		-5.5	-5.8	..

2. Area, demographic indicators and labour force share in agriculture

	Area		Demographic indicators						Labour force
Total	Share of arable land under permanent crops	Share covered by forestry and woodlands	Density	Average life expectancy at birth M	Average life expectancy at birth F	Average life expectancy at birth T	Infant mortality as share of live births	Share of population In urban areas	Share of population Economically active	Share in agriculture
	1984		1985	1982-1985			1980-1985		1985	
000 km2	Per cent		Pop/km2	Years			Per 1,000	Per cent		
2.8	42.7	46.9	56	..	..	65	33	22	..	75 b/c/

3. Origins and uses of output; investment

Years	Sectoral origin of GDP Agriculture	Mining	Manufacturing	Services	Uses of GDP Private consumption expenditure	Government consumption expenditure	Gross domestic savings	Investment
				Per cent of total GDP				
1980	46.2	..	5.5	42.0	86.9	17.7	-4.6	33.1
1985	51.1 d/	..	5.9 e/	36.7 e/	88.7	18.2	-6.9	31.2

4. Balance of payments, debt and external assistance

Years	Balance of payments Merchandise trade balance	Balance on services	Balance on current account	Debt service Amortization	Interest	Total	As ratio of exports of goods and services	Debt Amount outstanding at year-end	External assistance Total	of which: ODA
		Millions of dollars					Per cent	Millions of dollars		
1980	-39.6	-9.0	-29.9	1.5 d/	1.2 d/	2.6 d/	12.1 d/	63.5 d/	25.0	25.7
1985	-30.5	-2.6	- 9.5	3.3	1.6	4.9	18.2	74.8	20.1	19.2

5. Trade

Years and periods	Exports Value Mill. of dollars	Exports of which: share of Coconut oil Per cent	Imports Value Mill. of dollars	Imports of which: share of food Per cent	Terms of trade
1980	17	25.4 d/	63	24.8	100
1985	15	56.5 f/	51	23.5 e/	..

	Value	Volume	Purchasing power	Value	Volume	Index
			Growth rates, per cent per annum			
1980-1985	-2.5	..	-0.0	-4.1	-1.7	..
1984-1985	-21.1	..	-21.4	2.0	1.6	..
1985-1986	-20.0	..	-21.1	-5.9	-7.1	..

6. Other economic and social indicators

Energy Commercial energy consumption per capita	Transport & communication Commercial vehicles	Transport & communication Telephones	Education Adult literacy rate	Education School enrolment ratio share of relevant age group Primary M	Primary F	Primary T	Secondary M	Secondary F	Secondary T	Health Attendance at childbirth by trained personnel	Health Share of population Immunized against DPT (3 doses)	Share of population With access to safe water	Food and nutrition Cereals Consumption per capita	Self-sufficiency ratio	Average daily calorie intake per capita Total	Share of requirements
			Around 1985			1984				1982	1983	1985	1985		1985	Between 1982&1985
1984 kg of coal equiv.	1984 Per 1,000 pop.	1982							Per cent				kg	Per cent	Calories	Per cent
352	17.0	37.8	..	..	..	..	..	..	..	52.0	84.3	69	45	..	2389 b/	89

a/ 1980-1983.   b/ Year other than 1985.   c/ In subsistence agriculture.   d/ 1982.   e/ 1983.   f/ 1984.

ry, was lowered by 50 per cent. In addition, importers of motor vehicles have to make a non-interest-bearing advance deposit equal to the full import value with the Central Bank when the letter of credit is opened. Conversely, proceeds of all exports are required to be sold to an authorized bank within a certain period upon the shipment of goods. At present, the Government is undertaking a detailed review of the tax régime.

A joint exercise between the Government and Asian Development Bank to review and formulate a medium-term programme for the rationalization and privatization of parts of the public sector was expected to begin in early 1987.

2. *International support measures*

The country remains dependent on external assistance, which was reconfirmed at the second Round Table Meeting in April 1986. The donors at the Meeting expressed their support to the Government for its efforts in trying to accelerate growth by improved performance, particularly in the agricultural sector. It was also noted that external assistance on a continuing basis would be needed in the form of grants and loans on highly concessional terms to complement the Government's efforts to attain the objectives of the National Development Plan 1985-87.

31. Sao Tome and Principe

A. *Recent socio-economic developments*

1. *Overall economy*

The considerable fall in real GDP that had occurred over the period 1980-1984 appears to have been arrested. There was a recovery in 1985, and by 1986 real output had probably reverted to the 1983 level.

2. *Main sectors*

Economic activity continues to be dominated by cocoa, which in 1985 occupied 65 per cent of the cultivated land area. This sector has suffered a long-term decline due to a number of negative factors, such as the inadequate supply of inputs, organizational difficulties and the lack of motivation of workers. Although many of these problems persisted in 1985 and 1986, cocoa production recovered slightly from the low 1984 level (3,378 tonnes). In spite of the establishment or expansion of a number of industries (brewery, ceramics and garment factories), the share of value added by industry in GDP remained below 10 per cent in 1986. The performance of these industries has been erratic, owing to interruptions in the supply of electricity or of imported inputs (e.g. bottle caps for the brewery in 1986). Fishing, which is the main source of protein for the population, had developed rapidly since the mid-1970s.

The catch of small-scale fisheries continued to increase in 1985 and 1986, but the overall catch in these years was less than in 1983 and 1984 (4,266 tonnes for the latter year), owing to successive repairs overseas of the two modern trawlers. Fish licensing agreements have been signed with a number of countries, but the agreement with the EEC lapsed in 1986. A new 50-room hotel was officially opened in July 1986, but tourism remains underdeveloped, with a total capacity of only 100 rooms for the whole country. Air links have improved since December 1986 with the launching of a new joint-venture airline, which operates four times per week between Sao Tome and Libreville, Gabon, the closest country on the African mainland. This airline also serves Principe, regular air services to which had been discontinued in 1985.

3. *Trade and payments*

Cocoa still accounts for about 90 per cent of exports. The prices obtained declined in 1985 and 1986, in line with world prices, so that the recovery in terms of volume that occurred in 1986 was hardly reflected in increased earnings. Other exports are copra, coffee (11 tonnes in 1985), and fish (800 tonnes in 1985). Imports, consisting mostly of investment goods (one half of the total in 1985) and food, amounted to about two and a half times the value of exports in both 1985 and 1986. This, together with high payments for services, including freight and insurance, has led to a large

SAO TOME AND PRINCIPE

1. Population, total and per capita GDP, growth of agricultural and manufacturing output

Year and periods	Population Millions	GDP Total Millions of dollars	GDP Per capita Dollars	GDP Per capita Per cent of LDC average	Agricultural production Total	Agricultural production of which: Food	Manufacturing value-added Total
1985	0.1	35	324	150.7			
				Real growth rates, per cent per annum			
1980-1985	2.9	-3.6	-6.3		-2.9	-2.9	-2.0
1984-1985	2.9	8.5	5.4		1.2	1.3	49.0
1985-1986	2.2	..	..		0.2	0.2	..

2. Area, demographic indicators and labour force share in agriculture

Area Total 000 km2	Area Share of arable land under permanent crops 1984 Per cent	Area Share covered by forestry and woodlands 1984 Per cent	Density 1985 Pop/km2	Average life expectancy at birth M 1982-1985 Years	Average life expectancy at birth F 1982-1985 Years	Average life expectancy at birth T 1982-1985 Years	Infant mortality as share of live births 1980-1985 Per 1,000	Share of population In urban areas Per cent	Share of population Economically active 1985 Per cent	Labour force Share in agriculture 1985 Per cent
1.0	37.5	..	101	..	..	64	70	38	..	56 a/

3. Origins and uses of output; investment

Years	Sectoral origin of GDP Agriculture	Sectoral origin of GDP Mining	Sectoral origin of GDP Manufacturing	Services	Private consumption expenditure	Government consumption expenditure	Gross domestic savings	Investment
					Per cent of total GDP			
1980	44.7	0.3	9.1	35.4	91.3	23.6	-14.9	34.2
1985	27.6	0.3	9.4	50.7	80.7	37.4	-18.1	37.0

4. Balance of payments, debt and external assistance

Years	Merchandise trade balance	Balance on services	Balance on current account	Amortization	Interest	Total	As ratio of exports of goods and services	Debt Amount outstanding at year-end	External assistance Total	External assistance of which: ODA
	Millions of dollars						Per cent	Millions of dollars		
1980	1.6	-0.9	0.9	0.2 b/	0.2 b/	0.4 b/	3.6 b/	22.3 b/	3.9	3.9
1985	-12.8	-8.1	-21.1	0.8	2.5	3.3	34.7	31.2	12.8	12.8

5. Trade

Years and periods	Exports Value Mill. of dollars	Exports of which: share of Cocoa Per cent	Imports Value Mill. of dollars	Imports of which: share of food Per cent	Terms of trade
1980	20	..	19	36.2	100
1985	5	69.2 c/	13	36.3 c/	..

	Value	Volume	Purchasing power	Value	Volume	Index
			Growth rates, per cent per annum			
1980-1985	-24.2	..	-22.3	-7.3	-5.0	..
1984-1985	-28.6	..	-28.9	8.3	7.9	..
1985-1986	0.0	..	-1.3	15.4	13.9	..

6. Other economic and social indicators

Commercial energy consumption per capita 1984 kg of coal equiv.	Commercial vehicles 1984 Per 1,000 pop.	Telephones 1984	Adult literacy rate Around 1985 Per cent	School enrolment ratio Primary M 1984	Primary F	Primary T	Secondary M	Secondary F	Secondary T	Attendance at childbirth by trained personnel 1984	Immunized against DPT (3 doses) 1983 Per cent	With access to safe water 1985	Cereals Consumption per capita 1985 kg	Self-sufficiency ratio 1985 Per cent	Average daily calorie intake per capita Total 1985 Calories	Share of requirements Between 1982&1985 Per cent
181	..	26.7	56	..	..	..	..	..	..	..	28.0	41	79	8	2511 a/	97

a/ Year other than 1985.   b/ 1982.   c/ 1983.

and increasing current account deficit (46 per cent of GDP in 1985 as compared to 26 per cent in 1984). In 1985 this deficit was not covered by capital inflows, so that gross reserves fell to a level corresponding to only six weeks' imports at the end of 1985, while substantial external arrears had accumulated. The country's external total debt has increased rapidly in the 1980s, and was estimated at $31 million at the end of 1985, which compares with the country's GDP of $35 million. Debt servicing reached 65 per cent of the exports of goods and services in 1985 and will probably have amounted to about 67 per cent in 1986 in spite of the rescheduling of some debt obligations to Portuguese commercial banks in March 1986.

4. *Budget*

The ambitious public sector investment programme in the period 1982-85, coupled with the decline of revenue arising directly or indirectly from cocoa exports, have led to continued large fiscal deficits. For 1986, a balanced budget had been forecast based on increased revenues derived from trade, including petroleum products, but according to preliminary indications these increased revenues were only partly achieved.

B. *Recent policy developments*

1. *Macro-economic policies*

The 1986-1990 Plan contains the main orientations of the Government and a central Public Investment Programme. Since 1985, the Government has embarked on a series of new policies.

Thus, the monopolies of ECOMEX and ECOMIN, the State organizations for external and internal trade, respectively, have been disbanded; the management of several State agricultural enterprises has been handed over to foreign companies, and these enterprises have been given more autonomy. Small farmers are encouraged to own their own plot of land. A new Investment Code was enacted in 1986, providing for the possibility of foreign investment. These policies were confirmed and expanded by way of an official statement published in October 1986, which announced that the agricultural plantation companies would have the right to market their own crops abroad directly, and bring in their own imports. Important changes were made in the Council of Ministers in January 1987, but it is believed that most of the economic measures announced will continue to be implemented.

2. *International support measures and SNPA follow-up*

The first Round Table co-sponsored by UNDP and the Government, which assembled the country's main development partners, was held at Brussels in December 1985. This was followed by an in-country review meeting in May 1986, where problems in the main sectors were reviewed. A special conference for non-governmental organizations was also held in November 1986 in Sao Tome, at which many small-scale projects were submitted for funding. President Mario Soares of Portugal made an official visit to Sao Tome and Principe in December 1986, accompanied by officials and businessmen. At the end of the visit he stated that Portugal intended to regain its former position as the leading source of development aid to the country.

32. Sierra Leone

A. *Recent socio-economic developments*

1. *Overall economic performance*

Economic stagnation in Sierra Leone over the last decade persisted in FY 1985/86,[153] when real GDP is estimated to have fallen by 1.4 per

---

[153] The fiscal year (FY) ends on 30 June.

cent, as compared to a growth of 0.8 per cent in FY 1984/85, implying a 3.4 per cent drop in real per capita GDP. Output of all sectors fell, except for mining, which recorded an increase in the production of diamonds. Currency devaluation and the removal of subsidies on rice and petrol caused inflation (as measured by the consumer price index for Freetown) to accelerate from about 62 per cent in FY 1984/85 to about 73 per cent in FY 1985/86.

SIERRA LEONE

1. Population, total and per capita GDP, growth of agricultural and manufacturing output

Year and periods	Population Millions	GDP a/ Total Millions of dollars	GDP a/ Per capita Dollars	GDP a/ Per capita Per cent of LDC average	Agricultural production Total	Agricultural production of which: Food	Manufacturing value-added Total
1985	3.6	1168	324	150.7			
			Real growth rates, per cent per annum				
1980-1985	1.8	1.8	0.0		0.1	0.1	-1.2
1984-1985	1.7	0.8	-0.9		0.0	-3.7	-5.2
1985-1986	2.0	..	..		10.8	10.9	..

2. Area, demographic indicators and labour force share in agriculture

Area Total	Area Share of arable land under permanent crops	Area Share covered by forestry and woodlands	Density	Average life expectancy at birth M	Average life expectancy at birth F	Average life expectancy at birth T	Infant mortality as share of live births	Share of population In urban areas	Share of population Economically active	Labour force Share in agriculture
		1984	1985		1980-1985		1980-1985		1985	
000 km2	Per cent		Pop/km2		Years		Per 1,000		Per cent	
71.7	24.7	29.1	50	33	36	34	180	25	38	66

3. Origins and uses of output; investment

Years	Sectoral origin of GDP Agriculture	Mining	Manufacturing	Services	Uses of GDP Private consumption expenditure	Government consumption expenditure	Gross domestic savings	Investment
					Per cent of total GDP			
1980	33.0	11.7	5.5	44.8	83.5	13.8	2.8	16.2
1985	37.2	9.7	5.1	42.9	86.8	6.7	6.5	7.3

4. Balance of payments, debt and external assistance

Years	Balance of payments Merchandise trade balance	Balance on services	Balance on current account	Debt service Amortization	Interest	Total	As ratio of exports of goods and services	Debt Amount outstanding at year-end	External assistance Total	External assistance of which: ODA
	Millions of dollars						Per cent	Millions of dollars		
1980	-172.5	-45.2	-209.4	13.8 b/	23.4 b/	37.2 b/	24.3 b/	615.0 b/	92.7	92.6
1985	-9.3	-3.0	-9.0	16.5	22.1	38.6	24.1	693.2	76.3	75.1

5. Trade

Years and periods	Exports Value Mill. of dollars	Exports of which: share of Diamonds Per cent	Imports Value Mill. of dollars	Imports of which: share of food Per cent	Terms of trade
1980	204	58.9	414	23.7	100
1985	112	30.0 c/	156	32.6	96

	Value	Volume	Purchasing power	Value	Volume	Index
			Growth rates, per cent per annum			
1980-1985	-11.3	-7.8	-8.5	-17.7	-15.2	-0.8
1984-1985	-24.3	-22.6	-24.4	-6.0	-6.1	-2.3
1985-1986	0.0	-9.0	-0.8	2.6	1.7	8.9

6. Other economic and social indicators

Energy Commercial energy consumption per capita	Transport & communication Commercial vehicles	Telephones	Education Adult literacy rate	School enrolment ratio share of relevant age group Primary M	Primary F	Primary T	Secondary M	Secondary F	Secondary T	Health Attendance at childbirth by trained personnel	Share of population Immunized against DPT (3 doses)	With access to safe water	Food and nutrition Cereals Consumption per capita	Self-sufficiency ratio	Average daily calorie intake per capita Total	Share of requirements
1984	1984	1982	Around 1985		1982					1984	1984	1985		1985	1985	Between 1982&1985
kg of coal equiv.	Per 1,000 pop.							Per cent					kg	Per cent	Calories	Per cent
67	2.8	5.5	..	68	48	58	23	11	17	25.0	28.6	26	189	83	1817	91

a/ Years ending 30 June.   b/ 1982.   c/ 1984.

2. *Main sectors*

Agriculture, which accounts for about 40 per cent of GDP, registered an upswing in 1986, mainly due to incentives given to boost production. Producer prices for rice and the major export crops, namely coffee and cocoa, were raised substantially and at frequent intervals between 1983 and 1986. However, high domestic inflation and the rapid currency devaluation on the parallel market have caused even these increased nominal prices to be depressed in real terms and to remain uncompetitive as compared to producer prices prevailing in neighbouring countries. The industrial sector registered a decline of 5 per cent in 1985 affecting both manufacturing and construction, where critical shortages of foreign exchange have constrained imports and thereby output. The Dodo hydroelectric dam is now in operation, providing electricity to two towns.

3. *Trade and payments*

In FY 1985/86 recorded exports covered about 87 per cent of recorded c.i.f. imports on average, which represented a significant improvement over FY 1982/83, when this ratio stood at about 55 per cent. However, the country's official export receipts have been severely affected by rampant smuggling, especially of diamonds and gold. In FY 1985/86 recorded exports fell by 8.6 per cent in dollar terms over the previous fiscal year, whereas imports grew marginally (by 3.6 per cent), but remained well below (by 55 per cent) the average level registered in the period 1980-1982. These negative trends caused the trade deficit to widen from $1.4 million in FY 1984/85 to $19.3 million in the subsequent fiscal year. Due to the severe external payments difficulties, the authorities had to meet the critical shortage of imported fuel by paying for oil prices which (after including financial charges) were above market prices, inasmuch as these imports were financed under *ad hoc* arrangements, including the mortgaging of future export proceeds of the Sierra Leone Produce and Marketing Board. This contributed to the deterioration of the terms of trade, which had been improving between FY 1982/83 and FY 1984/85, but which worsened again by about 9 per cent in FY 1985/86, owing to a fall in the dollar-based average export unit value which outweighed that of the corresponding import unit value. The balance-of-payments position remains a severely constraining factor on the country's development. Sierra Leone was able to reduce drastically its untenable annual current account deficit (which had been well over $100 million in the early 1980s) to

$9.0 million in 1985 through a sharp cutback in imports as well as reduced expenditures on services. However, the marked outflow of recorded long-term capital since 1983 (approaching $68 million in 1985) has caused a succession of growing deficits on capital account. As in past years, the overall deficit – now caused exclusively by the capital account – has been financed by "exceptional" resources (e.g., commercial and other arrears). The country's external debt obligations will continue to exert considerable pressure on its balance of payments. Its total external debt (including use of IMF credit and short-term debts) at the end of 1985 was equal to about 51 per cent of GDP and total debt service payments due in 1985 were the equivalent of about 40 per cent of the level of recorded exports. Sierra Leone's difficult external payments situation led to the fourth rescheduling of its debts at the Paris Club in November 1986, the details of which are described below.

4. *Budget*

The fiscal deficit as a percentage of GDP rose to 14.5 per cent in FY 1985/86 from 11.5 per cent in FY 1984/85. This is largely owing to the marked increase in current and extra-budgetary expenditures (mainly for oil subsidies). The sharp depreciation in the exchange rate also led to a six-fold increase in foreign interest payments between FY 1985/86 and FY 1986/87. Revenue growth, on the other hand, has been sluggish, because of a slowdown in economic activity.

B. *Recent policy developments*

1. *Macro-economic policies*

In preparation for and following upon a one-year stand-by arrangement signed with the IMF in November 1986, a series of measures were adopted to correct the internal and external imbalances of the economy. They included the devaluation and flotation of the currency in June 1986, reduction of subsidies on consumer items such as rice and petrol, the liberalization of the import licensing régime and the abolition of foreign-exchange retention facilities previously accorded to various exporters. Two new rural banks were established to mobilize savings in the rural areas and to provide quick-disbursing credit facilities for farmers. Energy policies were geared towards the development of local sources of supply in order to reduce the oil import bill. Since mining, particularly the production of diamonds and gold, accounts for about three-quarters of the total value of exports, intensified efforts were made to ensure that production of these two items were directed through official channels, so as to raise their contribution to the country's official foreign-exchange income. Plans are under way to raise diamond production with the development of an underground kimberlite mine estimated at a cost of $100 million. The Government's strategy to promote the directly productive sectors was reflected in the Public Investment Programme covering the three-year period FY 1986/87 to FY 1988/89, in which 23.3 per cent of public investment was allocated to agriculture, 29 per cent to power and water and 32.5 per cent to transport and communications.

2. *International support measures*

Total net official development assistance to Sierra Leone in 1985 was $65 million, as compared to $90.9 million in 1980. About 70 per cent of the aid was in the form of grants. In November 1986 the Government obtained the agreement of the IMF on a financing package worth SDR 50.36 million which consisted of a 12 month stand-by credit of SDR 23.16 million and concessional funding amounting to SDR 27.2 million over a three-year period under the Structural Adjustment Facility. The programme aims to reduce the current-account deficit on the balance of payments from 3 per cent of GDP in FY 1985/86 to 2 per cent in FY 1986/87. The debt rescheduling agreed to at the Paris Club in November 1986 has given the country relief on all maturities due in the subsequent 18 months, which were postponed by 9 years and 8 months including 6 years and 2 months of grace.

3. *SNPA follow-up*

UNDP is planning to organize a Round Table meeting at the end of 1987 to seek external assistance for the Public Investment Programme, which envisages a foreign financing component of 90 per cent.

33. Somalia

A. *Recent socio-economic developments*

1. *Overall economy*

The improved level of agricultural production and the recovery of livestock exports were the main contributors to Somalia's growth in 1985, which is estimated at 3.5 per cent. In 1986, when climatic conditions continued to be favourable, the officially reported growth rate was 6 per cent. The high rate of inflation in Somalia declined substantially from over 90 per cent in 1984 to 38 and to 36 per cent in 1985 and 1986 respectively. Developments in 1987 have taken a negative turn, however, as late rains produced drought conditions. These ended with torrential rains and floods, causing extensive loss of property and life in the form of buildings, crops and livestock.

2. *Main sectors*

Harvests in 1985 were good, in particular of sorghum and maize, which reached record levels. The dollar value of banana exports in 1985 ($13.5 million) recovered from their extremely low 1984 levels to exceed their previous record achieved in 1982. Cereal production in 1986 by far exceeded the high 1982 level, making the country self-sufficient in sorghum and maize. Sugar production in 1986 regained a very good level, after having suffered from insufficient irrigation in 1984. However, harvest forcasts for 1987 are gloomy, since the first rainy season was delayed by six weeks.

Somalia has the longest coastline of Africa, but only a relatively small part of the potential fish catch is brought to land. The Government wishes to diversify Somalia's food production, and to this end it stimulates fishing. The fishing fleet has been

SOMALIA

1. Population, total and per capita GDP, growth of agricultural and manufacturing output

Year and periods	Population Millions	GDP Total Millions of dollars	GDP Per capita Dollars	GDP Per capita Per cent of LDC average	Agricultural production Total	Agricultural production of which: Food	Manufacturing value-added Total
1985	5.4	(1403)	261 a/	121.4			
			Real growth rates, per cent per annum				
1980-1985	2.9	4.1	1.2		0.9	1.0	-0.8 b/
1984-1985	2.9	3.5	0.6		6.5	6.5	..
1985-1986	2.9	..	..		1.2	1.2	..

2. Area, demographic indicators and labour force share in agriculture

Area Total	Area Share of arable land under permanent crops 1984	Area Share covered by forestry and woodlands 1984	Density 1985	Average life expectancy at birth M 1980-1985	Average life expectancy at birth F 1980-1985	Average life expectancy at birth T 1980-1985	Infant mortality as share of live births 1980-1985	Share of population In urban areas	Share of population Economically active 1985	Labour force Share in agriculture 1985
000 km2	Per cent	Per cent	Pop/km2	Years	Years	Years	Per 1,000	Per cent	Per cent	Per cent
637.7	1.7	14.0	8	39	43	41	155	34	43	74

3. Origins and uses of output; investment

Years	Sectoral origin of GDP Agriculture	Mining	Manufacturing	Services	Uses of GDP Private consumption expenditure	Government consumption expenditure	Gross domestic savings	Investment
				Per cent of total GDP				
1980	46.0	0.5	6.5	41.9	85.0	30.2	-15.2	5.9
1985	50.0 c/	0.5 c/	5.9 c/	38.8 c/	78.3 c/	23.6 c/	-1.9 c/	20.0 c/

4. Balance of payments, debt and external assistance

Years	Balance of payments Merchandise trade balance	Balance on services	Balance on current account	Debt service Amortization	Interest	Total	As ratio of exports of goods and services	Debt Amount outstanding at year-end	External assistance Total	External assistance of which: ODA
	Millions of dollars						Per cent	Millions of dollars		
1980	-268.2	-67.8	-278.8	11.2 c/	12.6 c/	23.8 c/	9.3 c/	1265.9 c/	530.4	443.7
1985	-240.1	-80.2	-300.9	48.1	42.6	90.7	71.1	1725.0	378.8	361.1

5. Trade

Years and periods	Exports Value Mill. of dollars	Exports of which: share of Live animals Per cent	Imports Value Mill. of dollars	Imports of which: share of food Per cent	Terms of trade
1980	133	85.1	348	32.5	100
1985	91	72.8	112	..	149

	Value	Volume	Purchasing power	Value	Volume	Index
			Growth rates, per cent per annum			
1980-1985	-7.3	-11.7	-4.4	-20.3	-17.8	8.3
1984-1985	102.2	60.7	103.0	2.8	3.2	26.4
1985-1986	-1.1	9.6	-7.0	2.7	-3.4	-15.1

6. Other economic and social indicators

Energy Commercial energy consumption per capita	Transport & communication Commercial vehicles	Transport & communication Telephones	Education Adult literacy rate	Education School enrolment ratio share of relevant age group Primary M	Primary F	Primary T	Secondary M	Secondary F	Secondary T	Health Attendance at childbirth by trained personnel	Health Share of population Immunized against DPT (3 doses)	With access to safe water	Food and nutrition Cereals Consumption per capita	Self-sufficiency ratio	Average daily calorie intake per capita Total	Share of requirements
1984	1984	1981	Around 1985	1983						1982	1984	1985	1985		1985	Between 1982&1985
kg of coal equiv.	Per 1,000 pop.					Per cent							kg	Per cent	Calories	Per cent
102	..	1.6	..	32	18	25	23	12	17	2.0	10.0	31	140	60	2072	89

a/ 1984.   b/ 1980-1982.   c/ 1982.

extended, and fish production almost doubled between 1982 and 1984 from 8,700 tonnes to 17,000 tonnes per year.

3. *Trade and payments*

Exports of livestock, which dominate the country's foreign trade, suffered a very serious setback in 1983, when Saudi Arabia closed its borders to cattle, goats and sheep from Africa. This obliged Somalia to look for other export markets. The country has partly succeeded in this, inasmuch as the dollar value of cattle exports in 1985 recovered to $66 million, i.e. to 40 per cent of the level prior to the ban (from 20 per cent of this level in 1984). In 1984 Saudi Arabia reopened its borders to sheep and goats, but cattle were still excluded as of July 1987. However, Government officials estimated that all cattle available for export in 1985-86 could be exported in fact.

While the positive factors affecting exports of livestock and bananas in 1985 contributed to the doubling of overall exports, merchandise imports only increased by 3 per cent. The trade deficit was therefore reduced markedly, while the service account remained virtually unchanged. However, the improved trade deficit was almost nullified by a fall of over $140 million in private inward transfers, reflecting a cutback of emigrants employed in the Gulf States after the oil price collapse. As a result, the sharp import cutback was only moderately reflected in the current account deficit, which improved by no more than $35 million (to $96.6 million) in 1985. The trade deficit was further narrowed in 1986 by reduced grain imports and the continued recovery of livestock exports.

Somalia's long- and medium-term debt at the end of 1985 amounted to $1.5 billion, an increase of about 2 per cent over the 1984 figure. Debt service payments in 1985 came close to $90 million but these are projected to surpass $150 million in 1987, which would equal normal merchandise export receipts. Therefore, the Paris Club was convened in July 1987 to reschedule Somalia's debt. Repayments on existing debt were rescheduled over 20 years, including a 10-year grace period.

4. *Budget*

The share of public expenditures in GDP reached a peak in 1983. Since then expenditure in absolute terms kept growing, but declined as a percentage of GDP. The recurrent budget expenditures for 1987 are projected to rise to SoSh.17.9 billion ($198 million), which constitutes a 14 per cent nominal increment over the 1986 budget figure, but probably a fall in real terms. Attaining this target would imply an accelerated decline of the Government expenditure/GDP ratio.

B. *Recent policy developments*

1. *Macro-economic policies*

At the most recent Consultative Group meeting (Paris, April 1987) Somalia presented its new Five-Year Development Plan, covering the period 1987-1991. The Government has changed the direction of its policies in favour of the private sector. Moreover, the Government intends to withdraw from productive activities. Concomitant objectives include the mobilization of savings, the liberalization of prices and exchange rates, and a cut in effective consumption to reduce inflation and pressure on the balance of payments.

In 1982 the Government set up a commission to examine the operations of public enterprises with a view to reducing their number. Since its recommendations did not lead to a real improvement, the Government decided to take more energetic action in 1985. Somalia counts about 50 State enterprises, few of which make a contribution to the budget. They have been classified into three groups: enterprises that should stay in the Government's hands, enterprises that are to be partly or entirely sold to the private sector, and companies that will be closed because they are considered non-viable. The Plan notes that installed industrial capacity in the public sector exceeds that of the private sector, as a result of which an improved performance by public enterprises would have a major impact on the unit cost of manufacturing output.

A restrictive monetary policy with high interest rates aims at limiting demand by curtailing credits and stimulating savings. In the first half of 1986 price inflation was 31 per cent, while the money supply rose by only 11 per cent and domestic credit by 4 per cent. To achieve this degree of monetary restraint the discount rate was raised from 8 to 12 per cent in January 1985, and the commercial bank lending rate from 12 to 20 per cent.

Prices of several agricultural products such as sorghum, maize and bananas were decontrolled in 1985, leading to producer's price increases for all these products. This is one important factor that explains Somalia's rapid agricultural growth in 1985 and 1986.

2. *International support measures*

Somalia received credits from Belgium and the IDA for rural development. The Belgian credit of $5.3 million will fund an agricultural development project, which focuses principally on irrigation and education of the rural population. An IDA credit of $12.7 million is to finance a project designed to improve crop yields by introducing new varieties and hybrids of traditional local plant species, particularly of maize and sorghum.

Following the Consultative Group Meeting, the IMF gave its support with an SDR 33.15 million stand-by credit and an SDR 20.77 million credit under the Structural Adjustment Facility. These credits are in support of and conditioned by the pursuance of the present policies aiming at the reduction of budget and balance-of-payments deficits as well as the continued reduction of inflation to a rate of less than 10 per cent by 1989.

3. *SNPA follow-up*

A Consultative Group Meeting was convened in Paris in March 1987, the results of which were satisfactory for Somalia. Aid requirements for 1987 and 1988 were estimated at $428 million and $407 million respectively, including programme aid and debt relief. Agreement was reached on a planned five-year investment programme of $1,025 million, with a disbursement level of $720 million over the period 1987-1989.

34. Sudan

A. *Recent socio-economic developments*

1. *Overall economy*

After four years of decline mainly due to the adverse effects of drought on agricultural production, the economy experienced a moderate recovery as real GDP increased by 4.2 per cent between FY 1984/85 and FY 1985/86.[154] In FY 1986/87 real GDP increased by 7.5 per cent, its highest level since FY 1981/82. This was brought about mainly by a 12 per cent increase in agricultural production during that fiscal year. The rate of inflation as measured by the consumer price index continued to be high and is estimated to have amounted to 35 per cent in FY 1985/86.

2. *Main sectors*

The good rains, the higher producer prices and the timely availability of agricultural inputs in the 1985/86 and 1986/87 crop years boosted agricultural production, particularly in the rain-fed sub-sector, where the main food crops are grown.

With sorghum production increasing by 14 per cent between 1985/86 and 1986/87, the country achieved self-sufficiency in its main food crop and is exporting the surplus. Output of cotton, the main export crop, is estimated to have increased by 9 per cent in 1986/87, while production of groundnuts and gum arabic increased by 50 and 100 per cent respectively. However, production of textiles and cement declined by 25 and 14 per cent respectively between FY 1984/85 and FY 1985/86. Sugar production in the five refineries was estimated at only 70 per cent of installed capacity, but aid worth $180 million provided by Kuwait, Saudi Arabia and the World Bank is designed to rehabilitate this industry. Further gold reserves estimated at 33 tonnes have been discovered in the eastern region. The construction sector has continued its decline for the fifth consecutive year for lack of finance as well as shortages of skilled manpower and imported raw materials.

3. *Trade and payments*

Although export earnings recovered slightly in 1986, they are still far below the 1981-1985 average. They were adversely affected by the fall in cotton prices and the ban on livestock and meat

---

[154] The fiscal year (FY) ends on 30 June.

SUDAN

1. Population, total and per capita GDP, growth of agricultural and manufacturing output

Year and periods	Population Millions	GDP a/ Total Millions of dollars	GDP a/ Per capita Dollars	GDP a/ Per capita Per cent of LDC average	Agricultural production Total	Agricultural production of which: Food	Manufacturing value-added Total
1985	21.6	8752	406	188.8			
			Real growth rates, per cent per annum				
1980-1985	2.9	-1.3	-4.1		3.6	3.1	..
1984-1985	2.7	-9.1	-11.5		20.0	23.5	..
1985-1986	3.1	..	..		4.2	6.6	..

2. Area, demographic indicators and labour force share in agriculture

Area Total 000 km2	Area Share of arable land under permanent crops 1984 Per cent	Area Share covered by forestry and woodlands 1984 Per cent	Demographic indicators Density 1985 Pop/km2	Demographic indicators Average life expectancy at birth M 1980-1985 Years	Demographic indicators Average life expectancy at birth F 1980-1985 Years	Demographic indicators Average life expectancy at birth T 1980-1985 Years	Demographic indicators Infant mortality as share of live births 1980-1985 Per 1,000	Demographic indicators Share of population In urban areas Per cent	Demographic indicators Share of population Economically active 1985 Per cent	Labour force Share in agriculture Per cent
2505.8	5.0	19.0	9	47	49	48	118	21	32	68

3. Origins and uses of output; investment

Years	Sectoral origin of GDP Agriculture	Sectoral origin of GDP Mining	Sectoral origin of GDP Manufacturing	Sectoral origin of GDP Services	Uses of GDP Private consumption expenditure	Uses of GDP Government consumption expenditure	Uses of GDP Gross domestic savings	Investment
					Per cent of total GDP			
1980	33.9	0.1	6.9	52.5	80.6	16.0	3.4	15.1
1985	25.5	0.1	9.4	56.9	92.4	11.0	-3.5	7.0

4. Balance of payments, debt and external assistance

Years	Balance of payments Merchandise trade balance	Balance of payments Balance on services	Balance of payments Balance on current account	Debt service Amortization	Debt service Interest	Debt service Total	Debt service As ratio of exports of goods and services	Debt Amount outstanding at year-end	External assistance Total	External assistance of which: ODA
	Millions of dollars						Per cent	Millions of dollars		
1980	-438.5	-107.9	-337.0	103.9 b/	42.5 b/	146.5 b/	16.0 b/	6366.8 b/	836.5	709.9
1985	-128.1	-73.9	45.2	49.8	133.9	183.7	22.0	6484.1	1023.0	1020.2

5. Trade

Years and periods	Exports Value Mill. of dollars	Exports of which: share of Cotton Per cent	Imports Value Mill. of dollars	Imports of which: share of food Per cent	Terms of trade
1980	543	44.9	1576	25.9	100
1985	367	44.3	757	19.7	99

	Value	Volume	Purchasing power	Value	Volume	Index
			Growth rates, per cent per annum			
1980-1985	-7.5	-4.5	-4.7	-13.6	-11.0	-0.2
1984-1985	-41.7	-41.6	-41.6	-34.0	-33.9	0.1
1985-1986	3.5	8.8	1.5	-12.8	-14.5	-6.7

6. Other economic and social indicators

Energy Commercial energy consumption per capita 1984 kg of coal equiv.	Transport & communication Commercial vehicles 1984 Per 1,000 pop.	Transport & communication Telephones 1985 Per 1,000 pop.	Education Adult literacy rate Around 1985	Education School enrolment ratio share of relevant age group Primary M 1983	Education Primary F 1983	Education Primary T 1983	Education Secondary M 1983	Education Secondary F 1983	Education Secondary T 1983	Health Attendance at childbirth by trained personnel 1984 Per cent	Health Share of population Immunized against DPT (3 doses) 1984 Per cent	Health Share of population With access to safe water 1983 Per cent	Food and nutrition Cereals Consumption per capita 1985 kg	Food and nutrition Cereals Self-sufficiency ratio 1985 Per cent	Food and nutrition Average daily calorie intake per capita Total 1985 Calories	Food and nutrition Average daily calorie intake per capita Share of requirements Between 1982&1985 Per cent
77	..	3.6	..	57	41	49	23	16	19	20.0	4.0	48	282	81	1737	90

a/ Years ending 30 June.   b/ 1982.

exports imposed by the Government in 1986, the combined effect of which is estimated at about $124 million. Imports, on the other hand, decreased by 13 per cent to $660 million. The large trade deficit coupled with increased debt service payments and the decline of workers' remittances was reflected in a deterioration in the current account balance (excluding official grants), which moved from a small surplus of $43 million in 1985 into a deficit of $262.4 million in 1986. Sudan's external debt was estimated at about $10.6 billion at the end of 1986. This figure includes arrears, which were estimated to have amounted to $2.6 billion at the end of June 1987. Debt service obligations for FY 1987/88 are expected to be about $782 million, equivalent to almost 95 per cent of projected earnings from exports of goods and services, which makes full payment unlikely. In 1986 the net international reserve position improved considerably: by the end of the year reserves had recovered to $58.5 million, the highest level since 1980, but a reversal during the first half of 1987 cut this figure by half to a level barely assuring one fortnight's imports.

4. *Budget*

The Government's current revenue doubled between FY 1985/86 and FY 1986/87 and exceeded projections by 4 per cent as a result of increases in tax and non-tax revenues. Total expenditures were estimated at LSd 5,542 million ($2,217 million), a decline of 9 per cent as compared to the previous year, of which 65.3 per cent was earmarked for current expenditure, 9.4 per cent for debt service payments and 24.9 per cent for development, with agriculture receiving a quarter of the development budget. In view of the increase in revenue and the decline in expenditure, the overall budgetary deficit for FY 1986/87 of LSd 2,742 million ($1,096 million) was 57 per cent below the previous year's level. In the FY 1987/88 budget, revenue is estimated at LSd 3,905 million ($1,562 million) as compared to LSd 2,800 million ($1,120 million) realized in the previous fiscal year. Expenditure is projected at LSd 6,790 million ($2,716 million), creating a projected deficit slightly higher than the one realized during the previous year; it is to be financed mainly by commodity aid and other grants.

B. *Recent policy developments*

1. *Macro-economic policies*

After 18 months of negotiations, Sudan and the IMF agreed on a new Economic Reform Programme in October 1987. The main elements of the agreement are: (*a*) the unification of the official and the commercial exchange rates, implying a devaluation of 44.5 per cent of the official exchange rate *vis-à-vis* the dollar, to which it is pegged; (*b*) elimination of budgetary subsidies for wheat and petroleum products, which would have cost an estimated LSd 907 million ($363 million at the previous official exchange rate) in FY 1987/88; and (*c*) reduction of the annual rate of monetary expansion from 32 per cent at present to 23 per cent. As a result of this agreement, the international community is expected to provide $4,845 million over the course of the Four-Year Programme for Salvation, Recovery and Development (FY 1987/88 – FY 1990/91). The Programme aims at providing a comprehensive framework for adjusting the structural imbalances facing the Sudanese economy. The Sudan has increasingly relied on countertrade deals to promote exports of the cotton carry-over stock and of sorghum surpluses, in order to help finance the import bill. Such deals have been signed with Bulgaria, the Islamic Republic of Iran, Saudi Arabia and the USSR. The Government has announced its intention of limiting debt service payments to a certain proportion of export earnings. The FY 1986/87 budget limits debt service payments to $212.2 million, which is about 25 per cent of expected exports of goods and services, as compared to projections for debt service payments of $1,348.8 million during the previous fiscal year, which could not be met. While the negotiations with the IMF were going on in 1987, the Government contacted creditors individually to obtain debt relief. Agreements were reached with Czechoslovakia, Japan, Poland and the OPEC Fund. Meanwhile the Government repaid $10.5 million of its $400 million arrears to the IMF.

2. *International support measures*

Concessional development assistance received from official sources was estimated at $1,020.2 million in 1985 as compared to $702.4 million in 1984. Although full figures for ODA are not yet available for 1986, grant aid more than doubled between 1985 and 1986 with a particular acceleration during the second half of 1986; this has continued during the first half of 1987.

35. Togo

A. Recent socio-economic developments

1. Overall economy

The favourable developments in Togo's economy that set in after the 1981-1983 drought period continued in 1985. Although the record harvest of 1984 was not matched in 1985, production was still far better than the 1980-1983 average. GDP measured in current prices grew by 7.1 per cent, to reach CFAF 312.9 billion ($696.5 million) in 1985. Although consumer prices declined (-1.5 per cent), the overall GDP deflator rose by 2.4 per cent, reducing the real growth rate to 4.7 per cent and the per capita growth rate to 1.8 per cent. Preliminary figures for 1986 indicate weaker GDP growth. Agricultural production was lower than in 1985, and real GDP will merely have kept pace with the 3 per cent population growth. The consumer price inflation rate in 1986 turned positive again to a rate of 4 per cent. First reports on 1987 indicate that agricultural production has suffered from the belated rainy season, which did not start until late May.

2. Main sectors

The three seasons since the 1981-1983 drought have had a satisfactory rainfall. During the course of this period agricultural production, particularly of cereals, was generally good. While production of most crops recovered to average pre-drought levels by 1984/85, cotton production in that year attained a record high equal to 2.5 times the 1981-1983 average. Agricultural production in 1985 generally improved further over the previous year. A 40 per cent improvement was recorded for cocoa, and cotton production continued its rising trend. Food production rose sufficiently to allow the President to report that Togo had become self-sufficient for food in 1986. The 1986 harvest showed a moderate decline from the relatively high levels of the previous year, with the exception of cotton, output of which improved again over the 1985/86 level, and of maize, output of which fell by 33 per cent.

The services sector has been gaining importance for the Togolese economy. Because of its good road network, the neighboring countries make increasing use of the Port of Lomé as a transshipment point. Togo's tourism sector also continues to grow. In 1986 a record number of 145,000 tourists were reported to have arrived, compared to 135,000 tourists in 1985. The estimated gross earnings on tourism ($23 million) in 1986 were the equivalent of 10 per cent of merchandise export revenues.

3. Trade and payments

By cutting down on imports, Togo succeeded in converting its long-standing trade deficit into a surplus in 1984. Between 1984 and 1986, however, the volume of imports kept constant, amounting to about one-half of the 1980 level. Exports in 1985 were marked by a fall of two-thirds in the volume of cocoa exports, and those of 1986 by falling commodity prices compounded by the appreciation of the CFA franc versus the dollar, the currency in which the major export commodities are denominated. The value of phosphate exports in 1985, measured in local currency, grew by 1.7 per cent. This was exclusively due to the strong rise in prices, which more than offset the decline of 12.5 per cent in volume. The downward trend for volume continued in 1986. In that year, however, falling phosphate prices measured in CFA francs compounded the decline in volume, causing phosphate exports measured in local currency to drop by 26 per cent (to CFAF 30.7 billion, or $88.65 million), even though the decline only amounted to 4.4 per cent in dollar terms.

Developments of the other main export commodities have been mixed. The volume of coffee exports more than tripled in 1985 accompanied by moderately strengthening prices, which made coffee the second export earner, ahead of cocoa. However, in 1986, prices and volume of coffee exports declined, while the volume of cocoa exports almost doubled, allowing cocoa to regain its traditional place as the second export earner. Prices of cocoa beans (measured in CFA francs) remained strong in 1985. Nevertheless, production of cocoa in 1985/86 was disappointing.

Estimates for the balance of payments in 1986 are sombre. The trade deficit of over $80 million compares with a deficit of $74 million in the previous year. This widening deficit is partly due to the fall of the dollar, the currency in which the country's major export products are denominated, and partly to increasing imports. The deficit

TOGO

1. Population, total and per capita GDP, growth of agricultural and manufacturing output

Year and periods	Population Millions	GDP Total Millions of dollars	GDP Per capita Dollars	GDP Per capita Per cent of LDC average	Agricultural production Total	Agricultural production of which: Food	Manufacturing value-added Total
1985	3.0	696	235	109.3			
				Real growth rates, per cent per annum			
1980-1985	3.0	-1.3	-4.2		1.5	1.1	-1.6
1984-1985	2.8	4.7	1.8		3.0	-0.4	7.1
1985-1986	3.3	..	..		-4.5	-4.8	..

2. Area, demographic indicators and labour force share in agriculture

Area Total	Area Share of arable land under permanent crops 1984	Area Share covered by forestry and woodlands 1984	Density 1985	Average life expectancy at birth M 1980-1985	Average life expectancy at birth F 1980-1985	Average life expectancy at birth T 1980-1985	Infant mortality as share of live births 1980-1985	Share of population In urban areas	Share of population Economically active 1985	Labour force Share in agriculture 1985
000 km2	Per cent	Per cent	Pop/km2	Years	Years	Years	Per 1,000	Per cent	Per cent	Per cent
56.8	25.1	26.4	52	49	52	51	102	23	42	71

3. Origins and uses of output; investment

Years	Sectoral origin of GDP Agriculture	Sectoral origin of GDP Mining	Sectoral origin of GDP Manufacturing	Sectoral origin of GDP Services	Uses of GDP Private consumption expenditure	Uses of GDP Government consumption expenditure	Uses of GDP Gross domestic savings	Investment
				Per cent of total GDP				
1980	27.5	9.8	6.9	47.7	70.1	15.0	15.0	29.9
1985	29.8	9.9	7.0	46.6	71.0	13.8	15.2	26.2

4. Balance of payments, debt and external assistance

Years	Balance of payments Merchandise trade balance	Balance of payments Balance on services	Balance of payments Balance on current account	Debt service Amortization	Debt service Interest	Debt service Total	Debt service As ratio of exports of goods and services	Debt Amount outstanding at year-end	External assistance Total	External assistance of which: ODA
	Millions of dollars						Per cent	Millions of dollars	Millions of dollars	
1980	-48.3	-132.8	-180.7	22.1 a/	36.9 a/	59.0 a/	13.1 a/	1045.7 a/	180.9	90.9
1985	-7.6	-71.7	-79.0	47.6	46.3	93.9	27.1	1009.8	97.4	113.8

5. Trade

Years and periods	Exports Value Mill. of dollars	Exports of which: share of Phosphates Per cent	Imports Value Mill. of dollars	Imports of which: share of food Per cent	Terms of trade
1980	335	39.6	550	16.5	100
1985	190	55.1 b/	264	27.8 b/	87

	Value	Volume	Purchasing power	Value	Volume	Index
			Growth rates, per cent per annum			
1980-1985	-10.7	-5.8	-8.4	-13.7	-11.4	-2.7
1984-1985	-3.6	-2.0	-3.6	-5.0	-5.1	-1.7
1985-1986	0.0	4.2	2.7	2.3	5.0	-1.5

6. Other economic and social indicators

Energy Commercial energy consumption per capita 1984 kg of coal equiv.	Transport & communication Commercial vehicles 1983	Transport & communication Telephones 1983	Education Adult literacy rate Around 1985	Education School enrolment ratio share of relevant age group Primary M 1984	Education Primary F 1984	Education Primary T 1984	Education Secondary M 1984	Education Secondary F 1984	Education Secondary T 1984	Health Attendance at childbirth by trained personnel 1984	Health Share of population Immunized against DPT (3 doses) 1981	Health Share of population With access to safe water 1985	Food and nutrition Cereals Consumption per capita 1985 kg	Food and nutrition Cereals Self-sufficiency ratio 1985 Per cent	Food and nutrition Average daily calorie intake per capita Total 1985 Calories	Food and nutrition Average daily calorie intake per capita Share of requirements Between 1982&1985 Per cent
	Per 1,000 pop.							Per cent						Per cent		Per cent
71	0.3	4.3	41	118	75	97	32	10	21	..	9.0	57	163	85	2236	94

a/ 1982.   b/ 1984.

on services is likely to have been of the same order of magnitude as the trade deficit, boosting the deficit on current account to a level twice as high as the maximum registered so far during the 1980s. As a result, Togo's total external debt continued to grow, exceeding $1 billion by the end of 1985. Debt service payments in 1985 amounted to $94 million, which equalled about two-fifths of Togo's export revenues. Although Togo has been able to manage its external accounts without debt rescheduling, there is considerable doubt whether it will be able to do so much beyond 1987.

4. *Budget*

Government expenditures in 1986 are reported to have amounted to CFAF 90.6 billion ($261 million), which was CFAF 3.5 billion ($10.1 million) higher than budgeted. On the basis of estimated disbursements, the overall budget deficit grew from CFAF 23.9 billion in 1985 to CFAF 27 billion ($78 million) in 1986, equivalent to 7.6 and 8.0 per cent of GDP respectively. The 1987 budget provides for a 2.7 per cent expenditures increase (equivalent to CFAF 2.41 billion, or $6.4 million) over the 1986 budget. Expenditure on salaries will rise, as the wage freeze in the public sector, which had been in force for five years, was lifted in January 1987. The increase in Government expenditure is to be financed from several sources, including a contribution of CFAF 8.25 billion ($24 million) by State enterprises (which contributed nothing in 1986), higher customs revenues, and higher non-fiscal receipts from the petroleum refinery and the post and telecommunications monopoly. Partly offsetting items, however, are the reduced contributions of two other parastatals: the Phosphate Office (O.T.P.) and the State Marketing Board (O.P.A.T.).

B. *Recent policy developments*

1. *Macro-economic policies*

Since 1982 Togo has changed its policy towards the private sector. By the end of the 1970s there was a tendency for the Government to take over loss-making companies to save them from bankruptcy. The current trend is a reversal of this movement. A selection is being made among the 40 State-owned enterprises to determine which are to be privatized, which are to stay in Government hands, and which are to be closed down. Togo has been successful in selling several companies to the private sector. Among them are the steel mill (S.T.S.), which has become a profit-making company, two textile factories (Togotex and ITT), a dairy processing plant (Soprolait) and a marble-quarrying and processing plant (Sotoma). The tax system has been reorganized to stimulate the private sector. Export duties and taxes on industrial products have been abolished, import taxes on raw materials and semi-finished products have been reduced by 75 per cent, and import taxes on finished products have been cut by 50 per cent.

2. *International support measures*

In 1986 Togo received loans from the World Bank ($17.9 million) and the French *Caisse centrale de coopération économique* (CFAF 2.05 billion, equiva- lent to $6.7 million) for the development of coffee and cocoa production. For 1987 the World Bank plans to extend loans totalling $146.5 million via IDA, including a structural adjustment loan ($50 million) and several project loans, among which agricultural development projects will receive $51.5 million.

3. *SNPA follow-up*

After the 1985 Round Table Conference of Lomé, sectoral meetings were planned, of which the last one was convened in October 1986 in Lomé. The latter dealt principally with socio-economic development and the economic infrastructure. The Government aims at rehabilitating and strengthening of the latter, rather than expanding it. The water supply in rural and urban areas is to be improved, while rain and sewerage-collecting systems are planned in urban areas. Other objectives include the strengthening of Togo's transit role as well as self-sufficiency in food and energy. An important step in the direction of the last objective will be taken with the approaching completion of work on the Nangbeto hydroelectric dam, scheduled for early 1988. A second hydroelectric plant at Adjarra on the Mono River is under consideration, with a feasibility study already under way. Like the Nangbeto dam, construction of this dam would be undertaken in co-operation with Benin. This dam would raise Togo's self-sufficiency in energy from 30 to 50 per cent.

36. Tuvalu

A. *Recent socio-economic developments*

1. *Overall economy*

Tuvalu is among the most remote LDCs. It is extremely handicapped by its geographical isolation and peripheral position in the world economy as well as by its internal fragmentation, compounded by extremely poor transportation and communication links. The tiny indigenous population of about 8,200 lives on nine widely dispersed coral atolls with a total land area of 24 km^2. The almost total lack of resources confines the larger part of the population to a semi-subsistence existence.

GDP was expected to decline in 1985 largely owing to depressed demand for the principal export goods. A significant rise in the population caused by Tuvaluans returning from neighbouring island countries during the first half of the 1980s, aggravated the effects of a shrinking GDP. In 1985, GDP per capita of the indigenous population was estimated at $245, i.e. one-fifth lower than the 1981-83 average. The rate of inflation, at 3.5 per cent in 1984, tended to fall even further mainly owing to a wage freeze dictated by budgetary restraint.

2. *Main sectors*

Agriculture is mainly subsistence-oriented. Copra production for export is hampered by the superannuation of coconut palms and parasite infestation as well as by volatile, but downward-tending, copra prices on the world market. The latter were almost 50 per cent lower in 1986 than in 1985 and 72 per cent lower than in 1984. Only a small fraction of potential fish resources is used for commercial purposes. Manufacturing is almost non-existent.

3. *Trade and payments*

Tuvalu's terms of trade deteriorated steadily during the past few years. Export revenue derives mainly from postal stamps, fish and copra. In September 1985 Tuvalu started exporting coconut oil on an experimental basis. However, limited cargo volumes render services by ocean-going vessels expensive and compound the problem of finding a market outlet.

Major import items are food, manufactured goods and fuel. The trade balance displays a chronic deficit. Substantial amounts of external assistance as well as remittances from wages of Tuvaluans employed on merchant vessels abroad or in the phosphate industry of Nauru help to balance the trade deficit. Fees for granting fishing rights in the country's exclusive economic zone represent a potentially important source of revenue and they did, in fact, more than double in 1985 to $410,000 compared to the previous year.

4. *Budget*

Internally-generated Government revenue amounted to $A 2.63 million [155] ($2.31 million) in 1984, representing an increase of 13 per cent on the trough in the preceding year. However, the Government could only cover about three-quarters of its recurrent expenditure during the period 1981-1985. The remaining 25 per cent, about $A 0.9 million ($0.8 million) per year during 1981-1985, were provided by the United Kingdom as a direct budgetary contribution. This assistance is to be scaled down by at least $A 100,000 (about $70,000) annually from 1987 onwards. Following a 25 per cent increase in public spending in 1984, mainly owing to local costs incurred in connection with a rise in externally-financed development expenditure, a much more moderate rise of 2 to 3 per cent was expected for 1985.

B. *Recent policy developments*

1. *Macro-economic policies*

The Government is committed to developing and diversifying the Tuvaluan economy. It planned to implement a $A 29.2 million ($25.7 million) capital development programme in 1984-87, which was to be almost entirely funded externally. A financial institution attached to the Ministry of Finance and designed to provide venture

---

[155] The value of the Tuvalu dollar is pegged at par to the value of the Australian dollar, which is also legal tender in Tuvalu.

TUVALU

1. Population, total and per capita GDP, growth of agricultural and manufacturing output

Year and periods	Population Millions	GDP Total Millions of dollars	GDP Per capita Dollars	GDP Per capita Per cent of LDC average	Agricultural production Total	Agricultural production of which: Food	Manufacturing value-added Total
1985	0.0	2	245[a]	114.0			
			Real growth rates, per cent per annum				
1980-1985	1.2	..	..		..	..	..
1984-1985	0.2	..	..		..	..	..
1985-1986	1.2	..	..		..	..	..

2. Area, demographic indicators and labour force share in agriculture

Area Total 000 km2	Area Share of arable land under permanent crops 1984 Per cent	Area Share covered by forestry and woodlands 1984 Per cent	Density 1985 Pop/km2	Average life expectancy at birth M 1980-1985 Years	Average life expectancy at birth F 1980-1985 Years	Average life expectancy at birth T 1980-1985 Years	Infant mortality as share of live births 1980-1985 Per 1,000	Share of population In urban areas 1985 Per cent	Share of population Economically active 1985 Per cent	Labour force Share in agriculture 1985 Per cent
0.2	..	..	51	..	..	60	40	..	..	..

3. Origins and uses of output; investment

Years	Sectoral origin of GDP Agriculture	Sectoral origin of GDP Mining	Sectoral origin of GDP Manufacturing	Sectoral origin of GDP Services	Uses of GDP Private consumption expenditure	Uses of GDP Government consumption expenditure	Uses of GDP Gross domestic savings	Investment
				Per cent of total GDP				
1980	8.0[b]	..	1.2[b]	82.2[b]	..	..	..	..
1985	10.8	..	2.1	75.7	..	..	..	..

4. Balance of payments, debt and external assistance

Years	Balance of payments Merchandise trade balance	Balance of payments Balance on services	Balance of payments Balance on current account	Debt service Amortization	Debt service Interest	Debt service Total	Debt service As ratio of exports of goods and services	Debt Amount outstanding at year-end	External assistance Total	External assistance of which: ODA
	Millions of dollars						Per cent	Millions of dollars		
1980	..	..	..	- [c]	- [c]	- [c]	- [c]	0.0 [c]	4.9	4.9
1985	..	..	..	-	0.1	0.1	..	0.1	3.4	3.4

5. Trade

Years and periods	Exports Value Mill. of dollars	Exports of which: share of Copra Per cent	Imports Value Mill. of dollars	Imports of which: share of food Per cent	Terms of trade
1980	..	78.4	..	29.7	100
1985	..	78.6[d]	..	25.8[d]	..

	Value	Volume	Purchasing power	Value	Volume	Index
			Growth rates, per cent per annum			
1980-1985	..	..	..	..	..	..
1984-1985	..	..	..	..	..	..
1985-1986	..	..	..	..	..	..

6. Other economic and social indicators

Energy Commercial energy consumption per capita 1984 kg of coal equiv.	Transport & communication Commercial vehicles 1984 Per 1,000 pop.	Transport & communication Telephones 1985 Per 1,000 pop.	Adult literacy rate Around 1985	Education School enrolment ratio share of relevant age group Primary M 1984	Education Primary F 1984	Education Primary T 1984	Education Secondary M 1984	Education Secondary F 1984	Education Secondary T 1984	Health Attendance at childbirth by trained personnel 1984 Per cent	Health Share of population Immunized against DPT (3 doses) 1982	Health Share of population With access to safe water 1985	Food and nutrition Cereals Consumption per capita 1985 kg	Food and nutrition Cereals Self-sufficiency ratio 1985 Per cent	Food and nutrition Average daily calorie intake per capita Total 1985 Calories	Food and nutrition Average daily calorie intake per capita Share of requirements Between 1982&1985 Per cent
..	..	18.8	..	..	..	..	..	..	..	..	72.0	100	51	..	..	..

a/ Income accruing to indigenous population.   b/ 1981.   c/ 1982.   d/ 1983.

capital to Tuvaluans for the establishment of micro-enterprises has proved to function well. However, these activities are mainly confined to the service sector and concentrate on the main island of Funafuti.

2. International support policies

Upon carefully considering the options available for financing recurrent and development expenditures, particularly after the withdrawal of budget support from the United Kingdom which is expected to take place in 1995, the Government put forward a proposal in 1985 to establish a Tuvalu Trust Fund. It is suggested that potential donors and the Government of Tuvalu should jointly contribute at least $20.0 million to that Fund. The interest earned would be used as a substitute for the existing budget assistance . Negotiations on this project with potential contributors are still under way. Another unsettled problem in Tuvalu's development efforts is the need to cover increasing recurrent costs associated with the implementation of development projects. Given the budgetary constraints, these expenditures represent a formidable hardship for the Government, which hopes that donors will assume responsibility for recurrent costs of projects financed by them.

37. Uganda

A. Recent socio-economic developments

1. Overall economy

Uganda's economic performance in 1985 must be seen against the background of civil war which raged in the country during much of 1985. The resulting events made rational economic planning impossible, leading to neglect in the maintenance of existing facilities and infrastructure and preventing the execution of recurrent and development programmes. GDP per capita, like other data for the period, reflects the exceptional circumstances prevailing in the country in 1985, with a fall of 2.7 per cent against 1984. It was in particular the informal sector, whose 40 per cent share of GDP traditionally weighs heavily in the country's overall economic performance, that was affected. Following the stabilization of the political situation since the new Government took over in January 1986, GDP is estimated to have recovered by 12 per cent in 1986 as against 1985. Again it was the informal sector whose revival was decisive for the improvement of the general economic situation.

2. Main sectors

The exceptional circumstances prevailing in the country are a main cause for the high volatility in the development of the major economic sectors and for, sometimes, conflicting data on their performance. According to information from FAO, agricultural production increased markedly in 1985, recovering from a steep decline in the previous year. The growth of food processing by 11 per cent is closely related to that recovery. However, other industries experienced a sharp decline. Other sectors which declined were transport and communications, construction, electricity and mining and quarrying, while services grew by 7 per cent. The poor performance of the informal sector in 1985 was mainly due to an 11 per cent decline in subsistence agriculture.

3. Trade and payments

Total export earnings fell by 5 per cent in 1985 against 1984, owing to a drop in export receipts from coffee, tea, tobacco and maize. Imports, which had declined by 13 per cent in 1984 following drastic restrictions on imports of consumer goods, stagnated in 1985. The net services deficit (which includes interest payments) deteriorated to $98.9 million from $44 million in 1984. The sharp curbing of imports has again resulted in a surplus (of $77.1 million) in the current-account balance, albeit smaller than the $107.1 million achieved in 1984. In 1986, Ugandan exports improved, reflecting the buoyant coffee prices on world markets. Imports recovered slightly. At the end of 1985, total external debt amounted to $1,076 million, of which $774 million was me-

UGANDA

1. Population, total and per capita GDP, growth of agricultural and manufacturing output

Year and periods	Population Millions	GDP Total Millions of dollars	GDP Per capita Dollars	GDP Per capita Per cent of LDC average	Agricultural production Total	Agricultural production of which: Food	Manufacturing value-added Total
1985	15.5	(3401)	220[a/]	102.3			
				Real growth rates, per cent per annum			
1980-1985	3.4	5.0	1.6		8.3	8.2	0.5
1984-1985	3.4	0.6	-2.7		52.5	55.0	-11.0
1985-1986	3.4	..	..		3.6	4.1	..

2. Area, demographic indicators and labour force share in agriculture

Area Total 000 km2	Area Share of arable land under permanent crops 1984 Per cent	Area Share covered by forestry and woodlands 1984 Per cent	Density 1985 Pop/km2	Average life expectancy at birth M 1980-1985 Years	Average life expectancy at birth F 1980-1985 Years	Average life expectancy at birth T 1980-1985 Years	Infant mortality as share of live births 1980-1985 Per 1,000	Share of population In urban areas Per cent	Share of population Economically active 1985 Per cent	Labour force Share in agriculture Per cent
236.0	27.5	24.8	66	47	51	49	112	10	46	84

3. Origins and uses of output; investment

Years	Sectoral origin of GDP Agriculture	Sectoral origin of GDP Mining	Sectoral origin of GDP Manufacturing	Sectoral origin of GDP Services	Uses of GDP Private consumption expenditure	Uses of GDP Government consumption expenditure	Uses of GDP Gross domestic savings	Investment
				Per cent of total GDP				
1980	75.6	0.0	4.0	23.3	..	..	..	6.1
1985	..	..	..	..	..	..	..	8.5[b/]

4. Balance of payments, debt and external assistance

Years	Balance of payments Merchandise trade balance	Balance of payments Balance on services	Balance of payments Balance on current account	Debt service Amortization	Debt service Interest	Debt service Total	Debt service As ratio of exports of goods and services Per cent	Debt Amount outstanding at year-end Millions of dollars	External assistance Total Millions of dollars	External assistance of which: ODA Millions of dollars
	Millions of dollars									
1980	..	..	..	54.5 [c/]	11.6 [c/]	66.1 [c/]	17.3 [c/]	879.3 [c/]	135.9	112.3
1985	..	..	..	94.0	23.8	117.8	29.6	1075.6	229.4	185.8

5. Trade

Years and periods	Exports Value Mill. of dollars	Exports of which: share of Coffee Per cent	Imports Value Mill. of dollars	Imports of which: share of food Per cent	Terms of trade
1980	345	97.9	293	(11.2)	100
1985	380	93.6	375	(10.8)	95

	Value	Volume	Purchasing power	Value	Volume	Index
			Growth rates, per cent per annum			
1980-1985	2.0	5.0	3.8	5.1	7.0	-1.1
1984-1985	-4.8	-3.4	-6.2	1.1	-0.4	-2.9
1985-1986	5.3	-25.8	-2.0	2.7	-4.4	32.1

6. Other economic and social indicators

Energy Commercial energy consumption per capita 1984 kg of coal equiv.	Transport & communication Commercial vehicles 1984 Per 1,000 pop.	Transport & communication Telephones 1983 Per 1,000 pop.	Education Adult literacy rate Around 1985	Education School enrolment ratio share of relevant age group Primary 1982 M	Education Primary 1982 F	Education Primary 1982 T	Education Secondary 1982 M	Education Secondary 1982 F	Education Secondary 1982 T	Health Attendance at child-birth by trained personnel 1984 Per cent	Health Share of population Immunized against DPT (3 doses) 1983 Per cent	Health Share of population With access to safe water 1985 Per cent	Food and nutrition Cereals Consumption per capita 1985 kg	Food and nutrition Cereals Self-sufficiency ratio 1985 Per cent	Food and nutrition Average daily calorie intake per capita Total 1985 Calories	Food and nutrition Average daily calorie intake per capita Share of requirements Between 1982&1985 Per cent
24	..	3.8	..	66	50	58	11	5	8	..	2.0	2.1	88	99	2083 [d/]	101

[a/] GNP per capita in 1984.   [b/] 1983.   [c/] 1982.   [d/] Year other than 1985.

dium- and long-term in nature. Debt service absorbed about one-third per cent of merchandise export earnings in 1985. Total net disbursed ODA increased by 13 per cent (to $185.8 million) from 1984 to 1985. The small fall in bilateral aid from DAC countries (due to the civil strife and the resulting political insecurity) was more than offset by multilateral aid, which rose by nearly 19 per cent to a record of $140 million in 1985. For the first time in 10 years the level of ODA loans ($98.4 million) came to exceed that of grants in 1985.

4. *Budget*

The budgetary revenues anticipated for FY 1985/86 [156] have not been realized, mainly because the proceeds from the coffee export duty, which traditionally account for the bulk of revenues, fell short of expectations. Realized expenditures in FY 1985/86 were also below the budgeted targets. This shortfall ranged from about 10 per cent for recurrent expenditures to about 67 per cent for development expenditures. A large share of the former went to defence, while the major part of the latter financed investments in parastatal enterprises. Education received an estimated 15 per cent, while less than 3 per cent was spent for health. In fact, in May 1986 the new President stated that the Government only had $1 per capita available for health services.

As in previous years, the budget deficit, which during FY 1985/86 amounted to USh 85.7 billion ($78.9 million), was mainly financed by borrowing from the banking system. Largely as a result of that, money supply increased by 90 per cent, which, together with the drastic fall in domestic production and imports, was responsible for rates of inflation of 133 per cent in 1985 and 177 per cent in 1986.

B. *Recent policy developments*

1. *Macro-economic developments*

Government policy set out in a Ten-Point Programme stresses the establishment of a mixed economy. The Government has established a committee to identify the parastatals to be sold to the private sector and announced a relaxation of Governmental control of industrial production. Producer prices were raised for coffee, tea, cocoa beans and tobacco, and interest rates were in-

creased in order to attract savings back into the formal economy. Measures are being taken to widen the tax base, and an entirely new system of tax regulations has been instituted, including a revision of specific tax rates to bring them into line with inflation. The Government has concluded countertrade agreements with the United Republic of Tanzania, Rwanda, Zimbabwe and Yugoslavia to obtain manufactures in exchange for agricultural products. To ensure that enough products are channelled towards fulfilling these obligations, the Government has taken over the marketing of the country's produce, providing about $7 million (USh 10 billion) in local currency to the Produce Marketing Board for purchases from the peasants. The Government has also taken over the importation of essential commodities to prevent their sale at excessive profit rates.

The two-tier exchange-rate system (USh 1,400 and USh 5,000 per dollar), which was introduced in May 1986, was abolished after three months in favour of a single rate of USh 1,400 per dollar. Although the new exchange rate of 60 cranes to the dollar represented an effective devaluation of 76.7 per cent, the rate on the parallel market was still three times as high. The overvalued currency and foreign-exchange shortages coupled with low producer prices to peasants have continued to stimulate unofficial exports across the borders; this applies in particular to coffee, which fetches 10 times more across the border than at home. Such unofficial exports have fuelled the informal economy by making imported goods available for which no foreign exchange is officially granted.

2. *International support policies*

In November 1986 the World Bank suspended the remaining 10 per cent of a $35 million Structural Adjustment Loan, but unfroze it at the beginning of 1987 in support of the rehabilitation of the country's sugar industry. In April 1986, agreement was reached with the IMF on a $29 million drawing. Under the Lomé III Convention, Uganda will receive ECU 125 million ($141 million) in aid during the period 1986-1990.

3. *SNPA follow-up*

In June 1987 Uganda held its most recent Consultative Group Meeting under World Bank chairmanship in Paris, after having come to terms with the IMF about a policy framework for the country's rehabilitation efforts.

---

[156] The fiscal year (FY) ends 30 June.

The Rehabilitation and Development Plan, which covers the period 1987 to 1991 and is costed at $2,866.87 million, received the full support of donors, who pledged around $300 million for the first year of the programme. About one half of total commitments will go towards general balance-of-payments support designed to ease the country's crippling foreign exchange shortages, which had threatened to bring the formal economy to a virtual halt. The other half is committed to investments in the context of the Rehabilitation and Development Plan.

A few days after that meeting the Government met with its major official creditors for its first rescheduling exercise in the framework of the Paris Club. As a result, the amortization and interest payments due between 1 July 1987 and 30 June 1988 were rescheduled for repayment in 18 equal instalments between 1994 and 2002 after a six-year grace period. It is expected that a further $45 million will be rescheduled by non-member countries of the Paris Club, which would raise the total rescheduled debt to slightly over $110 million.

38. United Republic of Tanzania

A. Recent socio-economic developments

1. Overall economy

In 1986, GDP in real terms grew by an estimated 3 per cent as compared to 1985. With an annual population growth of 3.5 per cent, this resulted in a slight fall in per capita GDP. Consumer price inflation between 1985 and 1986 was estimated to have reached 44 per cent. In 1986, agriculture was affected by locust swarms.

2. Main sectors

The performance of the economy in FY 1985/86 [157] was seriously affected by the foreign currency shortage, due to which essential inputs for agriculture and industry, such as spare parts and fuel, could not be imported. Cash crop farming, manufacturing, mining, transportation and construction activities, all of which rely heavily on imported inputs, have been adversely affected. The production of cash crops was again disappointing in FY 1985/86, while the output of food crops, largely produced by subsistence farming, seemed to have recovered owing to sufficient rains and good climatic conditions. The industrial sector continued its decline by a further 6.4 per cent in that year, with industrial plants operating at an estimated average capacity utilization of only 40 per cent. As consumer goods industries account for

about 70 per cent of industrial value added, this resulted in acute shortages of essential supplies for the population. The performance of the tiny tourism sector improved, e.g. wildlife lodges earned $2.9 million in 1985 as against $1.96 million in 1984.

3. Trade and payments

Export earnings measured in United States dollars declined by 25 per cent in 1985 as compared to 1984, the main causes being the reduction in the volume of exports of agricultural commodities and their price decline on world markets. Exports of coffee, the main currency earner, fell by 21.3 per cent in value terms and by 11 per cent in volume terms (from 55,000 tonnes to 49,000 tonnes) between 1984 and 1985. The fact that nearly 60 per cent of coffee exports were concentrated in the first quarter of 1985 precluded the United Republic of Tanzania from benefiting from the price increases on world coffee markets that occurred later that year. Export earnings of cotton, whose prices declined by 38 per cent on world markets, fell by 42 per cent in 1985 as compared to 1984. The volume of imports also fell, but expenditures for them grew by 21 per cent in dollar terms. In 1986 exports seem to have recovered by 11 per cent in balance-of-payments terms, while imports similarly measured declined by 3.4 per cent. The 1985 trade deficit rose by more than 58 per cent (to $742 million) over its 1984 level, with exports only covering 32 per cent of CIF imports. Services registered declines on both the receipts

---

[157] The fiscal year (FY) ends 30 June.

UNITED REPUBLIC OF TANZANIA

1. Population, total and per capita GDP, growth of agricultural and manufacturing output

Year and periods	Population Millions	GDP Total Millions of dollars	GDP Per capita Dollars	GDP Per capita Per cent of LDC average	Agricultural production Total	Agricultural production of which: Food	Manufacturing value-added Total
1985	22.2	6211	279	129.8			
				Real growth rates, per cent per annum			
1980-1985	3.5	1.3	-2.1		1.5	2.0	-4.8
1984-1985	3.5	1.0	-2.4		0.7	1.5	-5.1
1985-1986	3.5	..	..		2.7	2.9	..

2. Area, demographic indicators and labour force share in agriculture

Area Total	Area Share of arable land under permanent crops 1984	Area Share covered by forestry and woodlands 1984	Demographic indicators Density 1985	Average life expectancy at birth M 1980-1985	Average life expectancy at birth F 1980-1985	Average life expectancy at birth T 1980-1985	Infant mortality as share of live births 1980-1985	Share of population In urban areas	Share of population Economically active 1985	Labour force Share in agriculture
000 km2	Per cent	Per cent	Pop/km2	Years	Years	Years	Per 1,000	Per cent	Per cent	
945.1	5.5	45.3	24	49	53	51	115	14	49	83

3. Origins and uses of output; investment

Years	Sectoral origin of GDP Agriculture	Mining	Manufacturing	Services	Uses of GDP Private consumption expenditure	Government consumption expenditure	Gross domestic savings	Investment
				Per cent of total GDP				
1980	44.4	0.9	10.9	38.6	78.0	12.8	9.2	22.5
1985	58.5	0.3	5.2	33.2	85.0	12.3	2.7	14.5

4. Balance of payments, debt and external assistance

Years	Balance of payments Merchandise trade balance	Balance on services	Balance on current account	Debt service Amortization	Interest	Total	As ratio of exports of goods and services	Debt Amount outstanding at year-end	External assistance Total	of which: ODA
	Millions of dollars						Per cent	Millions of dollars		
1980	..	..	..	33.2[a]	59.4[a]	92.6[a]	17.4[a]	2740.3[a]	838.4	670.0
1985	..	..	..	48.5	53.5	102.0	23.1	3374.2	550.7	506.3

5. Trade

Years and periods	Exports Value Mill. of dollars	Exports of which: share of Coffee Per cent	Imports Value Mill. of dollars	Imports of which: share of food Per cent	Terms of trade
1980	508	26.7	1226	(13.3)	100
1985	284	40.2	1026	(10.1)[b]	90

	Value	Volume	Purchasing power	Value	Volume	Index
	Growth rates, per cent per annum					
1980-1985	-11.0	-7.0	-9.0	-3.5	-1.4	-2.2
1984-1985	-24.9	-21.2	-25.0	15.4	15.3	-4.8
1985-1986	12.7	-3.0	14.3	-4.5	3.1	17.8

6. Other economic and social indicators

Energy Commercial energy consumption per capita 1984 kg of coal equiv.	Transport & communication Commercial vehicles 1982 Per 1,000 pop.	Telephones 1985 Per 1,000 pop.	Education Adult literacy rate Around 1985	School enrolment ratio share of relevant age group Primary M 1983	Primary F 1983	Primary T 1983	Secondary M 1983	Secondary F 1983	Secondary T 1983	Health Attendance at childbirth by trained personnel 1983 Per cent	Share of population Immunized against DPT (3 doses) 1982 Per cent	With access to safe water 1985 Per cent	Food and nutrition Cereals Consumption per capita 1985 kg	Self-sufficiency ratio 1985 Per cent	Average daily calorie intake per capita Total 1985 Calories	Share of requirements Between 1982&1985 Per cent
43	2.5	5.1	..	91	84	87	4	2	3	74.0	58.0	49	175	93	2335	98

a/ 1982.   b/ 1983.

and expenditure sides. The current account deficit of $593.3 million was larger by 24 per cent than in 1984. The 1986 trade deficit appears to have been of the same order of magnitude as in the preceding year.

Total external debt at the end of 1985 exceeded $3.3 billion; this represented an increase of 11 per cent over the level one year earlier and equalled 54 per cent of GDP in 1985. Service on public long-term debt amounted to $85 million as against $80 million in 1984, despite a substantial decline of such payments to non-OECD creditor countries. However, the outflow to the IMF diminished considerably, causing overall debt service to decline in 1986. As public debt service was to rise to no less than $381.3 million in 1986, the United Republic of Tanzania resorted to the Paris Club for debt rescheduling. Partly as a result of this, international currency reserves recovered to over $60 million at the end of 1986 from their $16 million low one year earlier.

Despite the worsening external balance, total financial flows to the United Republic of Tanzania declined by 14 per cent from $614.5 million in 1984 to $527.9 million in 1985, largely reflecting the on-going decline of ODA from DAC countries, which account for over 90 per cent of total net financial inflows.

4. Budget

Government expenditures continued to mount in FY 1985/86, reflecting in particular a 13 per cent rise in recurrent expenditures over FY 1984/85. The increases were caused by higher costs in running public administration, increases in public debt service and by subsidies to local government and government-supported institutions. Recurrent revenues in nominal terms also rose through higher tax revenues, but since this improvement was much smaller than the rise in expenditures, the recurrent budget again showed a deficit. Development expenditures declined to TSh 6,828 million ($389 million), equivalent to only 29 per cent of recurrent expenditures. For FY 1986/87, the Government plans to increase development expenditures by over 130 per cent in nominal terms, to be financed by a fivefold increase of donor funding following agreement with the IMF. Recurrent expenditures are planned to increase by 53 per cent, partly reflecting the impact on the Government budget of the 63.6 per cent devaluation of the shilling against the United States dollar between FY 1985/86 and FY 1986/87.

B. Recent policy developments

1. Macro-economic policies

A three-year Economic Recovery Programme (ERP) was announced in June 1986 with the support of the World Bank and the IMF. Energy, manufacturing, and agriculture will receive the major shares of the planned rehabilitation expenditures. The Government aims to increase the production of basic manufactured consumer goods, such as soap, textiles and beverages. This forms an important part of its agricultural incentives package, designed to make goods available to agricultural producers receiving additional monetary income. The ERP also aims to raise capacity utilization of industry to 60 per cent over three years. In order to increase recurrent revenues and improve the poor state of tax collection, a number of tax reform measures have been introduced.

Between mid-April and end-June 1986 the Government devalued the currency by 56.3 per cent, raising the exchange rate from TSh 17.47 to TSh 40 per dollar. A crawling peg system of devaluations since then produced a further cumulative devaluation of 32 per cent (to TSh 58.14) by the end of April 1987.

There has been a substantial increase in producer prices for the country's export crops. In 1986 the Government broadened the export retention and import liberalization scheme, allowing exporters of certain goods to retain 50 per cent of export earnings for import purposes, a measure which has increased the supply of consumer goods on local markets. Since August 1986, there have been large increases in Government-controlled consumer prices. The price of maize meal, which is the staple food, was nearly doubled, while the sugar price was raised 52 per cent, flour 46 per cent and rice flour 31 per cent. This has closed the gap between goods sold at official prices and those sold on the black market, bringing more food items into official market channels.

2. International support measures

In August 1986 the IMF approved an 18-months stand-by arrangement amounting to SDR 64.2 million ($77.5 million) in support of the ERP. The amount is equivalent to 60 per cent of the country's IMF quota of SDR 107 million. The United Republic of Tanzania's arrears to the Fund were cleared with a $25 million bridging loan from a United States commercial bank. The Scandinavian countries also assisted in clearing this final obstacle. The United Republic of Tanzania has also started negotiations with the IMF on a loan from the Structural Adjustment Facility. Last September, it met with its official creditors under the aegis of the Paris Club for the rescheduling of official debt due between 1 October 1986 and 30 September 1987. The agreement covers principal, interest and arrears and amounted to at least $600 million.

3. *SNPA follow-up*

In June 1986, the United Republic of Tanzania had a Consultative Group Meeting under World Bank chairmanship in Paris. At the meet-ing, the Government presented its ERP to donors, who endorsed its broad lines. Under the new aid package, the World Bank is the largest source of new finance, increasing existing commitments to-talling $85 million by a multi-sector credit of $100 million for balance-of-payments support. Bilateral donors also increased their support, pledging $130 million per annum over three years above their current aid commitments. Aggregate multilateral and bilateral pledges amounted to about $800 million per annum over the next three years, which is about 68 per cent more than the $477.6 million which the United Republic of Tanzania received in 1985 as ODA from the same group of donors (ODA from other donors was marginal). However, the above agreements are conditional on its acceptance of the IMF package of economic policy measures.

---

39. Vanuatu

A. *Recent socio-economic developments*

1. *Overall economy*

Vanuatu's economy suffered considerable setbacks during the two years following the short-lived economic upswing in 1984. Falling prices for copra, the major cash and export product, adversely affected economic growth. While real GDP stagnated in 1985, real output decreased by 1 per cent in 1986. GDP per capita of the indigenous population fell by 4.6 per cent in 1985 (at current prices), to a level of $499 as compared to $523 in 1984. In an effort to adjust the exchange rate of the vatu to the domestic rate of inflation and to the devaluation of the currencies of the country's main trading partners, the Government devalued the national currency (by 8.5 per cent against the SDR) in 1985 and twice successively (by 9.8 per cent and 14.1 per cent) in 1986. Inflation was kept below 1 per cent in 1985, but rose again to 5 per cent in 1986. In addition to its economic hardships, the country had to overcome considerable damage caused by cyclones in 1985. In February 1987, another cyclone hit the country, damaging about 95 per cent of the housing in the capital and sinking three boats, which had secured the transportation link between the various parts of the archipelago.

2. *Main sectors*

The agricultural sector, which had suffered severely from cyclone damage in 1985, made a remarkable recovery during 1986. The effects of a domestic price stabilization scheme and the introduction of a pricing system, which allows prices to vary in accordance with differences in grade, resulted in higher copra yields and improved quality. Cocoa producers also responded positively to price incentives. While total cocoa production in 1986 rose by 30 per cent (to 1,281 tonnes), making this the second best crop since 1980, production of high-valued export grades increased by as much as 60 per cent. In late 1986, a foreign company, which is prospecting for diamonds, announced the discovery of a gold deposit. There is some external interest in the reopening of a cold-storage fishing base, which would restore abandoned jobs in the small manufacturing sector and enhance the country's bargaining power *vis-à-vis* potential licensees for the fish resources in Vanuatu's EEZ. The tourist industry experienced a further setback, as the number of visitors decreased for the second consecutive year. The loss in tourist arrivals was 22 per cent and 29 per cent in 1985 and 1986 respectively.

VANUATU

1. Population, total and per capita GDP, growth of agricultural and manufacturing output

Year and periods	Population Millions	GDP Total Millions of dollars	GDP Per capita Dollars	GDP Per capita Per cent of LDC average	Agricultural production Total	Agricultural production of which: Food	Manufacturing value-added Total
1985	0.1	66	499	232.1			
			Real growth rates, per cent per annum				
1980-1985	2.8	2.4	-0.4		4.1	4.2	..
1984-1985	2.8	0.4	-2.4		-4.1	-4.2	..
1985-1986	2.8	..	..		6.1	6.1	..

2. Area, demographic indicators and labour force share in agriculture

Area Total 000 km2	Area Share of arable land under permanent crops 1984 Per cent	Area Share covered by forestry and woodlands 1984 Per cent	Density 1985 Pop/km2	Average life expectancy at birth M 1980-1985 Years	Average life expectancy at birth F 1980-1985 Years	Average life expectancy at birth T 1980-1985 Years	Infant mortality as share of live births 1980-1985 Per 1,000	Share of population In urban areas 1985 Per cent	Share of population Economically active 1985 Per cent	Labour force Share in agriculture 1985 Per cent
14.8	6.4	1.1	9	..	..	55	94	25	..	79a/

3. Origins and uses of output; investment

Years	Sectoral origin of GDP Agriculture	Sectoral origin of GDP Mining	Sectoral origin of GDP Manufacturing	Sectoral origin of GDP Services	Uses of GDP Private consumption expenditure	Uses of GDP Government consumption expenditure	Uses of GDP Gross domestic savings	Investment
				Per cent of total GDP				
1980	38.7b/	..	3.0b/	54.9b/	56.0b/	37.2b/	23.5b/	26.9b/
1985	40.1	..	4.0	52.5	56.9	38.6	26.4	29.0

4. Balance of payments, debt and external assistance

Years	Balance of payments Merchandise trade balance	Balance of payments Balance on services	Balance of payments Balance on current account	Debt service Amortization	Debt service Interest	Debt service Total	Debt service As ratio of exports of goods and services Per cent	Debt Amount outstanding at year-end	External assistance Total	External assistance of which: ODA
	Millions of dollars						Per cent	Millions of dollars		
1980	..	..	..	1.2c/	1.0c/	2.2c/	4.1c/	13.9c/	42.3	44.0
1985	..	..	..	4.0	7.0	11.0	13.1	127.7	38.6	21.8

5. Trade

Years and periods	Exports Value Mill. of dollars	Exports of which: share of Copra Per cent	Imports Value Mill. of dollars	Imports of which: share of food Per cent	Terms of trade
1980	35	24.2	71	29.5	100
1985	31	40.9	71	25.8b/	..

	Value	Volume	Purchasing power	Value	Volume	Index
			Growth rates, per cent per annum			
1980-1985	-2.4	..	0.0	0.0	2.5	..
1984-1985	-29.5	..	-29.8	2.9	2.5	..
1985-1986	-54.8	..	-55.4	-19.7	-20.8	..

6. Other economic and social indicators

Energy Commercial energy consumption per capita 1984 kg of coal equiv.	Transport & communication Commercial vehicles 1984 Per 1,000 pop.	Transport & communication Telephones 1985	Education Adult literacy rate Around 1985	Education School enrolment ratio share of relevant age group Primary M 1984	Education Primary F 1984	Education Primary T 1984	Education Secondary M 1984	Education Secondary F 1984	Education Secondary T 1984	Health Attendance at childbirth by trained personnel 1983	Health Share of population Immunized against DPT (3 doses) 1984	Health Share of population With access to safe water 1985	Food and nutrition Cereals Consumption per capita 1985 kg	Food and nutrition Cereals Self-sufficiency ratio 1985 Per cent	Food and nutrition Average daily calorie intake per capita Total 1985 Calories	Food and nutrition Average daily calorie intake per capita Share of requirements Between 1982&1985 Per cent
				Per cent												
203	9.4	22.9	..	..	..	..	..	..	..	72.0	22.0	99	82	6	220a/	81

a/ Year other than 1985.   b/ 1983.   c/ 1982.

3. *Trade*

Despite a significant increase in the export volume of copra and cocoa – the country's principal export goods – Vanuatu experienced a dramatic 54.8 per cent decline (in dollar terms) of its export earnings in 1986. This drop in export income was mainly caused by a steep fall in prices for copra and tuna fish. While copra prices slumped by almost 50 per cent in 1986, following a decline of 46 per cent in the preceding year, the fall in tuna prices forced the closure of a fishing company, which had markedly contributed to export income since the 1950s. Imports dropped by 19.7 per cent in 1986, reflecting depressed demand due to the reduced number of tourist arrivals and the loss of income from copra exports. But despite the import reduction, the trade deficit widened further, reaching its highest level in the 1980s.

4. *Budget*

Although Government expenditure in 1986 was in line with initial projections, revenues were substantially lower than expected, mainly due to a marked reduction in commercial activity connected with reduced copra exports and tourism receipts. To redress the budget disequilibrium, the Government announced expenditure cutbacks and austerity measures for 1987. Simultaneously, the coverage of customs duties will be widened and the level of tariffs will be increased to expand revenue.

B. *Recent policy developments*

1. *Macro-economic policies*

With a view to restoring fiscal equilibrium, the Government initiated austerity measures, including a restriction on the expansion of the public sector, a freeze on recruitment for Government service and a squeeze on departmental expenditures. Monetary policy provides for a regular adjustment of the exchange rate to assist exports and attract tourism. The subsidy scheme for major export products will be maintained. Agreements were signed with the United States and the Soviet Union in 1986 and early 1987 respectively for the exploitation of the fish resources in the archipelago's EEZ.

2. *International support measures*

Vanuatu receives considerable international assistance, notably budget support from the two former co-administrating Powers: France ($1.74 million in 1985) and the United Kingdom ($0.94 million in 1985). However, this assistance has been declining in nominal terms and is likely to terminate in the near future. Given the limited internal revenue basis, the country faces the options either of cutting its budget expenditure or of finding new sources for external assistance.

40. Yemen Arab Republic

A. *Recent socio-economic developments*

1. *Overall economy*

The weak economic performance experienced during 1983 and 1984 continued in 1985, as real GDP grew by only 3 per cent. Given an annual population growth rate of 3 per cent, this implied a stagnation in per capita GDP. In 1986, growth is estimated to have been 4 per cent in real terms. As a result of the growth of the money supply by about 20 per cent, the devaluation of the rial against the dollar by 9.6 per cent and the administrative re-striction of imports, the Sana'a consumer price index increased by 27 per cent in 1985. It is estimated to have risen by 30 per cent in 1986.

2. *Main sectors*

A major development in the agricultural sector in 1986 was the opening of the first stage of the Marib Dam, which is expected to irrigate about 4,000 ha initially, increasing to 20,000 ha by 1988. Further projects initiated include a dam near Sana'a to irrigate 500 ha and the Wadi Siham agri-

YEMEN

1. Population, total and per capita GDP, growth of agricultural and manufacturing output

Year and periods	Population Millions	GDP[a] Total Millions of dollars	GDP[a] Per capita Dollars	GDP[a] Per capita Per cent of LDC average	Agricultural production Total	Agricultural production of which: Food	Manufacturing value-added Total
1985	8.0	(3832)	482[b]	224.2			
				Real growth rates, per cent per annum			
1980-1985	2.5	5.6	3.1		4.0	4.1	18.2[c]
1984-1985	2.5	3.0	0.5		7.8	7.8	..
1985-1986	2.5	..	..		14.6	14.8	..

2. Area, demographic indicators and labour force share in agriculture

Area Total	Area Share of arable land under permanent crops	Area Share covered by forestry and woodlands 1984	Demographic indicators Density 1985	Demographic indicators Average life expectancy at birth M 1980-1985	F	T	Demographic indicators Infant mortality as share of live births 1980-1985	Demographic indicators Share of population In urban areas	Economically active 1985	Labour force Share in agriculture
000 km2	Per cent		Pop/km2	Years			Per 1,000	Per cent		
195.0	6.9	8.2	41	47	50	48	135	19	24	65

3. Origins and uses of output; investment

Years	Sectoral origin of GDP Agriculture	Mining	Manufacturing	Services	Uses of GDP Private consumption expenditure	Government consumption expenditure	Gross domestic savings	Investment
				Per cent of total GDP				
1980	34.5	1.5	6.5	46.5	105.5	19.3	-24.8	40.7
1985	23.6[b]	1.3[b]	9.3[b]	55.7[b]	82.7[b]	39.8[b]	-22.4[b]	20.9[b]

4. Balance of payments, debt and external assistance

Years	Balance of payments Merchandise trade balance	Balance on services	Balance on current account	Debt service Amortization	Interest	Total	As ratio of exports of goods and services	Debt Amount outstanding at year-end	External assistance Total	of which: ODA
	Millions of dollars						Per cent	Millions of dollars		
1980	-1856.6	-45.6	-833.5	58.4[d]	23.5[d]	81.9[d]	24.2[d]	1541.4[d]	543.5	460.0
1985	-1228.8	-80.1	-437.1	154.0	53.1	207.2	92.0	2398.5	295.3	298.1

5. Trade

Years and periods	Exports Value Mill. of dollars	Exports of which: share of Hides and skins Per cent	Imports Value Mill. of dollars	Imports of which: share of food Per cent	Terms of trade
1980	23	..	1853	28.4	100
1985	106	6.4[e]	1598	33.1	..

	Exports Value	Volume	Purchasing power	Imports Value	Volume	Index
			Growth rates, per cent per annum			
1980-1985	35.7	..	39.1	-2.9	-0.5	..
1984-1985	63.1	..	62.4	-3.4	-3.8	..
1985-1986	-24.5	..	-25.5	-6.1	-7.4	..

6. Other economic and social indicators

Energy Commercial energy consumption per capita 1984 kg of coal equiv.	Transport & communication Commercial vehicles 1984 Per 1,000 pop.	Tele-phones 1981	Education Adult literacy rate Around 1985	School enrolment ratio share of relevant age group Primary M 1983	F	T	Secondary M 1983	F	T	Health Atten-dance at child-birth by trained personnel 1982	Share of population Immu-nized against DPT (3 doses) 1984	With access to safe water 1985	Food and nutrition Cereals Consumption per capita 1985 kg	Self-suffi-ciency ratio 1985 Per cent	Average daily calorie intake per capita Total 1985 Calories	Share of require-ments Between 1982&1985 Per cent
				Per cent						Per cent			kg	Per cent	Calories	Per cent
162	..	5.7	..	112	22	67	17	3	10	12.0	10.0	32	177	41	2250	92

a/ Years ending 30 June.   b/ 1984.   c/ 1980-1984.   d/ 1982.   e/ 1983.

cultural project. In the energy sector, oil is to be exported from the Alif field by the end of 1987 upon completion of the oil pipeline, representing the country's first oil exports. A second, substantial oil field has been discovered in the Marib/Jawf region. Gas has also been found in large quantities and studies are under way to estimate the reserves and its possible uses. IDA is financing the construction of a 62-km road to link Marib to the oil fields and to the oil refinery at Safer.

3. Trade and payments

The economy of Yemen is heavily dependent on external resources including workers' remittances and ODA flows. As compared to imports, exports have remained at a low level, covering about 5 per cent of merchandise imports. Import restrictions initiated in 1983 remained in force during the following years. These, together with three devaluations during 1985 and 1986 (amounting to a cumulative cut of 34.8 per cent vis-à-vis the dollar), caused imports in 1985 and 1986 to decline. Although workers' remittances ($745 million) were 17 per cent below their 1985 level, the current account deficit (excluding official unrequited transfers) fell from $437 million in 1985 to about $409 million in 1986. Since ODA and other long-term capital inflows more than doubled to well above their 1983-1985 average, the overall balance moved into surplus for the first time during the 1980s. As a result, net international reserves rose from less than $300 million at the end of 1985 to over $432 million one year later and stood at $527.6 million at the end of July 1987, which was equivalent to about six months' imports at their sharply-reduced current levels. Total external debt including short-term debt and use of IMF credits, was estimated at $2.4 billion at the end of 1986. Debt service payments represented 55.8 per cent of exports of goods and services in 1985 as against 26.6 per cent in 1984.

4. Budget

In view of the imposition of stabilization measures, revenues increased by 16 per cent, while expenditures declined by 7 per cent between 1985 and 1986, causing the overall budgetary deficit to drop by 41 per cent. However, even this reduced deficit still represents 26 per cent of total Government expenditure. The main features of the 1987 budget are a 20 per cent increase in expenditure accompanied by a 10 per cent increase in revenue as compared to the 1986 levels. The resulting pro-

jected budget deficit is estimated to rise to 32 per cent of expenditures, equivalent to 17 per cent of GDP as against 22.8 per cent effectively realized in 1985.

5. Social sectors

Efforts to expand the coverage of education and health services have remained a priority. The number of primary schools and of enrolled students increased by 36 and 50 per cent respectively between 1982 and 1985. The number of rural health units, health centres and hospitals increased by 38, 44 and 13 per cent respectively during the same period. The Government has announced plans to spend about $140 million during the period 1987-1991 to improve water supply and sewerage connections in cities and provincial towns.

B. Recent policy developments

1. Macro-economic policies

The implementation of stabilization programmes were continued in 1986 and 1987 involving: (a) import restrictions on luxury items; (b) adoption of a flexible exchange rate policy involving three devaluations during 1985 and 1986; (c) reduction of current expenditures, and (d) tightening investment priorities. The guidelines for the Third Five-Year Development Plan (1987-1991) published in March 1987 give high priority to: increasing agricultural production; full exploitation of the country's oil resources; restrictions of non-essential imports, including stricter control on illegal trading; increased domestic resource mobilization; and the development of human resources. Total Government expenditure during the Plan period is estimated at about $4 billion.

2. International support measures

The inflow of concessional development assistance in 1985, at $298.1 million, was about 13 per cent below the previous year's level. But in 1986, ODA receipts were close to $500 million, including about $220 million in grants from Saudi Arabia.

Annex

BASIC DATA ON THE LEAST DEVELOPED COUNTRIES

Annexe

DONNÉES DE BASE RELATIVES AUX PAYS LES MOINS AVANCÉS

Contents

Table des matières

Explanatory notes

A. Definition of country groupings

LEAST DEVELOPED COUNTRIES

In this document, the 40 countries identified by the United Nations as least developed are: Afghanistan, Bangladesh, Benin, Bhutan, Botswana, Burkina Faso, Burundi, Cape Verde, Central African Republic, Chad, Comoros, Democratic Yemen, Djibouti, Equatorial Guinea, Ethiopia, Gambia, Guinea, Guinea-Bissau, Haiti, Kiribati, Lao People's Democratic Republic, Lesotho, Malawi, Maldives, Mali, Mauritania, Nepal, Niger, Rwanda, Samoa, Sao Tome and Principe, Sierra Leone, Somalia, Sudan, Togo, Tuvalu, Uganda, United Republic of Tanzania, Vanuatu and Yemen. Except where otherwise indicated, the totals and the tables for least developed countries as a group refer to these 40 countries. The United Nations General Assembly at its forty-second session in December 1987 has approved the inclusion of Burma which will be covered in the next issue of the *Basic Data*.

MAJOR ECONOMIC AREAS

The classification of countries and territories according to main economic areas used in this document has been adopted for purposes of statistical convenience only and follows that in the UNCTAD *Handbook of International Trade and Development Statistics, Supplement 1986*. Countries and territories are classified according to main economic areas as follows:

Developed market-economy countries: United States, Canada, EEC (Belgium, Denmark, France, Germany, Federal Republic of, Greece, Ireland, Italy, Luxembourg, Netherlands, Portugal, Spain, United Kingdom), EFTA (Austria, Finland, Iceland, Norway, Sweden, Switzerland), Faeroe Islands, Gibraltar, Israel, Japan, Australia, New Zealand, South Africa.

Socialist countries of Eastern Europe: Albania, Bulgaria, Czechoslovakia, German Democratic Republic, Hungary, Poland, Romania, USSR.

Socialist countries of Asia: China, Democratic People's Republic of Korea, Mongolia, Viet Nam.

Developing countries and territories: All other countries, territories and areas in Africa, Asia, America, Europe and Oceania not specified above.

In some tables the group of *all developing countries* excludes, as indicated, *major petroleum exporters*. *Major petroleum exporters* are defined as those countries for which petroleum and petroleum products accounted for more than 50 per cent of their total exports in 1978, namely, Algeria, Angola, Bahrain, Brunei, Congo, Ecuador, Gabon, Indonesia, Iran (Islamic Republic of), Iraq, Kuwait, Libyan Arab Jama-hiriya, Mexico, Nigeria, Oman, Qatar, Saudi Arabia, Syrian Arab Republic, Trinidad and Tobago, United Arab Emirates and Venezuela.

OTHER COUNTRY GROUPINGS

DAC member countries: In this document, the countries members of the OECD Development Assistance Committee are Australia, Austria, Belgium, Canada, Denmark, Finland, France, Germany, Federal Republic of, Ireland, Italy, Japan, Netherlands, New Zealand, Norway, Sweden, Switzerland, United Kingdom and United States.

OPEC member countries: The countries members of the Organization of the Petroleum Exporting Countries are Algeria, Ecuador, Gabon, Indonesia, Iran (Islamic Republic of), Iraq, Kuwait, Libyan Arab Jamahiriya, Nigeria, Qatar, Saudi Arabia, United Arab Emirates and Venezuela.

B. Terms, definitions and sources used

The estimates of *population* are for mid-year and are primarily based on data from the Population Division of the Department of International Economic and Social Affairs of the United Nations Secretariat.

National accounts data are mainly based on information from the United Nations Statistical Office, the United Nations Economic Commission for Africa, the World Bank and national sources.

The estimates relating to *agricultural production, food* and *nutrition*, are derived mainly from information provided by FAO.

Trade data are estimates by the UNCTAD secretariat mainly derived from the UNCTAD *Handbook of International Trade and Development Statistics, Supplement 1986*. Unless otherwise indicated, trade data refer to merchandise trade. Exports are valued f.o.b. and imports c.i.f.

The figures concerning *aid flows* are mainly based on information provided by the OECD secretariat. Following the DAC definitions [1] *concessional assistance* refers to flows which qualify as official development assistance (ODA), i.e., grants or loans undertaken by the official sector, with promotion of economic development and welfare as main objectives, and at concessional financial terms (if a loan, at least 25 per cent grant element). *Non-concessional flows* include grants from private agencies (private aid) and transactions at commercial terms: export credits, bilateral portfolio investment (including bank lending) by residents or institutions in donor countries; direct investment (including reinvested earnings);

---

[1] See OECD *Development Co-operation, 1983 Review* (Paris, 1983), p. 176.

and purchases of securities of international organizations active in development. Figures for *commitments* reflect a firm obligation to furnish assistance specified as to volume, purpose, financial terms and conditions, while figures for *disbursements* represent the actual provision of funds. Unless otherwise specified, disbursement figures are shown net, i.e., less capital repayments on earlier loans. Grants, loans and credits for military purposes and loans and credits with a maturity of less than one year are excluded from aid flows.

The data for the years 1977-1985 concerning aid flows from OPEC member countries and multilateral agencies mainly financed by them have been supplied directly by the donors to the UNCTAD secretariat. In a few cases the figures represent estimates by the UNCTAD secretariat based on secondary sources.

Tables 34 and 46 present data for individual DAC and OPEC member countries respectively on the estimated amount of official development assistance provided to LDCs expressed as a percentage of the GNP of each donor. So as to give a clear picture of the total flow, an attempt has been made to estimate the share of multilateral flows to LDCs which is provided by each donor. In order to do so, the share of each agency's disbursements to LDCs, expressed as a percentage of its total disbursements to developing countries, was applied to the donor's contributions to the agency in question; the sum for all agencies thus calculated was then added to the donor's bilateral ODA and expressed as a percentage of its GNP.

Debt data cover total external long-term and medium-term debt (including private debt) and are based on information provided by the OECD secretariat.

With regard to other economic and social indicators, data on *area* are from the United Nations, *Demographic Yearbook 1985* [2] and the FAO, *Production Yearbook 1985*.

The estimates relating to *urban population* are not strictly comparable from country to country because of differences in definitions and coverage. They have been mainly derived from the United Nations, *World Population Chart 1985* [3] and the World Bank, *World Development Report 1987*.

The *labour force participation rate* refers to economically active population as a percentage of total population of sex(es) specified of all ages, as shown in the World Bank, *Social Indicators of Development 1986*.

Crude birth rates and *crude death rates* indicate respectively the number of births and deaths per thousand of population. Together with *life expectancy at birth* and *infant mortality rates, crude birth* and *death rates* have been derived mainly from the United Nations, *Demographic Yearbook 1985*, United Nations, *World Population Prospects: estimates and projections as assessed in 1984,* [4] and United Nations, *World Population Chart 1985.*

Life expectancy at birth indicates the average number of years the newly born children would live, if subject to the same mortality conditions in the year(s) to which the life expectancy refers, while the *infant mortality rate* is the number of infants who die before reaching one year of age per thousand live births in the reference year.

Under the heading *health at birth,* low birth weight directly reflects the nutritional status of mothers and indirectly, mediated through the status of women, that of the population in general. The figures are drawn from WHO, *World Health Statistics Annual 1986* and UNICEF, *The State of the World's Children 1987.*

The *percentage of women attended during childbirth by trained personnel* is a good indicator of the availability of medical services. It reflects the geographical distribution of the facilities and hence their accessibility, and indeed whether the hospitals had the equipment and supplies to dispense effective medical care. The percentage of women attended during childbirth by trained personnel also to a degree reflects the status of women. Data are drawn from WHO, *World Health Statistics Annual 1986.*

The *percentage of children immunized against DPT* (3 doses) refers to the vaccination coverage of children under one year of age for the target diseases of the Expanded Programme of Immunization (diphtheria, tetanus, whooping-cough, measles, poliomyelitis and tuberculosis). Data are drawn from WHO, *World Health Statistics Annual 1986.*

The estimates of *average daily calorie intake per capita* was calculated by dividing the calorie equivalent of the food supplies in an economy by the population. Food supplies comprise domestic production, imports less exports, and changes in stocks; they exclude animal feed, seeds for use in agriculture, and food lost in processing and distribution. The daily calorie requirements used as a basis for calculating average daily calorie intake as a *percentage of requirements* refer to the calories needed to sustain a person at normal levels of activity and health taking into account age and sex distributions, average body weights, and environmental temperatures. The data in this table are weighted by population and are taken from World Bank, *World Development Report 1987* and World Bank, *Social Indicators of Development 1986.*

The *percentage of population with access to safe water or adequate sanitation* are estimates by WHO. The percentage with access to safe water refers to the share of people with "reasonable" access to treated surface waters or untreated but uncontaminated water, such as that from protected boreholes, springs and sanitary wells, as a percentage of their respective populations. In an urban area a public fountain or standpost located not more than 200 metres from a house is considered as being within "reasonable" access to the house; in rural areas, "reasonable" access would imply that the housewife or members of the household do not spend a disproportionate part of the day in fetching the family's water needs.

The *percentage of population with access to adequate sanitation* includes the share of urban population served by connections to public sewers or by systems (pit privies, pour-flush latrines, septic tanks, communal toilets, etc.) and the share of rural population with adequate disposal such as pit privies, pour-flush latrines, etc.

With respect to both water and sanitation, the figures are derived from *The international drinking water supply and sanitation decade: review of national progress* (as at 31 December 1985).

Data relating to *education and literacy* are mainly derived from information provided by UNESCO. The *adult literacy rate* is the percentage of people aged 15 and over who

[2] ST/ESA/STAT/SER.R/15, United Nations Publication, Sales No. E/F.86.XIII.1.

[3] ST/ESA/SER.A/98/Add.1, United Nations Publication, Sales No. E.85.XIII.A.

[4] ST/ESA/SER.A/98, United Nations Publication, Sales No. E.86.XIII.3.

can read and write. The data on *school enrolment ratios* refer to estimates of total, male, and female enrolment of students of all ages in primary/secondary school, expressed as percentages of the total, male, and female population of primary/secondary school age.

Newsprint consumption is estimated from imports, except in Bangladesh, which also produces newsprint for domestic consumption. The estimates are based on data from UNESCO, *Statistical Yearbook 1986.*

Data on *mail traffic* cover letters, postcards, printed matter, merchandise samples, small packets and photopost packets. The figures are from the Universal Postal Union, *Statistiques des services postaux 1980* and *1984.*

Data on *circulation of daily newspapers per 1000 inhabitants*, refer to circulation of "daily general interest newspapers" and are based on data from UNESCO, *Statistical Yearbook 1986.*

Data on *telephones per 1000 inhabitants* are based on ITU, *Yearbook of Common Carrier Telecommunication Statistics* (14th edition).

Data on radio receivers per 1000 inhabitants are based on data from UNESCO, *Statistical Yearbook 1986.* The ratio uses the number of receivers in use and/or licences issued, depending on the method of estimation used in each reporting country.

Data on *energy consumption per capita* refer, on the one hand, to forms of primary energy, including hard coal, lignite, peat and oil shale, crude petroleum and natural gas liquids, natural gas, and primary electricity (nuclear, geothermal, and hydroelectric power) – often called "commercial energy" – and, on the other hand, to the use of fuelwood, charcoal and bagasse. All data are converted into coal equivalent and are based on information from United Nations, *Energy Statistics Yearbook 1984.*[5]

The data on *installed electricity capacity* are also derived from United Nations, *Energy Statistics Yearbook 1984.*

C. Other notes

"Dollars" ($) refer to United States dollars, unless otherwise stated.

Annual rates of growth and change refer to compound rates.

Details and percentages in tables do not necessarily add up to totals, because of rounding.

The following symbols have been used:

A dash (–) or a zero (0) indicates that the amount is nil or negligible.

Two dots (..) indicate that the data are not available or are not separately reported.

One dot (.) indicates that the data are not applicable.

---

[5] ST/ESA/STAT/SER.J/28, United Nations Publication, Sales No. E/F.86.XVII.2.

Use of a hyphen (-) between dates representing years, e.g. 1970-1980, signifies the full period involved, including the initial and final years.

D. Abbreviations used

AfDB	African Development Bank
AfDF	African Development Fund
AFESD	Arab Fund for Economic and Social Development
AsDB	Asian Development Bank
BADEA	Arab Bank for Economic Development in Africa
CMEA	Council for Mutual Economic Assistance
CRS	Creditor Reporting System (OECD)
DAC	Development Assistance Committee (of OECD)
DRS	Debtor Reporting System (World Bank)
EDF	European Development Fund
EEC	European Economic Community
EIB	European Investment Bank
FAO	Food and Agriculture Organization of the United Nations
IBRD	International Bank for Reconstruction and Development (World Bank)
IDA	International Development Association
IDB	Inter-American Development Bank
IFAD	International Fund for Agricultural Development
IFC	International Finance Corporation
IMF	International Monetary Fund
LDCs	Least Developed Countries
mill.	Millions
OAPEC	Organization of Arab Petroleum Exporting Countries
ODA	Official development assistance
OECD	Organisation for Economic Co-operation and Development
OPEC	Organization of the Petroleum Exporting Countries
SAAFA	Special Arab Aid Fund for Africa
SITC	Standard International Trade Classification, Revision 1
SNPA	Substantial New Programme of Action for the 1980s for the Least Developed Countries
UN	United Nations
UNDP	United Nations Development Programme
UNHCR	Office of the United Nations High Commissioner for Refugees
UNICEF	United Nations Children's Fund
UNTA	United Nations Technical Assistance
WFP	World Food Programme

Notes explicatives

A. – Définition des groupements de pays

PAYS EN DÉVELOPPEMENT LES MOINS AVANCÉS

Les 40 pays ainsi identifiés par l'Organisation des Nations Unies qui figurent dans ce document sont les suivants : Afghanistan, Bangladesh, Bénin, Bhoutan, Botswana, Burkina Faso, Burundi, Cap-Vert, Comores, Djibouti, Ethiopie, Gambie, Guinée, Guinée-Bissau, Guinée équatoriale, Haïti, Kiribati, Lesotho, Malawi, Maldives, Mali, Mauritanie, Népal, Niger, Ouganda, République centrafricaine, République démocratique populaire lao, République-Unie de Tanzanie, Rwanda, Samoa, Sao Tomé-et-Principe, Sierra Leone, Somalie, Soudan, Tchad, Togo, Tuvalu, Vanuatu, Yémen, Yémen démocratique. Les totaux et les tableaux concernant l'ensemble des pays les moins avancés se rapportent à ces 40 pays. L'Assemblée générale des Nations Unies, au cours de sa quarante-deuxième session en décembre 1987, a approuvé l'inclusion de la Birmanie, qui sera comprise dans la prochaine édition des *Données de base*.

GRANDES ZONES ÉCONOMIQUES

Le classement des pays et territoires par grandes zones économiques, utilisé dans ce document, n'a été adopté qu'aux fins de présentation des statistiques et il suit celui qui est utilisé dans le *Manuel de statistiques du commerce international et du développement, Supplément 1986*. Les pays et territoires sont classés en grandes zones économiques, constituées comme suit :

Les pays développés à économie de marché : Etats-Unis, Canada, Communauté économique européenne (Allemagne, République fédérale d', Belgique, Danemark, Espagne, France, Grèce, Irlande, Italie, Luxembourg, Pays-Bas, Portugal, Royaume-Uni), AELE (Autriche, Finlande, Islande, Norvège, Suède, Suisse), Gibraltar, îles Féroé, Israël, Japon, Australie, Nouvelle-Zélande, Afrique du Sud.

Les pays socialistes d'Europe orientale : Albanie, Bulgarie, Hongrie, Pologne, République démocratique allemande, Roumanie, Tchécoslovaquie, URSS.

Les pays socialistes d'Asie : Chine, Mongolie, République populaire démocratique de Corée, Viet Nam.

Les pays et territoires en développement : tous les autres pays, territoires et zones d'Afrique, d'Asie, d'Amérique, d'Europe et d'Océanie non mentionnés ci-dessus.

Dans certains tableaux, il est indiqué que l'*ensemble des pays en développement* ne comprend pas les *principaux pays exportateurs de pétrole*. Par *principaux pays exportateurs de pétrole*, on entend les pays pour lesquels les exportations de pétrole et de produits pétroliers ont représenté plus de 50 pour cent de leurs expotations totales en 1978, c'est-à-dire : Algérie, Angola, Arabie saoudite, Bahreïn, Brunéi, Congo, Emirats arabes unis, Equateur, Gabon, Indonésie, Iran (République islamique d'), Iraq, Jamahiriya arabe libyenne, Koweït, Mexique, Nigéria, Oman, Qatar, République arabe syrienne, Trinité-et-Tobago, Venezuela.

AUTRES GROUPEMENTS DE PAYS

Les pays membres du Comité d'aide au développement (CAD) qui figurent dans ce document sont les suivants : Allemagne, République fédérale d', Australie, Autriche, Belgique, Canada, Danemark, Etats-Unis, Finlande, France, Irlande, Italie, Japon, Norvège, Nouvelle-Zélande, Pays-Bas, Royaume-Uni, Suède, Suisse.

Les pays membres de l'Organisation des pays exportateurs de pétrole (OPEP) sont les suivants : Algérie, Arabie saoudite, Emirats arabes unis, Equateur, Gabon, Indonésie, Iran (République islamique d'), Iraq, Jamahiriya arabe libyenne, Koweït, Nigéria, Qatar, Venezuela.

B. – Définitions, terminologie et sources utilisées

Les estimations de la *population* sont des estimations de milieu d'année fondées essentiellement sur des données fournies par la Division de la population du Département des affaires économiques et sociales internationales de l'ONU.

Les données se rapportant aux *comptes nationaux* ont été établies principalement d'après des informations provenant du Bureau de statistique des Nations Unies, de la Commission économique pour l'Afrique et de la Banque mondiale, ainsi que de sources nationales.

Les estimations concernant la *production agricole*, l'*alimentation* et la *nutrition* sont surtout tirées d'informations communiquées par la FAO.

Les données se rapportant au *commerce* sont des estimations du secrétariat de la CNUCED tirées en grande partie du *Manuel de statistiques du commerce international et du développement, Supplément 1986*. Sauf indication contraire, les données du commerce se rapportent au commerce de marchandises. Les exportations sont données en valeur f.o.b. et les importations en valeur c.a.f.

Les chiffres se rapportant aux *apports d'aide* sont principalement fondés sur des informations communiquées par le secrétariat de l'OCDE. Suivant les définitions du CAD[1], l'*aide concessionnelle* désigne les apports qui sont considérés comme une "aide publique au développement" (APD), c'est-à-dire les

---

[1] Voir OCDE, *Coopération pour le développement, examen 1983* (Paris 1983), p. 200.

dons ou les prêts accordés par le secteur public, dans le but essentiel d'améliorer le développement économique et le niveau de vie, et assortis de conditions financières libérales (dans le cas des prêts, 25 pour cent au moins d'élément de don).

Les apports *non concessionnels* comprennent les dons des organismes privés (aide privée) et les transactions assorties de conditions commerciales : crédits à l'exportation, investissements bilatéraux de portefeuille (prêts bancaires compris) effectués par des résidents ou des institutions des pays donneurs; investissements directs (bénéfices réinvestis compris) et achats de titres d'organisations internationales s'occupant du développement. Les données concernant les *engagements* se rapportent au moment où le donneur prend l'engagement ferme de fournir une aide déterminée quant à son volume, sa destination, ses conditions financières et ses modalités, tandis que les données concernant les *versements* correspondent à la fourniture effective des fonds. Sauf indication contraire, les chiffres des versements sont indiqués "nets", c'est-à-dire déduction faite des remboursements effectués au titre de prêts antérieurs. Les dons, les prêts et les crédits de caractère militaire, ainsi que les prêts et les crédits dont la durée de remboursement est inférieure à un an, sont exclus.

Les données pour les années 1977-1985 concernant l'aide en provenance des pays membres de l'OPEP et des institutions multilatérales essentiellement financées par ceux-ci ont été généralement fournies directement par les donneurs eux-mêmes. Dans quelques cas, les chiffres sont des estimations du secrétariat de la CNUCED à partir de sources secondaires.

Les tableaux 34 et 46 présentent des estimations, pour les divers pays membres du CAD et de l'OPEP, sur le montant de l'aide publique au développement qui a été fourni aux PMA, exprimé en pourcentage du PNB de chaque donneur. Afin de donner un aperçu précis des apports totaux, on a essayé d'estimer la part des apports multilatéraux qui a été fournie par chaque donneur aux PMA. A cette fin, on a appliqué aux contributions du pays donneur à chacune des institutions multilatérales la part respective des versements nets de chacune de ces institutions aux PMA, exprimée en pourcentage des versements nets correspondant à l'ensemble des pays en développement. La somme ainsi obtenue pour l'ensemble des institutions est ajoutée à l'aide bilatérale du pays donneur et exprimée en pourcentage de son PNB.

Les données concernant la *dette* recouvrent la dette extérieure totale à long et moyen terme (y compris la dette privée) et sont fondées sur des renseignements communiqués par le secrétariat de l'OCDE.

En ce qui concerne les autres indicateurs économiques et sociaux, les données relatives aux *superficies* sont tirées de l'*Annuaire démographique 1985* des Nations Unies [2] et de l'*Annuaire de la production 1985* de la FAO.

Les estimations concernant la *population urbaine* ne sont pas toujours comparables d'un pays à l'autre en raison des différences qui existent dans les définitions et la couverture. Elles sont principalement tirées du *World Population Chart 1985* des Nations Unies [3] et du *Rapport sur le développement dans le monde 1987* de la Banque mondiale.

Le *taux d'activité* est le rapport (en pourcentage) entre la population active et la population du ou des sexes indiqués, tous âges confondus. Les chiffres sont tirés des *Social Indicators of Development 1986* de la Banque mondiale.

Les *taux bruts de natalité et de mortalit*é indiquent respectivement le nombre de naissances vivantes et de décès pour mille habitants. Ces taux, ainsi que l'*espérance de vie à la naissance* et les *taux de mortalité infantile*, sont principalement tirés de l'*Annuaire démographique 1985*, de *World Population Prospects: estimates and projections as assessed in 1984* [4] et de *World Population Chart 1985* des Nations Unies.

L'*espérance de vie à la naissance* indique le nombre moyen d'années que vivrait un nouveau-né pour autant que les conditions de mortalité ne changent pas, alors que le *taux de mortalité infantile* exprime le nombre de décès d'enfants de moins d'un an pour mille naissances vivantes survenus pendant l'année de référence.

Sous la rubrique *santé à la naissance*, le *poids insuffisant à la naissance* reflète directement le statut nutritionnel des mères et indirectement, compte tenu du statut de la femme, celui de la population en général. Les chiffres sont tirés de l'*Annuaire des statistiques sanitaires mondiales 1986* de l'OMS.

Le *pourcentage de femmes ayant reçu des soins prodigués par du personnel qualifié pendant l'accouchement* constitue un indicateur de la disponibilité des services médicaux. Il reflète la distribution géographique de l'équipement et par conséquent son accessibilité et dans quelle mesure les hôpitaux disposent du matériel et des fournitures qu'il faut pour offrir des soins médicaux efficaces. Le pourcentage de femmes ayant reçu des soins prodigués par du personnel qualifié pendant l'accouchement reflète aussi dans une certaine mesure le statut de la femme. Les données sont tirées de l'*Annuaire de statistiques sanitaires mondiales 1986* de l'OMS et de *La situation des enfants dans le monde* du FISE.

Le *pourcentage d'enfants vaccinés DTC (3 doses)* se rapporte à la couverture vaccinale des enfants de moins d'un an pour les maladies cibles du programme élargi de vaccination (diphtérie, tétanos, coqueluche, rougeole, poliomyélite et tuberculose). Les données sont tirées de l'*Annuaire de statistiques sanitaires mondiales 1986* de l'OMS.

On a calculé les *disponibilités alimentaires* en divisant l'équivalent en calories de l'offre de denrées alimentaires disponible dans un pays par sa population totale. Cette offre comprend la production intérieure, les importations diminuées des exportations et les variations de stocks; elle ne recouvre ni l'alimentation du bétail, ni les semences utilisées dans l'agriculture, ni les pertes en cours de traitement et de distribution. Les besoins caloriques par habitant et par jour ayant servi à calculer les *disponibilités alimentaires en pourcentage des besoins* expriment le nombre de calories nécessaires pour maintenir une population dans un état d'activité et de santé normal, compte tenu de sa structure par âge et par sexe, du poids moyen des habitants et des températures ambiantes. Les chiffres présentés dans ce tableau sont pondérés par la population. Les données sont tirées du *Rapport sur le développement dans le monde 1987* et des *Social Indicators of Development 1986* de la Banque mondiale.

---

[2] ST/ESA/STAT/SER.R./15, Publication des Nations Unies, no. de vente E/F.86.XIII.1.

[3] ST/ESA/SER.A/98/Add.1, Publication des Nations Unies, no. de vente E.85.XIII.A.

[4] ST/ESA/SER.A/98, Publication des Nations Unies, no. de vente E.86.XIII.3.

Les *pourcentages de la population disposant d'eau saine ou de mesures suffisantes d'hygiène du milieu* sont des estimations de l'OMS. Le *pourcentage de la population disposant d'eau saine* indique la part en pourcentage de personnes jouissant d'un accès "raisonnable" aux eaux superficielles traitées ou à une eau non traitée mais non contaminée, provenant par exemple de forages, de sources et de puits protégés, par rapport à la population en question. Dans une zone urbaine, une fontaine publique ou une borne-fontaine située dans un rayon de 200 mètres est considérée comme étant d'accès "raisonnable". Dans les zones rurales, pour que l'accès soit "raisonnable" il faut que la ménagère ou toute autre personne faisant partie du ménage ne passe pas une trop grande partie de la journée à se procurer l'eau nécessaire à la famille.

Le *pourcentage de la population disposant de mesures suffisantes d'hygiène du milieu* comprend la part de la population urbaine jouissant de raccordements aux égouts publics ou de systèmes ménagers (cabinets à fosse, latrines à entraînement par eau, fosses septiques, toilettes communales, etc.) et la part de la population rurale jouissant de moyens suffisants d'évacuation (cabinets à fosse, latrines à entraînement par eau, etc.)

Tant pour l'eau que pour l'hygiène du milieu, les données se basent sur *The international drinking water supply and sanitation decade: review of national progress (as at 31 December 1985)*.

Les données concernant l'*enseignement et l'alphabétisme* sont principalement tirées de renseignements fournis par l'UNESCO. Le *taux d'alphabétisation des adultes* est le pourcentage de la population âgée de 15 ans ou plus sachant lire et écrire. Les données concernant les *taux d'inscription scolaire* sont des estimations du nombre total de garçons et du nombre de filles inscrits à l'école primaire et secondaire, de tous âges, exprimées en pourcentage de la population totale, masculine et féminine, en âge de fréquenter l'école primaire ou secondaire.

La *consommation de papier journal* est estimée à partir d'importations, à l'exception du Bangladesh, qui produit, en outre des importations, du papier journal pour la consommation intérieure. Les estimations sont établies d'après des données de l'*Annuaire statistique 1986* de l'UNESCO.

Les données relatives au *trafic postal* couvrent les lettres, les cartes postales, les imprimés, les échantillons, les petits colis et les colis renfermant des travaux photographiques. Les données sont tirées des *Statistiques des services postaux, 1980* et *1984* de l'Union postale universelle.

Les données sur la *circulation des journaux quotidiens pour 1 000 habitants* se rapportent à la "circulation des journaux quotidiens d'information générale" et sont établies d'après des données de l'*Annuaire statistique 1986* de l'UNESCO.

Les *données sur les téléphones pour 1 000 habitants* se basent sur l'*Annuaire statistique des télécommunications du secteur public* (14e édition) de l'UIT.

Les *données sur les postes récepteurs de radio pour 1 000 habitants* sont établies d'après des données de l'*Annuaire statistique 1986* de l'UNESCO. Le rapport est calculé à partir du nombre de postes récepteurs en service et/ou de licences délivrées selon la méthode d'estimation employée dans chaque pays qui fournit des données.

Les données concernant la *consommation d'énergie par habitant* se rapportent, d'une part, aux formes d'énergie primaire (houille, lignite, tourbe et schiste bitumineux, pétrole brut et liquides extraits du gaz naturel, et électricité primaire [nucléaire, géothermique et hydraulique]) – souvent appelées "énergie commerciale" – et, d'autre part, à l'utilisation de bois de chauffage, de charbon de bois et de bagasse. Toutes les données sont converties en équivalent charbon et ont été établies d'après l'*Annuaire des statistiques de l'énergie 1984* des Nations Unies [5].

Les données sur la *puissance électrique installée* sont également tirées de l'*Annuaire des statistiques de l'énergie 1984* des Nations Unies.

C. – Autres notes

Sauf indication contraire, le terme "dollar" s'entend du dollar des Etats-Unis d'Amérique.

Les taux annuels de croissance et de variation sont des taux composés.

Les chiffres étant arrondis, les totaux indiqués ne correspondent pas toujours à la somme des composantes et des pourcentages portés dans les tableaux.

Les symboles suivants ont été utilisés:

Un tiret (–) ou un zéro (0) signifient que le montant est nul ou négligeable.

Deux points (..) signifient que les données ne sont pas disponibles ou ne sont pas montrées séparément.

Un point (.) signifie que les données ne sont pas applicables.

Le trait d'union (-) entre deux millésimes, par exemple (1970-1980), indique qu'il s'agit de la période tout entière (y compris la première et la dernière année mentionnée).

D. – Abréviations utilisées

AID	voir IDA
APD	aide publique au développement
ATNU	assistance technique des Nations Unies
BADEA	Banque arabe pour le développement économique de l'Afrique
BAfD	Banque africaine de développement
BAsD	Banque asiatique de développement
BEI	Banque européenne d'investissement
BID	Banque interaméricaine de développement
BIRD	Banque internationale pour la reconstruction et le développement (Banque mondiale)
CAD	Comité d'aide au développement (de l'OCDE)
CAEM	Conseil d'aide économique mutuelle
CEE	Communauté économique européenne
CTCI	Classification type pour le commerce international (révision 1)
FADES	Fonds arabe de développement économique et social
FAfD	Fonds africain de développement
FAO	Organisation des Nations Unies pour l'alimentation et l'agriculture

---

[5] ST/ESA/STAT/SER.J./28, Publication des Nations Unies, no. de vente E/F.86.XVII.2.

FED	Fonds européen de développement
FIDA	Fonds international de développement agricole
FISE	Fonds des Nations Unies pour l'enfance
FMI	Fonds monétaire international
FSAAA	Fonds spécial d'aide arabe à l'Afrique
HCR	Haut Commissariat des Nations Unies pour les réfugiés
IDA	Association internationale de développement
mill.	millions
NPSA	Nouveau programme d'action pour les années 80 en faveur des pays les moins avancés
OCDE	Organisation de coopération et de développement économiques

ONU	Organisation des Nations Unies
OPAEP	Organisation des pays arabes exportateurs de pétrole
OPEP	Organisation des pays exportateurs de pétrole
PAM	Programme alimentaire mondial
PMA	Pays les moins avancés
PNUD	Programme des Nations Unies pour le développement
SFI	Société financière internationale
SNPC	"Système de notification des pays créanciers" de l'OCDE
SNPD	"Système de notification des pays débiteurs" de la Banque mondiale
UNHCR	voir HCR
UNICEF	voir FISE

Table 1
Per capita GDP and population: levels and growth

Country	Per capita GDP in 1985 dollars PIB par habitant en dollars de 1985			
	Estimated Estimation	Actual Réel	Projected Projection 1990	
	1970	1985	A a/	B b/
Afghanistan d/	210	210 e/	210	262
Bangladesh f/	156	163	165	203
Benin	242	253	257	315
Bhutan g/	..	133	..	166
Botswana f/	225	855	1334	1066
Burkina Faso	132	134	135	167
Burundi	209	232	240	289
Cape Verde	278	353	382	440
Central African Rep.	301	259	246	323
Chad	212	128	108	160
Comoros	262	219	206	273
Democratic Yemen	565	420 h/	370	523
Djibouti	895	567 j/	487	707
Equatorial Guinea	..	192	..	239
Ethiopia k/	121	109	105	136
Gambia f/	201	213	217	265
Guinea	319	349	360	435
Guinea-Bissau	197	152	140	189
Haiti l/	288	350 h/	373	436
Kiribati	..	317 j/	..	395
Lao People's Dem. Rep.	337	386	404	481
Lesotho g/	100	167	198	208
Malawi	123	156	169	194
Maldives	..	432 h/	..	538
Mali	145	143	142	178
Mauritania	445	366	343	456
Nepal n/	135	141	143	176
Niger	360	258	231	322
Rwanda	226	274 h/	292	341
Samoa	..	539	..	672
Sao Tome and Principe	334	324	321	404
Sierra Leone f/	305	324	331	404
Somalia	281	261 h/	255	325
Sudan f/	465	406	388	506
Togo	242	235	233	293
Tuvalu	..	245 j/	..	305
Uganda	353	220 o/	188	274
Un. Rep. of Tanzania	279	279	279	348
Vanuatu	..	499	..	622
Yemen f/	210	482 h/	636	601
All LDCs	225	215	212	268
All developing countries	673	866	942	1079
Developed market economy countries	7954	10863	12052	n.a.
Socialist countries of Eastern Europe	..	..	..	..

Source:　UNCTAD secretariat calculations based on data from the United
Nations Statistical Office, the Economic Commission for Africa,
the World Bank and other international and national sources.

a/ At 1970-1985 growth rate.
b/ Based on the target rate of 4.5 per cent as called for by the
International Development Strategy for the third United Nations
Development Decade.
c/ Exponential trend function.
d/ Years beginning 21 March.
e/ 1981.
f/ Years ending 30 June.
g/ Years beginning 1 April.
h/ 1984.
i/ 1980-1984.
j/ Income accruing to indigenous population.
k/ Years ending 7 July.
l/ Years ending 30 September.

m/ 1974-1980.
n/ Years ending 15 July.
o/ GNP per capita in 1984.
p/ Net material product.

Tableau 1
PIB par habitant et population: niveaux et croissance

Annual average growth rates of per capita real product (%) Taux annuels moyens d'accroissement du PIB par habitant (%)		Population			Pays
		Level Niveau (mill.)	Annual average growth rates (%) Taux annuels moyens d'accroissement(%)		
1970-1980c/	1980-85	1985	1970-80c/	1980-85	
1.2	0.3	18.1	2.5	2.6	Afghanistan d/
1.0	1.7	98.7	2.7	2.2	Bangladesh f/
-0.4	1.0	4.0	2.7	3.1	Bénin
..	4.5	1.4	2.0	2.1	Bhoutan g/
9.5	6.6	1.1	3.9	3.9	Botswana f/
0.0	-0.2	6.9	2.0	2.4	Burkina Faso
1.4	0.3	4.7	1.7	2.9	Burundi
0.7	4.0	0.3	0.9	2.5	Cap-Vert
0.0	-1.8	2.6	2.1	2.4	Rép. centrafricaine
-0.3	-6.4	5.0	2.1	2.2	Tchad
-4.2	1.0	0.4	3.5	3.1	Comores
-0.5	-1.1 i/	2.3	3.1	3.1	Yémen démocratique
-3.8	-1.9	0.4	7.0	3.3	Djibouti
..	0.3	0.4	1.9	2.2	Guinée équatoriale
-0.1	-2.8	43.4	2.7	2.8	Ethiopie k/
1.9	-3.1	0.7	3.5	2.7	Gambie f/
2.2	-1.6	6.1	2.1	2.4	Guinée
-1.8	1.6	0.9	4.4	1.9	Guinée-Bissau
2.3	-1.8	5.3	1.4	1.4	Haïti l/
..	-2.0	0.1	2.0	2.0	Kiribati
-1.5	3.3	3.6	1.4	2.0	Rép.Dém.populaire lao
7.0	-2.4	1.5	2.4	2.6	Lesotho g/
3.1	-1.9	6.9	2.8	3.1	Malawi
10.2 m/	6.8	0.2	3.1	3.0	Maldives
1.6	-3.1	8.1	2.1	2.8	Mali
-1.3	-1.4	1.9	2.7	3.0	Mauritanie
0.2	1.6	16.6	2.5	2.5	Népal n/
-0.9	-5.2	6.1	2.5	2.9	Niger
1.8	0.9	6.0	3.3	3.2	Rwanda
..	-2.0	0.2	0.7	0.9	Samoa
2.8	-6.3	0.1	2.5	2.9	Sao Tomé-et-Principe
0.3	0.0	3.6	1.5	1.8	Sierra Leone f/
-0.3	1.2	5.4	3.0	2.9	Somalie
2.2	-4.1	21.5	3.0	2.9	Soudan f/
1.5	-4.2	3.0	2.4	3.0	Togo
..	..	0.0	2.0	1.2	Tuvalu
-5.2	1.6	15.5	2.9	3.4	Ouganda
1.1	-2.1	22.2	3.3	3.5	Rép.-Unie de Tanzanie
..	-0.4	0.1	3.0	2.8	Vanuatu
6.7	3.1	8.0	3.0	2.5	Yémen f/
0.9	-0.8	333.5	2.6	2.6	Ensemble des PMA
3.1	-0.9	2526.1	2.5	2.3	Ensemble des pays en développement
2.3	1.6	792.5	0.9	0.6	Pays développés à économie de marché
4.4 p/	2.5 p/	394.0	0.8	0.9	Pays socialistes d'Europe orientale

Source: Chiffres calculés par le secrétariat de la CNUCED d'après des données
du Bureau de statistique des Nations Unies, de la Commission
Economique pour l'Afrique, de la Banque mondiale et d'autres sources
internationales et nationales.

a/ D'après le taux de croissance 1970-1985.
b/ D'après l'objectif de 4,5 pour cent prévu dans la Stratégie
Internationale du développement pour la Troisième Décennie
de développement des Nations Unies.
c/ Fonction exponentielle de tendance.
d/ Années commençant le 21 mars.
e/ 1981.
f/ Années finissant le 30 juin.
g/ Années commençant le 1er avril.
h/ 1984.
i/ 1980-1984.
j/ Revenu afférent à la population locale.
k/ Années finissant le 7 juillet.

l/ Années finissant le 30 septembre.
m/ 1974-1980.
n/ Années finissant le 15 juillet.
o/ PNB par habitant en 1984.
p/ Produit matériel net.

Table 2
Real GDP, total and per capita : annual average growth rates

Percentages

Country	Total real product Produit réel total						
	1970-1980 a/	1980-1985	1980-1981	1981-1982	1982-1983	1983-1984	1984-1985
Afghanistan b/	3.7	2.9	1.8	2.0	4.8	2.1	3.7
Bangladesh c/	3.7	3.9	6.8	0.8	3.6	4.2	4.1
Benin	2.3	4.2	10.0	6.8	-2.2	2.3	4.3
Bhutan d/	..	6.6	9.0	10.8	6.1	2.6	5.0
Botswana c/	13.8	10.8	8.6	-2.4	23.8	20.2	5.9
Burkina Faso	1.9	2.2	8.8	1.1	-4.2	-0.9	6.7
Burundi	3.1	3.1	10.5	-3.2	1.1	0.1	7.7
Cape Verde	1.5	6.5	5.2	14.6	5.7	3.5	4.0
Central African Rep.	2.2	0.6	-2.3	0.4	-6.1	8.7	2.8
Chad	1.8	-4.4	-9.0	-7.3	-7.0	-4.6	6.9
Comoros	-0.9	4.1	3.6	5.9	3.7	3.9	3.4
Democratic Yemen	2.6	1.9 e/	6.6	-4.6	4.0	2.0	..
Djibouti	3.0	1.3	-8.0	13.6	0.9	0.5	0.6
Equatorial Guinea	..	2.5	2.3	3.8	-3.0	2.3	7.3
Ethiopia f/	2.6	-0.0	2.5	1.4	4.7	-1.2	-7.0
Gambia c/	5.4	-0.5	-8.3	9.6	14.6	-7.5	-8.7
Guinea	4.3	0.7	0.6	1.8	1.3	-2.7	2.6
Guinea-Bissau	2.5	3.5	18.2	4.2	-3.9	-1.1	1.5
Haiti g/	3.8	-0.4	-2.7	-3.9	0.3	2.7	1.7
Kiribati	..	-0.0	-5.0	7.6	-3.4	11.4	-9.3
Lao People's Dem.Rep.	-0.1	5.4	6.3	2.0	-2.1	14.5	7.2
Lesotho d/	9.6	0.1	-0.4	-3.6	-1.4	3.7	2.4
Malawi	6.0	1.2	-6.2	2.6	3.8	4.3	1.8
Maldives	13.6 h/	10.0	7.9	9.6	5.9	12.9	14.1
Mali	3.8	-0.4	-1.8	5.9	-4.1	-0.1	-1.6
Mauritania	1.4	1.5	3.7	-2.2	6.6	-3.3	3.1
Nepal i/	2.7	4.1	8.3	3.8	-1.4	7.4	2.8
Niger	1.6	-2.5	1.1	-0.8	-2.4	-16.1	7.1
Rwanda	5.2	4.2	6.4	4.3	4.0	2.9	3.4
Samoa	..	-1.1	-9.0	-1.0	0.4	2.1	2.6
Sao Tome and Principe	5.4	-3.6	-27.5	26.3	-8.7	-8.3	8.5
Sierra Leone c/	1.8	1.8	1.3	-1.4	0.5	8.1	0.8
Somalia	2.7	4.1	6.7	5.6	1.4	3.1	3.5
Sudan c/	5.3	-1.3	2.2	6.4	-3.1	-2.4	-9.1
Togo	3.9	-1.3	-3.3	-3.6	-5.4	1.3	4.7
Tuvalu	..	..	..	..	..	..	..
Uganda	-2.4	5.0	5.7	9.1	4.9	5.2	0.6
Un. Rep. of Tanzania	4.5	1.3	2.1	1.3	-0.4	2.5	1.0
Vanuatu	..	2.4	2.0	2.0	3.0	4.6	0.4
Yemen c/	9.9	5.6	9.6	10.0	3.5	2.4	3.0
All LDCs	3.5	2.0	3.6	2.5	1.3	1.7	1.1
All developing countries	5.6	1.4	0.8	0.7	0.7	2.4	2.2
Developed market economy countries	3.2	2.2	1.9	-0.5	2.2	4.6	2.8
Socialist countries of Eastern Europe j/	5.3	3.4	2.4	3.0	4.2	3.6	3.6

Source: UNCTAD secretariat calculations based on data from the
United Nations Statistical Office, the Economic Commission
for Africa, the World Bank and other international
and national sources.

a/ Exponential trend function.
b/ Years beginning 21 March.
c/ Years ending 30 June.
d/ Years beginning 1 April.
e/ 1980-1984.
f/ Years ending 7 July.
g/ Years ending 30 September.
h/ 1974-1980.
i/ Years ending 15 July.
j/ Net material product.

Tableau 2
Produit intérieur brut réel, total et par habitant :
taux annuels moyens d'accroissement

En pourcentage

Per capita real product / Produit réel par habitant					Pays
1980-1981	1981-1982	1982-1983	1983-1984	1984-1985	
-0.8	-0.5	2.1	-0.5	1.0	Afghanistan b/
4.7	-1.5	1.4	2.0	2.1	Bangladesh c/
6.6	3.6	-5.2	-0.8	1.2	Bénin
6.7	8.6	4.0	0.5	2.9	Bhoutan d/
4.3	-6.3	19.3	15.8	2.2	Botswana c/
6.1	-1.3	-6.5	-3.2	4.3	Burkina Faso
7.3	-6.0	-1.7	-2.6	4.9	Burundi
2.7	11.9	3.1	1.0	1.5	Cap-Vert
-4.6	-1.9	-8.3	6.1	0.4	Rép. centrafricaine
-11.0	-9.3	-9.0	-6.7	4.6	Tchad
0.2	2.7	0.0	1.2	0.7	Comores
3.4	-7.5	0.9	-1.1	..	Yémen démocratique
-11.9	9.9	-2.0	-2.0	-2.2	Djibouti
0.1	1.6	-5.1	0.2	5.1	Guinée équatoriale
-0.4	-1.4	1.8	-3.9	-9.6	Ethiopie f/
-10.6	6.7	11.7	-9.9	-11.0	Gambie c/
-1.9	-0.6	-1.0	-4.9	0.4	Guinée
15.9	2.2	-5.7	-2.9	-0.3	Guinée-Bissau
-4.1	-5.3	-1.1	1.2	0.3	Haïti g/
-6.9	5.5	-5.3	9.2	-11.1	Kiribati
4.2	0.0	-4.0	12.3	4.9	Rép. dém. pop. lao
-2.9	-6.1	-3.9	1.0	-0.2	Lesotho d/
-9.3	-0.6	0.6	1.3	-1.1	Malawi
4.7	6.4	2.8	9.5	10.7	Maldives
-4.6	2.9	-6.8	-2.8	-4.2	Mali
0.6	-5.1	3.6	-6.0	0.3	Mauritanie
5.8	1.2	-3.8	4.7	0.2	Népal i/
-1.9	-3.6	-5.1	-18.4	4.3	Niger
3.2	1.0	0.7	-0.3	0.2	Rwanda
-9.6	-1.9	-0.6	1.1	1.4	Samoa
-29.6	23.0	-11.3	-10.8	5.4	Sao Tomé-et-Principe
-0.5	-3.2	-1.2	6.2	-0.9	Sierra Leone c/
3.7	2.7	-1.4	0.2	0.6	Somalie
-0.9	3.4	-5.9	-5.1	-11.5	Soudan c/
-6.3	-6.5	-8.2	-1.5	1.8	Togo
..	..	..	..	..	Tuvalu
2.3	5.5	1.4	1.8	-2.7	Ouganda
-1.3	-2.1	-3.7	-1.0	-2.4	Rép.-Unie de Tanzanie
-0.8	-0.8	0.2	1.8	-2.4	Vanuatu
6.8	7.2	0.9	0.2	0.5	Yémen c/
1.0	-0.2	-1.3	-0.9	-1.4	Ensemble des PMA
-1.6	-1.6	-1.6	0.1	0.0	Ensemble des pays en développement
1.3	-1.1	1.6	4.0	2.2	Pays développés à économie de marché
1.6	2.2	3.3	2.7	2.7	Pays socialistes d'Europe orientale j/

Source: Chiffres calculés par le secrétariat de la CNUCED
d'après des données du Bureau de statistique des
Nations Unies, de la Commission économique pour
l'Afrique, de la Banque mondiale et d'autres
sources internationales et nationales.

a/ Fonction exponentielle de tendance.
b/ Années commençant le 21 mars.
c/ Années finissant le 30 juin.
d/ Années commençant le 1er avril.
e/ 1980-1984.
f/ Années finissant le 7 juillet.
g/ Années finissant le 30 septembre.
h/ 1974-1980.
i/ Années finissant le 15 juillet.
j/ Produit matériel net.

Table 3
Total agricultural production and food production:
annual average growth rates

Percentages

Country	Total agricultural production Production agricole totale							
	1970-1980a/	1980-1986	1980-1981	1981-1982	1982-1983	1983-1984	1984-1985	1985-1986
Afghanistan	2.4	-0.1	2.1	0.0	1.7	0.2	-0.5	-4.0
Bangladesh	2.2	2.4	-0.2	4.4	2.1	1.4	6.6	0.1
Benin	2.5	6.7	-0.8	3.0	4.8	23.4	5.1	6.6
Bhutan	2.4	2.3	1.7	2.6	2.8	2.2	2.2	2.2
Botswana	-2.0	1.8	18.9	-0.4	-6.1	-6.2	5.8	1.0
Burkina Faso	1.1	7.7	9.5	1.4	1.7	-0.9	23.6	12.6
Burundi	1.9	3.3	19.1	-7.3	4.2	-5.0	8.7	2.1
Cape Verde	2.2	-0.1	-23.1	-1.5	-10.2	18.4	-7.2	33.1
Central African Rep.	2.3	1.3	2.4	3.0	-0.9	-0.0	-5.3	9.1
Chad	1.7	2.8	-6.1	5.5	8.7	-11.9	23.4	0.6
Comoros	2.6	1.7	-7.0	5.6	6.0	-1.2	5.4	2.1
Democratic Yemen	2.5	0.2	1.9	-5.2	7.0	0.5	-0.7	-2.0
Djibouti	..	..	..	..	..	..	..	..
Equatorial Guinea	..	..	..	..	..	..	..	..
Ethiopia	1.6	0.8	-0.2	8.4	-5.5	-7.8	5.9	4.9
Gambia	-2.6	6.8	32.0	18.9	-30.3	10.4	23.5	-0.4
Guinea	1.5	0.9	1.8	2.0	-5.7	1.8	1.0	4.7
Guinea-Bissau	2.6	7.9	19.9	14.6	-12.0	15.7	4.3	8.2
Haiti	1.3	1.9	1.5	0.1	4.8	2.2	-0.6	3.4
Kiribati	..	..	..	..	..	..	..	..
Lao People's Dem.Rep.	2.1	6.4	9.6	0.3	4.1	11.2	9.3	4.1
Lesotho	0.8	-0.7	0.3	-11.7	5.0	-0.6	11.2	-6.7
Malawi	4.0	2.2	4.4	5.6	-2.9	3.7	0.5	2.2
Maldives	1.7	3.4	0.7	4.2	7.1	3.9	1.5	2.9
Mali	2.9	3.9	8.4	7.9	5.7	-6.6	-2.6	11.8
Mauritania	0.4	1.7	5.8	-6.0	-7.5	2.5	4.7	11.7
Nepal	1.3	1.5	3.3	-6.4	16.3	-0.6	1.4	-3.4
Niger	4.1	1.0	-1.3	-0.1	2.0	-20.0	27.2	3.7
Rwanda	4.2	1.6	9.9	3.6	7.4	-16.0	4.7	2.4
Samoa	1.3	-0.8	0.9	-2.7	-1.2	3.1	0.9	-5.5
Sao Tome and Principe	-3.5	-2.4	7.4	-7.5	-1.4	-13.0	1.2	0.2
Sierra Leone	1.6	1.8	0.5	9.8	1.5	-10.4	0.0	10.8
Somalia	0.9	1.0	0.6	4.3	-4.9	-1.3	6.5	1.2
Sudan	2.4	3.7	12.3	-8.5	3.8	-6.7	20.0	4.2
Togo	0.9	0.5	1.3	-1.1	-5.3	10.3	3.0	-4.5
Tuvalu	..	..	..	..	..	..	..	..
Uganda	0.4	7.5	10.7	7.8	6.4	-23.0	52.5	3.6
Un. Rep. of Tanzania	4.4	1.7	2.9	-4.0	2.9	5.0	0.7	2.7
Vanuatu	3.7	4.4	24.9	-14.2	4.8	13.4	-4.1	6.1
Yemen	3.2	5.7	6.5	2.4	-6.2	10.4	7.8	14.6
All LDCs b/	1.9	2.4	3.0	2.1	1.8	-2.1	7.4	2.5
All developing countries	2.8	2.8	4.7	1.1	3.0	2.4	4.6	1.0

Source: UNCTAD secretariat calculations, based on data from FAO.

a/ Exponential trend function.

b/ Excluding Djibouti, Equatorial Guinea, Kiribati,
    Mauritania and Tuvalu.

Tableau 3
Production agricole totale et production vivrière totale:
taux annuels moyens d'accroissement

En pourcentage

Total food production Production vivrière totale								
1970-1980a/	1980-1986	1980-1981	1981-1982	1982-1983	1983-1984	1984-1985	1985-1986	Pays
2.4	-0.1	2.5	0.6	0.9	0.2	-0.5	-4.3	Afghanistan
2.3	2.5	0.1	3.6	2.3	1.7	4.3	2.9	Bangladesh
2.8	6.0	-0.8	2.1	4.0	22.0	5.3	4.9	Bénin
2.5	2.3	1.7	2.6	2.9	2.2	2.3	2.2	Bhoutan
-2.0	1.9	19.1	-0.4	-6.1	-6.3	5.9	1.0	Botswana
0.9	7.4	10.0	0.6	1.6	-0.9	23.1	11.9	Burkina Faso
1.8	2.9	11.0	-0.2	-1.0	-2.7	7.5	3.5	Burundi
2.2	-0.1	-23.6	-1.5	-9.8	18.5	-7.1	32.9	Cap-Vert
2.5	1.2	3.0	1.7	0.7	-2.1	-5.4	9.8	Rép. centrafricaine
1.9	3.0	-5.5	3.6	5.3	-9.0	24.2	2.6	Tchad
2.8	1.6	-7.2	5.1	6.4	-1.3	5.3	2.2	Comores
2.8	-0.1	1.8	-5.4	5.4	0.6	-0.7	-2.2	Yémen démocratique
..	..	..	..	..	..	..	..	Djibouti
..	..	..	..	..	..	..	..	Guineé équatoriale
1.6	0.6	-1.0	9.4	-6.6	-9.8	9.9	3.2	Ethiopie
-2.8	6.8	31.2	19.5	-30.1	10.0	23.7	-0.4	Gambie
1.5	0.9	1.9	2.0	-6.1	1.8	1.0	4.9	Guinée
2.6	7.9	19.9	14.6	-12.0	15.7	4.3	8.2	Guinée-Bissau
1.5	1.7	0.7	0.2	4.1	2.8	-0.6	3.3	Haïti
..	..	..	..	..	..	..	..	Kiribati
2.1	6.4	9.6	0.2	4.4	11.4	9.3	4.0	Rép. dém. pop. lao
1.5	-0.9	0.2	-12.8	4.4	-0.7	12.5	-7.3	Lesotho
3.5	1.3	4.4	3.6	-2.9	1.0	0.2	1.7	Malawi
1.7	3.4	0.7	4.2	7.1	3.9	1.5	2.9	Maldives
2.6	3.9	10.6	8.4	4.8	-7.3	-3.6	11.8	Mali
0.4	1.7	5.8	-6.0	-7.5	2.5	4.7	11.7	Mauritanie
1.3	1.6	3.6	-6.0	16.5	-0.3	1.3	-3.9	Népal
4.1	1.0	-1.3	-0.1	1.9	-20.0	27.2	3.7	Niger
3.9	1.3	8.0	5.6	7.0	-18.5	5.8	2.8	Rwanda
1.3	-0.8	0.9	-2.9	-1.2	3.3	0.9	-5.8	Samoa
-3.5	-2.4	7.4	-7.6	-1.4	-13.1	1.3	0.2	Sao Tomé-et-Principe
1.5	1.8	1.0	10.5	3.0	-9.4	-3.7	10.9	Sierra Leone
0.9	1.0	0.7	4.2	-4.9	-1.3	6.5	1.2	Somalie
3.3	3.7	14.0	-11.3	1.9	-8.3	23.5	6.6	Soudan
0.9	0.1	1.6	-1.2	-5.3	11.9	-0.4	-4.8	Togo
..	..	..	..	..	..	..	..	Tuvalu
1.0	7.5	11.6	6.9	6.5	-24.6	55.0	4.1	Ouganda
5.3	2.2	2.9	-2.5	3.4	4.9	1.5	2.9	Rép.-Un. de Tanzanie
3.8	4.5	25.1	-13.8	4.5	13.8	-4.2	6.1	Vanuatu
3.3	5.8	6.5	2.5	-6.3	10.8	7.8	14.8	Yémen
2.2	2.4	3.5	1.4	1.4	-2.8	7.5	3.5	Ensemble des PMA b/
3.0	2.9	4.6	1.7	3.0	2.2	4.2	2.0	Ensemble des pays en développement

Source: Chiffres calculés par le secrétariat de la CNUCED, d'après
des données de la FAO.

a/ Fonction exponentielle de tendance.

b/ Non compris Djibouti, la Guinée équatoriale, Kiribati,
la Mauritanie et Tuvalu.

Table 4
The agricultural sector

Country	Labor force (% in agri.) Main d'oeuvre (% dans l'agri.) 1985	% share of agri. in GDP Part en % de l'agri. dans le PIB 1985	Agricultural production Annual average growth rates per capita (%) Production agricole Taux annuels moyens d'accroissement par habitant (%)						
			1970-1980a/	1980-1981	1981-1982	1982-1983	1983-1984	1984-1985	1985-1986
Afghanistan	58	(58)	-0.1	-0.5	-2.5	-0.9	-2.4	-3.1	-6.4
Bangladesh	71	50	-0.5	-2.1	2.0	-0.2	-0.8	4.5	-2.0
Benin	64	48	-0.1	-3.8	-0.2	1.6	19.6	1.9	3.4
Bhutan	91	50 d/	0.4	-0.4	0.6	0.8	0.1	0.2	0.0
Botswana	60	5	-5.6	14.2	-4.3	-9.5	-9.6	2.2	-3.0
Burkina Faso	86	46	-0.9	6.8	-1.1	-0.7	-3.2	20.8	9.5
Burundi	92	57	0.1	15.6	-10.0	1.3	-7.5	5.9	-1.0
Cape Verde	45	20	1.3	-25.0	-3.9	-12.3	15.6	-9.5	30.0
Central Afr.Rep.	66	37	0.1	0.0	0.6	-3.2	-2.4	-7.5	6.6
Chad	79	47	-0.4	-8.1	3.3	6.3	-13.8	20.8	-1.6
Comoros	81	42	-0.9	-10.1	2.5	2.2	-3.8	2.7	-0.5
Democratic Yemen	36	10 d/	-0.6	-1.2	-8.0	3.7	-2.5	-3.7	-4.9
Djibouti	(2)	6	..	..	..	..	..	..	..
Eq. Guinea	61	46	..	..	..	..	..	..	..
Ethiopia	77	44	-1.1	-3.0	5.4	-8.1	-10.4	3.1	2.0
Gambia	83	33	-5.9	28.6	15.8	-32.1	7.5	20.4	-3.1
Guinea	78	44	-0.6	-0.7	-0.4	-7.9	-0.5	-1.2	2.0
Guinea-Bissau	81	42 b/	-1.7	17.5	12.4	-13.7	13.6	2.4	5.9
Haiti	68	(32)d/	-0.1	0.1	-1.3	3.3	0.7	-2.0	1.8
Kiribati	..	37 d/	..	..	..	..	..	..	..
Lao P.D.R.	74	(62)	0.7	7.4	-1.6	2.1	9.0	6.9	2.1
Lesotho	84	20	-1.6	-2.3	-14.0	2.3	-3.1	8.4	-9.0
Malawi	78	38 d/	1.2	1.1	2.3	-5.9	0.6	-2.4	-1.4
Maldives	46	29 d/	-1.3	-2.3	1.1	3.9	0.9	-1.5	0.0
Mali	83	46	0.8	5.3	4.9	2.7	-9.2	-5.2	8.4
Mauritania	59	29	-2.3	2.6	-8.8	-10.1	-0.4	1.9	8.1
Nepal	93	56 b/	-1.2	0.9	-8.7	13.4	-3.1	-1.2	-5.8
Niger	89	47	1.5	-4.2	-3.0	-0.8	-22.1	23.9	0.5
Rwanda	92	46 e/	0.8	6.6	0.3	4.0	-18.6	1.4	-0.8
Samoa	75b/c/	51 f/	0.7	0.3	-3.6	-2.2	2.1	-0.3	-6.5
Sao Tome & Prin.	(56)	28	-5.9	4.3	-9.9	-4.2	-15.4	-1.6	-2.0
Sierra Leone	66	37	0.0	-1.4	7.8	-0.3	-12.0	-1.7	8.6
Somalia	74	50 f/	-2.1	-2.2	1.4	-7.6	-4.1	3.5	-1.7
Sudan	68	26	-0.6	8.9	-11.1	0.9	-9.3	16.8	1.0
Togo	71	30	-1.4	-1.8	-4.0	-8.1	7.2	0.2	-7.6
Tuvalu	..	11	..	..	..	..	..	..	..
Uganda	84	82 e/	-2.4	7.1	4.3	2.9	-25.6	47.6	0.2
U.R. of Tanzania	83	58	1.0	-0.5	-7.2	-0.5	1.4	-2.7	-0.8
Vanuatu	(79)	40	0.7	21.5	-16.5	2.0	10.3	-6.7	3.2
Yemen	65	24 d/	0.3	3.8	-0.1	-8.5	8.0	5.2	11.8
All LDCs g/	76	45	-0.7	0.4	-0.6	-0.8	-4.6	4.8	-0.2
All developing countries	57	(20)	0.4	2.3	-1.3	0.6	0.0	2.3	-1.2

Source: UNCTAD secretariat calculations based on data from FAO,
the Economic Commission for Africa, the World Bank and
other international and national sources.

a/ Exponential trend function.
b/ 1983.
c/ In subsistence agriculture.
d/ 1984.
e/ 1981.
f/ 1982.
g/ Excluding Djibouti, Equatorial Guinea, Kiribati,
Mauritania and Tuvalu.

Tableau 4
Le secteur agricole

Food production Annual average growth rates per capita (%) Production vivrière Taux annuels moyens d'accroissement par habitant (%)							Pays
1970-1980a/	1980-1981	1981-1982	1982-1983	1983-1984	1984-1985	1985-1986	
-0.1	-0.1	-1.9	-1.6	-2.4	-3.1	-6.7	Afghanistan
-0.4	-1.9	1.2	0.0	-0.5	2.3	0.6	Bangladesh
0.2	-3.8	-1.0	0.8	18.3	2.1	1.8	Bénin
0.4	-0.4	0.6	0.8	0.1	0.2	0.0	Bhoutan
-5.7	14.4	-4.3	-9.6	-9.7	2.2	-3.0	Botswana
-1.1	7.2	-1.8	-0.8	-3.2	20.3	8.9	Burkina Faso
0.1	7.7	-3.0	-3.7	-5.3	4.7	0.4	Burundi
1.3	-25.5	-3.9	-11.9	15.7	-9.3	29.7	Cap-Vert
0.4	0.6	-0.6	-1.7	-4.4	-7.7	7.3	Rép. centrafricaine
-0.2	-7.5	1.3	3.1	-11.0	21.5	0.4	Tchad
-0.7	-10.3	2.0	2.6	-3.9	2.6	-0.5	Comores
-0.3	-1.3	-8.2	2.2	-2.4	-3.7	-5.1	Yémen démocratique
..	..	..	..	..	..	..	Djibouti
							Guineé équatoriale
..	..	..	..	..	..	..	
-1.1	-3.7	6.4	-9.1	-12.2	6.9	0.4	Ethiopie
-6.0	27.9	16.3	-31.9	7.1	20.5	-3.1	Gambie
-0.6	-0.6	-0.4	-8.2	-0.5	-1.2	2.2	Guinée
-1.7	17.6	12.4	-13.7	13.6	2.4	5.9	Guinée-Bissau
0.1	-0.6	-1.2	2.6	1.3	-2.0	1.7	Haïti
							Kiribati
..	..	..	..	..	..	..	
0.7	7.4	-1.8	2.4	9.2	7.0	2.0	Rép. dém. pop. lao
-0.9	-2.3	-15.0	1.8	-3.2	9.6	-9.7	Lesotho
0.7	1.1	0.4	-5.8	-2.0	-2.7	-1.9	Malawi
-1.3	-2.3	1.1	3.9	0.9	-1.5	0.0	Maldives
0.5	7.4	5.4	1.9	-9.8	-6.1	8.4	Mali
-2.3	2.6	-8.8	-10.1	-0.4	1.9	8.1	Mauritanie
-1.1	1.2	-8.3	13.6	-2.8	-1.3	-6.3	Népal
1.6	-4.2	-3.0	-0.9	-22.2	23.9	0.5	Niger
0.6	4.7	2.3	3.6	-21.1	2.5	-0.4	Rwanda
0.7	0.3	-3.8	-2.2	2.2	-0.3	-6.7	Samoa
-5.9	4.3	-10.0	-4.2	-15.5	-1.6	-2.0	Sao Tomé-et-Principe
0.0	-0.8	8.6	1.2	-10.9	-5.3	8.7	Sierra Leone
-2.1	-2.2	1.3	-7.6	-4.0	3.5	-1.7	Somalie
0.3	10.7	-13.9	-1.0	-10.8	20.2	3.4	Soudan
-1.4	-1.5	-4.1	-8.1	8.8	-3.2	-7.8	Togo
..	..	..	..	..	..	..	Tuvalu
-1.9	7.9	3.4	3.1	-27.0	50.0	0.7	Ouganda
1.9	-0.5	-5.8	0.0	1.4	-1.9	-0.6	Rép.-Un. de Tanzanie
0.8	21.7	-16.2	1.6	10.7	-6.8	3.2	Vanuatu
0.3	3.9	-0.1	-8.6	8.4	5.2	12.0	Yémen
-0.4	0.8	-1.2	-1.2	-5.3	4.8	0.8	Ensemble des PMA g/
0.5	2.1	-0.7	0.6	-0.1	1.9	-0.2	Ensemble des pays en développement

Source: Chiffres calculés par le secrétariat de la CNUCED, d'après
des données de la FAO, de la Commission économique pour
l'Afrique, de la Banque mondiale, et d'autres sources
internationales et nationales.

a/ Fonction exponentielle de tendance.
b/ 1983.
c/ Dans l'agriculture de subsistence.
d/ 1984.
e/ 1981.
f/ 1982.
g/ Non compris Djibouti, la Guinée équatoriale, Kiribati,
la Mauritanie et Tuvalu.

Table 5
The manufacturing sector

Tableau 5
Le secteur manufacturier

Country	Pays	% share in GDP / Part en % dans le PIB 1985	Annual average growth rates a/ / Taux annuels moyens d'accroissement a/						
			1970–1980 b/	1980–1985	1980–1981	1981–1982	1982–1983	1983–1984	1984–1985
Afghanistan	Afghanistan	..		..	..	..	-1.6	..	..
Bangladesh	Bangladesh	8	11.8	2.4	5.4	1.6	-9.7	3.7	3.2
Benin	Bénin	4	-1.3	7.4	-6.1	63.0	16.1	-12.1	17.5
Bhutan	Bhoutan	4 d/		..	..	-1.5	-7.4	4.8	..
Botswana	Botswana	6	16.0	9.5	26.7	23.8	8.1	3.8	4.5
Burkina Faso	Burkina Faso	14	2.1	2.9	1.1	3.0	6.6	-1.2	3.9
Burundi	Burundi	12	3.7	7.5	14.1	-2.9	..	4.1	16.6
Cape Verde	Cap-Vert	..	..	..	..	..	..	1.4	..
Central African Rep.	Rép. centrafricaine	7	..	-2.3	-9.8	-5.4	1.4	-5.2	1.4
Chad	Tchad	9	0.5	-5.5	-12.6	-6.8	-7.6	4.5	5.4
Comoros	Comores	6	-4.9	4.7 i/	6.5	5.0	4.0	..	3.6
Democratic Yemen	Yémen démocratique	11 d/	..	4.4 i/	22.6	-11.2	0.9	-1.6	..
Djibouti	Djibouti	10	6.3	0.6	-0.3	3.3	-6.4	6.8	0.9
Equatorial Guinea	Guineé équatoriale	5	..	4.9	3.7	3.3	4.9	..	18.7
Ethiopia	Ethiopie	11 e/	2.3	4.1 i/	4.1	3.4	5.8	-0.8	..
Gambia	Gambie	10	..	..	..	35.8	3.0	5.6	-11.8
Guinea	Guinée	2	0.8	1.2	0.8	-2.0	-1.7	1.0	-1.0
Guinea-Bissau	Guinée-Bissau	4 e/	2.1	0.3	-4.0	3.0	5.6	-1.6	3.4
Haiti	Haïti	(17) d/	8.5	-3.1 k/	-11.6	-3.9	..	..	..
Kiribati	Kiribati	2 d/	..	..	..	..	..	..	..
Lao People's Dem.Rep.	Rép. dém. pop. lao	(4)	..	2.2	0.9	1.1	-3.3	-8.5	23.9
Lesotho	Lesotho	7	17.3	4.9	-3.4	27.5	-25.4	25.9	10.0
Malawi	Malawi	12 d/	6.0	2.7	3.4	-0.2	6.8	2.7	1.3
Maldives	Maldives	5 d/	..	14.6 k/	26.2	21.9	6.3	5.5	..
Mali	Mali	7 d/	..	..	..	..	..	..	..
Mauritania	Mauritanie	6 d/	4.2	3.0	2.2	-0.8	3.4	5.0	5.5
Nepal	Népal	4 e/	..	..	..	..	..	..	..
Niger	Niger	4	..	..	..	..	..	..	..
Rwanda	Rwanda	16 f/	9.5 h/	..	6.5	3.6	..	..	..
Samoa	Samoa	6 e/	..	9.4 j/	7.2	13.6	17.7	..	..
Sao Tome and Principe	Sao Tomé-et-Principe	9	2.3	-2.0	-26.4	1.9	2.5	-29.3	49.0
Sierra Leone	Sierra Leone	5	4.6	-1.2	6.9	-0.7	-3.2	-5.9	-5.2
Somalia	Somalie	6 g/	3.1	-0.8 i/	-0.8	..	..	..	..
Sudan	Soudan	9	3.9	..	..	..	..	..	..
Togo	Togo	7	-10.0	-1.6	9.1	4.2	-7.4	-18.2	7.1
Tuvalu	Tuvalu	2	..	..	..	..	..	..	..
Uganda	Ouganda	4 f/	-9.1	0.5	-5.4	14.2	2.8	3.4	-11.0
Un. Rep. of Tanzania	Rép.-Unie de Tanzanie	5	6.0	-4.8	-10.7	-3.0	-3.4	-1.4	-5.1
Vanuatu	Vanuatu	4	..	..	..	..	..	..	..
Yemen	Yémen	9 d/	12.2	18.2 k/	19.2	20.4	23.2	10.6	..
All LDCs c/	Ensemble des PMA c/	8	(4.6)	1.1	1.0	2.6	-1.4	1.1	2.4

Table 5 (continued)

Source: UNCTAD secretariat calculations based on data from the United Nations Statistical Office, the Economic Commission for Africa, the World Bank and other international and national sources.

a/ Value added at constant prices.
b/ Exponential trend function.
c/ Growth rates relate to countries for which data are available for the years 1980 to 1985.

d/ 1984.
e/ 1983.
f/ 1981.
g/ 1982.
h/ 1972-1980.
i/ 1980-1982.
j/ 1980-1983.
k/ 1980-1984.

Tableau 5 (suite)

Source: Chiffres calculés par le secrétariat de la CNUCED d'après des données du Bureau de statistique des Nations Unies, de la Commission économique pour l'Afrique, de la Banque mondiale et d'autres sources internationales et nationales.

a/ Valeur ajoutée aux prix constants.
b/ Fonction exponentielle de tendance.
c/ Les taux de croissance se rapportent à l'ensemble des pays pour lesquels les données sont disponibles de 1980 à 1985.

d/ 1984.
e/ 1983.
f/ 1981.
g/ 1982.
h/ 1972-1980.
i/ 1980-1982.
j/ 1980-1983.
k/ 1980-1984.

Table 6
Investment a/

Tableau 6
Investissement a/

Country	Pays	Per capita levels ($) / Niveaux par habitant ($) 1985	% share in GDP / Part en % dans le PIB 1985	Annual average growth rates b/ / Taux annuels moyens d'accroissement b/ 1970-1980 c/	1980-1985	1980-1981	1981-1982	1982-1983	1983-1984	1984-1985
Afghanistan	Afghanistan	..	..	..	..	..	..	..	..	..
Bangladesh	Bangladesh	19	12	0.3	2.7	2.8	-5.7	-6.2	11.7	12.4
Benin	Bénin	35	14	11.4	-12.5	13.8	7.0	-53.4	-20.9	14.0
Bhutan	Bhoutan	..	..	..	..	..	..	..	..	..
Botswana	Botswana	225	26	6.9	-3.4	1.8	-3.5	-30.7	-2.1	26.0
Burkina Faso	Burkina Faso	11	8	3.9	-10.3	-19.1	-1.4	-26.2	-26.5	34.4
Burundi	Burundi	36	16	16.2	22.0 i/	37.6	-25.0	75.8	..	..
Cape Verde	Cap-Vert	178	50	-9.7	10.4	56.7	4.3	5.9	-9.6	4.8
Central African Rep.	Rép. centrafricaine	39	15	-0.8	13.2	21.7	-8.9	47.8	10.3	2.7
Chad	Tchad	8	7	-1.0	-16.1	-32.6	-29.4	-13.6	-5.5	7.1
Comoros	Comores	90	41	..	5.1	-16.2	1.4	11.6	58.7	-14.6
Democratic Yemen	Yémen démocratique	132	..	-1.4	5.3	27.8	10.1	1.8	-6.1	-3.8
Djibouti	Djibouti	28	23	..	1.4	5.2	3.6	-7.0	3.3	2.6
Equatorial Guinea	Guineé équatoriale	11	14	-1.1	-0.3	3.4	9.2	0.7	11.2	-22.0
Ethiopia	Ethiopie	46	10	-1.1	-6.2	-2.3	-17.6	7.6	-32.6	24.3
Gambia	Gambie	33	22	31.4	-7.8	-9.1	-1.3	..	..	..
Guinea	Guinée	9	9	-1.4	4.3	-16.5	28.3	2.8	-23.1	-6.1
Guinea-Bissau	Guinée-Bissau	61	40	-1.7	0.9 j/	0.7	-6.8	-3.9	3.8	15.5
Haiti	Haïti	55 e/	16 e/	13.6	4.3	..	-6.8	5.4	4.8	..
Kiribati	Kiribati	..	..	..	..	..	..	..	..	..
Lao People's Dem.Rep.	Rép. dém. pop. lao	96	25	23.3	2.7	-2.4	-2.1	4.3	9.5	..
Lesotho	Lesotho	61	36	..	-5.8 j/	-32.8	..	4.3	..	-0.1
Malawi	Malawi	24	16	3.2	..	..	33.4	14.9	9.5	..
Maldives	Maldives	133 e/	31 e/	..	..	..	0.9	62.4	-23.6	..
Mali	Mali	47	33	..	..	..	..	..	-6.8	..
Mauritania	Mauritanie	87	24	19.8	-3.5	23.4	26.2	-60.2	23.0	9.9
Nepal	Népal	29	21	..	6.7	4.3	-0.6	18.4	3.0	9.5
Niger	Niger	35	14	7.6	-6.2 i/	3.6	-15.4	-5.7	..	..
Rwanda	Rwanda	53 f/	23 f/	15.7	..	10.5	..	..	..	..
Samoa	Samoa	168	31	..	-13.1 i/	5.3	-33.7	-5.9	..	..
Sao Tome and Principe	Sao Tomé-et-Principe	120	37	15.8	1.7	-6.7	36.6	-34.9	59.8	-18.2
Sierra Leone	Sierra Leone	24	7	-1.5	-13.2	-15.9	-13.9	-7.6	-10.3	-17.9
Somalia	Somalie	70 g/	20 g/	-4.7	88.3 k/	261.8	..	..	..	..
Sudan	Soudan	29	7	8.4	-15.3	4.1	7.8	-7.3	-18.1	-48.8
Togo	Togo	62	26	11.9	-4.3	-3.9	-16.3	-18.9	-0.4	23.8
Tuvalu	Tuvalu	..	..	..	..	..	..	..	..	..
Uganda	Ouganda	18 h/	8 h/	-11.1	21.4 k/	22.3	20.5	..	..	..
Un. Rep. of Tanzania	Rép.-Unie de Tanzanie	41	15	2.5	0.1	12.3	-4.7	-19.2	-10.6	30.1
Vanuatu	Vanuatu	145	29	..	-14.9 j/	-13.9	-6.8	-28.7	-8.2	..
Yemen	Yémen	101 e/	21 e/	24.9	-13.9	..	-28.7	..	..	..
ALL LDCs d/	Ensemble des PMA d/	30	14	(4.5)	-2.5	3.6	-0.3	-12.4	-2.9	0.2

Table 6 (continued)

Source: UNCTAD secretariat calculations based on data from the United Nations Statistical Office, the Economic Commission for Africa, the World Bank and other international and national sources.

a/ Gross fixed capital formation plus increase in stocks.

b/ Real investment.
c/ Exponential trend function.
d/ Growth rates relate to countries for which data are available for the years 1980 to 1985.

e/ 1984.
f/ 1981.
g/ 1982.
h/ 1983.
i/ 1980-1983.
j/ 1980-1984.
k/ 1980-1982.

Tableau 6 (suite)

Source: Chiffres calculés par le secrétariat de la CNUCED d'après des données du Bureau de statistique des Nations Unies, de la Commission économique pour l'Afrique, de la Banque mondiale et d'autres sources internationales et nationales.

a/ Formation brute de capital fixe plus variation des stocks.

b/ Investissements réels.
c/ Fonction exponentielle de tendance.
d/ Les taux de croissance se rapportent à l'ensemble des pays pour lesquels les données sont disponibles de 1980 à 1985.

e/ 1984.
f/ 1981.
e/ 1982.
f/ 1983.
i/ 1980-1983.
j/ 1980-1984.
k/ 1980-1982.

Table 7
Exports and imports : basic comparisons

	Exports in 1985 Exportations en 1985			Annual average growth rates of purchasing power per capita (%)	
	Total ($ million)	% of GDP	Per capita ($)	Taux annuels moyens d'accroissement du pouvoir d'achat des exportations par habitant (%)	
Country	Totale (millions de dollars)	En % du PIB	Par habitant (dollars)	1970-80a/	1980-86
Afghanistan	557	(14.6)	30.7	5.3	-4.4
Bangladesh	927	5.8	9.4	-8.6	3.0
Benin	40	3.9	9.9	-12.5	-8.6
Bhutan	..	..	..	..	..
Botswana	727	76.8	656.7	14.1	2.8
Burkina Faso	66	7.1	9.5	3.1	-6.0
Burundi	110	10.0	23.3	1.7	22.5
Cape Verde	5	4.2	15.0	-9.1	3.2
Central African Rep.	88	13.0	33.7	-1.1	-0.9
Chad	80	12.5	15.9	-0.7	2.2
Comoros	25	25.7	56.3	-3.6	2.6
Democratic Yemen	690	(71.6)	300.8	0.6	-3.2
Djibouti	26	12.6	71.4	-19.6	3.3
Equatorial Guinea	20	26.5	51.0	-17.2	5.8
Ethiopia	333	7.0	7.7	-3.5	5.1
Gambia	43	27.3	58.3	-4.7	5.8
Guinea	430	20.3	70.8	11.0	1.1
Guinea-Bissau	14	10.4	15.7	-1.7	5.2
Haiti	174	(9.4)	33.0	4.1	-4.3
Kiribati	5	22.0	69.6	..	..
Lao People's Dem.Rep.	29	2.1	8.0	3.7	-0.7
Lesotho	21	8.2	13.7	8.7	-16.2
Malawi	252	23.3	36.3	0.4	-4.4
Maldives	32	(40.8)	176.2	-7.8	18.7
Mali	170	14.7	21.0	4.9	-2.3
Mauritania	374	54.2	198.1	-8.6	5.4
Nepal	161	6.9	9.7	-5.4	11.5
Niger	223	14.1	36.5	15.8	-19.1
Rwanda	112	(6.8)	18.6	4.2	-0.9
Samoa	15	17.1	92.0	-0.6	-4.8
Sao Tome and Principe	5	14.3	46.3	-3.3	-21.3
Sierra Leone	112	9.6	31.1	-7.6	-8.9
Somalia	91	(6.5)	16.9	-1.6	-7.5
Sudan	367	4.2	17.0	-8.7	-6.4
Togo	190	27.3	64.2	4.2	-9.4
Tuvalu	..	..	..	..	..
Uganda	380	(11.2)	24.6	-10.2	-0.5
Un. Rep. of Tanzania	284	4.6	12.8	-8.5	-8.7
Vanuatu	31	47.3	236.1	-2.1	-15.0
Yemen	106	(2.8)	13.3	0.0	22.3
All LDCs	7314	10.2	22.0	-3.0	-1.7
All developing countries b/	267910	20.7	131.8	2.9	3.9

Source: UNCTAD secretariat estimates mainly based on
UNCTAD Handbook of International Trade and
Development Statistics, Supplement 1987 and table 10.

a/ Exponential trend fucntion.
b/ Excluding major petroleum exporters.

Tableau 7
Exportations et importations : comparaisons de base

Imports in 1985 Importations en 1985			Annual average growth rates of import volume per capita (%)		
Total ($ million)	% of GDP	Per capita ($)	Taux annuels moyens d'accroissement du volume des importations par habitant (%)		
Totale (millions de dollars)	En % du PIB	Par habitant (dollars)	1970-80a/	1980-86	Pays
999	(26.2)	55.1	3.7	8.5	Afghanistan
2170	13.5	22.0	0.0	-0.6	Bangladesh
400	39.2	98.9	2.7	2.2	Bénin
..	..	..	..	..	Bhoutan
596	63.0	538.4	8.9	-4.0	Botswana
225	24.3	32.4	6.1	-7.8	Burkina Faso
186	17.0	39.4	6.2	2.4	Burundi
113	95.7	338.3	-2.2	8.5	Cap-Vert
109	16.2	41.8	-5.0	5.5	Rép. centrafricaine
190	29.6	37.9	-6.4	16.5	Tchad
30	30.8	67.6	-4.6	-2.7	Comores
1290	(133.8)	562.3	-1.1	8.6	Yémen démocratique
110	53.3	302.2	-9.7	-2.7	Djibouti
30	39.8	76.5	-19.3	2.1	Guineé équatoriale
996	21.1	23.0	-1.5	6.2	Ethiopie
93	59.1	126.2	6.8	-9.2	Gambie
420	19.8	69.1	2.6	7.5	Guinée
60	44.5	67.5	-10.6	1.4	Guinée-Bissau
470	(25.4)	89.1	6.4	4.5	Haïti
13	63.6	201.1	-1.1	-2.2	Kiribati
160	11.4	44.2	-10.8	3.2	Rép. dém. pop. lao
250	97.2	162.6	12.7	-9.9	Lesotho
284	26.3	40.9	1.0	-10.6	Malawi
53	(67.5)	291.8	7.3	·10.0	Maldives
410	35.5	50.7	6.7	-4.0	Mali
234	33.9	123.9	2.0	-3.7	Mauritanie
460	19.6	27.7	2.1	4.0	Népal
400	25.4	65.4	10.4	-6.6	Niger
343	(20.8)	56.9	8.6	4.5	Rwanda
51	58.0	312.9	3.9	-3.6	Samoa
13	37.1	120.4	-4.9	-4.7	Sao Tomé-et-Principe
156	13.4	43.3	-2.8	-14.1	Sierra Leone
112	(8.0)	20.8	3.5	-17.9	Somalie
757	8.6	35.1	1.8	-14.1	Soudan
264	37.9	89.2	9.2	-11.5	Togo
..	..	..	..	..	Tuvalu
375	(11.0)	24.2	-11.7	1.6	Ouganda
1026	16.5	46.1	-2.8	-5.0	Rép.-Unie de Tanzanie
71	108.4	540.8	0.3	-4.5	Vanuatu
1598	(41.7)	200.9	33.1	-4.0	Yémen
15517	21.7	46.7	2.0	-1.9	Ensemble des PMA
290496	22.5	142.9	3.3	-0.1	Ensemble des pays en développement b/

Source: Estimations du secrétariat de la CNUCED principalement d'après le Manuel de statistiques du Commerce International et du Développement, Supplément 1987, de la CNUCED et le tableau 10.

a/ Fonction exponentielle de tendance.
b/ Non compris les principaux pays exportateurs de pétrole.

Table 8
Export value and purchasing power : annual average growth rates a/

Tableau 8
Valeur et pouvoir d'achat des exportations : taux annuels moyens d'accroissement a/

Percentages / En pourcentage

Country	Export value / Valeur des exportations							Purchasing power of exports / Pouvoir d'achat des exportations							Pays
	1970–1980	1980–1981	1981–1982	1982–1983	1983–1984	1984–1985	1985–1986	1970–1980	1980–1981	1981–1982	1982–1983	1983–1984	1984–1985	1985–1986	
Afghanistan	21.2	3.6	2.0	3.0	-13.2	-12.0	-3.6	7.9	10.9	6.3	6.2	-13.1	-12.8	-6.3	Afghanistan
Bangladesh	6.3	-10.3	0.8	3.4	35.4	-0.7	-2.9	-6.1	-4.9	5.1	5.2	-36.3	-0.3	-5.1	Bangladesh
Benin	1.8	-46.0	-29.4	33.3	3.1	21.2	0.0	-10.2	-43.0	-27.1	38.1	5.4	20.7	-3.8	Bénin
Bhutan	.	.	.	.	.	.	.	.	.	.	.	.	.	.	Bhoutan
Botswana	34.4	-24.9	20.9	39.2	6.0	7.9	-7.8	18.6	-21.2	25.2	43.6	7.4	7.4	-9.1	Botswana
Burkina Faso	18.4	-16.7	-25.3	1.8	38.6	-16.5	-1.5	5.2	-12.1	-22.7	5.4	40.0	-16.9	-3.8	Burkina Faso
Burundi	17.2	-5.4	23.9	-6.2	24.1	12.2	111.8	5.2	-14.6	28.3	-6.2	24.1	11.8	109.0	Burundi
Cape Verde	4.0	-25.0	33.3	-31.3	14.7	0.0	0.0	-8.3	-21.3	38.1	-29.0	1.3	-0.4	-1.3	Cap-Vert
Central African Rep.	13.4	-31.3	38.0	-31.2	14.7	2.3	36.4	1.0	-26.8	42.4	-29.5	15.1	1.3	27.4	Rép. centrafricaine
Chad	14.0	16.9	-30.1	27.6	48.6	-27.3	6.3	1.4	23.0	-28.0	32.0	48.7	-28.1	3.5	Tchad
Comoros	13.0	-20.0	25.0	5.0	-4.0	19.0	0.0	3.7	-16.1	29.4	3.2	-3.0	18.6	-1.3	Comores
Democratic Yemen	17.5	-22.1	31.0	-15.0	0.0	0.0	0.0	-3.7	-18.2	35.6	-12.5	6.4	6.5	-1.3	Yémen démocratique
Djibouti	-2.6	10.5	-4.8	25.0	4.0	0.0	-3.8	-14.0	16.0	-1.4	29.0	5.4	-0.4	-5.1	Djibouti
Equatorial Guinea	-4.4	14.3	6.2	17.6	0.0	0.0	77.2	-15.6	19.9	10.0	21.4	1.3	-0.4	-1.3	Guineé équatoriale
Ethiopia	13.3	-8.5	3.9	-0.5	3.7	-20.1	77.2	-0.9	-7.2	6.6	3.9	5.7	-20.3	83.5	Ethiopie
Gambia	11.9	-12.9	63.0	9.1	-2.1	-8.5	4.7	-1.4	-6.4	70.6	12.4	0.0	-8.5	0.0	Gambie
Guinea	28.5	25.6	-16.3	-2.4	7.5	-8.5	0.0	13.4	31.8	-13.4	0.7	8.9	-0.4	-1.3	Guinée
Guinea-Bissau	16.3	27.3	91.7	-21.7	-22.2	2.2	7.1	2.6	33.5	-11.2	97.8	-20.7	-22.5	5.7	Guinée-Bissau
Haiti	19.6	-33.2	-14.3	-5.5	16.2	-2.8	-2.3	5.5	-29.9	11.8	-2.5	17.8	-3.2	-3.6	Haïti
Kiribati	19.1	44.4	-46.2	57.1	224.2	-57.9	3.4	5.1	51.6	-44.2	62.2	228.6	-58.1	2.1	Kiribati
Lao People's Dem.Rep.	26.1	6.5	21.2	-35.0	-53.8	141.7	-3.6	11.3	11.7	25.5	-32.9	-53.2	140.7	-1.3	Rép. dém. pop. lao
Lesotho	16.4	-13.8	-30.0	-45.7	10.5	-19.5	-3.6	3.2	-9.6	-27.5	-44.0	12.0	-20.4	-5.7	Lesotho
Malawi	7.7	-5.3	-8.9	36.7	31.6	-28.0	-6.3	-1.5	-3.4	-6.9	38.3	27.5	-20.3	-7.5	Malawi
Maldives	21.1	10.0	27.3	35.7	31.6	27.5	12.9	-5.0	15.4	31.8	40.1	33.3	27.5	11.0	Maldives
Mali	5.9	-24.9	-5.2	13.0	18.2	-12.8	-25.1	7.2	-21.1	-2.4	17.5	19.1	-13.7	-27.8	Mali
Mauritania	9.8	34.5	-11.1	31.5	-2.6	25.9	-0.6	-6.2	43.1	-7.2	35.7	-0.5	26.4	-1.9	Mauritanie
Nepal	33.8	75.0	-37.1	6.8	36.2	25.8	-25.1	-3.1	83.6	-34.9	10.3	38.0	25.3	-24.1	Népal
Niger	21.3	-19.6	-27.0	-10.2	-23.5	-22.8	-26.0	18.7	-16.9	-24.6	-6.3	-23.0	-22.9	2.0	Niger
Rwanda	13.3	-1.8	-6.4	17.5	19.8	-22.8	5.4	7.7	4.4	-2.7	19.7	20.0	-22.4	-21.1	Rwanda
Samoa	12.4	-35.3	46.2	0.0	16.7	-28.6	-20.0	-0.0	-32.1	22.4	50.9	1.3	-21.4	-21.1	Samoa
Sao Tome and Principe	6.4	-30.0	-33.3	3.4	60.9	-24.3	0.0	-0.8	-26.6	-31.2	18.2	64.5	-28.9	-0.8	Sao Tomé-et-Principe
Sierra Leone	15.0	-25.0	-41.8	-48.2	-56.3	102.2	-1.1	-6.2	-20.9	-39.3	7.2	64.5	-24.4	-7.0	Sierra Leone
Somalia	7.0	14.3	30.9	-48.2	-56.3	102.2	3.5	1.4	23.4	37.1	-47.5	-55.8	103.0	1.5	Somalie
Sudan	21.1	21.2	-24.2	25.1	0.8	-41.7	3.5	-5.9	27.8	-21.0	29.6	-41.6	2.7	0.0	Soudan
Togo	.	-36.7	-16.5	-8.5	21.6	-3.6	0.0	6.7	-34.7	-13.4	-4.4	24.0	-3.6	2.7	Togo
Tuvalu	.	.	.	.	.	.	.	.	.	.	.	.	.	.	Tuvalu
Uganda	4.6	-29.9	43.4	7.2	7.3	-4.8	5.3	-7.5	-26.1	45.7	10.1	8.3	-6.2	-2.0	Ouganda
Un. Rep. of Tanzania	7.5	20.7	-25.8	-19.6	3.3	-24.9	12.7	-5.5	23.3	-23.8	-16.1	5.4	-25.0	14.3	Rép.-Un. de Tanzanie
Vanuatu	14.3	-8.6	-28.1	26.1	51.7	-29.5	-54.8	0.9	-4.1	-25.6	-30.1	53.7	-29.8	-55.4	Vanuatu
Yemen	16.7	104.3	-17.0	-30.8	140.7	63.1	-24.5	3.0	114.4	-14.1	-28.5	143.9	62.4	-25.5	Yémen
All LDCs	12.8	-6.4	-3.9	1.1	7.3	-5.7	2.7	-0.4	-1.8	-0.4	4.3	8.8	-6.1	1.3	Ensemble des PMA
All developing countries b/	20.7	5.3	-4.8	3.5	12.6	-0.6	6.4	5.3	7.8	-1.4	7.5	14.2	-0.4	10.6	Ensemble des pays en développement b/

For source and notes, see table 7.

Pour la source et les notes, se reporter au tableau 7.

Table 9
Import value and volume : annual average growth rates a/

Tableau 9
Valeur et volume des importations : taux annuels moyens d'accroissement a/

Percentages — En pourcentage

Country	| Import value / Valeur des importations |							| Import volume / Volume des importations |							Pays
	1970–1980	1980–1981	1981–1982	1982–1983	1983–1984	1984–1985	1985–1986	1970–1980	1980–1981	1981–1982	1982–1983	1983–1984	1984–1985	1985–1986	
Afghanistan	19.4	12.7	11.7	-24.5	120.2	-13.6	-4.9	6.3	20.6	16.5	-22.1	120.3	-14.4	-7.6	Afghanistan
Bangladesh	16.4	-8.1	-4.2	-8.6	28.7	6.3	-10.1	2.8	-2.6	0.0	-7.1	29.6	6.8	-12.2	Bangladesh
Benin	19.5	64.4	-14.7	-31.0	-3.1	29.0	2.5	5.4	73.5	-11.9	-28.6	-1.0	28.5	-1.4	Bénin
Bhutan	..	..	..	..	..	..	..	..	..	..	..	..	..	..	Bhoutan
Botswana	28.2	15.6	-14.1	7.3	-7.7	-12.2	2.3	13.2	21.3	-11.1	10.7	-6.5	-12.6	1.0	Botswana
Burkina Faso	21.8	-5.6	2.4	-16.8	-28.1	8.7	2.2	8.2	-0.4	6.0	-13.8	-27.4	8.1	-0.2	Burkina Faso
Burundi	22.4	-4.2	32.9	-14.5	1.6	0.0	10.8	8.0	0.5	37.6	-11.7	3.0	-0.4	9.3	Burundi
Cape Verde	11.8	2.9	0.0	14.3	5.0	34.5	1.8	-1.4	8.0	3.6	18.0	6.4	34.0	0.4	Cap-Vert
Central African Rep.	8.9	17.3	33.7	-33.1	2.4	25.3	12.8	-3.0	25.0	38.0	-31.4	2.8	24.1	5.4	Rép. centrafricaine
Chad	7.5	45.9	0.0	7.3	46.2	11.1	2.6	-4.4	53.6	4.0	11.1	46.3	9.8	0.0	Tchad
Comoros	11.8	3.0	-5.9	0.0	-6.3	0.0	0.0	-1.3	-2.5	3.2	-5.0	0.9	-0.4	-1.3	Comores
Democratic Yemen	15.6	3.2	137.6	-7.3	4.0	-16.4	-10.9	-2.0	8.3	146.0	-4.3	5.4	-16.7	-12.0	Yémen démocratique
Djibouti	9.4	-4.0	-4.2	-2.0	-4.3	0.0	4.5	-3.4	0.7	-0.8	3.2	-3.1	-0.4	3.2	Djibouti
Equatorial Guinea	-6.8	19.2	35.5	-28.6	0.0	0.0	0.0	-17.8	25.1	40.3	-26.3	1.3	-0.4	-1.3	Guineé équatoriale
Ethiopia	15.7	2.4	6.5	11.6	7.5	5.7	7.4	1.2	3.8	9.4	16.2	9.6	5.5	11.3	Ethiopie
Gambia	25.5	-25.2	-20.5	18.6	-14.8	-5.1	2.2	10.5	-19.6	-16.9	22.2	-13.0	-5.1	-2.5	Gambie
Guinea	18.7	18.5	-3.1	-3.2	20.0	16.7	2.4	4.8	24.4	0.3	-0.1	21.6	16.2	-1.0	Guinée
Guinea-Bissau	5.8	-9.1	0.0	30.0	-26.2	25.4	0.0	-6.6	-4.6	3.6	34.2	-25.2	24.5	-1.3	Guinée-Bissau
Haiti	22.3	26.6	-13.6	13.7	7.3	-0.4	-4.3	7.9	32.8	-10.5	17.4	8.7	-0.8	-5.5	Haïti
Kiribati	14.4	-17.6	0.0	0.0	0.0	-7.1	15.4	0.9	-13.6	3.6	3.2	4.9	-7.5	13.9	Kiribati
Lao People's Dem.Rep.	2.4	-4.6	4.0	7.7	3.6	10.3	4.0	-9.6	0.1	11.2	7.7	1.9	-9.9	-1.3	Rép. dém. pop. lao
Lesotho	30.8	13.8	-0.2	11.4	-46.8	-19.9	4.0	15.4	19.4	15.0	3.4	-46.1	-20.2	2.6	Lesotho
Malawi	17.1	-20.5	-11.1	0.0	-13.5	5.6	-11.3	3.8	-17.3	-9.2	3.7	-12.5	4.6	-13.3	Malawi
Maldives	25.3	6.9	38.7	32.6	-7.0	0.0	3.8	10.6	12.2	43.6	36.8	-5.8	-0.4	2.4	Maldives
Mali	23.2	-12.5	-13.8	3.9	8.7	9.3	-9.8	9.0	-8.1	-11.2	8.1	9.6	8.3	-11.3	Mali
Mauritania	18.2	-7.3	3.0	-16.8	8.4	-4.9	-2.2	4.7	-1.4	7.6	-14.2	10.7	-4.5	-1.1	Mauritanie
Nepal	18.6	-14.1	7.0	17.5	-10.3	10.6	2.5	13.2	-9.2	10.8	21.2	-5.6	10.1	5.1	Népal
Niger	27.5	7.9	-8.6	-30.5	1.9	21.2	2.6	12.2	12.0	-5.6	-27.4	2.5	20.7	5.1	Niger
Rwanda	26.4	5.3	7.8	-2.5	9.7	16.3	5.9	12.2	-6.7	-0.7	9.8	16.0	1.6	-0.7	Rwanda
Samoa	18.5	-11.1	-10.7	12.0	-10.7	2.0	-5.4	4.6	-6.1	-7.5	15.6	-9.5	2.0	-5.9	Samoa
Sao Tome and Principe	10.5	-10.5	-11.8	-33.3	20.0	8.3	15.4	-2.5	-8.6	-19.7	-31.2	21.6	7.9	13.9	Sao Tomé-et-Principe
Sierra Leone	12.0	-24.6	-23.1	-30.8	-6.0	2.6	2.6	-1.3	-20.5	-19.7	-28.3	-6.1	1.7	1.7	Sierra Leone
Somalia	21.0	47.1	-35.5	-45.5	-39.4	2.8	2.7	6.7	58.9	-32.5	-44.7	-38.7	3.2	-3.4	Somalie
Sudan	19.2	-0.1	-18.6	5.4	-15.3	-34.0	-12.8	4.9	5.6	-15.1	9.2	-13.4	-33.9	-14.5	Soudan
Togo	26.9	-20.9	-10.1	-27.4	-2.1	-5.0	2.3	11.8	-18.4	-6.8	-24.1	-0.1	-5.1	5.0	Togo
Tuvalu	..	..	..	..	..	..	..	..	..	..	..	..	..	..	Tuvalu
Uganda	2.9	32.4	10.1	0.2	-13.3	1.1	2.7	-9.1	39.5	11.8	3.0	-12.5	-0.4	-4.4	Ouganda
Un. Rep. of Tanzania	14.2	-1.1	-6.7	-27.3	8.2	15.4	-4.5	0.4	1.0	-4.2	-24.2	10.4	15.3	-3.1	Rép.-Un. de Tanzanie
Vanuatu	17.1	-18.3	1.7	6.8	9.5	2.9	-19.7	3.3	-14.3	5.3	10.2	11.0	2.5	-20.8	Vanuatu
Yemen	55.3	-5.1	-13.5	4.7	3.9	-3.4	-6.1	37.1	-0.5	-10.4	8.1	5.3	-3.8	-7.4	Yémen
All LDCs	18.7	0.9	-1.0	-6.3	4.5	-1.5	-3.5	4.7	5.9	2.5	-3.3	5.9	-1.9	-4.8	Ensemble des PMA
All developing countries b/	21.2	5.7	-8.1	-3.3	4.5	-3.8	3.2	5.8	8.2	-4.8	0.5	6.0	-3.6	7.3	Ensemble des pays en développement b/

For source and notes, see table 7.

Pour la source et les notes, se reporter au tableau 7.

Table 10 / Tableau 10

Unit value indices of imports / Indices de valeur unitaire des importations

(1980 = 100)

Country	1970	1971	1972	1973	1974	1975	1976	1977	1978	1979	1981	1982	1983	1984	1985	1986	Pays
Afghanistan	30.9	32.8	34.9	43.2	56.2	57.8	58.4	64.2	71.3	87.1	93.4	89.6	86.9	86.9	87.7	90.2	Afghanistan
Bangladesh	28.6	30.2	32.7	41.7	57.9	59.8	59.5	65.4	72.3	85.0	94.3	90.4	88.9	88.3	87.9	90.0	Bangladesh
Benin	28.7	30.3	32.9	41.0	54.0	58.4	58.8	64.5	72.5	86.2	94.7	91.7	88.5	86.7	87.0	90.4	Bénin
Burkina Faso	30.1	32.2	34.5	42.8	55.3	58.1	59.0	64.7	72.3	87.0	94.8	91.5	88.4	87.5	88.0	90.1	Burkina Faso
Central African Rep.	31.7	33.9	37.0	45.2	58.7	61.2	61.8	67.6	76.5	90.1	93.8	92.2	89.1	88.3	89.2	95.4	Rép. centrafricaine
Chad	30.3	32.6	34.1	41.1	54.5	56.6	57.1	65.6	70.4	86.5	95.0	92.2	92.0	89.0	90.1	92.4	Tchad
Ethiopia	25.8	27.8	30.1	37.2	51.7	55.9	56.9	62.0	69.0	83.5	98.6	96.1	86.2	90.2	90.4	87.3	Ethiopie
Gambia	28.2	29.7	32.3	40.7	54.7	58.5	58.9	64.5	72.3	86.0	93.0	88.9	90.8	84.5	84.5	88.6	Gambie
Malawi	29.2	32.0	34.6	42.6	54.4	58.3	59.0	64.7	72.7	87.5	96.2	94.2	90.8	89.7	90.6	92.7	Malawi
Mali	29.2	31.2	33.5	41.6	55.5	57.6	58.3	64.1	71.0	86.4	95.2	92.4	88.8	88.1	89.0	90.6	Mali
Mauritania	29.2	31.5	34.3	42.4	54.8	58.6	58.1	64.5	72.3	85.4	94.0	90.0	87.2	85.4	85.1	88.2	Mauritanie
Niger	29.7	31.6	34.2	41.8	55.0	57.1	58.1	63.9	70.0	86.2	96.7	93.7	89.7	89.1	89.5	87.3	Niger
Rwanda	30.4	32.2	34.5	42.9	56.3	58.6	59.5	65.3	72.3	87.6	94.1	90.6	88.9	88.8	89.0	91.9	Rwanda
Sierra Leone	27.8	29.5	32.2	40.2	53.1	56.9	57.4	62.7	70.1	84.1	94.8	90.8	87.5	85.6	85.7	86.4	Sierra Leone
Somalia	28.7	30.4	32.8	41.6	56.0	59.9	59.9	65.6	73.5	87.0	92.6	88.4	87.2	86.1	85.7	91.1	Somalie
Sudan	28.4	30.3	32.8	41.0	56.0	60.5	60.7	66.5	75.4	88.0	94.8	91.0	87.8	85.9	85.8	87.5	Soudan
Togo	28.5	30.2	32.8	41.0	54.8	59.2	59.7	65.4	73.6	87.2	96.9	93.4	89.5	87.7	87.8	85.5	Togo
Uganda	29.9	32.1	34.4	42.0	57.3	60.8	61.6	67.4	76.3	90.4	94.9	93.4	90.9	90.0	91.4	98.1	Ouganda
Un. Rep. of Tanzania	27.3	29.5	32.1	39.3	53.9	58.1	58.6	63.9	71.7	85.0	97.9	95.3	91.4	89.5	89.6	88.3	Rép.-Un.de Tanzanie
All LDCs a/	28.6	30.5	33.0	41.0	55.3	58.8	59.2	64.8	72.4	86.2	95.3	92.0	89.2	88.0	88.4	89.5	**Ensemble des PMA a/**
All developing countries b/	25.4	27.4	29.4	36.6	52.0	55.9	56.5	62.0	68.5	83.1	97.7	94.3	90.8	89.5	89.3	85.9	**Ensemble des pays en développement b/**
All developing countries c/	26.4	28.5	30.8	38.5	53.2	57.6	58.4	64.1	71.6	85.3	96.2	93.3	90.2	88.7	88.8	88.7	**Ensemble des pays en développement c/**

Source: UNCTAD secretariat estimates. / Source: Estimations du secrétariat de la CNUCED.

a/ This index is based on the indices for individual countries shown above. It has been applied to obtain the data on import volume, export purchasing power and aid in constant prices in the case of individual LDCs for which such index was not available.

b/ Excluding major petroleum exporters.

c/ Including major petroleum exporters.

a/ Cet indice est basé sur les indices pour les pays individuels qui figurent ci-dessus. On l'a utilisé pour obtenir les données concernant le volume des importations, le pouvoir d'achat des exportations et l'aide en prix constants dans les cas des PMA pour lesquels un tel indice n'était pas disponible.

b/ Non compris les principaux pays exportateurs de pétrole.

c/ Y compris les principaux pays exportateurs de pétrole.

Table 11
Leading exports of LDCs as a group in 1983 a/

Tableau 11
Principales exportations de l'ensemble des PMA en 1983 a/

SITC CTCI	Item	Value ($ million) Valeur (millions de dollars)	As a per cent / En pourcentage			Produit
			of all LDCs' total du total des PMA	of all developing countries des pays en développement	of world du monde	
	All commodities	6654.6	100.00	1.48	0.37	Ensemble des produits
071	Coffee	1029.9	15.48	11.38	10.27	Café
332	Petroleum products	739.5	11.11	1.88	0.80	Produits dérivés du pétrole
283	Ores and concentrates of non-ferrous base metals	430.4	6.47	10.92	5.92	Minerais de métaux communs non ferreux et concentrés
263	Cotton	353.9	5.32	13.39	5.80	Coton
001	Live animals	350.8	5.27	32.80	6.96	Animaux vivants
031	Fish, fresh and simply preserved	252.6	3.80	5.23	2.25	Poisson frais ou conservé de façon simple
286	Ores and concentrates of uranium & thorium	237.0	3.56	99.78	39.24	Minerais,concentrés d'uranium & de thorium
653	Textile fabrics other than cotton	211.5	3.18	5.84	1.48	Tissus autres que les tissus de coton
341	Gas, natural and manufactured	206.4	3.10	1.68	0.56	Gaz naturel et gaz manufacturé
121	Tobacco, unmanufactured	150.9	2.27	8.51	3.94	Tabacs bruts
074	Tea and mate	139.8	2.10	11.60	9.68	Thé et maté
656	Made-up articles of textile materials	138.2	2.08	11.12	4.41	Articles façonnés en textiles
044	Maize (corn), unmilled	136.7	2.05	8.13	1.39	Maïs, non moulu
281	Iron ore and concentrates	130.9	1.97	4.47	1.89	Minerai de fer et concentrés
221	Oil seeds, nuts and kernels	123.6	1.86	10.44	1.35	Graines, noix et amandes oléagineuses
292	Crude vegetable materials, n.e.s.	121.4	1.82	9.96	2.60	Matières brutes d'origine végétale,n.d.a.
264	Jute	121.0	1.82	91.98	88.81	Jute
611	Leather	97.0	1.46	9.19	2.84	Cuirs
051	Fruit, fresh and nuts, fresh or dried	92.9	1.40	2.37	1.03	Fruits frais et noix fraîches ou sèches
667	Pearls, precious and semi-precious stones	85.7	1.29	4.55	0.80	Perles fines, pierres gemmes et similaires
271	Fertilizers, crude	69.0	1.04	6.65	4.31	Engrais bruts
081	Feeding stuff for animals	68.8	1.03	1.80	0.62	Nourriture destinée aux animaux
072	Cocoa	64.5	0.97	2.70	2.05	Cacao
657	Floor coverings, tapestries, etc.	63.6	0.96	5.19	1.64	Tapis et tapisseries, etc.
211	Hides and skins, undressed	61.5	0.92	24.85	2.37	Cuirs et peaux, non-apprêtés
841	Clothing, (except fur clothing)	51.6	0.77	0.30	0.15	Vêtements, à l'exclusion des fourrures
054	Vegetables,fresh,frozen or simply preserved	49.9	0.75	1.99	0.70	Légumes frais, congelés ou en conserve
061	Sugar and honey	48.6	0.73	0.59	0.43	Sucre et miel
682	Copper	44.4	0.67	1.47	0.45	Cuivre
075	Spices	41.1	0.62	6.02	4.92	Epices
711	Power generating machinery, non-electrical	36.0	0.54	1.65	0.12	Machines génératrices non-électriques
661	Lime, cement and fabricated building materials	34.9	0.52	3.08	0.80	Chaux, ciment et matériaux de construction fabriqués
291	Crude animal materials, n.e.s.	32.4	0.49	8.73	2.72	Matières brutes d'origine animale,n.d.a.
651	Textile yarn and thread	27.5	0.41	0.87	0.23	Filés et fils textiles

Source: UNCTAD secretariat computations based on data from the United Nations Statistical Office.

Source: Calculs du secrétariat de la CNUCED basés sur des données du Bureau de statistique des Nations Unies.

a/ Data for 33 LDCs (excluding Benin, Bhutan, Botswana, Chad, Lao People's Dem.Rep., Lesotho and Yemen) accounting for over 90 per cent of the total exports of LDCs. "Leading exports" refer to exports exceeding 25 millions of dollars in 1983.

a/ Les données se rapportent à 33 PMA (non compris le Benin, le Bhoutan, le Botswana, le Tchad, la Rép.dém. populaire lao, le Lesotho et le Yémen) dont les exportations représentent plus de 90 pour cent du total des exportations des PMA. Par "principales exportations", on entend les exportations de produits atteignant plus de 25 millions de dollars en 1983.

Table 12

Leading exports of individual LDCs, 1983
(or latest year available)

Tableau 12

Principales exportations des PMA, par pays individuels, 1983
(ou année la plus récente disponible)

SITC CTCI	Country and leading export commodity[a]	Value of exports in $ million[b] Valeur des exportations en millions de dollars [b]	As % of country total En % du total du pays	As % of all developing countries En % de l'ensemble des pays en développement	As % of World En % du Monde	Pays et principaux produits exportés[a]
		(1)	(2)	(3)	(4)	
	Afghanistan					**Afghanistan**
	All commodities	730.0	100.00	0.16	0.04	Ensemble des produits
341	Gas, natural	200.0	27.40	1.63	0.54	Gaz, naturel
657	Floor coverings, tapestries	50.3	6.89	4.10	1.30	Tapis et tapisseries
051	Fruit,fresh & nuts, fresh or dried	38.4	5.26	0.98	0.43	Fruits frais & noix fraîches ou sèches
	Bangladesh					**Bangladesh**
	All commodities	788.9	100.00	0.18	0.04	Ensemble des produits
653	Woven textiles, non-cotton	203.7	25.82	5.62	1.43	Tissus autres que les tissus de coton
656	Textiles, etc. products	123.6	15.66	9.95	3.94	Articles en textiles, etc.
264	Jute	113.4	14.37	86.18	83.22	Jute
031	Fish, fresh and simply preserved	74.3	9.42	1.54	0.66	Poisson frais ou conservé de façon simple
611	Leather	73.5	9.32	6.97	2.16	Cuirs
074	Tea and mate	58.8	7.46	4.88	4.07	Thé et maté
	Burkina Faso					**Burkina Faso**
	All commodities	57.0	100.00	0.01	0.00	Ensemble des produits
263	Cotton	31.2	54.80	1.18	0.51	Coton
221	Oil seeds, nuts, kernels	8.3	14.61	0.70	0.09	Graines, noix, amandes oléagineuses
045	Cereals, n.e.s., unmilled	3.5	6.17	0.53	0.20	Céréales, n.d.a., non moulues
001	Live animals	3.1	5.50	0.29	0.06	Animaux vivants
	Burundi					**Burundi**
	All commodities	99.4	100.00	0.02	0.01	Ensemble des produits
071	Coffee	74.2	74.58	0.82	0.74	Café
667	Pearls,precious & semi-precious stones	10.4	10.47	0.55	0.10	Perles fines, pierres gemmes et similaires
	Cape Verde					**Cap-Vert**
	All commodities	3.2	100.00	0.00	0.00	Ensemble des produits
031	Fish, fresh and simply preserved	1.8	56.76	0.04	0.02	Poisson frais ou conservé de façon simple
032	Fish etc. tinned, prepared	0.7	22.77	0.07	0.03	Préparation et conserves de poissons
051	Fresh fruit	0.3	8.54	0.01	0.00	Fruits frais
	Central African Republic					**République centrafricaine**
	All commodities	109.4	100.00	0.02	0.01	Ensemble des produits
071	Coffee	38.2	34.89	0.42	0.38	Café
667	Pearls, precious and semi-precious stones (diamonds)	34.0	31.06	1.80	0.32	Perles fines, pierres gemmes et similaires (diamants)
291	Crude animal materials, n.e.s.	10.4	9.50	2.80	0.87	Matières brutes d'origine animale, n.d.a.
263	Cotton	10.0	9.10	0.38	0.16	Coton
242	Wood rough	5.7	5.24	0.25	0.12	Bois bruts
	Chad					**Tchad**
	All commodities	58.0	100.00	0.01	0.00	Ensemble des produits
263	Cotton	43.2	74.46	1.74	0.70	Coton
652	Cotton fabrics, woven	10.0	17.16	0.47	0.15	Tissus de coton
	Comoros					**Comores**
	All commodities	18.9	100.00	0.00	0.00	Ensemble des produits
075	Spices	14.8	78.23	2.17	1.77	Epices
551	Essential oils, perfumes, etc.	2.8	14.74	1.39	0.18	Huiles essentielles, produits utilisés en parfumerie, etc.
	Democratic Yemen					**Yémen démocratique**
	All commodities	674.0	100.00	0.15	0.04	Ensemble des produits
332	Petroleum products	655.0	97.18	1.66	0.71	Produits dérivés du pétrole
	Djibouti					**Djibouti**
	All commodities	33.6	100.00	0.01	0.00	Ensemble des produits
841	Clothing (except fur clothing)	7.4	21.99	0.04	0.02	Vêtements (à l'exclusion des vêtements de fourrure)
061	Sugar and honey	4.4	13.18	0.05	0.04	Sucre et miel
732	Road motor vehicles	2.6	7.84	0.08	0.00	Véhicules automobiles routiers
042	Rice	2.2	6.49	0.12	0.06	Riz
332	Petroleum products	1.7	5.11	0.00	0.00	Produits dérivés du pétrole
	Equatorial Guinea					**Guinée équatoriale**
	All commodities	25.4	100.00	0.01	0.00	Ensemble des produits
072	Cocoa	13.6	53.59	0.57	0.43	Cacao
242	Wood rough	7.3	28.95	0.32	0.15	Bois bruts
283	Non-ferrous metal ores	1.3	5.15	0.03	0.02	Minerais de métaux communs non-ferreux

Table 12 (continued)   Tableau 12 (suite)

Leading exports of individual LDCs, 1983   Principales exportations des PMA, par pays individuels, 1983
(or latest year available)   (ou année la plus récente disponible)

SITC CTCI	Country and leading export commodity[a]	Value of exports in $ million[b] / Valeur des exportations en millions de dollars [b]	As % of country total / En % du total du pays	As % of all developing countries / En % de l'ensemble des pays en développement	As % of World / En % du Monde	Pays et principaux produits exportés[a]
		(1)	(2)	(3)	(4)	
	Ethiopia					**Ethiopie**
	All commodities	422.5	100.00	0.09	0.02	Ensemble des produits
071	Coffee	261.8	61.96	2.89	2.61	Café
711	Power generating machinery, other than electric	29.9	7.08	1.37	0.10	Machines génératrices à l'exception des machines électriques
292	Crude vegetable materials,n.e.s.	28.7	6.79	2.36	0.62	Matières brutes d'origine végétale,n.d.a.
211	Hides, skins, undressed	26.3	6.21	10.61	1.01	Cuirs et peaux non apprêtés
	Gambia					**Gambie**
	All commodities	45.0	100.00	0.01	0.00	Ensemble des produits
221	Oil seeds, nuts, kernels	22.0	48.94	1.86	0.24	Graines, noix, amandes oléagineuses
421	Fixed vegetable oils, soft	7.6	16.99	0.59	0.20	Huiles végétales fixes, fluides
667	Pearls, precious and semi-precious stones	6.4	14.24	0.34	0.06	Perles fines, pierres gemmes et similaires
	Guinea					**Guinée**
	All commodities	420.5	100.00	0.09	0.02	Ensemble des produits
283	Non-ferrous metal ores	399.3	94.96	10.13	5.50	Minerais de métaux communs non-ferreux
	Guinea-Bissau					**Guinée-Bissau**
	All commodities	11.7	100.00	0.00	0.00	Ensemble des produits
221	Oil seeds, nuts, kernels	5.6	47.53	0.47	0.06	Graines, noix, amandes oléagineuses
031	Fish, fresh and simply preserved	2.0	17.12	0.04	0.02	Poisson frais ou conservé de façon simple
051	Fruit,fresh & nuts, fresh or dried	1.0	8.14	0.02	0.01	Fruits frais et noix fraîches ou sèches
275	Natural abrasives	0.9	7.79	1.12	0.16	Abrasifs naturels
	Haiti					**Haïti**
	All commodities	154.0	100.00	0.03	0.01	Ensemble des produits
071	Coffee	53.9	34.98	0.60	0.54	Café
612	Manufactures of leather, n.e.s.	24.5	15.88	6.56	2.41	Articles manufacturés en cuir, n.d.a.
894	Toys, sporting goods, etc.	18.0	11.69	0.49	0.21	Jouets, articles pour divertissements, etc.
851	Footwear	10.2	6.66	0.21	0.09	Chaussures
551	Essentials oils, perfumes, etc.	9.2	5.99	4.60	0.59	Huiles essentielles, produits utilisés en parfumerie, etc.
841	Clothing (except fur clothing)	9.2	5.97	0.05	0.03	Vêtements (à l'exclusion des vêtements de fourrure)
831	Travel goods, handbags and similar articles	8.7	5.65	0.50	0.30	Articles de voyage, sacs à mains et articles similaires
221	Oil seeds, nuts, kernels	8.1	5.24	0.68	0.09	Graines, noix, amandes oléagineuses
	Kiribati					**Kiribati**
	All commodities	4.5	100.00	0.00	0.00	Ensemble des produits
221	Oils seeds, nuts, kernels	4.1	91.71	0.34	0.04	Graines, noix, amandes oléagineuses
	Malawi					**Malawi**
	All commodities	239.2	100.00	0.05	0.01	Ensemble des produits
121	Tobacco, unmanufactured	123.0	51.43	6.94	3.21	Tabacs bruts
074	Tea and mate	47.2	19.75	3.92	3.27	Thé et maté
061	Sugar and honey	23.0	9.60	0.28	0.20	Sucre et miel
044	Maize (corn), unmilled	17.9	7.49	1.07	0.18	Maïs non moulu
	Maldives					**Maldives**
	All commodities	19.9	100.00	0.00	0.00	Ensemble des produits
841	Clothing (except fur clothing)	9.2	46.40	0.05	0.03	Vêtements (à l'exception des vêtements de fourrure)
031	Fish, fresh and simply preserved	8.9	44.70	0.18	0.08	Poisson frais ou conservé de façon simple
	Mali					**Mali**
	All commodities	165.0	100.00	0.04	0.01	Ensemble des produits
263	Cotton	68.4	41.45	2.59	1.12	Coton
001	Live animals	55.0	33.33	5.14	1.09	Animaux vivants
	Mauritania					**Mauritanie**
	All commodities	304.7	100.00	0.07	0.02	Ensemble des produits
031	Fish, fresh and simply preserved	145.7	47.82	3.02	1.30	Poisson frais ou conservé de façon simple
281	Iron ore and concentrates	130.9	42.94	4.47	1.89	Minerai de fer et concentrés

Table 12 (continued)

Leading exports of individual LDCs, 1983
(or latest year available)

Tableau 12 (suite)

Principales exportations des PMA, par pays individuels, 1983
(ou année la plus récente disponible)

SITC / CTCI	Country and leading export commodity[a] / Valeur des exportations en millions de dollars [b]	Value of exports in $ million [b] / En % du total du pays	As % of country total / En % de l'ensemble des pays en développement	As % of all developing countries / En % du Monde	As % of World	Pays et principaux produits exportés[a]
		(1)	(2)	(3)	(4)	
	Nepal					**Nepal**
	All commodities	78.8	100.00	0.02	0.00	Ensemble des produits
657	Floor coverings, tapestries	11.1	14.07	0.90	0.29	Tapis et tapisseries
611	Leather	6.9	8.76	0.65	0.20	Cuirs
264	Jute	6.8	8.68	5.20	5.02	Jute
656	Textiles, etc. products	6.8	8.66	0.55	0.22	Articles en textiles, etc.
653	Woven textiles, non-cotton	5.8	7.39	0.16	0.04	Tissus autres que les tissus de coton
332	Petroleum products	4.9	6.16	0.01	0.01	Produits dérivés du pétrole
001	Live animals	4.7	6.02	0.44	0.09	Animaux vivants
221	Oil seeds, nuts, kernels	4.1	5.23	0.35	0.05	Graines, noix, amandes oléagineuses
532	Dyeing and tanning extracts,etc.	4.1	5.15	4.15	1.32	Extraits utilisés pour la teinture et le tannage, etc.
081	Animal feeding stuff	4.1	5.14	0.11	0.04	Nourriture destinée aux animaux
	Niger					**Niger**
	All commodities	320.0	100.00	0.07	0.02	Ensemble des produits
286	Ores and concentrates of uranium and thorium	237.0	74.07	99.78	39.24	Minerais et concentrés d'uranium et de thorium
001	Live animals	58.5	18.28	5.47	1.16	Animaux vivants
	Rwanda					**Rwanda**
	All commodities	96.9	100.00	0.02	0.01	Ensemble des produits
071	Coffee	79.3	81.81	0.88	0.79	Café
074	Tea and mate	6.7	6.89	0.55	0.46	Thé et maté
	Samoa					**Samoa**
	All commodities	17.3	100.00	0.00	0.00	Ensemble des produits
422	Other fixed vegetable oils	7.6	44.22	0.27	0.23	Autres huiles végétales fixes
072	Cocoa	2.9	16.64	0.12	0.09	Cacao
054	Vegetables, fresh, frozen or simply preserved	1.6	9.40	0.06	0.02	Légumes frais, congelés ou simplement en conserve
221	Oil seeds, nuts, kernels	1.4	8.38	0.12	0.02	Graines, noix, amandes oléagineuses
053	Fruit, preserved and fruit preparations	1.2	7.10	0.08	0.03	Préparations et conserves de fruits
	Sao Tome and Principe					**Sao Tomé-et-Principe**
	All commodities	7.4	100.00	0.00	0.00	Ensemble des produits
072	Cocoa	5.1	69.17	0.21	0.16	Cacao
221	Oil seeds, nuts, kernels	1.5	19.65	0.12	0.02	Graines, noix, amandes oléagineuses
	Sierra Leone					**Sierra Leone**
	All commodities	90.7	100.00	0.02	0.01	Ensemble des produits
667	Pearls, precious and semi-precious stones	29.1	32.08	1.54	0.27	Perles fines, pierres gemmes et similaires
283	Non-ferrous metal ores	20.1	22.18	0.51	0.28	Minerais de métaux communs non-ferreux
072	Cocoa	17.6	19.38	0.74	0.56	Cacao
275	Natural abrasives	7.3	8.03	8.95	1.30	Abrasifs naturels
071	Coffee	4.6	5.12	0.05	0.05	Café
	Somalia					**Somalie**
	All commodities	149.9	100.00	0.03	0.01	Ensemble des produits
001	Live animals	114.7	76.55	10.73	2.28	Animaux vivants
051	Fresh fruit (bananas)	19.7	13.12	0.50	0.22	Fruits frais (bananes)
	Sudan					**Soudan**
	All commodities	601.1	100.00	0.13	0.03	Ensemble des produits
263	Cotton	154.5	25.70	5.84	2.53	Coton
044	Maize (corn), unmilled	117.0	19.47	6.96	1.19	Maïs non moulu
001	Live animals	105.5	17.55	9.87	2.09	Animaux vivants
292	Crude vegetable materials, n.e.s.	67.7	11.26	5.55	1.45	Matières brutes d'origine végétale, n.d.a.
221	Oil seeds, nuts, kernels	35.4	5.89	2.99	0.39	Graines, noix, amandes oléagineuses
	Togo					**Togo**
	All commodities	162.5	100.00	0.04	0.01	Ensemble des produits
271	Fertilizers, crude	68.2	41.99	6.58	4.26	Engrais bruts
661	Lime, cement and fabricated building materials	34.7	21.38	3.07	0.80	Chaux, ciment et matériaux de construction fabriqués
263	Cotton	17.5	10.74	0.66	0.29	Coton
072	Cocoa	14.5	8.92	0.61	0.46	Cacao
071	Coffee	12.8	7.88	0.14	0.13	Café
	Tuvalu					**Tuvalu**
	All commodities	0.07	100.00	0.00	0.00	Ensemble des produits
223	Copra	0.06	78.57	0.06	0.06	Coprah

Table 12 (continued)   Tableau 12 (suite)

Leading exports of individual LDCs, 1983   Principales exportations des PMA, par pays individuels, 1983
(or latest year available)   (ou année la plus récente disponible)

SITC / CTCI	Country and leading export commodity[a]	Value of exports in $ million [b] / Valeur des exportations en millions de dollars [b]	As % of country total / En % du total du pays	As % of all developing countries / En % de l'ensemble des pays en développement	As % of World / En % du Monde	Pays et principaux produits exportés[a]
		(1)	(2)	(3)	(4)	
	Uganda					**Ouganda**
	All commodities	360.1	100.00	0.08	0.02	Ensemble des produits
071	Coffee	336.9	93.55	3.72	3.36	Café
	United Republic of Tanzania					**République-Unie de Tanzanie**
	All commodities	425.0	100.00	0.09	0.02	Ensemble des produits
071	Coffee	152.2	35.81	1.68	1.52	Café
263	Cotton	45.6	10.73	1.73	0.75	Coton
682	Copper	43.7	10.29	1.45	0.44	Cuivre
074	Tea and mate	22.4	5.26	1.86	1.55	Thé et maté
121	Tobacco, unmanufactured	21.6	5.09	1.22	0.57	Tabacs bruts
	Vanuatu					**Vanuatu**
	All commodities	17.9	100.00	0.00	0.00	Ensemble des produits
221	Oil seeds, nuts, kernels	13.1	73.43	1.11	0.14	Graines, noix, amandes oléagineuses
072	Cocoa	1.8	10.30	0.08	0.06	Cacao
011	Meat, fresh, chilled or frozen	1.4	7.94	0.07	0.01	Viande fraîche, réfrigérée ou congelée

Source : UNCTAD Secretariat computations based on data from the United Nations Statistical Office.

Note : Column (1) shows export values f.o.b. in millions of dollars. Column (2) shows for each commodity presented its percentage share in the individual country export total, while columns (3) and (4) show the relative importance of each commodity shown expressed as a percentage of the relevant total group for that commodity (i.e. "all developing countries" and "world" respectively).

a/ A "leading export commodity" is one which accounts for at least 5 per cent of the country's total exports.

b/ The figures shown refer in general to special or national trade. They may therefore differ from those used in other tables.

Source : Calculs du secrétariat de la CNUCED d'après les données du Bureau de statistiques des Nations Unies.

Note : La colonne (1) montre la valeur des exportations f.o.b. en millions de dollars. La colonne (2) montre, pour chaque produit indiqué, sa part en pourcentage dans le total des exportations du pays concerné, alors que les colonnes (3) et (4) montrent l'importance relative de chaque produit indiqué présenté comme part en pourcentage du total du groupe de produits auquel il se rapporte (total se référant respectivement à "l'ensemble des pays en développement" et au "monde").

a/ Par "principaux produits exportés" on entend les produits équivalent chacun à 5 pour cent au moins du total des exportations du pays concerné.

b/ Les données présentées correspondent en général au commerce spécial ou national. Elles peuvent par conséquent, dans certains cas, être différentes de celles utilisées dans les autres tableaux.

Table 13

Tableau 13

Commodity structure of exports of LDCs by main category
(1985 or latest year available)

Composition des exportations des PMA, par principales catégories de produits
(1985 ou année disponible la plus récente)

Country / Pays (SITC / CTCI)	Year / Année	Total value ($ million) / Valeur totale (million de $)	All food items / Produits alimentaires (0+1+22+4)	Agricultural raw materials / Matières premières d'origine agricole (2-22-27-28)	Fuels / Combustibles (3)	Ores and metals / Minerais et métaux (27+28+67+68)	Manufactured goods / Produits manufacturés (5+6+7+8-67-68)	Un-allocated / Non-distribués (9)	Textiles fibres, yarn and clothing / Fibres textiles, filés, tissus et vêtements (26+65+84)
Afghanistan	1985	557	17.0	6.8	55.6	-	4.8	15.8	10.6
Bangladesh	1985	927	17.9	13.3	2.6	-	65.8	0.4	67.5
Benin	1985	40	..	..	..	..	..	..	-
Bhutan	1983	14	25.2	6.8	0.0	..	46.8	21.2	-
Botswana	1985	727	7.1	0.8	-	8.7	77.8	5.6	2.1
Burkina Faso	1983	57	33.5	56.0	-	0.4	10.1	-	56.8
Burundi	1985	110	89.9	3.6	2.8	0.2	5.7	0.6	3.4
Cape Verde	1984	5	84.3	1.4	-	8.7	2.9	0.0	0.0
Central African Rep.	1985	88	(31.4)	(26.9)	-	..	(24.1)	(17.6)	(11.5)
Chad	1984	110	(18.7)	(81.3)	-	..	-	-	(81.3)
Comoros	1985	25	(87.0)	0.7	..	-	(9.3)	(3.7)	..
Democratic Yemen	1983	674	1.0	0.1	97.4	0.1	0.6	0.1	0.6
Djibouti	1983	25	39.4	5.8	5.2	1.8	45.3	2.7	25.0
Equatorial Guinea	1984	20	69.8	24.4	-	-	-	5.8	..
Ethiopia	1985	333	71.2	17.7	..	0.2	0.9	10.0	0.5
Gambia	1983	48	74.3	3.4	0.3	2.1	17.3	2.6	3.2
Guinea	1983	400	3.4	0.4	-	95.0	0.5	0.7	0.0
Guinea-Bissau	1985	14	94.0	3.4	..	..	..	2.6	..
Haiti	1984/85	227	52.7	0.2	..	..	47.1	0.0	..
Kiribati	1983	5	94.3	0.1	0.0	0.0	5.3	(0.2)	1.4
Lao People's Dem.Rep.	1985	29	(7.6)	(18.0)	(57.4)	8.8	..	(8.2)	..
Lesotho	1982	35	12.1	12.1	0.1	-	71.5	4.2	16.0
Malawi	1985	252	76.6	3.0	-	..	..	20.4	3.0
Maldives	1983	19	45.9	0.3	0.0	0.1	53.1	0.6	47.1
Mali	1984	195	34.7	49.8	-	-	3.1	12.4	49.7
Mauritania	1985	374	59.8	-	-	40.2	-	-	(45.3)
Nepal	1985	161	(35.1)	(5.6)	2.5	(0.3)	(59.0)	(0.0)	0.1
Niger	1983	298	18.9	0.6	0.1	76.7	0.8	0.5	0.0
Rwanda	1984	145	84.4	4.7	0.0	10.1	0.7	-	0.0
Samoa	1983	19	95.4	2.1	0.1	0.4	2.2	0.0	0.3
Sao Tome & Principe	1983	6	91.3	2.2	..	0.2	6.3	0.0	1.0
Sierra Leone	1985	112	37.2	0.1	..	39.0	18.7	5.0	..
Somalia	1985	91	87.7	..	..	..	..	12.3	..
Sudan	1985	367	33.2	52.1	..	-	4.6	10.1	44.3
Togo	1984	197	28.8	..	1.4	55.1	20.0	14.8	..
Tuvalu	1983	0.1	78.6	-	-	-	-	1.4	..
Uganda	1985	380	94.8	4.1	2.0	-	..	1.1	4.1
Un. Rep. of Tanzania	1982	455	70.8	18.3	..	2.5	5.3	1.0	18.9
Vanuatu	1985	31	76.1	4.2	(0.4)	-	..	19.6	..
Yemen	1983	27	(75.0)	(4.7)	..	-	(11.6)	(8.2)	(4.2)
All LDCs / Ensemble des PMA	1984	295546	36.4	10.8	13.6	13.3	21.0	4.9	17.4
All developing countries a/ / Ensemble des pays en développement a/	1984		20.6	5.1	19.1	8.0	45.2	2.0	..

Source : UNCTAD Handbook of International Trade and Development Statistics, Supplement 1987; IMF, International Financial Statistics, October 1987, and other international and national sources.

Source : CNUCED, Manuel de statistiques du commerce international et du développement, Supplément 1987; FMI, Statistiques financières internationales, Octobre 1987, et autres sources internationales et nationales.

a/ Excluding OPEC countries.

a/ Non compris les pays de l'OPEP.

Table 14
Commodity structure of imports of LDCs by main category
(1985 or latest year available)

Tableau 14
Composition des importations des PMA, par principales catégories de produits
(1985 ou année la plus récente disponible)

Country / Pays	Year / Année	Total value ($mill.) / Valeur totale (mill. de $)	All food items 0+1+22+4	Agricultural raw materials 2-22-27-28	Fuels 3	Ores and metals 27+28+67+68	Manufactured goods 5+6+7+8 -67-68	Un-allocated 9	Cereals 04	Crude and manufactured fertilizers 271+56	Transport equipment 73
Afghanistan	1981	622	12.1	-	21.4	-	56.3	10.2	-	0.5	(30.8)
Bangladesh	1985	2170	24.3	5.2	16.5	9.6	44.3	0.2	10.4	6.1	4.5
Bénin	1983	320	14.8	2.5	5.2	1.8	75.5	0.3	3.6	0.5	5.0
Bhoutan	1983	36	15.3	-	23.0	3.1	48.2	10.4	6.5	0.0	16.2
Botswana	1985	596	17.5	3.2	11.5	9.1a/	46.9	11.7	..	..	12.8
Burkina Faso	1983	288	25.5	2.1	17.1	4.1	51.2	..	10.9	2.0	11.3
Burundi	1985	186	16.4	2.1	18.1	12.2	47.9	3.3	8.0	0.5	7.9
Cap-Vert	1983	80	32.6	0.8	13.9	2.2	50.3	0.2	8.5	0.0	8.4
Rép.centrafricaine	1983	85	18.0	1.2	1.6	2.1	75.7	0.4	6.5	0.1	16.1
Tchad	1983	117	(18.1)	(1.0)	(1.2)	(1.5)	(77.9)	(0.2)	(9.7)	(4.3)	(21.4)
Comores	1983	32	(22.2)	(1.0)	(7.2)	(3.1)	(61.8)	(4.7)	(14.7)	(0.0)	(13.4)
Yémen démocratique	1983	1483	(24.3)	(0.8)	(37.5)	(2.6)	(34.6)	(0.2)	(7.0)	(0.0)	(6.6)
Djibouti	1983	115	(24.5)	(7.1)	(29.1)	(1.1)	(37.7)	(0.5)	(4.2)	-	(6.7)
Guinée équatoriale	1984	30	23.5	..	16.8	..	44.5	15.2	..	-	..
Ethiopie	1985	996	29.8	3.0	14.8	3.2	49.3	0.8	18.9	1.4	14.2
Gambie	1984/85	90	40.3	0.5	14.5	0.8	43.1	0.8	11.8	-	6.6
Guinée	1983	300	12.8	0.7	29.2	2.9	53.9	0.5	5.3	0.3	7.8
Guinée-Bissau	1983	65	39.7	1.2	10.5	0.9	47.1	0.6	31.3	0.0	9.4
Haïti	1984/85	449	28.1	2.7	14.2	-	54.1	0.9	..	..	18.4
Kiribati	1983	14	(18.7)	(0.6)	(9.9)	(2.1)	(60.0)	(8.8)	(6.6)	(0.2)	(22.3)
Rép.dém.populaire lao	1981	125	(20.8)	(0.1)	(18.9)	(3.6)	(53.5)	(3.1)	(16.2)	(3.3)	(14.1)
Lesotho	1982	527	25.1	0.4	7.6	2.8	61.5	2.6	7.1	1.5	10.0
Malawi	1983	311	8.2	1.5	18.0	4.2	67.8	0.3	2.4	8.7	7.5
Maldives	1983	57	16.9	1.7	25.0	(2.6)	52.9	1.0	4.7	-	2.4
Mali	1983	345	15.4	0.7	17.6	2.6	63.1	0.4	5.4	7.0	10.0
Mauritanie	1985	234	36.3	2.2	13.9	..	64.7	-	..	4.7	9.7
Népal	1985	460	14.0	1.3	11.6	7.5	(49.8)	0.0	0.8	5.2	5.2
Niger	1981	510	23.5	11.6	14.8	4.0	55.5	0.8	11.8	0.4	8.1
Rwanda	1984	295	16.5	0.8	17.0	14.0	40.8	0.1	5.5	0.7	8.4
Samoa	1983	56	23.5	0.5	17.5	3.7	54.5	0.1	5.7	0.7	9.6
Sao Tomé-et-Principe	1983	10	36.3	1.0b/	1.8	4.4	56.8	0.2	15.3	0.1	10.7
Sierra Leone	1985	156	32.6	6.3	21.3	..	41.0c/	4.1	13.3	0.3	23.3d/
Somalie	1981	512	20.3	..	2.2	1.5	69.0	0.7	..	0.3	22.2
Soudan	1985	757	19.7	..	18.7	..	61.6	-	..	..	10.3
Togo	1984	278	27.8	1.6	10.4	0.6	44.8	16.4	2.4	0.1	7.9
Tuvalu	1983	3	25.8	-	13.2	1.6	45.1	12.7	11.5	-	2.5
Ouganda e/	1985	375	(10.8)	(1.1)	-	(1.9)	(71.8)	(15.5)	(6.3)	0.1	(9.0)
Rep. Unie de Tanzanie	1983	822	(10.1)		(10.8)	(7.3)	(69.4)	(1.3)		(1.4)	(14.4)
Vanuatu	1983	63	25.8	0.7	11.0	1.8	58.1	2.5	7.8	0.1	7.8
Yémen	1985	1598	33.1	0.3	6.7	7.2	52.3	0.4	9.2	0.7	9.9
Ensemble des PMA / All LDCs			22.4	2.1	15.6	4.7	53.1	2.1	7.1	1.8	10.7
Ensemble des pays en développement f/ / All developing countries f/	1984	306099	11.5	3.5	21.3	6.1	54.0	3.8	..	..	..

Source : UNCTAD Handbook of International Trade and Development Statistics, Supplement 1987, and other international and national sources.

Source : CNUCED, Manuel de statistiques du commerce international et du développement, Supplément 1987, et autres sources internationales et nationales.

a/ Including metal products.   b/ SITC 2.   c/ SITC 5+6+7+8   d/ SITC 7.
e/ The percentage distribution excludes imports financed through loans or grants.
f/ Excluding OPEC countries.

a/ Y compris les produits métalliques.   b/ CTCI 2.   c/ CTCI 5+6+7+8.
d/ CTCI 7.   e/ La distribution en pourcentage ne comprend pas les importations financées par des prêts ou par des dons.
f/ Non compris les pays de l'OPEP.

Table 15

Tableau 15

Main markets for exports of LDCs : relative shares in 1985 (or latest year available)

Principaux marchés aux exportations des PMA : parts relatives en 1985 (ou année disponible la plus récente)

Percentages — En pourcentage

Country / Pays	Year / Année	Developed market economy countries / Pays développés à économie de marché					Socialist countries / Pays socialistes		Developing countries / Pays en développement			Un‑allocated / Non‑distribués
		Total	EEC / CEE	Japan / Japon	USA and Canada / Etats‑Unis et Canada	Other a/ / Autres a/	Eastern Europe / Europe orientale	Asia / Asie	Total	OPEC / OPEP	Other / Autres	
Afghanistan	1985	18.2	15.3	0.4	1.0	1.5	68.3	0.0	4.4	0.5	3.9	9.1
Bangladesh	1985	48.6	16.8	7.2	21.9	2.7	6.0	1.2	44.2	8.6	35.6	0.0
Benin / Bénin	1982	70.6	58.4	12.2	0.0	0.0	–	–	28.8	11.1	17.7	0.6
Bhutan / Bhoutan	1984/85	–	–	–	–	–	–	–	100.0	–	100.0	–
Botswana	1984	94.7	5.7	0.1	8.2	80.7	–	–	4.7	–	4.7	0.6
Burkina Faso	1984	48.0	38.1	7.2	1.1	1.6	–	4.7	30.0	0.4	29.6	17.3
Burundi	1985	77.1	41.6	1.1	5.9	28.5	–	–	21.9	0.1	21.8	1.0
Cape Verde / Cap‑Vert	1984	48.4	47.4	0.0	1.1	–	–	–	47.9	21.3	26.6	3.7
Central African Rep. / Rép. centrafricaine	1985	92.2	90.8	0.0	0.0	1.4	..	–	7.8	0.4	7.4	–
Chad / Tchad	1984	(52.6)	(47.2)	(3.1)	0.1	(2.2)	–	–	(12.2)	–	(12.2)	(35.2)
Comoros / Comores	1983	97.5	72.5	–	23.1	1.9	–	–	2.5	0.6	1.9	0.0
Democratic Yemen / Yémen démocratique		..	..	..	..	..	..	..	..	..	..	..
Djibouti		..	..	..	..	..	..	..	..	..	..	..
Equatorial Guinea / Guinée équatoriale	1985	96.4	94.9	–	–	1.5	–	–	3.7	0.0	3.7	–
Ethiopia / Ethiopie	1985	66.9	41.7	10.4	11.8	3.0	9.0	0.3	23.3	4.1	19.2	0.5
Gambia / Gambie	1982	68.7	52.9	–	0.4	15.4	–	–	31.3	1.4	29.9	–
Guinea / Guinée	1985	85.5	56.5	0.2	27.9	0.9	1.4	–	13.2	0.2	13.0	–
Guinea‑Bissau / Guinée‑Bissau	1984	51.9	51.3	–	0.6	–	35.9	9.4	2.8	–	2.8	–
Haiti / Haïti	1984/85	94.6	37.8	0.4	55.2	1.3	–	–	5.3	–	5.3	0.1
Kiribati	1984	64.6	35.4	–	28.8	0.4	–	–	33.8	–	33.8	1.7
Lao People's Dem.Rep. / Rép.dém.populaire lao	1984	32.8	9.7	4.5	15.9	2.7	–	38.7	23.1	4.7	18.4	5.4
Lesotho	1982	94.9	14.2	–	0.4	80.3	–	–	5.1	–	5.1	–
Malawi	1984	75.9	58.1	3.0	9.1	5.7	–	–	22.4	0.1	22.3	1.7
Maldives	1984	53.2	1.6	6.1	39.0	6.5	–	–	46.8	0.4	46.4	–
Mali		..	..	..	..	..	..	..	..	..	..	..
Mauritania / Mauritanie	1984	95.4	73.5	21.5	0.3	0.1	–	–	4.6	0.1	4.5	0.0
Nepal / Népal	1985	39.1	15.2	0.5	21.9	1.5	4.2	2.6	54.2	0.0	54.2	–
Niger	1985	82.6	77.1	1.4	4.0	0.1	–	–	15.1	11.9	3.2	2.3
Rwanda	1985	95.2	87.4	1.4	5.3	1.1	–	–	4.8	0.1	4.7	–
Samoa	1984	85.7	11.2	0.1	35.7	38.7	–	–	14.3	–	14.3	–
Sao Tome & Principe / Sao Tomé‑et‑Principe	1985	100.0	92.2	–	–	7.8	–	–	–	–	–	–
Sierra Leone	1984	65.4	56.1	–	8.8	0.5	–	–	5.7	3.9	1.8	28.9
Somalia / Somalie	1985	24.2	21.9	0.3	1.8	0.2	0.0	4.2	71.6	41.2	30.4	0.0
Sudan / Soudan	1985	33.0	19.9	8.1	3.3	1.7	19.8	0.1	46.6	20.1	26.5	0.5
Togo	1985	72.4	58.6	0.2	8.2	5.4	3.6	0.0	15.6	0.6	15.0	8.4
Tuvalu		..	..	..	..	..	..	..	..	..	..	..
Uganda / Ouganda	1985	83.7	50.8	2.5	27.1	3.3	–	–	16.3	1.3	15.0	–
Un. Rep.of Tanzania / Rép. Unie de Tanzanie	1985	70.8	57.7	3.8	2.9	6.4	1.1	0.7	24.5	7.7	16.7	2.9
Vanuatu	1985	58.4	40.3	11.0	–	7.1	–	–	8.2	–	8.2	33.4
Yemen / Yémen	1984	34.6	21.4	1.1	11.9	0.2	–	0.2	62.6	17.2	45.4	2.8
All LDCs / Ensemble des PMA	1984	65.7	37.6	4.0	12.4	11.7	8.9	0.5	21.7	4.5	17.2	3.2
All developing countries b/ / Ensemble des pays en développement b/	1984	63.6	16.7 c/	8.9	32.0	6.0 c/	4.8	2.6	27.5	6.6	20.9	1.5

Source : United Nations, 1985 International Trade Statistics Yearbook; IMF, Direction of Trade Yearbook 1987 and other international and national souces.

a/ Including EFTA.
b/ Excluding OPEC countries.
c/ Spain and Portugal are included with "other developed market economy countries".

Source : Nations Unies, Annuaire Statistique du Commerce International 1985; FMI, Direction of Trade Yearbook 1987 et autres sources internationales et nationales.

a/ Y compris l'AELE.
b/ Non compris les pays de l'OPEP.
c/ L'Espagne et le Portugal sont compris avec les "autres pays développés à économie de marché".

Table 16

Main sources of imports of LDCs : relative shares in 1985
(or latest year available)

Tableau 16

Principales sources d'importation des PMA : parts relatives en 1985
(ou année disponible la plus récente)

Percentages / En pourcentage

Country / Pays	Year / Année	Developed market economy countries / Pays développés à économie de marché — Total	EEC / CEE	Japan / Japon	USA and Canada / Etats-Unis et Canada	Other a/ / Autres a/	Socialist countries / Pays socialistes — Eastern Europe / Europe orientale	Asia / Asie	Developing countries / Pays en développement — Total	OPEC / OPEP	Other / Autres	Un-allocated / Non-distribués
Afghanistan	1985	22.1	8.2	13.0	0.5	0.4	46.1	2.3	18.8	0.2	18.6	10.7
Bangladesh	1985	42.9	12.5	12.2	14.1	4.1	3.9	4.1	49.1	10.9	38.2	-
Benin	1985	(66.2)	(38.8)	(5.6)	(14.7)	(7.1)	(2.4)	(1.9)	(28.1)	(4.3)	(23.8)	(1.4)
Bhutan	1984/85	-	-	-	-	-	-	-	87.9	-	87.9	12.1
Botswana	1984	89.3	8.6	0.3	2.2	78.3	-	-	8.9	-	8.9	1.8
Burkina Faso	1984	(55.8)	(39.9)	(3.8)	(11.8)	(0.3)	(0.4)	(3.2)	(39.2)	(2.3)	(36.9)	(1.4)
Burundi	1985	62.0	48.2	6.4	5.7	1.7	0.2	3.1	32.3	15.7	16.6	2.4
Cape Verde	1985	81.3	78.2	-	-	3.1	2.7	-	15.2	2.5	12.7	0.8
Central African Rep.	1985	62.9	56.9	3.0	2.6	0.4	0.2	0.5	20.6	0.2	20.4	15.8
Chad	1985	(50.9)	(37.6)	(0.3)	(12.1)	(0.9)	-	(0.7)	(45.0)	(0.0)	(45.0)	(3.4)
Comoros	1985	58.9	54.6	0.8	3.4	0.1	-	-	40.7	-	40.7	0.4
Democratic Yemen	..	..	..	..	..	..	:	:	..	..	..	..
Djibouti	..	..	..	..	..	..	:	:	..	..	..	..
Equatorial Guinea	1984	81.5	73.8	0.8	0.7	6.2	-	9.3	9.1	0.9	8.2	0.1
Ethiopia	1984	60.1	33.7	6.5	15.3	4.6	26.8	0.4	12.7	0.6	12.1	-
Gambia	1984	64.9	43.5	4.3	14.3	2.8	4.5	7.9	18.6	0.2	18.4	4.1
Guinea	1985	79.0	55.7	1.2	18.9	3.2	1.0	0.3	19.4	0.1	19.3	0.3
Guinea-Bissau	1985	71.6	64.5	0.9	-	6.2	2.5	2.3	21.0	0.0	21.0	2.6
Haiti	1984/85	77.8	12.6	6.5	54.4	4.3	-	-	22.1	-	22.1	0.1
Kiribati	1983	(86.9)	(2.7)	(17.9)	(6.1)	(60.2)	-	-	13.0	-	13.0	0.1
Lao People's Dem.Rep.	1982	32.8	18.2	12.4	0.4	1.8	-	-	66.0	-	66.0	1.2
Lesotho	1982	99.4	0.9	-	-	98.1	-	-	0.6	-	0.6	-
Malawi	1985	38.9	25.8	7.1	2.1	3.9	-	-	59.1	-	59.1	2.0
Maldives	1983	16.2	4.8	11.2	-	0.2	-	0.8	83.1	0.1	83.1	-
Mali	1985	64.9	54.2	1.4	8.1	1.2	0.6	2.6	30.9	0.1	30.8	1.0
Mauritania	1984	82.6	70.4	1.5	9.6	1.1	-	3.4	14.0	0.1	13.9	-
Nepal	1985	22.2	7.0	11.8	1.5	1.9	0.7	5.4	71.7	0.1	71.6	-
Niger	1985	63.3	54.3	3.0	4.1	1.9	0.5	2.1	27.2	13.1	14.1	6.9
Rwanda	1984	55.1	37.5	8.7	7.4	1.5	0.2	9.1	35.6	-	35.6	-
Samoa	1985	72.0	3.5	13.5	3.7	51.3	0.1	1.6	24.3	-	24.3	2.0
Sao Tome & Principe	1985	82.2	78.3	0.8	-	3.1	-	-	17.8	-	17.8	-
Sierra Leone	1985	56.9	45.7	5.2	4.4	1.6	0.7	4.6	30.0	22.7	7.3	7.8
Somalia	1981	72.4	66.0	1.8	4.3	0.3	0.1	1.3	26.2	11.2	15.0	-
Sudan	1983	53.6	38.3	3.2	9.6	2.5	5.1	2.4	36.8	18.8	18.0	2.1
Togo	1984	77.0	63.3	5.3	6.0	2.4	0.9	2.0	18.2	2.4	15.8	1.9
Tuvalu	1983	60.0	2.5	2.1	0.5	54.9	-	0.5	40.0	-	40.0	-
Uganda	1985	(51.4)	(40.0)	(7.2)	(1.9)	(2.3)	-	(0.9)	(47.4)	(2.3)	(45.1)	(0.3)
Un. Rep. of Tanzania	1985	64.9	42.6	9.4	5.4	7.5	1.1	1.6	32.3	15.7	16.6	0.1
Vanuatu	1985	75.7	31.6	11.8	-	32.3	-	1.5	11.8	-	11.8	11.0
Yemen	1985	58.8	39.8	8.5	3.7	6.8	1.1	3.0	32.2	9.9	22.3	4.9
All LDCs / Ensemble des PMA		57.7	31.9	6.7	8.7	10.4	6.1	2.3	31.7	6.7	25.0	2.2
All developing countries b/ / Ensemble des pays en développement b/	1984	56.6	17.3 c/	14.3	18.7	6.3 c/	7.1	3.2	33.2	14.2	19.0	-

Source : United Nations, 1985 International Trade Statistics Yearbook; IMF, Direction of Trade Yearbook 1987 and other international and national sources.

Source : Nations Unies, Annuaire Statistique du Commerce International 1985; FMI, Direction of Trade Yearbook 1987 et autres sources internationales et nationales.

a/ Including EFTA.
b/ Excluding OPEC countries.
c/ Spain and Portugal are included with "other" developed market economy countries.

a/ Y compris l'AELE.
b/ Non compris les pays de l'OPEP.
c/ L'Espagne et le Portugal sont compris avec les "autres" pays développés à économie de marché.

Table 17
External assistance (net disbursements), exports
and imports, 1984

$ million

| | Technical assistance DAC | Concessional assistance a/ / Aide concessionnelle a/ | | |
| | | All sources | of which/dont: | |
Country	Assistance technique CAD	Toutes provenances	DAC b/ CAD b/	OPEC c/ OPEP c/
Afghanistan	12.4	236.1	7.5	-0.7
Bangladesh	157.7	1237.2	1174.7	26.5
Benin	28.1	79.0	77.3	0.3
Bhutan	8.8	17.9	17.6	0.3
Botswana	34.8	102.6	91.8	10.8
Burkina Faso	71.4	178.2	178.6	-0.6
Burundi	42.7	137.6	128.3	9.3
Cape Verde	17.0	68.6	59.9	3.8
Central African Rep.	38.5	114.5	111.7	2.1
Chad	18.8	114.9	114.6	0.3
Comoros	9.4	41.4	33.9	5.9
Democratic Yemen	9.9	192.6	46.2	51.1
Djibouti	29.8	115.7	59.0	48.0
Equatorial Guinea	6.7	15.1	15.1	-0.0
Ethiopia	80.9	525.2	363.1	-0.2
Gambia	14.8	52.8	51.5	1.3
Guinea	17.9	130.7	88.8	34.4
Guinea-Bissau	11.8	62.0	52.9	3.3
Haiti	33.0	134.8	134.4	0.4
Kiribati	3.7	11.9	11.9	-
Lao People's Dem.Rep.	12.3	103.1	33.0	1.1
Lesotho	34.0	101.1	95.4	5.0
Malawi	39.7	158.5	158.6	-0.1
Maldives	3.6	7.3	6.5	0.8
Mali	59.9	341.3	310.1	15.0
Mauritania	31.3	207.3	109.5	96.7
Nepal	68.4	198.2	199.1	-0.9
Niger	61.1	165.6	155.5	10.1
Rwanda	50.1	164.6	158.7	5.9
Samoa	6.9	20.2	20.2	0.0
Sao Tome and Principe	2.3	12.3	10.9	0.4
Sierra Leone	19.4	63.5	44.5	17.1
Somalia	107.4	408.9	333.8	75.1
Sudan	121.8	702.4	500.3	170.3
Togo	29.9	109.8	106.4	3.4
Tuvalu	1.4	5.5	5.5	-
Uganda	32.4	164.4	165.3	-1.4
Un. Rep. of Tanzania	138.7	563.3	543.2	17.6
Vanuatu	13.1	24.5	24.5	-
Yemen	61.5	341.5	135.4	183.5
All LDCs	1543.3	7434.8	5935.2	798.3
All developing countries e/	7182.5	28720.1	23643.9	2719.8

Source: UNCTAD secretariat estimates mainly based on
data from the OECD/DAC secretariat, the World Bank,
and UNCTAD Handbook of International Trade and
Development Statistics, Supplement 1987.

a/ Including technical assistance.

b/ Including multilateral agencies mainly financed by
DAC member countries.

c/ Including multilateral agencies mainly financed by
OPEC member countries.

d/ Including private flows from DAC member countries.

e/ Excluding major petroleum exporters.

Tableau 17
Aide extérieure (versements nets), exportations
et importations, 1984

Millions de dollars

Non-concessional assistance from all sources d/ Aide non-concessionnelle de toutes provenancesd/	Exports Exporta-tions (f.o.b.)	Imports Importa-tions (c.i.f.)	Concessional assistance from all sources as % of imports Aide concessionnelle de toutes prove-nances en % des importations	Pays
-1.0	633	1156	20.4	Afghanistan
59.2	934	2042	60.6	Bangladesh
91.2	33	310	25.5	Bénin
-	..	..	..	Bhoutan
78.4	674	679	15.1	Botswana
0.6	79	207	86.1	Burkina Faso
15.1	98	186	74.0	Burundi
0.7	5	84	81.7	Cap-Vert
1.4	86	87	131.6	Rép. centrafricaine
-2.0	110	171	67.2	Tchad
1.8	21	30	138.2	Comores
-3.9	645	1543	12.5	Yémen démocratique
28.6	26	110	105.2	Djibouti
2.8	20	30	50.3	Guineé équatoriale
53.8	417	942	55.8	Ethiopie
7.6	47	98	53.9	Gambie
5.4	430	360	36.3	Guinée
6.8	18	48	129.2	Guinée-Bissau
0.2	179	472	28.6	Haïti
-0.5	11	14	85.3	Kiribati
1.1	12	145	71.1	Rép. dém. pop. lao
-4.5	21	312	32.4	Lesotho
2.2	313	269	58.9	Malawi
-0.1	25	53	13.8	Maldives
-6.3	195	375	91.0	Mali
6.5	297	246	84.3	Mauritanie
3.2	128	416	47.6	Népal
-22.0	228	330	50.2	Niger
-2.6	145	295	55.8	Rwanda
-6.6	19	50	40.4	Samoa
-	7	12	102.5	Sao Tomé-et-Principe
11.7	148	166	38.3	Sierra Leone
12.5	45	109	375.1	Somalie
71.9	629	1147	61.2	Soudan
5.9	197	278	39.5	Togo
-	..	..	..	Tuvalu
2.0	399	371	44.3	Ouganda
48.1	378	889	63.4	Rép.-Unie de Tanzanie
20.9	44	69	35.5	Vanuatu
0.1	65	1655	20.6	Yémen
490.1	7761	15756	47.2	Ensemble des PMA
33136.9	269468	301838	9.5	Ensemble des pays en développement e/

Source: Estimations du secrétariat de la CNUCED principalement d'après
des données du secrétariat de l'OCDE/CAD , de la Banque mondiale, et
du Manuel de statistiques du Commerce International et
du Développement, Supplément 1987, de la CNUCED.

a/ Y compris l'assistance technique.

b/ Y compris les institutions multilatérales essentiellement
financées par les pays membres du CAD.

c/ Y compris les institutions multilatérales essentiellement
financées par les pays membres de l'OPEP.

d/ Y compris les apports privés en provenance des pays membres du CAD.

e/ Non compris les principaux pays exportateurs de pétrole.

Table 17 (continued)
External assistance (net disbursements), exports
and imports, 1985

$ million

Country	Technical assistance DAC	Concessional assistance a/ Aide concessionnelle a/		
		All sources	of which/dont:	
	Assistance technique CAD	Toutes provenances	DAC b/ CAD b/	OPEC c/ OPEP c/
Afghanistan	15.4	257.7	18.3	-0.7
Bangladesh	165.1	1162.4	1139.7	9.9
Benin	29.9	95.7	91.7	4.0
Bhutan	10.3	24.2	21.3	2.9
Botswana	33.9	99.8	92.3	5.0
Burkina Faso	67.3	207.4	190.7	16.7
Burundi	45.1	139.9	135.6	4.1
Cape Verde	19.1	73.5	63.8	5.7
Central African Rep.	33.9	109.2	103.1	1.7
Chad	42.4	182.0	180.8	0.9
Comoros	10.6	47.5	38.5	8.5
Democratic Yemen	12.5	348.3	48.3	63.8
Djibouti	29.5	77.7	62.4	15.3
Equatorial Guinea	6.0	20.4	17.4	-0.2
Ethiopia	103.7	884.1	706.0	-0.2
Gambia	17.3	49.0	49.1	-0.1
Guinea	18.9	135.8	112.0	7.8
Guinea-Bissau	14.7	65.0	54.8	2.9
Haiti	39.7	152.6	151.7	0.9
Kiribati	4.8	12.1	12.1	-
Lao People's Dem.Rep.	13.8	126.9	36.9	0.0
Lesotho	29.5	94.5	89.0	5.1
Malawi	33.4	113.0	113.1	-0.1
Maldives	4.9	10.1	10.4	-0.3
Mali	59.2	389.0	349.0	27.2
Mauritania	35.8	198.0	142.9	54.9
Nepal	68.3	237.1	237.9	-0.8
Niger	73.0	316.8	303.5	0.2
Rwanda	58.4	181.5	175.9	5.6
Samoa	7.6	19.2	19.2	-0.0
Sao Tome and Principe	3.1	12.8	12.2	0.3
Sierra Leone	21.6	75.1	61.0	4.6
Somalia	131.5	361.1	315.3	32.1
Sudan	203.0	1020.2	913.4	106.8
Togo	28.9	113.8	104.5	9.3
Tuvalu	1.5	3.4	3.4	-
Uganda	36.6	185.8	182.7	0.9
Un. Rep. of Tanzania	135.6	506.3	477.6	9.4
Vanuatu	11.7	21.8	21.8	-
Yemen	56.4	298.1	136.3	154.9
All LDCs	1733.9	8431.1	6995.6	561.0
All developing countries e/	7373.6	30651.9	25512.6	2590.6

For sources and notes, see table 17, p. A-40.

Tableau 17 (suite)
Aide extérieure (versements nets), exportations
et importations, 1985

Millions de dollars

Non-concessional assistance from all sources d/ Aide non-con-cessionnelle de toutes provenancesd/	Exports Exporta-tions (f.o.b.)	Imports Importa-tions (c.i.f.)	Concessional assistance from all sources as % of imports Aide concessionnelle de toutes prove-nances en % des importations	Pays
-22.6	557	999	25.8	Afghanistan
-48.9	927	2170	53.6	Bangladesh
79.7	40	400	23.9	Bénin
-	..	..	..	Bhoutan
61.8	727	596	16.7	Botswana
-1.9	66	225	92.2	Burkina Faso
17.9	110	186	75.2	Burundi
0.9	5	113	65.1	Cap-Vert
7.6	88	109	100.2	Rép. centrafricaine
0.7	80	190	95.8	Tchad
3.2	25	30	158.4	Comores
2.3	690	1290	27.0	Yémen démocratique
21.7	26	110	70.6	Djibouti
0.4	20	30	67.9	Guineé équatoriale
69.0	333	996	88.8	Ethiopie
9.4	43	93	52.7	Gambie
4.8	430	420	32.3	Guinée
5.4	14	60	108.3	Guinée-Bissau
-7.9	174	470	32.5	Haïti
-0.1	5	13	93.1	Kiribati
27.1	29	160	79.3	Rép. dém. pop. lao
25.2	21	250	37.8	Lesotho
-1.5	252	284	·39.8	Malawi
-0.1	32	53	19.1	Maldives
1.7	170	410	94.9	Mali
17.2	374	234	84.6	Mauritanie
10.0	161	460	51.5	Népal
-15.6	223	400	79.2	Niger
4.5	112	343	52.9	Rwanda
0.9	15	51	37.6	Samoa
-	5	13	98.5	Sao Tomé-et-Principe
1.2	112	156	48.2	Sierra Leone
17.7	91	112	322.4	Somalie
2.8	367	757	134.8	Soudan
-16.4	190	264	43.1	Togo
-	..	..	..	Tuvalu
43.6	380	375	49.6	Ouganda
44.4	284	1026	49.3	Rép.-Unie de Tanzanie
16.8	31	71	30.7	Vanuatu
-2.8	106	1598	18.7	Yémen
380.0	7314	15517	54.3	Ensemble des PMA
13474.5	267910	290496	10.6	Ensemble des pays en développement e/

Pour les sources et les notes, se reporter au tableau 17, p. A-41.

Table 18
External assistance (net disbursements), exports
and imports per capita, 1984

$

| | Technical assistance | Concessional assistance a/ Aide concessionnelle a/ | | |
| | | All sources | of which/dont: | |
Country	Assistance technique	Toutes provenances	DAC b/ CAD b/	OPEC c/ OPEP c/
Afghanistan	0.7	13.4	0.4	-0.0
Bangladesh	1.6	12.8	12.1	0.3
Benin	7.2	20.1	19.7	0.1
Bhutan	6.3	12.9	12.7	0.2
Botswana	32.6	96.0	85.9	10.1
Burkina Faso	10.5	26.3	26.3	-0.1
Burundi	9.3	29.9	27.9	2.0
Cape Verde	52.2	210.6	183.8	11.7
Central African Rep.	15.1	45.0	43.9	0.8
Chad	3.8	23.4	23.3	0.1
Comoros	21.7	95.9	78.4	13.6
Democratic Yemen	4.4	86.6	20.8	23.0
Djibouti	84.2	326.9	166.7	135.6
Equatorial Guinea	17.4	39.3	39.3	-0.0
Ethiopia	1.9	12.5	8.6	-0.0
Gambia	20.6	73.5	71.7	1.8
Guinea	3.0	22.0	14.9	5.8
Guinea-Bissau	13.5	71.0	60.6	3.8
Haiti	6.3	25.9	25.9	0.1
Kiribati	58.4	188.5	188.5	-
Lao People's Dem.Rep.	3.5	29.1	9.3	0.3
Lesotho	22.7	67.5	63.7	3.3
Malawi	5.9	23.5	23.5	-0.0
Maldives	20.4	41.4	36.9	4.5
Mali	7.6	43.4	39.4	1.9
Mauritania	17.0	112.9	59.6	52.6
Nepal	4.2	12.2	12.3	-0.1
Niger	10.3	27.8	26.1	1.7
Rwanda	8.6	28.2	27.2	1.0
Samoa	42.8	125.4	125.4	0.0
Sao Tome and Principe	21.9	117.1	103.8	3.8
Sierra Leone	5.5	17.9	12.6	4.8
Somalia	20.5	78.1	63.8	14.3
Sudan	5.8	33.5	23.9	8.1
Togo	10.4	38.1	37.0	1.2
Tuvalu	172.8	665.8	665.8	-
Uganda	2.2	11.0	11.0	-0.1
Un. Rep. of Tanzania	6.5	26.2	25.3	0.8
Vanuatu	102.6	191.8	191.8	-
Yemen	7.9	44.0	17.4	23.6
All LDCs	4.7	22.9	18.2	2.5
All developing countries e/	3.6	14.4	11.9	1.4

For sources and notes, see table 17, p. A-40.

Tableau 18
Aide extérieure (versements nets), exportations
et importations par habitant, 1984

Dollars

Non-concessional assistance from all sources d/ Aide non-concessionnelle de toutes provenancesd/	Exports Exporta-tions (f.o.b.)	Imports Importa-tions (c.i.f.)	Pays
-0.1	35.8	65.4	Afghanistan
0.6	9.7	21.1	Bangladesh
23.3	8.4	79.1	Bénin
-	..	..	Bhoutan
73.3	630.5	635.2	Botswana
0.1	11.6	30.5	Burkina Faso
3.3	21.3	40.5	Burundi
2.1	15.3	257.7	Cap-Vert
0.5	33.8	34.2	Rép. centrafricaine
-0.4	22.4	34.8	Tchad
4.2	48.6	69.4	Comores
-1.8	289.9	693.5	Yémen démocratique
80.8	73.4	310.7	Djibouti
7.3	52.1	78.1	Guineé équatoriale
1.3	9.9	22.3	Ethiopie
10.6	65.5	136.5	Gambie
0.9	72.4	60.6	Guinée
7.8	20.6	55.0	Guinée-Bissau
0.0	34.4	90.8	Haïti
-7.9	168.9	221.0	Kiribati
0.3	3.4	40.9	Rép. dém. pop. lao
-3.0	14.0	208.3	Lesotho
0.3	46.4	39.9	Malawi
-0.6	141.8	300.7	Maldives
-0.8	24.8	47.6	Mali
3.5	161.7	133.9	Mauritanie
0.2	7.9	25.7	Népal
-3.7	38.3	55.4	Niger
-0.4	24.8	50.5	Rwanda
-41.0	117.9	310.4	Samoa
-	66.7	114.3	Sao Tomé-et-Principe
3.3	41.8	46.9	Sierra Leone
2.4	8.6	20.8	Somalie
3.4	30.0	54.7	Soudan
2.0	68.4	96.6	Togo
-	..	..	Tuvalu
0.1	26.7	24.8	Ouganda
2.2	17.6	41.4	Rép.-Unie de Tanzanie
163.6	344.5	540.2	Vanuatu
0.0	8.4	213.2	Yémen
1.5	23.9	48.7	Ensemble des PMA
16.7	135.4	151.7	Ensemble des pays en développement e/

Pour les sources et les notes, se reportér au tableau 17, p. A-41.

Table 18 (continued)
External assistance (net disbursements), exports
and imports per capita, 1985

$

| Country | Technical assistance | Concessional assistance a/ Aide concessionnelle a/ | | |
| | | All sources | of which/dont: | |
	Assistance technique	Toutes provenances	DAC b/ CAD b/	OPEC c/ OPEP c/
Afghanistan	0.8	14.2	1.0	-0.0
Bangladesh	1.7	11.8	11.6	0.1
Benin	7.4	23.7	22.7	1.0
Bhutan	7.3	17.1	15.0	2.0
Botswana	30.6	90.2	83.4	4.5
Burkina Faso	9.7	29.9	27.5	2.4
Burundi	9.6	29.6	28.7	0.9
Cape Verde	57.2	220.1	191.0	17.1
Central African Rep.	13.0	41.9	39.5	0.7
Chad	8.4	36.3	36.0	0.2
Comoros	23.9	107.0	86.7	19.1
Democratic Yemen	5.4	151.8	21.1	27.8
Djibouti	81.0	213.5	171.4	42.0
Equatorial Guinea	15.3	52.0	44.4	-0.5
Ethiopia	2.4	20.4	16.3	-0.0
Gambia	23.5	66.5	66.6	-0.1
Guinea	3.1	22.4	18.4	1.3
Guinea-Bissau	16.5	73.1	61.6	3.3
Haiti	7.5	28.9	28.8	0.2
Kiribati	74.3	187.2	187.2	-
Lao People's Dem.Rep.	3.8	35.1	10.2	0.0
Lesotho	19.2	61.5	57.9	3.3
Malawi	4.8	16.3	16.3	-0.0
Maldives	27.0	55.6	57.3	-1.7
Mali	7.3	48.1	43.2	3.4
Mauritania	19.0	104.9	75.7	29.1
Nepal	4.1	14.3	14.3	-0.1
Niger	11.9	51.8	49.6	0.0
Rwanda	9.7	30.1	29.2	0.9
Samoa	46.6	117.8	117.8	-0.0
Sao Tome and Principe	28.7	118.5	113.0	2.8
Sierra Leone	6.0	20.9	16.9	1.3
Somalia	24.4	67.1	58.6	6.0
Sudan	9.4	47.3	42.4	5.0
Togo	9.8	38.4	35.3	3.1
Tuvalu	182.3	413.2	413.2	-
Uganda	2.4	12.0	11.8	0.1
Un. Rep. of Tanzania	6.1	22.8	21.5	0.4
Vanuatu	89.1	166.0	166.0	-
Yemen	7.1	37.5	17.1	19.5
All LDCs	5.2	25.3	21.0	1.7
All developing countries e/	3.6	15.1	12.6	1.3

For sources and notes, see table 17, p. A-40.

Tableau 18 (suite)
Aide extérieure (versements nets), exportations
et importations par habitant, 1985

Dollars

Non-concessional assistance from all sources d/ Aide non-con-cessionnelle de toutes provenancesd/	Exports Exporta-tions (f.o.b.)	Imports Importa-tions (c.i.f.)	Pays
-1.2	30.7	55.1	Afghanistan
-0.5	9.4	22.0	Bangladesh
19.7	9.9	98.9	Bénin
-	..	..	Bhoutan
55.8	656.7	538.4	Botswana
-0.3	9.5	32.4	Burkina Faso
3.8	23.3	39.4	Burundi
2.7	15.0	338.3	Cap-Vert
2.9	33.7	41.8	Rép. centrafricaine
0.1	15.9	37.9	Tchad
7.2	56.3	67.6	Comores
1.0	300.8	562.3	Yémen démocratique
59.6	71.4	302.2	Djibouti
1.0	51.0	76.5	Guineé équatoriale
1.6	7.7	23.0	Ethiopie
12.8	58.3	126.2	Gambie
0.8	70.8	69.1	Guinée
6.1	15.7	67.5	Guinée-Bissau
-1.5	33.0	89.1	Haïti
-1.5	69.6	201.1	Kiribati
7.5	8.0	44.2	Rép. dém. pop. lao
16.4	13.7	162.6	Lesotho
-0.2	36.3	40.9	Malawi
-0.6	176.2	291.8	Maldives
0.2	21.0	50.7	Mali
9.1	198.1	123.9	Mauritanie
0.6	9.7	27.7	Népal
-2.6	36.5	65.4	Niger
0.7	18.6	56.9	Rwanda
5.5	92.0	312.9	Samoa
-	46.3	120.4	Sao Tomé-et-Principe
0.3	31.1	43.3	Sierra Leone
3.3	16.9	20.8	Somalie
0.1	17.0	35.1	Soudan
-5.5	64.2	89.2	Togo
-	..	..	Tuvalu
2.8	24.6	24.2	Ouganda
2.0	12.8	46.1	Rép.-Unie de Tanzanie
128.0	236.1	540.8	Vanuatu
-0.4	13.3	200.9	Yémen
1.1	22.0	46.7	Ensemble des PMA
6.6	131.8	142.9	Ensemble des pays en développement e/

Pour les sources et les notes, se reporter au tableau 17, p. A-41.

Table 19 / Tableau 19

Foreign exchange receipts and import volume expressed in constant 1980 dollars a/ per capita

Rentrées de devises et volume des importations, en dollars constants de 1980 a/ par habitant

A. Export purchasing power per capita

A. Pouvoir d'achat des exportations, par habitant

Country	1975	1976	1977	1978	1979	1980	1981	1982	1983	1984	1985	Pays
Afghanistan	27.5	35.5	33.1	29.8	36.5	42.0	45.4	47.1	48.7	41.2	35.0	Afghanistan
Bangladesh	6.4	9.0	8.3	9.0	8.7	8.3	7.8	8.0	8.2	10.9	10.7	Bangladesh
Benin	18.1	12.6	19.9	11.4	15.9	18.2	10.0	7.1	9.5	9.7	11.4	Bénin
Bhutan												Bhoutan
Botswana	319.8	377.8	339.0	360.4	572.8	549.7	416.2	500.5	692.5	716.5	743.2	Botswana
Burkina Faso	13.5	16.1	14.6	10.0	14.6	14.6	12.5	9.5	9.7	13.3	10.8	Burkina Faso
Burundi	14.5	24.3	35.3	24.1	29.9	15.9	17.6	22.0	20.1	24.2	26.4	Burundi
Cape Verde	12.0	11.8	16.1	9.5		13.5	10.4	14.0	17.6	17.4	16.9	Cap-Vert
Central African Rep.	38.1	44.6	56.1	42.6	38.8	49.7	35.5	49.4	34.0	38.3	37.8	Rép. centrafricaine
Chad	21.0	24.8	40.1	32.6	23.1	15.8	19.0	13.4	17.3	25.2	17.7	Tchad
Comoros	52.8	45.5	40.2	34.8	53.4	52.5	42.6	53.5	53.3	55.2	63.7	Comores
Democratic Yemen	173.0	171.6	155.3	143.9	283.6	395.6	313.7	412.7	350.3	329.4	340.4	Yémen démocratique
Djibouti	286.0	262.2	232.6	91.1	43.5	61.3	68.0	64.9	81.7	83.5	80.8	Djibouti
Equatorial Guinea	138.6	52.0	65.0	69.3	97.5	39.8	46.6	50.2	59.7	59.2	57.7	Guinée équatoriale
Ethiopia	13.0	15.2	16.2	12.6	13.6	11.3	10.2	10.5	10.7	11.0	8.5	Ethiopie
Gambia	153.5	107.1	129.1	90.0	108.5	48.0	43.8	72.7	79.6	77.5	69.0	Gambie
Guinea	50.1	73.9	78.4	78.3	69.4	72.1	92.8	78.5	77.2	82.2	80.1	Guinée
Guinea-Bissau	19.0	12.7	22.0	18.8	21.0	13.6	17.8	15.5	30.1	23.4	17.8	Guinée-Bissau
Haiti	30.1	45.5	46.8	46.0	35.4	46.0	31.8	35.0	33.7	39.1	37.3	Haïti
Kiribati	6.1	6.5	4.9	5.2	12.6	9.5	68.6	12.8	8.4	3.8	9.1	Kiribati
Lao People's Dem.Rep.	18.6	23.6	17.3	34.5	39.7	42.9	10.4	26.7	14.6	15.9	15.5	Rép. dém. pop. lao
Lesotho	46.2	52.8	56.4	45.2	44.0	47.9	37.8					Lesotho
Malawi	50.6	48.8	54.0	37.5	45.9	64.0	45.6	41.1	38.5	51.7	40.1	Malawi
Maldives							71.7	91.6	124.6	161.2	199.4	Maldives
Mali	14.9	22.6	29.6	23.4	24.6	29.2	22.4	21.2	24.2	28.1	23.6	Mali
Mauritania	208.6	206.7	161.7	109.9	108.3	118.9	165.1	148.6	195.9	189.4	232.9	Mauritanie
Nepal	13.1	11.2	11.8	8.7	8.8	5.5	9.8	6.2	6.7	9.0	11.0	Népal
Niger	34.2	48.1	50.9	80.0	100.3	106.6	85.9	62.9	57.3	43.0	40.7	Niger
Rwanda	16.4	30.1	30.8	20.0	27.0	21.8	22.0	20.8	24.1	28.0	20.9	Rwanda
Samoa	78.9	77.9	151.5	98.9	135.1	109.3	73.8	89.6	133.6	134.0	104.1	Samoa
Sao Tome and Principe	137.4	151.2	392.0	316.7	275.3	213.2	152.1	98.6	65.9	75.8	52.4	Sao Tomé-et-Principe
Sierra Leone	69.8	57.4	61.3	71.9	75.4	61.9	48.1	28.7	30.2	48.8	36.3	Sierra Leone
Somalia	36.3	37.6	22.2	32.8	28.3	28.5	34.1	45.5	23.2	10.0	19.7	Somalie
Sudan	45.2	55.1	58.2	40.2	33.5	29.1	36.0	27.7	34.8	34.9	19.8	Soudan
Togo	94.5	76.1	102.5	134.5	100.3	131.2	83.0	69.7	64.7	78.0	73.1	Togo
Tuvalu												Tuvalu
Uganda	39.3	50.5	70.6	37.3	38.0	26.3	18.8	26.5	28.3	29.6	26.9	Ouganda
Un. Rep. of Tanzania	40.2	50.8	49.9	37.8	33.1	27.1	32.3	23.8	19.3	19.6	14.2	Rép.-Un. de Tanzanie
Vanuatu	172.1	249.0	529.7	537.5	490.0	306.0	285.6	206.8	261.8	391.5	267.2	Vanuatu
Yemen	3.1	2.2	2.6	1.5	2.4	3.3	6.8	5.7	4.0	9.5	15.1	Yémen
All LDCs	24.6	29.3	31.0	26.5	27.9	27.2	26.0	25.2	25.7	27.2	24.9	Ensemble des PMA
All developing countries b/	100.2	117.1	123.2	123.9	126.6	126.7	133.5	128.7	135.3	151.2	147.5	Ensemble des pays en développement b/

For source and notes, see end of table.

Pour la source et les notes, se reporter à la fin du tableau.

Table 19 (continued)
Foreign exchange receipts and import volume expressed in constant 1980 dollars a/ per capita

Tableau 19 (suite)
Rentrées de devises et volume des importations, en dollars constants de 1980 a/ par habitant

B. External assistance per capita c/
B. Aide extérieure, par habitant c/

Country	1975	1976	1977	1978	1979	1980	1981	1982	1983	1984	1985	Pays
Afghanistan	13.0	14.2	13.3	12.6	12.4	21.0	19.0	11.9	24.2	15.3	14.8	Afghanistan
Bangladesh	24.3	11.9	12.1	16.7	16.0	14.1	12.8	16.8	14.5	15.2	12.8	Bangladesh
Benin	33.8	29.4	31.6	32.6	34.3	113.5	35.1	58.3	33.2	50.1	49.9	Bénin
Bhutan	3.1	4.6	3.7	3.6	5.5	6.5	7.9	9.2	10.6	14.7	19.3	Bhoutan
Botswana	193.7	116.1	75.1	34.6	184.3	58.4	121.8	129.7	141.4	192.4	165.2	Botswana
Burkina Faso	27.5	26.0	30.4	37.8	41.8	38.1	37.0	42.8	33.4	30.1	33.6	Burkina Faso
Burundi	24.0	20.6	24.3	26.3	30.0	32.3	34.0	40.3	46.5	37.8	37.8	Burundi
Cape Verde	51.7	151.2	142.4	167.6	135.8	211.4	180.9	227.1	242.1	241.7	252.2	Cap-Vert
Central African Rep.	46.1	31.5	29.7	30.3	42.2	55.0	46.8	46.4	45.9	51.6	50.2	Rép. centrafricaine
Chad	36.0	26.8	33.5	45.6	22.2	7.5	12.3	13.8	21.9	25.8	40.4	Tchad
Comoros	105.6	129.5	144.8	49.1	54.0	112.3	133.5	98.8	114.9	113.7	129.3	Comores
Democratic Yemen	84.6	213.4	118.1	75.7	68.6	129.9	77.4	118.6	96.2	96.4	173.0	Yémen démocratique
Djibouti	266.9	206.8	334.8	483.3	86.7	229.4	212.8	190.7	223.0	463.3	309.1	Djibouti
Equatorial Guinea	2.1	-7.3	-13.8	5.4	6.4	28.4	33.8	36.1	36.1	53.0	60.0	Guinée équatoriale
Ethiopia	7.3	-7.5	-5.5	5.9	8.0	7.2	9.1	9.5	11.0	15.2	24.3	Ethiopie
Gambia	26.2	34.6	71.8	90.0	85.7	133.7	138.7	75.9	63.0	99.5	93.7	Gambie
Guinea	12.1	7.2	13.9	24.8	15.2	28.4	23.6	15.7	15.9	26.0	26.2	Guinée
Guinea-Bissau	53.9	74.0	89.0	102.3	86.7	111.2	92.8	83.1	87.8	89.6	89.6	Guinée-Bissau
Haiti	22.2	26.6	28.8	26.9	30.3	24.0	23.9	28.0	27.6	29.5	31.1	Haïti
Kiribati	182.4	127.0	176.0	261.0	184.7	327.7	405.6	271.3	301.6	205.2	210.1	Kiribati
Lao People's Dem.Rep.	27.1	30.1	28.9	48.7	34.0	26.8	28.9	42.5	40.3	33.4	48.2	Rép. dém. pop. lao
Lesotho	43.5	41.9	48.7	57.1	56.5	69.7	81.3	74.3	84.2	73.2	88.1	Lesotho
Malawi	29.6	25.1	32.2	29.8	41.3	31.6	32.4	22.4	17.7	26.6	17.7	Malawi
Maldives	68.3	67.0	54.0	91.1	52.0	145.9	112.0	13.7	62.3	46.4	62.3	Maldives
Mali	40.0	24.9	29.9	38.1	37.2	38.3	36.6	30.9	32.7	48.3	54.3	Mali
Mauritania	59.4	240.8	127.9	187.9	124.7	89.7	132.0	137.2	144.4	136.4	134.0	Mauritanie
Nepal	6.0	6.3	13.1	7.7	11.4	11.0	12.6	14.3	14.1	14.1	16.8	Népal
Niger	57.0	59.9	44.2	62.1	59.5	47.4	70.1	55.5	40.4	27.1	55.0	Niger
Rwanda	35.6	32.4	32.3	35.8	36.9	30.3	30.8	31.0	32.7	31.3	34.7	Rwanda
Samoa	154.7	130.2	246.6	209.5	250.6	160.8	165.9	164.1	219.4	95.9	139.6	Samoa
Sao Tome and Principe	17.7	221.1	75.0	133.8	37.5	41.6	66.3	108.4	138.3	133.1	134.1	Sao Tomé-et-Principe
Sierra Leone	15.6	21.6	22.7	23.7	22.9	28.1	21.0	29.7	22.4	24.8	24.7	Sierra Leone
Somalia	79.9	50.1	146.2	72.9	65.8	113.5	83.5	141.6	71.9	93.5	82.1	Somalie
Sudan	58.1	40.2	35.3	37.0	40.8	44.8	38.2	43.8	64.4	43.0	55.3	Soudan
Togo	41.9	51.6	77.7	150.3	97.4	70.8	19.7	37.8	43.9	45.8	37.5	Togo
Tuvalu	12.1	697.5	505.8	533.4	628.8	634.9	712.6	794.2	575.8	756.6	467.6	Tuvalu
Uganda	8.9	6.5	4.0	-14.7	3.4	10.4	11.9	13.1	11.4	12.3	16.2	Ouganda
Un. Rep. of Tanzania	46.5	35.7	40.0	40.9	47.5	44.7	44.3	39.2	30.8	31.8	27.6	Rép.-Un. de Tanzanie
Vanuatu	283.9	682.4	244.3	303.3	450.4	369.9	263.3	289.5	312.3	403.9	332.7	Vanuatu
Yemen	56.2	71.4	86.5	66.7	59.4	77.2	61.8	74.9	70.6	50.0	42.0	Yémen
All LDCs	28.4	24.0	25.3	26.2	26.6	28.5	26.1	28.6	27.8	27.7	29.9	Ensemble des PMA
All developing countries b/	43.3	42.4	37.1	45.7	43.1	37.0	41.6	37.9	32.8	34.7	24.3	Ensemble des pays en développement b/

For source and notes, see end of table.

Pour la source et les notes, se reporter à la fin du tableau.

Table 19 (continued)
Foreign exchange receipts and import volume expressed in
constant 1980 dollars a/ per capita

Tableau 19 (suite)
Rentrées de devises et volume des importations, en dollars
constants de 1980 a/ par habitant

C. Total receipts d/, per capita
C. Total des rentrées de devises d/, par habitant

Country	1975	1976	1977	1978	1979	1980	1981	1982	1983	1984	1985	Pays
Afghanistan	40.5	49.7	46.4	42.4	48.9	63.0	64.4	58.9	72.9	56.5	49.8	Afghanistan
Bangladesh	30.7	20.8	20.5	25.7	24.7	22.5	20.6	24.7	22.7	26.1	23.5	Bangladesh
Benin	51.9	42.0	51.5	43.9	50.2	131.7	45.1	65.4	42.7	59.8	61.2	Bénin
Bhutan												Bhoutan
Botswana	513.4	494.0	414.1	395.0	757.1	608.1	537.9	630.2	833.9	908.9	908.5	Botswana
Burkina Faso	41.0	42.2	45.0	47.8	56.4	52.7	49.6	52.2	43.1	43.4	44.4	Burkina Faso
Burundi	38.5	45.0	59.6	50.4	59.9	48.1	51.7	62.3	66.5	62.0	64.2	Burundi
Cape Verde	63.7	163.0	158.5	177.1	143.7	224.9	191.3	241.1	259.7	259.2	269.1	Cap-Vert
Central African Rep.	84.2	76.1	85.9	72.9	80.9	104.7	82.3	95.7	79.9	89.8	88.1	Rép. centrafricaine
Chad	56.9	51.6	73.6	78.2	45.3	23.3	31.3	27.2	39.2	51.0	58.1	Tchad
Comoros	158.4	175.0	185.1	84.0	107.5	164.8	176.2	152.3	168.1	168.9	193.0	Comores
Democratic Yemen	257.6	385.0	273.5	219.6	352.2	525.5	391.1	531.3	446.5	425.8	513.4	Yémen démocratique
Djibouti	552.9	469.0	567.3	574.4	130.2	290.6	280.8	255.6	304.3	546.7	389.9	Djibouti
Equatorial Guinea	140.7	44.7	51.6	74.7	103.9	68.2	80.4	86.3	95.7	112.2	117.7	Guinée équatoriale
Ethiopia	20.3	22.6	21.7	18.4	21.6	18.4	19.2	20.0	21.7	26.2	32.8	Ethiopie
Gambia	179.8	141.8	200.9	180.0	194.2	181.6	182.4	148.6	142.7	177.0	162.7	Gambie
Guinea	62.2	81.0	92.3	103.2	84.7	100.6	116.3	94.2	93.1	108.3	106.3	Guinée
Guinea-Bissau	72.8	86.7	111.1	121.0	107.7	124.8	110.6	98.6	117.9	113.0	107.4	Guinée-Bissau
Haiti	52.2	72.0	75.6	72.9	65.7	70.0	55.7	63.1	61.3	68.6	68.4	Haïti
Kiribati		36.7	33.8	53.9	46.6	373.8	474.2	308.7	361.2	397.1	288.9	Kiribati
Lao People's Dem.Rep.	62.2	65.5	66.0	91.6	96.1	36.3	39.3	55.2	48.7	37.3	57.2	Rép. dém. pop. lao
Lesotho	75.7	77.9	88.6	75.0	85.3	112.7	119.1	101.0	98.8	89.2	103.6	Lesotho
Malawi	118.9	115.8	108.0	128.6	97.9	79.5	78.1	63.6	56.2	78.3	57.8	Malawi
Maldives						209.8	183.7	105.4	186.9	207.6	261.7	Maldives
Mali	54.9	47.6	59.5	61.6	61.8	67.5	59.0	52.2	57.0	76.4	77.9	Mali
Mauritania	268.0	447.5	289.6	297.8	233.0	208.7	297.0	285.8	340.3	325.7	366.9	Mauritanie
Nepal	19.1	17.5	24.9	16.4	20.2	16.5	22.4	20.5	20.8	23.1	27.8	Népal
Niger	91.2	108.0	95.0	142.1	159.8	154.0	156.1	118.4	97.7	70.0	95.8	Niger
Rwanda	52.1	62.5	63.1	55.9	64.0	52.1	52.8	51.8	56.8	59.2	55.6	Rwanda
Samoa	233.6	208.1	397.8	308.4	385.7	270.1	239.6	253.6	353.0	230.0	243.7	Samoa
Sao Tome and Principe	155.1	372.3	466.9	450.5	312.8	254.8	218.3	207.0	204.2	208.9	186.5	Sao Tomé-et-Principe
Sierra Leone	85.4	79.0	84.0	95.6	98.3	90.0	69.1	58.4	52.6	73.6	61.0	Sierra Leone
Somalia	116.3	87.7	168.4	105.7	94.1	141.9	117.6	187.1	95.1	103.5	101.8	Somalie
Sudan	103.4	95.3	93.5	77.2	74.3	73.8	74.3	71.5	99.2	77.9	75.2	Soudan
Togo	136.4	127.7	180.2	284.8	197.7	202.0	102.7	107.6	108.6	123.8	110.6	Togo
Tuvalu												Tuvalu
Uganda	48.1	57.0	74.6	22.6	41.4	36.7	30.7	39.6	39.7	41.9	43.1	Ouganda
Un. Rep. of Tanzania	86.7	86.5	89.9	78.6	80.6	71.8	76.5	62.9	50.1	51.4	41.9	Rép.-Un. de Tanzanie
Vanuatu	456.0	931.4	774.0	840.8	940.5	675.9	548.8	496.2	574.1	795.4	599.9	Vanuatu
Yemen	59.2	73.5	89.1	68.1	61.7	80.5	68.6	80.7	74.6	59.5	57.1	Yémen
All LDCs	52.9	53.1	56.2	52.6	54.4	55.6	52.0	53.7	53.3	54.8	54.7	Ensemble des PMA
All developing countries b/	143.4	159.5	160.2	169.6	169.7	163.7	175.1	166.6	168.1	186.0	171.8	Ensemble des pays en développement b/

For source and notes, see end of table.   Pour la source et les notes, se reporter à la fin du tableau.

Table 19 (continued)
Foreign exchange receipts and import volume expressed in
constant 1980 dollars a/ per capita

Tableau 19 (suite)
Rentrées de devises et volume des importations, en dollars
constants de 1980 a/ par habitant

D. Import volume per capita
D. Volume des importations par habitant

Country	1975	1976	1977	1978	1979	1980	1981	1982	1983	1984	1985	Pays
Afghanistan	43.0	39.8	52.5	54.7	50.6	34.6	40.7	46.2	35.1	75.3	62.8	Afghanistan
Bangladesh	18.5	16.4	21.9	22.0	20.8	22.2	21.2	20.7	18.9	23.9	25.0	Bangladesh
Benin	111.4	119.8	119.5	131.4	110.4	95.6	160.8	137.3	95.1	91.2	113.7	Bénin
Bhutan	...	...	...	...	...	...	...	...	...	...	...	Bhoutan
Botswana	490.9	448.7	519.7	573.1	684.4	755.2	879.7	751.3	801.3	721.8	609.3	Botswana
Burkina Faso	46.4	43.0	55.6	52.3	57.3	58.1	56.5	58.4	49.1	34.9	36.8	Burkina Faso
Burundi	28.1	28.8	29.4	34.2	43.8	41.0	40.0	53.5	45.9	46.0	44.6	Burundi
Cape Verde	240.3	177.2	235.6	204.2	162.3	230.0	242.5	245.0	282.0	292.9	382.9	Cap-Vert
Central African Rep.	54.8	41.5	43.9	32.6	34.4	35.0	42.7	57.5	38.6	38.7	46.9	Rép. centrafricaine
Chad	58.1	49.6	70.8	71.5	22.3	16.4	24.7	25.1	27.3	39.1	42.0	Tchad
Comoros	121.4	65.8	80.5	73.5	88.0	86.6	90.5	85.6	85.2	78.8	76.5	Comores
Democratic Yemen	324.9	399.3	466.9	428.7	238.7	331.1	347.0	830.0	770.7	788.0	636.4	Yémen démocratique
Djibouti	1167.8	830.2	642.6	475.7	411.7	403.2	388.6	373.0	373.6	353.1	342.0	Djibouti
Equatorial Guinea	106.6	20.8	46.5	36.7	63.9	73.9	90.3	124.0	89.5	88.8	86.6	Guinée équatoriale
Ethiopia	16.1	18.5	18.2	21.2	18.5	19.1	19.3	20.5	23.2	24.8	25.4	Ethiopie
Gambia	191.9	226.5	209.8	230.7	263.7	252.3	197.8	160.3	190.8	161.5	149.3	Gambie
Guinea	57.8	43.9	50.8	62.4	55.4	49.9	60.6	59.4	57.9	68.8	78.2	Guinée
Guinea-Bissau	100.2	94.1	68.1	78.8	91.5	68.0	63.6	64.6	85.1	62.5	76.4	Guinée-Bissau
Haiti	53.1	75.3	68.1	63.9	63.7	72.1	94.4	83.2	96.3	103.2	100.9	Haïti
Kiribati	385.3	375.3	363.8	344.1	303.4	290.6	246.1	249.9	252.8	251.1	227.6	Kiribati
Lao People's Dem.Rep.	23.9	22.0	29.0	33.0	33.8	40.0	39.3	41.5	45.2	46.5	50.0	Rép. dém. pop. lao
Lesotho	229.2	287.1	282.6	294.0	317.2	343.5	399.7	402.5	451.0	236.7	184.1	Lesotho
Malawi	83.4	65.6	65.7	82.5	78.5	73.9	59.2	52.0	52.3	45.1	45.1	Malawi
Maldives	37.9	36.6	43.2	112.6	153.0	185.5	201.9	281.5	373.7	341.7	330.2	Maldives
Mali	48.8	40.0	37.7	59.7	60.1	62.7	55.9	48.2	50.7	54.0	57.0	Mali
Mauritania	212.2	209.1	214.2	161.8	190.9	175.4	167.6	174.9	145.8	156.9	145.7	Mauritanie
Nepal	22.4	27.1	27.5	21.8	20.6	23.3	25.8	27.9	32.9	29.2	31.3	Népal
Niger	37.9	45.6	62.3	86.5	103.5	111.8	96.3	88.3	62.3	62.2	73.1	Niger
Rwanda	37.5	38.3	37.3	51.5	44.0	47.2	51.3	55.6	53.5	56.9	64.0	Rwanda
Samoa	417.2	333.8	414.0	476.5	547.8	405.1	375.6	344.0	393.7	352.7	354.1	Samoa
Sao Tome and Principe	215.9	170.1	238.6	331.8	250.3	202.6	184.6	164.3	109.8	129.9	136.2	Sao Tomé-et-Principe
Sierra Leone	106.8	87.2	91.7	116.1	108.7	125.6	98.0	77.3	54.5	54.8	50.5	Sierra Leone
Somalia	63.3	61.7	80.2	73.8	62.1	74.5	115.0	75.5	40.6	24.2	24.3	Somalie
Sudan	106.7	97.5	95.0	90.2	69.5	84.4	86.4	71.2	75.6	63.7	40.9	Soudan
Togo	130.5	134.8	183.0	251.2	238.3	215.3	170.3	154.1	113.5	110.1	101.6	Togo
Tuvalu	...	...	...	...	...	...	...	...	...	...	...	Tuvalu
Uganda	29.4	23.9	23.7	27.2	17.2	22.4	30.2	32.6	32.5	27.5	26.5	Ouganda
Un. Rep. of Tanzania	83.5	66.9	68.7	90.6	69.8	65.4	63.8	59.1	43.3	46.2	51.5	Rép.-Un. de Tanzanie
Vanuatu	585.1	498.1	765.2	793.5	761.1	620.8	517.6	530.4	568.7	613.0	612.0	Vanuatu
Yemen	82.3	110.7	249.0	267.2	253.3	263.2	255.5	223.2	235.2	242.2	227.3	Yémen
All LDCs	48.9	46.9	55.0	59.3	53.2	55.1	56.9	56.8	53.5	55.3	52.9	Ensemble des PMA
All developing countries b/	145.1	145.2	152.5	157.3	159.3	168.8	178.5	166.2	163.3	169.4	160.0	Ensemble des pays en développement b/

For source and notes, see end of table.   Pour la source et les notes, se reporter à la fin du tableau.

Tableau 19 (fin)

Source: Estimations du secrétariat de la CNUCED d'après le Manuel de statistiques du Commerce International et du Développement, Supplément 1987, de la CNUCED.

a/ Les recettes d'exportations, les rentrées au titre de l'aide extérieure et le total des rentrées de devises pour toutes les années sont exprimés en pouvoir d'achat à l'importation au prix de 1980. (Pour les déflateurs utilisés, se reporter au tableau 10).

b/ Non compris les principaux pays exportateurs de pétrole.

c/ Total des apports financiers comme au tableau 23A.

d/ Pouvoir d'achat des exportations plus aide extérieure.

Table 19 (end)

Source: UNCTAD secretariat estimates mainly based on UNCTAD Handbook of International Trade and Development Statistics, Supplement 1987.

a/ Exports, external assistance and total receipts in all years are expressed in terms of their command over imports at 1980 prices. (For the deflators used, see table 10).

b/ Excluding major petroleum exporters.

c/ Total financial flows as in table 23A.

d/ Export purchasing power plus external assistance.

Table 20
Percentage distribution of financial flows to all LDCs and to all developing countries, by type of flow

Percentages

Tableau 20
Répartition en pourcentage des apports financiers à l'ensemble des PMA et à l'ensemble des pays en développement, par catégorie d'apports

En pourcentage

	Least developed countries / Pays les moins avancés							All developing countries / Ensemble des pays en développement							
	1975	1980	1981	1982	1983	1984	1985	1975	1980	1981	1982	1983	1984	1985	
Concessional loans & grants, of which:	87.1	85.9	91.8	89.8	93.4	93.8	95.7	39.9	44.9	37.1	38.6	44.4	37.0	71.0	Prêts concessionnels et dons Dont:
DAC	64.9	65.8	71.6	68.3	69.1	74.9	79.4	25.5	30.5	25.7	28.7	33.6	29.5	58.2	CAD
- Bilateral	42.8	41.7	44.5	43.8	41.8	43.9	47.8	18.3	21.3	18.3	20.3	23.6	20.9	41.3	- Apports bilatéraux
- Multilateral a/	22.1	24.1	27.1	24.6	27.3	31.0	31.6	7.3	9.3	7.4	8.4	10.0	8.6	16.8	- Apports multilatéraux a/
- Grants	40.5	58.3	56.9	50.9	51.2	53.5	60.5	15.6	20.8	17.2	19.1	23.1	20.9	42.6	- Dons
- Loans	24.4	7.5	14.8	17.4	17.8	21.4	18.9	9.9	9.7	8.6	9.6	10.5	8.6	15.6	- Prêts
- Tech. assistance	14.7	17.9	21.0	18.9	20.1	19.5	19.7	7.8	9.1	7.9	8.8	10.9	9.1	17.1	- Assistance technique
- Other	50.2	48.0	50.7	49.4	49.0	55.4	59.7	17.7	21.4	17.9	19.9	22.7	20.4	41.1	- Autres
OPEC	16.5	13.0	12.8	14.0	13.0	10.1	6.4	11.5	11.6	8.8	7.0	7.3	4.7	7.2	OPEP
- Bilateral	14.6	11.4	9.9	11.8	11.0	8.8	5.4	11.1	11.2	8.5	6.6	6.9	4.5	6.9	- Apports bilatéraux
- Multilateral b/	1.9	1.7	2.9	2.2	2.0	1.3	0.9	0.3	0.3	0.4	0.4	0.4	0.2	0.3	- Apports multilatéraux b/
- Grants	10.1	5.3	3.4	7.1	8.1	6.1	3.7	6.3	5.1	3.7	3.6	3.5	4.0	5.5	- Dons
- Loans	6.4	7.8	9.4	7.0	5.0	4.0	2.6	5.2	6.5	5.1	3.4	3.9	0.7	1.6	- Prêts
Non-concessional flows	12.9	14.1	8.2	10.2	6.6	6.2	4.3	60.1	55.1	62.9	61.4	55.6	63.0	29.0	Courants financiers non-concessionnels
of which: DAC	9.7	13.5	7.7	11.1	6.2	5.9	4.5	54.0	55.5	63.2	61.8	55.5	62.7	28.2	Dont: CAD
- Bilateral official	0.1	2.7	2.1	2.3	2.8	3.3	1.6	3.5	5.6	4.4	6.3	4.9	6.3	8.4	- Apports publics bilatéraux
- Multilateral a/	2.0	1.1	1.2	1.3	1.5	0.8	1.7	4.9	5.8	5.8	7.6	9.9	9.3	15.3	- Apports multilatéraux a/
- Export credits c/	4.9	10.3	2.6	2.3	1.3	1.1	1.4	8.3	14.0	9.3	6.8	9.8	5.2	3.6	- Crédits à l'exportation c/
- Direct investment	1.3	0.6	1.4	2.1	0.4	0.4	0.3	20.9	12.7	17.2	14.2	12.8	13.0	15.7	- Investissements directs
- Other d/ e/	1.4	-1.2	0.5	3.2	0.2	0.3	-0.4	16.3	17.5	26.5	25.9	21.1	29.0	-14.8	- Autres d/ e/
TOTAL FINANCIAL FLOWS	100	100	100	100	100	100	100	100	100	100	100	100	100	100	TOTAL DES APPORTS FINANCIERS

For sources and notes, see table 21A.

Pour les sources et les notes, se reporter au tableau 21A.

Table 21A / Tableau 21A
Composition of total financial flows in current dollars- all LDCs /
Composition des courants financiers en dollars courants- ensemble des PMA

Net disbursements in $ million / Versements nets en millions de dollars

	1975	1976	1977	1978	1979	1980	1981	1982	1983	1984	1985
Concessional loans & grants / Prêts concessionnels et dons	3757	3338	3919	4945	5772	7184	6875	7305	7333	7435	8431
of which: DAC / Dont: CAD	2798	2369	2666	3858	4677	5508	5361	5557	5424	5935	6996
– Bilateral a/ / – Apports bilatéraux	1845	1464	1669	2380	2936	3491	3333	3559	3284	3479	4210
– Multilateral a/ / – Apports multilatéraux a/	953	904	998	1478	1741	2017	2028	1998	2140	2456	2786
– Grants / – Dons	1748	1556	1766	2947	3561	4881	4257	4142	4024	4236	5334
– Loans / – Prêts	1051	812	900	911	1117	627	1105	1415	1400	1699	1661
– Technical assistance / – Assistance technique	635	658	672	913	1165	1495	1569	1539	1578	1543	1734
– Other / – Autres	2163	1710	1994	2945	3512	4012	3792	4018	3846	4392	5262
OPEC / OPEP	711	755	1020	872	857	1089	961	1139	1022	798	561
– Bilateral / – Apports bilatéraux	630	656	903	759	760	950	742	963	863	698	479
– Multilateral b/ / – Apports multilatéraux b/	81	99	117	113	97	140	219	176	160	100	82
– Grants / – Dons	436	396	742	386	243	440	257	574	633	481	330
– Loans / – Prêts	274	359	278	486	614	650	704	565	390	317	231
Non-concessional flows / Courants financiers non-concessionnels	554	420	532	353	783	1181	612	829	521	490	380
of which: DAC / Dont: CAD	420	372	528	394	757	1131	580	906	486	471	400
– Bilateral official / – Apports publics bilatéraux	6	38	33	18	121	228	161	190	218	261	140
– Multilateral a/ / – Apports multilatéraux a/	85	22	42	66	91	89	88	103	116	65	147
– Export credits c/ / – Crédits à l'exportation c/	213	245	343	238	389	863	193	187	103	91	122
– Direct investment / – Investissements directs	57	45	117	50	34	52	102	168	30	32	23
– Other d/ e/ / – Autres d/ e/	59	22	-6	22	123	-101	37	258	19	21	-31
TOTAL FINANCIAL FLOWS / TOTAL DES APPORTS FINANCIERS	4311	3758	4451	5297	6556	8365	7487	8134	7853	7925	8811

Source: UNCTAD secretariat calculations mainly based on OECD/DAC and UNCTAD data.

a/ From multilateral agencies mainly financed by DAC member countries.
b/ From multilateral agencies mainly financed by OPEC member countries.
c/ Guaranteed private.
d/ Bilateral financial flows originating in DAC countries and their capital markets in the form of bond lending and bank lending (either directly or through syndicated "Eurocurrency credits").
e/ Only flows allocated by individual recipient country.

Source: Chiffres calculés par le secrétariat de la CNUCED d'après des données de l'OCDE/CAD et de la CNUCED.

a/ En provenance des institutions multilatérales essentiellement financées par les pays membres du CAD.
b/ En provenance des institutions multilatérales essentiellement financées par les pays membres de l'OPEP.
c/ Privés garantis.
d/ Apports financiers bilatéraux provenant des pays membres du CAD ou passant par leurs marchés de capitaux, sous forme d'émissions d'obligations et de prêts bancaires (soit directement, soit comme crédits consortiaux en euromonnaies).
e/ Uniquement les apports alloués par pays bénéficiaires.

Table 21B
Composition of total financial flows in current dollars-
all developing countries

Tableau 21B
Composition des courants financiers en dollars courants-
ensemble des pays en développement

Net disbursements in $ million / Versements nets en millions de dollars

	1975	1976	1977	1978	1979	1980	1981	1982	1983	1984	1985	
Concessional loans & grants	20166	19095	18539	25757	29440	35693	34788	32204	31311	31471	32924	Prêts concessionnels et dons
of which : DAC												Dont: CAD
– Bilateral a/	12919	12079	12635	16743	20604	24250	24117	23954	23704	25057	26976	– Apports bilatéraux
	9247	8660	8980	11874	14788	16887	17154	16943	16660	17745	19167	– Apports multilatéraux a/
– Multilateral a/	3672	3419	3655	4869	5817	7363	6963	7010	7044	7312	7809	
– Grants	7894	7533	8213	10920	13770	16534	16100	15957	16319	17782	19731	– Dons
– Loans	5024	4546	4422	5823	6835	7715	8017	7997	7385	7275	7244	– Prêts
– Technical assistance	3971	3808	4077	5000	6252	7255	7383	7364	7702	7745	7926	– Assistance technique
– Other	8947	8271	8558	11743	14352	16995	16734	16589	16002	17313	19050	– Autres
OPEC	5797	5579	4518	7548	7155	9186	8280	5851	5183	3963	3322	OPEP
– Bilateral	5638	5160	4277	7248	6907	8912	7930	5525	4886	3818	3176	– Apports bilatéraux
– Multilateral b/	159	418	241	300	249	274	350	326	297	145	146	– Apports multilatéraux b/
– Grants	3166	2602	3017	2262	3751	4045	3502	3013	2454	3401	2559	– Dons
– Loans	2631	2977	1501	5286	3404	5142	4778	2839	2728	562	763	– Prêts
Non-concessional flows	30433	30172	31638	45506	48397	43737	58947	51289	39237	53563	13430	Courants financiers non-concessionnels
of which : DAC	27335	27893	31784	46191	48636	44095	59221	51572	39150	53324	13066	Dont: CAD
– Bilateral official	1780	2057	1848	2951	2605	4415	4105	5220	3445	5315	3881	– Apports publics bilatéraux
– Multilateral a/	2480	2468	2625	2878	3838	4574	5414	6381	7018	7913	7112	– Apports multilatéraux a/
– Export credits c/	4222	6037	8310	9494	8410	11159	8752	6501	4793	4391	1659	– Crédits à l'exportation c/
– Direct investment	10597	7881	9321	10974	11633	10084	16111	11841	9035	11064	7272	– Investissements directs
– Other d/ e/	8256	9450	9679	19894	22150	13863	24838	21628	14858	24641	-6858	– Autres d/ e/
TOTAL FINANCIAL FLOWS	50600	49267	50177	71263	77837	79431	93735	83493	70547	85035	46354	TOTAL DES APPORTS FINANCIERS

For sources and notes, see table 21A.

Pour les sources et les notes, se reporter au tableau 21A.

Table 22A
Composition of total financial flows in constant dollars- all LDCs

Tableau 22A
Composition des courants financiers en dollars constants- ensemble des PMA

Net disbursements in millions of 1980 dollars / Versements nets en millions de dollars de 1980

	1975	1976	1977	1978	1979	1980	1981	1982	1983	1984	1985
Concessional loans & grants	6387	5639	6045	6832	6695	7184	7213	7937	8223	8449	9542
of which: DAC	4758	4002	4112	5330	5425	5508	5625	6038	6083	6745	7917
- Bilateral	3137	2474	2573	3288	3405	3491	3497	3867	3683	3953	4764
- Multilateral a/	1620	1528	1538	2042	2020	2017	2128	2171	2400	2791	3153
- Grants	2971	2629	2723	4072	4130	4881	4466	4500	4513	4814	6037
- Loans	1787	1372	1388	1258	1295	627	1159	1537	1570	1931	1880
- Technical assistance	1080	1112	1036	1261	1351	1495	1646	1672	1769	1754	1962
- Other	3678	2889	3076	4068	4074	4012	3979	4366	4314	4991	5955
OPEC	1208	1276	1573	1204	994	1089	1008	1238	1147	907	635
- Bilateral	1071	1108	1392	1049	882	950	779	1047	968	793	542
- Multilateral b/	137	167	181	155	112	140	230	191	179	114	93
- Grants	742	669	1144	533	282	440	270	623	710	547	374
- Loans	467	607	429	671	712	650	739	614	437	360	261
Non-concessional flows	943	710	820	487	909	1181	642	900	584	557	430
of which: DAC	714	629	815	545	878	1131	608	984	545	535	452
- Bilateral official	10	65	50	25	140	228	169	206	244	297	159
- Multilateral a/	144	38	65	91	106	89	92	112	130	74	166
- Export credits c/	363	414	529	329	451	863	202	203	115	103	138
- Direct investment	97	76	180	69	40	52	107	183	34	37	26
- Other d/ e/	100	37	-10	30	142	-101	38	280	22	24	-36
TOTAL FINANCIAL FLOWS	7330	6348	6865	7319	7604	8365	7855	8837	8807	9006	9972

French row labels (as printed): Prêts concessionnels et dons; Dont: CAD; - Apports bilatéraux; - Apports multilatéraux a/; - Dons; - Prêts; - Assistance technique; - Autres; OPEP; - Apports bilatéraux; - Apports multilatéraux b/; - Dons; - Prêts; Courants financiers non-concessionnels; Dont: CAD; - Apports publics bilatéraux; - Apports multilatéraux a/; - Crédits à l'exportation c/; - Investissements directs; - Autres d/ e/; TOTAL DES APPORTS FINANCIERS.

For sources and notes, see table 21A.

Pour les sources et les notes, se reporter au tableau 21A.

Table 22B
Composition of total financial flows in constant dollars—
all developing countries
Net disbursements in millions of 1980 dollars

Tableau 22B
Composition des courants financiers en dollars constants—
ensemble des pays en développement
Versements nets en millions de dollars de 1980

	1975	1976	1977	1978	1979	1980	1981	1982	1983	1984	1985	
Concessional loans & grants of which:	34993	32713	28912	35988	34514	35693	36155	34532	34705	35497	37081	Prêts concessionnels et dons Dont:
DAC	22417	20694	19705	23394	24155	24250	25065	25685	26274	28262	30382	CAD
- Bilateral	16045	14836	14004	16591	17336	16887	17828	18168	18466	20015	21587	- Apports bilatéraux
- Multilateral a/	6372	5858	5701	6803	6819	7363	7237	7517	7808	8248	8795	- Apports multilatéraux a/
- Grants	13698	12906	12808	15258	16143	16534	16732	17110	18088	20057	22223	- Dons
- Loans	8719	7788	6897	8136	8013	7715	8332	8575	8186	8205	8159	- Prêts
- Technical assistance	6891	6523	6358	6987	7330	7255	7674	7897	8536	8735	8926	- Assistance technique
- Other	15526	14170	13347	16407	16826	16995	17391	17788	17737	19527	21455	- Autres
OPEC	10059	9557	7046	10547	8389	9186	8606	6274	5744	4470	3741	OPEP
- Bilateral	9784	8841	6671	10127	8097	8912	8242	5924	5415	4306	3577	- Apports bilatéraux
- Multilateral b/	275	716	375	419	292	274	364	350	329	164	164	- Apports multilatéraux b/
- Grants	5493	4457	4706	3161	4398	4045	3640	3230	2720	3836	2882	- Dons
- Loans	4566	5100	2340	7386	3991	5142	4966	3044	3024	634	859	- Prêts
Non-concessional flows	52808	51691	49342	63583	56737	43737	61262	54996	43490	60415	15125	Courants financiers non-concessionnels
of which: DAC	47432	47787	49569	64540	57018	44095	61547	55299	43394	60145	14716	Dont: CAD
- Bilateral official	3089	3525	2883	4123	3054	4415	4267	5598	3819	5995	4371	- Apports publics bilatéraux
- Multilateral a/	4303	4228	4094	4021	4499	4574	5627	6843	7779	8925	8010	- Apports multilatéraux a/
- Export credits c/	7326	10343	12961	13265	9860	11159	9096	6971	5313	4952	1868	- Crédits à l'exportation c/
- Direct investment	18387	13502	14537	15333	13638	10084	16744	12697	10015	12479	8190	- Investissements directs
- Other d/ e/	14326	16190	15095	27797	25967	13863	25814	23191	16469	27793	-7724	- Autres d/ e/
TOTAL FINANCIAL FLOWS	87801	84404	78255	99571	91251	79431	97417	89527	78195	95911	52206	TOTAL DES APPORTS FINANCIERS

For sources and notes, see table 21A.

Pour les sources et les notes, se reporter au tableau 21A.

Table 23A
Composition of total financial flows in constant dollars per capita- all LDCs

Net disbursements in 1980 dollars

Tableau 23A
Composition des courants financiers en dollars constants par habitant- ensemble des PMA

Versements nets en dollars de 1980

		1975	1976	1977	1978	1979	1980	1981	1982	1983	1984	1985
Prêts concessionnels et dons	Concessional loans & grants	24.8	21.3	22.2	24.5	23.4	24.5	24.0	25.7	25.9	26.0	28.6
Dont:	of which :											
CAD	DAC	18.4	15.1	15.1	19.1	19.0	18.8	18.7	19.5	19.2	20.7	23.7
– Apports bilatéraux	– Bilateral	12.2	9.3	9.5	11.8	11.9	11.9	11.6	12.5	11.6	12.2	14.3
– Apports multilatéraux a/	– Multilateral a/	6.3	5.8	5.7	7.3	7.1	6.9	7.1	7.0	7.6	8.6	9.5
– Dons	– Grants	11.5	9.9	10.0	14.6	14.4	16.6	14.8	14.6	14.2	14.8	18.1
– Prêts	– Loans	6.9	5.2	5.1	4.5	4.5	2.1	3.9	5.0	5.0	5.9	5.6
– Assistance technique	– Technical assistance	4.2	4.2	3.8	4.5	4.7	5.1	5.5	5.4	5.6	5.4	5.9
– Autres	– Other	14.3	10.9	11.3	14.6	14.3	13.7	13.2	14.1	13.6	15.3	17.9
OPEP	OPEC	4.7	4.8	5.8	4.3	3.5	3.7	3.4	4.0	3.6	2.8	1.9
– Apports bilatéraux	– Bilateral	4.2	4.2	5.1	3.8	3.1	3.2	2.6	3.4	3.1	2.4	1.6
– Apports multilatéraux b/	– Multilateral b/	0.5	0.6	0.7	0.6	0.4	0.5	0.8	0.6	0.6	0.3	0.3
– Dons	– Grants	2.9	2.5	4.2	1.9	1.0	1.5	0.9	2.0	2.2	1.7	1.1
– Prêts	– Loans	1.8	2.3	1.6	2.4	2.5	2.2	2.5	2.0	1.4	1.1	0.8
Courants financiers non-concessionnels	Non-concessional flows	3.7	2.7	3.0	1.7	3.2	4.0	2.1	2.9	1.8	1.7	1.3
Dont:	of which :											
CAD	DAC	2.8	2.4	3.0	2.0	3.1	3.9	2.0	3.2	1.7	1.6	1.4
– Apports publics bilatéraux	– Bilateral official	0.0	0.2	0.2	0.1	0.5	0.8	0.6	0.7	0.8	0.9	0.5
– Apports multilatéraux a/	– Multilateral a/	0.6	0.1	0.2	0.3	0.4	0.3	0.3	0.4	0.4	0.2	0.5
– Crédits à l'exportation c/	– Export credits c/	1.4	1.6	1.9	1.2	1.6	2.9	0.7	0.7	0.4	0.3	0.4
– Investissements directs	– Direct investment	0.4	0.3	0.7	0.2	0.1	0.2	0.4	0.6	0.1	0.1	0.1
– Autres d/ e/	– Other d/ e/	0.4	0.1	-0.0	0.1	0.5	-0.3	0.1	0.9	0.1	0.1	-0.1
TOTAL DES APPORTS FINANCIERS	TOTAL FINANCIAL FLOWS	28.4	24.0	25.3	26.2	26.6	28.5	26.1	28.6	27.8	27.7	29.9

For sources and notes, see table 21A.

Pour les sources et les notes, se reporter au tableau 21A.

Table 23B
Composition of total financial flows in constant dollars
per capita- all developing countries
Net disbursements in 1980 dollars

Tableau 23B
Composition des courants financiers en dollars constants
par habitant- ensemble des pays en développement
Versements nets en dollars de 1980

	1975	1976	1977	1978	1979	1980	1981	1982	1983	1984	1985
Concessional loans & grants / Prêts concessionnels et dons	17.5	16.0	13.8	16.7	15.7	15.9	15.7	14.6	14.4	14.4	14.7
of which: / Dont: DAC / CAD	11.2	10.1	9.4	10.9	11.0	10.8	10.9	10.9	10.9	11.4	12.0
- Bilateral / Apports bilatéraux	8.0	7.2	6.7	7.7	7.9	7.5	7.7	7.7	7.6	8.1	8.5
- Multilateral a/ / Apports multilatéraux a/	3.2	2.9	2.7	3.2	3.1	3.3	3.1	3.2	3.2	3.3	3.5
- Grants / Dons	6.9	6.3	6.1	7.1	7.3	7.3	7.3	7.2	7.5	8.1	8.8
- Loans / Prêts	4.4	3.8	3.3	3.8	3.6	3.4	3.6	3.6	3.4	3.3	3.2
- Technical assistance / Assistance technique	3.4	3.2	3.0	3.3	3.3	3.2	3.3	3.3	3.5	3.5	3.5
- Other / Autres	7.8	6.9	6.4	7.6	7.6	7.6	7.5	7.5	7.3	7.9	8.5
OPEC / OPEP	5.0	4.7	3.4	4.9	3.8	4.1	3.7	2.7	2.4	1.8	1.5
- Bilateral / Apports bilatéraux	4.9	4.3	3.2	4.7	3.7	4.0	3.6	2.5	2.2	1.7	1.4
- Multilateral b/ / Apports multilatéraux b/	0.1	0.3	0.2	0.2	0.1	0.1	0.2	0.1	0.1	0.1	0.1
- Grants / Dons	2.7	2.2	2.2	1.5	2.0	1.8	1.6	1.4	1.1	1.6	1.1
- Loans / Prêts	2.3	2.5	1.1	3.4	1.8	2.3	2.2	1.3	1.3	0.3	0.3
Non-concessional flows / Courants financiers non-concessionnels	26.4	25.2	23.5	29.6	25.8	19.4	26.6	23.3	18.0	24.5	6.0
of which: / Dont: DAC / CAD	23.7	23.3	23.6	30.0	25.9	19.6	26.7	23.4	18.0	24.3	5.8
- Bilateral official / Apports publics bilatéraux	1.5	1.7	1.4	1.9	1.4	2.0	1.9	2.4	1.6	2.4	1.7
- Multilateral a/ / Apports multilatéraux a/	2.2	2.1	2.0	1.9	2.0	2.0	2.4	2.9	3.2	3.6	3.2
- Export credits c/ / Crédits à l'exportation c/	3.7	5.1	6.2	6.2	4.5	5.0	3.9	3.0	2.2	2.0	0.7
- Direct investment / Investissements directs	9.2	6.6	6.9	7.1	6.2	4.5	7.3	5.4	4.1	5.1	3.2
- Other d/ e/ / Autres d/ e/	7.2	7.9	7.2	12.9	11.8	6.2	11.2	9.8	6.8	11.2	-3.1
TOTAL FINANCIAL FLOWS / TOTAL DES APPORTS FINANCIERS	44.0	41.2	37.3	46.3	41.5	35.3	42.3	37.9	32.4	38.8	20.7

For sources and notes, see table 21A.

Pour les sources et les notes, se reporter au tableau 21A.

Table 24
Share of LDCs in flows to all developing countries, by type of flow

Tableau 24
Part des PMA dans les apports financiers à l'ensemble des pays en développement, par catégories d'apports

Percentages — En pourcentage

	1975	1976	1977	1978	1979	1980	1981	1982	1983	1984	1985
Concessional loans & grants — Prêts concessionnels et dons	18.6	17.5	21.1	19.2	19.6	20.1	19.8	22.7	23.4	23.6	25.6
of which : — Dont:											
DAC — CAD	21.7	19.6	21.1	23.0	22.7	22.7	22.2	23.2	22.9	23.7	25.9
– Bilateral — Apports bilatéraux	20.0	16.9	18.6	20.0	19.9	20.7	19.4	21.0	19.7	19.6	22.0
– Multilateral a/ — Apports multilatéraux a/	26.0	26.4	27.3	30.4	29.9	27.4	29.1	28.5	30.4	33.6	35.7
– Grants — Dons	22.1	20.7	21.5	27.0	25.9	29.5	26.4	26.0	24.7	23.8	27.0
– Loans — Prêts	20.9	17.9	20.4	15.6	16.3	8.1	13.8	17.7	19.0	23.4	22.9
– Technical assistance — Assistance technique	16.0	17.3	16.5	18.3	18.6	20.6	21.3	20.9	20.5	19.9	21.9
– Other — Autres	24.2	20.7	23.3	25.1	24.5	23.6	22.7	24.2	24.0	25.4	27.6
OPEC — OPEP	12.3	13.5	22.6	11.5	12.0	11.9	11.6	19.5	19.7	20.1	16.9
– Bilateral — Apports bilatéraux	11.2	12.7	21.1	10.5	11.0	10.7	9.4	17.4	17.7	18.3	15.1
– Multilateral b/ — Apports multilatéraux b/	50.9	23.7	48.8	37.5	38.8	51.0	62.5	53.9	53.8	68.8	56.4
– Grants — Dons	13.8	15.2	24.6	17.1	6.5	10.9	7.3	19.0	25.8	14.2	12.9
– Loans — Prêts	10.4	12.1	18.5	9.2	18.0	12.6	14.7	19.9	14.3	56.4	30.2
Non-concessional flows — Courants financiers non-concessionnels	1.8	1.4	1.7	0.8	1.6	2.7	1.0	1.6	1.3	0.9	2.8
of which: — Dont:											
DAC — CAD	1.5	1.3	1.7	0.9	1.6	2.6	1.0	1.8	1.2	0.9	3.1
– Bilateral official — Apports publics bilatéraux	0.3	1.9	1.8	0.6	4.6	5.2	3.9	3.6	6.3	4.9	3.6
– Multilateral a/ — Apports multilatéraux a/	3.4	0.9	1.6	2.3	2.4	1.9	1.6	1.6	1.7	0.8	2.1
– Export credits c/ — Crédits à l'exportation c/	5.1	4.1	4.1	2.5	4.6	7.7	2.2	2.9	2.1	2.1	7.3
– Direct investment — Investissements directs	0.5	0.6	1.3	0.5	0.3	0.5	0.6	1.4	0.3	0.3	0.3
– Other d/ e/ — Autres d/ e/	0.7	0.2	..	0.1	0.6	..	0.1	1.2	0.1	-	..
TOTAL FINANCIAL FLOWS — TOTAL DES APPORTS FINANCIERS	8.5	7.6	8.9	7.4	8.4	10.5	8.0	9.7	11.1	9.3	19.0

Note : No percentage is shown when either the net flow to all LDCs or the net flow to all developing countries in a particular year is negative. For other notes and sources, see table 21A.

Note : Aucune donnée n'est indiquée dans les cas où dans une année quelconque, les versements nets, soit aux PMA soit aux pays en développement dans leur ensemble, sont négatifs. Pour les autres notes et sources, se reporter au tableau 21A.

Table 25A
Bilateral ODA from DAC member countries and total financial
flows from multilateral agencies a/ to all LDCs

Tableau 25A
APD bilatérale des pays membres du CAD et apports financiers totaux
des institutions multilatérales a/ à l'ensemble des PMA

Net disbursements in $ million
Versements nets en millions de dollars

	1975	1976	1977	1978	1979	1980	1981	1982	1983	1984	1985
A. Bilateral donors / A.Donneurs bilatéraux											
Australia / Australie	30.2	15.2	19.4	33.2	55.6	38.0	62.7	89.0	56.6	72.0	39.0
Austria / Autriche	0.6	1.5	2.4	3.1	3.0	5.8	9.1	7.1	7.1	5.5	7.2
Belgium / Belgique	53.0	54.6	59.7	76.0	102.6	96.6	85.6	69.8	56.0	55.6	91.5
Canada	167.3	127.6	116.1	171.1	186.7b/	166.9b/	169.3	226.7	230.4	236.6	282.5
Denmark / Danemark	48.7	47.2	60.9	77.3	94.4	116.0	74.6	84.9	98.4	78.3	109.6
Finland / Finlande	12.6	15.9	11.3	10.6	14.9	22.1	23.9	21.7	32.8	37.8	43.6
France	260.6	254.2	230.2	273.6	388.0b/	450.8	519.2	437.6	412.1	526.3	538.3
Germany, Fed.Rep.of / Allemagne, Rép. Féd. d'	254.8	240.1	262.0	399.9	535.2	592.4	535.9	554.6	458.5	420.4	450.7
Ireland / Irlande	0.2	0.4	0.7	2.0	3.2	5.1	5.6	6.2	6.8	6.8	8.0
Italy / Italie	12.3	9.9	11.5	13.1	17.0	37.3	60.6	112.4	165.5	250.8	344.6
Japan / Japon	69.9	59.9	107.8	217.7	331.1	364.9	297.7	418.6	271.6	282.6	331.4
Netherlands / Pays-Bas	62.8	81.6	156.5	219.4	261.4	312.8	289.7	255.6	205.8	238.6	202.1
New Zealand / Nouvelle-Zélande	10.3	4.8	5.4	5.9	6.8	7.0	6.2	5.1	5.5	5.8	6.3
Norway / Norvège	38.2	39.1	61.8	77.4	90.8	94.6	90.4	121.9	120.7	100.0	121.8
Sweden / Suède	120.9	115.3	142.0	149.8	216.5	198.5	180.7	167.5	147.7	124.8	131.0
Switzerland / Suisse	13.7	11.8	20.4	42.6	29.4	57.9	56.1	59.0	66.8	69.8	68.3
United Kingdom / Royaume-Uni	122.2	114.9	135.2	222.4	288.6	370.8	317.1	271.0	228.5	208.0	244.8
United States / Etats-Unis	567.0	270.0	265.0	385.0	394.0	573.0	548.0	651.0	713.0	759.0	1189.0
Total bilateral concessional / Total des apports bilatéraux concessionnels	1845.4	1464.0	1668.2	2380.2	3019.2	3510.3	3332.5	3559.5	3283.7	3478.7	4209.7
B. Multilateral donors / B.Donneurs multilatéraux											
1. Concessional / 1.Apports concessionnels											
AfDF / FAfD	3.9	10.5	23.3	35.7	54.3	86.0	77.9	85.8	119.5	77.8	137.1
AsDB / BAsD	26.6	15.6	24.0	56.7	58.7	75.5	64.6	59.1	81.7	122.1	195.2
EEC/EDF / CEE/FED	305.7	192.8	224.5	320.3	424.3	452.1	508.1	404.2	383.9	472.2	445.4
IBRD / BIRD	-	0.1	6.1	13.3	19.5	18.7	9.8	3.0	2.5	0.5	0.4
IDA / AID	272.8	357.1	364.3	378.4	476.8	497.6	578.5	701.2	742.3	884.9	909.1
IDB / BID	14.6	15.7	21.3	16.9	15.9	8.9	10.0	12.5	14.9	16.2	10.7
IFAD / FIDA	-	-	-	-	1.1	12.9	22.6	28.0	50.8	51.6	91.0
IMF Trust fund / Fonds fiduciaire du FMI	-	-	39.3	245.0	201.6	253.0	2.6	-	-	-	-
UN / ONU	329.0	312.4	294.7	411.7	489.2	612.4	754.0	704.1	744.8	830.9	996.7
of which:UNDP / dont : PNUD	94.3	97.0	91.5	115.1	143.7	179.7	270.5	233.9	202.2	207.0	231.3
UNHCR	9.0	10.0	18.0	18.0	35.8	96.9	100.9	88.6	111.1	133.2	183.1
UNICEF	26.9	24.1	32.8	49.7	67.2	72.3	65.9	62.6	78.6	80.7	99.4
UNTA / ATNU	15.3	17.4	21.8	27.4	24.2	7.0	31.5	29.1	42.4	32.6	50.9
WFP / PAM	122.5	98.1	118.0	153.6	175.5	174.2	221.5	220.8	236.8	298.9	340.7
Total	952.6	904.1	997.5	1477.9	1741.4	2017.0	2028.2	1997.9	2140.3	2456.2	2785.6
2. Non-concessional / 2.Apports non-concessionnels											
AfDB / BAfD	14.6	16.3	21.4	18.1	25.6	31.6	27.1	44.0	52.2	37.6	71.6
AsDB / BAsD	1.1	0.0	-0.1	-0.7	-0.7	0.2	-0.6	-1.0	-0.7	-0.7	-0.6
EEC/EDF / CEE/FED	-	-	-0.1	12.5	15.2	18.9	17.3	14.4	17.2	5.2	5.8
IBRD / BIRD	83.2	0.3	14.1	19.8	37.7	31.8	41.7	38.2	39.5	5.7	52.2
IFC / SFI	-13.9	5.6	6.6	16.2	13.2	6.4	2.5	7.7	7.5	17.1	17.9
Total	84.9	22.2	41.9	65.9	91.0	88.9	87.9	103.3	115.7	64.9	146.9
Total concessional (A + B.1) / Total des apports concessionnels (A + B.1)	2798.0	2368.2	2665.6	3858.1	4760.7	5527.3	5360.7	5557.4	5424.0	5934.9	6995.3
GRAND TOTAL / TOTAL GENERAL	2882.9	2390.3	2707.5	3924.0	4851.7	5616.1	5448.6	5660.6	5539.7	5999.8	7142.2

For source and notes, see p. A-64.

Pour la source et les notes, se reporter p. A-64.

Table 25B
Bilateral ODA from DAC member countries and total financial flows from multilateral agencies a/ to all LDCs

Net disbursements in millions of 1980 dollars c/

Tableau 25B
APD bilatérale des pays membres du CAD at apports financiers totaux des institutions multilatérales a/ à l'ensemble des PMA

Versements nets en millions de dollars constants de 1980 c/

	1975	1976	1977	1978	1979	1980	1981	1982	1983	1984	1985
A. Bilateral donors / A. Donneurs bilatéraux											
Australia / Australie	51.4	25.7	29.9	45.9	64.5	38.0	65.8	96.7	63.4	81.8	44.1
Austria / Autriche	1.0	2.5	3.7	4.3	3.5	5.8	9.5	7.7	8.0	6.3	8.1
Belgium / Belgique	90.1	92.6	92.1	105.0	119.0	96.6	89.8	75.8	62.8	63.2	103.6
Canada / Canada	284.4	215.6	179.0	236.4	216.6b/	166.9b/	177.6	246.3	258.4	268.9	319.7
Denmark / Danemark	82.8	79.8	93.9	106.7	109.5	116.0	78.2	92.2	110.3	89.0	124.0
Finland / Finlande	21.4	26.8	17.4	14.7	17.2	22.1	25.1	23.5	36.8	42.9	49.3
France / France	443.1	429.5	355.0	378.0	450.1b/	450.8	544.4	475.4	462.2	598.0	609.2
Germany, Fed.Rep.of / Allemagne, Rép. Féd. d'	433.3	405.7	404.0	552.5	620.9	592.4	562.3	602.5	514.2	477.7	510.1
Ireland / Irlande	0.3	0.7	1.1	2.8	3.7	5.1	5.9	6.7	7.6	7.7	9.1
Italy / Italie	20.9	16.7	17.7	18.1	19.7	37.3	63.6	122.1	185.6	285.0	390.0
Japan / Japon	118.9	101.2	166.2	300.8	384.1	364.9	312.3	454.8	304.6	321.1	375.1
Netherlands / Pays-Bas	106.7	137.8	241.3	303.2	303.2	312.8	304.0	277.7	230.7	271.1	228.7
New Zealand / Nouvelle-Zélande	17.5	8.1	8.1	8.1	7.9	7.0	6.5	5.6	6.1	13.6	7.1
Norway / Norvège	65.0	66.0	95.3	107.0	105.3	94.6	94.9	132.4	135.3	113.6	137.8
Sweden / Suède	205.5	194.8	219.0	207.0	251.2	198.5	189.6	182.0	165.7	141.8	148.3
Switzerland / Suisse	23.3	19.9	31.5	58.9	34.1	57.9	58.9	64.1	74.9	79.3	77.3
United Kingdom / Royaume-Uni	207.8	194.2	208.5	307.2	334.7	370.8	332.7	294.5	256.3	236.4	277.0
United States / Etats-Unis	964.0	456.2	408.7	531.9	457.0	573.0	575.0	707.3	799.6	862.5	1345.6
Total bilateral concessional / Total des apports bilatéraux concessionnels	3137.4	2473.5	2572.7	3288.5	3502.2	3510.3	3496.5	3867.3	3682.5	3953.1	4764.3
B. Multilateral donors / B. Donneurs multilatéraux											
1. Concessional / 1. Apports concessionnels											
AfDF / FAfD	6.6	17.7	36.0	49.3	63.0	86.0	81.8	93.3	134.0	88.5	155.2
AsDB / BAsD	45.2	26.4	37.0	78.3	68.1	75.5	67.7	64.3	91.6	138.8	220.9
EEC/EDF / CEE/FED	519.7	325.8	346.3	442.5	492.1	452.1	533.2	439.2	430.5	536.6	504.1
IBRD / BIRD	-	0.2	9.4	18.4	22.7	18.7	10.3	3.3	2.8	0.6	0.5
IDA / AID	463.8	603.3	561.9	522.8	553.1	497.6	607.0	761.9	832.5	1005.5	1028.9
IDB / BID	24.8	26.4	32.8	23.4	18.4	8.9	10.5	13.5	16.7	18.4	12.1
IFAD / FIDA	-	-	-	-	1.3	12.9	23.7	30.4	56.9	58.6	103.0
IMF Trust fund / Fonds fiduciaire du FMI	-	-	60.7	338.4	233.9	253.0	2.8	-	-	-	-
UN / ONU	559.3	527.8	454.4	568.8	567.5	612.4	791.1	765.0	835.3	944.2	1128.0
of which:UNDP / dont : PNUD	160.4	163.8	141.0	159.0	166.7	179.7	283.8	254.1	226.7	235.2	261.8
UNHCR / UNHCR	15.3	16.9	11.7	24.9	41.5	96.9	105.9	96.3	124.6	151.4	207.2
UNICEF / UNICEF	45.6	40.6	50.5	68.6	77.9	72.3	69.1	68.0	88.2	91.7	112.5
UNTA / ATNU	26.0	29.4	33.6	37.8	28.1	7.0	33.1	31.7	47.6	37.0	57.6
WFP / PAM	208.3	165.7	181.9	212.2	203.5	174.2	232.4	239.9	265.6	339.6	385.6
Total	1619.4	1527.5	1538.4	2041.8	2020.0	2017.0	2128.0	2170.7	2400.3	2791.1	3152.6
2. Non-concessional / 2. Apports non-concessionnels											
AfDB / BAfD	24.8	27.5	33.0	25.0	29.7	31.6	28.4	47.8	58.5	42.8	81.0
AsDB / BAsD	1.9	0.0	-0.2	-0.9	-0.9	0.2	-0.6	-1.0	-0.7	-0.8	-0.7
EEC/EDF / CEE/FED	-	-	-0.1	17.2	17.6	18.9	18.1	15.6	19.3	5.9	6.6
IBRD / BIRD	141.4	0.5	21.7	27.4	43.7	31.8	43.8	41.5	44.3	6.5	59.1
IFC / SFI	-23.6	9.5	10.2	22.4	15.3	6.4	2.6	8.4	8.4	19.4	20.3
Total	144.4	37.5	64.6	91.1	105.6	88.9	92.3	112.2	129.8	73.8	166.3
Total concessional (A + B.1) / Total des apports concessionnels (A + B.1)	4756.8	4001.0	4111.1	5330.3	5522.2	5527.3	5624.5	6038.0	6082.7	6744.2	7916.8
GRAND TOTAL / TOTAL GENERAL	4901.2	4038.4	4175.7	5421.3	5627.8	5616.1	5716.7	6150.2	6212.5	6818.0	8083.1

For source and notes, see p. A-64.   Pour la source et les notes, se reporter p. A-64.

Table 25C
Bilateral ODA from DAC member countries and total financial flows from multilateral agencies a/ to all LDCs- main recipients in 1985 d/

	Main recipients in 1985 d/
A. Bilateral donors	
Australia	Ethiopia, Samoa, Vanuatu, U.-R. of Tanzania, Bangladesh.
Austria	Ethiopia, Cape Verde, Sudan.
Belgium	Rwanda, Burundi, Bangladesh.
Canada	Bangladesh, Ethiopia, U.-R.of Tanzania
Denmark	Bangladesh, U.-R. of Tanzania.
Finland	U.-R. of Tanzania, Ethiopia.
France	Mali.
Germany,Fed.Rep.of	Sudan, Bangladesh.
Ireland	Lesotho, U.-R. of Tanzania, Sudan.
Italy	Ethiopia, Sudan, Somalia, U.-R.of Tanzania.
Japan	Bangladesh, Nepal.
Netherlands	Bangladesh,U.-R. of Tanzania, Sudan.
New Zealand	Samoa, Vanuatu, Kiribati.
Norway	U.-R. of Tanzania, Bangladesh.
Sweden	U.-R.of Tanzania,Ethiopia,Bangladesh.
Switzerland	Rwanda, Nepal.
United Kingdom	Sudan, Bangladesh, Ethiopia.
United States	Sudan, Bangladesh, Ethiopia.
B. Multilateral donors	
1.Concessional	
AfDF	Ethiopia.
AsDB	Bangladesh, Nepal.
EEC/EDF	Ethiopia, Sudan.
IBRD	U.-R. of Tanzania.
IDA	Bangladesh, Uganda.
IDB	Haïti.
IFAD	Bangladesh.
UN	Sudan, Ethiopia.
of which:UNDP	Bangladesh.
UNHCR	Sudan, Somalia, Ethiopia.
UNICEF	Ethiopia, Bangladesh.
UNTA	-
WFP	Ethiopia, Chad, Sudan, Somalia.
2. Non-concessional	
AfDB	Botswana, Uganda, Lesotho.
AsDB	Bangladesh.
EEC/EDF	Botswana, Guinea, Burkina Faso, Mauritania.
IBRD	Uganda, U.-R. of Tanzania, Botswana.
IFC	Yemen,Uganda,Nepal,U.-R.of Tanzania.

For source and notes, see p. A-64.

Tableau 25C
APD bilatérale des pays membres du CAD et apports financiers totaux des institutions multilatérales a/ à l'ensemble des PMA- principaux bénéficiaires en 1985 d/

	Principaux bénéficiaires en 1985 d/
A.Donneurs bilatéraux	
Australie	Ethiopie, Samoa, Vanuatu, R.-U. de Tanzanie,Bangladesh.
Autriche	Ethiopie, Cap-Vert, Soudan.
Belgique	Rwanda, Burundi, Bangladesh.
Canada	Bangladesh,Ethiopie,R.-U.de Tanzanie.
Danemark	Bangladesh, R.-U. de Tanzanie.
Finlande	R.-U. de Tanzanie, Ethiopie.
France	Mali.
Allemagne, Rép. Féd. d'	Soudan, Bangladesh.
Irlande	Lesotho, R.-U. de Tanzanie, Soudan.
Italie	Ethiopie, Soudan, Somalie, R.-U. de Tanzanie.
Japon	Bangladesh, Népal.
Pays-Bas	Bangladesh,R.-U. de Tanzanie,Soudan.
Nouvelle-Zélande	Samoa, Vanuatu, Kiribati.
Norvège	R.-U. de Tanzanie, Bangladesh.
Suède	R.-U.de Tanzanie,Ethiopie,Bangladesh.
Suisse	Rwanda, Népal.
Royaume-Uni	Soudan, Bangladesh, Ethiopie.
Etats-Unis	Soudan, Bangladesh, Ethiopie.
B.Donneurs multilatéraux	
1.Apports concessionnels	
FAfD	Ethiopie.
BAsD	Bangladesh, Népal.
CEE/FED	Ethiopie, Soudan.
BIRD	R.-U. de Tanzanie.
AID	Bangladesh, Ouganda.
BID	Haïti.
FIDA	Bangladesh.
ONU	Soudan, Ethiopie.
dont : PNUD	Bangladesh.
UNHCR	Soudan, Somalie, Ethiopie.
UNICEF	Ethiopie, Bangladesh.
ATNU	-
PAM	Ethiopie, Tchad, Soudan, Somalie.
2.Apports non-concessionnels	
BAfD	Botswana, Ouganda, Lesotho.
BAsD	Bangladesh.
CEE/FED	Botswana, Guinée, Burkina Faso, Mauritanie.
BIRD	Ouganda, R.-U. de Tanzanie, Botswana.
SFI	Yémen,Ouganda,Népal,R.-U.de Tanzanie.

Pour la source et les notes, se reporter p. A-64.

Tableau 25 (suite)

Source: Secrétariat de la CNUCED, d'après des renseignements du secrétariat de l'OCDE/CAD.

a/ Institutions multilatérales essentiellement financées par les pays du CAD.

b/ Y compris les apports aux PMA non alloués par pays bénéficiaires.

c/ Les versements effectifs ont été convertis aux prix de 1980 en utilisant l'indice pour les PMA qui figure au tableau 10.

d/ Recevant individuellement 10 pour cent ou davantage du total accordé à l'ensemble des PMA.

Table 25 (continued)

Source: UNCTAD secretariat, based on information from the OECD/DAC secretariat.

a/ Multilateral institutions mainly financed by DAC countries.

b/ Including flows to LDCs not allocated by recipient country.

c/ Actual disbursements were converted to 1980 prices using the index for LDCs in Table 10.

d/ Accounting each for 10 per cent or more of the total provided to all LDCs.

Table 26 / Table 26

Concessional assistance to LDCs from individual DAC member countries and multilateral agencies mainly financed by them: relative importance and relative shares as compared to all developing countries

Percentages

Aide concessionnelle aux PMA en provenance des pays membres du CAD et des institutions multilatérales essentiellement financées par ceux-ci: importance relative et parts relatives par rapport à l'ensemble des pays en développement

En pourcentage

Relative importance of individual DAC countries and multilateral agencies in all their ODA flows to LDCs — Importance relative des différents pays du CAD et institutions multilatérales dans l'ensemble de leurs apports concessionnels aux PMA

Share of LDCs in ODA flows to all developing countries — Parts des PMA dans le total des apports concessionnels aux pays en développement

Bilateral donors / Donneurs bilatéraux	1975	1980	1981	1982	1983	1984	1985	1975	1980	1981	1982	1983	1984	1985
Australia — Australie	1.1	0.7	1.2	1.6	1.0	1.2	0.6	7.0	7.8	11.5	15.8	10.7	12.0	7.5
Austria — Autriche	0.0	0.1	0.2	0.1	0.1	0.1	0.1	1.2	4.0	5.8	4.4	5.8	4.1	4.2
Belgium — Belgique	1.9	1.7	1.6	1.3	1.0	0.9	1.3	21.2	21.8	23.9	24.5	19.3	22.0	34.5
Canada — Canada	6.0	3.0	3.2	4.1	4.2	4.0	4.0	27.3	25.4	22.7	27.6	27.3	22.9	28.8
Denmark — Danemark	1.7	2.1	1.4	1.5	1.8	1.3	1.6	45.7	45.8	36.9	41.6	42.6	35.7	50.0
Finland — Finlande	0.4	0.4	0.4	0.4	0.6	0.6	0.6	51.4	40.0	35.9	28.1	38.6	36.4	36.4
France — France	9.3	8.2	9.7	7.9	7.6	8.9	7.7	14.6	13.1	14.7	13.2	13.2	16.7	16.6
Germany, Fed.Rep.of — Allemagne, Rép.féd.d'	9.1	10.7	10.0	10.0	8.5	7.1	6.4	23.4	27.6	24.4	26.6	23.8	24.4	24.7
Ireland — Irlande	0.0	0.0	0.1	0.1	0.1	0.1	0.1	22.2	52.0	53.8	50.8	48.6	46.6	46.8
Italy — Italie	0.4	0.7	1.1	2.0	3.1	4.2	4.9	21.4	44.8	36.6	37.7	37.9	40.8	45.0
Japan — Japon	2.5	6.6	5.6	7.5	5.0	4.8	4.7	8.2	18.2	13.3	21.0	13.1	13.9	15.3
Netherlands — Pays-Bas	2.2	5.7	5.4	4.6	3.8	4.0	2.9	17.6	25.7	25.9	24.4	25.7	27.5	26.8
New Zealand — Nouvelle-Zélande	0.4	0.1	0.1	0.1	0.1	0.1	0.1	20.5	13.4	12.3	10.3	11.6	13.2	14.7
Norway — Norvège	1.4	1.7	1.7	2.2	2.2	1.7	1.7	43.1	35.0	36.1	38.3	37.7	34.6	37.6
Sweden — Suède	4.3	3.6	3.4	3.0	2.7	2.1	1.9	36.2	32.0	34.3	32.6	31.0	27.0	24.6
Switzerland — Suisse	0.5	1.0	1.0	1.1	1.2	1.2	1.0	19.8	33.0	34.6	32.3	30.8	32.1	30.2
United Kingdom — Royaume	4.4	6.7	5.9	4.9	4.2	3.5	3.5	22.0	28.2	23.9	28.2	26.6	26.8	29.5
United States — Etats-Unis	20.3	10.4	10.2	11.7	13.1	12.8	17.0	22.4	16.3	15.6	16.0	16.7	14.5	19.3
Total bilateral — Total bilatéraux	66.0	63.5	62.2	64.0	60.5	58.6	60.2	20.0	20.8	19.4	21.0	19.7	19.6	22.0
Multilateral donors / Donneurs multilatéraux														
AfDF — FafD	0.1	1.6	1.5	1.5	2.2	1.3	2.0	100.0	89.8	86.1	70.2	75.7	69.9	65.2
AsDB — BAsD	1.0	1.4	1.2	1.1	1.5	2.1	2.8	35.0	53.1	45.3	33.4	36.8	40.2	49.9
EEC/EDF — CEE/FED	10.9	8.2	9.5	7.3	7.1	8.0	6.4	42.4	43.5	35.6	35.6	31.9	37.2	34.6
IBRD — BIRD	-	0.3	0.2	0.6	0.0	0.0	0.0	-	17.5	11.1	5.2	5.3	1.2	1.2
IDA — AID	9.8	9.0	10.8	12.6	13.7	14.9	13.0	25.1	32.4	30.3	29.7	32.8	37.5	38.2
IDB — BID	0.5	0.2	0.2	0.3	0.3	0.3	0.2	4.6	2.7	2.3	3.4	4.1	3.7	3.0
IFAD — FIDA	-	0.2	0.4	0.5	0.9	0.9	1.3	-	24.0	30.2	27.8	36.0	32.2	36.3
IMF Trust Fund — Fonds fiduciaire du FMI	-	4.6	0.0	-	-	-	-	-	15.5	9.5	-	-	-	-
UN — ONU	11.8	11.1	14.1	12.7	13.7	14.0	14.2	22.7	25.7	27.7	26.5	28.5	31.8	34.6
Total multilateral — Total multilatéraux	34.0	36.5	37.8	36.0	39.5	41.4	39.8	25.9	27.4	29.1	28.5	30.4	33.6	35.7
GRAND TOTAL — TOTAL GENERAL	100.0	100.0	100.0	100.0	100.0	100.0	100.0	21.7	22.8	22.2	23.2	22.9	23.7	25.9

Source: UNCTAD secretariat, based on information from the OECD/DAC secretariat.

Source: Secrétariat de la CNUCED, d'après des renseignements du secrétariat de l'OCDE/CAD.

Table 27
Concessional assistance from DAC member countries and multilateral agencies a/ to individual LDCs

Net disbursements in $ million

Tableau 27
Aide concessionelle reçue par chacun des PMA en provenance des pays du CAD et des institutions multilatérales a/

Versements nets en millions de dollars

Country	1975	1976	1977	1978	1979	1980	1981	1982	1983	1984	1985	Pays
Afghanistan	53.5	63.9	75.3	76.4	99.5	30.8	2.6	9.0	15.9	7.5	18.3	Afghanistan
Bangladesh	956.4	521.2	586.0	961.8	1132.0	1208.0	1014.9	1197.8	957.6	1174.7	1139.7	Bangladesh
Benin	52.0	50.9	45.0	57.7	81.1	86.3	77.6	76.0	80.1	77.3	91.7	Bénin
Bhutan	2.1	3.2	2.9	3.2	5.9	8.3	9.8	11.3	12.9	17.6	21.3	Bhoutan
Botswana	45.9	47.6	47.5	68.8	99.1	103.9	96.5	92.9	91.3	91.8	92.3	Botswana
Burkina Faso	86.1	83.1	107.4	157.9	193.4	205.4	208.3	201.0	181.3	178.6	190.7	Burkina Faso
Burundi	47.1	44.5	46.8	71.4	88.6	109.2	118.0	120.7	132.0	128.3	135.6	Burundi
Cape Verde	8.7	13.1	24.4	32.5	32.5	60.4	49.3	53.2	59.9	59.0	63.8	Cap-Vert
Central African Rep.	55.4	38.1	40.4	51.3	82.3	108.9	101.6	88.7	92.7	111.7	103.1	Rép. centrafricaine
Chad	57.1	60.9	81.9	117.8	79.7	35.3	59.8	60.9	95.2	114.6	180.8	Tchad
Comoros	21.7	11.6	8.6	7.6	13.5	25.4	32.1	26.1		33.9	38.5	Comores
Democratic Yemen	20.2	23.2	32.1	47.0	39.7	38.6	36.1	57.4	57.3	46.2	48.3	Yémen démocratique
Djibouti	34.4	28.1	34.5	32.0	23.1	40.6	50.1	54.9	52.3	59.0	62.4	Djibouti
Equatorial Guinea	0.7	0.4	0.4	0.6	2.7	9.3	9.8	13.0	10.7	15.1	17.4	Guinée équatoriale
Ethiopia	119.2	140.5	111.7	137.1	174.3	211.8	226.7	199.9	269.3	363.1	706.0	Ethiopie
Gambia	7.7	9.8	17.8	26.7	30.0	40.2	45.3	43.0	40.9	51.5	49.1	Gambie
Guinea	9.4	11.5	17.1	48.3	48.5	84.9	79.6	60.2	67.4	88.8	112.0	Guinée
Guinea-Bissau	15.5	18.7	35.9	47.7	49.8	55.6	63.7	59.7	57.7	52.9	54.8	Guinée-Bissau
Haiti	59.3	71.7	84.5	92.9	92.7	105.1	105.6	125.7	132.3	134.4	151.7	Haïti
Kiribati	5.7	4.1	6.2	10.7	9.1	19.2	15.3	15.1	16.8	11.9	12.1	Kiribati
Lao People's Dem.Rep.	38.9	28.4	30.2	71.8	49.9	40.1	34.9	37.9	29.3	33.0	36.9	Rép. dém. pop. lao
Lesotho	27.4	30.2	37.3	51.2	65.9	94.3	103.2	90.6	99.7	95.4	89.0	Lesotho
Malawi	63.9	63.3	79.4	98.5	141.7	142.0	137.3	121.2	116.9	158.6	113.1	Malawi
Maldives	3.0	1.5	2.0	4.8	2.5	5.5	5.0	3.0	6.9	6.5	10.4	Maldives
Mali	115.3	86.0	97.1	151.4	179.7	224.5	210.2	159.3	168.6	310.1	349.0	Mali
Mauritania	37.1	38.0	48.6	86.9	109.8	86.8	110.5	93.2	107.4	109.5	142.9	Mauritanie
Nepal	45.4	50.0	71.4	75.1	133.3	156.3	169.2	195.3	200.2	199.1	237.9	Népal
Niger	124.1	125.4	91.0	134.9	167.6	161.6	164.3	167.6	157.9	155.5	303.5	Niger
Rwanda	81.6	78.9	90.5	121.1	145.4	148.2	145.3	149.0	148.4	158.7	175.9	Rwanda
Samoa	13.4	11.7	19.0	19.7	29.4	24.9	24.0	21.9	27.0	20.2	19.2	Samoa
Sao Tome and Principe	0.3	1.7	3.0	4.0	3.0	3.9	5.6	9.4	11.1	10.9	12.2	Sao Tomé-et-Principe
Sierra Leone	16.3	15.0	25.1	40.0	48.3	84.0	58.0	80.8	64.5	44.5	61.0	Sierra Leone
Somalia	72.7	67.4	68.2	88.0	101.9	290.2	307.2	279.0	283.3	333.8	315.3	Somalie
Sudan	110.3	115.6	109.5	224.3	261.9	441.6	484.0	554.8	599.4	500.3	913.4	Soudan
Togo	39.8	40.5	64.2	102.4	109.7	87.4	62.4	73.4	106.4	106.4	104.5	Togo
Tuvalu	0.1	3.0	2.4	2.9	4.1	4.9	5.4	6.2	4.2	5.5	3.4	Tuvalu
Uganda	13.3	20.1	14.1	17.1	41.3	112.1	135.5	127.4	124.4	165.3	182.7	Ouganda
Un. Rep. of Tanzania	288.2	267.3	327.4	422.4	584.2	647.1	650.2	658.1	565.1	543.2	477.6	Rép.-Un. de Tanzanie
Vanuatu	12.6	31.0	14.7	18.8	38.4	44.0	30.5	26.0	26.9	24.5	21.8	Vanuatu
Yemen	36.7	47.5	64.6	73.0	81.7	121.2	115.8	136.6	124.2	135.4	136.3	Yémen
All LDCs	2798.4	2368.5	2666.1	3857.7	4677.2	5507.8	5361.2	5557.2	5424.2	5935.2	6995.6	Ensemble des PMA
All developing countries	12919	12079	12635	16743	20604	24250	24117	23954	23704	25057	26976	Ensemble des pays en développement

Source: UNCTAD secretariat, based on information from the OECD/DAC secretariat.

Source: Secrétariat de la CNUCED, d'après des renseignements du secrétariat de l'OCDE/CAD.

a/ Multilateral institutions mainly financed by DAC countries.

a/ Institutions multilatérales essentiellement financées par les pays du CAD.

Table 27 (continued)
Concessional assistance from DAC member countries and
multilateral agencies a/ to individual LDCs -
leading donors b/ in 1985

Country	Leading donors
Afghanistan	UNDP, France, UNTA.
Bangladesh	IDA, USA, AsDB, Japan.
Benin	IDA, Germany, Fed.Rep.of, France.
Bhutan	UNDP, AsDB.
Botswana	WFP, Germany, Fed.Rep.of, Norway, USA.
Burkina Faso	USA, France, IDA.
Burundi	France, Belgium, IDA.
Cape Verde	Italy, Sweden.
Central African Rep.	France, IDA.
Chad	WFP, France, Italy, EEC, USA.
Comoros	France, EEC, IDA, AfDF.
Democratic Yemen	IDA, WFP.
Djibouti	France.
Equatorial Guinea	France, IDA, WFP, UNDP.
Ethiopia	USA, EEC, Italy.
Gambia	USA, Germany, Fed. Rep. of.
Guinea	France, IDA, Canada.
Guinea-Bissau	IDA, Sweden, EEC.
Haiti	USA, IDA, France.
Kiribati	U.K., Japan, Australia.
Lao People's Dem.Rep.	Japan, UNDP, Sweden, IDA, AsDB.
Lesotho	USA, WFP.
Malawi	IDA, U.K., Germany, Fed. Rep. of.
Maldives	Japan, USA.
Mali	France, USA.
Mauritania	USA, France.
Nepal	Japan, AsDB, IDA.
Niger	USA, France.
Rwanda	IDA, Germany, Fed.Rep.of, Belgium.
Samoa	Australia, New Zealand.
Sao Tome and Principe	WFP, EEC, France.
Sierra Leone	Germany, Fed.Rep.of, USA, IDA, EEC.
Somalia	Italy, USA, UNHCR, IDA, WFP.
Sudan	USA, UNHCR.
Togo	IDA, France, Germany, Fed. Rep.of.
Tuvalu	U.K., Australia, New Zealand.
Uganda	IDA.
United Rep.of Tanzania	Sweden.
Vanuatu	U.K., France, Australia.
Yemen	USA, IDA.

Source: UNCTAD secretariat, based on information from the
OECD/DAC secretariat.

a/ Multilateral institutions mainly financed by
   DAC countries.
b/ Accounting for 10 per cent or more of total
   concessional assistance received by the given LDC.

Tableau 27 (suite)
Aide concessionelle reçue par chacun des PMA en provenance des pays
du CAD et des institutions multilatérales a/ -
principaux donneurs b/ en 1985

Pays	Principaux donneurs
Afghanistan	PNUD, France, ATNU.
Bangladesh	AID, Etats-Unis, BAsD, Japon.
Bénin	AID, Allemagne, Rép. féd. d', France.
Bhoutan	PNUD, BAsD.
Botswana	PAM, Allemagne, R.F.d', Norvège, Etats-Unis.
Burkina Faso	Etats-Unis, France, AID.
Burundi	France, Belgique, AID.
Cap-Vert	Italie, Suède.
Rép. centrafricaine	France, AID.
Tchad	PAM, France, Italie, CEE, Etats-Unis.
Comores	France, CEE, AID, FAfD.
Yémen démocratique	AID, PAM.
Djibouti	France.
Guinée équatoriale	France, AID, PAM, PNUD.
Ethiopie	Etats-Unis, CEE, Italie.
Gambie	Etats-Unis, Allemagne, Rép. féd. d'.
Guinée	France, AID, Canada.
Guinée-Bissau	AID, Suède, CEE.
Haïti	Etats-Unis, AID, France.
Kiribati	Royaume-Uni, Japon, Australie.
Rép. dém. pop. lao	Japon, PNUD, Suède, AID, BAsD.
Lesotho	Etats-Unis, PAM.
Malawi	AID, Royaume-Uni, Allemagne, Rép. féd. d'.
Maldives	Japon, Etats-Unis.
Mali	France, Etats-Unis.
Mauritanie	Etats-Unis, France.
Népal	Japon, BAsD, AID.
Niger	Etats-Unis, France.
Rwanda	AID, Allemagne, Rép. féd. d', Belgique.
Samoa	Australie, Nouvelle-Zélande.
Sao Tomé-et-Principe	PAM, CEE, France.
Sierra Leone	Allemagne, Rép.féd.d', Etats-Unis, AID, CEE.
Somalie	Italie, Etats-Unis, UNHCR, AID, PAM.
Soudan	Etats-Unis, UNHCR.
Togo	AID, France, Allemagne, Rép. féd. d'.
Tuvalu	Royaume-Uni, Australie, Nouvelle-Zélande.
Ouganda	AID.
Rép.-Un. de Tanzanie	Suède.
Vanuatu	Royaume-Uni, France, Australie.
Yémen	Etats-Unis, AID.

Source: Secrétariat de la CNUCED, d'après des renseignements du
secrétariat de l'OCDE/CAD.

a/ Institutions multilatérales essentiellement financées
   par les pays du CAD.
b/ Donnant 10 pour cent ou davantage de l'aide
   concessionnelle totale reçue par le PMA en question.

Table 28
Bilateral ODA from DAC member countries to individual LDCs

Tableau 28
APD bilatérale reçue par chacun des PMA en provenance des pays membres du CAD

Net disbursements in $ million   Versements nets en millions de dollars

Country	Pays	1975	1976	1977	1978	1979	1980	1981	1982	1983	1984	1985
Afghanistan	Afghanistan	32.5	34.8	27.6	32.0	47.0	11.4	-7.9	0.4	5.4	-1.0	6.9
Bangladesh	Bangladesh	703.9	319.9	384.0	666.6	774.8	850.2	672.0	822.0	582.5	674.6	621.6
Benin	Bénin	29.1	27.5	26.6	30.3	48.6	35.7	45.0	40.9	41.3	39.7	47.7
Bhutan	Bhoutan	0.6	1.0	0.6	0.7	1.2	1.7	2.6	3.2	2.9	4.8	6.6
Botswana	Botswana	38.5	40.6	38.1	55.1	73.6	83.5	75.9	83.2	74.6	64.9	59.1
Burkina Faso	Burkina Faso	53.1	60.1	71.7	96.6	132.0	151.1	158.1	147.0	128.0	122.2	122.2
Burundi	Burundi	26.4	25.9	28.8	38.6	44.1	59.8	65.0	75.3	69.3	70.4	77.1
Cape Verde	Cap-Vert	2.1	6.8	15.8	25.0	27.2	39.0	36.2	42.6	45.3	39.3	40.8
Central African Rep.	Rép. centrafricaine	33.3	25.7	30.2	29.7	51.2	75.1	72.8	68.8	64.8	68.3	61.6
Chad	Tchad	28.2	43.2	49.6	70.9	49.4	20.2	31.3	35.3	51.4	58.9	95.8
Comoros a/	Comores a/	17.5	8.4	1.8	1.8	6.3	13.4	17.8	14.2	15.1	18.2	18.0
Democratic Yemen	Yémen démocratique	6.1	9.0	6.9	12.9	4.7	4.1	4.7	9.7	6.6	5.3	10.5
Djibouti	Djibouti	34.1	28.1	32.7	29.3	19.0	32.0	36.3	44.5	41.4	48.5	46.4
Equatorial Guinea	Guinée équatoriale	-	-	-	-	0.1	1.2	4.3	5.1	4.0	8.0	6.9
Ethiopia	Ethiopie	73.0	72.8	59.0	56.0	70.5	91.4	76.2	77.0	93.1	187.2	416.3
Gambia	Gambie	3.5	5.4	12.6	14.8	13.2	16.5	19.3	23.6	21.4	32.3	31.2
Guinea	Guinée	5.5	4.4	5.1	9.9	14.2	32.5	31.4	26.8	26.6	42.2	59.8
Guinea-Bissau	Guinée-Bissau	8.1	11.8	26.1	36.8	33.9	34.4	41.4	33.7	32.1	30.5	24.3
Haiti	Haïti	24.8	32.1	39.6	49.8	48.5	62.8	67.0	78.7	78.8	71.0	102.4
Kiribati	Kiribati	5.5	3.8	6.0	10.0	8.8	18.6	13.7	14.4	14.4	10.4	10.9
Lao People's Dem.Rep.	Rép. dém. pop. lao	32.6	24.0	26.7	42.6	26.4	16.7	16.8	21.3	12.6	13.8	15.5
Lesotho	Lesotho	14.7	18.1	21.1	30.3	45.7	63.7	62.3	57.2	64.7	66.0	51.5
Malawi	Malawi	47.1	46.2	54.1	56.4	92.0	75.6	82.1	65.0	56.2	51.7	52.9
Maldives	Maldives	2.0	0.6	1.2	3.7	0.9	1.9	2.8	0.9	3.2	3.4	6.9
Mali	Mali	55.7	53.3	60.9	93.0	93.9	131.4	133.0	96.3	96.9	223.7	251.3
Mauritania	Mauritanie	12.8	17.8	24.8	39.6	35.4	53.5	66.7	61.8	72.2	68.7	100.3
Nepal	Népal	28.6	29.2	37.5	39.6	82.4	84.0	88.0	111.4	109.5	98.4	123.5
Niger	Niger	80.2	80.1	59.4	77.7	116.7	105.0	122.5	123.6	107.0	101.9	206.4
Rwanda	Rwanda	53.7	56.6	61.4	78.9	88.4	96.7	102.7	99.1	94.7	96.0	103.1
Samoa	Samoa	8.8	7.3	11.1	11.3	20.7	13.7	14.2	15.4	16.6	11.0	13.2
Sao Tome and Principe	Sao Tomé-et-Principe	-	0.7	1.6	1.8	1.4	1.2	1.8	3.8	3.4	4.0	3.0
Sierra Leone	Sierra Leone	9.8	7.5	12.1	13.5	28.5	56.8	33.8	55.7	35.6	22.6	30.3
Somalia	Somalie	23.3	20.1	25.2	46.8	49.8	139.3	139.8	141.6	151.4	193.0	163.5
Sudan	Soudan	60.2	54.4	55.9	113.1	149.5	272.1	295.9	357.7	438.6	309.0	647.2
Togo	Togo	23.5	20.5	42.4	66.5	68.9	52.1	36.9	50.4	48.8	53.0	53.2
Tuvalu	Tuvalu	-	2.9	2.4	2.5	4.1	4.5	4.5	5.5	3.8	5.2	3.2
Uganda	Ouganda	4.7	9.6	3.8	7.5	16.1	42.3	78.6	52.8	43.7	47.4	42.7
Un. Rep. of Tanzania	Rép.-Un. de Tanzanie	234.7	212.3	257.4	332.8	458.1	523.7	485.6	485.2	429.4	409.8	372.6
Vanuatu	Vanuatu	12.1	30.5	12.6	18.4	37.7	43.3	24.4	23.3	24.4	22.2	18.9
Yemen	Yémen	15.1	11.3	34.2	37.1	51.0	78.5	77.4	85.1	72.1	82.2	84.3
All LDCs	Ensemble des PMA	1845.4	1464.3	1668.6	2379.9	2935.9b/	3490.7c/	3332.8	3559.5	3283.9	3478.8	4209.9
All developing countries	Ensemble des pays en développement	9246.6	8659.7	8979.6	11874	14788	16887	17154	16943	16660	17745	19167

Table 28 (continued)

Source: UNCTAD secretariat, based on information from the OECD/DAC secretariat.

a/ Excluding grants from France to Mayotte.

b/ Excluding $31.8 million and $69.7 million from Canada and France respectively, not allocated by recipient country.

c/ Excluding $19.5 million from Canada, not allocated by recipient country.

Tableau 28 (suite)

Source: Secrétariat de la CNUCED, d'après des renseignements du secrétariat de l'OCDE/CAD.

a/ Non compris l'aide versée au titre de dons par la France à Mayotte.

b/ Non compris 13,8 millions de dollars et 69,7 millions de dollars, en provenance du Canada et de la France respectivement, non alloués par pays bénéficiaires.

c/ Non compris 19,5 millions de dollars en provenance du Canada, non alloués par pays bénéficiaires.

Table 29
Bilateral grants from DAC member countries
to individual LDCs

Tableau 29
Dons reçus par chacun des PMA en provenance des pays membres
du CAD

Net disbursements in $ million   Versements nets en millions de dollars

Country	1975	1976	1977	1978	1979	1980	1981	1982	1983	1984	1985	Pays
Afghanistan	19.6	18.8	27.9	31.8	42.7	17.5	1.9	7.0	11.8	5.4	8.4	Afghanistan
Bangladesh	255.1	147.5	222.4	531.3	538.4	1044.7	542.7	617.7	480.6	573.1	543.2	Bangladesh
Benin	22.4	16.1	16.9	36.4	33.3	42.0	41.3	36.4	33.4	37.1	39.0	Bénin
Bhutan	0.6	1.0	0.6	0.7	1.2	1.7	2.6	3.2	2.9	4.8	6.6	Bhoutan
Botswana	24.8	31.5	31.6	86.2	69.9	81.3	76.4	83.9	75.9	66.4	60.3	Botswana
Burkina Faso	47.0	48.1	62.0	91.8	165.9	133.2	161.4	125.9	105.7	110.4	114.3	Burkina Faso
Burundi	26.5	26.0	27.5	36.5	42.7	57.1	64.8	60.7	59.2	61.9	59.7	Burundi
Cape Verde	2.1	6.8	15.8	25.0	27.2	38.9	35.8	42.5	45.3	39.3	38.3	Cap-Vert
Central African Rep.	33.4	24.0	30.8	29.0	52.9	71.9	58.5	60.7	50.8	65.1	47.5	Rép. centrafricaine
Chad	27.4	40.3	45.7	64.7	51.3	20.4	46.5	35.3	50.0	59.7	91.0	Tchad
Comoros a/	16.9	8.0	1.1	0.6	7.5	14.0	22.7	11.9	13.6	14.7	14.2	Comores a/
Democratic Yemen	4.1	8.5	6.0	6.6	4.9	7.6	5.8	5.8	5.2	3.6	9.1	Yémen démocratique
Djibouti	25.6	26.3	29.7	30.3	20.5	34.1	37.8	44.4	37.0	41.8	52.1	Djibouti
Equatorial Guinea	-	-	-	-	0.1	1.2	4.3	5.1	4.0	8.0	6.9	Guinée équatoriale
Ethiopia	42.6	47.2	55.1	60.9	65.7	87.6	78.3	71.8	95.3	157.7	401.9	Éthiopie
Gambia	1.9	3.8	10.4	11.4	10.8	23.9	17.7	20.8	21.9	30.3	28.4	Gambie
Guinea	0.2	0.3	2.6	9.2	12.7	14.7	21.8	17.4	14.3	29.5	44.3	Guinée
Guinea-Bissau	8.1	11.8	25.2	34.9	33.5	31.8	39.7	33.3	31.9	29.5	29.8	Guinée-Bissau
Haiti	21.8	24.7	26.5	32.5	35.7	48.2	53.8	64.1	66.8	57.6	86.8	Haïti
Kiribati	5.5	3.8	6.0	10.0	8.8	18.6	13.7	14.4	14.4	10.4	10.9	Kiribati
Lao People's Dem.Rep.	27.3	13.8	14.0	28.7	23.9	16.8	17.0	22.0	13.3	15.0	16.8	Rép. dém. pop. lao
Lesotho	14.8	17.9	21.1	30.3	42.6	64.0	62.2	57.1	64.8	66.0	51.6	Lesotho
Malawi	16.4	27.3	21.3	78.8	120.3	58.2	78.3	64.2	56.5	50.3	54.7	Malawi
Maldives	0.8	0.6	1.2	2.6	0.6	1.9	3.0	2.3	3.6	3.7	6.2	Maldives
Mali	52.0	42.4	49.1	74.7	146.3	120.0	133.0	90.7	91.2	122.1	155.5	Mali
Mauritania	14.8	20.4	22.1	30.2	35.3	53.0	56.0	51.4	60.5	62.9	89.3	Mauritanie
Nepal	25.9	27.6	38.7	40.5	69.8	95.3	84.3	108.8	103.9	90.8	112.8	Népal
Niger	61.4	58.7	41.4	91.8	125.9	86.9	104.9	116.9	101.6	87.8	187.1	Niger
Rwanda	52.4	50.4	56.5	75.6	101.3	91.8	92.6	93.9	92.3	93.9	95.6	Rwanda
Samoa	7.6	7.2	11.0	11.3	21.7	13.6	14.2	15.4	16.6	11.0	13.2	Samoa
Sao Tome and Principe	-	0.7	1.6	1.8	1.4	1.2	1.8	3.8	3.4	4.0	3.0	Sao Tomé-et-Principe
Sierra Leone	6.5	6.9	8.9	12.8	22.1	27.5	22.9	22.7	22.2	18.0	76.8	Sierra Leone
Somalia	24.4	18.5	25.9	27.2	39.4	157.0	117.1	105.2	109.2	107.9	138.4	Somalie
Sudan	27.4	27.5	43.2	93.1	112.3	377.4	274.8	337.4	369.0	269.1	568.2	Soudan
Togo	19.9	19.9	24.8	25.1	32.0	31.0	33.2	31.8	36.1	38.5	160.5	Togo
Tuvalu	-	2.9	2.4	2.5	4.1	4.5	4.5	5.5	3.8	5.2	3.2	Tuvalu
Uganda	3.5	3.1	4.0	8.6	27.5	41.3	90.9	54.2	69.1	47.1	40.0	Ouganda
Un. Rep. of Tanzania	152.0	169.6	192.0	420.7	439.3	608.0	443.0	429.3	377.6	363.6	344.9	Rép.-Un. de Tanzanie
Vanuatu	10.6	29.3	12.0	17.9	36.3	43.7	25.0	23.8	24.8	21.9	18.8	Vanuatu
Yemen	11.1	8.1	22.4	30.3	44.0	150.8	54.6	59.8	77.7	70.1	66.4	Yémen
All LDCs	1114.2	1047.3	1257.4	2234.3	2671.7	3834.5	3040.1	3058.5	2918.0	2955.2	3895.7	Ensemble des PMA
All developing countries	5753.5	5896.5	6397.7	8581.1	10795	13192	12151	12351	12653	13969	15517	Ensemble des pays en développement

Source: UNCTAD secretariat, based on information from the
OECD/DAC secretariat.
a/ Excluding grants from France to Mayotte.

Source: Secrétariat de la CNUCED, d'après des renseignements du
secrétariat de l'OCDE/CAD.
a/ Non compris l'aide versée au titre de dons par la France
à Mayotte.

Table 30
Concessional assistance from multilateral agencies
mainly financed by DAC member countries to individual LDCs

Tableau 30
Aide concessionnelle reçue par chacun des PMA en provenance
des institutions multilatérales essentiellement financées par
les pays membres du CAD

Net disbursements in $ million   Versements nets en millions de dollars

Country	1975	1976	1977	1978	1979	1980	1981	1982	1983	1984	1985	Pays
Afghanistan	21.0	29.1	47.7	44.4	52.5	19.4	10.5	8.6	10.5	8.5	11.4	Afghanistan
Bangladesh	252.5	201.3	202.0	295.2	357.5	357.8	342.9	375.8	375.0	500.1	517.8	Bangladesh
Benin	22.9	23.4	18.4	27.4	32.5	50.6	32.6	35.1	38.8	37.6	44.0	Bénin
Bhutan	1.5	2.2	2.3	2.5	4.7	6.6	7.2	8.1	10.0	12.8	14.7	Bhoutan
Botswana	7.4	7.0	9.4	13.7	25.5	20.4	20.6	9.7	16.7	26.9	33.2	Botswana
Burkina Faso	33.0	23.0	35.7	61.3	61.4	54.3	50.2	54.0	53.3	56.4	68.5	Burkina Faso
Burundi	20.7	18.6	18.0	32.8	44.5	49.4	53.0	45.4	62.7	57.9	58.5	Burundi
Cape Verde	6.6	6.3	8.6	7.5	21.4	21.4	13.1	10.6	14.6	20.6	23.0	Cap-Vert
Central African Rep.	22.1	12.4	10.2	21.6	31.1	33.8	28.8	19.9	27.9	43.4	41.5	Rép. centrafricaine
Chad	28.9	17.7	32.3	46.9	30.3	15.1	28.5	25.6	43.8	55.7	85.0	Tchad
Comoros	4.2	3.2	6.8	5.8	7.2	12.0	14.3	11.9	13.8	15.7	20.5	Comores
Democratic Yemen	14.1	14.2	25.2	34.1	35.0	34.5	31.4	47.7	50.7	40.0	37.8	Yémen démocratique
Djibouti	0.3	-	1.8	2.7	4.1	8.6	13.8	10.4	10.9	10.5	16.0	Djibouti
Equatorial Guinea	0.7	0.4	0.6	0.6	2.6	8.1	5.5	7.9	6.7	7.1	10.5	Guinée équatoriale
Ethiopia	46.2	67.7	52.7	81.1	103.8	120.4	150.5	122.9	176.2	175.9	289.7	Ethiopie
Gambia	4.2	4.4	5.2	11.9	16.8	23.7	26.0	19.4	19.5	19.2	17.9	Gambie
Guinea	3.9	7.1	12.0	38.4	34.3	52.4	48.4	33.4	40.8	46.6	52.2	Guinée
Guinea-Bissau	7.4	6.9	9.8	10.9	15.9	21.2	22.3	26.0	25.6	22.4	30.5	Guinée-Bissau
Haiti	34.5	39.6	44.9	43.1	44.2	42.3	38.6	47.0	53.5	63.4	49.3	Haïti
Kiribati	0.1	0.3	0.2	0.7	0.3	0.6	1.6	0.7	2.4	1.6	1.2	Kiribati
Lao People's Dem.Rep.	6.3	4.4	3.5	29.2	23.5	23.4	18.1	16.6	16.7	19.2	21.4	Rép. dém. pop. lao
Lesotho	12.7	12.1	16.2	20.9	20.2	30.6	40.9	33.4	35.0	29.4	37.5	Lesotho
Malawi	16.8	17.1	25.3	42.1	49.7	66.4	55.2	56.2	60.7	106.9	60.2	Malawi
Maldives	1.0	0.9	0.8	1.1	1.6	2.2	2.2	2.1	3.7	3.1	3.5	Maldives
Mali	59.6	32.7	36.2	58.4	85.8	93.1	77.2	63.0	71.7	86.4	97.7	Mali
Mauritania	24.3	20.2	23.8	47.4	74.3	33.2	43.8	31.4	35.1	40.8	42.6	Mauritanie
Nepal	16.8	20.8	33.9	35.5	50.9	72.3	81.2	83.9	90.7	100.7	114.4	Népal
Niger	43.9	45.3	31.6	57.2	50.9	56.6	41.8	44.0	50.8	53.6	97.1	Niger
Rwanda	27.9	22.3	29.1	42.2	57.0	51.5	42.6	49.9	53.7	62.7	72.8	Rwanda
Samoa	0.6	4.4	7.9	8.4	8.7	11.2	9.8	6.5	10.4	9.2	6.0	Samoa
Sao Tome and Principe	0.3	1.0	1.4	2.2	1.6	2.7	3.8	5.6	7.7	6.9	9.2	Sao Tomé-et-Principe
Sierra Leone	6.5	7.5	13.0	26.5	19.8	27.2	24.2	25.1	28.9	21.9	30.7	Sierra Leone
Somalia	49.4	47.3	43.0	41.2	52.1	150.9	167.4	137.4	131.9	140.7	151.8	Somalie
Sudan	50.1	61.2	53.6	111.2	112.4	169.5	188.1	197.1	160.8	191.3	266.2	Soudan
Togo	16.3	20.0	21.8	35.9	40.8	35.3	25.5	23.0	57.6	53.4	51.3	Togo
Tuvalu	0.1	0.0	0.0	0.3	0.1	0.4	0.9	0.8	0.4	0.3	0.2	Tuvalu
Uganda	8.6	10.5	10.3	9.6	25.2	69.8	56.9	74.6	80.7	117.9	140.0	Ouganda
Un. Rep. of Tanzania	53.5	55.0	70.0	89.6	126.1	123.4	164.6	172.9	135.7	133.4	105.0	Rép.-Un. de Tanzanie
Vanuatu	0.5	0.5	2.1	0.4	0.7	0.7	6.1	2.7	2.5	2.3	2.9	Vanuatu
Yemen	21.6	36.2	30.4	35.9	30.7	42.7	38.4	51.5	52.1	53.2	52.0	Yémen
All LDCs	953.0	904.2	997.5	1477.8	1741.3	2017.1	2028.5	1997.7	2140.2	2456.4	2785.7	Ensemble des PMA
All developing countries	3672.1	3419.2	3655.2	4868.9	5816.7	7362.7	6963.2	7010.5	7044.1	7312.3	7809.1	Ensemble des pays en développement

Source: UNCTAD secretariat, based on information from the OECD/DAC secretariat.

Source: Secrétariat de la CNUCED, d'après des renseignements du secrétariat de l'OCDE/CAD.

Table 31
Grants from multilateral agencies mainly financed by
DAC member countries to individual LDCs

Tableau 31
Dons reçus par chacun des PMA en provenance des institutions
multilatérales essentiellement financées par les pays
membres du CAD

Net disbursements in $ million   Versements nets en millions de dollars

Country	1975	1976	1977	1978	1979	1980	1981	1982	1983	1984	1985	Pays
Afghanistan	16.4	13.5	20.2	21.9	34.0	9.4	9.5	9.2	11.0	9.2	11.7	Afghanistan
Bangladesh	107.4	82.3	87.4	107.8	105.2	95.7	130.6	153.3	123.0	169.6	85.3	Bangladesh
Benin	17.3	16.9	10.4	17.5	23.4	24.9	19.3	17.1	15.6	17.8	17.4	Bénin
Bhutan	1.5	2.2	2.3	2.5	4.7	6.6	6.9	7.4	9.3	12.1	11.0	Bhoutan
Botswana	6.2	5.5	7.4	11.0	20.8	16.8	17.4	9.6	16.1	21.4	30.3	Botswana
Burkina Faso	26.6	15.7	17.4	37.3	32.2	27.3	32.6	40.4	32.2	41.4	41.3	Burkina Faso
Burundi	20.4	17.4	12.0	16.6	24.9	26.9	38.6	18.9	25.9	22.7	24.8	Burundi
Cape Verde	6.6	6.3	8.6	7.5	5.1	10.9	9.3	8.5	12.9	17.7	17.7	Cap-Vert
Central African Rep.	21.4	12.1	9.1	11.2	18.0	18.0	20.7	14.0	18.3	24.3	19.5	Rép. centrafricaine
Chad	23.6	12.5	13.6	21.6	19.4	13.1	26.7	25.1	42.8	49.7	76.4	Tchad
Comoros	4.2	3.2	6.8	5.2	4.8	7.1	11.2	9.6	9.6	7.1	10.8	Comores
Democratic Yemen	12.3	7.3	17.2	15.1	17.3	19.0	22.2	29.6	24.0	19.4	20.1	Yémen démocratique
Djibouti	0.3	-	1.8	2.7	3.7	8.0	13.0	9.4	9.6	9.4	9.7	Djibouti
Equatorial Guinea	0.7	0.4	0.4	0.6	2.6	2.2	5.5	7.8	6.0	6.5	6.3	Guinée équatoriale
Ethiopia	27.5	30.7	18.3	33.0	42.4	81.1	111.0	87.9	117.5	127.8	215.8	Ethiopie
Gambia	3.3	3.4	2.2	7.5	11.2	16.0	22.0	14.6	10.2	13.5	10.0	Gambie
Guinea	3.9	5.9	5.7	18.5	17.1	28.9	21.5	20.0	16.9	23.0	19.1	Guinée
Guinea-Bissau	7.4	6.9	9.8	10.6	14.4	16.9	13.0	13.2	11.2	15.6	14.2	Guinée-Bissau
Haiti	10.9	9.3	7.6	13.1	13.7	14.3	12.7	18.5	13.1	19.5	15.8	Haïti
Kiribati	0.1	0.3	0.2	0.2	0.3	0.6	1.6	0.7	2.4	1.6	1.1	Kiribati
Lao People's Dem.Rep.	3.8	4.0	3.6	20.3	16.6	13.2	11.5	8.2	8.2	10.2	12.0	Rép. dém. pop. lao
Lesotho	10.9	9.8	10.4	14.8	14.4	20.1	28.1	16.1	22.9	20.3	24.3	Lesotho
Malawi	5.3	4.8	9.0	13.8	17.4	26.7	25.6	21.9	17.5	24.5	17.9	Malawi
Maldives	1.0	0.9	0.8	1.1	1.6	2.0	1.7	2.0	2.6	2.6	2.7	Maldives
Mali	45.1	17.0	19.7	31.9	49.0	56.4	49.3	39.0	39.6	61.3	56.0	Mali
Mauritania	22.6	15.9	15.7	35.6	65.8	18.1	36.1	23.6	26.1	31.5	33.7	Mauritanie
Nepal	10.7	10.5	14.7	13.6	20.1	33.9	32.1	29.8	36.3	31.5	35.1	Népal
Niger	41.6	41.6	24.1	41.2	38.0	24.9	26.5	30.6	29.5	34.2	63.7	Niger
Rwanda	22.3	13.7	17.6	28.1	32.3	30.6	32.3	32.6	25.9	28.6	36.6	Rwanda
Samoa	1.8	2.5	4.0	2.4	4.3	5.1	5.2	3.8	5.2	4.0	4.2	Samoa
Sao Tome and Principe	0.3	1.0	1.4	2.2	1.6	2.7	1.8	3.0	6.0	6.7	8.4	Sao Tomé-et-Principe
Sierra Leone	4.1	5.5	7.9	6.6	7.9	14.1	17.7	13.5	18.3	12.4	16.5	Sierra Leone
Somalia	39.7	39.2	32.6	30.5	43.8	125.6	146.0	112.4	105.0	109.1	104.1	Somalie
Sudan	35.0	22.3	28.3	34.5	56.5	104.5	105.4	102.2	96.1	108.0	223.6	Soudan
Togo	14.2	15.6	11.7	16.1	14.0	13.0	14.5	8.7	23.0	26.4	16.6	Togo
Tuvalu	0.1	0.0	0.0	0.3	0.1	0.4	0.9	0.8	0.4	0.2	0.2	Tuvalu
Uganda	5.9	7.9	9.3	8.1	24.2	39.9	43.2	30.8	41.1	51.4	44.3	Ouganda
Un. Rep. of Tanzania	36.0	26.3	23.5	36.3	48.4	50.3	66.4	60.9	52.3	65.8	63.1	Rép.-Un. de Tanzanie
Vanuatu	0.5	0.5	2.1	0.4	0.7	0.7	6.1	2.3	2.4	1.7	2.3	Vanuatu
Yemen	14.5	18.3	13.6	13.7	17.0	20.5	20.9	26.7	20.4	21.0	15.0	Yémen
All LDCs	633.4	509.1	508.5	712.9	888.9	1046.3	1216.5	1083.6	1106.3	1280.7	1438.6	Ensemble des PMA
All developing countries	2140.7	1636.5	1815.0	2339.2	2974.8	3342.2	3949.0	3605.9	3666.0	3813.3	4214.2	Ensemble des pays en développement

Source: UNCTAD secretariat, based on information from the OECD/DAC secretariat.

Source: Secrétariat de la CNUCED, d'après des renseignements du secrétariat de l'OCDE/CAD.

Table 32
Non-concessional assistance from multilateral agencies
mainly financed by DAC member countries to individual LDCs

Net disbursements in $ million

Tableau 32
Aide non-concessionnelle reçue par chacun des PMA en provenance
des institutions multilatérales essentiellement financées par
les pays membres du CAD

Versements nets en millions de dollars

Country	1975	1976	1977	1978	1979	1980	1981	1982	1983	1984	1985	Pays
Afghanistan	55.9	-	-	-	-	-	-	-	-	-	-	Afghanistan
Bangladesh	0.1	0.2	0.0	-0.5	-0.5	1.3	-0.3	0.4	-0.7	-0.7	-0.8	Bangladesh
Benin	-	1.1	3.5	2.5	1.2	3.4	2.5	-0.4	0.1	-0.4	-1.4	Bénin
Bhutan	-	-	-	-	-	-	-	-	-	-	-	Bhoutan
Botswana	2.7	2.1	2.9	2.5	5.5	3.3	9.7	16.6	18.5	23.0	37.7	Botswana
Burkina Faso	-	1.0	-0.2	0.7	-0.5	0.0	-0.5	-0.4	2.6	1.8	2.3	Burkina Faso
Burundi	0.3	1.5	1.1	0.2	-0.2	0.3	0.3	0.9	9.9	10.5	4.9	Burundi
Cape Verde	-	-	-	-	-	-	-	7.0	4.1	0.7	1.2	Cap-Vert
Central African Rep.	0.6	0.2	-	0.0	-0.1	0.2	0.0	-0.1	0.8	1.6	3.1	Rép. centrafricaine
Chad	-	-	-	-	-	-	-	-	-	-	-	Tchad
Comoros	-	-	-	-	-	-	-	1.1	2.6	2.6	3.4	Comores
Democratic Yemen	-	-	-	-	-	-	-	-	-	-	-	Yémen démocratique
Djibouti	-	-	-	-	-	-	-	-	-	-	-	Djibouti
Equatorial Guinea	-	-	-	-	-	-	-	-	-	-	-	Guinée équatoriale
Ethiopia	2.1	-1.8	-3.7	-3.9	-4.0	0.7	1.5	2.6	1.2	-1.8	-0.3	Ethiopie
Gambia	-	-	0.0	0.1	0.8	-2.2	-1.3	-1.9	-1.3	-1.8	-3.1	Gambie
Guinea	1.3	-2.1	-0.3	-1.8	-1.4	5.7	2.1	1.3	1.2	4.1	1.5	Guinée
Guinea-Bissau	-	-	-	-	-	-2.5	-2.4	0.6	2.1	12.9	-0.3	Guinée-Bissau
Haiti	-	-	-	-	-	0.0	0.4	2.0	4.0	2.8	1.2	Haïti
Kiribati	-	-	-	-	-	-	7.9	-	0.7	-	-	Kiribati
Lao People's Dem.Rep.	-	-	-	-	-	-	-	-	-	-	-	Rép. dém. pop. lao
Lesotho	0.4	3.0	8.7	0.3	-	-	0.2	2.1	2.4	4.7	10.7	Lesotho
Malawi	-	-	-	11.9	21.8	15.8	26.7	22.0	2.5	1.4	4.2	Malawi
Maldives	-	-	-	-	-	-	-	-	-	-	-	Maldives
Mali	-0.1	-0.1	0.5	2.6	1.6	1.1	0.4	1.6	0.8	-1.1	-0.9	Mali
Mauritania	-21.6	-0.4	1.2	0.0	0.3	-0.5	16.1	38.7	34.1	-	-5.8	Mauritanie
Nepal	0.1	-0.1	2.1	0.5	-0.2	-0.3	-0.4	-0.3	-	2.4	2.5	Népal
Niger	0.2	-0.1	-0.1	0.9	7.4	6.8	3.8	0.7	14.5	0.6	-1.0	Niger
Rwanda	-	-	0.3	0.2	-	0.2	0.1	1.2	0.6	-0.3	-0.4	Rwanda
Samoa	-	-	-	-	-	-	-	-	-	-	-	Samoa
Sao Tome and Principe	-	-	-	-	-	-	-	-	-	-	-	Sao Tomé-et-Principe
Sierra Leone	3.9	1.3	0.8	-0.1	2.1	3.3	1.3	0.3	-0.9	-3.6	-0.6	Sierra Leone
Somalia	1.5	0.1	0.0	0.0	-0.2	-	0.2	-0.1	-0.4	0.6	2.3	Somalie
Sudan	-2.9	0.4	-3.1	3.7	2.7	-2.4	-0.5	-3.1	-5.4	-8.5	-4.9	Soudan
Togo	-0.1	0.8	1.8	29.8	29.0	31.8	-2.6	-2.5	-1.1	-1.0	-2.7	Togo
Tuvalu	-	-	-	-	-	-	-	-	-	-	-	Tuvalu
Uganda	0.9	2.6	2.5	0.5	3.1	1.8	4.8	6.0	6.6	5.4	49.0	Ouganda
Un. Rep. of Tanzania	39.6	11.7	24.0	16.0	20.2	21.0	17.8	6.9	17.3	7.5	34.0	Rép.-Un. de Tanzanie
Vanuatu	-	-	-	-	-	-	-	-	-	-	-	Vanuatu
Yemen	-	-	-	-	2.4	-	-	-	-0.9	-0.5	11.1	Yémen
All LDCs	84.9	22.2	42.0	66.1	91.0	88.8	87.8	103.2	115.9	65.0	146.9	Ensemble des PMA
All developing countries	2480.0	2467.6	2625.2	2878.1	3837.7	4574.1	5414.1	6381.4	7017.9	7913.3	7112.2	Ensemble des pays en développement

Source: UNCTAD secretariat, based on information from the OECD/DAC secretariat.

Source: Secrétariat de la CNUCED, d'après des renseignements du secrétariat de l'OCDE/CAD.

Table 33
Technical assistance disbursements a/

Tableau 33
Versements au titre de l'assistance technique a/

$ million   Millions de dollars

Country	1975	1976	1977	1978	1979	1980	1981	1982	1983	1984	1985	Pays
Afghanistan	25.1	20.3	28.1	31.1	37.8	21.8	14.8	13.9	15.2	12.4	15.4	Afghanistan
Bangladesh	58.3	60.1	27.4	99.8	148.3	158.9	147.2	133.2	176.0	157.7	165.1	Bangladesh
Benin	19.8	16.0	13.7	16.9	20.4	25.9	25.1	27.9	25.5	28.1	29.9	Bénin
Bhutan	1.8	2.7	2.1	2.2	4.8	6.0	7.4	6.2	7.2	8.8	10.3	Bhoutan
Botswana	13.7	15.5	18.0	23.0	36.4	47.5	48.0	42.8	40.5	34.8	33.9	Botswana
Burkina Faso	32.6	37.5	37.6	49.1	60.7	73.0	72.1	73.7	65.2	71.4	67.3	Burkina Faso
Burundi	23.2	23.0	25.6	30.4	35.7	45.1	44.2	46.9	43.3	42.7	45.1	Burundi
Cape Verde	1.0	2.2	2.8	5.6	6.2	11.9	11.4	20.6	17.3	17.0	19.1	Cap-Vert
Central African Rep.	19.5	19.4	20.8	24.6	32.9	34.1	33.6	31.2	28.9	38.5	33.9	Rép. centrafricaine
Chad	25.4	22.0	24.6	29.2	21.4	11.9	16.8	15.3	21.7	18.8	42.4	Tchad
Comoros	7.0	2.2	2.3	1.3	2.9	7.0	10.1	9.6	9.9	9.4	10.6	Comores
Democratic Yemen	9.2	11.3	10.6	10.8	7.9	11.6	12.6	14.8	14.3	9.9	12.5	Yémen démocratique
Djibouti	11.1	14.0	15.2	14.3	19.0	27.8	29.8	30.9	29.3	29.8	29.5	Djibouti
Equatorial Guinea	0.7	0.4	0.4	0.6	2.2	2.0	4.5	4.1	3.9	6.7	6.0	Guinée équatoriale
Ethiopia	36.1	31.5	30.3	26.5	29.2	44.2	63.9	53.1	63.6	80.9	103.7	Ethiopie
Gambia	2.7	4.3	3.3	6.8	9.6	12.7	13.8	17.4	15.8	14.8	17.3	Gambie
Guinea	3.4	5.5	6.0	10.3	11.1	18.7	21.4	20.5	14.4	17.9	18.9	Guinée
Guinea-Bissau	2.5	7.0	4.6	6.7	9.0	12.1	12.7	15.2	16.1	11.8	14.7	Guinée-Bissau
Haiti	11.8	13.5	13.6	20.5	24.0	32.3	32.8	34.1	31.0	33.0	39.7	Haïti
Kiribati	2.3	2.7	2.7	3.6	3.4	5.5	4.5	5.0	4.4	3.7	4.8	Kiribati
Lao People's Dem.Rep.	15.0	4.5	5.0	11.8	12.0	14.0	13.3	11.3	10.7	12.3	13.8	Rép. dém. pop. lao
Lesotho	8.7	12.1	12.8	16.6	21.2	32.0	33.4	34.7	34.7	34.0	29.5	Lesotho
Malawi	16.3	17.4	17.6	24.0	30.0	36.4	38.1	37.2	34.7	39.7	33.4	Malawi
Maldives	0.8	1.0	1.0	1.5	2.2	2.8	2.5	3.6	3.8	3.6	4.9	Maldives
Mali	24.6	23.2	25.6	35.4	49.5	76.9	63.0	55.0	52.8	59.9	59.2	Mali
Mauritania	11.4	13.3	13.8	18.6	24.5	28.8	37.7	33.7	32.6	31.3	35.8	Mauritanie
Nepal	24.7	20.4	26.0	30.6	38.1	50.5	52.7	63.8	68.0	68.4	68.3	Népal
Niger	29.2	27.9	30.5	38.4	47.3	62.1	59.2	68.3	60.8	61.1	73.0	Niger
Rwanda	31.4	32.3	41.2	42.8	50.9	54.6	53.3	49.7	53.9	50.1	58.4	Rwanda
Samoa	4.7	4.7	5.6	6.8	6.0	9.8	10.8	7.6	7.3	6.9	7.6	Samoa
Sao Tome and Principe	0.3	0.5	0.9	1.5	1.3	1.3	1.4	2.8	1.6	2.3	3.1	Sao Tomé-et-Principe
Sierra Leone	7.9	10.4	10.4	13.2	14.9	21.4	21.7	21.3	19.2	19.4	21.6	Sierra Leone
Somalia	19.6	16.0	19.4	21.5	32.1	92.9	103.2	92.0	113.5	107.4	131.5	Somalie
Sudan	28.1	30.9	37.8	60.4	69.3	102.6	131.6	118.0	127.9	121.8	203.0	Soudan
Togo	16.9	16.9	18.9	21.9	25.0	28.9	30.4	30.3	27.5	29.9	28.9	Togo
Tuvalu	0.1	0.2	1.0	0.7	0.6	1.4	1.8	1.8	1.5	1.4	1.5	Tuvalu
Uganda	9.0	8.4	7.7	12.0	16.4	21.0	33.8	29.5	34.0	32.4	36.6	Ouganda
Un. Rep. of Tanzania	60.2	77.0	80.2	106.5	138.6	172.9	176.8	181.2	173.9	138.7	135.6	Rép.-Un. de Tanzanie
Vanuatu	2.1	14.5	2.3	2.7	22.4	24.7	17.2	16.1	16.0	13.1	11.7	Vanuatu
Yemen	17.0	15.7	25.2	32.8	39.5	50.4	60.6	64.7	59.9	61.5	56.4	Yémen
All LDCs	635.1	658.4	671.8	913.0	1164.7	1495.3	1569.2	1539.0	1577.8	1543.3	1733.9	Ensemble des PMA
All developing countries	3971.3	3807.7	4076.7	5000.4	6252.1	7255.2	7383.5	7364.4	7701.6	7744.7	7925.7	Ensemble des pays en développement

Source: UNCTAD secretariat, based on information from the OECD/DAC secretariat.
   a/ Bilateral contributions from DAC member countries plus contributions from multilateral agencies mainly financed by them.

Source: Secrétariat de la CNUCED, d'après des renseignements du secrétariat de l'OCDE/CAD.
   a/ Somme des contributions bilatérales des pays membres du CAD et des contributions des institutions multilatérales essentiellement financées par ceux-ci.

Table 34

Tableau 34

Net ODA as per cent of donor's GNP from individual DAC member countries to LDCs as a group

Apports nets de l'APD accordée par chaque pays membre du CAD à l'ensemble des PMA, en pourcentage du PNB du pays donneur

Percentages / En pourcentage

Bilateral ODA / APD bilatérale

Country / Pays	1976	1977	1978	1979	1980	1981	1982	1983	1984	1985
Australia / Australie	0.02	0.02	0.03	0.05	0.03	0.04	0.06	0.04	0.04	0.03
Austria / Autriche	0.00	0.01	0.01	0.00	0.01	0.01	0.01	0.01	0.01	0.01
Belgium / Belgique	0.08	0.08	0.08	0.09	0.06	0.09	0.08	0.07	0.07	0.11
Canada / Canada	0.07	0.06	0.08	0.09	0.06	0.09	0.08	0.07	0.07	0.09
Denmark / Danemark	0.11	0.13	0.14	0.15	0.18	0.13	0.16	0.18	0.15	0.20
Finland / Finlande	0.05	0.04	0.03	0.04	0.04	0.05	0.04	0.07	0.08	0.08
France / France	0.07	0.06	0.06	0.06	0.07	0.09	0.08	0.08	0.11	0.11
Germany, Fed.Rep. of / Allemagne, Rép.féd.d'	0.05	0.05	0.06	0.07	0.07	0.08	0.08	0.07	0.07	0.07
Ireland / Irlande	0.01	0.01	0.02	0.02	0.03	0.08	0.08	0.04	0.04	0.05
Italy / Italie	0.01	0.01	0.01	0.01	0.01	0.02	0.03	0.05	0.07	0.10
Japan / Japon	0.01	0.02	0.02	0.03	0.04	0.03	0.04	0.02	0.02	0.02
Netherlands / Pays-Bas	0.09	0.14	0.16	0.17	0.19	0.21	0.19	0.16	0.19	0.16
New Zealand / Nouvelle-Zélande	0.04	0.04	0.04	0.03	0.03	0.03	0.02	0.02	0.03	0.03
Norway / Norvège	0.13	0.18	0.20	0.20	0.17	0.16	0.22	0.23	0.19	0.22
Sweden / Suède	0.15	0.17	0.16	0.20	0.16	0.16	0.17	0.16	0.14	0.13
Switzerland / Suisse	0.02	0.03	0.05	0.03	0.05	0.06	0.06	0.07	0.07	0.07
United Kingdom / Royaume-Uni	0.05	0.05	0.07	0.07	0.07	0.06	0.06	0.05	0.05	0.05
United States / Etats-Unis	0.02	0.01	0.02	0.02	0.02	0.02	0.02	0.02	0.02	0.03
Total DAC countries / Total pays du CAD	0.03	0.04	0.04	0.05	0.05	0.05	0.05	0.04	0.04	0.05

Total ODA a/ / APD totale a/

Country / Pays	1976	1977	1978	1979	1980	1981	1982	1983	1984	1985
Australia / Australie	0.03	0.03	0.08	0.10	0.07	0.06	0.10	0.08	0.07	0.08
Austria / Autriche	0.02	0.01	0.03	0.04	0.01	0.04	0.04	0.03	0.03	0.05
Belgium / Belgique	0.12	0.11	0.14	0.14	0.13	0.17	0.15	0.13	0.14	0.18
Canada / Canada	0.11	0.13	0.15	0.15	0.11	0.11	0.12	0.13	0.13	0.15
Denmark / Danemark	0.18	0.20	0.23	0.25	0.30	0.25	0.29	0.27	0.29	0.31
Finland / Finlande	0.08	0.06	0.06	0.07	0.07	0.08	0.08	0.10	0.12	0.13
France / France	0.10	0.08	0.08	0.08	0.11	0.13	0.13	0.12	0.15	0.15
Germany, Fed.Rep. of / Allemagne, Rép.féd.d'	0.09	0.09	0.10	0.12	0.13	0.13	0.12	0.12	0.12	0.13
Ireland / Irlande	0.01	0.01	0.02	0.02	0.03	0.03	0.04	0.08	0.09	0.09
Italy / Italie	0.03	0.03	0.04	0.02	0.06	0.06	0.07	0.08	0.09	0.13
Japan / Japon	0.03	0.04	0.05	0.06	0.08	0.05	0.05	0.06	0.06	0.06
Netherlands / Pays-Bas	0.17	0.20	0.21	0.25	0.27	0.30	0.29	0.24	0.30	0.26
New Zealand / Nouvelle-Zélande	0.06	0.06	0.05	0.05	0.04	0.04	0.04	0.04	0.04	0.04
Norway / Norvège	0.23	0.28	0.32	0.33	0.29	0.29	0.37	0.35	0.31	0.35
Sweden / Suède	0.23	0.27	0.27	0.31	0.23	0.26	0.31	0.25	0.22	0.22
Switzerland / Suisse	0.04	0.06	0.07	0.06	0.08	0.09	0.08	0.10	0.10	0.10
United Kingdom / Royaume-Uni	0.08	0.11	0.13	0.14	0.11	0.12	0.11	0.10	0.10	0.10
United States / Etats-Unis	0.04	0.03	0.05	0.02	0.05	0.03	0.05	0.04	0.04	0.04
Total DAC countries / Total pays du CAD	0.06	0.07	0.08	0.08	0.09	0.08	0.08	0.08	0.08	0.08

Source: UNCTAD secretariat, based on information from the OECD/DAC secretariat.
a/ Including imputed flows to LDCs through multilateral channels.

Source: Secrétariat de la CNUCED, d'après des renseignements du secrétariat de l'OCDE/CAD.
a/ Y compris le montant imputé de l'APD fournie aux PMA à travers les voies multilatérales.

Table 35
ODA commitments from individual DAC member countries
and individual multilateral agencies a/
to all LDCs

Tableau 35
Engagements de l'APD de chaque pays membre du CAD
et de chaque institution multilatérale a/
en faveur de l'ensemble des PMA

$ million / Millions de dollars

	1975	1976	1977	1978	1979	1980	1981	1982	1983	1984	1985
A.Bilateral donors / A.Donneurs bilatéraux											
Australia / Australie	28.3	10.8	52.4	48.5	37.3	53.3	76.7	64.1	58.9	51.8	47.5
Austria / Autriche	0.5	0.9	0.3	2.4	0.3	0.9	1.1	6.3	5.7	4.9	7.4
Belgium / Belgique	62.9	68.4	76.1	101.0	105.9	112.9	89.8	72.1	65.3	51.4	91.5
Canada	191.3	141.9	356.1	511.5	198.2	121.7	204.1	238.2	306.9	342.5	305.5
Denmark / Danemark	34.4	46.2	49.7	217.9	117.5	108.5	58.2	115.6	88.7	153.8	135.4
Finland / Finlande	20.7	10.6	9.7	8.3	41.4	38.8	38.4	35.0	21.2	42.6	108.5
France	309.6	305.6	235.3	233.5	364.2	599.8	608.1	534.3	574.7	648.9	609.9
Germany,Fed.Rep.of / Allemagne, Rép. Féd. d'	310.9	373.5	352.1	514.0	1027.8	1842.8	731.0	487.4	504.6	494.1	709.1
Ireland / Irlande	0.2	0.4	0.7	2.0	3.2	5.1	5.6	6.2	6.8	6.8	8.0
Italy / Italie	14.7	12.1	16.5	15.7	19.4	43.9	225.5	214.2	284.5	296.3	444.3
Japan / Japon	154.9	108.6	165.3	349.3	332.3	405.2	373.6	455.8	324.8	397.7	367.1
Netherlands / Pays-Bas	107.9	148.1	257.4	418.4	328.8	365.6	317.2	204.6	253.8	203.7	204.6
New Zealand / Nouvelle-Zélande	7.0	1.9	3.6	8.6	5.3	9.8	9.8	4.4	3.7	5.4	11.4
Norway / Norvège	47.6	34.9	57.0	71.5	68.4	67.9	121.0	101.8	86.0	108.1	128.0
Sweden / Suède	151.1	130.0	265.3	224.8	285.7	164.3	192.5	167.6	145.2	145.5	146.7
Switzerland / Suisse	14.4	7.8	34.6	41.5	24.5	56.6	101.8	36.0	80.9	51.2	103.6
United Kingdom / Royaume-Uni	223.1	249.1	126.9	437.0	499.0	437.7	235.1	156.4	192.5	235.6	197.5
United States / Etats-Unis	527.4	387.4	387.4	448.9	519.7	641.2	652.6	719.7	789.1	1061.0	1074.8
Total bilateral concessional / Total des apports bilatéraux concessionnels	2207.2	2038.0	2446.4	3654.6	3979.0	5076.0	4041.7	3619.6	3793.3	4301.1	4700.8
B.Multilateral donors / B.Donneurs multilatéraux											
AfDB/AfDF / BAfD/FAfD	95.2	80.0	121.9	144.5	164.1	190.3	224.4	210.1	243.6	173.5	293.3
AsDB / BAsD	70.9	127.4	128.2	130.9	178.5	204.3	241.2	256.7	378.1	390.8	372.8
EEC/EDF / CEE/FED	173.7	384.0	472.4	380.9	483.1	495.2	590.8	605.0	479.2	536.0	421.8
IBRD / BIRD	-	62.7	31.5	-	-	-	-	-	-	-	-
IDA / AID	607.3	540.7	610.7	769.8	686.3	1237.3	1004.8	1194.5	1295.5	1362.5	1158.6
IDB / BID	41.1	5.0	15.7	43.5	4.1	9.1	-	32.6	17.4	-	24.7
IFAD / FIDA	-	-	-	62.3	120.1	144.6	154.8	60.5	82.8	89.7	83.1
UN / ONU	329.0	312.4	294.7	411.7	489.2	612.3	754.0	704.1	744.8	830.9	996.7
Total multilateral concessional / Total des apports multilatéraux concessionnels	1317.1	1512.1	1675.1	1943.6	2125.3	2893.2	2970.0	3063.5	3241.4	3383.4	3351.0
GRAND TOTAL / TOTAL GENERAL	3524.3	3550.1	4121.4	5598.2	6104.3	7969.2	7011.8	6683.1	7034.7	7684.5	8051.8

Source: UNCTAD secretariat based on information from the
OECD/DAC secretariat.

Source: Secrétariat de la CNUCED, d'après des renseignements du
secrétariat de l'OCDE/CAD.

a/ Multilateral agencies mainly financed by
DAC member countries.

a/ Institutions multilatérales essentiellement financées
par les pays membres du CAD.

Table 36
ODA commitments from DAC member countries
and multilateral agencies mainly financed by them
to individual LDCs

$ million

Tableau 36
Engagements de l'APD à chacun des PMA, en provenance des pays
membres du CAD et des institutions multilatérales
essentiellement financées par ceux-ci

Millions de dollars

Country	1975	1976	1977	1978	1979	1980	1981	1982	1983	1984	1985	Pays
Afghanistan	71.8	117.3	112.1	134.8	148.0	17.3	13.9	14.5	17.1	13.9	19.4	Afghanistan
Bangladesh	1215.5	877.6	892.5	1411.3	1216.2	2007.0	1455.1	1511.6	1354.6	1618.2	1477.6	Bangladesh
Benin	47.3	57.7	73.7	120.7	78.8	99.0	125.7	154.6	61.7	151.2	89.2	Bénin
Bhutan	1.8	3.6	3.0	3.1	5.3	15.4	11.8	12.4	24.8	28.2	47.4	Bhoutan
Botswana	54.0	52.7	58.1	153.8	123.6	126.5	113.2	101.0	101.7	108.1	113.1	Botswana
Burkina Faso	111.6	134.2	139.7	202.0	255.5	244.8	322.0	268.6	195.3	202.3	249.9	Burkina Faso
Burundi	61.2	68.4	75.9	78.4	127.5	171.0	222.0	97.8	169.0	114.3	201.6	Burundi
Cape Verde	16.7	20.1	36.9	47.6	59.3	56.5	71.2	59.5	74.0	93.3	62.0	Cap-Vert
Central African Rep.	57.2	32.4	61.6	62.4	85.3	129.9	85.4	145.8	142.0	97.0	105.0	Rép. centrafricaine
Chad	73.6	113.5	86.4	134.5	50.6	35.2	96.1	67.9	99.3	136.5	210.6	Tchad
Comoros	20.9	11.6	15.8	15.7	22.0	35.4	56.2	43.9	33.3	49.2	26.9	Comores
Democratic Yemen	37.2	17.4	25.4	45.3	31.4	56.4	56.5	114.0	55.6	53.2	66.5	Yémen démocratique
Djibouti	34.8	26.4	32.7	23.6	31.5	46.2	58.0	71.8	74.8	76.3	60.9	Djibouti
Equatorial Guinea	0.7	-1.5	0.4	0.6	3.2	19.7	18.5	13.6	17.2	25.3	41.0	Guinée équatoriale
Ethiopia	195.2	132.1	177.5	117.9	145.3	227.2	295.9	295.7	428.1	597.2	621.7	Ethiopie
Gambia	9.2	29.3	13.6	35.2	66.9	72.7	64.6	48.3	59.9	80.9	33.2	Gambie
Guinea	36.4	17.4	45.8	95.9	90.1	148.5	69.7	106.4	121.0	175.3	177.3	Guinée
Guinea-Bissau	23.8	41.8	47.2	65.6	64.3	63.5	59.8	57.8	91.2	75.1	50.0	Guinée-Bissau
Haiti	95.8	102.1	104.7	130.3	86.6	76.5	136.8	195.9	153.9	134.3	155.5	Haïti
Kiribati	6.4	8.5	12.5	11.9	46.1	12.6	10.9	16.3	16.6	9.9	13.7	Kiribati
Lao People's Dem.Rep.	37.3	30.6	36.1	68.7	65.5	81.0	46.6	19.4	53.9	37.8	25.4	Rép. dém. pop. lao
Lesotho	38.4	53.3	81.4	60.2	127.0	123.0	111.6	71.6	98.9	123.5	91.8	Lesotho
Malawi	85.4	69.5	145.8	266.7	185.2	143.4	210.8	84.1	270.3	143.9	222.1	Malawi
Maldives	2.4	1.8	8.3	2.9	6.5	5.9	4.8	7.2	15.6	13.7	8.8	Maldives
Mali	146.7	163.1	154.1	165.6	249.2	158.8	264.9	210.1	280.2	378.9	425.8	Mali
Mauritania	42.7	59.8	49.6	74.9	148.6	117.8	109.9	115.8	97.9	140.6	171.9	Mauritanie
Nepal	53.7	161.9	128.7	184.5	207.0	270.1	249.6	210.0	282.5	393.3	352.9	Népal
Niger	109.6	180.4	117.3	171.0	250.0	184.7	239.4	209.2	241.4	308.0	240.0	Niger
Rwanda	97.9	116.2	147.1	141.1	161.4	207.2	207.7	196.8	192.8	163.3	196.8	Rwanda
Samoa	17.8	8.0	21.9	32.0	29.1	24.9	45.7	14.1	17.6	21.1	30.9	Samoa
Sao Tome and Principe	0.3	1.6	3.8	14.1	3.6	4.4	7.9	7.4	9.6	13.9	13.8	Sao Tomé-et-Principe
Sierra Leone	33.6	17.2	51.6	42.7	108.1	67.4	114.8	74.0	58.3	66.3	103.3	Sierra Leone
Somalia	78.5	100.4	79.9	109.1	184.0	366.5	457.5	307.4	313.6	341.0	373.7	Somalie
Sudan	167.0	129.3	155.8	413.7	428.5	967.8	535.4	515.1	662.0	619.6	947.5	Soudan
Togo	43.1	66.8	150.9	61.7	77.9	137.2	80.4	111.7	148.4	114.5	234.2	Togo
Tuvalu	0.1	2.1	5.1	3.2	12.5	3.5	6.3	4.4	3.3	4.5	3.3	Tuvalu
Uganda	9.1	17.8	17.1	17.2	75.5	209.9	195.5	199.3	295.4	294.8	141.5	Ouganda
Un. Rep. of Tanzania	307.1	404.4	626.3	757.5	847.9	891.1	638.4	707.8	512.4	502.1	482.7	Rép.-Un. de Tanzanie
Vanuatu	15.6	26.3	12.6	22.0	39.7	72.9	30.9	32.5	30.7	22.7	29.0	Vanuatu
Yemen	65.8	77.2	112.7	98.9	159.7	270.4	110.5	188.0	159.0	140.9	133.7	Yémen
ALL LDCs	3524.2	3550.3	4121.4	5598.2	6104.2	7969.3	7011.8	6683.0	7034.8	7684.8	8051.6	Ensemble des PMA

Source: UNCTAD secretariat, based on information from the
OECD/DAC secretariat.

Source: Secrétariat de la CNUCED, d'après des renseignements du
secrétariat de l'OCDE/CAD.

Table 37

ODA commitments from DAC member countries and multilateral agencies a/ to LDCs as a group, by purpose, average 1983–1985

Tableau 37

Engagements de l'APD de chaque pays membre du CAD et de chaque institution multilatérale, a/ en faveur de l'ensemble des PMA, par objet, moyenne 1983–1985

Donors / Donneurs	Agriculture / Agriculture	Industry, mining, construction / Industries manufacturières, extraction, construction	Energy / Energie	Transport and communication / Transports et communications	Health / Santé	Education / Enseignement	Social infra-structure / Infrastructure sociale	Trade, banking, tourism and other services / Commerce, banques, tourisme et autres services	General economic support b/ / Soutien économique général b/	Other c/ / Autres c/	Total (in $ m. / en m.$)
	Per cent of total — En pourcentage du total										
A. Bilateral donors											
Australia	1.9	0.0	3.2	5.7	7.6	1.9	0.0	0.0	47.5	32.2	158
Austria	-	0.0	-	-	-	-	-	-	-	100.0	18
Belgium	1.4	1.4	11.6	15.5	1.0	-	1.7	-	8.7	87.5	208
Canada	15.2	8.3	15.2	12.9	5.4	3.2	0.2	0.5	0.9	37.7	955
Denmark	24.8	6.1	-	-	21.0	3.3	-	0.0	0.8	15.7	378
Finland	2.3	1.7	7.3	11.4	0.0	0.6	1.5	-	-	96.0	172
France	12.3	3.9	12.6	5.1	3.7	0.1	0.6	1.3	7.8	50.2	1833
Germany, Fed.Rep.of	6.6	0.3	7.2	10.2	6.0	0.5	-	-	30.2	38.5	1708
Italy	11.5	6.5	14.0	12.9	4.4	1.3	0.6	-	-	59.7	1025
Japan	17.7	0.3	0.0	3.9	11.8	0.1	0.7	-	30.1	11.3	1090
Netherlands	24.1	2.5	3.6	3.9	5.7	0.1	0.0	0.4	31.0	28.0	662
New Zealand	5.0	-	0.0	-	5.0	0.0	0.0	0.6	0.0	90.0	21
Norway	9.3	5.3	8.7	12.4	14.2	5.0	2.5	0.0	6.8	35.2	322
Sweden	18.9	8.4	3.4	8.0	8.2	11.2	2.5	1.6	32.2	7.2	437
Switzerland	22.4	1.6	0.8	7.2	12.8	13.6	6.0	0.1	0.4	33.6	236
United Kingdom	3.4	0.0	7.7	13.0	0.3	1.1	-	-	37.2	37.2	626
United States	13.0	-	1.5	3.4	5.8	2.3	1.6	0.8	41.8	29.8	2925
Total bilateral d/	12.8	2.4	6.9	8.0	6.3	2.0	1.2	0.5	23.7	36.2	12774
B. Multilateral donors											
AfDF	33.1	5.8	1.8	25.0	20.8	13.1	0.4	-	-	-	710
AsDB	30.6	2.4	35.1	11.4	3.3	3.2	-	0.3	3.5	10.2	1142
EEC/EDF	24.0	4.3	4.3	13.1	5.5	2.4	1.4	3.5	30.5	11.0	1437
IDA	28.3	2.3	16.8	17.3	4.5	10.2	5.0	0.2	11.1	4.3	3817
IDB	61.3	10.7	..	..	..	16.0	..	..	..	12.0	42
UN	..	..	..	..	..	..	..	..	..	100.0	2572
IFAD	100.0	-	-	-	..	..	..	..	..	-	256
Total multilateral	23.1	2.3	11.2	11.6	4.4	5.7	2.2	0.6	9.1	29.8	9976
GRAND TOTAL (A+B) d/	17.2	2.4	8.7	9.5	5.5	3.6	1.6	0.5	17.4	33.6	22749

Source : OECD "Creditor Reporting System".

Note : For technical reasons the amounts to sectors may be understated.

Source : "Système de notification des pays créanciers" de l'OCDE.

Note : Pour des raisons techniques les données pour les secteurs peuvent être sous-estimées.

a/ Multilateral agencies mainly financed by DAC member countries.
b/ Including current imports financing, food aid and other emergency and disaster relief, budget support, balance of payments support and debt re-organisation.
c/ Technical cooperation not allocated by sector and other unallocated commitments.
d/ Excluding Ireland.

a/ Institutions multilatérales essentiellement financées par les pays membres du CAD.
b/ Comprend les contributions destinées à financer des importations courantes, l'aide alimentaire et autres secours d'urgence, le soutien budgétaire, le soutien à la balance des paiements et le réaménagement de la dette.
c/ Coopération technique non-ventilée par secteur et autres engagements non-ventilés.
d/ Non compris l'Irlande.

Table 38

ODA commitments from DAC member countries a/ and multilateral agencies b/ to individual LDCs, by purpose, average 1983-1985

Tableau 38

Engagements de l'APD à chacun des PMA en provenance des pays membres du CAD a/ et des institutions multilatérales, b/ par objet, moyenne 1983-1985

Recipient country	Agriculture	Industry, mining, construction	Energy	Transport and communication	Health	Education	Social infrastructure	Trade, banking and other services	General economic support c/	Other d/	Total (in $ m.)	Pays bénéficiaire
	Agriculture	Industries manufacturières, extraction construction	Energie	Transports et communications	Santé	Enseignement	Infrastructure sociale	Commerce, banques, et autres services	Soutien économique général c/	Autres d/	en m.$	
	Per cent of total — En pourcentage du total											
Afghanistan	-	-	-	-	1.9	0.0	1.9	-	13.2	83.0	50	Afghanistan
Bangladesh	21.9	3.0	21.3	5.4	4.6	4.1	0.2	0.6	23.5	15.4	4450	Bangladesh
Benin	17.5	3.5	16.8	15.2	7.3	1.3	5.1	0.6	3.2	29.5	302	Bénin
Bhutan	15.0	17.0	6.0	1.0	3.0	1.0	5.1	3.0	-	54.0	100	Bhoutan
Botswana	7.3	1.8	6.7	7.3	7.6	10.4	1.2	0.9	8.6	48.2	323	Botswana
Burkina Faso	19.3	1.7	9.3	5.8	10.1	5.5	0.0	-	6.1	42.2	647	Burkina Faso
Burundi	15.0	0.0	17.7	12.7	8.2	7.2	2.7	1.0	3.1	32.4	484	Burundi
Cape Verde	6.6	10.9	2.6	14.4	2.6	1.3	0.4	1.7	21.8	37.7	229	Cap-Vert
Central African Rep.	20.9	1.2	1.5	7.0	3.5	6.4	2.3	1.2	7.6	48.4	344	Rép. centrafricaine
Chad	9.4	3.4	0.2	3.6	3.8	1.3	2.0	0.4	16.8	59.1	446	Tchad
Comoros	16.4	1.8	6.4	10.0	4.5	0.9	0.0	0.9	6.4	52.7	110	Comores
Democratic Yemen	20.0	4.4	-	10.0	15.0	6.1	-	-	1.1	43.4	175	Yémen démocratique
Djibouti	3.3	0.0	9.9	13.2	8.0	3.3	4.2	-	4.2	53.9	212	Djibouti
Equatorial Guinea	21.7	..	6.0	2.4	4.8	8.4	..	0.0	3.6	49.4	83	Guinée équatoriale
Ethiopia	15.0	3.5	1.9	16.3	2.4	1.8	1.5	2.4	23.9	33.7	1647	Ethiopie
Gambia	28.7	..	2.9	9.2	0.0	1.7	6.9	1.1	10.3	39.2	174	Gambie
Guinea	14.0	6.6	5.9	28.3	3.6	3.0	7.4	0.0	12.3	18.9	474	Guinée
Guinea-Bissau	14.9	5.3	5.7	13.2	3.9	3.1	2.6	0.9	20.6	29.8	216	Guinée-Bissau
Haiti	20.9	1.5	6.2	6.2	6.0	9.6	8.1	2.1	13.5	25.9	444	Haïti
Kiribati	24.4	2.4	-	4.9	7.3	..	..	-	17.1	41.5	40	Kiribati
Lao People's Dem.Rep.	23.7	0.8	5.3	10.7	8.4	0.0	-	-	7.6	43.5	117	Rép.dém.populaire lao
Lesotho	11.1	1.0	4.1	19.0	10.2	7.0	2.5	0.3	9.5	35.3	305	Lesotho
Malawi	17.9	1.0	0.3	16.5	6.7	6.3	2.6	1.0	15.9	29.6	636	Malawi
Maldives	18.8	-	..	7.7	12.8	5.1	..	-	10.3	43.5	38	Maldives
Mali	13.1	0.4	1.8	11.4	8.3	2.5	2.6	0.1	16.9	37.2	1085	Mali
Mauritania	25.9	3.2	3.9	6.6	4.1	1.5	4.4	-	20.7	42.5	410	Mauritanie
Nepal	19.4	3.4	17.9	9.7	4.7	3.4	0.5	0.0	1.7	32.8	1029	Népal
Niger	14.1	1.1	3.0	13.7	7.8	3.5	1.6	1.6	12.1	36.2	789	Niger
Rwanda	2.9	1.8	7.2	11.4	8.9	2.0	3.6	2.2	6.9	41.9	552	Rwanda
Samoa	21.1	2.9	1.4	18.6	10.0	0.0	0.0	5.7	1.4	57.1	70	Samoa
Sao Tome & Principe	16.3	-	-	7.9	-	5.3	2.6	-	28.9	34.2	37	Sao Tomé-et-Principe
Sierra Leone	12.6	-	4.0	1.8	1.8	10.6	0.9	-	37.0	27.6	228	Sierra Leone
Somalia	17.7	0.4	2.8	8.9	4.7	1.2	0.2	0.3	17.2	51.7	1028	Somalie
Sudan	15.5	0.4	4.1	6.1	2.7	0.9	0.3	0.0	34.2	33.6	2227	Sudan
Togo	..	1.7	6.6	1.1	8.7	2.8	1.3	0.2	40.9	21.2	497	Togo
Tuvalu	20.6	..	..	..	..	..	..	-	30.0	50.0	11	Tuvalu
Uganda	10.7	1.9	5.3	14.3	10.1	4.4	2.6	1.2	18.2	21.4	732	Ouganda
Un. Rep. of Tanzania	18.6	5.8	11.7	14.6	6.1	3.7	0.7	0.1	12.2	34.4	1490	Rép. Unie de Tanzanie
Vanuatu	17.2	2.3	-	3.5	0.0	1.2	-	1.2	12.8	60.4	82	Vanuatu
Yemen	17.5	1.6	6.5	2.6	8.1	9.3	3.4	1.0	8.3	42.0	434	Yémen
All LDCs	17.5	2.4	8.9	9.7	5.6	3.6	1.6	0.5	17.8	32.4	22749	**Ensemble des PMA**

Source : OECD "Creditor Reporting System".
Note : For technical reasons the amounts to sectors may be understated.

a/ Excluding Ireland.
b/ Multilateral agencies mainly financed by DAC member countries.
c/ Including current imports financing, food aid and other emergency and disaster relief, budget support, balance of payments support and debt re-organisation.
d/ Technical cooperation and other unallocated commitments.

Source : "Système de notification des pays créanciers" de l'OCDE.
Note : Pour des raisons techniques les données pour les secteurs peuvent être sous-estimées.

a/ Non compris l'Irlande.
b/ Institutions multilatérales essentiellement financées par les pays membres du CAD.
c/ Comprend les contributions destinées à financer des importations courantes, l'aide alimentaire et autres secours d'urgence, le soutien budgétaire, le soutien à la balance des paiements et le réaménagement de la dette.
d/ Coopération technique non-ventilée par secteur et autres engagements non-ventilés.

Table 39

Grant element of ODA commitments from individual DAC member
countries to LDCs and to all developing countries

Tableau 39

Elément de libéralité des engagements de l'APD
de chaque pays membre du CAD aux PMA et à
l'ensemble des pays en développement

Country		1975	1976	1977	1978	1979	1980	1981	1982	1983	1984	1985		Pays
Australia	A	100.0	100.0	100.0	100.0	100.0	100.0	100.0	100.0	100.0	100.0	100.0	A	Australie
	B	100.0	100.0	100.0	100.0	100.0	100.0	100.0	100.0	100.0	100.0	100.0	B	
Austria	A	100.0	100.0	35.5	99.0	95.9	93.2	94.1	94.9	99.4	100.0	100.0	A	Autriche
	B	94.8	97.3	67.5	65.8	86.1	70.3	55.1	58.8	61.1	81.8	(92.1)	B	
Belgium	A	100.0	99.0	98.7	98.9	98.4	98.1	98.5	98.3	96.4	98.2	95.4	A	Belgique
	B	98.1	98.2	98.3	98.6	98.0	97.9	97.6	98.6	97.3	97.6	..	B	
Canada	A	94.7	98.3	100.0	100.0	100.0	100.0	100.0	100.0	100.0	100.0	100.0	A	Canada
	B	(96.4)	97.3	97.5	96.6	97.2	98.0	97.2	98.8	99.3	98.6	99.6	B	
Denmark	A	88.6	91.5	94.9	96.4	96.8	93.5	95.2	96.9	99.1	100.0	98.7	A	Danemark
	B	96.0	96.6	97.3	95.3	96.7	97.3	95.4	95.7	96.4	98.0	95.8	B	
Finland	A	87.8	84.8	100.0	100.0	100.0	100.0	95.0	99.0	100.0	100.0	100.0	A	Finlande
	B	91.5	90.8	97.5	99.0	97.7	97.5	95.6	95.9	99.7	95.6	98.0	B	
France	A	97.0	87.9	94.6	(95.0)	(95.0)	79.2	89.0	82.5	79.9	77.1	76.8	A	France
	B	(90.9)	90.9	93.4	92.3	(93.5)	90.0	89.5	90.0	89.3	89.6	89.1	B	
Germany, Fed.Rep.of	A	93.0	91.1	93.8	92.7	97.8	98.8	99.0	99.4	96.2	99.4	99.6	A	Allemagne, Rép.féd.d'
	B	88.3	(86.8)	86.0	86.6	85.1	89.3	84.9	88.9	88.8	84.6	89.1	B	
Italy b/	A	100.0	100.0	100.0	100.0	100.0	90.0	54.7	70.3	89.6	80.3	94.6	A	Italie b/
	B	98.4	(97.3)	99.2	98.7	99.6	98.8	91.4	91.4	(90.7)	91.2	93.1	B	
Ireland	A	100.0	100.0	100.0	100.0	100.0	100.0	100.0	100.0	100.0	100.0	100.0	A	Irlande
	B	100.0	100.0	100.0	100.0	100.0	100.0	100.0	100.0	100.0	100.0	100.0	B	
Japan	A	86.0	72.7	72.5	76.2	75.4	80.2	85.7	82.3	88.1	89.1	91.4	A	Japon
	B	(69.5)	75.8	70.2	75.0	77.7	74.3	75.3	74.2	79.8	73.7	73.6	B	
Netherlands	A	95.0	93.1	97.2	99.3	98.5	99.8	98.2	99.5	99.1	100.0	97.5	A	Pays-Bas
	B	93.8	86.5	90.8	93.3	92.5	91.6	95.1	93.9	95.1	93.4	96.5	B	
New Zealand	A	100.0	100.0	100.0	100.0	100.0	100.0	100.0	100.0	100.0	100.0	100.0	A	Nouvelle-Zélande
	B	99.1	97.4	99.8	100.0	100.0	100.0	100.0	100.0	100.0	100.0	100.0	B	
Norway	A	100.0	100.0	100.0	100.0	100.0	100.0	100.0	100.0	99.9	99.5	99.6	A	Norvège
	B	100.0	100.0	100.0	100.0	100.0	100.0	99.7	99.2	98.1	99.7	99.7	B	
Sweden	A	100.0	100.0	100.0	100.0	100.0	100.0	100.0	100.0	100.0	100.0	100.0	A	Suède
	B	99.2	99.9	99.8	99.9	100.0	99.0	99.7	99.8	99.8	100.0	100.0	B	
Switzerland	A	100.0	98.2	100.0	100.0	100.0	100.0	100.0	100.0	100.0	100.0	100.0	A	Suisse
	B	93.0	92.1	96.9	95.1	95.8	96.9	97.0	96.6	98.5	98.1	98.9	B	
United Kingdom	A	99.0	99.7	93.6	(99.2)	99.0	99.7	100.0	100.0	100.0	100.0	100.0	A	Royaume-Uni
	B	(96.9)	97.5	96.7	93.9	96.1	96.4	96.9	98.5	98.3	98.6	99.5	B	
United States	A	92.0	82.7	90.0	92.1	96.5	95.0	96.4	97.6	95.7	97.5	96.5	A	Etats-Unis
	B	85.7	86.4	89.9	89.4	91.5	90.5	93.4	93.8	94.7	93.7	96.0	B	
Total DAC countries	A	95.4	92.1	94.2	93.9	95.7	94.7	93.5	92.8	93.9	93.5	95.1	A	Total des pays du CAD
	B	89.4	89.3	89.4	89.9	90.8	89.9	89.6	90.5	91.3	90.1	91.4	B	

Source : OECD, Development Co-operation (various issues)
and information from the OECD/DAC secretariat.

A = Commitments to LDCs excluding Djibouti, Equatorial Guinea,
Kiribati, Mauritania, Sao Tome and Principe, Sierra Leone,
Togo, Tuvalu and Vanuatu (1975-1980); Guinea-Bissau
(1975-1978); Bangladesh, Central African Republic,
Gambia and Democratic Yemen (1975-1976); and Cape Verde
and Comoros (1975). The DAC target norm for LDCs is 90
per cent. The SNPA, para. 70(a), calls upon donor
countries and institutions to provide as a general rule
assistance to LDCs as grants.

B = Commitments to all developing countries and territories,
as well as to Gibraltar, Greece, Israel, Portugal,
Yugoslavia and Viet Nam. The DAC target norm for all
developing countries is 84 per cent.

a/ Excluding debt reorganisation.

b/ Italy has not subscribed to the 1972 DAC Terms
Recommendation.

Source : OCDE, Coopération pour le développement (divers numéros)
et renseignements du secrétariat de l'OCDE/CAD.

A = Engagements aux PMA, non compris Djibouti, la Guinée
équatoriale, Kiribati, la Mauritanie, Sao Tomé-et-
Principe, Sierra Leone, le Togo, Tuvalu et Vanuatu (1975-
1980); la Guinée-Bissau (1975-1978); le Bangladesh,
la République centrafricaine, la Gambie et le Yémen démocratique (1975-1976); et le Cap-Vert et les Comores
(1975). L'objectif du CAD pour les PMA a pour norme 90
pour cent. Le NPSA, au paragraphe 70(a), demande aux pays
donateurs de fournir, en règle générale, sous forme de
dons l'aide aux PMA.

B = Engagements à l'ensemble des pays en développement, ainsi
qu'à Gibraltar, la Grèce, Israël, le Portugal,
la Yougoslavie et le Viet-Nam. L'objectif du CAD pour
l'ensemble des pays en développement a pour norme 84 pour
cent.

a/ Non compris la réorganisation de la dette.

b/ L'Italie n'a pas souscrit à la Recommandation sur les
Conditions de l'Aide du CAD de 1972.

Table 40A
Bilateral ODA from OPEC member countries and total financial flows from multilateral agencies mainly financed by them, to LDCs as a group

Net disbursements in $ million

Tableau 40A
APD bilatérale des pays membres de l'OPEP at apports financiers totaux des institutions multilatérales essentiellement financées par ceux-ci. en faveur de l'ensemble des PMA

Versements nets en millions de dollars

	1975	1976	1977	1978	1979	1980	1981	1982	1983	1984	1985
A. Bilateral donors / A. Donneurs bilatéraux											
Algeria / Algérie	4.5	2.2	2.5	0.5	14.5	20.0	9.6	0.2	-	-	-
Iran (Islamic Rep.) / Iran (Rép. Islamique)	3.1	6.6	-	15.0	-	-	-	-	-	-	-
Iraq / Iraq	71.7	39.0	25.0	42.5	47.5	48.8	-	-	-	-3.6	-19.6
Kuwait / Koweït	55.8	73.1	136.0	118.4	137.8	190.9	180.1	138.5	158.9	153.9	207.5
Libyan Arab Jamahiriya / Jamahiriya arabe Libyenne	59.6	19.7	0.9	10.4	0.0	8.2	24.5	-	-	-	10.0
Nigeria / Nigéria	2.2	0.2	1.4	-	0.1	0.1	-	-	-	-	-
Qatar / Qatar	20.3	14.6	5.0	8.5	5.7	41.5	23.2	7.7	7.4	2.0	5.1
Saudi Arabia / Arabie saoudite	296.4	398.2	608.7	405.5	441.9	487.5	417.9	741.6	645.6	513.0	233.4
United Arab Emirates / Emirats arabes unis	116.3	102.4	123.2	158.4	113.1	152.8	86.7	75.1	51.0	32.9	42.0
Total bilateral concessional / Total des apports bilatéraux concessionnels	629.9	656.0	902.7	759.2	760.6	949.8	742.0	963.1	862.9	698.2	478.7
B. Multilateral donors / B. Donneurs multilatéraux											
1. Concessional / 1. Apports concessionnels											
BADEA	-	-	4.6	19.7	16.0	18.5	15.1	15.6	20.6	12.1	9.2
AFESD / FADES	15.8	31.2	32.4	69.9	34.4	45.7	58.5	43.8	48.1	33.1	24.1
Islamic Dev. Bank / Banque islamique de dév.	-	-	-	4.9	11.4	5.4	18.3	10.5	15.9	24.1	28.3
OPEC Fund / Fonds de l'OPEP	-	-	80.6	18.1	34.8	70.2	127.1	106.2	75.2	30.9	20.9
OAPEC Special Account / Compte spécial de l'OPAEP	-	36.9	-	-	-	-	-	-	-	-	-
SAAFA / FSAAA	64.9	31.0	-	-	-	-	-	-	-	-	-
Total	80.7	99.1	117.6	112.6	96.6	139.8	219.0	176.1	159.8	100.2	82.5
2. Non-concessional / 2. Apports non-concessionnels											
BADEA	-	-	-	8.2	4.3	8.8	1.2	2.3	-0.5	0.5	9.6
Islamic Dev. Bank / Banque Islamique de dév.	-	-	5.0	8.8	110.4	97.4	105.3	-56.3	10.8	16.8	-37.4
OPEC Fund / Fonds de l'OPEP	-	-	-	-	-	0.5	-	-	0.4	-0.1	-0.1
Total	-	-	5.0	17.0	114.7	106.7	106.5	-54.0	10.7	17.2	-27.9
Total concessional (A+B1) / Total des apports concessionnels (A+B1)	710.6	755.1	1020.3	871.8	857.2	1089.6	961.0	1139.2	1022.7	798.4	561.2
GRAND TOTAL a/ / TOTAL GENERAL a/	710.6	755.1	1027.5	888.8	971.9	1196.3	1067.5	1095.1	1063.4	818.1	537.8

Source: UNCTAD secretariat estimates.
For 1975-1976: OECD secretariat estimates.
Note: The figures include only those amounts allocated to a specific country and therefore understate financial flows to the extent that certain donors have recorded disbursements in favour of groups of countries including some LDCs.
For abbreviations, see p. A-9.
a/ Including bilateral non-concessional flows.

Source: Estimations du secrétariat de la CNUCED.
Pour 1975-1976: estimations du secrétariat de l'OCDE.
Note: Les données ne comprennent que les montants imputables à un pays bénéficiaire déterminé. Par conséquent, les apports financiers sont sous-estimés dans la mesure où certains donneurs ont alloué des versements à des groupes de pays comprenant des PMA.
Pour les abréviations, se reporter p. A-12.
a/ Y compris des apports bilatéraux non-concessionnels.

Table 40B
Bilateral ODA from OPEC member countries and total financial flows from multilateral agencies mainly financed by them, to LDCs as a group

Tableau 40B
APD bilatérale des pays membres de l'OPEP at apports financiers totaux des institutions multilatérales essentiellement financées par ceux-ci, en faveur de l'ensemble des PMA

Net disbursements in millions of constant 1980 dollars a/ — Versements nets en millions de dollars constants de 1980 a/

	1975	1976	1977	1978	1979	1980	1981	1982	1983	1984	1985
A. Bilateral donors / Donneurs bilatéraux											
Algeria / Algérie	7.7	3.7	3.9	0.7	16.8	20.0	10.1	0.2	-	-	-
Iran (Islamic Rep.) / Iran (Rép. Islamique)	5.3	11.2	-	20.7	-	-	-	-	-	-	-
Iraq / Iraq	121.9	65.9	38.6	58.7	55.1	48.8	-	-	-	-4.1	-22.2
Kuwait / Koweit	94.9	123.5	209.7	163.6	159.8	190.9	189.0	150.5	178.2	174.9	235.2
Libyan Arab Jamahiriya / Jamahiriya arabe Libyenne	101.3	33.3	1.4	14.4	0.0	8.2	25.7	-	-	-	11.3
Nigeria / Nigéria	3.7	0.3	2.2	-	0.1	0.1	-	-	-	-	-
Qatar / Qatar	34.5	24.7	7.7	11.7	6.6	41.5	24.3	8.4	8.3	2.3	5.8
Saudi Arabia / Arabie saoudite	503.7	672.7	938.8	560.2	512.6	487.5	438.5	805.7	724.0	583.0	264.1
United Arab Emirates / Emirats arabes unis	197.7	173.0	190.0	218.8	131.2	152.8	91.0	81.6	57.2	37.4	47.5
Total bilateral concessional / Total des apports bilatéraux concessionnels	1071	1108	1392	1049	882.3	949.8	778.5	1046	967.7	793.4	541.8
B. Multilateral donors / Donneurs multilatéraux											
1. Concessional / Apports concessionnels											
BADEA	-	-	-	27.2	18.6	18.5	15.8	16.9	23.1	13.7	10.4
AFESD / FADES	26.9	52.7	50.0	96.6	39.9	45.7	61.4	47.6	53.9	37.6	27.3
Islamic Dev. Bank / Banque islamique de dév.	-	-	-	6.8	13.2	5.4	19.2	11.4	17.8	27.4	32.0
OPEC Fund / Fonds de l'OPEP	-	-	124.3	25.0	40.4	70.2	133.4	115.4	84.3	35.1	23.7
OAPEC Special Account / Compte special de l'OPAEP	110.3	62.3	-	-	-	-	-	-	-	-	-
SAAFA / FSAAA	-	52.4	-	-	-	-	-	-	-	-	-
Total	137.2	167.4	181.4	155.6	112.1	139.8	229.8	191.3	179.2	113.9	93.4
2. Non-concessional / Apports non-concessionnels											
BADEA	-	-	-	11.3	5.0	8.8	1.3	2.5	-0.6	0.6	10.9
Islamic Dev. Bank / Banque Islamique de dév.	-	-	7.7	12.2	128.1	97.4	110.5	-61.2	12.1	19.1	-42.3
OPEC Fund / Fonds de l'OPEP	-	-	-	-	-	0.5	-	-	0.4	-0.1	-0.1
Total	-	-	7.7	23.5	133.0	106.7	111.7	-58.7	12.0	19.5	-31.6
Total concessional (A+B1) / Total des apports concessionnels (A+B1)	1208.1	1276	1574	1204	994.3	1090	1008	1238	1147	907.3	635.1
GRAND TOTAL b/ / TOTAL GENERAL b/	1208.1	1276	1585	1228	1127	1196	1120	1190	1193	929.7	608.6

Source: Table 40A.

a/ Actual disbursements were converted to 1980 prices using the index for LDCs in table 10.

b/ Including bilateral non-concessional flows.

Source: Tableau 40A.

a/ Les versements effectifs ont été convertis aux prix de 1980 en utilisant l'indice pour les PMA qui figure au tableau 10.

b/ Y compris des apports bilatéraux non-concessionnels.

Table 41
Concessional assistance from OPEC member countries
and multilateral agencies mainly financed by them
to individual LDCs

Net disbursements in $ million

Tableau 41
Aide concessionnelle reçue par chacun des PMA, en provenance
des pays membres de l'OPEP et des institutions multilatérales
essentiellement financées par ceux-ci

Versements nets en millions de dollars

Country	1975	1976	1977	1978	1979	1980	1981	1982	1983	1984	1985	Pays
Afghanistan	21.6	14.7	4.3	15.5	8.3	1.4	20.4	0.3	-2.2	-0.7	-0.7	Afghanistan
Bangladesh	73.8	6.9	39.7	45.7	23.6	55.2	78.5	148.6	122.9	26.5	9.9	Bangladesh
Benin	2.4	0.0	4.6	5.4	3.4	2.4	3.9	1.6	6.4	0.3	4.0	Bénin
Bhutan	-	-	-	-	-	-	-	-	-	0.3	2.9	Bhoutan
Botswana	5.4	0.1	3.0	0.1	0.5	2.2	0.4	8.4	11.7	10.8	5.0	Botswana
Burkina Faso	3.5	0.1	1.2	2.7	5.8	7.9	11.1	8.6	2.7	-0.6	16.7	Burkina Faso
Burundi	1.0	11.0	2.2	2.8	6.1	7.3	3.9	6.4	4.9	9.3	4.1	Burundi
Cape Verde	0.1	1.4	1.7	0.6	1.0	2.0	1.3	0.1	-0.1	3.8	5.7	Cap-Vert
Central African Rep.	1.4	0.8	1.6	-	1.3	2.1	0.6	1.0	0.3	2.1	1.7	Rép. centrafricaine
Chad	13.0	-	-	7.5	6.0	0.0	0.6	0.5	0.2	0.3	0.9	Tchad
Comoros	-	13.8	22.5	2.6	3.0	16.4	12.9	10.4	9.8	5.9	8.5	Comores
Democratic Yemen	32.1	148.6	93.1	43.2	32.4	65.5	62.7	68.8	39.9	51.1	63.8	Yémen démocratique
Djibouti	-	-	19.7	64.0	-	30.6	13.2	3.6	14.8	48.0	15.3	Djibouti
Equatorial Guinea	1.5	-	0.5	-	0.9	0.1	0.5	0.9	0.4	-0.0	-0.2	Guinée équatoriale
Ethiopia	15.4	1.1	3.3	2.6	6.4	14.2	10.2	-0.0	-0.2	-0.2	-0.1	Ethiopie
Gambia	0.4	0.2	2.6	8.9	12.2	4.5	16.2	3.7	1.4	1.3	-0.1	Gambie
Guinea	15.4	0.2	15.6	14.0	2.8	3.8	2.5	2.5	0.6	34.4	7.8	Guinée
Guinea-Bissau	3.3	6.8	2.2	2.5	2.8	-	1.8	3.8	6.9	3.3	2.9	Guinée-Bissau
Haiti	-	-	3.1	-	-	-	1.2	1.8	1.3	0.4	0.9	Haïti
Kiribati	-	-	-	-	-	-	-	-	-	-	-	Kiribati
Lao People's Dem.Rep.	-	-	2.1	-	4.2	0.7	0.0	0.3	0.3	1.1	0.0	Rép. dém. pop. lao
Lesotho	2.8	-	1.9	0.0	0.3	0.0	1.0	2.7	7.4	5.0	5.1	Lesotho
Malawi	-	-	-	-	-	1.3	-0.1	-0.1	-0.1	-0.1	-0.1	Malawi
Maldives	-	-	-	-	-	-	-	2.5	4.5	-0.8	-0.3	Maldives
Mali	0.2	2.6	1.5	3.3	4.0	17.4	7.3	2.5	48.0	15.0	27.2	Mali
Mauritania	28.8	2.7	16.8	11.9	24.7	29.3	21.7	32.5	67.3	96.7	54.9	Mauritanie
Nepal	31.2	159.5	60.4	134.7	65.2	65.7	75.6	70.8	1.1	-0.9	-0.8	Népal
Niger	0.0	0.2	41.5	1.6	3.5	6.8	11.2	5.2	17.5	10.1	0.2	Niger
Rwanda	17.3	3.6	8.8	21.4	7.1	8.1	32.6	82.4	1.2	5.9	5.6	Rwanda
Samoa	9.2	0.3	5.8	4.0	2.7	7.2	8.3	1.7	-0.2	-0.0	-0.0	Samoa
Sao Tome and Principe	0.6	10.0	0.1	0.1	-	0.8	0.5	1.0	0.5	0.4	-0.3	Sao Tomé-et-Principe
Sierra Leone	1.8	0.2	1.0	0.3	5.2	6.6	2.1	1.2	2.7	17.1	4.6	Sierra Leone
Somalia	80.4	35.0	213.8	113.9	106.2	143.7	57.8	182.3	53.7	75.1	32.1	Somalie
Sudan	154.6	120.1	129.8	115.9	303.9	241.6	203.7	161.5	354.0	170.3	106.8	Soudan
Togo	2.0	2.6	0.1	0.5	3.5	3.5	0.1	2.7	5.1	3.4	9.3	Togo
Tuvalu	-	-	-	-	-	-	-	-	-	-	-	Tuvalu
Uganda	35.0	2.2	9.5	7.2	7.4	0.2	0.2	5.6	10.7	-1.4	0.9	Ouganda
Un. Rep. of Tanzania	7.3	0.6	12.8	2.0	4.7	19.7	24.0	28.7	32.3	17.6	9.4	Rép.-Un. de Tanzanie
Vanuatu	-	-	-	-	-	-	-	-	17.6	-	-	Vanuatu
Yemen	149.4	210.3	289.3	234.2	201.5	320.1	270.4	285.5	193.6	183.5	154.9	Yémen
All LDCs	710.6	755.1	1020.1	871.7	857.0	1089.5	961.0	1139.2	1022.5	798.3	561.0	Ensemble des PMA
All developing countries	5797.0	5578.6	4470.0	7549.4	7157.0	9199.8	8280.4	5851.5	5182.6	3860.5	3302.4	Ensemble des pays en développement

For sources and notes, see p. A-85.

Pour les sources et les notes, se reporter p. A-85.

Table 42
Concessional assistance from OPEC member countries to individual LDCs a/

Net disbursements in $ million

Tableau 42
Aide concessionnelle reçue par chacun des PMA, en provenance des pays membres de l'OPEP a/

Versements nets en millions de dollars

Country	1975	1976	1977	1978	1979	1980	1981	1982	1983	1984	1985	Pays
Afghanistan	21.6	14.7	0.6	15.5	8.3	1.4	20.4	0.4	-2.1	-0.6	-0.7	Afghanistan
Bangladesh	73.8	6.9	25.8	44.6	13.2	51.1	47.2	126.8	110.0	14.4	6.9	Bangladesh
Benin	–	0.0	1.2	–	2.1	1.8	1.2	0.0	2.1	-0.3	3.0	Bénin
Bhutan	–	–	–	–	–	–	–	–	–	–	2.9	Bhoutan
Botswana	0.8	0.1	0.1	0.9	–	0.0	–	6.1	8.1	10.1	3.6	Botswana
Burkina Faso	–	0.1	0.4	–	0.9	1.0	2.0	–	0.3	1.4	13.5	Burkina Faso
Burundi	–	0.5	0.7	2.0	1.7	2.8	2.0	5.9	3.3	9.4	3.3	Burundi
Cape Verde	0.1	1.4	–	–	–	–	–	–	0.2	1.2	1.8	Cap-Vert
Central African Rep.	0.2	–	–	–	–	2.1	0.0	1.1	0.3	0.5	0.7	Rép. centrafricaine
Chad	8.6	0.8	0.4	6.0	1.3	0.0	–	0.2	0.2	0.0	–	Tchad
Comoros	–	3.3	22.3	2.1	6.0	15.8	11.4	7.9	6.3	3.0	3.8	Comores
Democratic Yemen	31.9	141.9	88.6	28.9	2.8	53.2	44.2	56.5	23.2	38.9	44.4	Yémen démocratique
Djibouti	–	–	19.7	64.0	23.8	30.6	12.4	1.6	11.5	38.5	8.4	Djibouti
Equatorial Guinea	1.2	–	–	–	–	–	–	–	–	–	–	Guinée équatoriale
Ethiopia	1.2	–	–	0.2	0.9	0.1	10.1	–	–	0.7	–	Ethiopie
Gambia	–	1.1	0.9	7.5	4.1	7.0	14.0	2.3	0.9	0.7	-0.3	Gambie
Guinea	15.4	0.2	1.0	9.1	9.2	0.1	-0.2	0.7	-0.5	29.7	2.3	Guinée
Guinea-Bissau	3.3	6.8	13.2	1.9	1.8	1.3	0.0	2.7	6.1	3.2	2.9	Guinée-Bissau
Haiti	–	–	0.6	–	–	–	–	–	–	–	–	Haïti
Kiribati	–	–	–	–	–	–	–	–	–	–	–	Kiribati
Lao People's Dem.Rep.	–	–	–	–	–	–	–	–	–	–	–	Rép. dém. pop. lao
Lesotho	–	–	–	0.0	0.3	0.0	0.2	–	2.5	2.9	2.9	Lesotho
Malawi	–	–	–	–	–	–	–	0.0	–	–	0.0	Malawi
Maldives	0.2	2.6	1.3	3.1	3.6	16.6	5.7	1.6	3.9	0.3	-0.4	Maldives
Mali	24.9	2.7	12.4	5.2	21.3	19.0	7.0	20.4	32.3	10.2	22.6	Mali
Mauritania	31.2	143.4	50.5	112.5	65.1	63.0	68.3	54.2	43.0	79.1	48.7	Mauritanie
Nepal	0.0	0.2	37.4	1.6	3.5	6.8	8.7	0.0	-0.9	-0.9	-0.8	Népal
Niger	14.6	3.6	5.9	16.1	0.7	1.6	23.7	82.1	18.1	11.7	0.4	Niger
Rwanda	8.2	0.3	5.0	1.1	0.5	1.2	0.5	0.0	1.6	5.9	5.5	Rwanda
Samoa	–	–	–	–	–	–	–	–	–	–	–	Samoa
Sao Tome and Principe	0.1	–	–	–	–	–	–	–	–	–	–	Sao Tomé-et-Principe
Sierra Leone	0.0	0.2	0.0	0.0	4.0	4.0	0.0	0.2	1.0	14.5	0.0	Sierra Leone
Somalia	72.9	30.8	208.2	106.0	95.7	127.6	38.1	160.7	31.9	65.4	30.2	Somalie
Sudan	140.5	91.6	114.3	97.5	288.2	218.7	175.0	141.5	352.8	166.0	105.8	Soudan
Togo	2.0	2.6	0.1	–	0.0	0.0	0.1	2.7	2.3	1.9	9.0	Togo
Tuvalu	–	–	–	–	–	–	–	–	–	–	–	Tuvalu
Uganda	29.3	2.2	5.0	7.2	7.4	0.1	0.0	1.0	2.4	-1.5	0.6	Ouganda
Un. Rep. of Tanzania	0.2	0.6	6.9	1.0	3.5	15.5	15.3	14.3	18.2	10.9	10.0	Rép.-Un. de Tanzanie
Vanuatu	–	–	–	–	–	–	–	–	–	–	–	Vanuatu
Yemen	147.8	197.7	278.8	223.9	189.4	306.2	233.3	271.4	182.6	180.3	146.6	Yémen
All LDCs	629.9	656.0	902.7	759.2	760.5	949.8	742.1	963.2	862.9	698.2	478.6	Ensemble des PMA
All developing countries	5638.3	5160.4	4277.4	7248.2	6906.6	8912.4	7930.1	5525.0	4885.8	3818.0	3175.9	Ensemble des pays en développement

For sources and notes, see p. A-85.

Pour les sources et les notes, se reporter p. A-85.

Table 41 and 42 (continued)

Source: UNCTAD secretariat estimates.
For 1975-1976 : OECD secretariat estimates.

Note: The figures relating to LDCs include only those amounts allocated to a specific recipient country and therefore understate financial flows to the extent that certain donors have recorded disbursements in favour of groups of countries including some LDCs.

a/ The members of OPEC and the multilateral agencies financed by them included here and providing assistance to LDCs are listed in table 40A.

Tableau 41 et 42 (suite)

Source: Estimations du secrétariat de la CNUCED.
Pour 1975-1976 : estimations du secrétariat de l'OCDE.

Note: Les données se rapportant aux PMA ne comprennent que les montants imputables à un pays bénéficiaire déterminé. Par conséquent, les apports financiers sont sous-estimés dans la mesure où certains donneurs ont alloué des versements à des groupes de pays comprenant des PMA.

a/ La liste des membres de l'OPEP et des institutions multilatérales financées par ceux-ci qui sont inclus ici et qui fournissent de l'aide aux PMA figure au tableau 40A.

Table 43
Grants from OPEC member countries to individual LDCs

Tableau 43
Dons reçus par chacun des PMA, en provenance des pays membres de l'OPEP

Net disbursements in $ million

Versements nets en millions de dollars

Country	1975	1976	1977	1978	1979	1980	1981	1982	1983	1984	1985	Pays
Afghanistan	13.8	2.7	0.1	5.0	-	20.4	1.0	90.6	-	0.2	0.3	Afghanistan
Bangladesh	10.7	2.5	10.8	6.7	-	-	5.8	-	80.0	10.5	8.1	Bangladesh
Benin	-	-	0.5	-	-	-	-	-	0.1	0.1	0.1	Bénin
Bhutan	-	-	-	-	-	-	-	-	-	-	-	Bhoutan
Botswana	-	-	-	-	-	-	-	-	-	-	-	Botswana
Burkina Faso	0.2	1.0	0.1	0.9	0.9	0.0	2.0	-	0.3	0.0	0.1	Burkina Faso
Burundi	-	0.0	0.0	-	-	-	-	-	0.1	0.1	0.1	Burundi
Cape Verde	0.1	1.3	0.7	-	-	1.0	-	-	0.2	-	0.0	Cap-Vert
Central African Rep.	-	-	-	-	-	-	-	-	-	-	-	Rép. centrafricaine
Chad	3.7	1.5	0.4	6.0	6.0	0.0	-	-	0.2	0.0	-	Tchad
Comoros	-	2.3	19.7	0.6	1.1	1.9	7.5	0.7	1.9	1.3	0.3	Comores
Democratic Yemen	27.6	128.8	76.5	8.8	17.6	34.2	20.4	31.1	13.2	21.2	47.1	Yémen démocratique
Djibouti	-	-	19.7	64.0	-	25.0	12.2	0.1	5.7	25.0	0.5	Djibouti
Equatorial Guinea	1.2	-	-	-	0.9	-	-	-	-	-	-	Guinée équatoriale
Ethiopia	1.2	-	-	0.2	0.0	0.0	3.1	-	0.4	0.1	-	Ethiopie
Gambia	-	2.1	0.9	0.2	0.0	0.1	0.0	0.9	0.7	0.1	0.1	Gambie
Guinea	1.9	0.4	0.2	2.1	0.3	0.0	-	-	0.5	25.1	-	Guinée
Guinea-Bissau	1.2	3.8	0.6	-	0.0	-	-	0.0	-	-	0.5	Guinée-Bissau
Haiti	-	-	-	-	-	-	-	-	-	-	-	Haïti
Kiribati	-	-	-	-	-	-	-	-	-	-	-	Kiribati
Lao People's Dem.Rep.	-	-	-	-	-	-	-	-	-	-	-	Rép. dém. pop. lao
Lesotho	-	-	-	-	-	-	-	-	-	-	-	Lesotho
Malawi	0.2	1.8	1.2	0.0	1.0	1.1	1.2	0.0	0.8	-	0.0	Malawi
Maldives	-	3.0	5.1	1.0	11.5	5.1	0.0	0.1	0.8	0.8	0.0	Maldives
Mali	24.5	-	37.1	5.2	9.5	11.1	10.2	0.0	0.5	1.5	0.3	Mali
Mauritania	-	-	33.0	-	-	-	-	16.7	8.6	16.2	35.7	Mauritanie
Nepal	0.4	0.2	3.0	-	-	1.6	1.9	-	0.0	0.0	0.0	Népal
Niger	14.1	3.1	0.6	15.9	0.4	-	0.1	1.7	0.8	3.9	0.1	Niger
Rwanda	5.2	0.1	-	-	-	-	-	-	0.1	0.0	0.0	Rwanda
Samoa	-	-	-	-	-	-	-	-	-	-	-	Samoa
Sao Tome and Principe	0.1	0.2	0.0	0.0	0.1	4.0	0.0	0.2	-	-	-	Sao Tomé-et-Principe
Sierra Leone	0.0	-	-	-	-	-	-	-	1.0	14.5	-	Sierra Leone
Somalia	52.3	14.4	191.3	50.7	32.4	78.7	24.0	148.7	9.8	16.0	2.2	Somalie
Sudan	120.1	42.4	82.9	36.9	12.1	27.8	15.7	104.9	338.3	163.5	103.9	Soudan
Togo	2.0	2.6	0.1	-	-	0.0	-	0.0	0.0	0.0	0.0	Togo
Tuvalu	-	-	-	-	-	-	-	-	-	-	-	Tuvalu
Uganda	20.0	2.2	0.0	4.8	-	0.0	0.0	0.0	0.2	0.2	0.0	Ouganda
Un. Rep. of Tanzania	0.2	-	-	0.0	0.1	-	-	0.0	0.0	0.0	0.0	Rép.-Un. de Tanzanie
Vanuatu	-	-	-	-	-	-	-	-	-	-	-	Vanuatu
Yemen	135.4	179.7	255.5	175.9	148.1	226.8	149.6	175.4	166.1	177.3	121.0	Yémen
All LDCs	436.2	395.9	741.8	385.6	242.6	439.6	255.8	571.8	630.5	477.6	320.3	Ensemble des PMA
All developing countries	3164.7	2594.1	3015.4	2261.5	3750.3	4043.3	3499.7	3008.7	2447.4	3393.9	2529.2	Ensemble des pays en développement

Source: UNCTAD secretariat estimates.
For 1975-1976 : OECD secretariat estimates.

Source: Estimations du secrétariat de la CNUCED.
Pour 1975-1976 : estimations du secrétariat de l'OCDE.

Table 44
Concessional assistance from multilateral agencies a/
mainly financed by OPEC countries,
to individual LDCs

Net disbursements in $ million

Tableau 44
Aide concessionnelle reçue par chacun des PMA, en provenance
des institutions multilatérales a/ essentiellement financées
par les pays membres de l'OPEP

Versements nets en millions de dollars

Country	1975	1976	1977	1978	1979	1980	1981	1982	1983	1984	1985	Pays
Afghanistan	-	-	3.7	-	-	-	31.3	-0.1	-0.1	-0.1	-	Afghanistan
Bangladesh	-	-	13.9	1.1	10.4	4.1	2.7	21.8	12.9	12.1	3.0	Bangladesh
Benin	2.4	-	3.4	5.4	1.3	0.6	-	1.6	4.3	0.6	1.0	Bénin
Bhutan	-	-	-	-	-	-	-	-	-	-	-	Bhoutan
Botswana	5.4	-	-	0.1	0.5	2.2	0.4	2.3	3.6	0.7	1.4	Botswana
Burkina Faso	2.7	-	2.9	1.8	4.9	6.9	9.1	8.6	2.4	-2.0	3.2	Burkina Faso
Burundi	1.0	-	0.8	0.8	4.4	4.5	1.9	0.5	1.6	-0.0	0.8	Burundi
Cape Verde	-	10.5	1.5	0.6	1.0	2.0	1.3	-0.1	-0.3	2.6	3.9	Cap-Vert
Central African Rep.	1.2	-	1.7	1.5	-	-	-	-0.1	-0.0	1.6	1.0	Rép. centrafricaine
Chad	4.4	-	1.2	0.5	0.2	0.0	0.6	-0.5	-0.0	0.3	0.9	Tchad
Comoros	-	10.5	0.2	14.3	8.6	0.6	1.5	2.5	3.5	2.9	4.7	Comores
Democratic Yemen	0.2	6.7	4.5	-	-	12.3	18.5	12.3	16.7	12.2	19.4	Yémen démocratique
Djibouti	-	-	-	-	-	-	0.8	2.0	3.3	9.5	6.9	Djibouti
Equatorial Guinea	-	-	-	-	-	-	0.5	0.9	0.4	-0.0	-0.2	Guinée équatoriale
Ethiopia	0.3	-	0.5	2.4	2.3	0.0	0.1	-0.0	-0.2	-0.2	-0.2	Ethiopie
Gambia	14.2	-	2.4	1.4	3.0	7.2	2.2	1.4	-0.2	-0.2	-0.2	Gambie
Guinea	0.4	-	1.6	4.9	1.0	4.4	2.7	1.8	1.1	4.7	5.5	Guinée
Guinea-Bissau	-	-	2.4	0.6	-	2.5	1.8	1.1	0.8	0.1	0.0	Guinée-Bissau
Haiti	-	-	3.1	-	-	-	1.2	1.8	1.3	0.4	0.9	Haïti
Kiribati	-	-	-	-	4.2	-	-	-	-	-	-	Kiribati
Lao People's Dem.Rep.	-	-	2.1	-	-	0.7	0.0	0.3	0.3	1.1	0.0	Rép. dém. pop. lao
Lesotho	2.8	-	1.9	0.0	-	-	0.8	2.7	4.9	-0.1	2.2	Lesotho
Malawi	-	-	-	-	0.4	1.3	-0.1	-0.1	-0.1	-0.1	-0.1	Malawi
Maldives	-	-	-	0.2	3.4	0.8	1.6	-0.9	-0.6	-0.5	-0.1	Maldives
Mali	3.9	-	0.2	6.7	0.1	10.3	14.7	12.1	15.7	4.8	4.6	Mali
Mauritania	-	16.1	4.4	22.2	-	2.7	7.3	16.6	24.3	17.6	6.2	Mauritanie
Nepal	-	-	9.9	-	6.4	-	2.5	5.2	2.0	-	-0.0	Népal
Niger	2.7	-	4.1	5.3	2.2	6.5	8.9	0.3	-0.6	-1.6	-0.2	Niger
Rwanda	1.0	-	2.9	2.9	0.5	6.0	7.8	1.7	-0.4	0.0	-0.1	Rwanda
Samoa	-	-	0.8	0.5	-	0.8	1.0	1.0	-0.2	0.0	-0.0	Samoa
Sao Tome and Principe	0.5	10.0	1.6	0.1	1.2	-	0.5	0.5	0.5	0.6	0.3	Sao Tomé-et-Principe
Sierra Leone	1.8	-	0.1	0.3	10.5	2.6	2.1	1.0	1.7	2.6	4.6	Sierra Leone
Somalia	7.5	4.2	5.6	7.9	15.7	16.1	19.7	21.6	21.8	9.7	1.9	Somalie
Sudan	14.1	28.5	15.5	18.4	-	22.9	28.7	20.0	1.2	4.3	1.0	Soudan
Togo	-	-	-	-	0.0	3.5	-	-	2.8	1.5	0.3	Togo
Tuvalu	-	-	-	-	-	-	-	-	-	-	-	Tuvalu
Uganda	5.7	-	4.5	0.0	1.2	0.1	0.2	4.6	8.3	0.1	0.3	Ouganda
Un. Rep. of Tanzania	7.1	0.0	5.9	1.0	12.1	4.2	8.7	14.4	14.1	6.7	-0.6	Rép.-Un. de Tanzanie
Vanuatu	-	-	-	-	-	-	-	-	-	-	-	Vanuatu
Yemen	1.6	12.6	10.5	10.3	12.1	13.9	37.1	14.1	11.0	3.2	8.3	Yémen
All LDCs	80.7	99.1	117.4	112.5	96.5	139.7	218.9	176.0	159.6	100.1	82.4	Ensemble des PMA
All developing countries	158.7	418.2	240.5	300.0	248.9	274.0	350.3	326.5	296.8	145.4	146.0	Ensemble des pays en développement

Source: UNCTAD secretariat estimates.
For 1975-1976: OECD secretariat estimates.
a/ For the list of multilateral agencies included here, providing concessional assistance to LDCs, see table 40A.

Source: Estimations du secrétariat de la CNUCED.
Pour 1975-1976: estimations du secrétariat de l'OCDE.
a/ Pour la liste des institutions multilatérales qui sont incluses ici et qui fournissent l'aide concessionnelle aux PMA, se reporter au tableau 40A.

Table 45
Non-concessional flows from multilateral agencies a/ mainly financed by OPEC countries to individual LDCs.

Tableau 45
Apports non-concessionnels reçus par chacun des PMA, en provenance des institutions multilatérales a/ essentiellement financées par les pays membres de l'OPEP

Net disbursements in $ million   Versements nets en millions de dollars

Country	1977	1978	1979	1980	1981	1982	1983	1984	1985	Pays
Afghanistan	-	-	-	-	-	-	-	-	-	Afghanistan
Bangladesh	-	-	37.1	-14.7	34.1	-11.4	38.9	13.3	-32.1	Bangladesh
Benin	-	0.1	1.7	1.8	0.7	2.1	-0.0	-0.3	0.8	Bénin
Bhutan	-	-	-	-	-	-	-	-	-	Bhoutan
Botswana	-	-	-	-	-	-	-	-	-	Botswana
Burkina Faso	-	-	-	0.5	-	-	0.4	-0.1	2.2	Burkina Faso
Burundi	-	-	-	2.6	2.5	0.3	0.2	-2.3	-0.4	Burundi
Cape Verde	-	-	-	-	-	-	-	-	1.2	Cap-Vert
Central African Rep.	-	-	-	-	-	-	-	-	-	Rép. centrafricaine
Chad	-	-	-	-	-	-	-	-	0.4	Tchad
Comoros	-	-	-	-	3.7	-0.4	-2.4	-0.7	-0.1	Comores
Democratic Yemen	-	-	-	12.8	1.2	5.0	-20.4	-	-	Yémen démocratique
Djibouti	-	-	-	-	-	-	-	-	-	Djibouti
Equatorial Guinea	-	-	-	-	-	-	-	-	-	Guinée équatoriale
Ethiopia	-	-	-	-	-	-	-	-	-	Ethiopie
Gambia	-	-	-	-	6.6	-2.3	1.1	-1.2	-	Gambie
Guinea	-	2.3	10.5	18.0	3.6	-8.6	-2.3	-2.0	0.4	Guinée
Guinea-Bissau	-	-	-	8.5	5.0	-	-	1.0	1.7	Guinée-Bissau
Haiti	-	-	-	-	-	-	-	-	-	Haïti
Kiribati	-	-	-	-	-	-	-	-	-	Kiribati
Lao People's Dem.Rep.	-	-	-	-	-	-	-	-	-	Rép. dém. pop. lao
Lesotho	-	-	-	-	-	-	-	-	-	Lesotho
Malawi	-	-	-	-	-	-	-	-	-	Malawi
Maldives	-	-	-	-	3.3	-	-	-	-	Maldives
Mali	-	-	2.7	-0.3	-2.0	-	-	-	-	Mali
Mauritania	-	-	6.4	2.4	10.0	-0.8	-7.9	-	10.0	Mauritanie
Nepal	-	-	-	-	-	-	-	-	-	Népal
Niger	-	4.6	10.1	7.1	14.6	-14.6	-4.0	-0.0	1.0	Niger
Rwanda	-	-	-	-	-	-	-	-	-	Rwanda
Samoa	-	-	-	-	-	-	-	-	-	Samoa
Sao Tome and Principe	-	-	-	-	-	-	-	-	-	Sao Tomé-et-Principe
Sierra Leone	-	-	-	-	-	-	-	-	-	Sierra Leone
Somalia	4.9	1.7	3.9	15.0	12.6	-6.2	-4.6	-7.7	-9.8	Somalie
Sudan	-	2.2	39.0	32.6	7.2	-2.9	-7.2	-0.3	-	Soudan
Togo	-	-	1.0	0.0	-	-0.1	-0.1	-	1.0	Togo
Tuvalu	-	-	-	-	-	-	-	-	-	Tuvalu
Uganda	-	5.8	1.4	0.5	0.0	0.4	2.5	-0.2	1.4	Ouganda
Un. Rep. of Tanzania	-	-	-	-	-	0.5	-0.0	0.3	-	Rép.-Un. de Tanzanie
Vanuatu	-	-	-	-	-	-	-	-	-	Vanuatu
Yemen	-	-	0.4	19.8	3.4	-15.0	16.7	17.4	-5.6	Yémen
ALL LDCs	4.9	16.9	114.7	106.7	106.5	-54.0	10.7	17.1	-27.9	Ensemble des PMA
All developing countries	41.3	162.5	258.1	120.1	368.6	9.0	141.1	255.0	261.6	Ensemble des pays en développement

Source: UNCTAD secretariat estimates.
a/ For the list of multilateral agencies included here, providing concessional assistance to LDCs, see table 40A.

Source: Estimations du secrétariat de la CNUCED.
a/ Pour la liste des institutions multilatérales qui sont incluses ici et qui fournissent de l'aide concessionnelle aux PMA, se reporter au tableau 40A.

Table 46 / Tableau 46

Net ODA as per cent of donor's GNP from individual OPEC member countries to LDCs as a group

Apports nets de l'APD accordée par chaque pays membre de l'OPEP à l'ensemble des PMA, en pourcentage du PNB du pays donneur

Percentages / En pourcentage

Bilateral ODA / APD bilatérale

Country / Pays	1976	1977	1978	1979	1980	1981	1982	1983	1984	1985
Algeria / Algérie	0.01	0.01	0.00	0.05	0.05	0.02	0.00	–	–	–
Iran (Islamic Rep. of) / Iran (Rép. islamique)	0.01	–	0.02	–	–	–	–	–	–	–
Iraq / Iraq	0.24	0.13	0.19	0.14	0.12	–	–	–	-0.02	-0.08
Kuwait / Koweït	0.50	0.85	0.65	0.50	0.59	0.57	0.52	0.59	0.58	0.78
Libyan Arab Jamahiriya / Jamahiriya arabe libyenne	0.13	0.00	0.06	0.00	0.02	0.09	–	–	–	0.04
Nigeria / Nigéria	0.00	0.00	–	0.00	0.00	–	–	–	–	–
Qatar	0.50	0.16	0.24	0.11	0.63	0.32	0.12	0.12	0.03	0.09
Saudi Arabia / Arabie saoudite	0.85	1.03	0.62	0.58	0.42	0.26	0.48	0.58	0.51	0.23
United Arab Emirates / Emirats arabes unis	0.89	0.85	1.14	0.59	0.55	0.28	0.26	0.19	0.12	0.16
Venezuela	–	–	–	–	–	–	–	–	–	–
Total OPEC countries / Total des pays l'OPEP	**0.25**	**0.29**	**0.23**	**0.18**	**0.18**	**0.13**	**0.17**	**0.15**	**0.13**	**0.09**

Total ODA a/ / APD totale a/

Country / Pays	1976	1977	1978	1979	1980	1981	1982	1983	1984	1985
Algeria / Algérie	0.03	0.10	0.07	0.10	0.11	0.09	0.08	0.06	0.07	0.03
Iran (Islamic Rep. of) / Iran (Rép. islamique)	0.01	0.04	0.05	0.01	0.02	0.00	0.00	0.00	0.00	0.00
Iraq / Iraq	0.38	0.21	0.24	0.17	0.17	0.06	0.07	0.01	-0.01	-0.08
Kuwait / Koweït	0.81	1.31	1.06	0.76	0.79	0.77	0.96	1.03	1.04	1.10
Libyan Arab Jamahiriya / Jamahiriya arabe libyenne	0.23	0.18	0.32	0.16	0.12	0.22	0.09	0.19	0.03	0.06
Nigeria / Nigéria	0.09	0.11	0.03	0.02	0.01	0.12	0.03	0.03	0.04	0.03
Qatar	0.54	0.30	0.50	0.24	0.82	0.43	0.31	0.25	0.12	0.10
Saudi Arabia / Arabie saoudite	0.94	1.12	0.76	0.85	0.51	0.34	0.61	0.76	0.71	0.38
United Arab Emirates / Emirats arabes unis	0.93	0.93	1.30	0.78	0.64	0.35	0.39	0.28	0.13	0.16
Venezuela	0.02	0.06	0.04	0.03	0.04	0.05	0.04	0.07	0.01	0.01
Total OPEC countries / Total des pays de l'OPEP	**0.32**	**0.39**	**0.33**	**0.28**	**0.24**	**0.21**	**0.25**	**0.24**	**0.21**	**0.15**

Source: UNCTAD secretariat estimates. For 1976, the estimates are based on information from the OECD secretariat.

a/ Including imputed flows to LDCs through multilateral channels.

Source: Estimations du secrétariat de la CNUCED. Pour 1976, les estimations sont établies d'après des renseignements du secrétariat de l'OCDE.

a/ Y compris le montant imputé de l'APD fournie aux PMA à travers les voies multilatérales.

Table 47
ODA commitments from individual OPEC member countries and individual multilateral agencies mainly financed by them, to LDCs as a group

Tableau 47
Engagements de l'APD de chaque pays membre de l'OPEP et de chaque institution multilatérale essentiellement financée par ceux-ci, en faveur de l'ensemble des PMA

$ million / Millions de dollars

		1977	1978	1979	1980	1981	1982	1983	1984	1985
A. Bilateral donors	**A. Donneurs bilatéraux**									
Algeria	Algérie	2.5	0.5	34.5	–	20.0	0.2	–	–	100.0
Iran (Islamic Rep.)	Iran (Rép. Islamique)	–	–	–	–	–	–	–	–	–
Iraq	Iraq	1.3	75.5	327.5	289.5	145.8	37.4	165.6	142.0	–
Kuwait	Koweit	158.7	116.8	175.8	215.0	272.7	295.5	–	10.0	185.0
Libyan Arab Jamahiriya	Jamahiriya arabe Libyenne	0.9	25.4	6.0	42.8	24.5	–	–	–	–
Nigeria	Nigéria	0.1	1.0	1.7	2.5	–	–	–	–	–
Qatar	Qatar	4.7	10.8	4.8	40.5	22.6	7.6	7.4	2.0	5.1
Saudi Arabia	Arabie saoudite	842.5	912.9	463.8	407.1	432.9	896.9	1056.2	495.4	306.5
United Arab Emirates	Emirats arabes unis	282.5	141.0	93.7	294.4	46.1	94.8	8.7	102.9	20.1
Total bilateral concessional	Total des apports bilatéraux concessionnels	1293.2	1283.9	1107.8	1291.8	964.6	1332.4	1237.9	752.3	616.7
B. Multilateral donors	**B. Donneurs multilatéraux**									
BADEA	BADEA	29.9	22.6	8.2	44.8	10.0	32.0	20.5	0.3	11.0
AFESD	FADES	95.1	0.5	50.7	43.7	68.7	76.6	172.6	137.2	79.6
Islamic Dev. Bank	Banque islamique de dév.	31.2	13.6	18.3	17.9	19.0	45.1	23.5	92.9	65.4
OPEC Fund	Fonds de l'OPEP	91.3	59.7	93.5	115.3	180.2	163.9	74.1	74.7	36.0
OAPEC Special Account	Compte spécial de l'OPAEP	–	–	–	–	–	–	–	–	–
SAAFA	FSAAA	–	–	–	–	–	–	–	–	–
Total	Total	247.5	96.4	170.7	221.7	277.9	317.6	290.7	305.1	192.0
GRAND TOTAL	TOTAL GENERAL	1540.7	1380.3	1278.5	1513.5	1242.5	1650.0	1528.6	1057.4	808.7

Source: UNCTAD secretariat estimates.

For abbreviations, see p. A-9.

Source: Estimations du secrétariat de la CNUCED.

Pour les abréviations, se reporter p. A-12.

Table 48
ODA commitments from OPEC member countries
and multilateral agencies mainly financed by them
to individual LDCs

$ million

Tableau 48
Engagements de l'APD à chacun des PMA, en provenance des pays
membres de l'OPEP et des institutions multilatérales
essentiellement financées par ceux-ci

Millions de dollars

Country	1977	1978	1979	1980	1981	1982	1983	1984	1985	Pays
Afghanistan	42.3	20.0	3.6	-	1.0	-	-	0.1	0.4	Afghanistan
Bangladesh	85.4	75.0	50.0	78.4	227.5	301.2	334.2	38.8	53.4	Bangladesh
Benin	2.5	9.7	4.5	4.5	6.0	-	9.4	14.2	6.9	Bénin
Bhutan	-	-	-	-	-	-	10.3	7.1	6.6	Bhoutan
Botswana	1.0	-	4.2	25.6	3.9	24.1	-	2.0	-	Botswana
Burkina Faso	4.5	8.1	14.4	7.0	12.0	20.3	16.1	36.2	0.0	Burkina Faso
Burundi	11.8	6.0	4.5	9.5	30.4	9.0	14.6	14.0	8.3	Burundi
Cape Verde	1.5	1.9	1.0	17.7	1.0	2.5	14.5	0.2	-	Cap-Vert
Central African Rep.	2.8	-	3.6	1.6	2.5	8.4	5.8	-	12.1	Rép. centrafricaine
Chad	2.8	20.0	1.6	2.1	-	-	0.0	8.1	6.1	Tchad
Comoros	20.1	1.9	34.5	4.5	11.9	34.3	5.9	2.0	0.1	Comores
Democratic Yemen	80.8	21.9	63.6	100.8	66.4	79.1	40.8	52.9	141.8	Yémen démocratique
Djibouti	19.7	64.0	0.5	62.6	29.8	52.6	52.2	35.8	15.7	Djibouti
Equatorial Guinea	0.5	-	1.0	-	1.0	-	4.7	1.6	-	Guinée équatoriale
Ethiopia	5.7	0.7	0.9	0.1	11.2	-	-	5.0	100.0	Ethiopie
Gambia	26.2	2.6	1.0	28.6	6.6	2.4	1.0	2.1	-	Gambie
Guinea	12.0	7.5	14.8	180.8	-	24.1	11.2	62.0	0.0	Guinée
Guinea-Bissau	2.1	14.0	1.0	5.2	2.5	1.5	24.6	1.0	8.5	Guinée-Bissau
Haiti	3.2	-	4.0	3.5	-	-	2.8	1.2	-	Haïti
Kiribati	-	-	-	-	-	-	-	-	-	Kiribati
Lao People's Dem.Rep.	2.2	5.0	-	1.5	4.0	-	-	3.1	-	Rép. dém. pop. lao
Lesotho	1.9	5.1	3.0	17.0	3.5	-	3.0	1.5	-	Lesotho
Malawi	1.8	-	-	-	1.0	-	-	-	-	Malawi
Maldives	1.5	12.2	2.1	33.7	8.2	0.0	1.4	4.6	0.0	Maldives
Mali	28.6	20.0	26.3	46.7	22.8	3.3	7.8	25.2	18.0	Mali
Mauritania	42.8	161.7	268.3	110.7	141.5	141.1	53.5	49.2	58.0	Mauritanie
Nepal	37.1	3.0	12.2	1.3	11.0	136.6	0.0	25.4	19.9	Népal
Niger	11.5	17.7	5.2	42.3	100.6	41.8	5.0	41.7	21.2	Niger
Rwanda	15.6	-	4.8	3.0	9.3	10.0	18.8	5.0	12.5	Rwanda
Samoa	-	1.0	-	0.8	1.0	2.0	0.5	5.0	-	Samoa
Sao Tome and Principe	0.4	-	-	-	1.0	-	1.2	1.3	-	Sao Tomé-et-Principe
Sierra Leone	7.1	0.0	5.6	13.9	7.0	7.5	2.9	19.0	7.0	Sierra Leone
Somalia	447.9	68.3	80.8	105.3	90.0	205.8	34.1	91.4	2.2	Somalie
Sudan	215.9	401.9	169.6	269.0	130.9	118.9	585.1	130.2	191.2	Soudan
Togo	0.1	-	8.4	8.3	7.4	-	21.1	11.4	0.0	Togo
Tuvalu	-	-	-	-	-	-	-	-	-	Tuvalu
Uganda	14.7	27.2	-	5.0	10.5	16.3	0.1	14.4	10.0	Ouganda
Un. Rep. of Tanzania	11.6	5.1	-	36.6	85.0	22.0	5.0	15.0	-	Rép.-Un. de Tanzanie
Vanuatu	-	-	-	-	-	-	-	-	-	Vanuatu
Yemen	376.4	397.5	482.2	284.6	193.0	384.3	239.1	328.2	107.0	Yémen
ALL LDCs	1540.7	1380.1	1278.3	1513.2	1242.4	1650.1	1528.5	1057.3	808.5	Ensemble des PMA

Source: UNCTAD secretariat estimates.

Source: Estimations du secrétariat de la CNUCED.

Table 49
Grant element of ODA commitments from individual OPEC member
countries and multilateral agencies mainly financed by them,
to LDCs as a group

Tableau 49
Elément de libéralité des engagements de l'APD de chaque pays
membre de l'OPEP et de chaque institution multilatérale essentiellement financée par ceux-ci, à l'ensemble des PMA

	1977	1978	1979	1980	1981	1982	1983	1984	1985	
Bilateral donors										**Donneurs bilatéraux**
Algeria	100.0	100.0	94.2	-	54.8	100.0	-	-	50.0	Algérie
Iran (Islamic Rep.)	-	-	-	-	-	-	-	-	-	Iran (Rép. Islamique)
Iraq	50.0	63.2	52.9	56.1	47.0	42.1	-	-	-	Iraq
Kuwait	68.3	74.8	66.5	71.6	69.8	68.2	68.5	63.5	79.4	Koweit
Libyan Arab Jamahiriya	100.0	70.5	50.0	79.9	76.5	-	-	61.8	-	Jamahiriya arabe Libyenne
Nigeria	50.0	100.0	100.0	98.0	-	-	-	-	-	Nigéria
Qatar	100.0	74.2	100.0	100.0	100.0	100.0	100.0	100.0	100.0	Qatar
Saudi Arabia	85.6	61.5	66.4	73.8	64.5	82.5	94.3	83.8	82.7	Arabie saoudite
United Arab Emirates	70.0	84.2	78.5	61.8	61.7	60.5	100.0	100.0	46.9	Emirats arabes unis
Total	80.1	65.6	64.4	67.8	64.2	76.7	91.0	81.9	75.4	Total
Multilateral donors										**Donneurs multilatéraux**
BADEA	47.4	60.1	39.5	35.7	31.3	32.3	33.3	100.0	47.3	BADEA
AFESD	41.2	100.0	36.9	35.1	39.5	37.5	36.7	37.7	41.0	FADES
Islamic Dev. Bank	56.3	49.5	53.0	54.6	53.2	61.8	59.8	70.7	64.3	Banque islamique de dév.
OPEC Fund	66.9	58.9	58.9	53.5	53.2	57.8	50.9	55.4	53.8	Fonds de l'OPEP
Total	53.4	58.1	50.8	46.4	49.0	50.9	41.9	52.2	51.7	Total
GRAND TOTAL	75.8	65.1	62.6	64.7	60.8	71.8	81.6	73.3	69.8	TOTAL GENERAL

Source : UNCTAD secretariat estimates.

For abbreviations, see p. A-9.

Source : Estimations du secrétariat de la CNUCED.

Pour les abréviations, se reporter p. A-12.

Table 50
ODA commitments from individual OPEC member countries and individual multilateral agencies mainly financed by them, to LDCs as a group, by purpose, average 1981-1985

Tableau 50
Engagements de l'APD de chaque pays membre de l'OPEP et de chaque institution multilatérale essentiellement financée par ceux-ci, en faveur de l'ensemble des PMA, par objet, moyenne 1981-1985

	Agriculture / Agriculture	Mining / Industries extractives	Manufacturing / Industries manufacturières	Electricity gas & water / Electricité gas et eau	Transport & storage / Transports et entrepôts	Other services / Autres services	Multi-purpose / Objet multiple	Balance of payments support / Soutien à la balance des paiements	Distress Relief / Secours d'urgence	Other & unallocated a/ / Autres et non-ventilés a/	Total in $m. / en m.$
	Per cent of total — En pourcentage du total										
Bilateral donors / Donneurs bilatéraux											
Algeria / Algérie	–	–	–	–	–	0.2	–	16.6	83.2	–	120
Iraq / Iraq	27.3	–	17.4	–	19.4	1.0	–	–	1.1	34.9	183
Kuwait / Koweit	9.5	–	6.8	23.9	22.8	–	5.4	–	–	30.4	1061
Libyan Arab Jamahiriya / Jamahiriya arabe libyenne	–	–	–	–	–	–	–	–	–	100.0	34
Qatar / Qatar	–	–	–	–	–	–	–	–	–	100.0	45
Saudi Arabia / Arabie saoudite	2.0	1.7	3.6	2.4	6.6	1.0	3.2	24.1	8.1	47.3	3188
United Arab Emirates / Emirats arabes unis	–	–	10.5	8.2	8.2	–	–	–	1.4	71.6	273
Total	4.3	1.1	5.1	7.2	10.4	0.7	3.3	16.1	7.6	44.2	4904
Multilateral donors / Donneurs multilatéraux											
BADEA / BADEA	5.4	–	13.6	6.8	68.8	–	–	–	–	5.4	74
AFESD / FADES	19.8	–	8.7	28.3	34.5	5.4	1.3	–	–	2.0	534
Islamic Dev. Bank / Banque islamique de développement	15.1	5.1	–	21.8	17.9	6.5	14.2	–	–	24.4	246
OPEC Fund / Fonds de l'OPEP	5.5	2.0	3.4	22.0	16.3	3.1	–	32.1	–	12.5	529
Total	12.7	2.0	5.4	23.6	26.4	4.5	3.0	12.3	–	10.1	1383
GRAND TOTAL / TOTAL GENERAL	6.2	1.3	5.1	10.8	13.9	1.5	3.2	15.2	5.9	36.8	6287

Source: UNCTAD secretariat estimates.

a/ Mainly budget support in the case of bilateral flows. Mainly technical assistance in the case of multilateral flows.

Source: Estimations du secrétariat de la CNUCED.

a/ Principalement soutien budgétaire dans les cas des apports bilatéraux. Principalement assistance technique dans les cas des apports multilatéraux.

Table 51A
Total external debt a/
$ million

Tableau 51A
Encours de la dette extérieure totale a/
Millions de dollars

Country	Pays	1975	1976	1977	1978	1979	1980	1981	1982b/	1983b/	1984b/	1985b/
Afghanistan	Afghanistan	819.0	930.5	1073.0	1221.0	1285.0	1195.0	1242.0	1410.4	1682.8	1329.4	1429.2
Bangladesh	Bangladesh	1600.7	1933.5	2307.4	2793.0	3348.4	3613.8	3938.2	4941.9	5617.0	5866.2	6844.7
Benin	Bénin	89.6	115.2	149.2	185.7	237.1	483.8	573.6	622.5	717.1	641.4	777.1
Bhutan	Bhoutan	-	-	-	-	-	-	-	9.4	2.1	5.3	5.7
Botswana	Botswana	278.1	294.5	303.8	285.9	295.0	282.8	285.8	340.5	359.7	377.4	441.0
Burkina Faso	Burkina Faso	62.2	83.9	130.5	197.1	260.5	295.0	311.6	390.1	440.9	439.6	551.1
Burundi	Burundi	16.8	19.8	43.7	68.1	112.4	150.8	175.2	252.3	316.4	353.0	461.0
Cape Verde	Cap-Vert	0.5	11.7	13.8	14.9	17.6	20.1	39.8	56.5	75.7	78.0	102.4
Central African Rep.	Rép. centrafricaine	82.2	88.6	111.7	126.8	131.9	164.1	188.4	261.8	279.6	267.6	349.4
Chad	Tchad	67.1	95.6	114.5	162.2	172.2	155.5	126.0	156.8	158.3	149.8	167.0
Comoros	Comores	5.0	17.6	23.2	27.0	39.2	49.7	53.2	81.0	86.5	104.8	135.1
Democratic Yemen	Yémen démocratique	119.8	157.6	256.6	354.0	427.2	549.3	797.6	842.5	1070.3	1167.3	1573.4
Djibouti	Djibouti	27.0	26.0	27.0	31.0	51.0	28.3	22.0	47.0	64.7	143.2	243.5
Equatorial Guinea	Guinée équatoriale	27.0	28.9	31.7	34.2	35.7	57.2	66.6	124.0	126.6	104.2	140.8
Ethiopia	Ethiopie	385.8	429.5	473.1	542.6	616.5	703.5	962.9	1239.3	1435.7	1651.1	1911.1
Gambia	Gambie	14.3	15.2	30.5	49.7	80.4	118.4	145.2	211.7	218.6	248.7	248.0
Guinea	Guinée	847.9	896.8	884.8	985.4	1064.1	1110.5	1300.9	1439.7	1345.4	1274.1	1432.5
Guinea-Bissau	Guinée-Bissau	7.0	18.7	24.5	42.4	65.8	103.9	111.4	151.5	167.5	180.9	253.3
Haiti	Haïti	56.8	86.4	136.1	184.8	226.5	268.9	356.4	667.5	716.0	759.3	833.1
Kiribati	Kiribati	-	-	-	-	-	-	-	8.5	8.6	9.6	10.6
Lao People's Dem.Rep.	Rép. dém. pop. lao	25.0	35.0	48.0	77.0	77.0	75.0	65.0	321.5	457.7	433.0	527.7
Lesotho	Lesotho	13.2	15.2	24.5	32.3	54.2	76.1	90.7	117.3	133.9	141.3	176.7
Malawi	Malawi	279.4	310.0	407.5	491.9	566.9	746.4	766.8	882.1	896.2	891.6	987.5
Maldives	Maldives	1.0	1.1	2.7	6.9	9.8	27.8	39.2	48.4	70.6	80.0	81.5
Mali	Mali	336.8	351.0	433.4	517.7	533.3	691.8	738.9	855.0	1017.7	1277.6	1503.7
Mauritania	Mauritanie	190.5	392.5	458.5	584.9	632.7	754.5	893.6	1200.6	1322.7	1336.0	1508.7
Nepal	Népal	37.7	45.1	73.1	105.7	154.6	184.8	242.7	352.4	451.8	475.1	588.7
Niger	Niger	117.1	157.5	207.1	309.6	406.2	608.2	703.4	891.2	914.9	930.1	1058.2
Rwanda	Rwanda	25.5	48.8	74.3	100.9	126.5	161.0	180.3	220.6	264.3	305.2	369.0
Samoa	Samoa	15.5	22.0	30.1	33.8	49.1	56.6	56.4	63.5	69.4	72.6	74.8
Sao Tome and Principe	Sao Tomé-et-Principe	-	-	-	-	-	-	-	22.3	30.2	27.1	31.2
Sierra Leone	Sierra Leone	168.7	166.8	211.9	299.4	359.9	389.4	392.3	615.0	685.2	706.4	693.2
Somalia	Somalie	236.0	292.5	408.9	548.6	678.7	749.1	906.0	1265.2	1542.4	1665.2	1725.0
Sudan	Soudan	1481.0	1820.7	2259.6	2759.7	3395.8	3953.0	4731.0	6366.8	6925.8	6605.6	6484.1
Togo	Togo	138.1	176.7	327.8	656.1	857.7	916.4	870.9	1045.7	976.2	855.2	1009.8
Tuvalu	Tuvalu	-	-	-	-	-	-	-	-	0.0	0.1	0.1
Uganda	Ouganda	213.4	251.6	280.9	354.5	492.4	609.2	592.7	879.3	1042.2	1054.1	1075.6
Un. Rep. of Tanzania	Rép.-Un. de Tanzanie	835.9	974.7	1201.8	1365.6	1592.2	1733.8	1950.6	2740.3	3001.0	3043.9	3374.2
Vanuatu	Vanuatu	6.0	7.0	7.0	10.0	12.0	10.0	7.0	13.9	77.7	93.0	127.7
Yemen	Yémen	247.8	270.7	341.5	500.2	626.6	983.8	1223.4	1541.4	1947.1	2113.3	2398.5
All LDCs	Ensemble des PMA	8875.4	10589	12934	16061	19092	22077	25148	32698	36717	37258	41706

Source: UNCTAD secretariat, based on information from the OECD secretariat.
a/ Disbursed outstanding at year-end including short-term debt and use of IMF credit.
b/ Data not strictly comparable with those for the years 1975-1981.

Source: Secrétariat de la CNUCED, d'après des renseignements du secrétariat de l'OCDE.
a/ Encours en fin d'année. (montants versés) y compris la dette à court terme et les crédits du FMI.
b/ Les données ne sont pas strictement comparables à celles qui se rapportent aux années 1975-1981.

Table 51B / Tableau 51B
Total debt a/ service payments / Paiements totaux au titre du service de la dette a/
$ million / Millions de dollars

Country	1975	1976	1977	1978	1979	1980	1981	1982b/	1983b/	1984b/	1985b/	Pays
Afghanistan	27.2	25.6	38.2	54.5	13.4	180.4	140.2	39.6	41.3	43.0	46.6	Afghanistan
Bangladesh	60.8	86.2	83.6	102.2	99.3	109.2	151.2	161.3	167.8	243.7	293.7	Bangladesh
Benin	9.2	7.2	10.6	14.1	16.2	24.2	54.8	30.1	70.9	47.0	41.3	Bénin
Bhutan	-	-	-	-	-	-	-	1.8	1.7	0.3	9.0	Bhoutan
Botswana	22.4	19.1	41.5	66.5	46.0	39.8	35.8	61.6	31.1	49.1	55.6	Botswana
Burkina Faso	7.7	5.8	6.8	9.0	10.3	17.5	15.3	26.8	23.2	25.7	33.0	Burkina Faso
Burundi	1.6	1.6	3.0	5.1	4.3	7.2	6.5	17.7	18.1	20.7	24.3	Burundi
Cape Verde	0.2	0.1	0.1	0.2	0.2	0.2	0.3	1.9	3.5	6.9	5.3	Cap-Vert
Central African Rep.	7.4	4.5	7.0	6.7	3.3	2.1	3.8	7.3	14.7	28.9	17.7	Rép. centrafricaine
Chad	6.2	6.1	9.5	13.3	15.4	12.0	8.5	2.1	1.6	8.0	9.1	Tchad
Comoros	0.5	0.5	0.6	1.0	2.3	1.7	0.7	2.1	2.5	2.8	2.5	Comores
Democratic Yemen	3.8	3.1	5.7	6.3	12.7	23.1	68.4	34.8	45.8	100.4	132.5	Yémen démocratique
Djibouti	4.3	3.8	4.0	3.0	11.4	6.2	4.9	4.0	6.7	16.8	34.7	Djibouti
Equatorial Guinea	1.9	1.9	1.6	0.4	1.2	3.1	4.3	4.0	9.6	2.1	4.4	Guinée équatoriale
Ethiopia	31.4	25.8	31.7	31.6	28.4	35.1	54.7	69.1	85.7	120.8	124.7	Ethiopie
Gambia	0.4	0.4	0.5	0.9	0.8	1.6	7.4	13.3	10.2	9.8	14.9	Gambie
Guinea	53.6	55.7	97.5	96.8	117.4	128.4	118.0	101.7	100.2	121.2	78.4	Guinée
Guinea-Bissau	-	0.4	0.4	0.9	3.6	4.4	4.3	3.4	3.2	6.6	18.6	Guinée-Bissau
Haiti	7.6	10.4	18.7	18.6	12.1	21.6	15.9	26.5	31.1	35.9	38.6	Haïti
Kiribati	-	-	-	-	-	-	-	0.0	0.0	0.2	0.5	Kiribati
Lao People's Dem.Rep.	2.1	2.0	3.0	2.2	3.3	2.3	1.8	2.4	4.2	6.1	25.8	Rép. dém. pop. lao
Lesotho	0.4	0.4	0.4	1.0	1.8	5.9	6.7	13.7	13.5	14.9	18.8	Lesotho
Malawi	20.1	26.2	28.0	37.1	45.6	69.8	91.3	75.8	72.9	79.9	85.6	Malawi
Maldives	-	-	-	0.1	0.2	0.4	1.0	2.3	6.2	26.1	12.7	Maldives
Mali	6.1	7.1	12.9	17.7	21.0	-16.6	13.0	33.4	15.3	24.0	51.8	Mali
Mauritania	41.6	38.1	52.0	51.2	50.7	40.5	59.2	55.3	54.2	55.5	95.9	Mauritanie
Nepal	4.5	1.8	2.4	3.0	5.4	13.2	8.1	13.5	18.6	16.5	18.3	Népal
Niger	9.5	11.2	17.7	28.1	46.0	87.3	115.5	171.9	128.3	105.6	95.8	Niger
Rwanda	1.0	0.9	2.2	2.6	2.5	3.2	4.1	9.8	7.8	21.0	24.0	Rwanda
Samoa	1.2	0.9	2.5	2.4	3.6	4.6	3.5	2.6	2.5	3.9	4.9	Samoa
Sao Tome and Principe	-	-	-	-	-	-	-	0.4	0.9	1.5	3.3	Sao Tomé-et-Principe
Sierra Leone	21.8	20.0	28.0	37.6	54.1	43.2	54.6	37.2	55.2	42.0	38.6	Sierra Leone
Somalia	5.1	4.7	5.5	7.9	9.4	20.1	31.0	23.8	35.3	49.3	90.7	Somalie
Sudan	165.7	158.7	146.4	118.9	96.2	100.4	134.7	146.5	108.9	134.4	183.7	Soudan
Togo	21.9	30.6	39.9	49.6	52.0	78.4	57.5	59.0	69.1	99.0	93.9	Togo
Tuvalu	-	-	-	-	-	-	-	-	-	0.0	0.1	Tuvalu
Uganda	20.0	16.1	31.6	14.4	17.0	15.1	61.4	66.1	84.9	108.8	117.8	Ouganda
Un. Rep. of Tanzania	39.7	36.0	47.9	52.6	107.6	114.8	93.2	92.6	138.0	100.1	102.0	Rép.-Un. de Tanzanie
Vanuatu	0.5	0.6	0.4	1.2	2.6	2.9	1.3	2.2	4.1	15.8	11.0	Vanuatu
Yemen	5.4	8.1	13.0	17.7	22.7	46.6	109.9	81.9	79.3	132.9	207.2	Yémen
All LDCs	612.5	621.7	795.0	876.4	939.7	1281.9	1542.8	1499.8	1568.0	1927.3	2267.2	Ensemble des PMA

Source: UNCTAD secretariat, based on information from the OECD secretariat.
a/ Total external including short-term but excluding the use of IMF credit.
b/ Data not strictly comparable with those for the years 1975-1981.

Source: Secrétariat de la CNUCED, d'après des renseignements du secrétariat de l'OCDE.
a/ Dette extérieure totale y compris la dette à court terme mais non compris les crédits du FMI.
b/ Les données ne sont pas strictement comparables à celles qui se rapportent aux années 1975-1981.

Table 52A
Long- and medium-term debt and total concessional debt

Tableau 52A
Dette à long et moyen terme et dette concessionnelle

$ million / Millions de dollars

Country	Long- and medium-term debt / Dette à long et moyen terme				Of which concessional / Dont dette concessionnelle				Pays
	1982	1983	1984	1985	1982	1983	1984	1985	
Afghanistan	1400.5	1674.3	1322.3	1424.1	1375.5	1650.5	1299.9	1418.1	Afghanistan
Bangladesh	4478.8	5079.8	5444.5	6372.5	4090.2	4362.2	4980.3	5925.1	Bangladesh
Benin	577.3	620.4	601.2	676.6	204.2	254.8	263.1	311.7	Bénin
Bhutan	8.4	2.1	3.3	5.3	1.4	1.8	2.1	5.3	Bhoutan
Botswana	298.7	312.9	362.5	417.5	101.6	106.5	115.0	128.2	Botswana
Burkina Faso	357.2	409.4	413.0	509.3	256.0	285.9	303.5	381.4	Burkina Faso
Burundi	225.8	301.6	341.3	435.2	193.2	260.0	286.1	354.6	Burundi
Cape Verde	56.5	75.5	77.7	101.3	29.8	34.9	43.9	61.6	Cap-Vert
Central African Rep.	226.4	239.5	229.9	302.8	123.3	137.5	150.4	210.8	Rép. centrafricaine
Chad	145.5	150.1	142.8	155.1	84.1	92.1	88.7	105.4	Tchad
Comoros	70.0	84.2	102.2	131.5	65.6	80.1	96.0	121.5	Comores
Democratic Yemen	813.5	989.1	1093.8	1431.8	759.5	901.8	1004.4	1285.6	Yémen démocratique
Djibouti	26.8	52.3	121.3	217.0	16.2	25.6	59.7	84.6	Djibouti
Equatorial Guinea	90.4	99.9	93.4	129.3	31.1	33.4	26.8	32.0	Guinée équatoriale
Ethiopia	1090.2	1294.2	1518.6	1790.5	878.4	1059.5	1163.2	1388.0	Ethiopie
Gambia	163.0	167.3	183.5	199.1	115.9	121.9	124.0	142.9	Gambie
Guinea	1339.3	1252.6	1218.2	1336.4	927.5	923.4	868.5	924.9	Guinée
Guinea-Bissau	148.0	159.3	164.7	222.8	106.1	118.2	131.7	154.6	Guinée-Bissau
Haiti	454.3	530.8	570.9	620.5	297.2	345.6	403.5	459.4	Haïti
Kiribati	8.5	8.5	8.5	10.4	0.5	0.6	0.5	0.7	Kiribati
Lao People's Dem.Rep.	307.2	439.1	398.8	457.7	305.6	435.4	396.1	452.7	Rép. dém. pop. lao
Lesotho	117.3	133.4	140.8	174.4	77.4	95.4	115.9	142.5	Lesotho
Malawi	722.1	722.6	740.7	774.8	393.6	415.8	483.5	531.9	Malawi
Maldives	44.1	54.4	58.9	68.2	35.4	39.6	35.9	37.9	Maldives
Mali	816.0	942.8	1155.1	1343.4	769.2	857.1	1001.7	1244.9	Mali
Mauritania	1045.4	1190.9	1238.6	1413.4	665.3	740.7	780.4	857.6	Mauritanie
Nepal	305.9	361.9	447.4	554.9	298.5	359.6	428.5	531.5	Népal
Niger	785.4	766.5	783.2	901.3	295.3	330.2	352.6	445.1	Niger
Rwanda	199.6	247.6	268.5	342.5	188.8	219.1	240.7	308.7	Rwanda
Samoa	59.4	60.4	64.4	65.2	45.4	48.7	54.0	55.7	Samoa
Sao Tome and Principe	18.3	26.2	25.0	29.9	16.4	19.3	20.5	22.9	Sao Tomé-et-Principe
Sierra Leone	445.8	415.3	458.8	434.1	244.3	254.3	247.2	242.3	Sierra Leone
Somalia	1189.3	1389.7	1525.5	1557.0	869.5	938.2	1063.4	1093.5	Somalie
Sudan	5152.6	5751.5	5501.4	5007.0	2160.0	2389.7	2733.6	2471.3	Soudan
Togo	923.8	858.4	746.8	845.8	289.3	336.4	353.0	318.6	Togo
Tuvalu	-	0.1	0.1	0.1	-	0.1	0.1	0.1	Tuvalu
Uganda	608.8	670.7	699.0	773.8	392.8	394.8	441.1	520.9	Ouganda
Un. Rep. of Tanzania	2482.1	2742.6	2855.4	3090.8	1554.1	1708.7	1732.3	1889.2	Rép.-Un. de Tanzanie
Vanuatu	10.7	45.9	59.3	106.0	3.9	2.7	3.2	4.7	Vanuatu
Yemen	1420.5	1744.6	1862.0	2124.3	1252.8	1534.8	1632.3	1720.8	Yémen
All LDCs	28633.5	32068.7	33043.5	36554.0	19515.2	21917.0	23527.8	26389.4	Ensemble des PMA

Source: UNCTAD secretariat, based on information from the OECD secretariat.

Source: Secrétariat de la CNUCED, d'après des renseignements du secrétariat de l'OCDE.

Table 52B
Long- and medium-term and concessional
debt service payments
$ million

Tableau 52B
Paiements au titre du service de la dette à long et moyen terme
et de la dette concessionnelle
Millions de dollars

Country	Long- and medium-term debt service Service de la dette à long et moyen terme				Of which concessional Dont service de la dette concessionnelle				Pays
	1982	1983	1984	1985	1982	1983	1984	1985	
Afghanistan	38.9	40.4	42.1	46.1	36.6	37.0	38.7	23.6	Afghanistan
Bangladesh	155.3	160.6	235.1	289.1	100.6	96.6	127.8	164.8	Bangladesh
Benin	18.1	63.9	39.7	35.6	4.4	4.7	4.9	8.0	Bénin
Bhutan	1.2	1.7	0.2	8.9	0.0	0.0	0.0	8.6	Bhoutan
Botswana	60.2	26.7	45.8	54.0	1.9	2.4	4.9	8.8	Botswana
Burkina Faso	25.9	20.0	22.6	30.3	4.4	3.6	8.4	6.9	Burkina Faso
Burundi	15.8	16.9	19.5	22.8	2.3	5.0	11.5	11.9	Burundi
Cape Verde	1.9	3.5	6.9	5.3	0.1	0.6	1.0	1.1	Cap-Vert
Central African Rep.	6.6	13.5	27.5	16.3	1.1	2.1	18.5	8.8	Rép. centrafricaine
Chad	0.8	1.4	7.8	8.9	0.2	0.2	4.8	2.9	Tchad
Comoros	2.1	1.8	2.6	2.3	0.8	1.2	2.1	1.1	Comores
Democratic Yemen	33.5	42.0	93.8	124.9	21.0	24.8	70.4	99.7	Yémen démocratique
Djibouti	3.7	5.0	14.9	32.7	1.8	2.1	2.5	13.3	Djibouti
Equatorial Guinea	3.9	8.2	1.4	4.2	0.1	0.1	0.1	0.3	Guinée équatoriale
Ethiopia	67.0	83.1	115.9	119.4	21.3	26.8	34.9	42.9	Ethiopie
Gambia	11.9	8.3	6.6	12.4	1.8	2.0	5.3	4.5	Gambie
Guinea	95.1	91.8	114.5	73.1	48.8	43.7	67.5	43.8	Guinée
Guinea-Bissau	3.4	2.9	5.6	17.0	0.9	1.3	1.8	14.0	Guinée-Bissau
Haiti	18.3	17.4	24.5	29.0	4.2	4.7	7.0	8.9	Haïti
Kiribati	0.0	-	0.1	0.5	-	-	0.1	0.5	Kiribati
Lao People's Dem.Rep.	2.3	3.9	4.5	21.9	2.1	2.5	2.2	20.2	Rép. dém. pop. lao
Lesotho	12.3	13.5	14.8	18.7	0.8	1.8	3.0	4.6	Lesotho
Malawi	68.5	65.3	74.0	80.8	7.6	7.4	11.8	17.7	Malawi
Maldives	2.2	5.2	24.1	11.3	1.6	2.5	4.8	3.8	Maldives
Mali	8.5	13.6	19.4	46.1	5.2	10.0	13.4	32.6	Mali
Mauritania	47.9	44.3	47.1	90.5	19.0	14.9	16.1	38.8	Mauritanie
Nepal	9.8	13.1	11.0	16.4	5.4	8.0	10.3	12.5	Népal
Niger	163.1	117.2	93.9	87.9	12.1	13.2	13.7	21.2	Niger
Rwanda	7.3	5.9	18.2	21.4	6.0	4.1	5.8	9.2	Rwanda
Samoa	2.6	2.4	3.8	4.9	0.7	1.0	1.4	1.8	Samoa
Sao Tome and Principe	0.3	0.5	1.2	3.2	0.0	0.0	-	2.0	Sao Tomé-et-Principe
Sierra Leone	20.6	39.0	21.9	24.1	2.7	2.3	5.2	7.4	Sierra Leone
Somalia	22.0	32.8	45.0	88.1	8.8	11.1	28.0	51.4	Somalie
Sudan	121.5	88.9	106.3	129.7	36.7	26.7	24.2	37.8	Soudan
Togo	52.3	61.3	91.8	87.4	2.8	12.0	19.7	33.9	Togo
Tuvalu	-	-	-	0.1	-	-	-	0.1	Tuvalu
Uganda	63.2	83.9	105.7	115.3	21.3	28.9	30.1	33.2	Ouganda
Un. Rep. of Tanzania	70.9	118.8	80.3	84.7	17.5	22.7	29.4	23.6	Rép.-Un. de Tanzanie
Vanuatu	1.8	2.3	12.3	8.7	0.7	0.6	0.3	0.7	Vanuatu
Yemen	74.2	60.8	108.4	186.6	46.4	30.3	46.5	105.4	Yémen
ALL LDCs	1315.1	1381.7	1710.9	2060.3	449.8	458.9	678.2	932.4	Ensemble des PMA

Source: UNCTAD secretariat, based on information from the OECD secretariat.

Source: Secrétariat de la CNUCED, d'après des renseignements du secrétariat de l'OCDE.

Table 53A
Non-concessional long- and medium-term debt

Tableau 53A
Dette non-concessionnelle à long et moyen terme

$ million / Millions de dollars

Country	Non-concessional debt / Dette non-concessionnelle				Of which official and officially guaranteed / Dont dette publique et dette garantie par l'Etat				Pays
	1982	1983	1984	1985	1982	1983	1984	1985	
Afghanistan	25.0	23.8	22.4	6.0	24.0	23.8	22.4	0.0	Afghanistan
Bangladesh	388.6	717.6	464.2	447.4	268.7	465.0	151.3	147.2	Bangladesh
Benin	373.1	365.6	338.1	365.0	163.9	215.1	190.3	233.6	Bénin
Bhutan	7.0	0.3	1.2	0.0	-	0.3	0.2	0.0	Bhoutan
Botswana	197.1	206.4	247.5	289.3	80.8	82.7	121.3	129.3	Botswana
Burkina Faso	101.2	123.5	109.5	127.9	44.0	53.4	45.3	62.2	Burkina Faso
Burundi	32.5	41.6	55.2	80.6	28.1	7.0	12.5	11.0	Burundi
Cape Verde	26.7	40.6	33.9	39.6	12.5	17.7	10.9	9.8	Cap-Vert
Central African Rep.	103.2	102.0	79.5	92.0	73.7	76.0	52.6	59.1	Rép. centrafricaine
Chad	61.4	58.0	54.1	49.7	24.0	20.8	20.9	25.0	Tchad
Comoros	4.4	4.1	6.2	10.0	1.5	1.2	0.9	1.1	Comores
Democratic Yemen	54.0	87.4	89.3	146.2	44.2	34.3	29.5	128.5	Yémen démocratique
Djibouti	10.6	26.6	61.6	132.4	3.8	19.7	24.0	34.0	Djibouti
Equatorial Guinea	59.3	66.5	66.6	97.3	44.7	51.4	45.4	77.0	Guinée équatoriale
Ethiopia	211.8	234.7	355.4	402.5	118.1	159.1	271.9	304.5	Ethiopie
Gambia	47.1	45.4	59.5	56.2	21.9	23.1	24.4	28.5	Gambie
Guinea	411.8	329.2	349.7	411.5	235.6	227.9	229.9	259.7	Guinée
Guinea-Bissau	41.8	41.2	32.9	68.2	14.8	9.2	8.8	25.8	Guinée-Bissau
Haiti	157.2	185.2	167.4	161.1	49.0	42.4	32.9	38.6	Haïti
Kiribati	7.9	7.9	7.9	9.7	-	-	-	-	Kiribati
Lao People's Dem.Rep.	1.5	3.7	2.6	5.0	0.5	3.2	2.6	5.0	Rép. dém. pop. lao
Lesotho	39.9	38.0	24.9	32.0	24.9	12.8	7.1	8.6	Lesotho
Malawi	328.5	306.8	257.2	242.9	87.6	60.5	59.2	75.6	Malawi
Maldives	8.7	14.8	22.9	30.3	0.9	0.6	1.0	2.0	Maldives
Mali	46.8	85.7	153.4	98.6	31.3	58.0	124.9	53.6	Mali
Mauritania	380.2	450.2	458.2	555.8	132.7	178.5	167.0	228.1	Mauritanie
Nepal	7.4	2.4	18.9	23.4	7.4	1.3	1.8	4.6	Népal
Niger	490.1	436.3	430.6	456.2	209.3	204.7	215.8	244.3	Niger
Rwanda	10.8	28.5	27.8	33.7	3.8	4.9	13.2	15.3	Rwanda
Samoa	14.0	11.7	10.4	9.5	4.9	3.8	3.2	4.4	Samoa
Sao Tome and Principe	1.9	6.9	4.5	7.0	1.9	6.9	4.5	4.2	Sao Tomé-et-Principe
Sierra Leone	201.5	161.0	211.6	191.8	153.8	122.4	135.4	106.0	Sierra Leone
Somalia	319.8	451.5	462.0	463.4	136.5	168.0	192.8	214.1	Somalie
Sudan	2992.6	3361.8	2767.8	2535.6	1176.4	1728.1	1239.5	1660.0	Soudan
Togo	634.5	522.0	393.7	527.2	452.4	398.3	263.8	403.7	Togo
Tuvalu	0.1	0.1	0.1	0.1	-	-	-	-	Tuvalu
Uganda	216.0	275.9	257.9	252.9	100.9	163.3	131.1	129.6	Ouganda
Un. Rep. of Tanzania	928.1	1033.9	1123.1	1201.6	453.3	385.2	414.9	492.8	Rép.-Un. de Tanzanie
Vanuatu	6.8	43.1	56.1	101.3	2.0	4.2	19.8	61.3	Vanuatu
Yemen	167.6	209.8	229.8	403.5	86.5	132.3	113.6	128.6	Yémen
ALL LDCs	9118.4	10151.7	9515.7	10164.6	4320.5	5167.5	4406.7	5416.9	Ensemble des PMA

Source: UNCTAD secretariat, based on information from the OECD secretariat.

Source: Secrétariat de la CNUCED, d'après des renseignements du secrétariat de l'OCDE.

Table 53B
Non-concessional long- and medium-term
debt service payments
$ million

Tableau 53B
Paiements au titre du service de la dette non-concessionnelle
à long et moyen terme
Millions de dollars

Country	Non-concessional debt service / Service de la dette non-concessionnelle				Of which official and officially guaranteed / Dont service de la dette publique et de la dette garantie par l'Etat				Pays
	1982	1983	1984	1985	1982	1983	1984	1985	
Afghanistan	2.3	3.4	3.4	22.4	1.2	2.1	3.4	22.4	Afghanistan
Bangladesh	54.7	63.9	107.3	124.2	28.6	31.8	46.2	69.8	Bangladesh
Benin	13.7	59.2	34.8	27.6	9.6	33.9	25.6	7.5	Bénin
Bhutan	1.2	1.7	0.2	0.3	-	0.2	0.2	0.1	Bhoutan
Botswana	58.3	24.2	40.9	45.2	2.2	6.6	11.2	15.5	Botswana
Burkina Faso	21.5	16.3	14.2	23.3	11.6	10.9	8.4	13.7	Burkina Faso
Burundi	13.5	11.9	8.0	10.8	3.3	4.2	3.2	2.4	Burundi
Cape Verde	1.7	2.9	5.9	4.2	0.9	1.0	2.3	1.1	Cap-Vert
Central African Rep.	5.5	11.3	9.0	7.5	4.5	9.1	7.7	4.3	Rép. centrafricaine
Chad	0.6	1.1	3.0	5.9	0.0	1.0	0.3	0.3	Tchad
Comoros	1.3	0.6	0.5	1.2	0.3	0.1	0.2	0.2	Comores
Democratic Yemen	12.5	17.3	23.4	25.3	9.8	15.1	11.6	13.0	Yémen démocratique
Djibouti	1.9	3.0	12.5	19.4	1.1	1.1	10.2	3.0	Djibouti
Equatorial Guinea	3.9	8.1	1.3	3.8	2.3	6.2	1.3	1.9	Guinée équatoriale
Ethiopia	45.8	56.4	81.0	76.5	22.7	35.6	52.9	50.7	Ethiopie
Gambia	10.1	6.2	1.2	7.9	2.3	0.5	0.1	4.7	Gambie
Guinea	46.3	48.1	47.0	29.3	24.8	26.1	25.4	14.9	Guinée
Guinea-Bissau	2.5	1.6	3.8	3.0	1.9	0.5	1.3	1.4	Guinée-Bissau
Haiti	14.1	12.7	17.5	20.1	7.2	6.3	6.4	5.7	Haïti
Kiribati	0.0	-	-	-	-	-	-	-	Kiribati
Lao People's Dem.Rep.	0.2	1.5	2.3	1.7	-	1.3	2.2	1.7	Rép. dém. pop. lao
Lesotho	11.4	11.7	11.8	14.2	2.4	2.6	8.5	5.8	Lesotho
Malawi	60.9	57.9	62.2	63.1	24.2	24.4	25.7	16.5	Malawi
Maldives	0.6	2.7	19.2	7.4	0.4	1.4	0.7	0.6	Maldives
Mali	3.3	3.7	5.9	13.5	2.3	2.0	4.6	9.7	Mali
Mauritania	28.9	29.4	31.0	51.7	17.0	10.0	12.7	11.9	Mauritanie
Nepal	4.4	5.1	0.6	3.9	4.1	5.1	0.4	1.7	Népal
Niger	151.4	104.0	80.2	66.7	85.8	68.5	54.6	37.8	Niger
Rwanda	1.3	1.8	12.4	12.1	0.7	1.1	4.0	6.1	Rwanda
Samoa	1.9	1.4	2.4	3.1	0.8	0.6	0.8	0.3	Samoa
Sao Tome and Principe	0.3	0.5	1.2	1.2	0.3	0.5	1.2	1.2	Sao Tomé-et-Principe
Sierra Leone	18.0	36.7	16.7	16.6	12.0	29.7	8.3	9.6	Sierra Leone
Somalia	13.2	21.7	17.1	36.7	0.6	4.9	12.7	8.7	Somalie
Sudan	84.8	62.3	82.1	91.9	26.6	-	23.1	69.0	Soudan
Togo	49.5	49.2	72.1	53.5	32.1	33.8	56.8	32.3	Togo
Tuvalu	-	-	-	-	-	-	-	-	Tuvalu
Uganda	41.9	55.0	75.6	82.2	3.9	14.0	33.2	17.0	Ouganda
Un. Rep. of Tanzania	53.4	96.1	50.8	61.1	21.0	54.6	11.6	12.0	Rép.-Un. de Tanzanie
Vanuatu	1.1	1.7	12.0	8.0	0.4	1.0	6.9	3.4	Vanuatu
Yemen	27.8	30.5	61.9	81.2	19.8	13.8	47.4	55.3	Yémen
ALL LDCs	865.3	922.7	1032.7	1127.9	388.6	461.0	533.2	533.4	Ensemble des PMA

Source: UNCTAD secretariat, based on information from the OECD secretariat.

Source: Secrétariat de la CNUCED, d'après des renseignements du secrétariat de l'OCDE.

Table 54A
Multilateral debt
$ million

Tableau 54A
Dette multilatérale
Millions de dollars

Country	Total multilateral debt / Dette multilatérale totale				Of which non-concessional / Dont dette non-concessionnelle				Pays
	1982	1983	1984	1985	1982	1983	1984	1985	
Afghanistan	109.8	109.1	108.5	119.0	-	-	-	-	Afghanistan
Bangladesh	1877.8	2114.0	2413.1	2886.0	31.2	13.7	14.0	3.2	Bangladesh
Benin	159.1	186.8	200.6	236.3	26.6	26.4	23.4	26.6	Bénin
Bhutan	1.0	1.8	1.8	4.9	-	-	-	-	Bhoutan
Botswana	116.5	135.1	158.3	200.1	76.7	91.9	112.0	148.2	Botswana
Burkina Faso	222.4	243.2	251.2	306.9	16.5	16.1	17.4	23.3	Burkina Faso
Burundi	121.7	169.8	209.0	258.1	4.4	14.1	23.6	32.4	Burundi
Cape Verde	29.0	33.7	39.7	52.6	7.1	10.8	10.8	13.2	Cap-Vert
Central African Rep.	73.5	82.1	98.1	134.6	3.0	3.9	3.9	10.6	Rép. centrafricaine
Chad	72.0	79.4	77.3	86.8	1.3	1.0	1.1	1.4	Tchad
Comoros	30.7	38.7	51.3	68.2	1.1	2.8	4.3	6.9	Comores
Democratic Yemen	160.4	195.0	220.3	267.5	-	-	-	-	Yémen démocratique
Djibouti	6.4	12.5	23.0	38.7	-	-	-	-	Djibouti
Equatorial Guinea	13.0	13.9	13.5	19.3	5.5	5.5	5.3	5.9	Guinée équatoriale
Ethiopia	442.4	489.8	522.0	609.3	34.3	35.2	35.7	36.7	Ethiopie
Gambia	67.6	73.8	78.5	90.8	12.3	9.7	10.3	13.8	Gambie
Guinea	193.8	207.5	226.8	268.0	58.5	59.4	59.4	59.2	Guinée
Guinea-Bissau	47.6	59.0	71.4	95.4	0.1	0.3	0.3	0.4	Guinée-Bissau
Haiti	208.9	246.6	286.5	320.8	-	-	-	-	Haïti
Kiribati	8.5	8.5	8.5	9.4	7.9	7.9	7.9	8.7	Kiribati
Lao People's Dem.Rep.	54.0	63.0	71.4	88.4	-	-	-	-	Rép. dém. pop. lao
Lesotho	75.0	92.4	115.0	151.1	1.4	2.6	7.6	21.0	Lesotho
Malawi	341.3	376.0	452.3	510.1	84.7	82.9	87.3	90.7	Malawi
Maldives	13.3	14.9	14.9	15.9	6.9	6.2	6.0	5.7	Maldives
Mali	288.8	340.2	364.7	413.2	6.8	6.3	7.6	8.8	Mali
Mauritania	252.9	314.2	328.7	341.4	94.3	126.9	122.1	110.7	Mauritanie
Nepal	251.2	307.3	372.7	455.7	-	-	-	-	Népal
Niger	192.3	224.0	239.2	276.1	30.7	42.5	42.7	48.7	Niger
Rwanda	134.2	161.8	188.4	238.3	1.2	2.0	1.7	1.7	Rwanda
Samoa	43.8	47.2	52.9	54.7	-	-	-	-	Samoa
Sao Tome and Principe	16.4	18.6	19.1	21.3	-	-	-	-	Sao Tomé-et-Principe
Sierra Leone	112.8	117.1	122.0	146.4	21.6	20.5	16.3	16.6	Sierra Leone
Somalia	383.5	432.3	435.4	499.4	131.0	144.5	132.5	129.4	Somalie
Sudan	868.9	903.5	966.0	989.5	186.8	157.1	132.6	92.6	Soudan
Togo	158.8	222.6	239.9	291.9	21.0	31.5	31.0	32.3	Togo
Tuvalu	-	-	-	0.1	-	-	-	-	Tuvalu
Uganda	191.1	241.8	333.8	458.9	21.8	29.2	62.2	70.5	Ouganda
Un. Rep. of Tanzania	807.4	896.5	1006.8	1065.4	212.7	231.5	277.6	274.6	Rép.-Un. de Tanzanie
Vanuatu	-	0.1	0.7	1.4	-	-	0.0	0.0	Vanuatu
Yemen	278.5	318.7	373.2	478.0	24.3	20.2	39.3	65.7	Yémen
ALL LDCs	8426.4	9591.5	10756.8	12570.3	1131.8	1202.7	1295.8	1359.6	Ensemble des PMA

Source: UNCTAD secretariat, based on information from the OECD secretariat.

Source: Secrétariat de la CNUCED, d'après des renseignements du secrétariat de l'OCDE.

Table 54B
Multilateral debt service payments

Tableau 54B
Paiements au titre du service de la dette multilatérale

$ million   Millions de dollars

Country	Multilateral debt service / Service de la dette multilatérale				Of which non-concessional / Dont service de la dette non-concessionnelle				Pays
	1982	1983	1984	1985	1982	1983	1984	1985	
Afghanistan	2.0	1.7	1.3	11.9	-	-	-	-	Afghanistan
Bangladesh	27.8	41.4	62.9	73.4	10.2	17.8	24.6	11.6	Bangladesh
Benin	5.3	6.7	6.7	11.8	3.0	3.7	3.0	5.6	Bénin
Bhutan	-	-	0.0	8.5	-	-	-	-	Bhoutan
Botswana	9.8	11.6	15.1	19.8	9.0	10.4	13.4	17.3	Botswana
Burkina Faso	5.7	3.9	8.5	7.9	2.1	1.3	1.4	2.8	Burkina Faso
Burundi	1.8	2.8	8.5	9.9	0.9	0.6	2.5	3.0	Burundi
Cape Verde	0.4	1.2	1.8	1.9	0.3	0.6	0.9	0.9	Cap-Vert
Central African Rep.	0.8	1.7	2.5	4.5	0.1	0.7	0.4	1.1	Rép. centrafricaine
Chad	0.8	0.2	0.5	2.9	0.6	-	0.0	0.0	Tchad
Comoros	0.5	0.7	1.3	1.4	0.0	0.1	0.3	0.5	Comores
Democratic Yemen	5.5	6.8	10.0	27.3	-	-	-	-	Yémen démocratique
Djibouti	0.0	0.3	0.8	1.3	-	-	-	1.2	Djibouti
Equatorial Guinea	0.1	0.1	0.1	1.6	-	0.0	-	5.1	Guinée équatoriale
Ethiopia	12.7	13.4	16.7	21.8	4.8	5.2	4.6	5.1	Ethiopie
Gambia	1.2	4.7	3.1	2.5	0.5	4.0	1.1	0.2	Gambie
Guinea	11.7	13.7	14.9	15.0	9.7	10.1	10.6	8.4	Guinée
Guinea-Bissau	0.8	0.1	0.4	0.6	-	-	-	-	Guinée-Bissau
Haiti	2.2	2.6	4.7	7.5	0.0	-	-	-	Haïti
Kiribati	0.0	-	0.1	0.5	-	-	-	-	Kiribati
Lao People's Dem.Rep.	0.6	1.2	0.3	11.4	0.0	-	-	-	Rép. dém. pop. lao
Lesotho	1.0	1.9	3.2	7.0	0.2	0.2	0.5	2.9	Lesotho
Malawi	12.8	18.0	18.6	17.6	8.8	12.4	12.0	9.3	Malawi
Maldives	0.1	1.0	0.5	1.4	-	0.8	-	0.9	Maldives
Mali	3.8	5.1	8.7	19.1	0.5	0.6	0.1	2.0	Mali
Mauritania	11.3	16.7	20.4	45.2	6.3	10.7	14.6	32.6	Mauritanie
Nepal	4.4	5.6	7.2	9.5	0.3	-	-	-	Népal
Niger	31.7	10.7	11.7	19.4	26.8	4.7	6.7	10.0	Niger
Rwanda	3.9	2.9	4.4	6.3	0.2	0.3	0.7	0.4	Rwanda
Samoa	0.7	1.0	1.3	1.8	0.0	-	-	-	Samoa
Sao Tome and Principe	0.0	0.0	-	2.0	-	-	-	-	Sao Tomé-et-Principe
Sierra Leone	2.7	3.5	10.5	3.3	1.9	1.7	6.7	0.9	Sierra Leone
Somalia	14.4	16.9	12.8	27.1	10.3	10.9	4.0	12.8	Somalie
Sudan	24.9	31.8	34.0	17.3	6.9	18.2	19.2	1.8	Soudan
Togo	11.3	7.4	9.8	14.9	10.0	3.6	3.2	7.4	Togo
Tuvalu	-	-	-	0.1	-	-	-	-	Tuvalu
Uganda	17.3	9.3	11.7	20.4	3.4	1.9	7.1	9.8	Ouganda
Un. Rep. of Tanzania	30.9	34.1	50.0	53.8	23.2	23.4	34.0	38.5	Rép.-Un. de Tanzanie
Vanuatu	-	-	0.0	0.0	-	-	-	-	Vanuatu
Yemen	9.2	14.8	25.9	26.4	0.2	4.9	13.5	10.8	Yémen
All LDCs	269.9	295.7	391.1	536.2	140.2	148.8	185.1	197.9	Ensemble des PMA

Source: UNCTAD secretariat, based on information from the OECD secretariat.

Source: Secrétariat de la CNUCED, d'après des renseignements du secrétariat de l'OCDE.

Table 55

Tableau 55

ODA debt and debt service payments to OECD countries

Dette d'APD et paiements au titre du service de la dette aux pays de l'OCDE

$ million

Millions de dollars

Country / Pays	Debt / Dette 1982	1983	1984	1985	Debt service / Service de la dette 1982	1983	1984	1985
Afghanistan / Afghanistan	157.4	145.2	133.0	141.3	9.6	10.3	9.9	4.6
Bangladesh / Bangladesh	1783.3	1755.1	2092.6	2558.9	38.6	39.3	48.9	50.1
Benin / Bénin	45.2	47.0	46.4	62.9	1.7	0.7	0.9	1.3
Bhutan / Bhoutan	-	-	-	-	-	-	-	-
Botswana / Botswana	55.7	48.9	45.0	45.9	1.0	1.0	2.4	2.3
Burkina Faso / Burkina Faso	34.4	43.9	48.9	71.5	0.7	0.9	1.1	1.8
Burundi / Burundi	19.0	24.2	28.8	57.2	0.2	1.0	1.3	1.5
Cape Verde / Cap-Vert	0.5	0.4	0.4	3.5	-	-	0.0	-
Central African Rep. / Rép. centrafricaine	36.7	41.9	39.4	66.7	0.4	1.0	16.0	4.6
Chad / Tchad	5.0	5.6	4.5	11.4	-	0.0	4.3	0.0
Comoros / Comores	1.9	2.8	5.7	11.7	0.0	0.0	0.1	0.2
Democratic Yemen / Yémen démocratique	15.4	15.4	15.9	19.3	0.7	0.6	0.9	1.2
Djibouti / Djibouti	9.8	10.1	14.9	12.1	1.8	1.8	1.6	11.7
Equatorial Guinea / Guinée équatoriale	-	-	-	-	-	-	-	-
Ethiopia / Ethiopie	183.4	174.9	187.0	222.6	8.8	10.6	10.8	11.4
Gambia / Gambie	13.9	11.3	14.0	20.1	0.1	0.3	0.7	0.7
Guinea / Guinée	123.3	127.3	132.4	164.8	9.3	4.3	3.9	5.5
Guinea-Bissau / Guinée-Bissau	6.4	5.5	5.8	0.7	0.1	0.0	0.0	6.1
Haiti / Haïti	88.3	99.1	117.0	138.6	2.0	2.1	2.2	1.4
Kiribati / Kiribati	-	-	-	-	-	-	-	-
Lao People's Dem.Rep. / Rép. dém. pop. lao	54.4	51.0	44.4	54.8	1.5	1.3	1.9	1.8
Lesotho / Lesotho	3.0	2.5	2.3	2.8	0.1	0.0	0.1	0.1
Malawi / Malawi	136.9	122.7	118.6	112.6	3.6	1.9	5.2	9.5
Maldives / Maldives	2.0	2.2	0.7	1.5	0.7	0.8	0.4	0.3
Mali / Mali	25.9	23.7	117.0	260.7	0.6	0.8	0.7	3.9
Mauritania / Mauritanie	41.1	45.9	45.6	70.2	2.6	1.6	1.4	1.5
Nepal / Népal	20.1	25.0	30.6	50.7	0.5	0.7	1.3	1.0
Niger / Niger	77.2	74.5	79.8	122.8	6.5	6.5	5.8	8.3
Rwanda / Rwanda	23.2	21.6	20.2	34.4	1.5	0.8	0.9	1.9
Samoa / Samoa	0.3	0.2	0.2	0.2	-	-	0.0	0.0
Sao Tome and Principe / Sao Tomé-et-Principe	-	-	-	-	-	-	-	-
Sierra Leone / Sierra Leone	118.8	123.2	116.7	81.9	1.9	0.4	1.4	5.1
Somalia / Somalie	120.0	150.5	220.2	267.1	3.5	3.8	5.9	9.5
Sudan / Soudan	164.1	169.4	319.8	426.9	5.2	2.1	5.2	4.0
Togo / Togo	148.6	141.0	137.0	42.8	1.5	8.2	13.0	26.2
Tuvalu / Tuvalu	-	-	-	-	-	-	-	-
Uganda / Ouganda	59.8	30.9	29.1	32.3	0.9	0.8	2.5	2.3
Un. Rep. of Tanzania / Rép.-Un. de Tanzanie	309.5	350.5	369.4	464.8	3.2	4.3	4.1	7.7
Vanuatu / Vanuatu	3.9	2.6	2.5	3.2	0.7	0.6	0.3	0.7
Yemen / Yémen	69.5	64.3	72.9	106.4	1.0	1.5	2.0	1.9
ALL LDCs / Ensemble des PMA	3958.2	3960.2	4658.6	5745.1	110.4	109.3	157.4	190.0

Source: UNCTAD secretariat, based on information from the OECD secretariat.

Source: Secrétariat de la CNUCED, d'après des renseignements du secrétariat de l'OCDE.

Table 56
Ratios : debt/GDP and debt service/exports
Tableau 56
Rapports : dette/PIB et service de la dette/exportations

Percentages / En pourcentage

Country	Debt/GDP / Dette/PIB				Debt service/exports a/ / Service de la dette/exportations a/				Pays
	1982	1983	1984	1985	1982	1983	1984	1985	
Afghanistan	(40.0)	(46.6)	(35.9)	(37.6)	4.6	5.8	6.1	6.7	Afghanistan
Bangladesh	37.4	46.3	41.8	42.6	15.9	17.2	20.2	22.9	Bangladesh
Benin	60.4	73.5	67.5	76.1	14.0	36.5	20.1	16.9	Bénin
Bhutan	5.8	1.2	3.1	3.0	6.2	5.9	0.9	23.7	Bhoutan
Botswana	40.2	38.1	33.6	46.6	9.6	3.7	5.6	6.3	Botswana
Burkina Faso	38.2	48.5	53.0	59.4	14.6	14.8	14.1	20.2	Burkina Faso
Burundi	24.7	29.3	36.4	42.0	16.4	17.9	18.2	20.1	Burundi
Cape Verde	52.6	67.8	70.1	86.8	6.3	10.3	18.2	13.6	Cap-Vert
Central African Rep.	39.8	42.4	42.0	51.8	4.3	9.1	19.0	9.5	Rép. centrafricaine
Chad	22.9	24.4	25.9	26.0	3.4	1.5	5.4	9.1	Tchad
Comoros	81.7	89.5	116.8	138.9	9.1	10.7	26.6	12.5	Comores
Democratic Yemen	111.5	126.1	124.9	(163.2)	18.1	25.6	62.5	83.9	Yémen démocratique
Djibouti	23.4	32.0	70.4	118.0	2.3	4.1	11.1	23.1	Djibouti
Equatorial Guinea	178.8	180.6	127.2	186.6	22.2	43.6	9.1	18.3	Guinée équatoriale
Ethiopia	28.0	30.3	34.8	40.4	11.9	15.0	19.4	22.3	Ethiopie
Gambia	102.2	102.8	121.1	157.6	16.4	12.6	9.2	18.2	Gambie
Guinea	82.3	70.4	63.8	67.7	22.4	19.6	23.4	15.1	Guinée
Guinea-Bissau	74.9	73.4	121.3	187.9	19.4	21.7	26.2	100.0	Guinée-Bissau
Haiti	45.2	43.9	41.7	(45.1)	9.7	10.6	11.3	11.0	Haïti
Kiribati	47.3	51.3	52.5	51.6		—	.	.	Kiribati
Lao People's Dem.Rep.	86.5	79.2	51.4	37.8	4.4	8.4	10.2	33.9	Rép. dém. pop. lao
Lesotho	33.9	36.8	49.0	68.7	3.3	2.9	3.6	6.3	Lesotho
Malawi	74.9	73.4	74.6	91.3	28.5	28.7	23.3	31.0	Malawi
Maldives	80.4	106.8	105.0	(103.8)	3.0	8.1	30.9	13.9	Maldives
Mali	68.2	91.9	118.7	130.3	17.6	7.3	10.3	22.7	Mali
Mauritania	160.0	168.4	185.0	218.5	18.1	15.3	16.8	23.2	Mauritanie
Nepal	15.1	18.5	19.0	25.1	5.1	6.6	5.6	5.7	Népal
Niger	45.6	51.7	66.0	67.1	39.0	33.1	29.4	31.4	Niger
Rwanda	15.4	17.0	19.1	(22.4)	6.2	4.8	11.5	14.1	Rwanda
Samoa	58.8	69.7	74.6	85.1	12.1	9.4	14.4	18.2	Samoa
Sao Tome and Principe	63.2	85.7	83.2	89.1	3.6	8.4	10.7	34.7	Sao Tomé-et-Principe
Sierra Leone	48.4	44.4	60.2	59.3	24.3	38.7	24.1	24.1	Sierra Leone
Somalia	73.1	101.1	122.1	(122.9)	9.3	19.9	46.2	71.1	Somalie
Sudan	72.8	91.8	77.5	74.1	16.0	13.4	17.0	22.0	Soudan
Togo	127.3	132.2	127.9	145.0	13.1	19.2	25.7	27.1	Togo
Tuvalu	-	2.1	4.4	5.5	-	-	-		Tuvalu
Uganda	27.1 b/	34.2 b/	32.0 b/	(31.6) b/	17.3	21.1	27.0	29.6	Ouganda
Un. Rep. of Tanzania	43.9	50.4	56.7	54.3	17.4	28.3	20.1	23.1	Rép.-Un. de Tanzanie
Vanuatu	(25.6)	139.2	139.2	194.9	4.1	6.5	18.9	13.1	Vanuatu
Yemen	44.3	51.7	56.5	(62.6)	24.2	26.1	52.9	92.0	Yémen
ALL LDCs	48.9	56.1	55.3	58.1	14.4	15.4	18.1	21.7	Ensemble des PMA

Source: UNCTAD secretariat, mainly based on information from the OECD secretariat, the World Bank and IMF.

Note: Debt and debt service are defined as in tables 51A et 51B.
a/ Exports of goods and all (factor and non-factor) services.
b/ As a percentage of GNP.

Source: Secrétariat de la CNUCED, principalement d'après des renseignements du secrétariat de l'OCDE, de la Banque mondiale et du FMI.

Note: La dette et le service de la dette sont définis comme aux tableaux 51A et 51B.
a/ Exportations de biens et de tous les services (facteurs et non-facteurs).
b/ En pourcentage du PNB.

Table 57A

Area and population: economic characteristics

Tableau 57A

Superficie et population: caractéristiques économiques

Country	Area / Superficie		Population						Pays
	Total Totale (000 km²)	% of arable land and land under permanent crops % de terres arables et sous cultures permanentes	Density Densité Pop./km²	Total Totale (mill.)	Urban Urbaine %	Actitivity rate[a] Taux d'activité[a] M	F	T	
		1984	1986	1986	1985	1982–1985			
Afghanistan	647.5	12.4	29	18.6	19	..	..	..	Afghanistan
Bangladesh	144.0	63.3	700	100.8	18	54	13	34	Bangladesh
Benin	112.6	16.1	37	4.2	35	49	38	43	Bénin
Bhutan	47.0	2.1	31	1.4	4	59	38	49	Bhoutan
Botswana	581.7	2.3	2	1.2	20	46	42	44	Botswana
Burkina Faso	274.2	9.6	26	7.1	8	54	49	51	Burkina Faso
Burundi	27.8	47.0	175	4.9	2	52	41	46	Burundi
Cape Verde	4.0	9.9	85	0.3	5	43	5	22	Cap-Vert
Central African Rep.	623.0	3.2	4	2.7	45	56	50	53	Rép. Centrafricaine
Chad	1284.0	2.5	4	5.1	27	58	18	38	Tchad
Comoros	2.2	43.3	210	0.5	25	44	23	34	Comores
Democratic Yemen	333.0	0.5	7	2.4	37	44	3	23	Yémen démocratique
Djibouti	22.0	0.0	17	0.4	77	..	..	..	Djibouti
Equatorial Guinea	28.1	8.2	14	0.4	60	57	3	29	Guinée équatoriale
Ethiopia	1221.9	11.4	36	44.6	15	52	26	39	Ethiopie
Gambia	11.3	14.6	67	0.8	20	53	41	47	Gambie
Guinea	245.9	6.4	25	6.2	22	52	35	43	Guinée
Guinea Bissau	36.1	8.0	25	0.9	27	52	2	26	Guinée-Bissau
Haiti	27.8	32.6	193	5.4	27	53	43	48	Haïti
Kiribati	0.7	52.1	91	0.1	34	..	..	..	Kiribati
Lao People's Dem.Rep.	236.8	3.8	16	3.7	16	49	40	45	Rép.dém.populaire lao
Lesotho	30.4	9.8	52	1.6	17	56	43	49	Lesotho
Malawi	118.5	19.8	61	7.2	12	51	30	40	Malawi
Maldives	0.3	10.0	628	0.2	20	55[b]	36[b]	46[b]	Maldives
Mali	1240.0	1.7	7	8.3	20	53	49	51	Mali
Mauritania	1030.7	0.2	2	2.0	31	56	3	29	Mauritanie
Nepal	140.8	16.5	121	17.0	7	56	37	47	Népal
Niger	1267.0	3.0	5	6.3	15	56	6	31	Niger
Rwanda	26.3	38.3	236	6.2	5	53	48	50	Rwanda
Samoa	2.8	42.7	58	0.2	22	41[b]	9[b]	25[b]	Samoa
Sao Tome & Principe	1.0	37.5	114	0.1	38	..	..	30	Sao Tomé-et-Principe
Sierra Leone	71.7	24.7	51	3.7	25	49	25	37	Sierra Leone
Somalia	637.7	1.7	9	5.5	34	54	22	38	Somalie
Sudan	2505.8	5.0	9	22.2	21	54	7	31	Soudan
Togo	56.8	25.1	54	3.1	23	48	32	39	Togo
Tuvalu	0.2	..	51	0.0	..	..	..	..	Tuvalu
Uganda	236.0	27.5	68	16.0	10	51	25	38	Ouganda
Un. Rep. of Tanzania	945.1	5.5	24	23.0	14	51	28	40	Rép. Unie de Tanzanie
Vanuatu	14.8	6.4	9	0.1	25	..	..	45[b]	Vanuatu
Yemen	195.0	6.9	42	8.2	19	48	3	24	Yémen
ALL LDCs	14432.4	6.2	24	342.4	17	53	23	38	Ensemble des PMA
All developing countries	66352.0	10.5	38	2582.6	34	50	22	36	Ensemble des pays en développement

Source: United Nations, Demographic Yearbook, 1985: United Nations, World Population Chart 1985: FAO, Production Yearbook 1985; World Bank, World Development Report 1987; World Bank, Social Indicators of Development 1986.

a/ Economically active population as a percentage of total population of sex(es) specified of all ages.

b/ Year other than 1982-1985.

Source: Nations Unies, Annuaire démographique 1985; Nations Unies, World Population Chart 1985; FAO, Annuaire de la production 1985; Banque Mondiale, Rapport sur le développement dans le monde 1987; Banque Mondiale Social Indicators of Development 1986.

a/ Population active en pourcentage de la population totale de tous âges du sexe ou des sexes précisés.

b/ Année autre que 1982-1985.

Table 57B

Birth and death rates, life expectancy

Tableau 57B

Taux de natalité et de mortalité, espérance de vie

Country	Infant mortality rate (per 1000 live births) Taux de mortalité infantile (pour 1000 naissance vivantes)		Average life expectancy at birth (Years) Espérance de vie moyenne à la naissance (années)						Crude bith rate (per 1000) Taux brut de natalité (pour 1000)		Crude death rate (per 1000) Taux brut de mortalité (pour 1000)		Pays
	1975–80	1980–85	1975–80			1980–85			1975–80	1980–85	1975–80	1980–85	
			M	F	T	M	F	T					
Afghanistan	194	194	37	37	37	37	37	37	48.6	48.9	27.2	27.3	Afghanistan
Bangladesh	137	128	47	46	47	48	47	48	47.2	44.8	19.0	17.5	Bangladesh
Benin	130	120	40	44	42	42	46	44	51.1	50.7	24.6	21.2	Bénin
Bhutan	147	139	45	43	44	47	45	46	40.0	38.4	19.8	18.1	Bhoutan
Botswana	82	76	51	54	53	53	56	55	50.6	49.9	14.0	12.6	Botswana
Burkina Faso	157	150	42	45	43	44	47	45	48.1	47.8	24.0	20.1	Burkina Faso
Burundi	130	124	43	47	45	45	48	47	48.2	47.2	20.5	19.0	Burundi
Cape Verde	87	75	55	58	57	57	61	59	32.9	30.9	9.7	11.4	Cap-Vert
Central African Rep.	145	142	40	44	42	41	45	43	44.9	44.6	23.5	21.8	Rép. centrafricaine
Chad	154	143	39	43	41	41	45	43	44.1	44.2	23.1	21.4	Tchad
Comoros	97	88	46	50	48	48	52	50	46.6	46.4	17.2	15.9	Comores
Democratic Yemen	150	135	45	47	46	47	50	48	47.6	47.0	20.9	17.4	Yémen démocratique
Djibouti	30a/	..	..	..	..	..	..	48d/	..	49.0d/	..	17.7d/	Djibouti
Equatorial Guinea	149	137	40	44	42	42	46	44	42.5	42.5	23.0	21.0	Guinée équatoriale
Ethiopia	155	155	39	43	41	39	43	41	48.3	49.7	23.0	23.2	Ethiopie
Gambia	185	174	32	35	34	34	37	35	48.3	48.4	30.4	29.0	Gambie
Guinea	171	159	37	40	38	39	42	40	46.9	46.8	25.3	23.5	Guinée
Guinea-Bissau	154	143	39	43	41	41	45	43	40.9	40.7	21.9	21.7	Guinée-Bissau
Haiti	139	128	49	52	51	51	54	53	41.8	41.3	15.7	14.2	Haïti
Kiribati	..	..	..	..	..	..	..	..	..	..	..	..	Kiribati
Lao P.D.R.	135	123	46	49	48	48	51	50	43.1	40.8	17.3	15.7	Rép. dém. pop. lao
Lesotho	123	111	44	50	47	46	52	49	41.9	41.8	17.9	16.5	Lesotho
Malawi	177	163	42	44	43	44	46	45	53.0	53.2	23.1	21.5	Malawi
Maldives	94b/	82	..	..	47b/	53	50	53	46.0b/	44.0	12.0b/	12.0	Maldives
Mali	191	180	39	42	40	40	44	42	50.9	50.6	24.5	22.5	Mali
Mauritania	149	137	40	44	42	42	46	44	50.0	50.1	22.5	20.9	Mauritanie
Nepal	147	139	45	43	44	47	45	46	44.6	41.7	20.5	18.4	Népal
Niger	157	146	39	42	41	41	44	43	50.9	51.0	25.0	22.9	Niger
Rwanda	140	132	43	47	45	45	48	47	51.1	51.9	18.1	18.9	Rwanda
Samoa	13b/	33	..	..	..	..	..	65d/	17.3b/	31.0	3.1b/	7.0	Samoa
Sao Tome & Principe	72c/	70	..	..	..	..	..	64d/	38.5c/	38.7	10.2c/	10.2	Sao Tomé-et-Principe
Sierra Leone	191	180	31	33	32	33	36	34	47.8	47.4	31.9	29.7	Sierra Leone
Somalia	155	155	39	43	41	39	43	41	48.5	47.9	22.8	23.3	Somalie
Sudan	131	118	44	46	45	47	49	48	47.1	45.9	19.4	17.4	Soudan
Togo	111	102	46	50	48	49	52	51	45.5	45.2	18.6	15.7	Togo
Tuvalu	..	40	..	..	..	..	..	60	..	22.0	..	16.0	Tuvalu
Uganda	114	112	46	50	48	47	51	49	50.3	50.3	17.6	16.8	Ouganda
U. R. of Tanzania	125	115	47	51	49	49	53	51	50.9	50.4	16.8	15.3	Rép.-Unie de Tanzanie
Vanuatu	..	94	..	..	..	..	..	55	..	45.0	..	12.0	Vanuatu
Yemen	150	135	45	47	46	47	50	48	48.6	48.6	24.1	18.4	Yémen
ALL LDCs	145	138	44	45	44	45	46	46	47.8	47.0	20.9	19.5	Ensemble des PMA
All developing countries	107	96	53	55	54	55	57	56	37.7	35.5	14.1	12.8	Ensemble des pays en développement

Source: United Nations, Demographic Indicators By Countries as assessed in 1984; United Nations, Demographic Yearbook 1981 and 1984; World Bank, Social Indicators of Development 1986: ESCAP, Statistical Yearbook for Asia and the Pacific 1984.

a/ 1978.
b/ 1980.
c/ 1979.
d/ Most recent estimates available between 1982 and 1985.

Source: Nations Unies, Indicateurs démographiques par pays estimés en 1984; Nations Unies, Annuaire démographique 1981 et 1984; Banque mondiale, Social Indicators of Development 1986; CESAP, Annuaire statistique pour l'Asie et le Pacifique 1984.

a/ 1978.
b/ 1980.
c/ 1979.
d/ Année la plus récente disponible entre 1982 et 1985.

Table 57C   Tableau 57C

Health at birth   Santé à la naissance

Country	Low-birth-weight infants (percentage) / Enfants de poids insuffisant à la naissance (pour cent) 1982-1983	Percentage of women attended during child-birth by trained personnel / Pourcentage des femmes ayant reçu des soins prodigués par du personnel qualifié pendant l'accouchement 1984	Percentage of children immunized against DPT (3 doses) / Pourcentage d'enfants vaccinés DTC (3 doses) 1984	Pays
Afghanistan	20.0	5.0	16.0	Afghanistan
Bangladesh	50.0	..	1.5 g/	Bangladesh
Benin	9.6	34.3 d/	15.8	Bénin
Bhutan	..	3.4	8.7	Bhoutan
Botswana	12.0	..	82.0 d/	Botswana
Burkina Faso	21.0	..	2.0 d/	Burkina Faso
Burundi	14.0	12.0	38.0 d/	Burundi
Cape Verde	..	10.0 e/	..	Cap-Vert
Central African Rep.	23.0	..	21.0 d/	République centrafricaine
Chad	11.0	..	1.1	Tchad
Comoros	..	24.0 f/	31.0	Comores
Democratic Yemen	12.0 b/	10.0 d/	7.0	Yémen démocratique
Djibouti	11.0 c/	73.0	20.0 c/	Djibouti
Equatorial Guinea	..	..	..	Guinée équatoriale
Ethiopia	10.4 b/	58.0	6.0 d/	Ethiopie
Gambia	14.0	80.0 e/	87.8 e/	Gambie
Guinea	18.0	..	4.0 e/	Guinée
Guinea Bissau	15.0 b/	..	24.0 e/	Guinée-Bissau
Haiti	17.0	20.0 e/	12.0	Haïti
Kiribati	..	..	53.0 d/	Kiribati
Lao People's Dem. Rep.	15.0	..	..	Rép. dém. pop. lao
Lesotho	10.5	28.0	69.0	Lesotho
Malawi	20.0 b/	58.6	66.0	Malawi
Maldives	26.0	..	23.0	Maldives
Mali	13.0	..	17.5 h/	Mali
Mauritania	10.0 b/	22.6	21.4	Mauritanie
Nepal	..	10.0 c/	26.4 g/	Népal
Niger	20.0	46.5 e/	5.0 e/	Niger
Rwanda	17.0	..	32.0 e/	Rwanda
Samoa	2.4	52.0 d/	84.3 e/	Samoa
Sao Tome and Principe	5.9	..	28.0 e/	Sao Tomé-et-Principe
Sierra Leone	17.0	25.0	28.6	Sierra Leone
Somalia	..	2.0 d/	10.0	Somalie
Sudan	15.0 b/	20.0	4.0	Soudan
Togo	16.9	..	9.0 f/	Togo
Tuvalu	..	..	72.0 d/	Tuvalu
Uganda	10.0	..	2.0 e/	Ouganda
Un. Rep. of Tanzania	12.0	74.0 e/	58.0 d/	Rép. Unie de Tanzanie
Vanuatu	4.7	72.0 e/	22.0	Vanuatu
Yemen	9.0	12.0 d/	10.0	Yémen
All LDCs a/	24.8	36.0	14.3	Ensemble des PMA a/
All developing countries a/	20.8	41.1	41.4	Ensemble des pays en développpement a/

Source: WHO, World Health Statistics Annual 1986 and UNICEF, The State of the World's Children 1987.

Source: OMS, Annuaire de statistiques sanitaires mondiales 1986 et FISE, La situation des enfants dans le monde 1987.

a/   Average of countries for which data are available.

b/   1984   c/   1985   d/   1982   e/   1983

f/   1981   g/   1983-1984   h/   1980

a/ Moyenne des pays pour lesquels les données sont disponibles.

b/   1984   c/   1985   d/   1982   e/   1983

f/   1981   g/   1983-1984   h/   1980

Table 57D
Food and Water

Tableau 57D
Alimentation et eau

Country / Pays	Average daily calorie intake per capita / Disponibilités alimentaires (calories par personne par jour)		Percentage of population with access to safe water or adequate sanitation / Pourcentage de la population disposant d'eau saine ou de mesures suffisantes d'hygiène du milieu							
			Urban / urbain				Rural			
		As % of requirements / En % des besoins	Water / Eau		Sanitation / Hygiène du milieu		Water / Eau		Sanitation / Hygiène du milieu	
	Average / Moyenne 1985	1982–1985	1980	1985	1980	1985	1980	1985	1980	1985
Afghanistan	..	..	28	38	..	5	8	17	..	..
Bangladesh	1899	81	26	24	21	24	40	49	1	3
Benin	2173	83	26	80	48	60	15	34	4	20
Bhutan	2571	..	50	..	..	..	5	19	..	1
Botswana	2219	93	..	84	..	93	31	46	..	28
Burkina Faso	1924	85	27	43	38	44	20	69	5	6
Burundi	2116	102	90	98	40	84	20	21	35	56
Cape Verde	2535 a/	111	100	83	34	32	21	50	10	9
Central African Rep.	2050	91	..	13	..	..	..	..	..	..
Chad	1504 a/	68	..	..	..	..	..	..	..	..
Comoros	2214 a/	91	85	73 a/	70	69 a/	25	39 a/	15	33 a/
Democratic Yemen	2337	94	50	50	43	78 a/	20	20	20	17
Djibouti	..	..	..	47 a/	..	99 a/	..	..	..	..
Equatorial Guinea	..	..	..	69	..	96	..	..	..	..
Ethiopia	1681 a/	93	85	97	..	..	..	9	..	..
Gambia	2257 a/	95	69	41	54	..	..	50	..	..
Guinea	1728	84	18	17	21	29	2	12	1	18
Guinea-Bissau	..	97	48	59	39	42	8	22	13	13
Haiti	1855	84	93	..	87	13 a/	8	30	10	13
Kiribati	2633 a/	..	21	28 a/	..	..	25	20 a/	80	4 a/
Lao People's Dem.Rep.	2228 a/	90	37	65	13	22	12	30	..	..
Lesotho	2358	104	77	97	100	75 a/	11	30	14	14
Malawi	2448	95	11	59	60	100	37	50	81	..
Maldives	..	91	37	46	79	8	3	12	1	1
Mali	1788	68	80	70	5	17	..	10	0	3
Mauritania	2078	98	41	35	16	36 a/	85	..	..	..
Nepal	2034	93	83	79	36	77	7	25	1	1
Niger	2250	97	48	..	60	88	32	49	3	3
Rwanda	1919	98	97	..	86	..	55	48	50	55
Samoa	2389 a/	89	..	75	..	2	94	67	83	83
Sao Tome & Principe	2511 a/	97	50	33	31	60	..	45	..	..
Sierra Leone	1817 a/	91	60	68	45	44	2	7	6	10
Somalia	2072	89	100	58	63	73 a/	20	22	5	5
Sudan	1737	90	70	100 a/	24	31 a/	31	31 a/	0	..
Togo	2236	94	..	100	100	81	31	41	10	9
Tuvalu	..	..	45	100	..	32	..	100	80	73
Uganda	2083 a/	101	..	37	40	93	8	18	10	30
Un. Rep. of Tanzania	2335 a/	98	65	90	95	99	..	42	..	58
Vanuatu	2206 a/	81	100	99	60	83	53	99	68	40
Yemen	2250	92	100	100	..	..	18	25	..	..
ALL LDCs b/ / Ensemble des PMA b/	1951	88	49	53	40	46	27	33	8	15
All developing countries b/ / Ensemble des pays en développement b/	2386	102	72	74	50	57	32	42	11	15

Source: FAO, Production Yearbook 1985 (Vol.39); WHO, The International Drinking Water Supply and Sanitation Decade: Review of National Progress (as at December 1985); World Bank, World Development Report 1987; World Bank, Social Indicators of Development 1986.

a/ Year other than 1985.
b/ Average of countries for which data are available.

Source: FAO, Annuaire de la production 1985 (vol.39); OMS, The International Drinking Water Supply and Sanitation Decade: Review of National Progress (as at December 1985); Banque Mondiale, Rapport sur le développement dans le monde 1987; Banque Mondiale, Social Indicators of Development 1986.

a/ Année autre que 1985.
b/ Moyenne des pays pour lesquels les données sont disponibles.

Table 57E — Education and literacy
Tableau 57E — Enseignement et alphabétisme

Country / Pays	Adult literacy rate (%) around/vers 1985 M	F	T	Number of illiterates (000) around 1985 M	F	T	Primary 1980 M	F	T	Primary 1984 M	F	T	Secondary 1980 M	F	T	Secondary 1984 M	F	T
Afghanistan	39	8	24	3114	4491	7605	54	12	34	22	10	16	16	4	10	10	5	8
Bangladesh	43	22	33	16313	20961	37274	76	46	62	70i/	50i/	60i/	26	9	18	26i/	10i/	18i/
Bénin	37	16	26	679	951	1630	88	40	64	86	42	64	24	9	16	28	11	19
Bhoutan	..	..	..	..	..	..	15f/	7f/	11f/	32	17	25	2f/	1f/	1f/	6	1	4
Botswana	73	69	71	56	83	139	82	100	91	94i/	104i/	99i/	18	21	19	26i/	30i/	28i/
Burkina Faso	21	6	13	1697	2079	3776	26	15	21	37	22	29	4	2	3	6	3	4
Burundi	43a/b/	26a/b/	34a/b/	..	..	..	35	22	29	58	40	49	5	2	3	5d/	3d/	4d/
Cap-Vert	61	39	47	..	..	..	117	108	112	113d/	107d/	110d/	9	7	8	13d/	10d/	11d/
Rép. centrafricaine	53	29	40	327	560	887	93	51	71	98a/	51a/	74a/	21	7	14	24a/	8a/	16a/
Tchad	..	..	..	..	..	..	..	..	..	55	21	38	..	..	..	11	2	6
Comores	..	..	..	..	..	..	109	78	93	..	..	..	31	16	24	..	..	..
Yémen démocratique	59	25	41	233	451	684	93	36	65	96d/	35d/	66d/	25	11	18	26d/	11d/	19d/
Djibouti	..	..	..	..	..	..	..	..	..	..	..	32k/	..	..	..	..	..	8k/
Guinée équatoriale	..	..	37c/	..	..	105c/	..	..	84	..	..	108d/	..	..	..	..	..	10a/
Ethiopie	..	..	55b/d/	..	..	..	46	25	35	48d/	29d/	39d/	11	6	9	14d/	8d/	11d/
Gambie	..	..	..	..	..	..	68	36	52	91	55	73	19	8	13	29	13	21
Guinée	..	..	..	..	..	..	42	21	31	44	20	32	21	8	14	20	7	13
Guinée-Bissau	46	17	31	101	160	261	95	41	67	84d/	40d/	62d/	10	2	6	19d/	4d/	11d/
Haïti	40	35	38	1080	1238	2318	72	62	67	81d/	72d/	76d/	13	12	13	16d/	16d/	16d/
Kiribati	..	..	..	..	..	..	..	..	..	..	..	..	..	..	..	..	..	..
Rép. dém. populaire lao	92e/	76e/	84e/	..	..	..	102	86	94	103d/	77d/	90d/	21	14	18	22d/	15d/	19d/
Lesotho	..	..	..	..	..	..	85	120	102	97d/	126d/	111d/	14	20	17	17d/	26d/	21d/
Malawi	..	..	..	..	..	..	74	49	61	71	53	62	6	2	4	6	2	4
Maldives	..	..	..	..	..	..	..	..	..	..	..	..	..	..	..	..	..	..
Mali	23	11	17	1625	1979	3604	32	18	25	30a/	17a/	24a/	12	5	8	10a/	4a/	7a/
Mauritanie	..	..	..	..	..	..	44	24	34	45a/	29a/	37a/	16	4	10	19a/	6a/	12a/
Népal	39	12	26	2892	4001	6893	115	48	83	104	47	77	33	9	21	35	11	23
Niger	..	..	..	..	..	..	35	19	27	..	..	28d/	7	3	5	3d/	1d/	2d/
Rwanda	61	33	47	562	1025	1587	66	60	63	64d/	60d/	62d/	2	1	2	3d/	1d/	2d/
Samoa	..	..	..	..	..	..	..	..	..	..	..	..	..	..	..	..	..	..
Sao Tomé-et-Principe	..	..	56	..	..	..	..	..	..	..	..	..	..	..	..	..	..	..
Sierra Leone	..	..	..	..	..	..	64	45	54	68a/	48a/	58a/	20	8	14	23a/	11a/	17a/
Somalie	..	..	..	..	..	..	43	24	34	32d/	18d/	25d/	11	4	8	23d/	12d/	17d/
Soudan	..	..	..	..	..	..	59	41	50	57d/	41d/	49d/	20	12	16	23d/	16d/	19d/
Togo	54	28	41	376	606	982	150	93	122	118	75	97	48g/	16g/	32g/	32	10	21
Tuvalu	..	..	..	..	..	..	..	..	..	..	..	..	..	..	..	..	..	..
Ouganda	..	..	..	..	..	..	56	43	50	66a/	50a/	58a/	7	3	5	11a/	5a/	8a/
Rép. Unie de Tanzanie	..	..	..	..	..	..	100	86	93	91d/	84d/	87d/	4	2	3	4d/	2d/	3d/
Vanuatu	..	..	..	..	..	..	..	..	..	..	..	..	..	..	..	..	..	..
Yémen	..	..	..	..	..	..	80	12	46	112d/	22d/	67d/	8	1	5	17d/	3d/	10d/
Ensemble des PMA j/	43	21	32	..	..	..	69	41	55	65	43	54	18	7	13	18	8	13
Ensemble des pays en développement j/	67	49	58	..	..	..	96	76	86	98	79	89	38	27	33	42	30	36

Source: UNESCO, Office of Statistics and Statistical Yearbook 1986; World Bank, Social Indicators of Development 1986.

Source: UNESCO, Office des Statistiques et annuaire statistique 1986; Banque Mondiale, Social Indicators of Development 1986.

a/ 1982. b/ Age group 10+. c/ 1980. d/ 1983. e/ Age group 15-45. f/ 1979. g/ 1981. h/ 1977. i/ 1985. j/ Average of countries for which data are available. k/ Most recent estimates available between 1982 and 1985.

a/ 1982. b/ Groupe d'âge 10+. c/ 1980. d/ 1983. e/ Groupe d'âge 15-45. f/ 1979. g/ 1981. h/ 1977. i/ 1985. j/ Moyenne des pays pour lesquels les données sont disponibles. k/ Année la plus récente disponible entre 1982 et 1985.

Table 57F
Communications and media

Tableau 57F
Communications et médias

Country	Newsprint consumption (Kg. per 1000 inhabitants) / Consommation de papier journal (Kg. pour 1000 habitants)		Mail traffic (number of items per 100 inhabitants) / Courrier postal (nombre d'envois pour 100 habitants) 1985			Circulation of daily news-papers per 1000 inhabitants / Tirage de journaux quotidiens pour 1000 habitants 1984	Telephones per 1000 inhabitants / Téléphones pour 1000 habitants 1985	Radio receivers per 1000 inhabitants / Postes récepteurs de radio pour 1000 habitants		Pays
	1980	1983	Domestic / Intérieur	Received / Reçu	sent / Envoyé			1980	1983	
Afghanistan	6	6	..	..	..	3.7	2.0b/	75	78	Afghanistan
Bangladesh	214	486	376	91	87	5.6	1.4j/	8c/	8c/	Bangladesh
Benin	29	26	449/	7	6	0.3	4.4j/	72	76	Bénin
Bhutan	..	..	..	..	..	..	1.3	5c/	9c/	Bhoutan
Botswana	..	..	4862	763	325	16.8	17.9j/	94	117	Botswana
Burkina Faso	..	..	75	203	52	0.3	2.1j/	18	19	Burkina Faso
Burundi	..	..	6f/	14f/	7f/	..	1.3e/	37	40	Burundi
Cape Verde	..	..	116	294	243	..	7.5j/	139	148	Cap-Vert
Central African Rep.	..	..	..	..	..	0.2	2.7	52	56	Rép. centrafricaine
Chad	..	..	5f/	10f/	6f/	..	0.6	167	219	Tchad
Comoros	..	..	..	..	..	..	7.9h/	110	133	Comores
Democratic Yemen	254	232	48	88	42	5.4	11.7j/	60	61	Yémen démocratique
Djibouti	..	..	63j/	232j/	192j/	2.6h/	22.2	68	67	Djibouti
Equatorial Guinea	..	..	102f/	12f/	9f/	0.9	3.1d/	284	306	Guinée équatoriale
Ethiopia	53	37	51f/	..	..	0.8	2.8	80	73	Ethiopie
Gambia	..	..	..	..	..	2.8	4.8	113	110	Gambie
Guinea	18	17	172f/j/	..	244f/j/	2.2	2.4h/	25	28	Guinée
Guinea-Bissau	124	117	..	..	..	6.9	2.7d/	31	33	Guinée-Bissau
Haiti	61	117	..	..	..	7.5	4.2d/	21	23	Haïti
Kiribati	..	..	..	44e/	13e/	..	17.4	195	213	Kiribati
Lao People's Dem. Rep.	61	58	10e/	656f/	508f/	..	2.1	107	124	Rép. dém. populaire lao
Lesotho	..	..	582f/	693	349	29.4	9.0	22	27	Lesotho
Malawi	84	92	599j/	150	594	4.7	5.8	46	47	Malawi
Maldives	..	..	..	..	..	..	13.7	45	88	Maldives
Mali	..	..	7f/	33j/	16j/	0.5	1.5h/	15	16	Mali
Mauritania	..	..	11j/	..	..	..	2.7e/	92	101	Mauritanie
Nepal	19	17	..	51j/	14j/	3.0	1.1j/	20	25	Népal
Niger	..	..	39j/	61	38	0.8	1.9	47	48	Niger
Rwanda	..	..	113	657f/	498f/	0.1	1.5	29	53	Rwanda
Samoa	..	..	..	133	75	..	37.8h/	205	438	Samoa
Sao Tome and Principe	..	..	22	541j/	191j/	..	26.7j/	245	245	Sao Tomé-et-Principe
Sierra Leone	61	58	141j/	..	..	2.8	5.5h/	137	201	Sierra Leone
Somalia	43	39	..	74	50	..	1.6d/	24	26	Somalie
Sudan	80	108	191	..	..	5.0	3.6	187	245	Soudan
Togo	..	..	..	..	..	3.5	4.3e/	215	211	Togo
Tuvalu	..	..	..	..	..	..	18.8	..	..	Tuvalu
Uganda	15	14	..	250f/	88f/	1.7	3.8e/	23	22	Ouganda
Un. Rep. of Tanzania	187	169	430	..	..	4.7	5.1	27	28	Rép. Unie de Tanzanie
Vanuatu	..	..	..	155	38	..	22.9	228	242	Vanuatu
Yemen	..	..	24	..	..	..	5.7d/	16	16	Yémen
All LDCs	123a/	224a/	263a/	120a/	77a/	3.8a/	2.8	49	55	Ensemble des PMA
All developing countries	1219	1243	1220	148	112	35.2	27.4	114	135	Ensemble des pays en développement

Source: UNESCO; Statistical Yearbook 1986; Universal Postal Union, Statistique des services postaux 1983, 1984 and 1985; ITU, Yearbook of Common Carrier Telecommunication Statistics (14th edition).

a/ Total of LDCs for which data are shown. b/ 1980. c/ The number of licences issued or sets declared. d/ 1981. e/ 1983. f/ Letters only. g/ Excluding "small packets". h/ 1982. i/ Excluding "Printed Matter". j/ 1984.

Source: UNESCO, Annuaire statistique 1986; Union Postale Universelle, Statistique des services postaux 1983, 1984 et 1985; UIT, Annuaire statistique des télécommunications du secteur public (14e édition).

a/ Total des PMA pour lesquels les données sont indiquées. b/ 1980. c/ Nombre de licences délivrées ou de postes déclarés. d/ 1981. e/ 1983. f/ Lettres seulement. g/ Non compris "petits paquets". h/ 1982. i/ Non compris "Imprimés". j/ 1984.

Table 57G / Tableau 57G

Energy / Energie

Country / Pays	Coal, oil, gas and electricity / Charbon, pétrole, gaz et électricité — Consumption per capita in kg. of coal equivalent / Consommation par habitant en kg. équivalent en charbon		Fuelwood, charcoal and bagasse / Bois de chauffage, charbon de bois et bagasse — kg. of coal equivalent / équivalant en charbon		Installed electricity capacity (kw./1000 inhabitants) / Puissance électrique installée (kw./1000 habitants)	
	1981	1984	1981	1984	1981	1984
Afghanistan	49	56	88	80	23	25
Bangladesh	45	54	93	95	11	13
Benin / Bénin	50	43	343	342	4	4
Bhutan / Bhoutan	11	11	751	707	12	12
Botswana	..	595	255	227	..	..
Burkina Faso	31	29	313	312	6	6
Burundi	18	16	249	248	2	2
Cape Verde / Cap-Vert	139	166	..	..	10	12
Central African Rep. / Rép. centrafricaine	37	38	357	350	13	12
Chad / Tchad	22	21	206	207	8	8
Comoros / Comores	46	42	..	..	10	9
Democratic Yemen / Yémen démocratique	572	796	42	41	64	67
Djibouti	284	263	..	..	108	107
Equatorial Guinea / Guinée équatoriale	83	91	397	388	19	18
Ethiopia / Ethiopie	18	17	237	236	9	8
Gambia / Gambie	112	113	449	351	17	15
Guinea / Guinée	75	72	189	174	32	29
Guinea-Bissau / Guinée-Bissau	42	42	171	162	8	8
Haiti / Haïti	67	65	351	360	25	24
Kiribati	217	206	..	..	34	32
Lao People's Dem. Rep. / Rép. dém. populaire lao	38	30	369	375	52	64
Lesotho	..	..	..	..	..	..
Malawi	52	43	323	320	24	24
Maldives	43	68	..	..	12	11
Mali	28	30	189	189	6	7
Mauritania / Mauritanie	169	158	1	1	33	30
Nepal / Népal	16	17	309	306	5	11
Niger	54	56	200	200	7	11
Rwanda	33	34	295	299	8	8
Samoa	327	348	167	161	83	106
Sao Tome & Principe / Sao Tomé-et-Principe	175	162	705	706	52	57
Sierra Leone	95	67	326	331	32	30
Somalia / Somalie	109	102	283	288	6	6
Sudan / Soudan	86	77	67	67	16	15
Togo	64	71	236	238	14	21
Tuvalu	..	..	..	..	..	..
Uganda / Ouganda	24	24	327	328	12	11
Un. Rep. of Tanzania / Rep. Unie de Tanzanie	46	43	68	63	22	20
Vanuatu	212	203	..	..	85	86
Yemen / Yémen	87	163	..	..	14	15
All LDCs / Ensemble des PMA	49	54	203	203	14	15
All developing countries / Ensemble des pays en développement	493	513	178	182	119	138

Source: United Nations, Energy Statistics Yearbook 1984; FAO, Yearbook of Forest Products 1973–1984, and World Bank, World Development Report 1986.

Source: Nations Unies, Annuaire des statistiques de l'énergie 1984; FAO, Annuaire des produits forestiers 1973–1984 et Banque Mondiale, Rapport sur le développement dans le monde 1986.